VOLUME I

Materials and Technology

A systematic encyclopedia
of the technology of materials used in industry and
commerce, including foodstuffs and fuels
Based upon a work originally devised
by the late Dr. J. F. van Oss

VOLUME I

Air, water, inorganic chemicals
and nucleonics

LONGMANS
J. H. DE BUSSY

Longmans, Green and Co Ltd
London and Harlow
Associated companies, branches and representatives
throughout the world

J. H. de Bussy
Rokin 62, Amsterdam

© Longmans, Green - J. H. de Bussy 1968

First published 1968

Set in 9 on 11 point Times
and printed in the Netherlands
by De Bussy Ellerman Harms N.V., Amsterdam

SBN 582 46201 0

Published in the United States
and the Philippines by Barnes
& Noble Inc. under the title

CHEMICAL TECHNOLOGY: AN
ENCYCLOPEDIC TREATMENT

661

Contents

Preface

The Encyclopedia of Materials and Technology provides up to date information for the layman and technologist alike, on the materials used in the world today. The term 'materials' covers all substances bought and sold by volume, weight, or area, and the encyclopedia describes the sources, manufacture, processing, and uses of both natural and synthetic materials. It has been written by specialists for people who want accurate information on materials, and care has been taken to present the information in a way which is acceptable to all readers. The layman with only slight technical knowledge will have no difficulty in following the text; on the other hand, the engineer or technologist is given the precise background information he requires. In addition, the encyclopedia will serve as a useful work of reference for those students in schools, colleges and universities, who are preparing for a career in Science and Technology.

More than 50 years ago this encyclopedia was written by the late Dr. J. F. van Oss and published as a single volume. Although this volume was written in Dutch its appeal was such that its publication ran to 5 editions in the succeeding 30 years and the work grew into a highly regarded 6 volume encyclopedia which was renowned for its lucid style of writing. In spite of the advanced information which was contained in it people with only a slight knowledge of science were able to use it.

Dr. van Oss planned a comprehensive revision of the work in English but unfortunately he died before the project could be completed. It has now been taken up as a joint venture by J. H. De Bussy of Amsterdam and Longmans of London who have set up an editorial board to continue Dr. van Oss's work. In his replanning of the encyclopedia, Dr. van Oss was assisted by Ir. A. Straub and after the death of Dr. van Oss the initial planning for this edition was completed by Ir. Straub and Drs. H. G. Roebersen. In recognition of his considerable services to this edition Ir. Straub was made an honorary member of the editorial board; Drs. Roebersen continued to be associated with the work as a member of the editorial board until his untimely death a few months before the first volume was scheduled for publication.

The editorial board would like to take this opportunity particularly to pay tribute to the work undertaken on this publication by the late Drs. Roebersen. He was personally involved in the reshaping of this edition to make it suitable for publication in English as a modern encyclopedia. The encyclopedia has benefited very considerably, although unobtrusively, from his knowledge, wise counsel and advise.

The TNO (The Central National Council for Applied Scientific Research in the Netherlands) has become associated with the work by giving help to the editorial board in the preparation of particular chapters, in finding subject experts to write other chapters and in co-ordinating most of the editorial work.

The arrangement of the encyclopedia is systematic rather than alphabetical. This arrangement, which was followed in the Dutch editions, ensures that related subjects are dealt with in proximity with each other rather than separated by the random vagaries of the alphabet. This is an advantage to the reader and also enables single volumes of the encyclopedia to be made available separately. No encyclopedia can expect to be entirely self sufficient and this is no exception. The aim of the editorial board has been to present a balanced picture of the fundamentals of each subject and this has been supplemented by a short bibliography of selected titles for further reading. The publishers have made arrangements whereby they hope to be able to answer any enquiries arising out of the use of this encyclopedia and these should be sent to Longmans, Green & Co. Ltd, Longman House, Burnt Mill, Harlow, Essex. They should be marked specifically 'For the attention of the Editor, Materials and Technology Encyclopedia'.

Finally, the editorial board would like to acknowledge their indebtedness to the many subject experts who have contributed individual chapters to this work. The names of the subject experts may be found in the list of authors for each volume. They would also like to acknowledge the valuable contribution made by the General Editor, Mr. T. J. W. van Thoor, who has been responsible for preparing much of the material for this volume in addition to co-ordinating the work of the many different people who have been associated with the various volumes of this encyclopedia.

THE EDITORS

Authors

The General Editor wishes particularly to thank the following who have written certain chapters in this volume:

S. C. CARSON, B.Sc. Ph. D.
Imperial Chemical Industries Ltd.,
(Reserarch Dept., Mond Division)

Sulphur, selenium,
tellurium and compounds

G. E. EDWARDS, B.Sc.
Imperial Chemical Industries Ltd.
(Research Dept., Mond Division)

Halogen compounds
Alkali metals and their compounds,
10.1-10.8
Alkaline earth metals and their compounds

IR. J. A. KNOBBOUT
Head of the department of refrigeration
and mechanical technology of the Central
Technical Institute TNO, Delft (Holland)

Elementary gases, 2.1

J. W. MINKEN, A.M.S.E.
Sometime head of the water treatment
department of the Central Technical
Institute TNO, Delft (Holland)

Water, 4.4-4.7

DR. IR. A. PASVEER
Deputy head of the water and soil
department of the Research Institute for
Public Health Engineering TNO, Delft
(Holland)

Water, 4.8

Acknowledgements

We are grateful to the following for their kind permission to reproduce the figures listed below;

Fig. 1.1: from Mellor's *Modern Inorganic Chemistry*, p. 154, London. Copyright 1951 Longmans, Green and Co. Ltd.

Fig. 1.2: from 'Zeitschrift für anorganische und allgemeine Chemie' *200* (1931) 57-73, Leipzig. Copyright Johann Ambrosius Barth Verlag.

Fig. 1.3: from 'Industrial and Engineering Chemistry' *32* (1940) 627, New York. Copyright The American Chemical Society.

Fig. 1.4, 1.9: from Bamforth, *Industrial Crystallization*, p. 42. London. Copyright Leonard Hill Books.

Fig. 1.5: from 'Chemical Engineering', Dec. 1965. New York. Copyright 1965 McGraw-Hill Book Company.

Fig. 1.8: by courtesy of Dead Sea Works Ltd., Beer-Sheba, Israel. Photograph by Shimon Fuchs.

Fig. 1.10: by courtesy of Lurgi Gesellschaften, Frankfurt/M., West-Germany.

Fig. 1.11, 1.22, 1.23: from Ullmanns *Encyklopädie der technischen Chemie*, Vol. 1, 3rd edn. Munich. Copyright 1960 Urban & Schwarzenberg.

Fig. 1.12: from 'Industrial and Engineering Chemistry' *40* (1948) 52. Copyright The American Chemical Society, Washington, DC.

Fig. 1.13, 1.24, 1.34: by courtesy of Dorr Oliver Company Ltd., Croydon, England.

Fig. 1.14: by courtesy of The Eimco Corporation, Salt Lake City, USA.

Fig. 1.17: by courtesy of T. Shriver and Company, Inc., Harrison. Copyright Interscience Publishers, New York (from Kirk-Othmer, *Encyclopedia of Chemical Technology*).

Fig. 1.19: from Perry, *Chemical Engineers' Handbook*, 3rd edn., p. 975. New York. Copyright McGraw-Hill Book Company.

Fig. 1.25, 1.26: from Kirk-Othmer, *Encyclopedia of Chemical Technology*. New York. Copyright Interscience Publishers.

Fig. 1.30: by courtesy of Benno Schilde AG, Bad Hersfeld, West-Germany.

Fig. 1.36: by courtesy of British 'Rema' Manufacturing Company, Ltd., Sheffield, England.

Fig. 1.37: by courtesy of Link-Belt, Chicago, USA.

Fig. 2.6, 2.11, 2.12, 2.14: by courtesy of N.V. Philips Gloeilampenfabrieken, Eindhoven, Holland.

Fig. 2.18, 2.23: by courtesy of Chicago Bridge & Iron Company, Oak Brook, Illinois, USA.

Fig. 2.19: by courtesy of The British Oxygen Company Ltd., London, England.

Fig. 2.28: by courtesy of Philipson Studios, Newcastle upon Tyne, England.

Fig. 3.4: by courtesy of Lurgi Gesellschaften, Frankfurt/M., West-Germany.

Fig. 3.6: from W. L. Faith, *Air Pollution Control*. Courtesy Ateliers de Construction Electriques de Charleroi S.A., Charleroi, Belgium.

Fig. 3.8: by courtesy of Schmelzbasaltwerk, Kaltenborn, West-Germany.

Fig. 3.9: by courtesy of Joseph Crosfield & Sons, Ltd., Warrington, England.

Fig. 3.10: from H. Spencer-Gregory and E. Rourke, *Hygrometry*. London. Copyright 1957 Crosby Lockwood & Son Ltd.

Fig. 3.11: by courtesy of Westinghouse Electric International Company, New York, USA.

Fig. 4.3: by courtesy of Infilco Inc., Chicago, USA.

Fig. 4.4: by courtesy of Infilco-Fuller Company, Tucson.

Fig. 4.7: by courtesy of Union Carbide Europa S.A., Geneva, Switzerland.

Fig. 4.11: by courtesy of Chicago Bridge & Iron Company, Illinois, USA.

Fig. 4.12: by courtesy of Shell Nederland N.V., Rotterdam, Holland.

Fig. 4.13: by courtesy of G. & J. Weir Holdings Ltd., Glasgow, Scotland.

Fig. 4.14: from 'Chemical Engineering', July 1960. New York. Copyright 1960 McGraw-Hill Book Company.

Fig. 4.15: from 'Chemical and Engineering News', June 10, 1963, p. 48. Washington, DC. Copyright American Chemical Society.

Fig. 4.20: by courtesy of The Central Technical Institute of the Netherlands Organisation for Applied Scientific Research (TNO), The Hague, Holland.

Fig. 4.22: from W. Rudolfs, *Industrial Wastes,* p. 110. Monograph series 118. Washington DC. Copyright American Chemical Society. Photograph by James E. Pepper and Company, Lexington, USA.

Fig. 4.25, 4.28: by courtesy of Prof. Dr. J. K. Baars of the Research Institute for Public Health Engineering (TNO), The Hague, Holland.

Fig. 4.26: by courtesy of Dienst Publieke Werken, Amsterdam, Holland.

Fig. 4.29: from F. Sierp, *Gewerbliche und Industrielle Abwässer,* p. 400. Berlin. Copyright 1953 Springer-Verlag.

Fig. 4.30: by courtesy of N.V. Nederlandse Staatsmijnen, Heerlen, Holland.

Fig. 6.3: by courtesy of Laporte Chemicals Ltd., Warrington, England.

Fig. 7.1, 7.3, 7.4, 7.5: from Rudge, *Manufacturing and uses of Fluorine and its Compounds*. London. Copyright Oxford University Press.

Fig. 7.7: by courtesy of Wuickfit & Quickfit & Quartz Ltd., Stone.

Fig. 8.3, 8.4: by courtesy of Freeport Sulphur Company, New York, USA.

Fig. 8.5: by courtesy of Pan American Sulphur Company, Houston, USA.

Fig. 8.7: by courtesy of Lurgi Gesellschaften, Frankfurt/M., West-Germany.

Fig. 8.8: by courtesy of Dorr-Oliver Inc., Croydon-Amsterdam, Holland.

Fig. 8.9: from 'Industrial and Engineering Chemistry', Nov. 1950, p. 2216. Washington, DC. Copyright The American Chemical Society.

Fig. 8.10: by courtesy of Imperial Chemical Industries Ltd., London, England.

Fig. 8.12, 8.13: by courtesy of Titlestad Corporation, New York, USA.

Fig. 9.4: by courtesy of English Steel Corporation Ltd., Sheffield, England.

Fig. 9.9: by courtesy of Pennsalt International, Philadelphia, USA.

Fig. 9.13, 9.15, 9.17: by courtesy of Staatsmijnen, Limburg, Heerlen, Holland.

Fig. 9.14: from 'Platinum Metals Review', Jan. 1959, p. 5. London. Copyright Johnson, Matthey & Co. Ltd.

Fig. 9.20, 9.21: by courtesy of Chilean Iodine Educational Bureau, London, England.

Fig. 9.23: by courtesy of W. R. Grace & Co., Memphis, Tennessee, USA.

Fig. 9.24: from 'Industrial and Engineering Chemistry', Vol. 48, No. 12, Dec. 1956, p. 41A. Washington DC. Copyright American Chemical Society.

Fig. 9.28: by courtesy of Tennessee Valley Authority, Knoxville, Tennessee, USA.

Fig. 9.29: by courtesy of Albright & Wilson Ltd., London, England.

Fig. 9.31: by courtesy of Engineering and Industrial Corporation, Luxemburg.

Fig. 9.33: from V. Sauchelli, *Chemistry and Technology of Fertilizers.* New York. Reinhold Publishing Corporation, 1960.

Fig. 9.37: by courtesy of Rönskärswerken, Sweden.

Fig. 10.2: by courtesy of U.S. Industrial Chemicals Co., Ashtabula, Ohio, USA.

Fig. 10.5: by courtesy of N.V. Koninklijke Nederlandsche Zoutindustrie, Hengelo, Holland.

Fig. 10.6: by courtesy of Leslie Salt Co., Newark, England.

Fig. 10.9: from Kaufmann, *Sodium Chloride,* ACS Monograph 145. New York. Reinhold Publishing Corporation, 1960.

Fig. 10.16: by courtesy of Davey, Paxman & Co. Ltd., Colchester, England.

Fig. 10.19: from *Electrochemical Engineering* by Mantell. New York. Copyright McGraw-Hill Book Company.

Fig. 10.21: by courtesy of Duisburger Kupferhütte, Duisburg, West-Germany.

Fig. 10.26, 10.28: by courtesy of N.V. Nederlandsche Kali-Import Maatschappij, Amsterdam, Holland.

Fig. 10.29: by courtesy of Palestine Potash Ltd., London, England.

Fig. 12.1: by courtesy of Borax Consolidated Ltd., London, England.

Fig. 13.1: by courtesy of Tennessee Valley Authority, Knoxville, Tennessee, USA.

Fig. 13.2: from 'Chemie-Ingenieur-Technik' 1956, p. 559/560. Weinheim. Copyright Verlag Chemie GmbH.

Fig. 13.3: by courtesy of Süddeutsche Kalkstickstoff-Werke AG, Trostberg, West-Germany.

Fig. 14.3: by courtesy of The New Jersey Zinc Company, New York, USA.

Fig. 15.1: by courtesy of N.V. Philips Gloeilampenfabrieken, Eindhoven, Holland.

Fig. 15.2: from H. London, *Separation of Isotopes.* London. Copyright 1961 George Newnes Ltd.

Fig. 15.11, 15.19: by courtesy of Union Carbide Corporation, New York, USA.

Fig. 15.13: from 'Electrical Review', 19 Oct. 1956. London. Copyright Iliffe Electrical Publications Ltd.

Fig. 15.16: from 'Industrial & Engineering Chemistry', Jan. 1957. Washington, DC. Copyright The American Chemical Society.

Fig. 15.17: by courtesy of 'The New Scientist', London, England.

Fig. 15.18: from 'Chemical Engineering'. July 1960. New York. Copyright McGraw-Hill Book Company.

Fig. 16.3: from G. F. J. Garlick, *Luminescent Materials*. London. Copyright 1949. Oxford University Press.

Table 16.1 and 16.2: largely based upon Ullmanns *Encyklopädie der technischen Chemie,* Vol. 11, 3rd ed. Munich. Copyright 1960 Urban & Schwarzenberg.

Symbols and Abbreviations

Symbol	Name of unit
*	radioactive
a	are (= 100 m²) (= 119.599 yd²)
A	ampere
Å	angström (= 10^{-8} m) (= 0.003 937 01 μ in)
a.c.	alternating current
at	technical atmosphere
atm	standard atmosphere (= 101.325 kN/m²) (= 14.2233 lbf/in²) (= 14.695q lbf/in²)
b	bar (10^5 N/m²) (= 14.5038 lbf/in²)
Bé	Beaumé's scale
BOD	biochemical oxygen demand
BP	boiling point
BPL	bone phosphate of lime
Btu	British thermal unit (= 1.05506 kJ)
bu	bushel (= 36.368 7 dm³)
c	centi (= 10^{-2})
C	coulomb
°C	degree Celsius (= 5/9 (°F – 32)) (temperature value)
cal	calorie (International table)
cal_{15}	15° C calorie
cd	candela
cg	centigram
Ci	Curie

Symbol	Name of unit
cm	centimetre (0.393 701 in)
c/s	cycles per second
cwt	hundred weight (= 50.8023 kg) (= 112 lb)
d	deci (= 10^{-1})
da	deca (– 10^1)
dag	decagram
d.c.	direct current
DDT	dichlorodiphenyl-trichloroethane
degC	degree Celsius (temperature interval)
degF	degree Fahrenheit (temperature interval)
dg	decigram
dm	decimetre
DTB crystal-lizer	draft-tube baffled crystallizer
dyn	dyne (= 10^{-5}N) (0.224829 x 10^{-5} lbf)
EDTA	ethylenediamine tetra-acetic acid
EDTA-OH	N-hydroxyethyl ethylenediamine triacetic acid
erg	erg (= 10^{-7}W) (= 0.737 562 x 10^{-7} ft lbf)
F	Farad

Symbol	Name of Unit
°F	degree Fahrenheit ($= \frac{9}{5}$ °C $+ 32$) (Temperature value)
fl oz	Fluid ounce ($= 28.4131$ cm³)
ft	foot ($= 0.3048$ m) ($= 12$ in)
ft H₂o	foot of water ($= 2989.07$ N/m²)
g	gram
G	giga ($= 10^9$)
gal	UK gallon ($= 54596$ litres) ($= 4.546$ og dm³) (cf. US gallon $= 3.78541$ dm³)
°GL	degree Gay-Lussac (alcohol content)
gr	grain ($= 64.798\ 9$ mg)
h	hecto ($= 10^2$)
H	henry
ha	hectare ($= 10.000$ m²) ($= 2.471\ 05$ acres)
HEDTA	$=$ EDTA-OH
hp	horsepower ($= 745.700$ W)
HTP	high test hydrogen peroxide
Hz	hertz
in	inch ($= 2.54$ cm)
in Hg	conventional inch of mercury ($= 3386.39$ N/m²) ($= 33.8639$ mb)
in H₂O	conventional inch of water ($= 249.089$ N/m²)
J	joule ($= 0.737562$ ft lbf)
K	kilo ($= 10^3$)
°K	degree kelvin ($=$ °C $+ 273$)
Kcal	kilocalorie
kg	kilogram
kgf	kilogram force ($= 9.806\ 65$ N) ($= 2.204\ 62$ lbf)
kJ	kilojoule
km	kilometre
kp	kilopond ($=$ Kgf)
kW	kilowatt
l	litre ($=$ approx 1 dm³) ($= 0.220\ 0$ gal) ($= 0.24642$ US gal)

Symbol	Name of unit
lb	pound ($= 0.45359237$ kg)
lbf	pound force ($= 4.44822$ N)
lm	lumen
lx	lux ($= 1$ lm per m²)
m	metre ($= 1.09361$ yd)
m	milli ($= 10^{-3}$)
M	mega ($= 10^6$)
mb	millibar ($= 100$ N/m²)
m.g.d.	million gallons per day
mile	mile ($= 1.60934$ km)
ml	millilitre
mm	millimetre
mmHg	conventional millimetre of mercury ($= 133.322$ N/m²) ($= 0.0393701$ in Hg)
mm H₂O	conventional millimetre of water ($= 9.80665$ N/m²)
money	£ ($=$ UK pound unless stated to the contrary) $ ($= US$ dollar unless stated to the contrary)
M.P.	melting point
μ	micro ($= 10^{-6}$)
μb	microbar ($= 0.1$ N/m²)
μ Hg	conventional micron of mercury ($= 0.133322$ N/m²)
μ in	microinch ($= 0.0254\ \mu$m) ($= 0.000001$ in)
μ m	micrometre (micron) (39.3701 m in)
μmHg	micron of mercury ($= 0.133322$ N/m²)
n	nano ($= 10^{-9}$)
N	newton ($= 0.224809$ lbf)
n mile	international nautical mile ($= 1852$ m) (cf. UK nautical mile $= 1853.18$ m)
oz	ounce ($= 28.3495$ g)
Oz apoth	apothecaries' ounce ($= 31.1035$ g) ($=$ oz tr)
ozf	ounceforce ($= 0.278014$ N)

Symbol	Name of unit	Symbol	Name of unit
oz tr	troy ounce (= 31.1035 g) (= oz apoth)	s	second
		sp. gr.	specific gravity
Ω	ohm	St	stokes (= 10^{-4} m²/s) (= 558.001 in²/h)
P	pico (= 10^{-12})		
P	poise (= 0.1 N s/m²) (= 2.08854 x 10^{-3} lbf s/ft²)	t	metric ton (= tonne) (= 1000 kg) (= 0.984207 tons) (= 2204.6 lb)
Pl	poiseville (= N m²/s)	T	tera (= 10^{12})
PS	Pferdestärke (ch)	ton	Imperial ton (= 1016.05 kg)
pH value	measure of acidity/alkalinity		(= 2240 lb) (= long ton)
p.p.m.	parts per million		(*cf.* US ton = 2000 lb = short
p.s.i.	poundweight per square inch (= 6894.76 N/m²) (= 68.9476 mb)		ton)
		tonf	tonforce (= 9964.02 N)
pt	pint (= 0.568261 dm³)	V	volt
pz	pieze (= 10^3 N/m²)		
PVC	polyvinylchloride	W	Watt (= J/s)
		Wb	Weber
q	quintal (= 100 kg)	wt	weight
qt	Imperial quart (1.13652 dm³)	w/w	weight for weight
°R	degree Rankine (°F + 459.67)	yd	yard (= 0.9144 m)
rad	radian		

Table of Chemical Elements

*These elements, like the transuranic elements (see below), have been produced by artificial means and do not occur naturally (at least, not in any appreciable amount).

Element	Symbol	Atomic Number	Atomic Weight	Element	Symbol	Atomic Number	Atomic Weight
Actinium	Ac	89	227	Gallium	Ga	31	69.72
Aluminium	Al	13	26.98	Germanium	Ge	32	72.60
Antimony	Sb	51	121.76	Gold	Au	79	197
Argon	A	18	39.944				
Arsenic	As	33	74.91	Hafnium	Hf	72	178.5
*Astatine	At	85	(210)	Helium	He	2	4.003
				Holmium	Ho	67	164.94
Barium	Ba	56	137.36	Hydrogen	H	1	1.008
Beryllium	Be	4	9.013				
(Glucinium)	(Gl)			Indium	In	49	114.76
Bismuth	Bi	83	209	Iodine	I	53	126.91
Boron	B	5	10.82	Iridium	Ir	77	192.2
Bromine	Br	35	79.916	Iron	Fe	26	55.85
Cadmium	Cd	48	112.41	Krypton	Kr	36	83.80
Caesium	Cs	55	132.91				
Calcium	Ca	20	40.08	Lanthanum	La	57	138.92
Carbon	C	6	12.01	Lead	Pb	82	207.21
Cerium	Ce	58	140.13	Lithium	Li	3	6.940
Chlorine	Cl	17	35.457	Lutetium	Lu	71	174.99
Chromium	Cr	24	52.01	(Cassiopeium)	(Cp)		
Cobalt	Co	27	58.94				
Copper	Cu	29	63.54	Magnesium	Mg	12	24.32
				Manganese	Mn	25	54.94
Dysprosium	Dy	66	162.46	Mercury	Hg	80	200.61
				Molybdenum	Mo	42	95.95
Erbium	Er	68	167.3				
Europium	Eu	63	152	Neodymium	Nd	60	144.27
				Neon	Ne	10	20.183
Fluorine	F	9	19	Nickel	Ni	28	58.7
Francium	Fr	87	223	Niobium	Nb	41	92.91
				(Columbium)	(Cb)		
Gadolinium	Gd	64	156.9	Nitrogen	N	7	14.008

Element	Symbol	Atomic Number	Atomic Weight	Element	Symbol	Atomic Number	Atomic Weight
Osmium	Os	76	190.2	Thallium	Tl	81	204.39
Oxygen	O	8	16	Thorium	Th	90	232.1
				Thulium	Tm	69	168.94
Palladium	Pd	46	106.7	Tin	Sn	50	118.70
Phosphorus	P	15	30.974	Titanium	Ti	22	47.90
Platinum	Pt	78	195.23	Tungsten	W	74	183.92
Polonium	Po	84	210	(Wolfram)			
(Radium F)							
Potassium	K	19	39.100	Uranium	U	92	238.07
Praseodymium	Pr	59	140.92				
*Prometheum	Pm	61	(145)	Vanadium	V	23	50.95
Protactinium	Pa	91	231				
				Xenon	Xe	54	131.3
Radium	Ra	88	226.05				
Radon	Rn	86	222	Ytterbium	Yb	70	173
(Niton)	(Nt)			Yttrium	Y	39	89
Rhenium	Re	75	186.31				
Rhodium	Rh	45	102.91	Zinc	Zn	30	65.38
Rubidium	Rb	37	85.48	Zirconium	Zr	40	91.22
Ruthenium	Ru	44	101.1				
Samarium	Sm	62	150.43				
Scandium	Sc	21	44.96				
Selenium	Se	34	78.96				
Silicon	Si	14	28.09				
Silver	Ag	47	107.873				
Sodium	Na	11	22.997				
Strontium	Sr	38	87.63				
Sulphur	S	16	32.066				
Tantalum	Ta	73	180.88				
*Technetium	Tc	43	(98.91)				
Tellurium	Te	52	127.61				
Terbium	Tb	65	158.9				

TRANSURANIC ELEMENTS

Atomic Number	Element	Symbol
93	Neptunium	Np
94	Plutonium	Pu
95	Americium	Am
96	Curium	Cm
97	Berkelium	Bk
98	Californium	Cf
99	Einsteinium	E
100	Fermium	Fm
101	Mendelevium	Mv
102	Nobellium	No

General references

Although a list of references is included in most chapters, additional information may be found in the following major reference works.

R. E. KIRK and D. F. OTHMER. *Encyclopedia of Chemical Technology,*
New York, Interscience, 1947-1960 (1st edition), 1963-1968 (2nd edition)

Ullmanns Encyklopädie der technischen Chemie
München - Berlin, Urban und Schwarzenberg, 1951-1968 (3rd edition)

P. PASCAL. *Nouveau traité de chemie minérale,*
Paris, Masson et Cie Editeurs, 1956

Comprehensive Inorganic Chemistry. M. C. SNEED, J. L. MAYNARD and R. C. BRACTED,
New York, Van Nostrand, 1958

Gmelins Handbuch der anorganischen Chemie, Gmelins-Institut für anorganische Chemie und Grenzgebiete in der Max-Planck-Gesellschaft zur Förderung der Wissenschaften,
Weinheim, Verlag Chemie, 1946-1968 (8th edition)

J. W. MELLOR. *Comprehensive Treatise on Inorganic and Theoretical Chemistry,*
London, Longmans, 1956-1968

THORPE'S *Dictionary of Applied Chemistry,*
London, Longmans, 1937-1954 (4th edition)

WINNACKER-KUCHLER. *Chemische Technologie,*
Hamburg, Carl Hanser Verlag, 1958-1962

Most of statistical data in this work has been taken from the following references. The most recent editions of these references should be consulted for more up to date statistics. In addition in most countries there is a government bureau of statistics which publishes annual volumes containing data on production, consumption and trade.

Periodicals (annual) of international production and trade statistics:

Statistical Summary of the Mineral Industry. World production, Exports and Imports. London, Mineral resources division of the Institute of geological sciences, overseas division.

Minerals Yearbook. Vol. I Metals and Minerals, Vol. II Fuels. Washington, U.S. Department of the interior. Bureau of mines.

Industrie und Handwerk Fachserie D.
Reihe 8 Industrie des Auslandes
         I Bergbau und Energiewirtschaft
         II Verarbeitende Industrie
Stuttgart, W. Kohlhammer.

Statistical Yearbook of the United Nations.
New York.

Fertilisers. An annual review of world production, consumption and trade. New York, Food and Agricultural organisation of the United Nations.

Les engrais en Europe. Production, consommation, prix et commerce. Paris, Organisation de coopération et de développement économique.

Commodity Yearbook.
New York, Commodity research bureau Inc.

Statistiques.
Paris, Minerais et métaux S.A.

Statistische Zusammenstellungen.
Frankfurt am Main, Metallgesellschaft A.G.

Periodicals (weekly and monthly) including international production and trade statistics:

Engineering and Mining Journal (Feb. number).
New York, McGraw-Hill Inc.

Oil, Paint and Drug Reporter.
New York, Schnell Publishing Company.

Chemical Age (Incorporating *Chemical Trade Journal*).
London, Benn Brothers.

Chemische Industrie.
Düsseldorf, Verlag Handelsblatt G.m.b.H.

Periodicals (annual) of production and trade statistics of the U.K. and U.S.A.:

United Kingdom:

Annual statement of the trade of the United Kingdom. Vol. II and III.
Imports and exports by commodity.
London, Her Majesty's Stationery Office.

Census of production of the Board of trade of the U.K. (a four year periodical).
London, H.M.S.O.

Annual Abstracts of Statistics.
London, H.M.S.O.

Accounts relating to Trade and Navigation of the U.K. (December number).
London, H.M.S.O.

U.S.A.:

Statistical Abstracts of the United States.
U.S. imports of merchandise for consumption.
U.S. exports of domestic merchandise.
U.S. Department of commerce.
Washington, Bureau of the census.

Mineral facts and problems Bulletin 630.
Washington, U.S. Department of the Interior. Bureau of mines.

Chemical and Engineering News (the first September number). An American Chemical
Society publication.
New York, Reinhold Corp.

CHAPTER 1

Some Industrial
Separation Processes

1.1 INTRODUCTION

Although most of the industrial processes described in this book involve chemical reactions of one kind or another, further physical separation processes are usually necessary. It is usually impossible to prepare any material directly in a pure state and free from side reaction products; unconverted starting materials and auxiliary substances such as solvents and catalysts must be removed in order to obtain a pure product.

Separation processes are also indispensable for obtaining any desired material from natural products (animal, vegetable or mineral) since these products usually consist of mixtures of various materials.

It therefore seems desirable to devote this first chapter to a brief consideration of some of the most important of these physical separation processes, with particular reference to the special types of equipment used in industry for carrying them out. The separation processes discussed in this chapter are listed below.

	Separation of	*from*
Crystallization	dissolved solids	liquid solvents
	solids	solid mixtures
Sedimentation and		
decantation	solids	liquids
Filtration	solids	liquids
Centrifuging	solids	liquids
	liquids	liquid mixtures
Drying	solids	liquids

This list comprises only processes for the separation of suspended or dissolved solids from liquids. Details of the separation processes mentioned in the table on the next page will be found in later chapters dealing with the manufacturing of individual substances.

Process	Separation of	from	reference	volume
Refrigeration	gases	gas mixture	Gases in general	I
Diffusion	gases	gas mixture	Separation of uranium isotopes	I
Gas absorption	gases	gas mixture	Production of coal gas	II
			Nitric acid production	I
Adsorption	gases	gas mixture		
	dissolved solids	liquid solvents	Adsorption and	II
	liquids	liquid mixtures	adsorbents	
Distillation	liquids	liquid mixtures	Petroleum refining	IV
Solvent extraction	liquids	liquid mixtures	Oils and fats	VIII
	dissolved solids	liquid solvents	Uranium purification	I
	solids	solid mixtures	Uranium ores	I
Flotation	solids	solid mixtures		
Size reduction and gravitation separation	solids	solid mixtures	Processing of ores	III
Magnetic separation	solids	solid mixtures		
Screening	solids	solid mixtures	Coal production	II
Dust collection	solids	gases	Air	I
Evaporation	dissolved solids	liquid solvents	Saline water conversion	I
			Boiler water	I
			Sodium chloride prod.	I

1.2 CRYSTALLIZATION

1.2.1 Principles of crystallization

Crystallization processes have been in use from ancient times. For example, some 5 000 years ago common salt was prepared by the Chinese, by evaporation and crystallization of brine.

Crystallization provides methods for (a) obtaining pure solids in attractive forms, often from impure solutions and (b) refining solutions by removing the dissolved impurities. Crystals can be formed by cooling a liquid below its melting point or by bringing the solution of a solid in a liquid below its saturation point.

Zone refining (see p. 544) and single-crystal production (see vol. II diamonds etc.) are important applications of crystallization from a melt. However crystallization of a solid from solution in a liquid is the most important process for the separation of dissolved solids (solute) from liquids (solvent) and for the separation and purification of solids.

a. Methods of crystallization from a solution. Crystallization from a solution is based on the equilibrium between a saturated solution and its solute. According to the principle of Le Chatelier and van 't Hoff the equilibrium in a saturated solution will automatically tend to alter so as to undo the effect of any change of concentration or temperature of the saturated solution. Thus a solid can be crystallized from a saturated solution by evaporating the solvent. The effect of evaporation is an increasing concentration of the dissolved product and the equilibrium alters to undo the effect of the increasing concentration by crystallization of a portion of the solid.

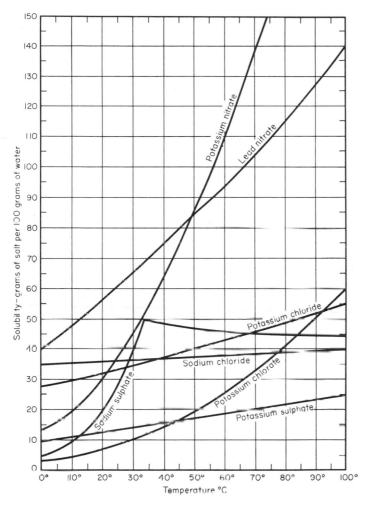

Fig. 1.1 Solubility curves of various inorganic salts.

Usually a solid can also be crystallized from a saturated solution by a change of the temperature. In some solutions crystallization proceeds on heating but usually solutions must be cooled to crystallize some solid. See the solubility curve for sodium sulphate in fig. 1.1. The solids which crystallize from a given saturated solution on cooling are those which develop heat during the crystallization process. The equilibrium system alters with the development of heat to undo the effect of the decreasing temperature.

The solids which crystallize from a given saturated solution on heating it are those which absorb heat during the crystallization process in that solution.

Solids which show little or no thermal effect on crystallization from a saturated solution cannot be crystallized from such a solution by simple heating or cooling. These solids (e.g. common salt in water) must be separated from the solvent by evaporating the solution. The solubility of various salts in water at different temperatures is shown in fig. 1.1.

A solute can also be crystallized from a saturated solution by the addition of a selected substance which reduces the solubility of the solid in the solvent. The added substance may be a solid, or a liquid which is miscible in all proportions with the solvent but in which the solid is rather insoluble. Salting-out gives rise to crystallization and dilution crystallization.

Salts which more or less dissociate into their ions in a solution may be crystallized from that solution by adding another salt which is very soluble in the same solution and which forms a large concentration of one common ion in the solution. In a salt solution the ions form an equilibrium with the portion of the dissolved salt which is not dissociated. If the concentration of one ion of the salt is increased the position of the dissociation equilibrium changes so as to undo the effect of the increasing ion concentration and the concentration of the undissociated salt tends to increase. However the equilibrium between the saturated solution and the solute also alters to undo the effect of the increasing solute concentration by crystallization of the solid. For example addition of sodium chloride 'salts out' ammonium chloride from its solutions.

b. Control of the crystal size. Basically the crystallization processes mentioned above are very simple. Industrial crystallization processes however, are usually complicated by the fact that crystals of predetermined and uniform size are desired, since these should have good flow, handling and storage characteristics in addition to an attractive appearance.

Control of the crystal size needs careful control of the crystallization process which in fact comprises two steps: (*a*) Formation of nuclei and (*b*) growth of the nuclei to the desired size. For example, a hot saturated solution of a solid which is less soluble at lower temperatures does not always crystallize by slow cooling. Often no crystallization occurs until the temperature has dropped considerably and then crystallization proceeds rapidly. Thus the equilibrium does not always change immediately with change in the temperature. This delay is caused by the fact that a number of unorientated molecules (or ions or atoms) in the solution have to form an agglomerate (nucleus) in which the molecules are orientated in a crystal structure. A number of molecules can agglomerate in many orientations but there is only one orientation (the orientation in a crystal structure) in which the agglomerate can direct further molecules to the correct positions so as to take them up more easily and rapidly. The probability of a relatively large number of molecules arranging themselves together in the correct positions is slight. For this reason some time is needed to form primary microcrystals (nuclei), but once

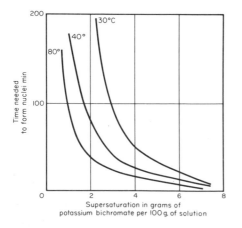

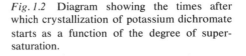

Fig. 1.2 Diagram showing the times after which crystallization of potassium dichromate starts as a function of the degree of supersaturation.

the nuclei have been formed they grow rapidly into macrocrystals and the equilibrium is restored.

The relatively slow formation of nuclei may cause the condition called supersaturation in which the concentration of a dissolved solid in a solution is higher than that corresponding with the equilibrium concentration at the same temperature. The time of nucleation and the number of nuclei formed in a supersaturated solution increase with increasing degree of supersaturation (see fig. 1.2) and thus the number of crystals increases and the dimensions of the crystals decrease.

For this reason large crystals can be obtained by limiting the number of nuclei either by limiting the degree of supersaturation or by limiting the portion of the solution in which excessive supersaturation occurs. The degree of supersaturation can be limited by agitating the solution in one section of the crystallizer (stirring promotes the formation of nuclei) or by adding small crystals of the same solid to the solution (seeding). The seeds act as a substitute for the nuclei and the equilibrium can then follow any change in the conditions (e.g. temperature) immediately.

Crystals of uniform size can be formed when the rate of crystal growth is high enough to allow the original nuclei to grow to the desired size before new nuclei are formed. A slightly supersaturated solution which is seeded usually satisfies these conditions. Crystals of uniform size may also be obtained from a slightly supersaturated solution which passes for a short time through a small zone in which nucleation is promoted followed by a zone which is less favourable for the formation of new nuclei. In the latter zone the crystals are allowed to grow to the desired size.

In the majority of modern crystallizers the crystal size is controlled by seeding with a portion of the crystal slurry already formed. (See for example the production of ammonium sulphate, p. 313.)

c. Habit control. In addition to size control it is also possible to control the general shape (also named the habit) of the crystals by inhibition of growth in one direction or the enhancement of growth in another. Thus the crystal structure remains the same but the crystals become longer or thicker. The general shape of a crystal can sometimes be modified by adjusting the degree of supersaturation and agitation and, in addition, by adding an impurity to the solution. Salts of trivalent ions and many complex dyes and surface-active agents have a habit modifying power. It is believed that they are selectively adsorbed on certain crystal surfaces and thus cause selective crystal growth in one direction. The general shape of crystals can also be modified by crystallization from a solution in another solvent.

d. Separation of solids by crystallization. Various solids usually show different properties in respect of their solubility, rate of nucleation, crystal growth etc. in the same solvent. Hence it is possible to separate solids from each other by dissolving the solid mixture (or a solid containing small quantities of an impurity) in a liquid to such an extent that one solid forms a saturated solution while the other solids do not. The first solid crystallizes partially on cooling, for example, before one of the other solids forms a saturated solution. See for example the separation of sodium carbonate, sodium nitrate, sodium sulphate, potassium chloride and potassium nitrate from naturally occurring salt mixtures (in chapter 10 on Alkali Metal Compounds).

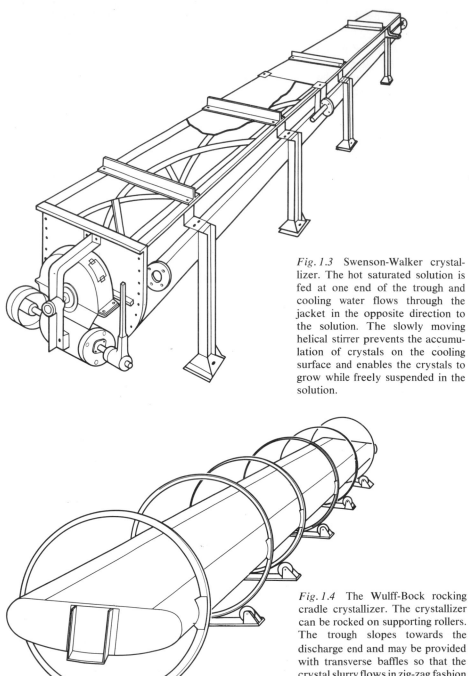

Fig. 1.3 Swenson-Walker crystallizer. The hot saturated solution is fed at one end of the trough and cooling water flows through the jacket in the opposite direction to the solution. The slowly moving helical stirrer prevents the accumulation of crystals on the cooling surface and enables the crystals to grow while freely suspended in the solution.

Fig. 1.4 The Wulff-Bock rocking cradle crystallizer. The crystallizer can be rocked on supporting rollers. The trough slopes towards the discharge end and may be provided with transverse baffles so that the crystal slurry flows in zig-zag fashion along the crystallizer. In this crystallizer corrosion problems are minimised since the crystallizer does not contain moving parts within the crystallization zone.

1.2.2 Classification of crystallizers

Very many types of industrial crystallizers are available (see, for example, literature reference 1.) A common classification is based on the method by which supersaturation is achieved and divides crystallizers into the following groups:

a. Cooling crystallizers operated at atmospheric pressure in which the saturated solution is cooled either by natural convection from the liquid surface to the air or by radiation to a cold liquid contained in a jacket or coil.

b. Evaporator crystallizers in which the solvent of the saturated solution is evaporated by heat supplied from hot air, steam, hot oil or electrical resistance. These crystallizers may be operated at atmospheric or diminished pressure. Examples are the open pan evaporator, the multiple effect evaporation crystallizer (see under sodium chloride, p. 418) and the submerged combustion crystallizer for the production of ferrous sulphate from pickle liquor (see p.586). The prilling tower for the production of ammonium nitrate 'prills' (see p. 319) by spraying is another modification of an evaporation crystallizer.

c. Vacuum crystallizers in which the saturated solution is simultaneously evaporated and cooled by applying a vacuum without cooling or heating. The heat necessary for evaporation comes only from the sensible heat of the feed solution and the heat of crystallization.

d. Salting-out crystallizers in which the solubility of the solute is decreased by adding a suitable liquid or a salt (see p. 337). This type of crystallizer usually comprises a simple agitated vessel provided with a cooling jacket.

e. Reaction crystallizers in which dissolved products are converted chemically into one or more other products one of which is less soluble in the solvent. Reaction and crystallization take place simultaneously. (See, for example, the saturator under ammonium sulphate, p. 314.) The principles of nucleation and crystal growth are important also in this method of crystallization.

Crystallizers may alternatively be classified into batch and continuous crystallizers, agitated and non-agitated crystallizers, circulating magma and circulating liquor crystallizers (in which the crystal slurry and clarified liquor are circulated respectively), crystallizers in which the degree of supersaturation is controlled and those in which it is not controlled and so on. Usually a particular crystallizer belongs to several of the above classes.

Many crystallizers consist basically of a horizontal or vertical vessel or trough (see for example the trough crystallizers in figs. 1.3 and 1.4). They may be provided with cooling or heating coils, a cooling or heating jacket, vacuum pumps, stirring equipment etc. In such crystallizers the degree of supersaturation is controlled by slow or rapid cooling, heating or evaporation in the presence of crystals already produced. Slow cooling for example diminishes the degree of supersaturation and thus few new nuclei (or none) are formed and the crystals which are already present in the crystallizer can grow to large crystals. Rapid cooling promotes the formation of more new nuclei and results in the formation of more small crystals.

Examples of more complicated crystallizers are discussed in detail below.

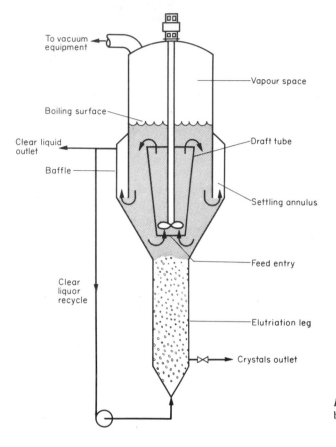

To vacuum equipment

Vapour space

Boiling surface

Clear liquid outlet

Draft tube

Baffle

Settling annulus

Feed entry

Clear liquor recycle

Elutriation leg

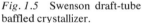

Crystals outlet

Fig. 1.5 Swenson draft-tube baffled crystallizer.

1.2.3 The draft-tube baffled vacuum crystallizer

The draft-tube baffled vacuum crystallizer (DTB crystallizer) consists of a vertical cylindrical vessel having an inner cylindrical baffle which forms an annular settling area (see fig. 1.5). The vessel is provided with a conical bottom section to which an elutriating tube is fitted. A tapered vertical draft-tube is located in the lower section of the vessel and surrounds a slowly moving agitator or propeller which induces a gentle circulating flow of the crystal slurry in the vessel. A vacuum is maintained in the vessel by means of a condenser and a vacuum pump which are fitted to the vapour outlet at the top of the vessel.

A saturated solution is fed into the crystal slurry at the base of the draft-tube and moves upward to the boiling liquor surface. Outside the draft-tube the slurry moves downward. The circular movement in the upper part of the vessel has the twofold advantage that (*a*) it brings growing crystals to the boiling surface where the super-saturation is the most intense and (*b*) it reduces the degree of supersaturation at this surface since the temperature difference between the surface liquid and the liquid below the surface is limited to 0.2-0.5° C. In this way the formation of new nuclei can be minimized.

In the annular space formed by the baffle agitation effects are absent, thus providing a settling zone from which mother liquor is withdrawn. This enables also the removal of excess of nuclei.

The larger crystals formed in the circulating zone move downward into the elutriating tube. The elutriating tube enables size classification of the crystals since the smallest crystals may be moved back to the circulating zone by a flow of saturated solution introduced at the bottom of the elutriation tube. The saturated solution may be a portion of the mother liquor withdrawn from the settling zone.

1.2.4 The Oslo-Kristal crystallizer

The Oslo-Kristal crystallizer is characterized by two features: (a) supersaturation is produced in a recycled stream and (b) the zone in which supersaturation is produced is separated from the zone in which the crystal growth proceeds.

One modification of this type, viz., the Oslo-Kristal vacuum crystallizer with recycled liquor (see fig. 1.6), comprises a vaporizer to which a vertical tube is fitted at the bottom extending downwards into a vessel containing a crystal suspension. The vessel is provided with an overflow from which clear mother liquor is withdrawn and pumped into the vaporizer below the level of the boiling liquor in the vaporizer. The latter is connected with a vacuum pump to maintain a diminished pressure above the

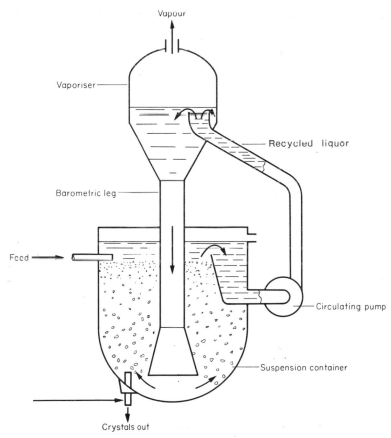

Fig. 1.6 Oslo-Kristal vacuum crystallizer with recycled liquor.

liquid. The supersaturated solution produced in the vaporizer moves downwards through the vertical tube into the crystal suspension in which crystal growth proceeds. The crystal suspension is kept under a higher pressure than the pressure in the vaporizer. The pressure difference is compensated by the difference of levels of the liquors in the vaporizer and in the suspension vessel which communicate by means of the vertical tube which for this reason is named a barometric leg.

The circular movement through the pump, the vaporizer and the barometric leg causes an upward flow of the liquor in the crystal slurry, thus forming a fluidized bed of crystals in which the large crystals collect near the bottom of the vessel and the small crystals at a certain level below the surface layer of clear mother liquor. Size classification of the crystals thus occurs. Fresh saturated solution is fed into the vessel in the clear mother liquor and a slurry of large crystals is withdrawn from the vessel near the bottom.

This type of Oslo-Kristal crystallizer has the great advantage that the crystal sizes are classified to a high degree because crystals withdrawn from any level have the same size. There is however the disadvantage that no small crystals are present at the boiling liquor surface where supersaturation is the most intense. Furthermore the production of large crystals of uniform size, limits the production capacity owing to the fact that the liquor velocity and the mass of crystals in the suspension must be kept low to avoid the transportation of small crystals in the circulation system.

The production capacity and the supersaturation control are considerably better in an Oslo-Kristal vacuum crystallizer with circulating magma. Basically it is the same crystallizer as that described above but owing to the increased liquor velocity the suspension of crystals is circulated through the vaporiser (see fig. 1.7). Owing to the circulation of the suspension, the classification of the crystals in the suspension vessel is less effective. For this reason the circulating magma crystallizer may be provided with an elutriation tube in which the settled crystal slurry is classified with clear saturated liquor introduced at the bottom of the tube.

The Oslo-Kristal vacuum crystallizer (and the draft-tube baffled crystallizer) may be operated at any desired temperature depending on the vacuum applied. If the temperature of the feed solution is higher than the temperature at which the solution would boil under the pressure existing in the vaporizer, the solution cools adiabatically to that boiling temperature. The heat liberated on cooling, and any additional heat of crystallization, cause the evaporation of the solvent.

The choice of the temperature of the saturated feed solution and the pressure in the vaporiser depend on the product to be crystallized. If a solution may be supersaturated to a large degree before nucleation occurs, the temperature in the crystallizer may be much lower than that of the feed solution. However, for the crystallization of saturated solutions which are very sensitive to nucleation the crystallizer must be operated at a temperature which is only slightly lower than the temperature of the feed solution.

The Oslo-Kristal crystallizer is not restricted to vacuum operation. In other modifications the circulating liquor or magma is heated to evaporate liquor or cooled to reduce the solubility of the solid (see the evaporation and cooled Oslo-Kristal crystallizers in the Alkali Metals chapter figs. 10.10 and 10.20). The Oslo-Kristal crystallizer may also be used as a reaction crystallizer. In this modification the feed solutions are introduced at separate places in the recirculating liquor or magma.

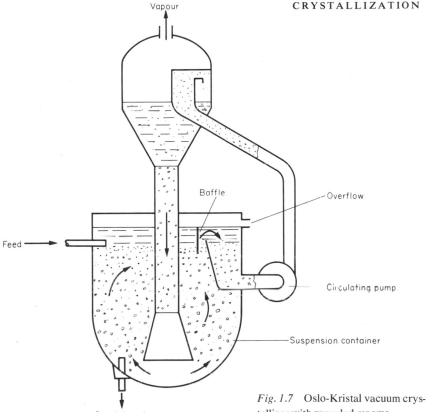

Fig. 1.7 Oslo-Kristal vacuum crystallizer with recycled magma.

Fig. 1.8 Four-stage Swenson D T B crystallizer for potash production installed at the Dead Sea Works Ltd., Sodom, Israel.

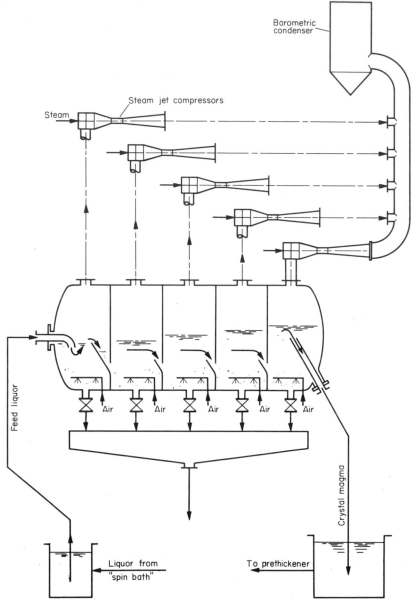

Fig. 1.9 Diagram of a multi-stage vacuum crystallizer.

1.2.5 Multi-stage crystallizer

If a very large difference is desired between the temperatures of feed solution and the crystal slurry the temperature of the feed solution may be decreased in stages in a multi-stage installation comprising two or more crystallizers of which the second is fed with the mother liquor of the first and so on. DTB crystallizers or Oslo-Kristal vacuum crystallizers may be used for this purpose (see fig. 1.8).

Such a crystallization process may also be performed in a so-called multi-stage or low temperature vacuum crystallizer which comprises a horizontal cylindrical vessel divided into a number of chambers by means of vertical partitions. The pressure decreases from chamber to chamber and the pressure in each chamber is controlled by means of steam jet pumps (see figs. 1.9 and 1.10).

The boiling crystal suspension from the surface level of each chamber is transported to the bottom of the following chamber in which the temperature is slightly lower by about 1-5° C. The temperature may drop from about 80° C for the feed solution to about 0° C and even − 10° C depending on the number of chambers or multi-stage crystallizers operated in series. The control of supersaturation is based on the presence of suspended crystals in the liquor.

The crystals are kept in suspension by the upward flow of liquor in each chamber and by the agitation provided by atmospheric air which is allowed to bubble through pipes in the bottom of each chamber. The largest crystals are collected from the bottom of each chamber.

The multi-stage vacuum crystallizer is widely used for the crystallization of sodium sulphate (see also fig. 10.21 in chapter 10 Alkali Metals) and ferrous sulphate from pickle liquor.

1.2.6 The choice of a crystallizer

The temperature-solubility relationship between the required product and the solvent is the first important factor in the choice of a crystallizer, since cooling crystal-

Fig. 1.10 A multi-stage vacuum crystallizer for the production of ferrous sulphate from pickle liquor.

lizers can be used only for products which deposit considerable quantities of crystals on cooling, i.e., those having a steep solubility curve.

Evaporator crystallizers and cooling crystallizers are less favourable for the crystallization of products which tend to form a hard crust of crystals on the heating or cooling surfaces. Vacuum crystallizers have no heat-exchange surface and do not suffer from this scaling problem, but the use of vacuum crystallizers is limited to solutions which do not show a high boiling-point elevation and they are less favourable for very dense crystal slurries.

Another factor of importance for the choice is the available floor area. Many cooling crystallizers and discontinuous evaporating crystallizers (such as evaporating pans) need much more floor space than the draft-tube baffled and Oslo-Kristal crystallizers for the same quantity of product.

The factors mentioned above are important for choosing the class of crystallizer. The choice of a specific unit belonging to any class involves other factors, e.g. the initial and operating costs, the required production capacity, the need for corrosion resistance, the price of the product and the desired habit and size of the crystals. DTB crystallizers and Oslo-Kristal crystallizers with circulating magma are particularly suitable for the production of large crystals; this may be difficult owing to rapid nucleation in slightly supersaturated solutions.

1.3 SEDIMENTATION AND DECANTATION

1.3.1 Principles of sedimentation

The term sedimentation generally means the gravitational settling of solid particles which are suspended in a liquid.

There are remarkable differences in the sedimentation characteristics of various suspensions. These differences are caused mainly by differences in the specific gravity of the solids, the size and structure of the particles and the concentration of the solid in the suspension.

The effect of the concentration is shown in fig. 1.11. At higher concentrations the settling of any particle is hindered by the surrounding particles and for this reason a concentrated suspension settles more slowly than a dilute suspension.

Relatively heavy particles settle rapidly, whereas voluminous, light or finely divided particles need a settling time up to several days. Very slow settling can be overcome by adding a soluble salt which forms a rather voluminous precipitate under the conditions in the liquid. (For coprecipitation or flocculation see clarification of water, p. 126).

Extremely small particles (between 0.0001 and 0.000001 mm in mean diameter) do not settle since the effect of gravity is balanced or over-balanced by the action of the moving molecules of the liquid. Such suspensions are named *colloids*. The particles in a colloid do not agglomerate to larger particles since they are surrounded by a protecting layer adsorbed on their surface. The layer consists either of liquid molecules (lyophilic colloids) or of positive or negative ions (lyophobic colloids). The second type of colloid is not very stable. The solid can be precipitated by adding small amounts of a salt which forms ions in the liquid; neutralization of the protecting ion layer is followed by agglomeration. The first type of colloid is very stable; sometimes the protecting liquid layer can be destroyed by adding large amounts of an ion forming salt to the liquid.

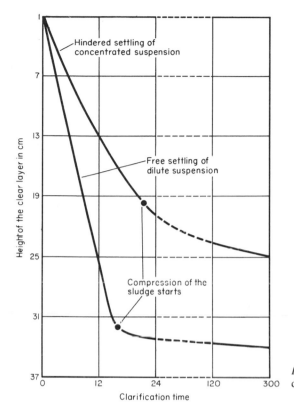

Fig. 1.11 Settling characteristic of a dilute and a concentrated suspension.

A large content of colloidal matter is usually present in solids which must be settled in clay washing processes and water treatment.

A group of liquid-solid systems which causes much trouble in sedimentation processes comprises the gels. If particles form a very loose and porous structure they can include much of the liquid in their pores and between the molecules. In these cases they can form a gel. For example gelatine, starch, rubber, soaps and pectin are materials which form gels in water. Gels are usually not separated from liquids by sedimentation.

Sedimentation includes the processes of clarification and thickening. The term clarification is used if the primary object is to produce a clear liquor from a dilute suspension; the corresponding equipment is named a clarifier. The term thickening is used if the recovery of the solids which have settled from a relatively concentrated suspension is the main object; the corresponding equipment is named a thickener.

Clarification and thickening processes and corresponding equipments differ only in detail.

Typical clarification operations in industry include the clarification of domestic and waste water (see ch. 4) and the removal of mud from hot sugar solutions (see vol. VII). Since recovery of the solid is not important in clarification, flocculants are often used to accelerate the settling of more or less colloidal particles. In thickening processes the use of flocculants is not common because they may lead to the introduction of impurities into the solid.

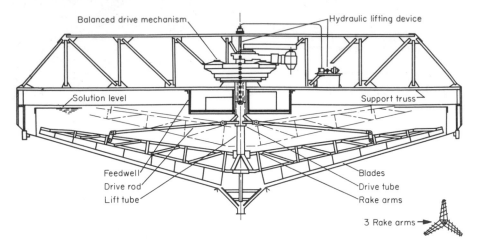

Fig. 1.12 Dorr thickener equipped with an automatic hydraulic lifting device to protect the moving parts against sudden overloads.

Very slow thickening velocities must be prevented by limiting the formation of colloidal particles and gels in the process in which the solid is produced.

Sedimentation is the simplest and cheapest method for the separation of solids from liquids. For this reason thickeners and clarifiers are often installed before a filtering or centrifuging operation so as to remove the bulk of the solid from the liquid before filtering or centrifuging it.

Another important operation in which thickeners are used is continuous counter-current decantation which is the name applied to a continuous process for washing finely divided solids by means of a series of thickeners. The solid is allowed to settle in the first thickener and withdrawn to disperse it in the second thickener and so on. The liquid flows through the system in the opposite direction.

1.3.2 Thickeners

Thickeners may be subdivided into mechanical and non-mechanical thickeners comprising thickeners with and without mechanical means to remove the settled sludge.

Examples of non-mechanical thickeners are the settling tank and the settling cone. The settling tank usually comprises a rectangular tank which is operated discontinuously. After filling and allowing time for settling, the clear liquid is removed by means of a siphon the level of which can be varied. After removal of the liquid the solid may be pumped out and the tank can be used again. The settling cone, which is usually operated continuously, consists of an inverted conical tank. The feed slurry is introduced through a submerged central well, clear liquid is removed at the top by means of a peripheral overflow trough and the solid settles in the apex of the cone from which it is removed by means of a discharge valve.

The most important thickeners are the continuous mechanical thickeners which are particularly important for the sedimentation of very large quantities of finely divided solids. A great number of varied types based on the same principle are available.

Continuous mechanical thickeners consist of a shallow cylindrical tank having a centrally located feed well, a peripheral overflow-collection trough, a central sludge

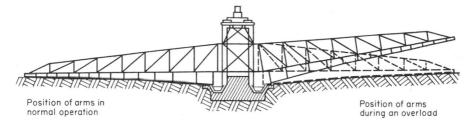

Position of arms in
normal operation

Position of arms
during an overload

Fig. 1.13 Hinged-arm construction of a Dorr thickener.

discharge outlet and a slowly rotating central shaft provided with radial arms and blades which move the settled sludge to the central sludge discharge outlet.

Fig. 1.12 is a diagram of a continuous mechanical thickener the central shaft of which, with its arms and blades, is protected against overloads by means of an automatic hydraulic lifting device. Another method to protect the thickener against overloads is the hinged arm construction shown in fig. 1.13. The arms are hinged at the centre so that they will rise when overloaded and return to the normal position when the load is reduced.

Thickeners of the types mentioned above and numerous varieties have been built

Fig. 1.14 A continuous mechanical thickener.

with diameters up to about 350 feet. An enormous thickener used in the treatment of ores is shown in fig. 1.14.

In addition to the single-compartment thickeners mentioned above, multicompartment thickeners have been designed. These consist of two or more superimposed settling compartments, each of which is provided with a set of raking arms and blades. Multicompartment thickeners are used if a large settling area on a small floor area is required. Similar multicompartment equipment is used for continuous countercurrent decantation.

Sedimentation tanks are usually made of mild steel, concrete or wood and may be lined with rubber or lead when the suspensions are corrosive.

1.4 FILTRATION

1.4.1 Principles of filtration

Filtration means the separation of solids from a liquid by passing the liquid through a porous medium which retains the solids on its surface in the form of a cake.

The porous medium (filter) may be a woven or non-woven fabric made of fibres or threads from materials such as cotton, wool, synthetic polymers, metals, glass and asbestos. Porous blocks made from graphite, silica, aloxite or ceramics and granular beds of sand or carbon are also widely used.

The diameters of the holes and pores in the filter must be small enough to prevent the passage of the larger solid particles. These diameters may, however, be larger than the diameters of the smallest solid particles in the liquid, since the filtering effect is based not only on the porosity of the filter but also on the porosity of the layer of solid (cake) collected on and in the filter. Smaller solid particles are retained in the holes and pores of the filter and thus the porosity of the filter is reduced and when a cake of solid has formed it acts as the filtering medium especially if the pores in the cake are smaller than those of the filter.

Thus the filtration velocity primarily decreases with the decreasing porosity of the filter. When a cake has ultimately been formed the filter resistance increases in proportion to the thickness of the cake (at constant porosity) and thus the filtration velocity decreases in inverse proportion to the increasing thickness of the cake (see line a in fig. 1.15). To avoid too low filtration velocities the cake must be removed from the filter periodically.

Suspensions which form compressible sludges, e.g. the precipitated metal hydroxide sludges and organic slimes, show other filtration characteristics since the pressure of the superposing layer may deform the particles plastically so as to fill the voids between the particles in the lower part of the cake. In this way the filter resistance increases much more than proportionally to the thickness of the cake. The result is a very low porosity and thus a very low filtration velocity (see curve b in fig. 1.15).

Low filtration velocities may also be caused by dilute suspensions of finely divided particles since particles of a size which can penetrate into the pores of the filters can plug up many pores almost completely. (In concentrated suspensions, too many small particles are forced towards a pore at the same time, but they can not easily enter the pore since they hinder each other.)

If the production of a clear liquid is the primary object of the filtration process, the

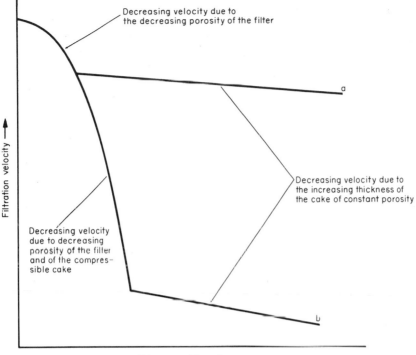

Decreasing velocity due to the decreasing porosity of the filter

a

Decreasing velocity due to the increasing thickness of the cake of constant porosity

Decreasing velocity due to decreasing porosity of the filter and of the compressible cake

b

Filtration velocity ⟶

Thickness of the cake ⟶

Fig. 1.15 Filtration velocity as a function of the thickness of the filter cake: a. for easily filtrable suspensions; b. for suspension of compressible particles and some dilute suspensions of finely divided particles.

filtration velocity can be accelerated by means of filter aids which prevent clogging of the filter or the cake. A filter aid should consist of relatively large particles which have a low specific gravity to keep them in suspension with the solid to be filtered.

The particles of a filter aid should also be relatively non-compressible and preferably porous so as to form a porous cake. The commonest and most widely used filter aid is diatomaceous earth. It is used for example in the filtration of sugar solutions, fruit juice beverages, vegetable oils and petroleum. Other suitable filter aids are paper pulp, fuller's earth, charcoal, activated carbon, asbestos, sawdust, magnesia and gypsum. Sometimes the flocculants, which are also used in sedimentation processes, may be used to agglomerate finely divided non-compressible particles.

A quite different problem is caused by colloids, since the particles of a colloid are too small to be collected on a normal filter. The solid particles of a colloid may be filtered by forcing the liquid through a membrane of a more or less porous synthetic polymer which retains the solid particles, but usually a colloid is precipitated by addition of a salt before filtration (see under sedimentation).

Filtration equipment is commonly classified according to its driving force into gravity filters, pressure filters, vacuum filters and centrifugal filters. Some examples of these groups are discussed below. The centrifugal filters are included under centrifuging.

1.4.2 Gravity filters

The simplest gravity filter comprises basically a tank with a discharge aperture in the bottom and a horizontal filter medium fitted in the tank near the bottom. The feed suspension is introduced above the filter medium and the clear liquid flows through the filter medium by gravity and is collected from the discharge aperture.

By far the largest number of large-scale gravity filters are equipped with a bed of sand as the filter medium to collect the solid, and are used in water clarification (see p. 125). The filter cake is removed periodically by passing water through the filter in the reverse direction (back-washing).

A small size modification of this gravity filter is the *Nutsche filter*. This filter may be operated by gravity just like the large scale units, but the filtration velocity is usually increased either by applying pressure above the filter layer or by applying a vacuum under the filter layer. These filters which are used for various small scale filtration processes are also operated discontinuously since the cake must periodically be removed from the filter.

A continuously operated gravity filter is the *band filter* in which the filter medium has the form of an endless conveyor band. The suspension is fed onto one end of the band and the filtrate drains through the band while travelling to the other end of the filter equipment from which the cake is discharged. Since the bulk of the liquid must be removed rapidly, only a thin cake or a cake of coarse particles can be allowed to form on a band filter. The filtration process is usually combined with a drying operation on the same band, e.g. by passing the band through a zone in which hot air is blown onto the cake. The band filter is widely used in the production of paper from suspensions of paper fibres (see vol. VI).

1.4.3 Pressure filters

The plate-and-frame filter press and the enclosed pressure filter are the commonest types of pressure filters.

A *plate-and-frame filter press* consists of a series of vertical plates which are ribbed and grooved on both faces and a series of hollow frames. The plates are covered with a filter cloth at both sides and a frame is set on one side of the plate which is covered with the filter. A series of these units is clamped together to form a multicell equipment of alternating plates and frames (see figs. 1.16 and 1.17). The plates and frames are provided with holes which form together one or more channels through which the feed suspension can be pressed into the chambers formed by the frames between the filter cloths, and through which clear liquid can be removed from the channels formed by the grooves of the plates at the opposite sides of the filter cloths.

When a filter cake has been formed on each filter cloth, wash liquid is forced into the frames between the cakes in the same manner as the feed suspension.

In another modification of the filter press it is also possible to feed the filter press with suspension until the frames are completely filled with filter cake. Washing of the cake is then performed by introducing wash liquid under pressure through the grooves of each alternate plate. This wash liquid passes through the filter cloth, the cake and the opposite filter cloth at each side of said plates and leaves the filter press through the grooves of the surrounding plates (see fig. 1.18). The cake is discharged from the filter press by dismounting it.

The *enclosed pressure filter* (also named batch-leaf filter) also comprises grooved

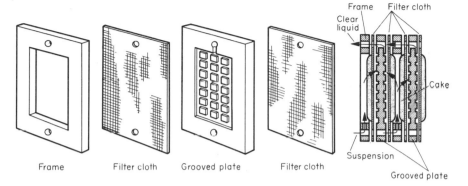

Fig. 1.16 Simplified layout of a set of elements of which several are clamped together to form a plate-and-frame filterpress.

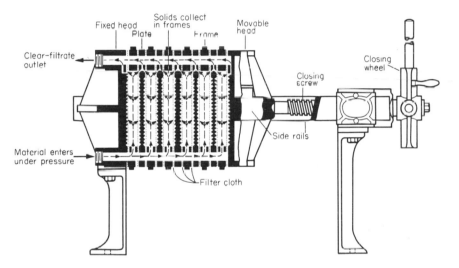

Fig. 1.17 Sectional drawing of a fully assembled filterpress.

plates (or other channelled or porous sheets) which are covered with a filter cloth at both sides forming filter leaves. However these leaves are not clamped together with frames but are immersed in the suspension which is kept in a vessel under a relatively high pressure.

Thus the enclosed pressure filter is similar to the plate-and-frame filter in that (*a*) a cake is deposited on each side of the leaves and (*b*) the clear liquid passes through the filter cloths into the grooves of the plates. The grooves of the plates communicate with the atmosphere by means of pipes so as to remove the clear liquid (see the diagram of the intermittent vacuum filter in fig. 1.19). The pipe system may also be formed by a hollow horizontal shaft on which a number of vertical leaves are mounted and which may rotate the leaves around their axis in the suspension as in the disc-type rotary vacuum filter discussed below.

The filter cake collected on the leaves is washed by lifting the leaves out of the suspension and immersing them in a pressure vessel filled with the wash liquid. Washing

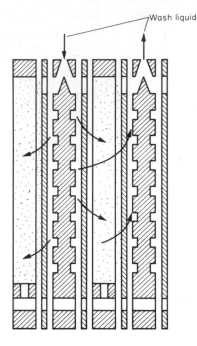

Fig. 1.18 Simplified section of a filterpress in which the frames are completely filled with a cake. The arrows show the flow direction of the wash liquid during washing of the cake.

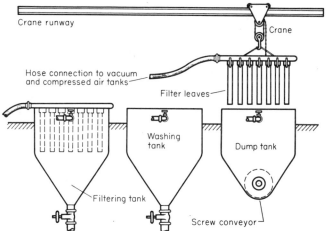

Fig. 1.19 Simplified drawing of the Moore intermittent vacuum filter.

may also be performed in a wash liquid at atmospheric pressure by applying vacuum on the liquid discharge pipe.

The intermittent operation is a disadvantage in all pressure filters. For this reason pressure filters are mainly used for relatively expensive products.

1.4.4 Vacuum filters

The construction of the *intermittent vacuum filter* is basically similar to the enclosed pressure filter. It differs in that (*a*) a vacuum is applied on the clear liquid outlet during the filtration cycle, and (*b*) no pressure is applied on the suspension to be filtered.

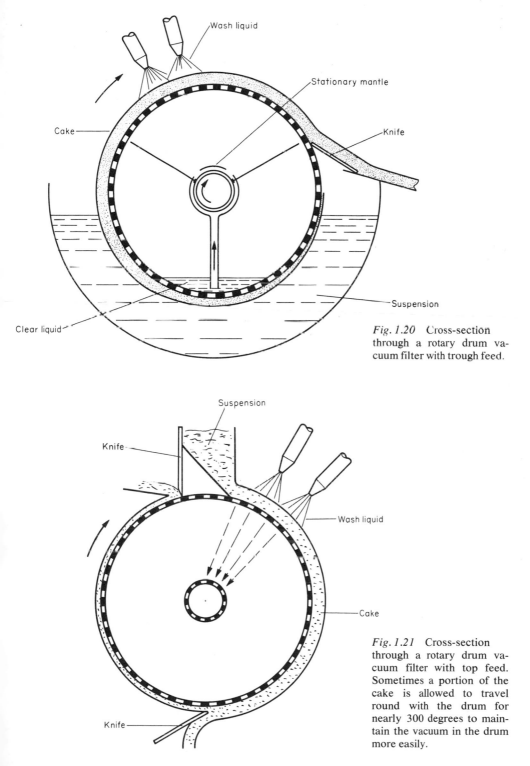

Fig. 1.20 Cross-section through a rotary drum vacuum filter with trough feed.

Fig. 1.21 Cross-section through a rotary drum vacuum filter with top feed. Sometimes a portion of the cake is allowed to travel round with the drum for nearly 300 degrees to maintain the vacuum in the drum more easily.

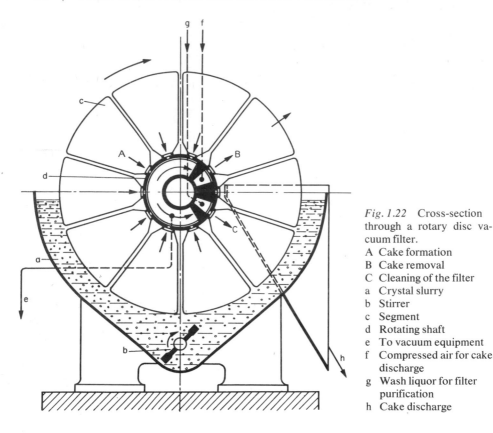

Fig. 1.22 Cross-section through a rotary disc vacuum filter.
A Cake formation
B Cake removal
C Cleaning of the filter
a Crystal slurry
b Stirrer
c Segment
d Rotating shaft
e To vacuum equipment
f Compressed air for cake discharge
g Wash liquor for filter purification
h Cake discharge

To wash the filter cake the leaves may be lifted out of the suspension and immersed in a washing tank (as in the Moore filter in fig. 1.19), or the suspension may be pumped out to enable filling of the same vessel with wash liquid (as in the Butters filter).

The *rotary drum vacuum filter* consists essentially of a horizontal cylindrical drum provided with a central horizontal shaft which allows rotation of the drum around its axis. The drum is perforated and may itself be the filter medium; alternatively it may be coated with a suitable filter cloth. The suspension is fed to the outside of the drum and is separated into a cake on the drum surface and a clear liquor which passes through the filter medium into the drum as a consequence of the vacuum which is maintained in the drum.

In one modification of the rotary drum vacuum filter the drum is partly immersed in the suspension to be filtered (trough feed) and the central shaft is surrounded with a stationary mantle which is provided with hollow side arms extending downwards into the clear liquid collected in the drum. In this way the liquid can be removed by means of a vacuum equipment connected to the mantle (see fig. 1.20). Washing is performed by spraying wash liquid on the ascending cake.

The washed cake is removed from the descending section of the drum by means of a knife. The stationary mantle is usually also provided with two longitudinal partitions which extend to the inner wall of the drum to enable the separate removal of clear liquid and wash liquid.

Fig. 1.23　A rotary disc vacuum filter.

Fig. 1.24　The Dorr-Oliver horizontal rotary filter.

A trough feed rotary drum filter has the disadvantage that it cannot retain very coarse particles on its surface when the drum travels upwards out of the suspension. For this purpose the top feed rotary drum filter is more suitable. This filter differs from the trough feed design in that the suspension is supplied through a hopper to the descending surface of the drum (fig. 1.21).

In still another modification of the rotary drum filter, the drum is divided into a relatively large number of segments which connect longitudinal sections of the filtering surface with the vacuum equipment (see the multicompartment rotary drum vacuum filter in fig. 9.30 of the Alkali Metals chapter).

The rotary disc vacuum filter is basically the same as the rotary drum vacuum filter with trough feed. It differs in that the drum is divided into a number of vertical hollow discs to increase the filter surface. Just like the multicompartment rotary drum filter each disc is divided into a number of segments (see figs. 1.22 and 1.23). Owing to the vertical position of the cake it is more difficult to keep the cake on the filter surface.

A quite different vacuum filter is the *horizontal rotary filter* (shown in fig. 1.24) in which a number of filters form a horizontal circular plane which rotates around its vertical axis. The clear liquid is sucked through the filters by applying a vacuum under a certain number of the filters. The cake is removed by means of a knife and a screw conveyor. A modification of this filter from which the cake is removed by turning the filter plates is shown in fig. 9.30 (see wet-process phosphoric acid, p. 373).

Horizontal rotary filters are especially used for coarse materials (over 3 mm) which cannot be retained on the surface of a rotary disc or drum filter.

Vacuum filters are the commonest filters for the filtration of heavy chemicals in the mining and chemical industries.

1.5 CENTRIFUGING

1.5.1 Principles of centrifuging

Centrifuging is the mechanical separation of the components of a mixture by subjecting the mixture to centrifugal forces. Industrial centrifuging equipment is usually intended to separate emulsified immiscible liquids and insoluble solids from a liquid medium. In a centrifuging process such a mixture is usually subjected to centrifugal forces by rotating a cylindrical vessel containing the mixture around its axis. Since the components of the moving mixture try to follow a rectilinear path they move away from the axis of rotation of the vessel as far as possible.

Since the component with the largest specific gravity is subjected to the largest centrifugal forces, the mixture is separated into concentric layers of which the outermost layer is formed by the component having the largest specific gravity. This process is named centrifugal sedimentation because of the analogy with a sedimentation process in which the components of a suspension or emulsion try to settle into layers; the lowest layer being formed by the component having the largest specific gravity.

Liquid solid mixtures may also be separated in a rotating vessel the cylindrical wall of which is perforated. The separation is then based on the fact that the liquid can leave the vessel through the perforations but the solid must form a cake on the perforated wall if it cannot pass through the perforations (centrifugal filtration).

Centrifugal forces have the same effect as gravitational forces on any matter but they differ in that they can be varied by changes in the speed of rotation of the matter by varying either the speed of rotation of the vessel or its dimensions. In industrial centrifuges the effect of centrifugal forces may reach 20000 times the effect of gravitational forces. For this reason centrifugal processes usually proceed much more rapidly than filtration or sedimentation processes and thus very small solid particles, gel-like and compressible sludges and emulsions can be separated more easily in centrifugal equipment.

Centrifugal equipment is usually divided into filtering centrifuges and sedimentation centrifuges. Some modifications of each group are discussed below.

1.5.2 Filtering centrifuges

Industrial filtering centrifuges or centrifugal filters are designed to separate solids from a liquid medium.

The *perforate-wall basket centrifuge* is the simplest form of centrifugal filter. It comprises basically a cylindrical vessel of which the cylindrical wall is perforated and, if necessary, lined with a suitable filter medium. The cylinder rotates around its axis and the feed slurry, introduced into the cylinder, is separated into a cake on the inner wall of the cylinder and a clear liquid which is collected outside the cylinder. The speed of rotation may vary from 600 rev/min for a cylinder of 60-inch diameter to 2 100 rev/min for a cylinder of 12-inch diameter.

In one modification of this centrifuge the cylinder rotates around its horizontal axis and the introduction of the feed slurry is stopped periodically to introduce wash liquid and to discharge the cake with a knife while the cylinder rotates at full speed (see the horizontal automatic short-cycle basket filtering centrifuge in fig. 9.9, p. 315 under ammonium sulphate. Modified types of basket centrifuges with vertical cylinders and centrifuges which must be stopped to enable the solid to be removed, are also used. (Compare the common centrifuge used in the household for laundry drying.)

Continuous cylindrical screen centrifuges are basically similar to the basket centrifuges. They differ in that the suspension is fed continuously at one end of the rotating cylinder and the cake is forced to the other end. While travelling the length of the cylinder the cake is washed by means of a spray of wash liquid. In one modification of this continuous type of centrifuge the cake is forced to the further end of the cylinder by means of a reciprocating piston (see fig. 9.10 under ammonium sulphate p 316). The diameter of the cylinder in continuous cylindrical screen centrifuges may vary from 10 to 50 inches and the equipment is operated at speeds up to 2 600 rev/min.

Another cake discharge equipment is used in the *conical screen conveyor discharge centrifuge*. The perforated vessel is more or less conical; it has a large end diameter, between 20 and 40 inches, and is operated at speeds up to 2 600 rev/min. The cake is scraped from the inner wall by means of a helical conveyor which rotates slightly more rapidly than the conical vessel. The feed suspension is introduced at the small end of the cone and the solids are discharged from the large end. Washing is performed by introducing wash liquid through the hollow shaft of the helical conveyor (see fig. 1.25).

1.5.3 Sedimentation centrifuges

The *imperforate-wall basket centrifuge* is used for the collection of fine solids which are difficult to collect on a filter medium. The construction differs from the perforate-wall basket centrifuges only in that the cylindrical wall of the rotating vessel is not perforated. The liquid is removed continuously by means of an overflow and the solid is removed periodically at low rotational speed by means of a skimmer.

The *continuous imperforate bowl conveyor discharge centrifuge* is used for the separation of fine or coarse solids from a liquid medium. This centrifuge comprises basically a horizontal cylindrical vessel having a diameter between 6 and 50 inches and provided with a central helical screw which has a slightly higher speed of rotation than the cylinder which rotates at 8 500-1 600 rev/min depending on the diameter. The

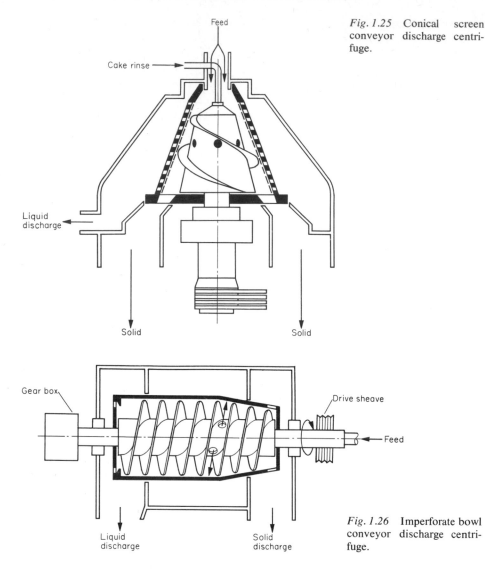

Fig. 1.25 Conical screen conveyor discharge centrifuge.

Fig. 1.26 Imperforate bowl conveyor discharge centrifuge.

feed suspension is introduced through the hollow screw (see fig. 1.26) and the cake which is collected on the inner wall of the cylinder is continuously moved to discharge apertures at one end of the cylinder. The clear liquid leaves the rotating cylinder at the other end through overflow apertures. The cake discharge end of the cylinder and the screw are more or less conical which makes it possible to locate the cake discharge apertures closer to the axis of rotation than those of the liquid, otherwise at least a part of the liquid would leave the cylinder together with the cake.

Solids discharged from a sedimentation centrifuge are not as dry as solids obtained from filtering centrifuges and efficient washing cannot be performed in the centrifuge. However the sedimentation centrifuges have the great advantage that they can separate very finely divided particles and gel-like particles from a liquid which can only be separated with difficulty or not at all in a filtering centrifuge. Owing to the facts that in general smaller particles are handled in it and that any cake remains in contact with the liquid, sedimentation centrifuges must usually be rotated at higher speeds than filtering centrifuges to produce a compact cake.

Liquid cyclones or hydrocyclones are used for the separation of a suspension into a more concentrated suspension and a clear liquid. The rotation of the suspension is not produced by rotating a cylindrical vessel, but by introducing the suspension radially at relatively high velocity into a stationary cylinder. The solid tends to concentrate near the wall and moves in a helical path to the conical bottom of the cyclone and the clear liquid moves upwards in the axis of the cyclone.

Thus the two fractions can be discharged separately. The construction and operation of the liquid cyclone is basically similar to that of a common cyclone for the separation of dust from gases. (See fig. 3.7, chapter 3.) Large diameter liquid cyclones are often provided with a number of superposed horizontal discs which rotate on the axis of the cyclone to accelerate the rotation velocity of the suspension without the risk of vertical turbulent flows which would decrease the separation efficiency.

Centrifuges which are suitable for the separation of emulsions are the *tubular*

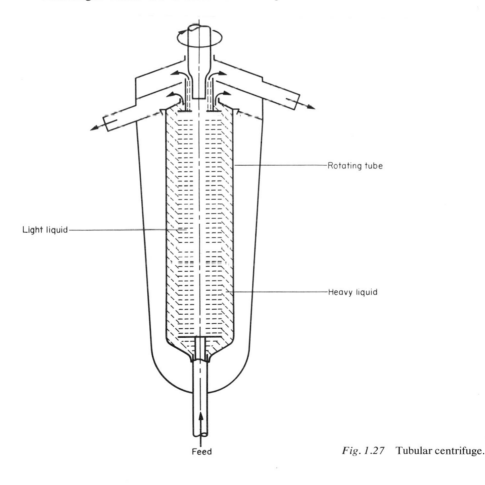

Rotating tube

Light liquid

Heavy liquid

Feed

Fig. 1.27 Tubular centrifuge.

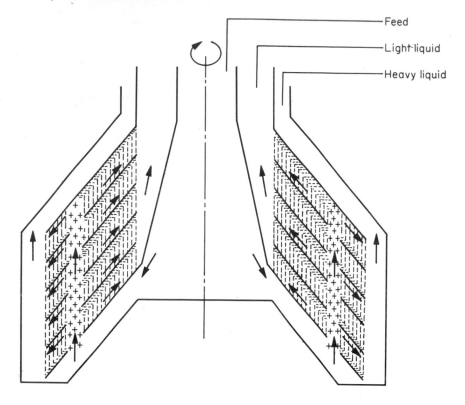

Fig. 1.28 Schematic diagram of a disc centrifuge for the separation of the constituents of an emulsion.

centrifuge and the *disc centrifuge*. Slightly modified designs of these types of centrifuges are used for the separation of small quantities of finely divided solids from large quantities of liquid.

The *tubular centrifuge* is shown in fig. 1.27. It comprises a long vertical tube having a diameter of 4 to 5 inches. The tube rotates around its axis at up to 15000 rev/min producing centrifugal forces up to 13000 times gravitational forces. The emulsion to be separated is introduced at the bottom and separated into two concentric liquid layers which flow upwards. When the two layers leave the tube at the top they are flung away radially by the centrifugal forces. The light liquid is flung away at a higher level than the heavy liquid owing to the presence of a short tube (with a smaller diameter) which is located concentrically to the long tube at the top.

In a *disc centrifuge* a number of conical discs are fitted into a rotating vessel (see fig. 1.28). The discs are provided with a series of passages at certain distances from the axis of rotation. The feed emulsion is introduced into the centrifuge through a hollow shaft and moves into the spaces between the discs through these passages. The heavier liquid moves outwards from the feed passages to the edge of the discs and the lighter one moves inwards. The two separated liquids are discharged by means of separate channels. The speed of rotation of industrial disc centrifuges ranges from 4000 to 8000 rev/min.

1.6 DRYING OF SOLIDS

1.6.1 Introduction

Drying is the removal of a liquid from a material by evaporating the liquid. Usually the liquid to be removed is water but it may be another volatile liquid.

Wet solids can be dried by accelerating the evaporation of the liquid either by applying a vacuum or by applying heat. Heat may be applied by contacting the material with hot air or another hot gas (indirect dryers) or by contacting with a hot surface, e.g. a metallic wall heated by means of steam, fuels etc. (in indirect dryers). In the latter type the drying time can be reduced by blowing air over the solids or by applying a vacuum, thus removing vapour over the solids. Solids can also be dried by means of radiant heat, e.g. in infrared dryers. An infrared dryer often consists of a tunnel provided with infrared incandescent lamps. The wet solid is passed through the tunnel by means of a conveyor.

In many cases the removal of a liquid from a solid is a simple process although care must be taken that the drying temperature is so chosen as to be below the temperature at which the solid decomposes.

In other cases drying is complicated by the fact that the solid material is more or less hygroscopic. A hygroscopic material is one which retains a certain percentage of water under given conditions of temperature and humidity of the ambient air. This retained water is in equilibrium with the water in the air. The equilibrium moisture may be held in the form of a solid solution, in or on the solid by adsorption in fine capillaries, or as a film on the solid particles. (For example calcium chloride and lithium chloride are hygroscopic substances.)

This equilibrium moisture can only be removed by heating at temperatures considerably above the boiling point of the liquid. Dried hygroscopic solids must be kept in carefully closed containers to avoid the adsorption of moisture from the air.

Care must also be taken in drying solids which contain chemically combined water (water of hydration). In these cases it is necessary to dry under closely controlled conditions of temperature and humidity so as to remove all the more or less free water but to retain all, or a desired quantity, of water of hydration (e.g. sodium sulphate and copper sulphate).

1.6.2 Direct dryers

The *direct rotary dryer* is one of the most extensively used dryers in the chemical industry, especially for crystals, granules, flakes, powders etc. A rotary dryer consists basically of a cylinder slightly inclined to the horizontal and rotating on bearings (see fig. 1.29). The length of the cylinder usually ranges from four to ten times its diameter which can vary from 1 to 10 ft. The wet solid is introduced into one end of the rotating cylinder, travels through it and is discharged from the other end in a dry state. A hot gas (air or combustion gases) is also passed through the cylinder either countercurrently or parallel with the solid to be dried. Owing to the rotation of the cylinder, the solid is continually mixed so as to contact all the material with the gas. Usually flights are attached to the interior surface of the dryer for lifting and showering the wet material through the hot gases, thus improving the contact. The shape of the flights depends upon the material to be dried. For sticky materials, straight radial flights are preferred. For free flowing materials the flights are often provided with lips (see fig. 1.30).

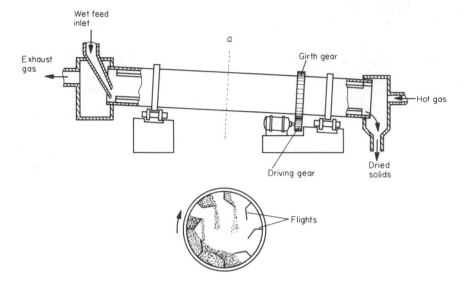

Fig. 1.29   Direct rotary dryer. The cross-section at (a) shows the flights.

A simplified construction of the direct rotary dryer is the *rotary kiln*. The material travels on the bottom of the rotating cylinder since it is not provided with flights. Usually rotary kilns are refractory-lined to make them suitable for calcining and roasting.

The spray dryer is also extensively used in the chemical industry. It consists basically of a chamber, e.g. a tower, equipped with a means for spraying a liquid into a hot gas stream (atomizer). The liquid may be a solution or dispersion of the solid to be dried or a melt containing water. The hot gas can flow counter to or parallel with the falling drops or solidified particles. A cyclonic flow of the hot gases may also be used (see fig. 1.31).

To promote rapid drying, the liquid must be sprayed in very small droplets (atomization). The most important types of atomizers are the centrifugal disc atomizer and the pressure nozzle. The former is common in the chemical industry but the latter is preferred in the food and soap industries.

The simplest form of centrifugal disc atomizer is a horizontal circular plate rotating on a vertical shaft. Drops falling on the plate near the shaft are discharged at high speed from the periphery of the rapidly rotating plate. Other centrifugal atomizers consist of a flat cylindrical box. Drops falling into the box are discharged through small openings in the cylindrical side wall of the box (see fig. 1.32 a). To get very fine atomization the centrifugal atomizer is sometimes provided with S shaped vanes which lengthen the liquid path to the periphery (see fig. 1.32 b).

A pressure nozzle consists basically of a pipe provided with a small orifice. Atomization of a liquid can be effected by placing a small worm in the orifice thus giving the liquid which is forced through it a high degree of spin. In this way the liquid is atomized by centrifugal forces. The liquid can also be atomized by means of air. In this case the nozzle is surrounded by a second pipe and air is blown through the annular space around the nozzle (or conversely air through the central opening and the liquid through the annular space). This air atomizes the liquid if it is blown either perpendicularly or tangentially to the liquid flow (see fig. 1.33a and b). The tangential air flow may be obtained by introducing air tangentially into the air feed pipe surrounding the nozzle (compare cyclones, p. 104).

In a *through-circulation dryer* hot air is blown through a permeable bed of wet material on a screen. Many materials can be dried without preliminary treatment in this dryer but sometimes the material must be crushed, flaked, briquetted, granulated, extruded or otherwise treated to make beds permeable to air. In a discontinuous or batch through-circulation dryer the wet material is dried on fixed screens. If air is blown through a bed of finely divided material at sufficient speed, the layer acquires the character of a boiling liquid. The particles dance in a turbulent layer; this is known as a *fluid bed*. In the fluidized zone there is a uniform temperature distribution and drying takes place more rapidly than in the dryers with fixed beds (see fig. 1.34).

A continuous through-circulation dryer which is widely used in the chemical industry

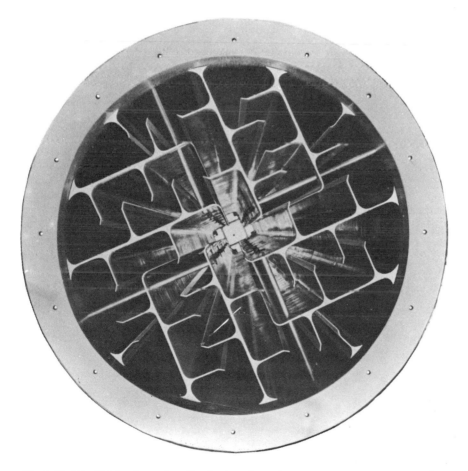

Fig. 1.30 The flights of a modern direct rotary dryer.

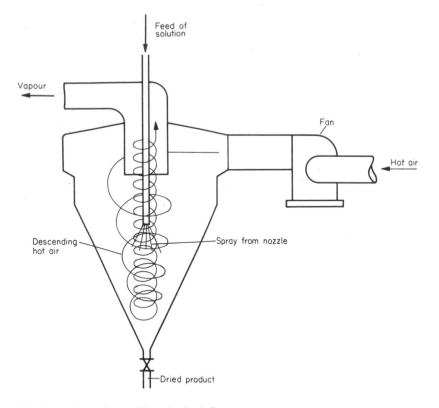

Fig. 1.31 Spray dryer with cyclonic air flow.

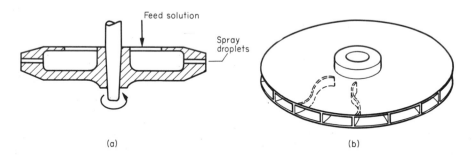

Fig. 1.32 (a) centrifugal disc atomizer; (b) centrifugal disc atomizer provided with S-shaped vanes to lengthen liquid travel to the periphery.

consists of a horizontal conveying screen, which moves through a tunnel-like drying chamber. The air is blown either upwards or downwards through the bed of wet material. The conveying screen through-circulation dryer is widely used to dry fibrous, granular and flaky materials which do not need any preliminary treatment. Examples are: cotton, rayon and cellulose acetate fibres, silica gel and sawdust. This dryer is also widely used for materials which need any pre-treatment, e.g. pigments, starch, insecticides etc.

Continuous through-circulation drying is also applied in one type of rotary dryer. A cylindrical screen formed by several louvres which are fixed concentrically in the rotary dryer. The wet material travels over the louvres through the inner cylinder. Hot air is blown into the annular space between the cylinder and passes through the wet material via the louvres (see fig. 1.35).

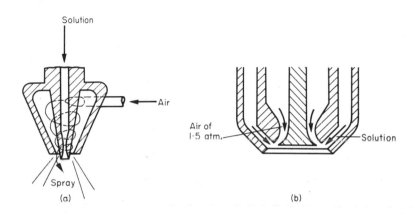

Fig. 1.33   (a) spray nozzle with perpendicular air flow; (b) spray nozzle with tangential air flow.

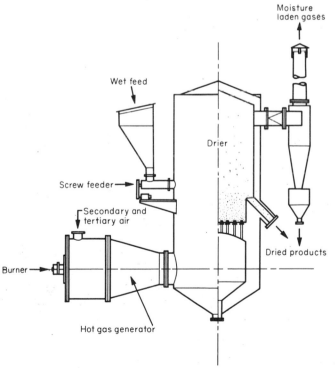

Fig. 1.34   Fluid bed dryer.

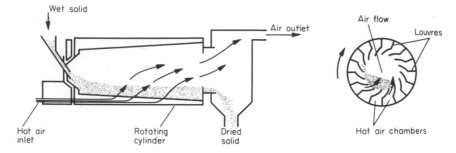

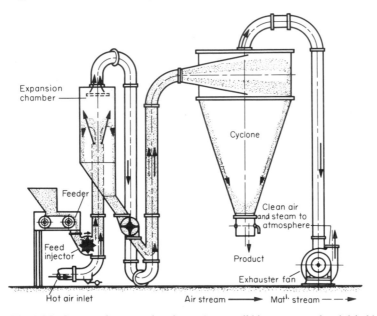

Fig. 1.35 Roto-louvre through circulation dryer.

Fig. 1.36 Pneumatic conveying dryer. A wet solid is transported and dried by fluidization in a hot air stream. The dried solid is separated from the air stream in a cyclone.

In *pneumatic conveying dryers* a wet solid is dried and transported at the same time in a high velocity stream of hot gas. Temperatures up to 750° C may be used and are often above the decomposition temperatures of the solids to be dried but this is permissible owing to the very short contact time (see fig. 1.36).

Tray and compartment dryers consist of simple drying rooms through which conditioned or hot air is blown. These dryers are provided with racks, hangers or trays for drying ceramics, sheet material (e.g. hides), granular materials etc. The tunnel dryer is a modification of this type of dryer. It consists of a tunnel through which the wet material is moved on cars (see also ceramics vol. II). A dryer which is basically the same as the multiple-hearth roasters used for sulphur-containing ores can also be used for granular or powdery materials (see roasters, p. 273).

The *direct sheeting dryer* is used to dry sheet material such as printed textiles, paper etc. Hot air is blown through and over the sheet which is passed through a drying room over rolls etc. (See paper and textiles in vol. VI.)

1.6.3 Indirect dryers

Apart from additional means for external heating and sometimes for applying a vacuum, the construction of indirect dryers is often substantially the same as that for direct dryers. An example of such a dryer is the *indirect rotary dryer* which may be surrounded with a combustion chamber. The most common indirect rotary dryer is the steam tube dryer. Steam-heated tubes running the full length of the cylinder are fastened in one or more concentric cylindrical layers to the inside of the cylinder and rotate with it. This dryer can be used for granular or powdery materials. Materials that tend to stick to hot surfaces cannot be dried in this dryer since a coating on the heat transfer surfaces rapidly decreases the drying capacity.

Vacuum dryers consist of vacuum-tight chambers capable of being evacuated. This type of dryer can be used at moderate temperatures and is particularly suitable for materials that cannot withstand high temperatures. Various types of vacuum dryers are in use. The *vacuum shelf dryer* consists of a vacuum-tight chamber equipped with hollow shelves of flat sheet plate which are fastened to the walls. The heating agent (e.g. hot water, oil or steam) is circulated through the hollow shelves. This dryer is usually operated at a pressure of 20 to 30 mm mercury (Hg) and between 0° C and 100° C.

The vacuum rotary dryer is basically an indirect rotary dryer consisting of a rotating vacuum-tight cylinder. Its distinguishing feature is that it is usually mounted horizontally. Thus it is a batch dryer wherein the material is mixed but not moved from one end to the other. It is usually operated at a pressure of 700 mm Hg. Another batch dryer of similar type consists of a stationary cylindrical shell mounted horizontally. The wet material is agitated by means of a stirrer which consists of agitator blades mounted on a revolving central shaft. The dryer is heated by circulating a hot liquid through a jacket around the shell or through the hollow central shaft.

In *vacuum freeze dryers* solids are freed from water which is brought into a frozen state. Thus drying occurs by sublimation in vacuum. The vacuum freeze dryer is used for drying food and other heat sensitive materials. The evaporating equipment consists of a shelf dryer, a vacuum rotary dryer or another indirect dryer, but a high vacuum is required to accelerate sublimation at low temperatures; for rapid drying at −25° C the maximum is 0.5 mm Hg. To avoid repeated evacuation of the equipment, the dryers are equipped with air locks for filling and discharging. The volume occupied by the water vapour under the expanded conditions of these very low pressures demands pumps of high volume capacity and large diameter piping to transport the vapour without large pressure drop. For this reason water vapour is condensed as ice in a device refrigerated with solid carbon dioxide, ammonia or freon. A temperature of −45° C is sufficiently low to condense water vapour to ice since the vapour pressure of saturated water vapour is 0.05 mm Hg at this temperature. (The pressure in the dryer is usually 0.5 to 1 mm Hg.) The refrigerator is placed between the dryer and the vacuum pump and is provided with scrapers to avoid the formation of thick layers of ice on the cooled surfaces. The scraped ice is discharged from the refrigerator at intervals by means of ice ejectors. Water vapour can also be removed by absorption on solid dehydrating agents or dehydrating solutions having an extremely low vapour pressure at the temperatures used in the dryer (see dehumidification of air, p. 111).

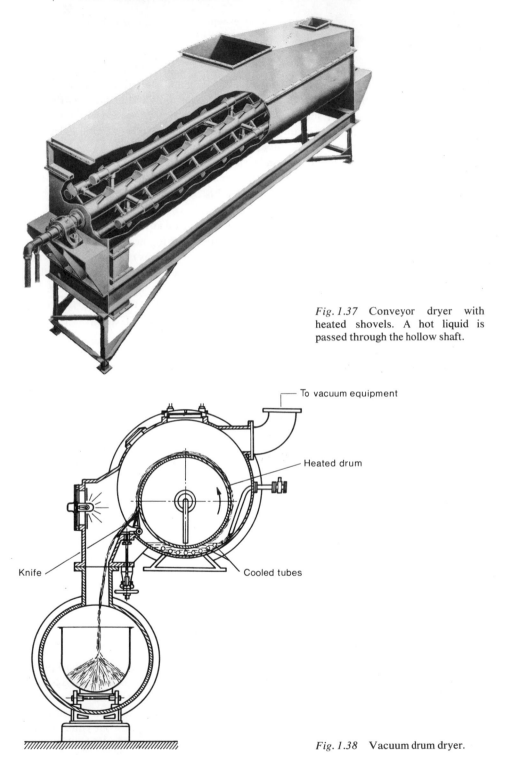

Fig. 1.37 Conveyor dryer with heated shovels. A hot liquid is passed through the hollow shaft.

To vacuum equipment

Heated drum

Cooled tubes

Knife

Fig. 1.38 Vacuum drum dryer.

The *screw conveyor dryer* is suitable for drying pastes to granular materials. It is said to be one of the cheapest continuous dryers in use, but is not widely used. It consists of a trough equipped with a screw conveyor or a series of shovels mounted on a horizontal shaft. The material is mixed, dried and transported at the same time. The trough is heated with water, steam or other heating medium. Frequently the screw conveyor is also heated by means of a hollow shaft (see fig. 1.37). The screw conveyor can also be mounted in a vacuum-tight cylinder for drying at diminished pressure (about 700 mm Hg).

The *drum dryer* consists of one or more rotating heated metal drums. The wet material (slurry, paste or liquid) is applied on the drum and forms a film which is evaporated to a cake of dry material which is scraped from the drum by a stationary knife (see fig. 1.38). Drum dryers occur both as single drum and double drum dryers, both of which can be operated at atmospheric pressure or at diminished pressure by enclosing them in a vacuum-tight casing. The drum is fed with wet material by dipping it in the wet material or by spraying the wet material on the drum. In double drum dryers, rotating towards the nip of the rolls, a reservoir of wet material can be formed between the drums.

Cylinder dryers are similar to drum dryers but are especially designed for drying wet sheet materials, e.g. sheets of paper pulp, textiles etc. (see under these headings, in vol. VI).

1.7 LITERATURE

1. A. W. BAMFORTH. *Industrial crystallisation*. London, Leonard Hill, 1965.
2. A. VAN HOOK. *Crystallisation. Theory and practice*. London, Chapman & Hall, 1961.
3. J. W. MULLIN. *Crystallisation*. London, Butterworths, 1961.
4. J. H. PERRY. *Chemical engineers handbook*, 4th edition. New York, McGraw-Hill, 1963.

CHAPTER 2

Some Elementary
Gases

2.1 GASES IN GENERAL

2.1.1 Physical properties

Gases (and vapours) are substances in a state in which their molecules, owing
to thermal agitation, tend to fly apart and fill the space in which they are confined.
Hence they can be stored only in containers whose walls are impervious to the molecules.

There is no fundamental difference between gases and vapours. A vapour can be
condensed into a liquid at constant temperature by increasing the pressure. Any gas
can be a vapour and can be condensed, but sometimes the required temperature is very
low (see also p. 42).

The physical behaviour of gases can be represented approximately by a few simple
formulae. Every gas (and every vapour) consists of rapidly moving molecules. Because
these moving molecules hit against the walls of the vessel in which the gas is contained
(and also against other molecules), the gas exerts a pressure on these walls. (The
average speed of the molecules is high; that of nitrogen for instance being about 1800
m/s). If the same amount of gas is introduced into a larger space at the same temperature,
fewer molecules per cm² will hit the wall; thus the pressure decreases as the gas occupies
a larger volume. The relation between pressure and volume is represented by the
formula:

$$PV = \text{constant},$$

where P represents the pressure, V the volume. This law which was formulated by
Boyle (1627-91) and independently by Mariotte (1620-84) thus proclaims the product
of these two magnitudes to be always the same.

This is only true however, so long as the temperature remains the same. For with an
increase of the temperature the speed of the molecules will increase also, so that the
number of collisions on the wall and therefore the force exerted on the wall at each
collision will be augmented. The combined effect of temperature and pressure may be
represented by the equation:

$$PV = RT.$$

In this formula T is the so-called absolute temperature, i.e. the temperature in °C +
273, and R is a constant, which is the same for all gases.

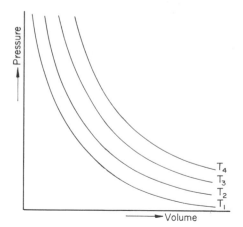

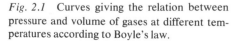

Fig. 2.1 Curves giving the relation between pressure and volume of gases at different temperatures according to Boyle's law.

Fig. 2.1 shows the relation between P and V according to this formula at various temperatures (each curve is a hyperbola).

It was later found that this formula is only approximately true, and that only for a few gases.

Van der Waals (1837-1923) proposed an equation which gives a better representation of the correlation between pressure, volume and temperature. In this equation both the natural volume of the molecules, which makes it impossible for them to be compressed to an unlimited extent, and the mutual attraction between the molecules, have been taken into account.

This equation is as follows:

$$(P + \frac{a}{V^2}) \; (V - b) = RT$$

In this formula a and b are constants, which are dependent on the nature of the gas. In fig. 2.2 again a number of curves representing the correlation between P (pressure) and V (volume) of a gas (carbonic acid gas) at various temperatures is shown.

If, starting on the curve for 10° C (i.e. 283° absolute) at A, the volume of the carbonic acid gas is decreased (for instance with the aid of a piston), the pressure will increase. As soon as the point B is reached, the pressure does not increase any more, but part of the gas starts condensing into liquid; condensation continues until the point C has been reached, where all the gas has been changed into liquid. As a liquid is much less compressible than a gas, a very large change in pressure beyond the point C is only accompanied by a small change in volume.

At higher temperatures the distance from B to C becomes progressively smaller; at 31.3° it has dwindled to a point (the critical point) and above this temperature carbonic acid gas cannot be liquefied. This temperature is called *the critical temperature*. A gas which is below its critical temperature but which has not yet been liquefied is often called 'vapour' (see also p. 41).

It appears from fig. 2.2 that, particularly when approaching the liquid range, the curves deviate from the curves obtained according to the simple gas law in fig. 2.1.

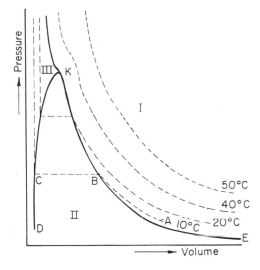

Fig. 2.2 Curves giving the relation between pressure and volume of carbon dioxide gas at different temperatures, according to van der Waals's law. II is the section in which the gas and liquid phase are in equilibrium. I is the gas phase section and III is the liquid phase section.

Therefore, the simple law is approximately valid only for gases which are at a considerable distance from the conditions under which they liquefy, but as the critical point is approached the van der Waals forces become more and more important and the modified gas equation of van der Waals gives a truer picture.

If a gas under pressure in a cylinder is allowed to expand against the pressure of the atmosphere (e.g. by moving a piston in the cylinder), it does work at the expense of the internal energy of the gas: if the process is carried out under such conditions that heat cannot enter from outside – under so-called *adiabatic* conditions – the temperature of the gas will fall. By using the cold gas to cool further quantities by expansion, a continuous process can be devised for reducing the temperature below the critical temperature and so causing liquefaction.

In the process described above, the heat lost will, by the law of the conservation of energy, be exactly equivalent to the work done by the gas in expanding against the pressure of the atmosphere. We have, however, so far failed to take into consideration the work done by the gas against the van der Waals forces – the forces which tend to hold the molecules together. The work so done causes a further loss of heat, the cooling effect produced in this way being known as the Joule-Thompson effect. It should be noted that this effect occurs even when no external work is done against the atmosphere (e.g. when a gas under pressure is allowed to expand into a vacuum).

The application of the Joule-Thompson effect forms the basis of modern methods for liquefying gases.

2.1.2 Liquefaction and separation of gas mixtures

As already shown, liquefaction of gases necessitates cooling them below the critical temperature. Mixtures of gases also have critical temperatures, depending on their composition.

Modern equipment is based largely on the *Linde* process, which virtually revolutionized gas liquefaction at the beginning of the twentieth century by taking advantage of the Joule-Thompson effect. Fig. 2.3 gives a highly simplified diagram of the Linde process.

The main stages of this process are:
1. Compression of the air.
2. Purification.
3. Heat exchange to ensure economical operation.
4. Liquefaction by cooling.
5. Distillation to obtain the constituents.

When gases of low boiling point are liquefied in such installations, care must be taken to purify them thoroughly beforehand, in order to avoid clogging the apparatus with impurities that would solidify at the low temperatures employed.

Let us take as an example the liquefaction of ordinary air, followed by separation into its components, mainly oxygen and nitrogen.

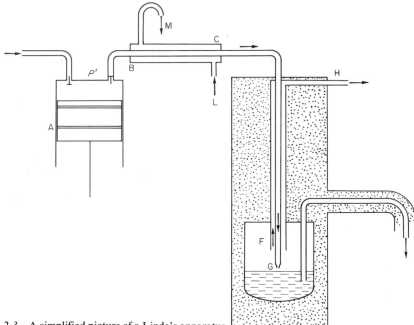

Fig. 2.3   A simplified picture of a Linde's apparatus.

Fig. 2.3 shows how the compressor P¹ compresses purified air entering the compressor cylinder at A. The pressure is raised to 135-280 atm. Heat produced by the rapid compression is removed by passage through a long, tubular coil BC located in a cooler in which water enters at L and leaves at M. The compressed, cooled air travels on through a very long tube and expands suddenly at G, where its temperature is greatly reduced owing to the Joule-Thompson effect. The cooled air, still at a slight pressure, enters a wide tube enclosing the tube which contains the compressed air. The temperature of the air in the latter is reduced by the cooled air in the outer tube, and when it expands it reaches such a low temperature that it liquefies and precipitates at F. The refrigerating air that has flowed around the inside tube can be fed to the compressor via H, thus making a partial cycle. Fresh purified and cooled air is supplied at A.

Fig. 2.4 shows a section (again greatly simplified and schematic) of a Linde unit. A high-capacity compressor forces air into the descending tube (at B). This air, at a pressure of 10 atm, enters an absorption tower, through which caustic soda solution percolates over a system of baffles or rings. Dust and practically all the carbon dioxide in the air are thereby removed. The air is sucked out again at the top of the tower by a multistage compressor A.

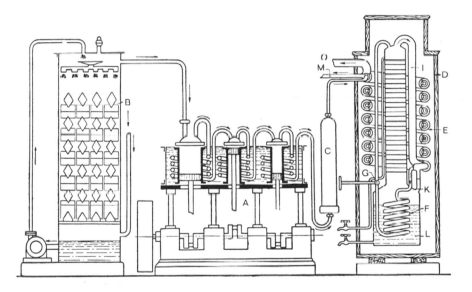

Fig. 2.4 Section of oxygen liquefaction plant.
A. Air compressor system; B. Carbon dioxide absorption tower, with circulating caustic soda solution at bottom; C. Absorption tank with silica gel to dry air; D. Linde air liquefaction unit; E. Triple-concentric coil; F. Coil for additional cooling; G. Reducing valve; I. Wide tube; K. Inlet for narrow tube; L. Liquefied oxygen; M. Outlet of the mixture rich in oxygen from L. This recycles to a point before the pumps; O. Nitrogen outlet.

This provides the requisite high pressure in at least three stages (preferably four or five). After each stage the air passes through a system of tubes coiled around the compressor cylinders and entirely surrounded by water, so that the heat generated by compression is carried off by the water. From the cooler of the final high pressure cylinder the air travels through a drier C, filled, for instance, with calcium chloride, activated aluminium hydroxide or silica gel. The latter absorbs nearly all the vapours formed from the compressor lubricants. In newer purification processes, the air, at a pressure of 10 atm, is purified as follows: Water is removed first in filters containing silica gel, or aluminium hydroxide and the dried air is passed through a dry bed containing the same absorbents at low temperature to remove carbon dioxide and less volatile hydrocarbons such as acetylene.

After this the compressed and purified air is further cooled and afterwards cooled until it liquefies. The liquid air produced is finally separated into liquid oxygen and gaseous nitrogen by distillation. This is effected in the following manner.

From the drying plant C the compressed air streams through the inner tube of the spiral E. This spiral is a heat exchanger, comprising three coaxial tubes. In the innermost tube the compressed air is strongly cooled by a low temperature and low pressure gas, which streams through the middle tube and comes from the evaporating liquid at the bottom of the apparatus and by cold gaseous nitrogen, which streams through the outer tube. These gases are discharged at the top of the fractionating column.

The air which has thus been cooled and compressed is led through the spiral F, immersed in liquid oxygen, in which it is still further cooled, and is subsequently expanded at the throttle valve G, whereby it partly liquefies as a result of the Joule-Thompson effect. This mixture is introduced into the fractionating column. This column occupies the central part of the installation. The column is provided with a large number of trays, similar to those in the fractionating columns employed in the oil industry (see also equipment for liquefaction of gases, p. 49). In this column the liquid air streaming downward is separated into liquid oxygen (boiling point $-183°$ C) which moves downward and is collected at L, and into cold gaseous nitrogen, which is discharged from the top of the fractionating column. As has been explained, this cold nitrogen serves to cool the compressed air entering the apparatus. After the low temperature of the nitrogen has thus been made use of, the nitrogen can be collected separately.

Part of the liquid oxygen present in L, which still contains a little nitrogen, is evaporated by heat absorbed from the spiral. As nitrogen is more volatile than oxygen, a relatively large amount of nitrogen evaporates, so that the purity of the remaining oxygen increases. From this cold vapour, part of the oxygen is condensed again in the fractionating column; the nitrogen discharged, however, still contains some oxygen. Part of this gas is led through the middle tube of the heat exchanger to cooperate in the cooling of the incoming compressed air, and is discharged at M.

The liquid oxygen is drained off by the tap N. Liquid air coming from the topmost tray of the fractionating column can, if desired, be drained off from the tap lying above the first one.

In a single column only about 70% of the oxygen in the air can be recovered. The resulting nitrogen still contains 7% oxygen. In order to recover a higher percentage of the oxygen a reflux of liquid nitrogen must be produced. For this purpose the impure nitrogen is liquefied again.

Liquid or gaseous oxygen with a large yield and pure gaseous nitrogen can also be produced in Linde double columns (see fig. 2.5).

In this apparatus very cold air, which is partially liquefied, is admitted into a heat exchanger at the bottom of the lower column. In this heat exchanger the air condenses and gives up heat to the boiling liquid in the column. The liquid air enters the lower column half way up and has a pressure of 4 to 5 atm. Nitrogen vaporizes and a liquid containing about 50% oxygen is collected at the bottom of the lower column. This nitrogen-oxygen mixture is expanded to atmospheric pressure, is admitted into the upper column and is fractionated.

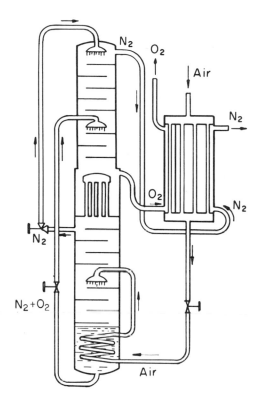

Fig. 2.5 Diagram of a double column for separating the oxygen and nitrogen in an air supply. This goes through tubes cooled in compartments through which cold oxygen and nitrogen flow. It is liquefied in the bottom of the lower column, and mainly nitrogen rises in a gaseous form. It is also greatly cooled in the tubes surrounded by liquid oxygen from the upper column. The oxygen rich liquid is conducted to the middle of the upper column, where condensation, mainly of oxygen occurs, the more volatile nitrogen rising to the compartment that cools the incoming air. The arrows show the route followed by the liquid and gases.

Liquid or gaseous oxygen is collected at the bottom of the upper column and gaseous nitrogen at the top of the upper column.

The nitrogen which vaporizes in the lower column is liquefied by the liquid oxygen in the column in a heat exchanger between the columns. This is possible as the nitrogen has a pressure of 4 to 5 atm. The liquefied nitrogen is partially refluxed in the lower column and partially collected at the top of the lower column. This liquid nitrogen is drawn off, expanded to atmospheric pressure and admitted into the upper column at the top. In this process the boiler of the upper column is at the same time the reflux condenser for both columns. High purity nitrogen (99.5% and even higher) and oxygen having a purity of 95% to 99.5% can be obtained in this process.

Fig. 2.6 gives some idea of the size of a modern oxygen plant supplying up to 6 tons of liquid oxygen an hour. Each tower contains a distillation column which may be 15 to 20 m high.

It used to be necessary to close down oxygen plants completely once every three weeks for removal of condensed water and carbon dioxide. Purification methods have been improved and modern installations are now able to operate for much longer runs (up to six months for instance).

Some plants differ from those described in that the air after removal of carbon dioxide and water vapour is precooled to − 30° C with refrigerating machines. This greatly improves the yield. It is also possible, and as a matter of fact advantageous, to process only part of the air at about 200 atm and the rest at lower pressures (6 to 7 atm).

Fig. 2.6 View of plant for separating air into its constituents and obtaining argon, etc. The equipment is inside the 15 m casing enclosing the tall distilling units.

Other gases such as helium and hydrogen are liquefied in similar liquefaction plants.

Units of similar design have also made it possible to separate mixtures of oxygen and argon, helium and nitrogen and mixtures of many other gases (water gas, coal gas, coke oven gas, etc.) into their components. Purification methods vary with the gases being treated and are discussed in the chapters on the specified gases.

Fig. 2.7 gives a diagram of the complex equipment required for separating acetylene, ethylene, methane, nitrogen and hydrogen from prerefined coke oven gas, by cooling and fractional distillation. Cooling is performed by cold nitrogen which is obtained by expansion of high pressure nitrogen. Coke oven gas is cooled in stages and each constituent which liquefies is drawn off, vaporized and passed separately through preceding stages for further cooling the gases which have to be separated. Nitrogen is fed to the last stage and passes all preceding stages. All components are drawn off between the heat exchangers A. Thus the low temperature is fully utilized and this makes the process economical (see also fig. 2.26 which is a simplified version of fig. 2.7).

A gas-separating plant is obviously an expensive and complex installation. It would require a large capital outlay and would be a paying proposition only for large gas and coke producing plants. All pipelines, tanks, etc. are heavily insulated against heat losses and heat absorption. The plant is usually installed in the open air.

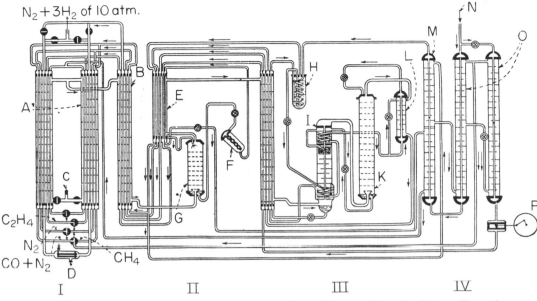

$N_2 + 3H_2$ of 10 atm.

C_2H_4

N_2

$CO + N_2$

CH_4

I   II   III   IV

Fig. 2.7 Diagram of an installation supplying a gas mixture for ammonia synthesis by cooling and separating purified coke oven gas.

I. A. Heat exchangers; B. Cold exchangers; C. Coke oven gas inlet (11 atm); D. Heater.
II. E. Ethylene condenser; F. Filter; G. Ethylene washing column.
III. H. Methane vaporizer; I. Fractionation column; K. Column for washing with nitrogen; L. Nitrogen cooler.
IV. M. Ethylene vaporizer; N. Nitrogen inlet (200 atm); O. Nitrogen exchange; P. Nitrogen expansion engine.

2.1.3 Equipment for liquefaction of gases

a. Heat exchangers. Nowadays several alternative forms of heat exchanger are used instead of Linde's triple-concentric coils.

One improved heat exchanger is the regenerator (or reversing exchanger) introduced into low temperature technology by Fränkl and used in Linde-Fränkl liquefaction plants. These regenerators are devices filled with rolls of aluminium tape. Each roll consists of two corrugated strips, the corrugations of one being at right-angles to those of the other (see fig. 2.8). Heat is exchanged in this regenerator by passing hot and cold gas alternately through it in such a way that, first a stream of, say, cold oxygen or nitrogen flows through it, cooling the rolls. Then a stream of compressed air flows through the regenerator depositing water and carbon dioxide in the rolls and heating them. Then a stream of cold gas is again passed through the rolls. Due to its much lower pressure this

gas first removes water and carbon dioxide and then cools the rolls again – and so on. These units thus transfer cold and at the same time remove traces of water, carbon dioxide and hydrocarbons from the cold gases. However, the oxygen or nitrogen is less pure, as it is mixed with the air in the regenerator by reversing the gas streams. The gas stream is reversed every two or three minutes.

Fig. 2.8 Tape for low temperature regenerator.

Fig. 2.9 A section of a flat-plate heat exchanger.

Another heat exchanger is the flat-plate exchanger (see fig. 2.9). This consists of a number of parallel brass plates alternated with corrugated plates. All points of contact can be soldered by dipping the laminate into a molten salt flux bath followed by dipping in a molten solder. The resulting laminate is fixed in a rectangular tank. The hot and cold gases flow in countercurrent in alternate channels of the laminate. The partitions are such good conductors of heat that rapid heat exchange takes place. It is calculated that 70 dm² heat exchanging surface is obtained per kg of brass. Ordinary air for lique-faction is cooled so rapidly by cold gas on the other side that water vapour and even carbon dioxide condense and are deposited at the bottom, being removed from the system by flushing with nitrogen. Such equipment is therefore usable for relatively long periods without shut-down for cleaning. At the present time such heat exchangers are also made of aluminium. These exchangers are also used as reversing exchangers (see above). Other typical heat exchangers, very often used, comprise systems of deoxidized copper tubes (see fig. 2.10) sometimes as long as 6000 m, into which the cold gases or liquids are compressed. The windings are secured between bronze plates in such a way that another gas or liquid can flow round them to ensure rapid heat exchange. The system of pipes is contained in a strong tank.

b. Distillation columns (fractionating columns). These columns must have as low a pressure drop as possible since increasing pressure drop causes increasing power

Fig. 2.10 Systems of thin copper tubing being assembled for use in compressed gas heat exchangers. They are placed in a strong well-insulated casing.

consumption. Bubble-cap plate towers are therefore preferably used. These towers are provided with a number of perforated plates or trays fixed horizontally one above the other. Each plate is bent upwards at the periphery of each perforation and caps of larger diameter than the perforations are placed above them.

All the equipment has to be carefully insulated. Only insulations which resist low temperatures can be used. Glass wool, balsa wood and some foamed plastics are suitable. Double shelled equipment with vacuum insulation or powder insulation between the walls may also be used.

Thus the vapours in the tower have to pass a layer of reflux liquid on all the plates and an intensive contact between vapour and reflux is ensured. Reflux passes down the tower from plate to plate by means of downflow pipes. Entry of heat from outside is minimized by reducing the tower dimensions. Small size bubble caps and close tray perforations are therefore employed (see also distillation columns in the petroleum industry, vol. IV).

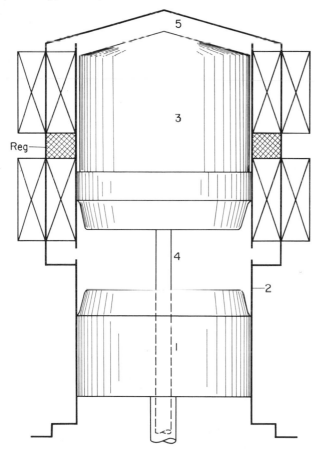

Fig. 2.11   The principle of the displacement unit.
1 = main piston moving in cylinder 2. 3 = displacement piston causing the gas to flow intermittently between chambers 4 and 5. The gas flows through the annular heat exchanger around the displacement piston.
Simplified sectional drawing.

c. Compressors. Compressors which operate without lubrication are required, since even traces of oils in the air will accumulate in the boilers of the distillation column. In addition, the higher the oxygen content of air, the better it supports combustion of oils. Moreover, at low temperatures oils lose their lubricating properties.

At present, non-lubricated centrifugal compressors or non-lubricated piston compressors are used for compressing gases.

In the case of non-lubricated piston compressors the space between the piston and

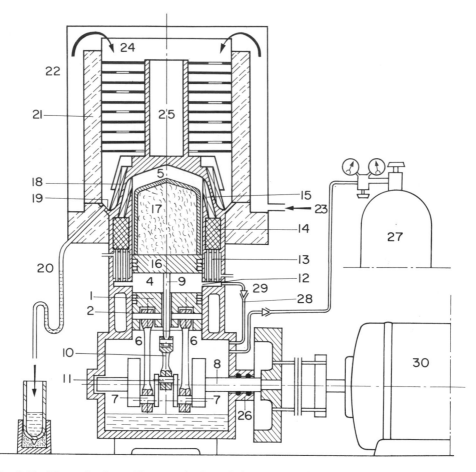

Fig. 2.12 The main piston (1) moves in the cylinder (2). The displacement piston (16 and 17) causes the medium to flow intermittently to and fro between the chambers (4) and (5). This gas flows through the annular exchangers around the displacement piston. Parallel rods (6) connect the pins (7) on the shafts (8) with the piston (1). The displacement piston rod (9) is connected with the rod (10) and pin (11) of the shaft (8). The channel (12) from heat exchanger to heat outlet (13) and regenerator (14) connect the compression chamber with the heat exchanger (15) for removing cold. Head (16) with hood of displacement piston (17). Condenser (18), where the gas liquefies, with annular channel (19) and outlet pipe (20) (swan-neck). Insulating jacket (21) surrounds the plates through which the incoming gas flows inside the outer casing (22). Air inlet (23). De-icer plates (24) are connected via tube (25) with the heat exchanger for removing cold (15). Gas-tight bearing (26). Gas cylinder (27) with medium (helium or hydrogen). Feed pipe (28) with check valve (29). Drive motor (30).

the cylinder wall is so small that air leakage is negligible, while the length of the piston rod and the piston rod stuffing box is made so that no oil can enter. In order to avoid rapid deterioration, gaskets of graphite are employed.

d. Materials. Many metals do not retain their strength sufficiently to allow their use at the low temperatures involved. Copper, low carbon nickel steel (stainless steel), aluminium, aluminium alloys, nickel and Monel metal can be used, as they remain resilient at extremely low temperatures, even at the welds. In general ferrous alloys and higher carbon steels cannot be used as they would be as brittle as glass at these temperatures.

2.1.4 Cold gas refrigerating machines

For very small quantities of liquefied gases, units known as 'cold gas refrigerating machines' are available. These supply about 100 litres a day (see figs. 2.11, 2.12, 2.13 and 2.14).

A main piston and a displacement piston move reciprocally in a cylinder. The space between the two pistons contains helium or hydrogen. The pistons move in such way that the gas is compressed, after which it is cooled by passing through a heat exchanger and a regenerator into a second space at the other side of the displacement piston. The

Fig. 2.13 Philips gas refrigerating machine with nitrogen column in operation for condensing nitrogen from the air at atmospheric pressure. Its capacity is approximately 600 litres of liquid nitrogen per six working days.

gas expands quickly in this space and is thus strongly cooled, thereby withdrawing heat from the walls and the surrounding system.

The gas is then forced back via the regenerator to the space between the two pistons for recompression. This repeated gas compression and expansion causes such a drop in temperature that ordinary air liquefies on the outside walls of the expansion chamber. The liquefied air is collected in a Dewar flask (see fig. 2.15).

Fig. 2.13 gives an idea of the small dimensions of such a unit. This picture shows the cold gas refrigerating machine and a nitrogen column for the separation of the liquefied air into nitrogen and oxygen. The principle of the nitrogen column is shown in fig. 2.14.

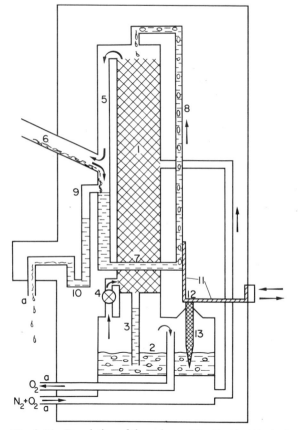

Fig. 2.14 Regulation of the column. The liquid at the bottom of the column (1) can pass to the re-boiler (2) only via the liquid seal (3). The oxygen evaporating in (2) is partly returned to the column via the adjusting valve (4), which functions as a variable resistor. This resistor is adjusted so that the pressure in (2) rises slightly above atmospheric pressure, as a result of which the excess oxygen vapour is blown off. The saturated nitrogen vapour escaping from the column at the top reaches the liquefier via the tubes (5) and (6) and, after being condensed, flows back to the lower section of tube (5), via (6). The vapour bubble pump (5, 7, 8), which lifts the reflux to the top, is heated by means of the copper strip (11). The point of the pin (13) fixed to the copper strip reaches well into the liquid in the re-boiler. If the reflux quantity is too large, the surface of the liquid in (2) rises, as a result of which the pin draws more heat from the strip (11) and the action of the pump is slowed down. The product to be drawn off leaves the column via the overflow (9) and the liquid seal (10). The use of a vapour bubble pump, coupled to the control system described above, offers the great advantage that the column contains no moving parts, so excluding the possibility of freezing-up.

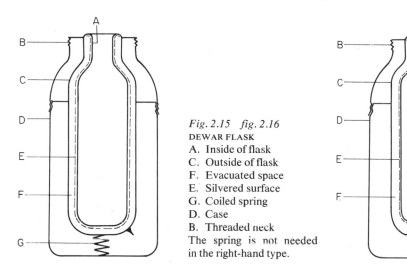

Fig. 2.15   fig. 2.16
DEWAR FLASK
A. Inside of flask
C. Outside of flask
F. Evacuated space
E. Silvered surface
G. Coiled spring
D. Case
B. Threaded neck
The spring is not needed
in the right-hand type.

2.1.5   Storage of liquefied gases

Gases which are difficult to liquefy can be stored in the liquid state for a long time in a *Dewar flask* (see fig. 2.15).

This is a double-walled flask. The space between the walls is evacuated and silvered. The vacuum prevents heat from being conducted inwards or outwards, while the silver surface avoids heat absorption by radiation.

Various improvements have been made to the original design of these flasks. For example, a depression may be made in the outside flask to prevent the point left after evacuation from protruding so that it will not be so liable to break. The bottom may be flat, so that the flask can be used without a case (see figs. 2.15 and 2.16). After filling, the open mouths of the flasks are stopped with a plug of cotton wool; the contents often take ten days to evaporate completely.

Silvered Dewar flasks are mass-produced as the well-known Thermos flasks. Unsilvered flasks are used round sodium vapour lamps, to keep the lamp itself at a temperature at which the sodium vapour pressure suffices to produce the required light radiation.

Dewar flasks are also used in connection with some types of photoelectric cells.

Large forms of Dewar flask for storing liquefied gases are made of stainless steel or copper. Fig. 2.17 shows how a big metal Dewar flask is built up. Coconut charcoal is often put in the evacuated space to absorb the final traces of gas remaining when the very low temperature is reached. The flasks are closed with extremely sensitive valves (see also fig. 2.18).

Flasks for the storage of liquid gases are also made without evacuating the intervening space, which is then filled with light mineral powders with good insulating properties. This method is applied especially for the big metal flasks used for storing large quantities of liquefied gas. These have an inner tank of stainless steel, the outer tank consisting of ordinary carbon steel. They may be as large as 9 to 60 ft in diameter.

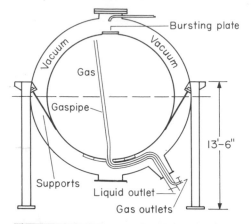

Fig. 2.17 Sectional diagram of two big concentric metal spheres functioning as a Dewar flask. The one sphere is suspended inside the outer on strong bands. The pipe inside is open at the top; from the point where it emerges from the inner sphere, it is enclosed in a wider, liquid discharge pipe. The entire system is firmly suspended in vertical supports.

Fig. 2.18 Building of a double walled sphere called Horton sphere, for storage of liquid gases. The 36 ft diameter aluminium inner sphere is lowered into the bigger carbon steel shell. The wide space between the shells is filled with an insulation to keep the temperature very low.

Dewar flasks with two or more outlets are made for carrying several kilograms of liquid oxygen in aircraft. Oxygen gas can thus escape in either position and the internal pressure cannot become excessive.

Aircraft pilots require two flasks of compressed oxygen containing 760 litres each (at normal pressure). These weigh at least 35 lb. But 3.5 litres liquefied oxygen is ample and this, including the Dewar flask, weighs only 15 lb.

For transporting large quantities (up to as much as 12 tons) of liquefied gas either cylindrical metal tanks with concave ends or spheres may be used. These tanks are fitted with an outer steel envelope. The gap of 35 cm in between the inner and outer shells is well insulated with slag wool and the small ones with a powder insulation (e.g. magnesium oxide) in a vacuum. Pipes with taps are fitted for filling and emptying the tank and there are narrow open tubes to allow the escape of evaporated gas. A bursting plate is fitted to prevent a particular internal pressure being exceeded. The tanks are placed, well sprung, on wagons or trucks (see fig. 2.19). Transport of liquefied gases by this means is much cheaper than transport in steel cylinders, which weigh 15 kg per m^3 of oxygen (1.4 kg).

Fig. 2.19 Bulk oxygen transport. This big Dewar flask can carry five tons of liquid oxygen. It is much cheaper than carriage in iron cylinders, which can take gaseous oxygen only.

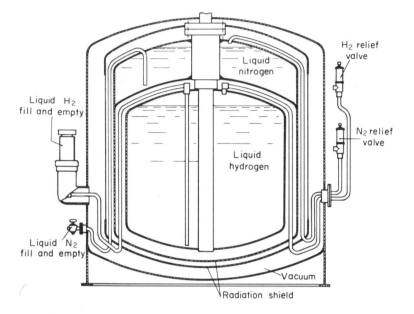

Fig. 2.20 A schematic diagram of a Dewar vessel for liquid hydrogen. The radiation shield is cooled by liquid nitrogen in the other container.

Transferring liquefied gas from the transport containers was always a very difficult matter, since normally flexible materials became brittle and broke quickly at the low temperatures. Flexible pipes are at present made in the form of a coil of stainless steel wire. This is wrapped alternately with layers of Terylene and plastic film, these in turn being wrapped with double layers of strong stainless steel mesh. Connecting pieces are secured to the pipe with a special plastic adhesive. The inside diameter is 10 cm. Pipes of this kind last at least six times as long as the older type.

The heat loss in a Dewar vessel is caused by the heat radiation between the cold wall and the surroundings. The loss through evaporation of, for instance, liquid hydrogen or helium can be reduced by placing a radiation screen between the said wall and surroundings. In fig. 2.20 there is represented a large Dewar vessel for 500 l of hydrogen, in which the aluminium radiation screen in the vacuum space is cooled with liquid nitrogen. Owing to the good heat conductivity of the aluminium the temperature of the screen substantially corresponds to the temperature of the liquid nitrogen. The loss through evaporation can also be considerably restricted by using a large number of radiation screens in the vacuum space. Insulation materials based on the principle of a large number of radiation screens are called multilayer insulations or super insulations. For very low temperature scientific research Dewar flasks are sometimes assembled from three or four coaxial flasks, all the spaces being silvered and evacuated (see also Helium, p. 91).

2.1.6 Containers for gas storage

Several gases (especially hydrogen, but also nitrogen, oxygen, carbon dioxide etc.) are also stored at atmospheric temperature.

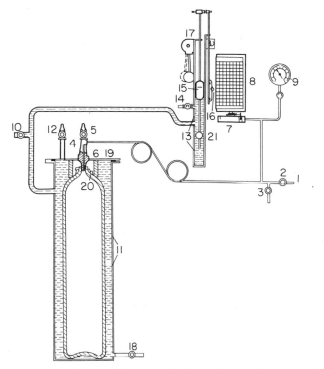

Fig. 2.21 Diagram of apparatus for inspecting steel compressed-air cylinders:
1. Feed pipe for compression fluid (2, 3, 4 and 5 are cocks); 6. Connection to cylinder; 7. Clock-work for rotating drum (8); 9 Manometer; 10. Tap in pipe supplying water to tank (11) enclosing steel cylinder; 12. 14 and 18. Drain taps; 13. Cylinder with piston (15), which is kept vertical by the counterweight 21 and holds the pen (16) via a right-angled rod to draw a curve on the rotating drum, from which changes in volume during compression of the cylinder and the causes thereof can be appraised; 17. Warning device in case the cylinder bulges too much.

The gases are compressed up to 150 atm. and put into steel cylinders made of seamless tubing; the top and bottom being in one piece with the body (see vol. II, p.   ) Before use (and then once every five years) they are filled with water under 240 atm. pressure and placed in a completely enclosed tank of water, so that any bulging can be carefully checked (see fig. 2.21). In some countries these cylinders are government inspected. For liquefied gases of relatively low vapour pressure cylinders are also being made of strong aluminium alloy, especially for liquefied petroleum gases (LPG) (see vol. IV). While a large steel cylinder may weigh 150 lb, a comparable cylinder of aluminium alloy weighs only 47 lb.

Spherical containers of fibre-glass reinforced epoxy resins (see vol. IV) are also being made. These can contain 2 m³ gas compressed to 200 atm. For the same capacity and strength these are many times lighter than metal containers, especially steel ones.

International standards are being proposed for cylinders to contain inflammable and non-inflammable gases, subdivided into three categories. Two categories of storage vessel are also being standardized for inflammable and non-inflammable liquefied gases.

Standards are moreover being agreed upon for connections, according to the type of gas.

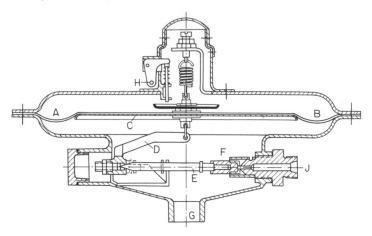

Fig. 2.22 Section of a reducing valve. The gas enters at J, being admitted in small quantities under the membrane AB which, when the pressure rises, is forced up in the space underneath. Its movement turns the bar D slightly, the rod E closing the inlet at F. When enough gas has left via G, reducing the pressure, the spring over AB (or a rod that can be moved by the angular lever H) will depress the valve again, a little compressed gas again being admitted via J.

In tracing defects in cylinders X-rays are used for structural photography; ultrasonic waves are also employed, and optical instruments exist for internal inspection.

The cylinders are emptied via a reducing valve (see fig. 2.22) bringing the high internal pressure down to a low working pressure. The pressure of the supplied gas is controlled by means of a membrane. When the pressure of this gas increases or decreases the membrane moves. This movement is transmitted to the top of the gas container which is closed or opened respectively. The membrane used to be made of leather or synthetic resin. Nowadays strong nylon fabric is coated on both sides with synthetic rubber and corrugated by compression; it is strong, impermeable to gases and unaffected by them. The rubber is thickened at the edges, ensuring a complete seal between the two parts of the metal casing. This makes the membrane – and the instrument as a whole – much more sensitive to slight changes in pressure.

Manometers for pressures below 1 atm. have evacuated chambers, two sides of which are made of thin beryllium copper, also having annular corrugations. These are calibrated with a sensitive liquid manometer and can then indicate pressures to a minimum of 0.01 mm mercury and a maximum of 75 mm.

Cylinders for hydrogen and other inflammable or dangerous gases usually have a left-hand thread to obviate mistakes.

Cylinders for 'medical' gases (e.g. for anaesthetics) are marked by international agreement with specified colours at the valve end to about one-third of the cylinder length. For mixed gases two colours are used, divided into four segments. It is to be hoped that before long all cylinders will be marked in this way.

These expensive containers are let out on hire by manufacturers to purchasers of the gases. The longer the cylinders are retained the more steeply the rental increases in order to stop them being held up through carelessness.

Those of normal capacity weigh about 40 kg, i.e. many times heavier than the 6 m³ of gas compressed into them. Carriage costs are high.

In many countries, filled returnable cylinders are not charged with import duties, while new ones are charged at a high rate.

Bulk storage of highly compressed hydrogen or other gases would be far too costly because of the size and strength of the steel vessels required. A system of spherical tanks may be used for quantities of about 400 m³ compressed to about 10 atm. A number of such spherical tanks can be welded together in the form of a polyhedron to provide one big storage tank (see fig. 2.23).

Fig. 2.23 Multisphere for storing 400 m³ of gas at about 10 atm. Its height is about 10 m. Where the spheres meet they are welded inside to plates with a large hole in them, making the unit very strong.

2.2 HYDROGEN (H_2, mole weight = 2.001 6)

2.2.1 Occurrence

Something has been known about this gas since the sixteenth century. Cavendish (1760) realized that it must be a definite substance and this was confirmed by Lavoisier (1783), who called it hydrogenium.

This element occurs in vast quantities in all the stars (the sun is 60% hydrogen) and in interstellar space. It does not occur in the free state on earth. It was once thought that it occurred free in the highest layers of the atmosphere; spectroscopic measurements of the aurora borealis, however, have shown that this is possible only to an extremely small degree.

Hydrogen is a constituent of water, carbohydrates, hydrocarbons, fats, etc., and of many other compounds. It is also a constituent of numerous synthetic gaseous fuels, such as coal gas, coke oven gas, water gas and synthesis gas.

2.2.2 Production of gases containing hydrogen

a. Steam re-forming of natural gas and refinery gas. Natural gas consists mainly of methane, and refinery gas (cracked gas) is a mixture of hydrocarbon gases such as methane, propane, butane, etc. These gases are treated with steam at a temperature of 700 to 800° C in the presence of nickel supported on an inert material. In this process the nickel accelerates the reaction without itself being consumed. (A substance behaving in this way is called 'a catalyst'.

The equation for the reaction of steam with methane is: $CH_4 + H_2O \rightarrow CO + 3H_2$. Sometimes, depending on the composition of the hydrocarbon mixture, the reaction is not complete in one step. The gas is then passed with air through a second reaction chamber in which a small part of the hydrogen and the residual hydrocarbons are burned (see also fig. 2.24). The resulting gas mixture contains by volume about 57% hydrogen, 21% nitrogen, 10% carbon dioxide, 11% carbon monoxide and some impurities such as oxygen, methane and argon.

This process is the most important method for the production of hydrogen containing gases. It is used in countries where natural gas has been found, such as the United States, Italy, France, Pakistan and Yugoslavia. Hydrogen rich refinery gases are produced in the United States and the Middle East. It is estimated that about 40% of the world's hydrogen comes from natural gas and refinery gas.

b. Water gas generation. Water gas is produced by passing steam over red-hot coke (see gas production, vol. II). The following reactions take place:
$C + H_2O \rightarrow CO + H_2$ and $C + 2H_2O \rightarrow CO_2 + 2H_2$. Water gas contains the following percentages by volume: hydrogen 44-51%, nitrogen 3.5-7%, carbon monoxide 33-34%, carbon dioxide 2.5-4% and some impurities such as oxygen, hydrogen sulphide and argon. Often a mixture of air and steam is used in water gas production. In this case water gas obtained contains less hydrogen (about 36-40%) and more nitrogen (about 20%), and is called semi-watergas. Unlike water gas, semi-watergas is produced in a continuous process. This process is an important source of hydrogen in the United Kingdom and is other countries, which have little or no natural gas or refinery gas sources.

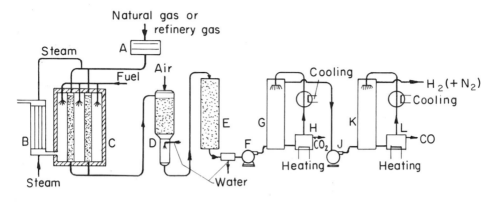

Fig. 2.24 Flow sheet of the production of hydrogen from natural gas.
A. Sulphur purifier; B. Heat exchanger; C. Methane reforming furnace; D. Secondary reformer;
E. Carbon monoxide converter (water-shift reactor); F. Compressor (10-20 atm); G. Carbon
dioxide absorber; H. Regeneration of absorbent and recovery of CO_2; J. Compressor (100 atm);
K. Carbon monoxide absorber; L. Regeneration of absorbent and recovery of CO.

c. Coal gas production. Coal gas and coke-oven gas are obtained by thermal decomposition of coal (see carbonization and coal gas, vol. II). Several by products are recovered before distribution. Coal gas contains about 50% by volume of hydrogen, 4% carbon monoxide, 25-30% methane and several impurities. This gas mixture is a source of hydrogen in the United Kingdom, France, Belgium, Germany and other countries which have an important coal industry.

d. Partial combustion of carbonaceous materials. This process was developed for natural gas but it is especially used for carbonaceous materials which can not be subjected to the steam treatment discussed under *a*. In the United States, United Kingdom, Canada, Finland, France and some other countries, this process is adapted to the partial combustion of coal and fuel oil. The carbonaceous materials are burned with a limited quantity of oxygen in the presence of steam at a temperature of about 1300-1500° C. Oxygen is used instead of air for the reaction. For this reason this process is profitable if byproduct oxygen can be cheaply obtained as, for instance, in the production of nitrogen from air. The partial combustion reaction may be represented by the following simplified reaction based on the paraffins present in fuel oils:
$CnH(2n + 2) + \frac{1}{2}nO_2 \rightarrow nCO + (n + 1)H_2$. The addition of steam is necessary to prevent the formation of carbon (soot) in a side reaction (compare water gas generation p. 62).

The partial combustion process demands careful control of the feed rates to the combustion chamber. Heat resisting materials are needed for the construction of the reaction vessels. These are made of steel with a lining of many layers of fire bricks.

The gas obtained from partial combustion of fuel oil contains about 48 volume % hydrogen, 48% carbon monoxide, 3% carbon dioxide, 0.2% nitrogen and some impurities such as methane and sulphur compounds.

e. In smaller quantities, for instance for filling small meteorological observation balloons, hydrogen is produced by dripping hydrocarbons on glowing coke, or by conducting coal gas through it. In America a mixture of hydrogen and carbon monoxide, known as 'electrolene', is produced as a gaseous fuel by passing coal gas and steam through an electric oven.

2.2.3 Separation of hydrogen from gas mixtures

The hydrogen content of gases containing much carbon monoxide, especially water gas, can be increased by making use of the 'water gas shift reaction', in which carbon monoxide is treated with steam in the presence of a mixture of iron oxide and chromium oxide as a catalyst to give carbon dioxide and hydrogen with 90% yield. A mixture of cobalt oxide or nickel oxide with chromium oxide may also be used as catalyst.

Fig. 2.25 shows a simplified diagram. In reality there are two stages, one at 500° C and one at 400° C. Heat exchangers are used because the reactions release a large amount of available heat.

Carbon dioxide is removed from the gas mixture by treatment with liquid absorbents in countercurrent. The absorbents may be an aqueous solution of an amine, such as mono ethanolamine, an aqueous solution of a carbonate or water. If water is used, the gas has to be compressed to a pressure of 15-50 atm. The solutions can be regenerated by heating. The large amounts of carbon dioxide obtained may be used for making urea (see p. 345) or for the production of liquid or solid carbon dioxide.

Most of the hydrogen sulphide present is also absorbed by the absorbents for carbon

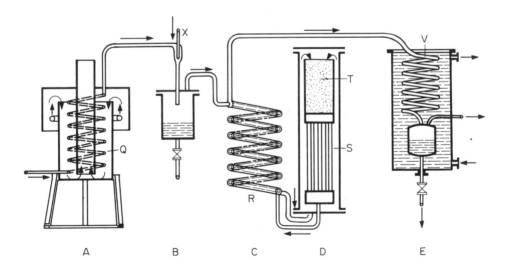

Fig. 2.25 Diagram of apparatus for converting carbon monoxide in water gas into carbon dioxide. Water gas is heated at A in a coil Q (with steam). B is a steam trap, in which steam enters at X, for extracting steam quickly from Q through the injector X. Heat exchange takes place at C and D in the coil R (made of coaxial tubes) and in the tube system S. The catalyst is in the top of tank D (at T). In tank E there is a water-cooled cooling coil (V); the steam that condenses in this runs into the steam trap under the coil and is removed.

dioxide. Remaining quantities can be removed by passing the gas, with some air, over a mixture of iron oxide and peat at about 30° C. Hydrogen sulphide is thus converted into sulphur and water. Hydrogen sulphide can also be removed in this way before the water gas shift reaction.

The remaining carbon monoxide can be removed by dissolving in an ammoniacal solution of a cuprous salt at a high pressure. This process is performed by counter-current extraction (see fig. 2.24).

The resulting gas mixture consists of hydrogen, nitrogen and small quantities of oxygen, argon, methane and sometimes other hydrocarbons. When used in ammonia synthesis (the largest single use of hydrogen) it is only necessary to remove oxygen, after which the mixed gas can be used directly. (Since coal gas contains much more methane the latter must be removed when coal gas is the starting material.)

There are several processes for further purification which may be used depending on the quantities and kinds of impurities. Thus hydrogen for ammonia production must be free from carbon monoxide and oxygen but the presence of small amounts of methane (up to about 1%) is permitted. Small quantities of carbon monoxide can be removed by contacting the gas with a nickel chromic oxide catalyst at a temperature of about 400° C. In this process carbon monoxide is converted to methane. At the same time most of the oxygen is converted to water.

If necessary, methane can be removed by drying the gas and cooling in stages with precooled nitrogen from air liquefaction plants. Several traces of impurities such as hydrocarbons and carbon dioxide liquefy in the first stages and can be drawn off. In the last stage most of the methane liquefies and can be recovered. The last traces of methane are removed by washing the cold gas with liquid nitrogen.

Small quantities of oxygen can be removed, either from hydrogen-nitrogen mixtures or from impure hydrogen, by conducting the gas over a palladium catalyst, which forms water from the oxygen and hydrogen. This is then entrained in the form of a vapour and can be removed by water-absorbents. This is very important in hydrogenation (i.e. addition of hydrogen to other molecules; see fats, coal, petroleum, resin, etc.).

In recent years there has been a tendency to purify hydrogen in one process by cooling gas mixtures in stages either with liquid or precooled nitrogen or in a refrigerating unit, after removal of water vapour, carbon dioxide and sulphur compounds. In the first stages traces of several hydrocarbons, carbon dioxide etc. liquefy and are drawn off. In the last stages carbon monoxide, oxygen, methane and a part of the nitrogen liquefy and can be removed by fractional distillation (see liquefaction and fractional distillation of air, fig. 2.7 and fig. 2.26; the latter is a simplified diagram of fig. 2.7).

Some installations using this method are almost fully automatic. A large number of safety valves and warning devices are installed, all connected to central control panels in air conditioned rooms.

Continuous flowmeters, hydrogen sulphide and oxygen content analysers and also a mass spectrograph (for checking the purity of the hydrogen) are connected with the control panels. In spite of the staff required at the various control points, the process is more economical than the decentralized control of the past.

If pure hydrogen is needed, the remaining gas is passed through silica gel cooled with liquid nitrogen. At this low temperature the nitrogen liquefies and cold hydrogen gas is obtained. The low temperature of this gas is used for precooling impure gases.

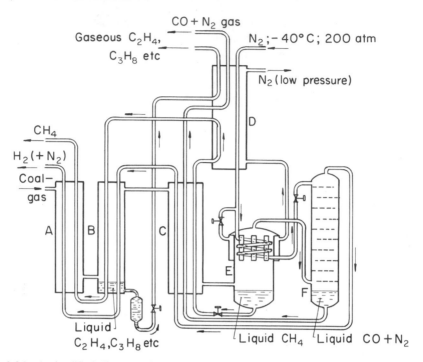

Fig. 2.26 A simplified diagram of an installation for separating hydrogen (and nitrogen) from coal gas by cooling and liquefaction with liquid nitrogen.
A, B, C and D are heat exchangers; E is a methane condenser; F is a nitrogen scrubber.
High pressure nitrogen is expanded and partially used for liquefying methane in E and partially for liquefying carbon monoxide in F. The liquefied products and the remaining cold hydrogen are passed through the heat exchangers thus precooling the feed gas in steps.

If liquid hydrogen is needed, cold hydrogen is compressed. cooled with liquid nitrogen and liquefied by expansion through a Joule-Thompson valve. The equipment is housed in large metal Dewar flasks, as extremely low temperatures are needed (−252° C). For this reason the main practical uses of liquid hydrogen are for military purposes (e.g. rocket fuel) and on a small scale for scientific experiments.

Very pure hydrogen is obtainable with a special unit. consisting substantially of a box divided in two by a palladium partition. The whole is heated to 250° C (at low temperature a brittle hydrogen-palladium compound would be produced). If impure hydrogen is fed at one end only pure hydrogen diffuses through the palladium screen. The other gases must be blown off periodically.

2.2.4 Electrolytic production of hydrogen

In principle electrolysis is effected as follows:
Two electrodes are placed in a vessel full of water. The cathode (negative) is an iron plate and the anode (positive) is a nickelled iron plate. A diaphragm of asbestos, metal wire mesh or a perforated nickel plate is positioned between the electrodes. About 25% by weight of sodium hydroxide or potassium hydroxide is dissolved in the water to make it conductive. Water decomposes at a voltage difference of from 2.0 to 2.3 V

between the electrodes, giving rise to hydrogen at the cathode and oxygen at the anode. The diaphragm prevents the mixing of the gases, which are collected separately. The presence of alkali greatly reduces the resistance of the liquid, so that even at the low voltage difference mentioned above the intensity of the current is considerable. According to the law of Faraday the amount of gas produced per unit of time is proportional to the current intensity (see also alkali electrolysis, p. 429).

Hydrogen is also recovered cheaply as a byproduct in alkali chloride electrolysis.

The great advantage of electrolysis is that it yields very pure hydrogen. With caustic soda electrolyte, the product contains only 0.1 to 0.5% of oxygen and some water vapour.

In practice two types of electrolytic cells are used, i.e. one type with a number of electrodes in parallel connection (called unipolar type) and another with a number of electrodes in series connection (called bipolar or filterpress type). The former is mainly applied in the United States and the latter is mainly used in Europe.

In the unipolar system a number of anodes, diaphragms and cathodes are placed in a large vessel as shown in fig. 2.27. Anodes and cathodes occur alternately all the anodes being connected with the positive pole and all the cathodes with the negative pole of the current source (parallel connection). The gases are collected by means of bells which are positioned as shown in fig. 2.27. An example of this type of electrolytic apparatus is the Knowles cell. The gases are collected separately in two undulating tubes which, in the wave troughs, are in connection with the bells that collect the gas. One tube is connected to those collecting oxygen, the other tube to those collecting hydrogen (see fig. 2.28). The hydrogen production amounts to about 0.2 m³ (of dry gas at 0° C and 760 mm Hg) per kWh. At the same time 0.1 m³ of oxygen is obtained as a byproduct. The purity of the hydrogen is 99.7% and that of the oxygen 99.5%. The current intensity may be from 3000 to 15000 amp. A complete hydrogen plant comprises a plurality of Knowles cells connected in series.

In the bipolar system the arrangement of electrodes can be the same as in the unipolar one. In this case, however, only the first and the last electrodes are connected to a current source, the voltage difference between the said two electrodes being much larger than from 2 to 2.3 V. Thus each electrode between the two outermost ones has a higher voltage than the preceding electrode and a lower voltage than the following electrode (series connection) and each of the electrodes (except the two outermost ones) acts as a cathode on one side and as anode on the other side, whence the name 'bipolar'. By choosing an adequate number of cells, a voltage difference of about 2 V between each pair of electrodes is obtained. An example of such an apparatus is the

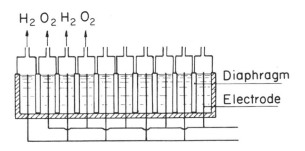

H₂ O₂ H₂ O₂

Diaphragm

Electrode

Fig. 2.27 Simplified diagram of an electrolysis cell for hydrogen production, with parallel connection of the electrodes.

Fig. 2.28 A hydrogen-oxygen plant with Knowles cells. Some of the 256 cells can be seen with their S-shaped pipes, hydrogen pipes, say, at the front and a series for oxygen at the back.

Zdansky Lonza unit (see fig. 2.29). This unit is built up as a filter press (see p. 21) by clamping on to one another a series of plate-electrodes and diaphragms with ring-shaped frames in between. The frames are provided with outlet channels for the gases. The Zdansky Lonza unit operates under a pressure of 30 atm, so that the volume can be smaller than in a cell operating under normal pressure. It contains from 400 to 600 cells and thus operates at a voltage difference of from 800 to 1 200 V. In units of considerable production capacity the current intensity is from 2 000 to 5 000 amp. The efficiency per kWh and the purity of the gases are about equal to those of the Knowles cell.

2.2.5 Other production methods

The oldest method for the commercial production of hydrogen gas is the reduction of steam by iron at temperatures from 750 to 1 000° C (by leading steam over red-hot iron helices).

Equation of reaction: $Fe + H_2O \rightarrow FeO + H_2$ and $3FeO + H_2O \rightarrow Fe_3O_4 + H_2$. Thus this reaction gives rise to iron oxide and hydrogen gas.

In some cases it is expedient to prepare hydrogen by heating ammonia in an electric oven in the presence of 'nickel shot' or nickel oxide as a catalyst. In this case a mixture of 75 % of hydrogen and 25 % of nitrogen is obtained. The remaining ammonia is washed out with water. This process is only economical when small quantities of hydrogen are

Fig. 2.29 A Zdansky Lonza unit for hydrogen production.

required and when the presence of nitrogen in the gas is no drawback. This hydrogen-nitrogen mixture is used in the reduction of metal oxides (for example, cleaning of metal surfaces of small objects, such as parts of radio valves). It may also be used as a protective atmosphere in the bright annealing of metals and in powder metallurgy.

For laboratory use, hydrogen may be produced by the action of sulphuric acid on zinc, hydrochloric acid on iron, caustic soda on aluminium, silicon or ferrosilicon, zinc etc., but these methods are too expensive for large scale use.

2.2.6 Properties

Hydrogen is the lightest of all gases and one litre weighs 0.0898 of a gram at 0° C and 76 cm pressure. Its critical temperature is −240° C and its boiling point is −252.7° C. Its heat of combustion is 34 000 cal per kg and hence about 3 000 cal per m³, at normal pressure and temperature. The solubility of hydrogen in water is low (2.1 cm³ in 100 cm³ water at 0° C, decreasing at higher temperatures).

Mixtures with air containing from 4% to 72.4% of hydrogen can be exploded by a flame or a spark, to form water with the oxygen in the air. Hydrogen also forms compounds with metals (see hydrides, p. 72).

Ordinary hydrogen contains also about 0.02% of another form of hydrogen which has almost the same chemical properties but different physical properties. This hydrogen is named heavy hydrogen or deuterium as it is twice as heavy as ordinary hydrogen (see isotopes, ch. 15 Nucleonics). A third kind of hydrogen is tritium, which is three times heavier than ordinary hydrogen. Tritium is a radioactive substance. Ordinary hydrogen contains one tritium atom in about 10^{17} hydrogen atoms (see radioactive isotopes, ch. 15 Nucleonics).

Ordinary hydrogen has a dual molecular structure in another respect. The electrons of the two atoms forming the molecule may rotate round their nuclei in the same direction; but they may circle in opposite directions instead. The former type we call *orthohydrogen* and the latter *parahydrogen*. Under normal and high temperatures ordinary hydrogen consists of 75% orthohydrogen and 25% parahydrogen. At very low temperatures orthohydrogen is slowly converted into parahydrogen. A fairly substantial amount of heat is released in converting orthohydrogen into parahydrogen. This was one of the reasons why keeping of hydrogen in liquefied condition was so difficult. At present, after the gas has been strongly cooled, it is passed over a chromium oxide or hydrous ferric oxide catalyst at $-250°$ C, whereupon conversion is almost complete. The gas (over 99% parahydrogen) is then liquefied and stored.

Only a small space is needed over the stored liquid; formerly the space over the liquid had to be much bigger because a small space would soon have been subjected to an excessive pressure due to rapid evaporation of hydrogen. Low-temperature storage of liquefied hydrogen is possible for relatively long periods. This is greatly encouraging its use, as liquid hydrogen can be used as rocket fuel. Especially in the United States, therefore, a number of hydrogen liquefaction plants have been built. The first big production plant making high purity liquid hydrogen is operated by the US Air Force and has a production capacity of 10 million lb/yr.

2.2.7 Uses

Large quantities of hydrogen are used for producing synthetic ammonia (see p. 305) and also in the hydrogenation of vegetable and animal oils and fats to produce margarine (see vol. VIII). Other oils and fats and hydrocarbons are hydrogenated for use in soaps, paints, varnishes, lubricants and several other products. Methanol and synthetic petrol are produced from carbon monoxide and hydrogen (see vol. IV.) Hydrochloric acid may be produced by combining chlorine and hydrogen. For the purposes mentioned before, hydrogen must be free of catalyst poisons as the processes are performed in the presence of catalysts. Large quantities of hydrogen are also used for hydro-treating of petroleum fractions, thus reducing their sulphur content (see vol. IV).

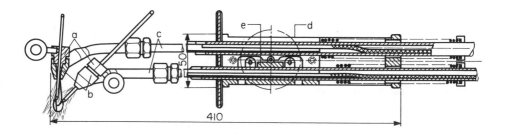

Fig. 2.30 Section of an atomic hydrogen burner.
a. Holders for carbon rods; b. Hydrogen and oxygen nozzles; c. Hydrogen and oxygen feed pipes; d. Grip; e. Electrode gap adjuster.

The consumption of hydrogen can largely be estimated from the production of synthetic ammonia and the hydrogenation of fats, oils and petroleum products. Large users produce it in their own plants.

Its low specific gravity (about one-eleventh of a gram per litre at normal temperature and pressure) makes hydrogen excellent for filling balloons. During the second world war Britain used large quantities of hydrogen for the balloon barrage against enemy aircraft. It is also used in meteorological and toy balloons. For big transport balloons (airships) it was increasingly replaced by helium, which is non-inflammable (but very expensive).

Its great heat of combustion makes it suitable for supplying very hot flames for melting precious metals and for oxyhydrogen cutting and welding. Hydrogen and oxygen are usually supplied through tubes with converging openings, shaped so that the flame comes to a sharp point. With correct adjustment, the oxyhydrogen flame may be hotter than 2 000° C. If a pattern is drawn on a sheet of iron the pointed flame can be guided along it, melting and burning the iron. An excess of oxygen is used for cutting and an excess of hydrogen for welding.

For some purposes hydrogen is used in electric arc welding. Hydrogen is blown into an electric arc formed by two tungsten electrodes. In the electric arc, molecular hydrogen absorbs much heat and dissociates into atomic hydrogen. At the outside of the arc atomic hydrogen recombines to molecular hydrogen and the absorbed heat is released. At the same time hydrogen burns with the surrounding air. Thus an excep tionally high temperature is formed (about 4000° C). This atomic welding (plasma torch welding) is used for high-speed mass production jobs. A diagram of the atomic hydrogen burner is shown in fig. 2.30.

A drawback of the welding methods described above is that hydrogen can form a kind of very hard, brittle alloy with iron and several other metals. For subsequent working of iron and steel after hydrogen welding, the metal has therefore to be heated red hot. Hence, it is preferable for welding to be done with acetylene or other hydro-carbon gases (see also welding, vol. II).

Atomic hydrogen has strong reducing properties. Hence the use of nascent hydrogen for difficult reductions. The compounds to be reduced are introduced into an acid or caustic soda and a metal powder, e.g. zinc is added. The metal dissolves and atomic hydrogen (nascent hydrogen) is released. This hydrogen can react with the compounds to be reduced before combining to molecular hydrogen (compare production of hydrogen, p. 68).

The great affinity of hydrogen for oxygen is used to reduce pure metal oxides to metals by passing hydrogen through them in a tall refractory tube heated to a high temperature from the outside. Even ordinary iron oxides can be reduced to a carbon free crude iron at 950° C.

Hydrogen is being increasingly used for cooling dynamos because of its low density, its relatively high heat conductivity and because coronas cannot produce ozone in it (this can happen in air, and the insulating material is then destroyed). Winding resistance (about 10% of that in air) is, as a result, lower and this has made it possible to raise the capacity of large generators from 40000 to over 90000 kVA. The generator is of course gas-tight, bearings, collectors and brushes being constructed to allow inspection without removing the entire supply of hydrogen. Only slight replenishment is required. Many modern generators are made so that hydrogen compressed to

10 atm can be used. The interior is built to allow easy circulation and rapid heat dispersion. It has been found that the temperature of hydrogen in the generator can increase by 50° C in one-fiftieth of a second. The hot hydrogen is cooled again with water circulating round the gas tubes.

Especially rapid cooling is ensured if the generator windings are made of copper tubing through which the cooling gas flows. The advantages of this are a much higher voltage with the use of much less copper and steel.

2.2.8 Hydrides

In both the molecular and the atomic state hydrogen can penetrate into a number of metals to form compounds known as hydrides.

Iron and steel, for instance, dissolve a relatively large amount of hydrogen, which may cause them to blister. In steel this may cause enamel to flake off later. In the atomic state hydrogen forms hydrides in steel, making it very brittle. Such steel must therefore be pretreated, for example by heating it in a vacuum. Hydrides are often formed in iron, etc. during electrolytic processing, because nascent hydrogen is released at the same time. This often happens with nickel, and especially during pickling of steel.

With other elements, such as Na, K, Li, Ca, Al, B, etc., hydrides may be formed by the action of hydrogen on emulsions containing them at high pressures and temperatures.

The hydrides are strong reducing agents, though their reducing capacity varies greatly. They may selectively attack certain places in organic molecules, a feature that has made them very important in organic chemistry.

Complex hydrides, such as lithium/aluminium hydride, sodium/boron hydride, etc., may also be formed.

The behaviour of palladium with hydrogen is quite different from that of most other metals.

Calcium hydride is used especially for producing hydrogen for smaller balloons.

Many hydrides form fine powders; they are self-igniting and explosive in that state, and are therefore stored under a rare gas (see also the various metallic elements, and boron, p. 516).

2.2.9 Statistics

The production figures published by several countries are not complete. Thus about 67500 million ft³ of hydrogen were produced in the United States during 1961, according to figures published by the US Department of Commerce and the US Bureau of Mines. However this figure excludes amounts consumed in synthetic ammonia production, methanol production and hydro-treating and amounts disposed of, as waste e.g. used as fuel, etc. The total hydrogen production of that country was estimated to be 640000 million ft³ in the same year (excluding the large quantities in gases which are burned as fuel).

It is estimated that about 350000 million ft³ were consumed in ammonia production, 175000 million ft³ in hydro-treating of petroleum fractions, 75000 million ft³ in methanol production and 20 million ft³ in hydrogenation of oils and fats. Only small quantities were used for other purposes.

Before the last world war, about 80% of the world's hydrogen was obtained from coal and coke. Nowadays about 40% is obtained from coal and coke, another 40% from refinery gas and natural gas and the remaining 20% from fuel oil and water (electrolytic). In the United States, about 75% of the hydrogen production comes from natural gas.

Hydrogen plants ranging from 50 thousand to 50 million ft^3 per day are furnishing hydrogen for a variety of industrial uses. The initial cost of a typical 50 million ft^3 per day hydrogen plant is now nearly $ 4 million.

The production cost of crude hydrogen in the US ranges from $ 0.38 to $ 0.51 per thousand ft^3 for steam reforming in plants having a capacity of 15 to 5 million ft^3 per day. The production cost of hydrogen produced by partial oxidation of fuel oil amounts to $ 0.50 to $ 0.70 per thousand ft.^{3}

The production cost of pure hydrogen is about twice the cost mentioned before and the production cost of pure electrolytic hydrogen in the United States amounts to about four times the same figures. Electrolytic hydrogen is cheaper in countries having cheap electric energy sources.

2.3 OXYGEN (O_2, mole weight = 32)

2.3.1 Occurrence

This gas occurs in a free state in air and dissolved in water. Combined with hydrogen, it accounts for 89% of the weight of water. It is found combined in many carbon compounds and in most minerals, acids, alkalis and salts. It is estimated that 48.6% (by weight) of the earth consists of oxygen. The rest is estimated to be 26.3% silicon, 7.7% aluminium, 4.8% iron, 3.5% calcium, 2.7% sodium, 2.5% potassium, 2.0% magnesium, 0.8% hydrogen and 0.4% titanium, less than 1% thus being left for all the other elements together.

The main source of oxygen is air. Air consists of four volumes of nitrogen to one of oxygen (see also constituents of air, p. 95). Their ratio by weight is about 3 : 1, the proportions being fairly constant in spite of the respiration of plants and animals, since green plants regularly discharge oxygen when exposed to light, forming it from absorbed carbon dioxide and water by catalytic processes.

Algae (see vol. V) exist which convert the carbon dioxide they absorb so rapidly that they discharge a thousand times as much as their volume of oxygen a day.

Oxygen is indispensable for respiration and 'combustion' in general. Thus its presence in air is the basis of animal and vegetable life.

Dissolved in water, it makes life possible for fish and other animals. All water discharged into public rivers and lakes must therefore contain sufficient oxygen (see effluent, p. 167).

2.3.2 Production

The most important method for producing oxygen is the liquefaction and fractionation of air according to the Linde process (see liquefaction of gases, p. 44).

For occasional use, transported and stored liquid oxygen is the obvious choice. If, as increasingly applies in the iron industry and the gas industry, oxygen is required almost continuously, it is preferable to use local plants supplying gaseous oxygen. These plants which are named 'tonnage oxygen' plants need a lower power consumption, as the liquid oxygen produced is gasified by heat exchange with the feed air. In this way a lower compression of the air feed is possible. The power consumption of tonnage oxygen plants is about 500 kWh per short ton of oxygen. The power consumption for the production of liquid oxygen is about 800 kWh per short ton. Tonnage oxygen plants are available in sizes ranging from 100 to 1 000 short tons per day, producing oxygen at about $ 16 to $ 8 per short ton respectively.

Modern heat exchangers, greatly improved turbines, pumps, etc. have made it possible for small units to work economically. A unit has been constructed weighing less than 70 kg for producing oxygen for aircraft in flight. Even in this case the oxygen need cost no more than about $ 12 to $ 13 per short ton.

Aircraft carriers nowadays have two plants for liquefying oxygen and nitrogen from the air. The oxygen can be used for respiration by men in aeroplanes flying at high altitudes and the nitrogen as a fire precaution, by storing petrol or other fuel under nitrogen and sending supplies up under pressure.

Such plants are expensive, mainly because the distilling equipment has to be specially built to operate normally during rolling of the ship.

Oxygen is also produced as a by-product in electrolytic hydrogen production (see p. 66). It usually contains about 4% hydrogen, which can be removed by catalytic combustion. It is not worth while setting up an electrolytic cell specifically for producing oxygen, ordinary air being a much cheaper source. About 3% of the world's oxygen is obtained in this way. The method may be used increasingly for producing oxygen in submarines now that a strong cell has been constructed which keeps the two gases quite separate, supplying them at a pressure of 225 atm, thus dispensing with the need for equipment for compression. The cell is constructed in such a way that the gases cannot mix even when the vessel is in violent motion. When this method is used the unwanted hydrogen is discharged into the sea.

For producing small amounts of oxygen, a chemical method is sometimes used that resembles the reaction by which oxygen is utilized by the human body. This method makes use of a cobalt chelate from organic compounds with a cobalt salt, such as 'salcomine' (= bis-salicylaldehyde ethylenediimine-cobalt). The red crystalline granules absorb up to 4.5% of their weight in oxygen, thereby turning black. The tube in which this compound absorbs oxygen is cooled to obtain a better effect. Heating the tube causes the black mass to discharge the oxygen again. This can be repeated 1 000 times before the chelate requires recrystallizing.

Where only very small amounts of oxygen are required, chlorate candles may be used; these are prepared by melting a mixture of barium peroxide, fibreglass, iron powder and a chlorate. The candles release oxygen when lighted. The iron powder acts as an accessory heat source and the barium peroxide prevents chlorine being released, since it forms barium chloride with the chlorine liberated from the chlorate.

2.3.3 Properties of oxygen

Oxygen is a colourless gas of which the molecules consist of two oxygen atoms. One litre of oxygen weighs 1.4 at 0° C and 76 cm pressure. Its critical temperature is − 119° C. Below this temperature it can be liquefied to a blue liquid (boiling point = −183° C). Oxygen is only slightly soluble in water at ordinary temperatures and pressures (4.9 cm³ in 100 cm³ water at 0° C).

Some metals can absorb large volumes of oxygen. The absorption of oxygen by palladium is important in some catalytic reactions (see catalysis, p. 62). The formation of blow holes in steel is caused by the absorption of oxygen in molten steel.

Oxygen and air rich in oxygen cause many inflammable substances (even road asphalt) to catch fire easily and burn fiercely. For this reason reducing valves of oxygen containers, oxygen pumps, etc. must not be lubricated with oils and fats (see also equipment for liquefaction of gases, p. 49).

If oxygen has to be compressed, diaphragm pumps are sometimes used. These contain a diaphragm instead of a moving piston, the cylinder being hermetically sealed.

Nowadays traces of hydrocarbons can be removed even from liquid oxygen by filters containing silica gel.

Special precautions are necessary during use and in 'transhipment' of oxygen in order to avoid sparks and flame. Organic substances, e.g. asphalt, can detonate if drops of liquid oxygen are absorbed in them.

Very low temperatures have a similar action on the skin to that of high temperatures: thus drops of liquefied oxygen may cause very nasty 'burns'.

Like other elements, oxygen contains small quantities of atoms, having the same chemical properties but not the same atomic weight. Normal oxygen is a mixture containing mainly atoms of atomic weight 16, 0.04% atoms having atomic weight 17 (O^{17}) and 0.2% oxygen having atomic weight 18 (O^{18}). The latter's chief importance is in investigating the role of oxygen in biological processes. The research is done by 'labelling' the oxygen of chemicals with O^{18} or by using 'labelled' oxygen for respirations (see isotopes, ch. 15).

Chemically, oxygen can combine with most of the elements to form oxides. The process is known as 'oxidation'. Oxygen is divalent in its compounds.

In most cases *oxidation* means increasing the oxygen content of a substance or combining oxygen with it. Substances which readily effect this are known as oxidizing agents (More generally oxidation means an increase of positive ionic charge or loss of electrons and reduction is a decrease of positive ionic charge or admitting electrons.) For example:

Chlorine reaction: $Cl_2 + H_2O \rightarrow 2HCl + O$
Nitric acid reaction: $HNO_3 \rightarrow HNO_2 + O$
Bleaching powder gives off free chlorine.
Sodium peroxide reaction: $Na_2O_2 \rightarrow Na_2O + O$
Hydrogen peroxide reaction: $H_2O_2 \rightarrow H_2O + O$
Sodium chlorite reaction: $NaClO_2 \rightarrow NaCl + 2O$
Chlorine dioxide reaction: $H_2O + 2 ClO_2 \rightarrow 2 HCl + 5 O$
Ozone reaction: $O_3 \rightarrow O_2 + O$

The efficiency of the most important oxidizing agents is given in the table on p. 76 showing, at the left, the amount of agent equivalent to 1 kg of ozone. The percentages show the purity of the commercial chemical. The prices are the average for 1963.

Kg	Oxidizing agents	Price per lb (1963) (US)	(UK) (approx)	
		$	s	d
0.56	Chlorine dioxide	–	–	
0.74	Sodium chlorate	0.10		9
0.85	Potassium chlorate	0.14	1	2
1.14	Sodium chlorite	0.58	4	1
1.34	Potassium chromate	0.50	3	6
1.40	Chromic acid (99.5%)	0.30	2	1
1.48	Chlorine	0.07		6
1.55	Nitric acid (42°Bé)	0.21		6
1.69	Sodium peroxide	0.07	1	6
2.02	Hydrogen peroxide (35%)	0.22	1	9
2.04	Potassium bichromate	0.18	1	4
2.07	Sodium chromate	0.15	1	3
2.13	Manganese dioxide (83-87%)	0.08		7
2.24	Potassium permanganate	0.38	2	8
4.93	Bleaching powder (30% Cl)	0.05		4
5.99	Potassium persulphate	0.20	1	5
5.01	Ammonium persulphate (pur)	0.40	–	–
5.98	Sodium perborate 4 aq	0.19	–	–

Besides the above, the following can be used as oxidizing agents: peroxide of lead (PbO$_2$), redlead (Pb$_3$O$_4$) and also many peroxides, perborates, perchlorates, persulphates and percarbonates of metals other than those mentioned above.

Reduction is the opposite of oxidation and consists in lowering the oxygen content of substances. The main *reducing agents* are hydrogen, hydrazine, hydrocarbons, aluminium, zinc dust, iron filings or iron shavings and especially carbon. In the form of coke, carbon is used in large quantities for reducing metal oxides to metals.

2.3.4 Determination of oxygen

The determination of the amount of oxygen contained in various gases is often of considerable importance, e.g. in submarines, for respiratory equipment, and for certain manufacturing purposes. It is often important to know also the amount of free oxygen contained in combustible gases.

Oxygen can be determined as follows: A gas sample is contacted with pyrogallol or with an alkaline solution of sodium hydrosulphite containing 2% anthraquinonebeta-sulphonic acid. These compounds are rapidly oxidized by oxygen. Thus the latter is removed from the gas sample. The oxygen content can be taken from measurements of the volume of the gas sample before and after contacting with pyrogallol or the anthra-quinone derivative. Chromic chloride in acetic acid, which is stable in storage, can be used in a similar way.

These substances may on occasion be used to remove oxygen from relatively small quantities of air, as for example in the case of large electrical transformers, when air drawn in for cooling might ignite the transformer oil. Chelates may also be used for such purposes (see p. 131).

Another method for the determination of oxygen is based on the fact that oxygen is relatively highly paramagnetic. Thus a non-homogeneous magnetic field changes with the oxygen content of a gas in this magnetic field. The change can be measured by means of a small diamagnetic body suspended on a stretched glass fibre wire (forming a torsion balance) in the magnetic field. The position of the test body changes with any change of the magnetic field.

There are also other devices based on the paramagnetic properties of oxygen, for example, if a paramagnetic gas is present in a magnetic field, a convection flow of this gas takes place. This flow cools an electrically heated wire, thus changing its resistance which can be measured. The cooling effect depends on the velocity of the gas and in turn the velocity of the gas depends on its oxygen content.

Small quantities of oxygen may be eliminated from many gases that are required to be oxygen-free (e.g. neutral gases for tempering hard steel) by ensuring that enough hydrogen is present to form water vapour with it by catalysis. Hydrogen can be removed from oxygen-containing mixtures in the same way. For every 0.1% oxygen so removed, the temperature rises by 10° C. Standard equipment is available commercially for this purpose. A similar process can also be used for eliminating small quantities of CO from gas mixtures (see p. 64).

2.3.5 Uses

Combustible gases burn so vigorously in oxygen that much higher temperatures can be reached than with air. These high temperatures are necessary for autogenous welding and cutting, for smelting various metals, for drilling in ore deposits, glass-blowing, etc.

Extremely high temperatures may be obtained by burning metal powders in the flame: mainly aluminium, magnesium and iron. The use of iron filings gives a very hot cutting flame, suitable for quick work, e.g. in working stainless steel.

The largest consumer of oxygen is the steel industry. This industry is using increasing quantities of oxygen in Martin furnaces and blast furnaces, converters, etc. In this way the carbon in the iron is oxidized more quickly than when air is used. Nowadays steel is also produced by blowing raw pig iron with a blast of pure oxygen (see iron and steel, vol. II). Large steel works operate one or more tonnage oxygen plants which continuously deliver gaseous oxygen of 95% purity. These plants have a capacity from 150 to 1 000 tons per day (see liquefaction of gases, p. 43).

Another large consumer of oxygen is the gas industry. Producer gas is manufactured by partial combustion of any carbonaceous fuel with oxygen (see producer gas, vol. II). Synthesis gas results from the treating of coal with oxygen and steam under pressure (see synthesis gas, vol. II and production of hydrogen, p. 62). Synthesis gas is a starting material for the production of ammonia and methanol.

Acetylene is produced by partial combustion of methane with oxygen.

Oxygen is also used for producing sulphur trioxide from sulphur dioxide and for processing low grade sulphide ores (for instance roasting of nickel). Together with a lower fuel consumption, a gas of up to 70% SO_2 is obtained which is more useful than the gas obtained by roasting with air and containing 1.5 to 8% SO_2.

Oxygen is also used in safety cartridges. Porous paper cartridges filled with cellulose and with certain metal powders having a high heat of combustion, or with finely divided carbon, are soaked in liquid oxygen. Many safety cartridges are precooled in liquid oxygen and then filled with it. They are exploded with electric detonators or fuses not more than fifteen minutes after charging with oxygen. After this time their effectiveness is greatly diminished and ultimately disappears. For this reason they are absolutely harmless if stolen. When used in mines they do not contaminate the atmosphere to anything like the same extent as other explosives. What is more, they are about 25% cheaper than other safety cartridges.

Liquefied oxygen is also being used in rockets, e.g. for very rapid combustion of fuels such as alcohol. Rapid combustion causes an extra thrust by the combustion products.

Oxygen containing 5% carbon dioxide (to stimulate the respiratory centre) is used medicinally and by fire brigades, in some mines and also for high-altitude flying. In this case, almost absolutely dry oxygen is used, breathed in through special masks. Oxygen highly compressed in steel cylinders is almost invariably used for this purpose. Hospitals in America already have special piped supplies of oxygen for all wards.

2.3.6 Statistics

Oxygen is produced in over 3000 plants around the world. A few hundred plants are large installations producing over 30 tons per day. The other plants are small. The world oxygen capacity was estimated at 72500 short tons per day in 1961 (about 1740 million ft^3 per day). Ninety-seven per cent of it is obtained from air and 3% by electrolysis of water. The estimated production capacity of several countries in 1961 is given in the following table (relating to plants of 20 or more short tons per day).

Country	Oxygen capacity in sh. tons per day
United States	22200
Germany, West	8300
Italy	4800
United Kingdom	3100
France	2500
Spain	1300
Netherlands	1400
Belgium	2100
Canada	1300
South Africa	1600
South America	500
USSR	17000
Others	6200
Total	72300

Oxygen capacity is increasing. It is estimated that the oxygen capacity of the United Kingdom will soon be 5000 short tons per day.

The production of oxygen is closely related to that of nitrogen. Nitrogen is produced by manufacturers of synthetic ammonia, nitric acid, etc. and oxygen can be considered to be a byproduct which is often difficult to dispose of. Conversely oxygen is consumed in the steel industry and produced in situ. Thus a large quantity of nitrogen is obtained as a by-product. This nitrogen must sometimes be wasted. It would be ideal if plants needing nitrogen were located close to those that could process large quantities of oxygen.

Actually, therefore, oxygen cannot be costed strictly. Where oxygen is considered

For production of	Short tons per day	Used in	Short tons per day
Ammonia	19 500	Missiles	5 000
Acetylene	6 000	Steel industry	29 600
Miscellaneous chemicals	4 300	Miscellaneous	
Gasoline	2 000	non-chemical	2 400
Ethylene oxide	1 500		
Town gas	1 000		
Methanol	500		
PPG oxidation products	500		
Acrolein and H₂O₂	200		
Chemicals total	35 500	Non-chemical total	37 000

Source = *Chem. and Eng. News*

as the main product it can be taken that almost one-third of the cost price of oxygen is due to interest and depreciation on the expensive equipment. The biggest plant in America has to allow only 25% for these items. Power nearly always accounts for 56-68%.

The price of very small quantities is determined by expensive containers and carriage.

Slightly less than half of the oxygen produced is used in making chemicals. The world consumption (estimated) of oxygen in 1961 is shown above.

2.4 OZONE

2.4.1 History and occurrence

Ozone (O₃) was discovered in 1840 by Schönbein. He proved that this gas is formed at the anode during electrolysis of dilute sulphuric acid. He called it ozone (derived from the Greek word for smell) because the gas has a peculiar smell.

As ozone is also formed by the action of ultraviolet light on oxygen, it occurs in relatively large quantities at high altitudes. Ozone filters out most of the harmful ultraviolet rays in the sunlight. Hence it forms a protective layer around the earth which extends from an altitude of about 50 000 to 100 000 feet (15-30 km).

Ozone is also formed by the action of electric discharges upon oxygen. In this way ozone is formed in thunderstorms.

The ozone content of the air at ground level is extremely small (0-5 p.p.m.) as ozone is rapidly destroyed under the influence of dust in the air.

2.4.2 Production

Ozone is produced commercially in ozonizers, in which it is formed by silent electric discharges through the dielectric of a condenser consisting partially of oxygen or air. (Silent discharges are discharges without sparks and without heat development.) Several industrial ozonizers, based on the principle mentioned before, have been developed. The first of them was built by Siemens in 1857.

An example of a modern industrial ozonizer is the Welsbach ozonizer. This is constructed of several units consisting of two coaxial tubes. The inner tube is a

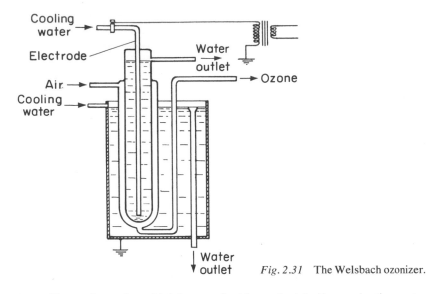

Fig. 2.31 The Welsbach ozonizer.

borosilicate glass tube which is coated with an electrically conductive material on the inside. The outer tube is made of steel. The steel tube and the coating of the glass tube are connected with a unit generating a high voltage alternating current of about 15000 V and 50 c/s. (The steel tube is earthed.) Dry air or oxygen passes through the annular space between the tubes. Several units are fastened into a stainless steel shell that is used as a cooling-water jacket. The cooling water flows in spaces between the outer tubes of the units (see fig. 2.31).

Before using, the feed gas is freed from dust in electrical precipitators (see purification of air, p. 102). Moisture is removed by intensive cooling followed by drying over activated aluminium oxide. During operation the feed gas is partially converted to ozone by electric discharges through the glass and gas layer which form the dielectric. The glass is a dielectric that acts as a stabilizing resistance.

On an average 1% ozone is formed in air and 2% in oxygen with the same electrical energy consumption. As eight to nine kWh of electrical energy are required to generate 1 lb of ozone from air at 1% concentration, four to five kWh are needed to produce 1 lb of ozone from oxygen at 2% concentration. Ozone-oxygen mixtures containing up to 10% ozone can be obtained by passing oxygen through several ozonizing units in series.

On a smaller scale ozone may be produced in an ozonizer consisting of a double-walled glass flask. An electrode is fastened in the flask which is filled with cooling water. The flask is put into a steel vessel filled with another mass of cooling water. A high voltage alternating current is applied to the electrode in the flask. The steel vessel is earthed. Ozone is thus produced in the air stream which flows between the glass walls of the flask. Fig. 2.32 shows a simplified diagram of the Siemens 10000 cycle ozonizer. This ozonizer produces about 4 lb of ozone per day from air. With dry oxygen the ozone production capacity is twice as great. Units containing several double walled flasks are in use.

Ozonizers of several other sizes are available. There are many variations in shape, dimensions, electrodes, etc. The dielectric and electrodes are flat plates in some ozonizers and concentric tubes in others. Multiple units producing up to 10 000 lb or more ozone per day are used in the United States. Small-scale ozone production is expensive, but large-scale production is cheap. Thus production cost in a small scale plant may be up to $ 1 per lb of ozone, but in a plant having a capacity of 1 000 lb per day, the cost may be only about $ 0.50. In very large plants where by-product oxygen is available, the cost may be $ 0.10 per lb of ozone. As ozonizers have no moving parts, the units can be in operation for as much as twenty-five years without renewal.

Dilute ozone can be concentrated by adsorbing it on refrigerated silica gel. At a temperature of −90° C about 6 lb of ozone are adsorbed on 100 lb of silica gel from oxygen containing 2% ozone at atmospheric pressure. Ozone can be desorbed by a stream of gas at room temperature. Air, nitrogen, oxygen, argon or other gases which are not strongly adsorbed on silica gel, may be used. Gases containing up to 25% ozone are produced.

Ozone adsorbed on silica gel can be stored and transported without loss at liquid oxygen or nitrogen temperature but it is still a problem to avoid dispersal of the desorbed ozone if refrigeration fails, as highly concentrated ozone is very explosive. Transportation of dilute ozone is too expensive, due to its dilution and its instability, and ozone is therefore only produced where it is to be used.

2.4.3 Properties

Ozone is a modification of oxygen having three oxygen atoms in its molecule (O_3). It is an unstable blue gas but at the concentrations at which it is normally available, the colour is not visible. Dilute ozone decomposes only slowly at ordinary temperatures but a gas containing over 30% ozone is very explosive. Ozone liquefies to a deep blue liquid at a temperature of −112° C.

Ozone can be separated from oxygen and other gases by cooling it with liquid air and separating the liquid ozone obtained from the remaining gas. Pure ozone may also be obtained by adsorbing gas containing it on silica gel, and desorbing it by reduction of pressure. These processes are dangerous, since liquid ozone is very explosive and even sensitive to mechanical shocks.

Nascent oxygen is formed when ozone decomposes. For this reason dilute ozone is a strong oxidizing agent. It oxidizes unsaturated organic compounds (such as unsaturated

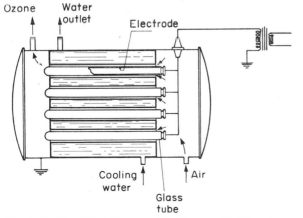

Fig. 2.32 Simplified diagram of the Siemens 10 000 cycle ozonizer.

fats) and turns them rancid: it bleaches dyestuffs and destroys micro-organisms: it has a destructive effect on natural rubber and many kinds of synthetic rubber. Only a few synthetic rubbers can withstand it. Even in small concentrations, ozone has a corrosive action on the respiratory organs. Its prolonged inhalation in concentrations above 0.1 p.p.m. is not without hazard.

As said, unsaturated organic compounds are oxidized by ozone, which is consequently itself decomposed. Various unsaturated compounds may therefore be used as *antiozonants*. Antiozonants, such as a solution of cyclohexene in carbon tetrachloride, may be used for treating the air in warehouses where rubber and other oxidizable substances have to be stored for protracted periods. Antiozonants can also be incorporated in rubber to increase its resistance to ozone.

2.4.4 Detection

Ozone can easily be detected in air. Its odour is detectable in air at concentrations less than 0.1 p.p.m. Ozone can also be detected with a spectrometer, since it absorbs light in the red and infrared spectrum and it has a strong absorption maximum in the ultraviolet at 2537 Ångstroms. The concentration of ozone can also be determined by its property of releasing iodine from a potassium iodide solution. Starch added to this is coloured blue by the iodine (see also starch, vol. VII). The iodine formed can be determined by adding a sodium thiosulphate solution of known strength until the blue colour disappears owing to reduction of iodine to iodide ions.

2.4.5 Uses

Air having an ozone content is used on a large scale for disinfecting filtered drinking water. At the same time several water soluble impurities, such as iron and manganese ions, are oxidized to insoluble compounds. In this way many unpleasant tastes, colours and odours are eliminated. For this reason ozone is sometimes preferred to chlorine for the disinfection of water. In the United States a very large plant, having an ozone capacity of 50 metric tons per day, is in operation. More than 10000 million gallons per year of presettled water are treated with ozonized air from this plant. (Ozonized air containing 1.5 p.p.m. ozone is employed.)

Ozonized air is also used in purification of waste water. Phenol-containing effluent (from coking plants, etc.) can be purified with ozone because ozone reduces the concentration of phenol by oxidation to harmless products. Twenty times as much chlorine would be needed because it reacts with other constituents in preference to the phenol, forming compounds with obnoxious odours and tastes.

In underground railways, tunnels, mines, big abbatoirs, etc. air having an ozone content is used for purifying the atmosphere. Minute amounts of ozone (0.05 p.p.m.) are effective in destroying odours in the air. It is also used for disinfection of air in cold storage rooms. Ozone concentrations of 1-3 p.p.m. inhibit the growth of moulds and bacteria in stored eggs, meat, vegetables and fruits. Ozone cannot be used in dairies because it imparts an unpleasant taste to milk.

Air with an ozone content is useful for bleaching cotton yarns and fabrics. Washing spread out to bleach is whitened by the bleaching effect of light, but it is said that bleaching is also effected by a small quantity of ozone that is formed from air under the influence of ultraviolet light. Washing has been bleached in this way since time immemorial.

The oxidizing properties of ozone are also utilized in numerous chemical reactions. One of the greatest advances in the chemical utilization of ozone has been the production of carboxylic acids by ozonation of compounds with ethylenic double bounds. In this way azelaic and pelargonic acid are produced from oleic acid on a large scale according to the equations:

$$CH_3-(CH_2)_7-CH=CH-(CH_2)_7COOH + O_3 \rightarrow CH_3-(CH_2)_7CH \overset{\displaystyle O}{\underset{\displaystyle O-O}{\diagup \diagdown}} CH-(CH_2)_7-COOH$$

The compound obtained is decomposed by water and oxygen to form the two organic acids, $CH_3-(CH_2)_7-COOH$ and $HOOC-(CH_2)_7-COOH$, pelargonic acid and azelaic acid respectively (see also organic chemistry, vol. IV). These acids are intermediates in the production of lubricants and plasticizers for vinyl compounds. Azelaic acid is a starting material in the production of a nylon type polymer.

Ozone may also be used for oxidizing linseed oil for paint making and for quick drying of lacquers and varnishes on mass produced goods.

Several pharmaceuticals, perfumes and flavours such as safrol, anisaldehyde, piperonal and vanillin can be produced from terpenes by methods using ozonation.

Air with an ozone content can also be used for rapidly maturing and aging spirits, vinegar, wood, etc. Oxidation then quickly forms the substance which would normally take years to produce. The method has the additional advantage of sterilizing the substance.

Liquid ozone-oxygen mixtures containing about 25 weight % ozone are used as a high energy oxidizing agent in rocket fuels.

2.4.6 Literature

Ozone chemistry and technology. Proceedings of the International Ozone Conference in Chicago. November 1956. Washington, American Society, 1959.

G. A. LUTZ. 'Ozone's role in chemistry and technology'. *Battelle technical review* **9** (June 1960), 9-15.

2.5 NITROGEN (N_2, mole weight = 28.016)

2.5.1 Introduction

Nitrogen was recognized as an element by Lavoisier at the same time as oxygen. He named it azote (without life), which is still the French name for nitrogen. The prefix 'az' is used as an indication for the presence of combined nitrogen in several compounds. For example: azide and azole. The English name nitrogen is derived from the Greek terms for nitre-forming.

Nitrogen occurs in the free state in vast quantities in air, accounting for four-fifths of its volume and three-fourths of its weight. Nitrogen also occurs combined in the proteins of all living organisms. Natural deposits of potassium nitrate in India and sodium nitrate in Chile also contain combined nitrogen.

2.5.2 Production

The bulk of the nitrogen produced is made by liquefying air and separating it into nitrogen and oxygen by fractional distillation (see liquefaction of gases, p. 43).

Sometimes, nitrogen is produced from combustion gases. A mixture of carbon dioxide, water vapour, carbon monoxide, hydrogen and nitrogen is obtained by combustion of carbonaceous material. Water vapour is removed by condensation. The ratio of air to carbonaceous material is chosen in such a way that the quantities of hydrogen and carbon monoxide formed are small. These gases may be removed by catalytic conversion to methanol. Carbon dioxide is recovered by liquefaction or by absorption in ethanolamine or other absorbents (see production of carbon dioxide, p. 534). The cost price of nitrogen obtained by this process is only $0.17-$0.20 per 1 000 ft.^{3}

On a laboratory scale nitrogen may be obtained by passing air over heated copper powder. Oxygen combines with copper to form copper oxide and nitrogen remains.

2.5.3 Properties

Nitrogen is a colourless diatomic gas which liquefies to a colourless liquid at a temperature of $-195.5°$ C below zero. At normal temperatures it is a very inert gas. This is due to the great force with which the atoms building up the molecules in pairs are linked together.

At higher temperatures the molecules split into atoms having a greater affinity for many elements. At high temperatures nitrogen combines with several metals to give nitrides. For example, calcium nitride (Ca_3N_2) and boron nitride (BN).

The commonest kind of nitrogen is N^{14} (having atomic weight 14). About 0.5% of normal nitrogen consists of N^{15}, having atomic weight 15 (see isotopes, ch. 15).

Nitrogen gas may be compressed to 200 atm. in steel cylinders and stored for transport. Large quantities of liquid nitrogen are stored and transported in large Dewar flasks (see storage of liquefied gases, p. 55).

2.5.4 Uses

Despite the low affinity of molecular nitrogen for other elements, research has made it possible to make ammonia and nitrogen compounds containing oxygen from nitrogen or air. The compounds obtained are starting materials for the production of fertilizers and several other nitrogen compounds (see nitrogen compounds, e.g. ammonia, nitric acid etc., p. 301). Production of ammonia and nitrogen compounds containing oxygen is the most important use of nitrogen. Nitrogen for ammonia production is not separated from nitrogen-hydrogen gas mixtures resulting from combustion gases, etc. (see production of hydrogen, p. 62 and ammonia, p. 302).

Important quantities of nitrogen are used in calcium cyanamide production. Calcium cyanamide is produced by reacting nitrogen with calcium carbide at high temperatures (see calcium cyanamide, p. 357).

Nitrogen is also used for applying pressure to liquids if they are dangerous with air or other gases, or deteriorate in the presence of oxygen. For example, it is used as an inert pressure medium for propellant feed systems.

Nitrogen is also suited as a protective atmosphere for bright hardening and annealing of steel, for arc welding, for chilling in aluminium foundries, for storing fat or fatty products and also for filling the space over the contents in canned foods to prevent them from being spoiled by atmospheric oxygen. The same is sometimes done with prepacked bacon, frozen fish, cheese, etc. These products are packed in gasproof paper or plastic bags which are evacuated and filled with nitrogen. Nitrogen is also used for expelling air during the drying of goods which might quickly be affected by oxygen at a high drying temperature.

If tanks or drums are likely to have a gas or vapour in them liable to form an explosive mixture with air, nitrogen is used to expel this.

Nitrogen can also be used for testing containers, pipes, etc. for leaks.

High-pressure nitrogen gas is used for agitating liquids, because of its low chemical activity, in place of compressed air. This is very important in photography, in order to keep the baths of uniform quality and produce better results than with still liquids.

Because of its low chemical activity, compressed nitrogen (72 atm) is also used in hydraulic apparatus. In a hydraulic apparatus a high pressure can be built up by compressing liquid in a vessel filled with a gas. Thus liquid under high pressure is obtained. This liquid can be used for applying high pressures, e.g. for moulding metals, etc. (see vol. II). To prevent the absorption of the gas in the liquid, cylindrical rubber bags of nitrile rubber placed in the pressure chamber of the hydraulic system are filled with nitrogen. When the hydraulic pressure in the system is raised, the pressure of the hydraulic liquid compresses the rubber bags to a smaller volume. If the pressure drops owing to a 'blow out', the bags expand again. The nitrile rubber is not attacked either by the nitrogen or by the hydraulic liquid.

2.5.5 Uses of liquid nitrogen

Liquid nitrogen, owing to its very low temperature, is used for freezing out gaseous impurities in electronic tubes. It is also of some importance for freeze drying although on account of cost carbon dioxide snow (temperature $-80°$ C) is frequently preferred for this purpose.

The use of liquid nitrogen to refrigerate frozen and perishable foods, during transit, is of growing importance.

Liquid nitrogen is also used in grinding valuable materials which are too tough at normal temperatures, or which are liable to overheat and deteriorate. They are precooled to $-80°$ C by carbon dioxide formed from the snow, then finely divided in a hammer mill cooled with liquid nitrogen. The unit is heavily insulated.

The same method of grinding is used for fats, waxes, glands, hormones, antibiotics, vitamins, vaccines, various synthetic resins, etc. These materials are so costly that the relatively high cost of cooling and grinding is not excessive. Herbs and spices, for instance nutmegs, which might lose aromatic constituents in ordinary grinding, are likewise ground by this method.

The low temperature rapidly attainable with liquid nitrogen may also be used for removing even minute quantities of methane (see p. 48) or unpleasant smelling impurities from other gases. The method can be used for exact analysis of gases.

2.5.6 Statistics

The world production of nitrogen is not precisely known, but a probable figure can be calculated from oxygen production, since an oxygen production plant producing 400 tons of oxygen per day produces 1 000 tons of gaseous nitrogen at the same time (see statistics for oxygen, p. 78). Only a portion of this nitrogen is recovered for use, the remaining part being blown off. In addition large quantities of nitrogen, present in gases obtained during the production of hydrogen, are available. This nitrogen is not separated from hydrogen but the mixture is converted to fixed nitrogen in ammonia plants (see hydrogen production, p. 62 and ammonia production, p. 302).

Figures showing the nitrogen production of various countries do not give a general picture of all available nitrogen. The incompleteness of the figures is shown by the following example. The United States production of synthetic ammonia was about 5 million tons in 1961. For this purpose 4 million tons of nitrogen (100 000 million ft³) were needed. However the US nitrogen production figure published was 25 000 million ft³ (1961).

2.6 THE RARE GASES

2.6.1 Introduction

The rare gases helium, neon, argon, krypton, xenon and radon are distinguished from all other elements by being chemically inert. For this reason they are also called the 'inert gases' or 'noble gases'.

This statement needs modification since a special type of 'compound' can be formed. Argon, krypton and xenon form clathrates with hydroquinone. Clathrates are compounds in which atoms or molecules of one substance (the guest) are enclosed in a crystalline cage formed by molecules of a second substance (the host). The atoms of the guest substance are bound by weak forces (van der Waals forces). The clathrates of the rare gases and hydroquinone are obtained by cooling a solution of hydroquinone in the presence of a rare gas under a pressure of 20 atm. These clathrates are relatively stable at room temperature, but the gases enclosed can be liberated by heating or by mechanical shock. Similar clathrates can be prepared with phenol or water (hydrates) at low temperatures and increased pressure, but these are not stable at normal temperatures and atmospheric pressure. Neon and helium do not form clathrates. Perhaps neon and helium atoms can escape from the host substance as they are too small (see also chelates, ch. 4 Water, p. 131).

The rare gases are colourless, odourless and tasteless. They are all monatomic gases and occur in atmospheric air, with the exception of radon, which comes from the radioactive decay of radium and which is itself an unstable radioactive element (see ch. 15 Nucleonics and radioactive elements). Atmospheric air contains about 1 mole % argon and about 5, 18, 1 and 0.09 parts per million by volume of helium, neon, krypton and xenon respectively. Small quantities of rare gases are occluded in several minerals and dissolved in water.

2.6.2 Argon (A, atomic weight = 39.9)

a. History. Argon was discovered as a component of atmospheric air by Sir William Ramsay and Lord Rayleigh in 1894. At that time it was characterized by the complete absence of any chemical affinity and it was called argon (derived from Greek words, meaning 'having no action'). The discovery was made by comparing atmospheric nitrogen with the residual gas of nitride formation from heated magnesium and nitrogen. It appeared that atmospheric nitrogen was less dense than the residual gas.

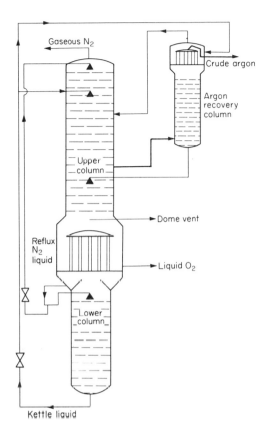

Fig. 2.33 Argon recovery system.

b. Production. As its boiling point is −185.7° C (87.3° K), argon can be obtained in oxygen liquefaction plants (see liquefaction of gases, p. 43). The boiling point is between those of oxygen and nitrogen. Accordingly gaseous oxygen, containing about 12% argon and some nitrogen, can be drawn off from the upper column of Linde's double column for oxygen production. This vapour is enriched in argon in a fractional distillation column. 'Crude argon gas' containing about 98% argon is obtained from the top of this column (see fig. 2.33). The impurities are nitrogen and oxygen.

Oxygen is removed by heating the crude argon gas to room temperature in a heat exchanger. Then hydrogen is added and the gas mixture is compressed to about 60 lb/in² (4 atm) and oxidized in the presence of a catalyst. The water formed is removed by an adsorbent such as silica gel. Nitrogen and excess of hydrogen are removed by cooling the gas mixture in the heat exchanger, mentioned before, liquefying and fractionally distilling. Liquid argon having a purity of 99.99% is obtained.

Alternatively oxygen may be removed by passing crude argon gas over heated copper powder, which is converted into copper oxide.

Nitrogen can afterwards be removed by passing the oxygen-free gas over a red-hot metal, which is converted into a nitride.

In another purification process oxygen may be removed by passing crude argon through a synthetic crystalline zeolite (a molecular sieve of specific pore size). This adsorbs the oxygen molecules in the pores, allowing the bigger argon atoms, which cannot enter into the pores, to pass. Intensely cooled crude argon passes two such columns in succession while in a third column any particles of adsorbent are retained.

Small quantities of argon are usually stored and transported as gas. For large quantities storing and transporting in liquid form are preferred (see storage of gases, p. 55).

c. Uses. The chief use of argon is for argon arc welding (i.e. inert-gas-shielded electric arc welding). In this welding process a limited hot area is obtained by an electric arc between a metal electrode (often made of tungsten) and the metal being welded. A metal wire is often fed at the correct rate as a filler metal for the weld. The hot area and the electrode are shielded with an inert argon gas stream, thus protecting the metal being welded and the electrode from atmospheric attack. The inert atmosphere must be maintained during cooling of the electrode after use and for this reason the supply of argon is not cut off until a few seconds after switching off the electric current. The following figures show the losses of argon: a large American plant was spending $ 120 000 per year on argon until automatic switching-gear was introduced, when the cost fell to $ 82 000. Besides argon, other inert gases such as helium and sometimes nitrogen may be used. The use of argon has many advantages. When a flux is used to keep the welded area clean it is difficult to remove it completely. With an argon atmosphere fluxes are superfluous and the weld is so neat that after polishing stainless steel welded in this way, no trace of the seam is left. If aluminium is welded, argon also breaks the film of oxide on the surface of the metal without any danger of its reforming.

The argon arc is used for welding stainless steel, aluminium, magnesium, aluminium and magnesium alloys and several other metals. In particular argon is useful for welding metals which form nitrides with nitrogen when the latter is used as a protective atmosphere. Argon is also more useful for welding of steel as nitrogen dissolves in steel. In other cases nitrogen, which is cheaper than argon, is often used, especially in Europe where the prices of argon or helium are a drawback.

Argon, which may contain some nitrogen, is used as a filling for incandescent electric lamps and electronic tubes. Argon must be free from oxygen and water to protect the filaments from attack. The presence of argon prevents evaporation of the hot filament. Before filling with argon or argon-nitrogen mixtures the lamps are evacuated and heated in an inert gas atmosphere to detach absorbed gases and vapours from the glass. Finally the lamps are filled and sealed off by a flame.

Argon is also used as a discharge gas in fluorescent lamps, mercury vapour lamps, Geiger-Muller counters, etc. (see Geiger-Muller counters, Nucleonics, ch. 15). Most fluorescent lamps are filled with argon or with an argon-krypton mixture. The luminous efficiency is greatest with krypton alone, but starting is troublesome on cold days.

Argon is also used as an inert atmosphere in metallurgy of several metals, e.g. in processing zirconium, titanium and other metals. A gastight building has been built (1959) in a larger building and filled with argon. The intention was that the men working in the gastight building should be dressed in 'space suits' and breathe air through tubes, supplied from outside. It was intended to use these buildings for working niobium, tantalum, molybdenum, tungsten and other metals in a process requiring such high temperatures that these metals would react with air. Airlocks were provided for personnel and materials to move in and out with a minimum loss of argon.

In the United States argon is especially used as an inert atmosphere in brazing 'honey-comb' panels, etc. for supersonic aircraft structures. These structures are high rigidity assemblies having low weight.

Molten metals such as steel, aluminium, titanium, etc. can be degassed with argon.

d. Statistics. The production of argon is increasing. The United States production in 1951 was 91 million ft.[3] In 1961 it was increased to 664 million ft.[3] The US production of 1962 is estimated at 720 million ft.[3] The capacity in the same year was 1 100 million ft.[3] It is estimated that about 75% of the US production is consumed in electric arc welding. About equal parts of the remaining 24% are used as a filling or discharge gas in lamps, etc. and as protective atmosphere in metallurgy.

2.6.3 *Helium* (He, at weight = 4.003)

a. History and occurrence. Helium was discovered by Ramsay in 1895. Ramsay collected an inert gas produced by heating an uranium mineral with an acid. A spectroscopic examination showed that the gas must be a mixture of argon and one or more other gases as a yellow line was observed that did not belong to the argon spectrum. It was found (by Lockyer) that this yellow line corresponds with a yellow line in the spectrum of the sun. Hence the new gas was called 'helium' (derived from the Greek word for the sun).

It is estimated that 6% of the sun's atmosphere consists of helium while young stars have even more. In the sun and other stars helium is presumably formed from hydrogen in a continuous process, the hydrogen thereby losing a part of its nuclear energy (see nuclear fission, nuclear fusion and mass defect, ch. 15). This is why the sun keeps its enormous temperature despite the emission of radiant energy. It is estimated that about 23% of the mass of the whole universe is helium and 76% is hydrogen. The remaining 1% is made up by all the other elements together.

In addition to its occurrence in air, helium also occurs in many natural gases. In the United States several natural gas sources containing 1-2 mole % are found. Some natural gas sources containing up to 9 mole % helium are found in the United States and South Africa. Recently natural gas containing up to 2% helium has been found in Canada and USSR. In other gas sources the percentage of helium is far smaller.

In the earth it is presumed that helium was and still is formed by the decomposition of several radioactive elements (see ch. Nucleonics and radioactive elements, ch. 15).

b. Production. In the United States nearly all helium is produced from natural gas. Natural gas is compressed to a pressure of 450 lb/in² (30 atm) and small quantities of carbon dioxide, water and hydrogen sulphide are removed by countercurrent treatment with a liquid absorbent in a bubble-cap tray tower. The last traces of water are removed by passing through towers filled with activated bauxite. The purified and compressed gas is cooled to a temperature of $-150°$ C ($123°$ K) in a liquefaction unit (see liquefaction of gases, p. 43). Most of the natural gas (methane) is liquefied. The gaseous fraction containing about 70% helium and 30% nitrogen is separated from the liquid. The helium-nitrogen mixture is compressed to a pressure of 2 700 lb/in² (180 atm) and cooled to $-196°$ C ($77°$ K) in a second liquefaction unit. Most of the nitrogen is liquefied and a gas containing about 98% helium can be separated from the liquid. In a third stage helium may be purified to 99.5% purity. High purity helium (99.995%) is obtained by passing the gas through adsorbers containing activated charcoal.

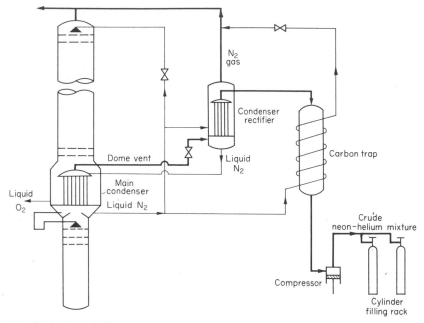

Fig. 2.34 Neon-helium recovery cycle.

In several countries, small quantities of helium (and neon) are recovered as a byproduct from plants separating oxygen and nitrogen from air. Helium and neon tend to concentrate at the top of the lower column of a Linde's double column (see fractionation of liquefied gases, p. 46 and fig. 2.5). Gaseous nitrogen containing about 2% neon and 0.8% helium may be drawn off from this place. This gas mixture is liquefied by cooling with liquid nitrogen and expansion in a liquefaction unit. Most of the nitrogen liquefies and a crude gaseous neon-helium mixture is obtained by separating the liquid from the gas. The remaining nitrogen is removed by adsorption on active carbon which is cooled with liquid nitrogen. Helium and neon are separated by adsorption of neon in a similar adsorption process with carbon cooled by liquid nitrogen. Helium is not adsorbed. Neon is recovered by heating the carbon.

Helium can also be isolated by diffusion processes. A gas mixture which flows through a porous wall is enriched in the component of lower molecular weight. For the separation of helium from other gases very thin layers of silica glass may be used. Borosilicate glass is an extremely selective porous wall, only helium being able to diffuse through it. Pressurized helium containing gas may be passed around the outside of capillary tubes, made from borosilicate glass, arranged in bundles. Helium passes through the tube walls and is collected in the capillary tubes. This process may be a potential commercial production process, although at present it is not in commercial operation.

c. Storage. Helium is usually stored as gas in steel vessels at a pressure of about 2 000 p.s.i. (130 atm) (see also storage of gases, p. 55). Sometimes storage of small quantities of liquid is necessary.

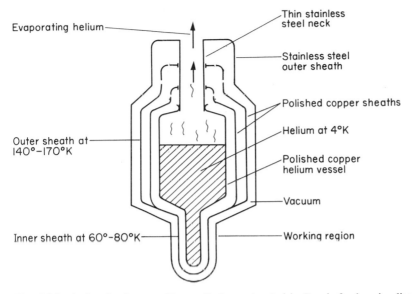

Fig. 2.35 A sketch of a new Dewar flask constructed in Russia for keeping liquid helium or other liquefied gases near to the absolute zero, with minimal losses.

As its boiling point is $-269°$ C ($4°$ K), helium is the most difficult gas to liquefy. Its liquefaction was achieved in 1907 by Kamerlingh Onnes, while Keesom solidified it in 1925. Both these feats were achieved in the cryogenic laboratories at Leiden (Netherlands).

Liquid helium boils off rapidly if kept in a simple Dewar vessel such as is used for liquid air or liquid nitrogen. For this reason supplementary cooling by liquid nitrogen is used, either by immersing the helium Dewar flask directly in liquid nitrogen or by filling the vacuum space with it. A new flask for keeping liquid helium has been developed in the USSR. Two polished copper shields surround the inner vessel of a Dewar flask. At the top of the vessel both shields are soldered to the stainless steel neck of the vessel (see fig. 2.35). In this way the neck of the vessel is cooled by liquid helium in the vessel and a part of the evaporating helium is refluxed. In such flask having a capacity of two litres, helium evaporates at the rate of 6 g per hour and one filling will last for forty hours. Liquid nitrogen kept in such a flask, needs six days to evaporate completely.

d. Uses. Helium having only twice the weight of hydrogen, is excellent for filling balloons, especially for high-altitude meteorological observation. As air and helium slowly diffuse in and out through the wall of the balloon, it is necessary to replace and to purify the helium from time to time. Mobile equipment is sometimes used for this purpose in the United States. Notwithstanding its high cost, helium is used mainly because fire risks are eliminated. Furthermore, the annual loss is only one or two charges, as compared with eight to ten when hydrogen is used.

In the United States, large quantities of helium are used in guided missiles for pressurizing liquid rocket fuels.

Two other important applications are in shielded arc welding (see argon, p. 88) and as a coolant in nuclear reactors (see nuclear reactors, ch. 15).

Like argon, helium is used as a protective atmosphere in the metallurgy of several metals.

Helium is also used in wind tunnels for aeronautic research with scale-models of aircraft and rockets. In wind tunnels the effects of surrounding atmosphere on an object moving at a high speed are imitated by passing the gas at high velocity round a stationary object. Higher gas velocities corresponding to twenty-eight times the speed of sound can be reached with helium than with air. The expensive gas is recovered by collecting in a large balloon.

Small quantities of helium are used for other purposes. Mixed with oxygen, helium can be used in diving equipment and caissons. As helium dissolves in blood far less than nitrogen, the time required for decompression of divers or caisson workers can be reduced without formation of gas bubbles in the blood of the workers when they come to the surface. There is thus much less risk of caisson disease ('the bends').

Even highly dilute helium can easily be detected by spectroscopic examination in a discharge tube. Hence it is suited as a tracer gas in oil and natural gas fields, for tracking down gas leaks, etc. For example, natural gas containing helium may be injected into oil-bearing sandstone and the helium content of the gases from surrounding wells can be measured. This method cannot be used when natural gas sources containing helium occur in the field to be searched. Helium is also used for leak detection in pipes, etc. The pipe to be tested is evacuated and a stream of helium is passed over the outside of the pipe. Any helium that is sucked in through a leak is detected. When helium is used as cooling gas in nuclear reactors it may be used for leak detection at the same time.

Helium is also used in cold gas refrigerating machines (see p. 53) for cooling and liquefying of air on a small scale.

The low temperature of liquid helium has made it possible to investigate the properties of several materials at temperatures closely approching the absolute zero ($-273°$ C). This led to the discovery of the very remarkable superconductivity of several materials at very low temperatures. The electric resistance of many metals falls continuously as their temperature is reduced. When the absolute zero is approached within a few degrees, a sudden disappearance of the electric resistance is observed in some metals such as lead, tin, mercury aluminium, niobium and tantalum. These metals can than conduct strong currents for unlimited periods without any heat generation. This phenomenon was discovered by the Dutch scientist Kamerlingh Onnes in 1911. Practical applications were not available before 1956. Nowadays the phenomena of superconductivity and the destruction of superconductivity by means of a magnetic field are utilized in an apparatus known as a *cryotron*.

Fig. 2.36 Scheme of a cryotron.

A cryotron consists of a tantalum wire wound with a coil of insulated niobium wire (see fig. 2.36) and immersed in a bath of liquid helium. Both tantalum and niobium are superconductive under these conditions. An electric current is passed through the tantalum wire. By passing an electric current through the niobium wire a magnetic field is obtained and the resistance of the tantalum changes suddenly from zero to a definite value, causing the electric current through the tantalum wire to decrease suddenly. Thus the cryotron might be used as a switch in computers. An advantage is the very small size (2 x 10 mm). The disadvantages are its relatively long switching time and its high cost. Recently a similar element, containing germanium, has been developed. It is called cryosar and had a switching time of 10^{-8} sec or less.

e. Statistics. The United States is the largest producer of helium. Before 1939 the US production amounted about 10 million ft^3. Since then the production has steadily increased, reaching 112 million ft^3 in 1951, 642 million ft^3 in 1960 and 727 million ft^3 in 1961.

It is estimated that the US natural gas reserves contain 200000 million ft^3 of helium, of which 160000 million ft^3 can be recovered. The US production of helium has exceeded sales in the last years. The excess is stored underground (about 447 million ft^3 at the end of 1961).

The US consumption in 1960 was about 522 million ft^3. Estimated consumption for various purposes in the same year is given in the following table:

Missiles	21%	Aeronautical research	9%
Atomic energy	19%	Air ships	5%
Arc welding	18%	other (incl. metallurgy)	14%
Meteorology	14%		

Only one large-scale helium plant is in operation in the United Kingdom. Production figures are not available.

The cost price of helium in 1961 was $ 15.5 per thousand ft^3. The commercial price which amounted to $ 19 per thousand ft^3 in 1961 rose to $ 35 at the end of that year.

2.6.4 Neon (Ne, atomic weight = 20.2)

Neon is recovered from air (see production of helium, p. 89). The helium neon mixture, obtained from air, may be separated either by adsorption of neon on activated carbon or by fractional distillation of the liquefied mixture. The latter method is possible as neon boils at −223° C and helium at −269° C, but this process is more expensive than the adsorption process.

Neon is used especially in glow discharge lamps, it emits a red light that can be turned blue by putting a little mercury vapour in the lamp. These lamps are used as advertising signs. A gas discharge only appears when the voltage exceeds a certain value. Thus gas discharge lamps can be used as voltage regulators (neon bulbs).

2.6.5 Krypton and xenon (Kr, atomic weight = 83.7 and Xe = 131.3)

Krypton and xenon are produced from air by washing air with liquid air. One volume of liquid air is needed for 20 to 30 volumes of gaseous krypton and xenon. As the boiling points of krypton and xenon are − 152° and − 109° C respectively, both gases liquefy and dissolve in the liquid air. They are then separated by fractional distillation.

Krypton is used as a filling gas for incandescent lamps. It gives a more efficient source of lighting than is obtained from lamps filled with argon. For the same reason, mixtures of argon and krypton are used as discharge gases in fluorescent lamps.

A mixture of xenon and oxygen, containing 20% oxygen has anaesthetic properties. Xenon penetrates into the nerve tissue.

Xenon is used in some discharge lamps. Mercury lamps are sometimes filled with xenon to a pressure of several atmospheres: Such lamps begin to emit light immediately on application of a high voltage. These lamps, which attain 20% of full lamp brightness within 5 sec are called Mercury-xenon short arc lamps.

2.6.6 Literature

G. A. COOK. *Argon, helium, and the rare gases.* 2 vols. New York, Interscience Publishers, 1961.

CHAPTER 3

Air

3.1 THE CONSTITUTION OF AIR

We are aware of the air around us from the wind, the shimmering of rising currents of hot air and the pressure upon a surface behind which the air is (partly or wholly) removed. The layer of air that surrounds the earth is probably 100 miles thick, but more than one half of the total weight of air is in the four miles just above the surface of the earth.

Air is a mixture of gases. Apart from incidental local impurities air consists of the same components in about the same ratio all over the world.

Dry air contains 20.95% (by volume) of oxygen, 78.08% nitrogen, 0.93% argon, 0.03% carbon dioxide and 0.01% other gases (neon, helium, krypton, xenon, methane, nitrous oxide (N_2O) and hydrogen). In addition to these, variable quantities of water vapour and several gaseous and solid impurities are contained in air. Among those are ozone, ammonia, nitric oxide, nitrogen dioxide, sulphur dioxide, hydrocarbons and dust. Although the percentages of impurities are very small, they represent in the aggregate a vast quantity, because the quantity of air is enormous. The nitrogen compounds are formed especially during thunder storms. They reach the soil by way of rain and are important fertilizers especially in the tropics.

Oxygen is the most important constituent of air since it makes living for most vegetable and animal life possible. Lavoisier showed for the first time that air contains oxygen, by the formation of mercuric oxide (HgO) from mercury heated in air.

Air is only slightly soluble in water. The concentration of oxygen in water is very low although it is higher than that of nitrogen. This and the consequent lack of facilities for oxidation is the reason why fish and other animals that have to obtain their oxygen from water can only exist because they are cold blooded and have the temperature of their environment. In densely populated aquaria it is necessary to pump oxygen (air) through the water to keep the oxygen concentration high enough. Animals with lungs have to rise regularly to the surface for breathing. They are protected against heat losses by a layer of fat.

It is the oxygen content in air which supports combustion. A given volume of air at a pressure of 5 atmospheres contains as much oxygen as the same volume of pure oxygen at atmospheric pressure, but compressed air is not as active as pure oxygen because the large quantity of nitrogen acts as ballast which also has to be heated in the combustion process.

Carbon dioxide (CO_2) present in ordinary air represents 0.03% by volume. Over the sea the amount is about 10% less because CO_2 dissolves in water. The presence of carbon dioxide in air is easily demonstrated by passing the air through lime water (a solution of calcium hydroxide in water). This becomes turbid owing to the formation of insoluble calcium carbonate

$$Ca(OH)_2 + CO_2 \rightarrow CaCO_3 + H_2O.$$

The turbidity disappears again if the supply of air is continued, the carbon dioxide and the carbonate forming calcium bicarbonate, which is soluble in water:

$$CaCO_3 + CO_2 + H_2O \rightarrow Ca(HCO_3)_2.$$

Carbon dioxide is ejected into the atmosphere by volcanoes, by decay of organic matter (e.g. rotting of humus in the soil), by respiration, and by the combustion of fuel. The annual production of carbon dioxide by respiration and decay is estimated to be 2×10^{11} metric tons. Thus each year 10% carbon dioxide is added to the total quantity of carbon dioxide which is about 2×10^{12} tons. In addition an estimated quantity of 7×10^9 tons per year is produced by the combustion of fuels. However, the carbon dioxide content of the atmosphere has only increased about 30 p.p.m. in the last fifty years. The remainder is mainly consumed by plants (carbon dioxide assimilation) and dissolved in the water of the seas. Carbon dioxide is converted by the chlorophyll of green leaves, acting in conjunction with light and an enzyme, into sugars and starch (carbohydrates) with simultaneous liberation of oxygen. The starch serves to build up the plant structure and also acts as a reserve. All animals use vegetable food either directly or indirectly. The carbon compounds derived from this food are again converted in the body into carbon dioxide which in turn is released into the atmosphere, completing a cycle through the plants and animals.

Due to this cycle the oxygen content of the air remains approximately constant. Oxygen is converted into carbon dioxide by respiration etc., and is reconverted into oxygen and carbohydrates by the carbon dioxide assimilation of plants.

As carbon dioxide transmits short wavelength radiation more easily than long wave radiation, it has been argued that the growing carbon dioxide content is increasingly preventing radiation from the earth and that the temperature will thus rise gradually, resulting in less rain, and so on.

At the same time combustion generates so much heat that the mean temperature is said to be rising by 1.5° F or 0.81° C every hundred years. If fuel consumption continues at its present rate, there will be $1\frac{1}{2}$ times as much atmospheric carbon dioxide by the year 2080.

The air we exhale contains about 4% carbon dioxide. We can easily see this high content by blowing through lime water; turbidity and clarification occur much quicker than when unbreathed air is passed through. If the air we breathe contains more than 4% carbon dioxide for any reason, the lungs can no longer discharge carbon into the atmosphere and suffocation follows immediately. However, careful experiments have shown that 'bad air' in places where a lot of people are congregated is harmful not so much because of carbon dioxide or foul-smelling products as because of excessive humidity and temperature.

3.2 ATMOSPHERIC DUST

3.2.1 Occurrence and sources of atmospheric dust

Dust is a general name for finely divided solid matter, which can be moved by air of normal wind velocity. In general the particle size ranges from 0.01 to 100 microns. All air in the lower atmosphere contains dust. Air is cleanest over the ocean where salt particles and marine micro-organisms are the major forms of dust. The dust content of rural air is about ten times greater than that of air above the ocean. The dust content of air in cities can be 35 to 150 times (and sometimes even 4000 times) the value found over the ocean. The air above large cities in the USA contains usually from 50 to 500 micrograms of dust per cubic metre. A common measurement of dust in air above cities is the amount which settles per square mile in a given time. In New York 33 to 67 tons per square mile (= 12-25 g per m²) per month come down to earth in the summer (measured in 1951).

In the winter months this amount is about two to three times higher. In the industrial centres of Manchester and Leeds (in the United Kingdom) the dust fall is 20 to 30 tons per square mile per month in the summer (measured in 1954). In the winter months it is slightly higher.

The dust sources may be classified as natural, industrial and domestic. Natural dust comes from seas (e.g., salt particles), deserts, volcanoes, forests and erosion areas. In certain seasons there may be much pollen in the atmosphere. The pollen content of air is far less than that of other natural dust but it has peculiarly irritating properties (it causes hay-fever). Spores and several micro-organisms are also present in dust.

Domestic and industrial dust comes from several sources: Carbon (soot) is formed by combustion of fuels especially from badly built or poorly managed fuel-burning plants, open fireplaces and motor vehicles. Soot is also formed by forest fires. Dust of various kinds is formed by handling of materials, e.g. loading and unloading, mixing, crushing, grinding, sawing, cutting etc. Thus dust is formed in cement factories, casting mills, metal producing or metal working industries, quarries, etc. Much dust is also formed by earth moving, e.g. in construction of roads, buildings, dams, etc. Dust is also whirled up from bad roads by motor cars. Large buildings in big cities often have their own incinerators which often function badly and the waste gases cause a great deal of dust and smoke.

3.2.2 Harmfulness of dust

All dust is bad for human and animal health. It is bad for plants, too, because it clogs the pores of the leaves and stops the pistils of flowers from collecting pollen. The effect of dust on lung complaints varies with the quantity of dust in air. Besides cigarette smoking, dust is said to be of significance in the incidence of lung cancer. The death rate of asthma patients also increases with increasing dust content of the air.

It is obvious that dust of poisonous and radioactive substances is very dangerous and precautions must be taken to avoid its distribution in air. Besides these, dust of some substances which are not poisonous in massive form, can also be very dangerous. For example, silica laden dust is dangerous if breathed in, and the silica must be removed completely. It occurs especially in mines (see vol. II, coal) and during cutting and working of stone, etc. If breathed in, the fresh silica surface causes chemical reactions in the lungs that destroy the tissue (silicosis).

Silicosis is caused mainly by breathing through the mouth, or when the nasal mucous membrane is not able to bind all the dust. Proper medical examination will almost invariably show which workers must be kept away from plants where there are dangerous dusts. In some countries (e.g. the Netherlands) the working of sandstone is prohibited owing to the danger of silicosis. In many countries (Britain for instance) there are special regulations regarding the wearing of masks during sandblasting and other operations involving risk of silicosis: the use of silicate-containing powders (for facing moulds for instance) is also forbidden.

Dust of asbestos contains very sharp crystal-needles that irritate the lungs and the intestine. It may cause asbestosis even many years afterwards.

Besides pollen which can cause hay-fever, there are several other kinds of dust causing allergic manifestations. This group includes synthetic resins, plastics, felt, kapok, leather, paper, wood dust, starch, wool etc. Dust of chemical compounds having an acid or alkaline character cause chemical irritation of the mucous membranes. In addition several kinds of dust irritate the skin and mucous membranes in a mechanical way.

A notorious consequence of air pollution is the formation of *smog*. Smog is much in evidence in areas having often a stagnant atmosphere (e.g. Los Angeles in California) and in areas having often a very moist (foggy) atmosphere (e.g. London). The London smog is sometimes very dangerous. The dense and dark smog of December 1952 lasted five days and caused 4000 deaths, principally among the old, the infirm and those with respiratory diseases.

Originally the word 'smog' was a combination of the words 'smoke' and 'fog' because the London smog, being the oldest air pollution problem, is formed when fog or mist mixes with smoke (soot particles and several liquid and gaseous substances). Nowadays the word smog has become descriptive of any air pollution accompanied by an important decrease in visibility (see the Los Angeles smog, p. 107).

Besides its harmfulness for vegetable, animal and human life, the London smog causes economic losses, since it makes almost all traffic impossible. It has been estimated that smog damage is costing Great Britain £ 250 million a year. Smokeless zones have been created in selected industrial areas and have demonstrated the possibilities of area-wide improvement.

3.2.3 Reducing dust formation

It is clear that dust formation must be reduced as far as possible. The suppression of smoke from combustion processes is very important. Coal can be burned in a relatively smokeless manner if sufficient air is supplied through the fuel bed. Gaseous fuels are the cleanest fuels available because they can easily be mixed with sufficient air for complete combustion. Oils and wood burn with smoky, sooty flames. An important process for reducing smoke from oil combustion is the mixing of steam or air with the hot waste gases before release in a high flare stack. The soot particles are burned in this way together with combustible gaseous constituents of the waste gases (see also gaseous pollutants). The formation of dust in factories is often suppressed by spraying water. It is recommended that a synthetic soap or some other wetting agent should be dissolved in the water; this makes only half the quantity of water necessary. A water spray is used for sawing and polishing stones, in many crushing equipments, etc. The dust distribution in factories is also avoided by means of industrial vacuum cleaners placed near the sources of dust.

On dusty roads regular wetting with water would be too expensive in view of the labour involved. Calcium chloride and magnesium chloride solutions are more effective because these hygroscopic substances retain water better; but rain washes them away again. Besides which, they are rather expensive.

In America, especially in Wisconsin where there are many sulphite wood pulp factories, an endeavour is being made to use these factory effluents for spraying country roads on which it would be uneconomical to lay a harder or better surface. The effluent can be used within a short range of the factory. Further away than, say, fifty miles it is no longer economical and effluent concentrated to 50% is used. This treatment binds and hardens the surface and reduces dust, with consequent benefit to traffic and to the surrounding fields. Another important thing is that good use is being made of a waste product that cannot be discharged into waterways as an effluent.

A better anti-dust agent, but a much dearer one, is crude oil containing asphalt, or a tar emulsion. These often keep roads free of dust for several years. Plants cultivated along dust-free roads yield much higher crops.

3.2.4 Removal of dust from air and other gases

Dust must often be removed from waste air which is laden with much dust in factories, or even from fresh air, to avoid troubles in chemical processes etc. There are several methods for removing dust from air and other gases. These processes are also used to separate solid particles from any other gas containing them, either to purify the gas or to recover valuable solids from a waste gas.

a. Filters. Dust filters may be divided into two types: the deep-bed or fibrous filters and the cloth filters. In the first dust is collected in the interstices of the bed of fibres. In the latter a layer of dust is formed on the surface of the cloth. This layer acts also as a further filter for smaller dust particles. Thus the efficiency increases as the dust layer builds up.

Dry layers of fibres are extensively used in air conditioning units etc. Fibres of wool, asbestos, cellulose, glass and several others may be used. Since waste gases often have a high temperature, filter beds of wool and cotton cannot always be used. Hence the success of glass fibres which can easily withstand temperatures above 200° C. In general the efficiency is not greater than 50%, but beds of glass fibres can be made with an efficiency of 99.99% for submicron particles at a pressure drop of 4 inches of water. Such filter beds are used for the removal of radioactive dust from air, and for the purification of air in plants producing photographic film. The efficiency of filter beds can be increased by wetting them with oil (viscous filters). This is achieved by mounting filter beds in metal frames and attaching the frames to chains which are mounted on sprockets at the top and bottom of the filter equipment. In this way a vertical conveyor belt is formed. In action the belt passes through an oil bath at the bottom of the house, thus wetting and cleaning the filter beds periodically. For purifying small quantities of air porous ceramic masses are sometimes used as filters.

Cloth filters consist of envelopes or long tubular bags. A bag filter equipment consists of a number of vertical bags which are suspended near each other in a filter house (see fig. 3.1). The upper ends of the tubes are closed. The lower ends are open and

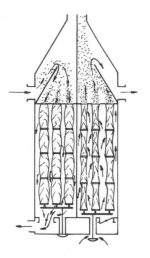

Fig. 3.1 Bag filter. In the right section dust is collected in the bags. The left section is cleaned by shaking the bags and by blowing air in reverse through the bags.

are attached to an inlet manifold. The dust laden gas is blown into the bags via the open ends, and dust deposits on the inside of the bags. Periodically the dust must be removed from the tubes. The dust can be removed by shaking the tubes. The tubes can also be constricted at regular intervals by means of a frame having openings which are a little smaller than the diameter of the tubes. This frame moves slowly up and down, thus squeezing each part of the tubes from time to time. The loosely adhering dust is released and falls into the hopper. The dust can also be removed from the tubes by reversing the direction of the air flow. The dust is then blown from the filter bag. This is shown in the left section of fig. 3.1.

An envelope filter equipment consists of a number of wide cloth envelopes which are mounted over frames. Air passes from the outside of the envelopes into the space formed by the frame and thus the dust deposits on the outside of the envelope. These envelopes are cleaned by reversing the direction of the air flow from time to time.

b. Scrubbers and washers. Dust can also be removed from air by means of scrubbers and washers which work with liquids. Fig. 3.2, for instance, is a diagram of a very large installation. This has large air cylinders filled with Raschig rings (see vol. II) that are regularly wetted with oil to retain all the dust, which is carried down to the bottom by the oil and pumped away. When the dust has settled and after other substances have been removed from it, the oil is used again for spraying the Raschig rings.

Instead of oil it is possible to use glycerine cleaned in the same way, or a synthetic detergent solution.

Dust in internal combustion and explosion engines is liable to cause extensive cylinder wear, and filters are therefore placed at the air intake.

These filters consist of a mass of oil-soaked metal gauze to which dust adheres. Oil bath filters are also used, the air bubbling through a layer of oil that also wets the gauze above it. Dust not trapped in the oil bath is retained by the gauze.

Another type of scrubber is the spray chamber in which water or another liquid is sprayed. The gas is passed countercurrently to the falling drops of liquid. The contact between liquid droplets and the dust particles can be increased by introducing the

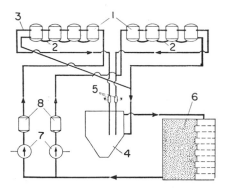

Fig. 3.2 Diagram of an air scrubber with continuous liquid (oil) purification, for large installations.

1. Cylindrical tanks filled with Raschig rings, through which air flows upwards.
2. Pipe for removing dirty oil.
3. Clean oil supply with overflow.
4. Collection tank for dirty oil, which is kept at 100°.
5. Sight glasses.
6. Settling tanks, in which all the heavier particles in the oil from (4) can settle in a vertical succession of trays.
7. Pumps compressing the oil from (6) through 8.
8. Cylinders of activated carbon which retains all adsorbable substances. The pumps return the clean oil to the jets at the top of the filters.

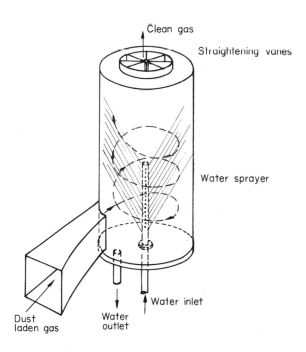

Fig. 3.3 The Pease-Anthony cyclonic spray scrubber.

Fig. 3.4 Dust-extracting plant for hot blast furnace gases. The gases first pass through a washing tower and are then freed from all dust in a horizontal type electrostatic dust separator.

impure air tangentially at the bottom. Thus the air moves spirally through the liquid droplets (see fig. 3.3). This type of scrubber may also be used for humidifying and dehumidifying air (see p. 111); conversely the open circuit dehumidifiers can be used for dust removal.

Dust is also removed from air by passing the air through a layer of water.

Of course, other chemicals or solutions can also be used as the scrubber liquid. This makes it possible to absorb gaseous impurities at the same time.

c. Electric dust precipitators. An electric (or electrostatic) dust precipitator consists basically of two series of electrodes: a series of earthed collecting electrodes having a large surface, and a series of ionizing electrodes, usually wires, on which a high voltage is applied. When air is blown between the electrodes it becomes ionized. The dust particles contained in it absorb the positive ions, are attracted to the large collecting electrodes, precipitate on the latter and fall down to the bottom of the equipment. The large collecting electrodes may have the form of small pipes. A wire is suspended in each pipe and supplied with a high potential. Collecting electrodes which consist of a number of concentric pipes are also used. A number of high potential wires is then placed in the annular spaces between the pipes (see figs. 3.4 and 3.5). Plate-type precipitators are also built. Dust-collecting plates are placed alternately with a number

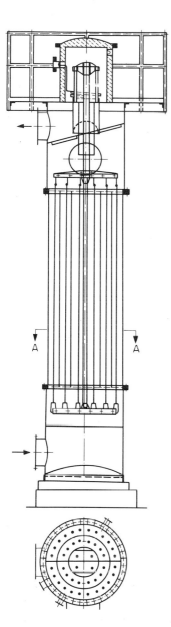

Fig. 3.5 Diagram of an electrostatic separator. The anodes consist of wires arranged as coaxial cylinders which are kept taut with a heavy ring. Underneath is a cross-section along the line AA. The wires can be shaken by means of a device at the top.

of high potential wires (see fig. 3.6). The electric precipitators previously described are single stage precipitators. They are also known as Cottrell precipitators. These precipitators are used for removing huge amounts of dust from air, e.g. in cement factories and carbon black factories. In sulphuric acid and phosphoric acid plants they are used for the collection of acid mist, and in fluidized bed catalyst plants of the oil industry for the collection of catalyst from the effluent gases.

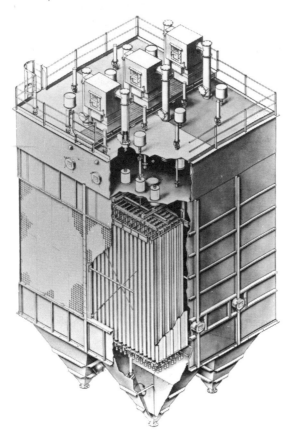

Fig. 3.6 A cutaway view of a plate-type electrostatic precipitator.

A modified type of the electric precipitator is the two stage precipitator, which consists of an ionizing section and a non-ionizing collecting section separated from each other. These precipitators are used for gases having a low dust content.

d. Centrifugal separators. The most common centrifugal separator is the *cyclone* which comprises a conical chamber provided with a cylindrical section at the top (see fig. 3.7, 3.8). The dust-laden gas enters the cylindrical section tangentially with as little turbulence as possible. Thus the gas rotates at relatively high velocity. Solid and liquid particles are subjected to great centrifugal forces, move towards the wall of the cyclone and fall into a dust receiver at the bottom of the cyclone. The clean gas forms a vortex in the centre of the cyclone, travels upwards and leaves the cyclone at the top through a fairly wide coaxial tube in the cylindrical section. This air collects a substantial quantity of the dust-laden air which enters near the central outlet of the clean gas, owing to the turbulent currents that are generated near this outlet. This can be diminished by removing dust from the annular space between the cyclone wall and the outlet pipe via a shave-off opening in the wall of the cyclone. This opening is connected to a by-pass

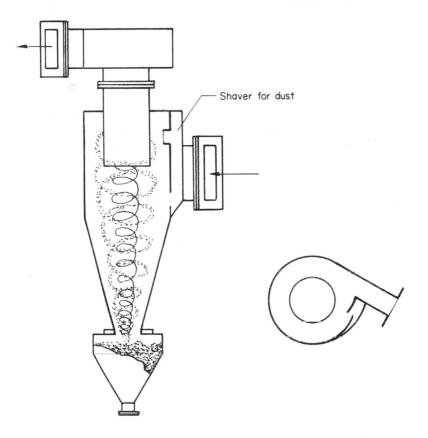

Shaver for dust

Fig. 3.7 Van Tongeren Cyclone Dust Collector. Air in the annular space above in the cyclone is removed by way of the shaver opening and is reintroduced in a lower section of the cyclone.

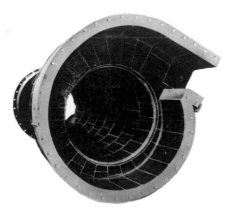

Fig. 3.8 Body and lid of a cyclone lined with cast basalt. Even with very sharp dust in rapid motion the cyclone wears well. The basalt lining is built up of pieces factory-made to fit exactly.

Fig. 3.9 A multiclone.

channel in the wall and reintroduces the dust in a lower section of the cyclone. This is realized in the 'van Tongeren cyclone'.

Cyclones are generally adapted to remove particles in the 10 to 200 μ range. Several modifications of the cyclone are available. One of them is the multiclone (see fig. 3.9), which consists of a number of individual cyclones in parallel with a single air-collector at the top and a single dust-collector at the bottom. Sometimes cyclones are provided with vanes in the inlet to impart a spiral motion to the gas, and others have helical plates in the cyclone body to guide the gases. Sometimes cyclones are lined (e.g. with soft rubber or a very hard cast basalt) to protect them against wear (see fig. 3.8).

Another centrifugal separator is the *mechanical centrifugal separator,* in which the centrifugal force is supplied by rotating paddles or blades.

3.3   GASEOUS POLLUTANTS IN AIR

Several gaseous pollutants are produced in industrial areas. Sulphur dioxide is formed in almost all combustion processes, especially in big boiler plants, since most fuels contain sulphur. This gas is also formed during the processing of sulphur-bearing ores. Besides sulphur dioxide, combustion gases nearly always contain the very poisonous carbon monoxide and several hydrocarbons, acids, aldehydes and nitrogen dioxide. In cities pollutant gases are introduced into the air by motor vehicles.

Hydrogen sulphide and other obnoxious sulphur compounds are released by the petroleum industry. Several other gases such as hydrogen fluoride, chlorine and ammonia are released incidentally in chemical processes. All these gases are poisonous, cause irritation of the mucous membranes or have a troublesome odour. Nowadays the harmful gases released by the petroleum industry and the chemical industry are often removed from air at the source by scrubbing with liquid absorbents or adsorption on porous solids. Thus, these gases play a less important role in air pollution than combustion gases do. The purification of waste gases from chemical processes are discussed with the specified products or processes.

It is clear that almost all gaseous pollutants are harmful to human, animal and vegetable life. An air pollution problem which threatens to affect several metropolitan areas is the Los Angeles smog, which is caused by combustion gases. It is said that nitrogen dioxide is decomposed to atomic oxygen and nitric oxide under the influence of ultraviolet light. These reaction products react with molecular oxygen and form ozone and nitrogen dioxide respectively. Thus nitrogen dioxide is continuously regenerated and although the concentration of nitrogen dioxide is low, considerable amounts of ozone can be formed. The ozone concentration can increase to 30-40 p.p.m. and oxidize vapours of organic compounds to peroxides and sulphur dioxide to sulphur trioxide. When the atmospheric conditions are stable these pollutants form a hazy layer which causes eye irritation and plant damage. This haze also prevents further pollutants from escaping, thus increasing pollution of the air. This is shown by comparision of the measured concentrations of pollutants in Los Angeles (in p.p.m. by volume).

Pollutant	Clear day (visibility 7 miles)	Day of smog (visibility less than 1 mile)
Carbon monoxide	3.5	23.0
Oxides of nitrogen	0.08	0.4
Sulphur dioxide	0.05	0.3
Total hydrocarbons	0.2	0.1
Aldehydes	0.07	0.4
Organic acids	0.07	0.4

Unlike London smog, Los Angeles smog has a relatively low dust (soot) content.

Several steps can be taken to diminish air pollution by combustion gases. The oldest method of diminishing air pollution is to build high chimneys. The highest concentration of injurious flue-gas constituents (at ground level) has been found at a distance of fifty chimney lengths. But the higher the chimney the greater is the dilution of the gases. The chimney-top temperature has a great influence on the rate of distribution of waste gases in the atmosphere. It is estimated that every additional degree Centigrade has the same effect as increasing the height of the chimney by $1\frac{1}{2}$ metres.

A smelter in Canada has built a concrete chimney 600 ft high. Its bottom diameter is 50 ft and its top diameter 30 ft. Its total weight is 15000 tons. It is lined inside with acid resistant brick and with stainless steel at the top. This expensive construction was necessary to reduce to a minimum the ground-level damage caused by waste gases bearing sulphur dioxide.

Many industrial plants and machines, for instance painting and lacquering plants (e.g. for wire enamelling), core ovens at iron foundries, fat rendering plants, oil refineries, asphalt factories and even motor vehicles discharge gases into the atmosphere. This can be prevented by passing the waste gases through a catalyst mass secured between perforated plates. Catalysts consisting of nickel or platinum gauzes are often used. All combustible constituents then oxidise without flaming at a temperature of 260° C and turn into water vapour and carbon dioxide, which can be discharged without causing any inconvenience. Sometimes so much heat is recovered that the method is profitable.

In the USA, tests are now being made on possible methods of reducing air pollution caused by motor vehicles. One method is to run exhaust gases through a catalyst which is claimed to burn completely nearly all the residual hydrocarbons. Another method is to ignite all the combustible matter in the exhaust gases with an electrical spark plug.

3.4 ATMOSPHERIC MOISTURE

3.4.1 Absolute and relative humidity

Water vapour is present in varying quantities in the air. It is, of course, found mostly over large areas of water and at elevated temperatures. Big lakes in hot regions may lose so much by evaporation that a water shortage is caused. Evaporation is sometimes reduced by distributing a little cetyl alcohol (which is liquid in the tropics) over the surface. At the same time mosquito larvae are suffocated when they come to the surface for breathing (for Cetyl alcohol see vol. V).

Porous soil, as found in big forests, also imparts a high water vapour content to the atmosphere. The spongy earth retains rain water for long periods and regularly supplies water vapour. Exhalation by animals and by plants (via their leaves) likewise increases the humidity of the atmosphere.

The water content of air is sometimes expressed in grains per cubic foot, grams per litre etc. (absolute humidity). The water vapour content is more frequently expressed in mm of mercury as the contribution of the water vapour to the total atmospheric pressure (normally 760 mm of mercury). This pressure of water vapour, which can never be greater than the saturation pressure of water vapour above a water surface at the particular temperature, is known as the partial pressure. The lower the partial pressure of water vapour in the air, the drier is the air. However, the humidity characteristics of moist air also depend on the temperature. Air behaves like drier air when the temperature increases although the absolute moisture content remains the same. For this reason the moisture content of air is customarily expressed as relative humidity.

The relative humidity is the ratio of the actual partial pressure of water to the maximum, or saturation, pressure at the same temperature. As the saturation pressure is greater at a higher temperature, one way to reduce the relative humidity of a room is to heat it. The other way is obviously to remove water vapour from the air.

If the atmosphere is very humid the water vapour may become saturated upon cooling and, if the air cools further still, may remain suspended in the form of very fine droplets. This phenomenon is the well known fog or mist.

At the present time an effort is being made to combat fog with rain-making methods. The idea is to spray silver iodide, or carbon dioxide snow mixed with finely divided wetting agents (e.g. synthetic soap), over fog banks from small aircraft: the fine particles are intended to act as condensation nuclei, causing the fine droplets to conglomerate and fall as rain. During the Second World War, fog was driven from airstrips by applying heat along them, but this method is too expensive for peacetime use.

3.4.2 Determination of the humidity of air

Determination of the humidity of air is very important in air-conditioning of factories etc. There are several ways of determining the humidity of air.

a. Determination of the dew-point. The dew-point is the temperature at which air, having a certain moisture content, becomes saturated. This temperature can be measured as follows:

A thermometer is suspended in a wider tube the outside of which is silvered or gilded underneath. Air is blown through the tube, which contains some ether.

The tube decreases gradually in temperature by the evaporation of the ether. At the moment the tube is cooled to a temperature where the saturation pressure is greater than the partial pressure of the surrounding air, water precipitates in fine droplets (dew) on the outside of the silvered tube. This temperature is then read from the thermometer. From tables in which the saturation pressure of water at various temperatures is given, the pressure of the water at the dew-point can be found (which is the partial pressure of the water in the air) and also the saturation pressure of water at the ambient temperature. The proportion of partial pressure to saturation pressure is the relative humidity.

In a more exact method for the determination of the dewpoint, use is made of the Peltier effect. The Peltier effect comprises the following phenomenon:

If an electric current is passed across the junction of two dissimilar metals, heat is absorbed or liberated at this junction depending on the direction of the current. For measuring the dew-point of air, two blocks of semi-conducting materials are joined at a small silver mirror. A parallel beam of light is reflected by the mirror on a photoelectric cell or photoresistor. The temperature of the mirror is lowered by passing a current across the junctions of the semi-conductors and the mirror. As soon as the temperature of the mirror drops below the dew-point, its surface mists over and the light beam is reflected diffusely. As a result less light reaches the photoelectric cell, and the current flowing through the cell decreases. The current of the photoelectric cell controls the current flowing through the Peltier element in such a way that the cooling diminishes when the reflector mists over. The temperature of the silver mirror then rises once more above the dew-point, the mist disappears and the process repeats itself. After one or two oscillations, the equilibrium is reached and the temperature of the silver mirror remains

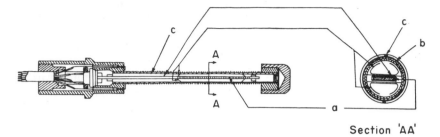

Section 'AA'

Fig. 3.10 Dew cell element. Temperature sensitive element (a) contained in a stainless steel tube (b) carrying a lithium chloride impregnated glass wick and silver conductors (c).

equal to the dew-point temperature. This temperature is measured by means of small thermocouples which are placed in small holes in the mirror.

The dew-point can also be determined by means of the *Dew cell* (see fig. 3.10). This cell is based on the behaviour of saturated solutions of hygroscopic salts. The measuring element of this instrument consists of a thermometer (e.g. a thermocouple) wound with glass fabric and two silver wires that are not in direct contact. The glass fabric contains a saturated solution of lithium chloride in addition to solid lithium chloride. A saturated solution of lithium chloride absorbs water from the surrounding atmosphere, since the water vapour pressure of the former is lower than the normally occurring water vapour pressures of the surrounding atmosphere. The absorption of water is suppressed by applying an alternating current between the silver wires. The flow of current through the solution generates enough heat to raise the temperature of the solution. The vapour pressure of the solution increases and less water is absorbed from the surrounding atmosphere. The temperature rises until the vapour pressures of the saturated solution and the atmosphere are equal. At this point the heat, generated in the solution, is entirely used for the evaporation of water. Thus the temperature of the solution remains constant and can be read from the thermometer. The dew-point temperature can be obtained from a table showing the vapour pressure of a saturated solution of lithium chloride and that of water as a function of the temperature.

b. Determination of the wet-bulb temperature. For measuring the wet-bulb temperature in a room the sling psychrometer is often used. This device consists of two thermometers mounted side by side in a sling which can be whirled to give the desired gas velocity around the bulbs of the thermometers. One thermometer is fixed with its bulb beyond the bulb of the other. The former bulb is covered with a very light fabric or gauze which is moistened with pure water. The other bulb is kept dry. When the sling thermometer is whirled and the evaporation of moisture causes the temperature of the wet bulb thermometer to decrease. When the temperature of the wet bulb thermometer has reached a constant value, readings are taken of both thermometers. The relative humidity of the air can be found by means of tables (psychrometric charts).

c. The hair-hygrometer. The hair-hygrometer is based on the change in length of a taut hair, or other hygroscopic material, with change of the relative humidity. A strip of polystyrene which is coated with a hygroscopic material or a strip of cellophane may also be used. The humidity sensitive material is stretched by means of a spring, and the change in length with the change in relative humidity is transmitted to a pointer that moves along a scale when the hygroscopic strip changes length. These measuring instruments are calibrated by means of an accurate indicating hygrometer. The hair hygrometer is not very exact.

d. Other hygrometers. Several hygrometers are based on the change of electric conductivity with relative humidity of materials which can absorb water from the atmosphere. These materials may be porous solids, solutions of hygroscopic compounds absorbed in porous solids, coatings of porous conductive materials on an insulator, etc.

The relative humidity can also be determined by means of compounds capable of changing colour upon absorbing water, e.g. paper impregnated with cobaltous chloride. This method is not very exact. It is often used for cheap weather indicators.

An optical hygrometer has also been constructed, based on the fact that infrared rays of certain wavelengths pass through water vapour, while others that may be only slightly different are absorbed. Two such different rays are passed through a quantity of air and the difference in absorption is measured, thus indicating the amount of water vapour.

Absolute humidity can be measured by drawing a quantity of air through a tube containing a hygroscopic substance (see below) and measuring the difference in weight of the tube before and after.

3.4.3 Dehumidifying of air (and other gases)

The humidity of air can be decreased by cooling air below its dew-point. Thus water is removed by condensation. The dried cold air is heated again to the desired temperature. Air can be cooled by spraying chilled water in a device packed with glass filaments or other materials that provide large areas of contact surface. The air is passed in countercurrent through the device. Air can also be cooled by passing it through a chamber in which chilled water is sprayed. Dehumidifiers in which air is directly contacted with the cold liquid are called open-circuit dehumidifiers. In other devices a cold liquid is indirectly contacted with moist air by passing air through a heat exchanger provided with cooling coils (closed-circuit dehumidifiers). An example of such a dehumidifier is shown in fig. 3.11. The cold liquid can be obtained from cold water wells or by means of refrigerating machines (see Cooling and ice, p. 185). Cold brines, liquid ammonia and liquid air or nitrogen may also be used as cooling agents if extremely low humidities are required. The air is then cooled below the freezing point of water and ice settles on the cooling parts of the equipment. Periodical de-icing is necessary in these cases.

Low humidities can also be reached with dehydration equipment which is provided with a liquid or solid dehydrating agent. Dehydrating agents are substances that can absorb water (hygroscopic substances). They can be subdivided into several groups.

One attracts water vapour from the atmosphere because the molecules retain water molecules with moderate force owing to more or less weak chemical action, leading to the formation of hydrates. The most common substances of this type are: calcium chloride, lithium chloride, lithium bromide, magnesium chloride and many substances

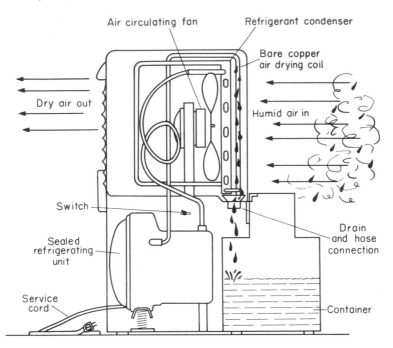

Fig. 3.11 Diagram of a dehumidifier.

that form crystals of a specific form with water. These may release the water again when moderately heated.

Materials such as $CaCl_2$ and $MgCl_2$ are often difficult to use as such, but they can be absorbed in dried wood. Especially brittle and porous woods (e.g. poplar, hemlock, plane, sassafras) are put in a solution of 20% calcium chloride, which soaks in along the grain. This may take several weeks. The wood is then thoroughly dried at 100° C. It can be used to extract water vapour from the atmosphere in closed premises. When it has absorbed water to saturation its hygroscopicity can be restored by heating. Such blocks may be used for keeping grain dry in closed elevators. Most of these substances can also be used in concentrated aqueous solutions, since the water vapour pressure of these solutions is often very low. Thus water in air having a higher water vapour pressure condenses in the solution. Dehumidifying with a combination of cooling and a concentrated solution of a dehydrating agent is effected by sprinkling cooling coils with a strong solution of lithium chloride.

The second group of dehydrating agents forms strong chemical compounds which do not readily release the water again. These include quicklime (CaO) and phosphorus pentoxide (P_2O_5) which form slaked lime ($Ca(OH)_2$ (and phosphoric acid (H_3PO_4) respectively. These compounds are more powerful dehydrating agents than the chlorides of calcium, magnesium or lithium.

There are also dehydrating agents such as silica gel, aluminium hydroxide etc. which absorb water vapour without forming any definite chemical compound. When heated, they release the water again. This group includes sulphuric acid, glycerols and glycols such as (see vol. IV) diethylene glycol and triethylene glycol. These are used mainly where large supplies of natural gas have to be conducted through pipelines. In the winter, the water vapour in the gas might block the pipelines where they dip, or might cause obstruction by freezing. The glycols are non-corrosive, an important point with steel pipelines. These materials are discussed further in vols. IV and V.

The periodical regeneration is necessary at intervals with all hygroscopic substances and it is thus difficult to use them for continuous working. It is often necessary to know when the dehydrating agent has to be regenerated. Silica gel, aluminium hydroxide etc. may be mixed with anhydrous cobaltous chloride ($CoCl_2$). When the dehydrating agent becomes exhausted the blue anhydrous cobaltous chloride absorbs the remaining water vapour and forms a hydrate which possesses a pink colour.

3.4.4 Humidifying of air

It is often necessary or advisable to increase the humidity of the atmosphere in houses and factories. Air may be humidified by means of open-circuit dehumidifiers (see above), but the water is not chilled for this purpose. Water may also be sprayed into an air stream by means of sprinkler equipment which supplies water in the form of mist. Simple equipment works by means of a fan driven by an enclosed electro-motor. This sucks water from a tank through a tube. The water is brought on to rapidly rotating discs and flung against a slatted wall. This turns the water into extremely fine droplets, which are sucked upwards by the fan and dispersed into the atmosphere. This unit may also be used for spraying disinfectants or deodorants in hospitals, cattle stalls, etc.

Air can also be humidified by ejecting steam into an air stream, or by passing air over water which is heated by means of steam coils.

3.5 SOME USES OF AIR

3.5.1 Air conditioning and its use

Air conditioning is the simultaneous control of at least three factors which affect the physical and chemical conditions of the atmosphere in enclosed areas. The most important factors are the temperature, humidity and motion of air. Other factors which often have also to be controlled are dust and toxic gases contained in air, and the odour of air. For this reason air conditioning equipment is often provided with filters etc. (see p. 99). If open circuit dehumidifiers are used dust and gases can be removed at the same time. (Gases can be removed by using a cold solution of an absorbent as dehumidifying liquid.)

As air must be transported to the conditioning equipment, the latter must be provided with fans. The motion of air can be controlled by controlling the speed and the position of the fans. The motion of air is also affected by the position of apertures in walls of the rooms to be conditioned and the pipes for supplying fresh air and removing waste air.

Air is dehumidified or humidified by the methods previously described and then heated or cooled in the usual ways, e.g. electrical heating, or heating and cooling with coils fed with steam or cold brines respectively. The temperature of air is controlled

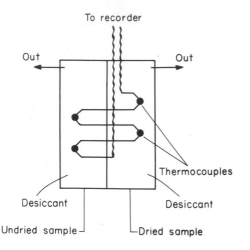

Fig. 3.12 Diagram of a continuous electric humidity control apparatus.

by means of thermostats. The humidity of air can be controlled by controlling the temperature of the cooling agent in the dehumidifier. (Dehydrating agents are mainly used to obtain air which is as dry as possible.) The humidity content of air is sometimes controlled by an automatic method depending on the fact that a dehydrating agent heats when it absorbs water and cools when the water is liberated (see fig. 3.12). A small sample is regularly drawn off from the liquid stream and divided into two portions. The two samples, one of which is carefully dried, go to two compartments containing a desiccant with thermocouples inserted in it. If the undried sample contains any moisture the temperature in that compartment will rise slightly and the thermocouple will give a signal. At certain times the dried and undried samples are automatically reversed. The dried sample then absorbs water from the desiccant and dries it again, while the undried sample can release water again.

A small conditioning plant as built in windows is shown in fig. 3.13. This conditioning

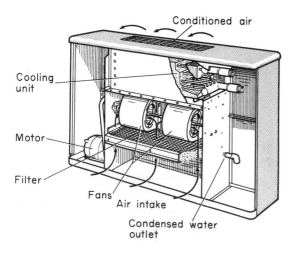

Fig. 3.13 A small air conditioning unit. Such units are often fitted in windows.

unit draws air in from outside with electric fans through a dust filter. The air passes over the pipes of a cooling unit, which reduces its temperature until all excess water vapour condenses and runs to a tank (the water level in which is indicated automatically after a certain point). The air is raised to the desired temperature again by heating it to 70° F, or by mixing it with uncooled air from outside.

Air conditioning is used either to improve human comfort in houses, theatres, office buildings, aircraft etc., or to improve the working conditions for materials and men in factories, laboratories, stores etc. The large installations used in big buildings and manufacturing plants almost invariably justify themselves because of their beneficial effect on working conditions.

Air conditioning is also applied in deep mines to control both temperature and humidity in order to facilitate work or, in fact, to make work possible. A Canadian nickel mine employs a special method. At a depth of 90 and 150 metres huge spaces have been made. In the icy cold winter, air enters the spaces, where it is sprinkled with mine water. The water freezes instantaneously. Ice pellets form, and so much heat is given off into the atmosphere that air enters the galleries at a good temperature. When the weather gets warmer, the hot outside air passes through the ice deposits that have formed and its temperature is greatly reduced, so that it can be used for cooling. It is estimated that in winter about 140 000 tons of ice are collected. During melting this can absorb over 11 000 million calories in total. To supply this quantity of heat would take about 1 600 tons of coal (without counting heat losses).

In South Africa galleries in the very deep gold mines are cooled with large refrigerating plants.

In factories air conditioning is used to control chemical and biochemical reactions that are affected by atmospheric conditions. Thus air conditioning is used in the textile industry, since the formation of cellulose xanthate in the manufacture of rayon and the viscosity of spinning solution, which affect the rate of reaction and coagulation during spinning, depend on atmospheric conditions, especially temperature and humidity. The properties of rayon are also affected by the temperature of the spinning bath. Fermentation processes and processes for the production of yeast and malt are also affected by atmospheric circumstances.

Air conditioning is also used to protect moisture- and heat-sensitive materials from drying out or from lumping, caking, sticking etc. For this reason stores for hygroscopic or other moisture sensitive materials, e.g. food products, must be provided with air conditioning equipment. A typical industry which uses air conditioning for this purpose is the pharmaceutical industry, for the production of pills and capsules. Lumping of hygroscopic pharmaceuticals must be prevented and at the same time the capsules (gelatin) must be kept at constant conditions. (Gelatin becomes soft and sticky at too high temperatures and humidity, and brittle at low temperatures and humidity.) For the same reason air conditioning is necessary in factories in which photographic materials are produced. The removal of dust is also particularly important in this industry to prevent dust particles from settling in gelatin emulsions.

Air conditioning is also necessary in drying chambers, e.g. for ceramic goods. Ceramic products must be uniformly dried before firing to standardize form and dimensions of the products and to prevent setting up strains which cause cracking, etc. The uniform drying can only be achieved by means of air conditioning.

Air conditioning also makes it possible to minimize the effect of static electricity, thus reducing fire hazard in explosives industries, in the rubber industry, in flour mills, and in plant for the production of photographic materials, and reducing friction of yarns, paper and plastic foils in the textile, paper and plastics industries respectively.

In many countries warehouses have been built with air conditioning installations capable of providing a tropical climate in enclosed areas. These are used for the cultivation of tropical plants and to ascertain how materials will behave under tropical conditions, in order to test their useful life and value.

The choice of air conditions is often difficult, since different conditions are often wanted for different purposes in one process, e.g. for the filling of capsules in the pharmaceutical industry and for the production of photographic materials. In the photographic industry, for example, gelatin must be kept under favourable conditions with regard to the strength and stability of thin layers of the product, but in general less favourable conditions must be chosen in order to reduce static electricity.

In aircraft carriers great inconvenience was caused by cigarette smoke in the workshops below deck. As a ban on smoking would have caused ill-feeling and hampered efficiency, it was decided to pass the air through filters capable of retaining even 0.1 micron tar particles in smoke. The air in a big room could be changed in four minutes. Such filters are now recommended for restaurants and particularly for hospitals, for the radical elimination of the many bacteria which include dangerous causes of infection.

In hospitals and in plants producing antibiotics or other fermentation products air must often be sterilized. Bacteria cannot withstand ultraviolet light and can thus be combated with mercury vapour lamps. Air can also be sterilized by filtering through fairly long tubes filled with absorbent granulated substances, or with fibrous substances, mainly glass wool and slag wool. At a fairly high velocity microbes are retained on the surface of the granules or fibres (oiling or any other form of wetting is unnecessary).

Bacteria can also be destroyed by intense heating of the air, but this is expensive for air conditioning purposes.

3.5.2 Some uses of compressed air

Under moderate pressure, air has since old times been obtained with a pair of bellows, for smithy fires for instance. Nowadays compressors are used that can go up to very high pressures and handle vast quantities of air. They very often work in stages to prevent overheating by rapid compression.

Compressed air is used for tunnel buildings and in mines for driving drills and cutters, etc. It provides ventilation at the same time. Large supplies of compressed air are used for riveting machines, for breaking concrete or other stone, and for pulverizing compact masses of salt and fertilizer. Compressed air is often produced by portable machines, especially for breaking up and for other purposes where mobile equipment is required. It acts as the motive power for tools operating on the piston and cylinder principle of steam or internal combustion engines. The excessive vibration of such tools was formerly injurious to the workers, but they are now constructed so that the reactive force of the expanding air is intercepted by a rubber bag, to which the handle is fixed, sliding in a cylinder: this damps out most of the vibration.

Some factories have compressed air installations for starting up heavy engines. Ships' diesel engines are started up in this way.

A recent application is that of raising vehicles and vessels from the ground or water with a downward jet of compressed air. This greatly reduces the resistance to forward propulsion.

Long central pneumatic tube systems are used for delivering messages. These go to central stations, whence the 'pneus' are delivered to the addressees just like telegrams. Many big office buildings have such systems of their own. Papers travel in small containers that almost exactly fit the tubes. Hitherto there has had to be an individual air compressor for each tube. (If all the tubes are connected to a central compressor, the air selects the one with the least resistance, which means that the busiest line will not function.) This is now changing since a valve system has been invented, which has such internal restriction that the air attains the speed of sound in it. An air mass with such a high speed is not affected by difference in the resistances after the valve systems, thus all the tubes (each provided with a valve system) can be connected to a central compressor.

Pneumatic conveying is also used for granular substances such as cereals, sugar, meal, etc., which meet an air blast at an outflow opening strong enough to fluidize them and allow them to be handled like liquids. They can be unloaded much more quickly than in the past and pneumatically raised into silos, for instance. More and more trucks are being constructed for transporting granular or powdered materials for fluidized handling. (Compare pneumatic conveying dryers, p. 36.)

Compressed air is being increasingly used for stopping arcing of electric switches.

Compressed air is used in paint and lacquer spray-guns. An electric heating equipment is sometimes applied so that such spray-guns can be used for molten metal. Agricultural use of compressed air is increasing for spraying crops with insecticides and fungicides.

An important application of compressed air is in wind tunnels for sonic speed tests at aircraft research stations. The usual method is to fill large tanks with high-pressure air, and use them to produce strong air currents in the wind tunnel proper. Scale-model aircraft, parts, etc. are placed inside to study or measure their behaviour in given air currents. The compressed air required for a single test is obtained fairly cheaply by this method. For research at extremely high velocities small scale models are used and the big tunnels are replaced by small-diameter tubes in which even ultrasonic speeds can be obtained.

A very remarkable use for compressed air is in fast military aircraft. Compressed air is let inside the pilot's clothing from a tank via a most ingenious valve the moment he changes flight direction rapidly. The air applies pressure to the body, preventing blood from flowing from the brain. The pilot reacts normally and does not lose consciousness.

Compressed air can be used for agitating liquids. In water purification plants the oxygen from finely dispersed air is able to dissolve quickly. The required fine dispersion is obtained by fixing a porous fabric bag over the end of the feed pipe. In a similar way compressed air is used in flotation processes (see vol. III) for causing fine air bubbles to rise to the surface.

Bubble breakwaters are sometimes used in harbours (e.g. at Dover). By means of perforated tubes at the harbour entrance vast numbers of air bubbles are periodically discharged into the water. These greatly reduce the height of the waves. This is also of great value for building harbours and the like in rough water.

In Lake Malaren in Sweden air is blown into a system of perforated tubes of $4\frac{1}{2}$ miles total length, thus producing air bubbles which bring the warmer water to the surface to prevent the formation of ice. Before this system was working, the ice was often 20 inches thick. In Lake St Peter, below Montreal, two systems of 16 miles long will be constructed.

In other places warmer water will be brought to the surface by means of propellers.

Another application of this principle was demonstrated near a dam. There was a danger that an explosion caused for breaking rocks under the water would damage the dam because of the sudden blast. When a large quantity of air was discharged into the water in front of the dam the underwater blast was reduced and damage was prevented.

3.6 LITERATURE

W. L. FAITH. *Air pollution control*. New York, John Wiley, 1959.

N. C. HARRIS. *Modern air conditioning practice*. New York, McGraw-Hill, 1959.

P. L. MAGILL, F. R. HOLDEN and C. A. ACKLEY. *Air pollution handbook*. New York, McGraw-Hill, 1956.

J. H. PERRY. *Chemical engineers handbook*. Section 12. New York, McGraw-Hill, 1953.

W. H. SEVERNS and J. R. FELLOW. *Air conditioning and refrigeration*. New York, John Wiley, 1958.

P. A. WHITE and S. E. SMITH, ed. *High efficiency air filtration*. London, Butterworth, 1964.

CHAPTER 4

Water

4.1 WATER IN GENERAL

4.1.1 The occurrence of water

Water is by far the most important liquid found on earth and is the substance most familiar to man. The amount of water present on the earth is so great that a layer of thickness about 2 500 m would be formed if it were uniformly distributed over the earth's surface. About five-sevenths of the earth's surface is covered with water. An average of less than 1% of the land is covered with water in various forms, such as rivers, lakes, etc. The remainder of the water occurs in the seas and oceans, which are the source of practically all the water found on the land. Large quantities of water evaporate, particularly in warmer regions, from the seas and oceans, and the water vapour in the atmosphere is carried by the wind and forms mists and clouds, from which the water again falls on the earth in the form of rain, snow or hail. To a small extent, water vapour condenses directly on to the surface of the earth in the form of dew. A portion of the precipitation is again evaporated on the spot, either directly or through the intermediary of plants, which have taken up the water from the soil. Another portion penetrates into the ground until it meets an impervious stratum, thus giving rise to surface water which, in part, through the intermediary of channels, ditches and rivers, flows into lakes, or back into the sea.

When water flows at a high level between two impervious strata, it tends to move between these strata to some lower level, and may then come to the surface through fissures and the like (see fig. 4.1). If the pressure on the water is sufficiently great to cause it to spurt out by itself, the result is a natural well. An artesian well of this type can be produced artifically by boring through the upper impervious strata at a suitable place and installing a pipe.

Hot springs are also found in certain parts of the world which are usually volcanic regions or regions in which volcanic activity has not become completely extinct. The water is heated, in such regions, at great depths by magmatic reservoirs or remains of such reservoirs at even greater depths. Examples of hot springs include that at Karlsbad in Germany (water temperature 75° C), the hot springs of the Yellowstone area in the USA and the geysers of Iceland. In general, the water of hot springs is derived from precipitation. In certain areas, this water is of purely magmatic origin, and is then

Fig. 4.1 A schematic geological section showing an artesian well in relation to the geological strata.

derived from water of crystallization, split off from minerals and rocks by the high temperatures existing at great depths, and then forced under pressure to the surface.

Sea water is used directly by man as a raw material on a far smaller scale than either surfacewater and spring water, on the one hand, or the water of streams, rivers and lakes on the other.

4.1.2 Composition and properties of water

Water is a compound of hydrogen and oxygen in the ratio of 1:8 by weight (chemical formula H_2O). Naturally occurring hydrogen and oxygen both consist essentially of one type of atom of atomic weights 1 and 16 respectively. In addition, both of these elements in the natural state contain small quantities of other types of atom (isotopes) of greater atomic weight but practically identical chemical properties (see hydrogen and oxygen, ch. 2, and isotopes, ch. 15). As a consequence, pure natural water always consists of a mixture of several types of water.

An important constituent of 'ordinary' water, apart from H_2O molecules, is heavy water (deuterium oxide, D_2O), which is present in a proportion of about 0.02% in ordinary water. Heavy water has the same chemical properties as ordinary water but different physical properties. For example, the freezing point is 3.8° C, instead of 0° C, the boiling point 101.42° C, instead of 100° C, and the density of heavy water is greatest at 11.3° C, instead of 4.0° C (see nucleonics, ch. 15).

A remarkable property of water is its variation of density with temperature. As already mentioned, the density of water is at a maximum at 4.0° C (it is then, by definition, equal to one) and decreases at both higher and lower temperatures, because water expands when heated above, or cooled below, this temperature. It expands still further on freezing. Thus the density of ice at 0° C is 0.918, hence icebergs float in water. This physical property is of great importance in the behaviour of large bodies of water. As a result of the variation in density, during the winter, with cooling of the water, for example in a lake at the surface, the colder surface layer sinks to the bottom until the entire body of water has reached a temperature of 4.0° C. Subsequently, only the water at the surface undergoes further cooling, at least initially, since it no longer sinks to the bottom, and forms a layer of ice on the surface when it freezes. If the cold weather continues, this layer gradually becomes thicker, but the temperature of the body of the water, close to the bottom of the lake, remains at 4.0° C for long periods. This is of great importance in ensuring the survival of the aquatic flora through the winter.

The expansion which occurs when water freezes has other important consequences. Thus it is responsible for the destruction of the tissues of living organisms when these are frozen, the break-up of lumps of soil as well as for the bursting of water-pipes and the shattering of rocks. In the last case, small cracks become enlarged as the result of the freezing of water in them, and the repetition of this process leads ultimately to the shattering of the rock.

Water is seldom, if ever, found in the pure state (dew is an exception to this rule). Even rain-water is not pure, since it always contains in solution, the gases present in the air, as well as sodium chloride in small quantities, depending on its proximity to the sea. Since water in the soil continuously comes into contact with soluble compounds all such water is a solution. Apart from common salt and other chlorides, water almost invariably contains the following substances: oxygen, nitrogen, nitrogen peroxide, carbonic acid, the bicarbonates of calcium, magnesium and iron, sulphates (including gypsum, $CaSO_4$) and silicates. In addition to the dissolved substances, water also contains in suspension clay particles and other solid materials, as well as micro-organisms, such as bacteria and algae.

Water also often contains organic waste materials which are not always due to the pollution of water by industry (see Fertilizers, vol. VII).

The so-called 'natural mineral waters' (medicinal springs) contain salts which are not normally present in water, e.g. iodides, sulphides, salts of heavy metals and sodium sulphate, or unusually large quantities of salts and other substances which are normally found only in extremely small amounts.

4.1.3 Hardness of water

Hard water is water in which fairly large amounts of calcium and magnesium salts are dissolved. Such water is called 'hard' because of the feeling produced on washing the hands in it. Water containing small amounts of these salts is called 'soft' water.

Hardness is expressed in terms of 'degrees'; unfortunately, the definition of a degree of hardness varies in different countries, as follows:

One German degree corresponds to 10 mg CaO per litre of water

One French degree corresponds to 10 mg $CaCO_3$ per litre of water

One English degree corresponds to 10 mg $CaCO_3$ per 0.7 litres of water.

In the USA and certain other countries, hardness is expressed in terms of p.p.m. of calcium carbonate (i.e. milligrams of $CaCO_3$ per litre of water).

1 German degree = 1.25 English degrees = 1.79 French degrees = 17.9 p.p.m. of calcium carbonate. Magnesium salts are expressed as the equivalent amounts of calcium salts on the basis of the ratio MgO:CaO = 1:1.4. Since the calcium hardness usually exceeds the magnesium hardness, the latter is often ignored in the determination of hardness.

The expressions 'temporary' and 'permanent' hardness are also used. Water treatment experts tend no longer to use these terms and use instead the terms 'alkaline' and 'non-alkaline', or 'carbonate' and 'non-carbonate' hardness.

Temporary hardness means that caused by the bicarbonates of calcium and magnesium which, when the water is boiled, decompose to give carbon dioxide and calcium and magnesium carbonates; these form a precipitate, since they are less soluble in water than the bicarbonates $Ca(HCO_3) = CaCO_3 + H_2O + CO_2$. The carbon dioxide evolved precipitates a further portion of the remaining calcium and magnesium salts, but in general, the quantity of bicarbonate present is not sufficient for all these salts to be precipitated. Some remains in solution, therefore, and this constitutes the permanent hardness.

Some typical examples of the hardness of various kinds of water are given in the following table:

	Total hardness (p.p.m. CaCO3)	Temporary hardness (p.p.m. CaCO3)	Permanent hardness (p.p.m. CaCO3)	Total salt content (mg/litre)
Hard surface water	400	310	90	425
Soft surface water	10	4	6	20
Hard well water	900	270	630	1180
Rain water	140-180	100-140	40	300

The hardness of water is one of the causes of the formation of scale in boilers (see boiler water, p. 149). Hard water is also objectionable in laundering, since it causes the decomposition of part of the soap used. Soap consists of the potassium and sodium salts of fatty acids; these salts form insoluble calcium and magnesium precipitates with calcium and magnesium salts. Not only do these compounds have no detergent effect, but they are also readily precipitated, during laundering, on to the fibres, which become grey and less flexible as a result (see also textiles, vol. VI and soap, vol. V). Water must therefore be softened before it is used for washing and rinsing, the cost of the softening being more than compensated for by the saving in soap. It is estimated that 1.5 kg of soap with a fat content of 60% are wasted per m^3 of water with a hardness of 180 p.p.m. CaCO3, which is a fairly low value for tap water.

Hard water is also less suitable than soft for a number of other applications, e.g. it is avoided, as far as possible, in factories producing food preserves since some of these are cooked more slowly when they are boiled in it.

Soft water is required also in the textile and paper-making industries and for the production of mineral waters. A softened water is less palatable than the original water because of removal of dissolved carbon dioxide and the substitution of dissolved sodium salts for calcium salts in the water. The presence of hardening salts does not affect the wholesomeness of the water; softening is not required to render the water safe to drink.

4.2   CATCHMENT OF WATER

The catchment of water is effected in various ways depending on the form in which it is present. Surface water derived from precipitation is an important source of water. The simplest method for the catchment of surface water is the boring of wells in which the water level is the same as that of the surface water, and from which the water is then simply drawn up. On a larger scale, pipes may be inserted into the ground to a considerable depth, and the water pumped up. The hand pumps formerly widely used for domestic purposes provide a simple example of this form of water catchment. With artesian wells, the use of pumps is not always necessary.

Reserves of surface water are very considerable although serious difficulties and water shortages nevertheless occur in certain localities. The average daily rainfall in the United Kingdom amounts to 80000 million gallons. Per head of population, this amounts to 1500 gallons per day, while actual requirements are only 30-40 gallons. The greater part of the rain water flows into the sea, and only a small proportion is retained in the earth as surface water.

After allowing for losses by evaporation, transpiration from plants, etc., the aggregate rainfall is much greater than is likely ever to be required by the community.

The extent of the reserves of surface water depends mainly on the character of the rock, and in particular, its porosity. Thus, a very large layer of impervious clay, which has the form of a bowl, is present at a great depth beneath the city of London, and this bowl is filled, to a large extent, with a porous layer of chalk 600 ft thick. The rain which falls on the surface of the ground in the London area collects within this porous layer. At the present time, the water must be pumped to the surface from a depth of about 200 ft, since the quantity required (nearly 500 million gallons per day in 1962, 1 gallon = 4.546 litres) is greater than that which falls on the area as rain. As a result of this continued withdrawal of water, salt water from the sea has penetrated nearly to the centre of the basin. In order to prevent any further penetration by salt water, large quantities of impure water are withdrawn from the Thames in winter and pumped into the chalk, where it is purified, and later pumped up again, in a purer condition, at other points in the layer.

A similar situation exists in some places in America. Attempts are being made to prevent the penetration of salt water by withdrawing water, sometimes over long distances by means of pipelines, from large rivers, and then spraying it over large areas of land; it then penetrates into the ground to a great depth and is completely purified at the same time.

The problems of the salting of the soil and the desalting of brackish water and sea water are also of great importance to agriculture. A special committee has been set up by the Organisation of European Economic Cooperation to study them. It is possible that in the Netherlands the problem of salting up could be solved, at least in part, by sealing off the mouths of the large rivers in the country, so as to form fresh-water lakes.

In many towns, either water is withdrawn from a nearby river or river water is used to supplement surface water. Care is then taken to ensure that the place from which the water is withdrawn is located upstream of the outlets of all sewers and factory drains. The water is almost invariably polluted, so that thorough treatment is necessary, together with chlorination (see p. 145). This treatment may result in a deterioration in the taste.

Another catchment procedure is to lay stoneware pipes in deep ditches at a distance of about 100 m from, and parallel to, a river; this method is adopted where the river bed consists of gravel or other highly porous rock. The river water then penetrates into the pipes, but all impurities in suspension are left behind, as shown diagrammatically in fig. 4.2. The pipes are connected to the suction pipe of a pumping station.

Sometimes the method of Ranney is used. In this method, a deep concrete-lined borehole of large diameter is sunk close to a river. Perforated pipes are then forced, by means of hydraulic presses, through special, closely fitting openings, in a horizontal direction under the river bed, sometimes for a distance of as much as 80 m. The sand surrounding these pipes is then displaced by means of compressed air or water under high pressure, so that they are embedded in a highly permeable material. The river water then penetrates into the pipes, from which it is pumped away. The water thus obtained does not need to be filtered, since all suspended matter has already been removed.

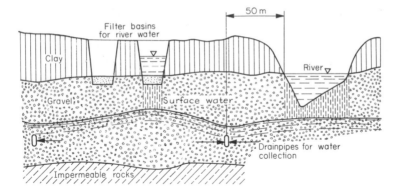

Fig. 4.2   Recovery of water from porous strata near a river.

Impure water is sometimes pumped directly out of rivers by large factories. Such water is first passed through screens consisting of steel grills and stainless steel gauze, which remove all fairly large impurities (pieces of wood, paper, food remains etc.). Horizontal rotary cylindrical filters are also used for this purpose, the part above the water level being sprayed with water in order to prevent blockage. The water, after filtration in this way, is pumped to a treatment plant for chemical treatment (see clarification of water, etc., p. 125).

In the coastal areas of the Netherlands, a number of large water supply undertakings obtain water from the sand dunes which are found in the areas. In the course of time a large amount of rain water has fallen on the dunes, so that, in spite of the losses due to run-off, they still contain large quantities of fresh water. A comparatively thin layer of clay is present under the dunes, and in the course of the centuries, the fresh water has percolated through this layer, so that fresh water is present underneath it, in the sand. This fresh water has largely displaced the salt water originating from the sea. Stoneware drain pipes are laid in the dunes, and discharge into a channel which carries the water away. In order to tap the water present underneath the layer of clay, long iron pipes, fitted at the lower end with a copper filter, are forced to considerable depths through the clay, so that the deep dune water is also made available.

An unusual method of collecting rain water is used in Gibraltar. The population makes use of rain water tanks, but the amount of water collected in such tanks is quite often inadequate. To meet the needs of the garrison, galvanised iron sheets, supported on posts, and having a total surface area of about 15 hectares, have been installed on the eastern face of the rock. The rain which falls on these sheets flows down into a channel running along the bottom of them. From here, the water is piped through a tunnel to the treatment plant and storage reservoir, which has been cut out of the rock. The reservoir, of volume 37 000 m^3, is large enough to provide an adequate supply of water for the garrison and its attached personnel, even in dry years.

Water supply has always provided a problem in fortresses. Even in antiquity, the city of Jerusalem possessed underground reservoirs large enough to provide a reliable supply of water for a number of years. This was one of the factors which contributed to the military strength of the city.

Water is often supplied to large towns from the artificial lakes formed by the construction of dams (see Energy, vol. II). In some places, demand has increased to such an extent that special measures have had to be taken to ensure the supply of adequate amounts of water to these lakes.

Another method of increasing the supply of water, which has been tried out in Japan, for example, is to spread enormous quantities of carbon black over the surface of snow fields in the mountains. Since the black surface thus produced readily absorbs the solar radiation, the snow melts more quickly. In this way, the rate of supply of water to the reservoirs can be made more regular, and flooding is avoided. In the USA, use has often been made of the services of volunteers in determining the surface area and depth of the snow, and it has then been possible to estimate, in advance, the amount of water which will be obtained from it. This has made it possible to advise farmers as to the crops they should plant, on the basis of the varying water requirements of such crops and the amounts of water likely to be available for irrigation.

In mountainous areas, relatively pure water is obtained from glaciers and mountain streams.

In tropical and sub-tropical countries (e.g. Australia, Israel) attempts are being made to reduce the amounts of water lost by surface evaporation. Use is made, for this purpose, of small amounts of cetyl alcohol (see vol. V). This compound is used because (a) it spreads over the surface of the water in the form of a compact monomolecular layer with strong cohesive forces between the paraffin chains of the cetyl alcohol molecules; and (b) its spreading rate and resealing ability when disturbed by wind, waves, fish etc. are good. Evaporation may be reduced by as much as 50% and at the same time mosquito larvae are destroyed.

In most industrial areas, the amounts of water required are very large since, in addition to water for domestic purposes, large quantities are used by the foodstuffs and consumer goods industries, the chemical industry, the dairy industry, public baths and swimming baths; for this reason, in such areas, the re-use of water is essential (see industrial wastes and effluents, p. 178; see also cooling water, p. 153).

4.3 CLARIFICATION OF WATER

Water is usually contaminated with solid impurities. The amount of such impurities can be greatly reduced by catchment of the water at suitable places e.g. by pumping up surface water from underneath a layer of sand or gravel which acts as a filter for the water percolating downwards. (See also the various methods of water catchment described above.) Large heavy solid particles in water can be removed simply by allowing the water to remain in large tanks until the particles have settled out.

With certain types of water, air may be passed through, as in the biological treatment of sewage (see p. 172). Another method, used mainly in the treatment of drinking water and water for domestic use, is slow filtration. In this process, the technique used is similar in character to the natural filtration of surface water by the soil; it is generally used without prior sedimentation. Slow filtration is usually carried out in three stages, with progressively decreasing filtration rates. The filters consist of large vessels with a total surface area of about 40 000 m² or more. Layers of gravel, the particle size of which decreases from the bottom upwards so that the uppermost layer may consist of a layer of sand 1 m thick, rest on a porous plate at the bottom; this is sometimes made of aloxite. While the first-stage filters may have a throughput of about 3 m³ of water per hour, that of the last-stage filters does not exceed 3 dm³ per hour.

The filtration process is essentially biological in character. Large numbers of bacteria are present in the sand layer; these are perfectly adapted to life in water, and extract the undesirable substances from it for use as nutrients. Algae and diatoms are also present in slow filters. Since the process is, in part, a biological one, dissolved organic material is also removed from the water. For the process to be effective, an adequate amount of oxygen must be present in the untreated water; if it is not present, the water must first be passed through large spray ponds to enable it to pick up the necessary oxygen from the air. At the same time, some of the free carbon dioxide, which is corrosive, is removed from the water, and any divalent iron present is oxidized, which is important from the point of view of iron removal.

When the biological mat of a filter becomes too thick, the filtration rate decreases so markedly that some form of cleaning becomes necessary. With first-stage filters, this is effected by means of backwashing; with a last-stage filter, however, a layer of sand of about 2 cm in thickness must be removed. If the layer is then too thin, fresh sand must be added. After biological examination, the cleaned filter can be used again. Filters are also sometimes cleaned with a 1% solution of sulphur dioxide.

In the USA and the UK use is made in the filtration of water of high grade anthracite, which has sharp angular grains, instead of sand the grains of which are usually rounded. The use of anthracite increases both the filtration rate and the length of time before backwashing becomes necessary. Specially tough grades of anthracite, which are resistant to attrition, are used, so that less damage is caused when the grains are rubbed against one another during backwashing. After filtration, the water is pumped into reservoirs, and thence to water towers or to the place of use.

Another process used is rapid filtration, in which sand and gravel are again used as the filter medium. The filters are smaller in size than those for slow filtration, and the flow rate is in the range 5-25 m³/hr. These filters retain only the larger solid particles, and they are therefore generally used only after the preliminary addition of chemical coagulants, to precipitate both colloidal and dissolved substances, followed by settling in tanks. They are otherwise suitable only for the treatment of water for industrial purposes, such as cooling water, or for agricultural use (irrigation).

Colloidal particles which do not settle out, or which pass through the filters, as well as certain dissolved substances, are precipitated by the addition of small amounts of aluminium salts, ferric salts or sodium silicate to which a little acid has been added.

As the result of hydrolysis, a flocculent precipitate of metal hydroxide is formed. This retains both colloids and organic substances which become mechanically trapped or are absorbed. A large number of salts can be added to the water for this purpose, including a mixture of aluminium sulphate and sodium aluminate, sodium silicate, magnesium sulphate, lime or caustic soda. The aim of the procedure is to control the pH value of the water since the properties of the floc (settling velocity and ease of filtration) depend on its acidity. For the precipitation of aluminium hydroxide (formed from aluminium sulphate), the optimum pH value of the water is in the range 5.5-7. For ferric hydroxide (formed from ferric chloride), the optimum values are between 5.5 and 6, and 8 and 9. Too high a pH value can be reduced by passing sulphur dioxide into the water. The taste of chlorinated water can also be removed in this way.

The flocculent precipitate can be removed by settling or filtration. To obtain

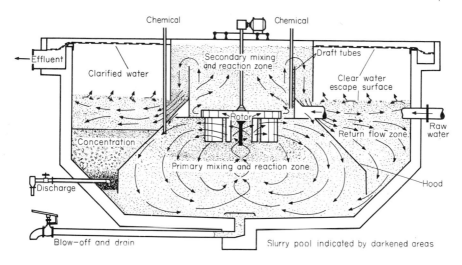

Fig. 4.3 Diagram of an 'accelerator' for the clarification of water.

thorough mixing of the coagulant with the water, and also to achieve rapid settling of the precipitate formed, special settling tanks are used. An example of such a settler is the 'Accelerator' shown in figs 4.3 and 4.4, from which the method of operation can be seen. (See also effluent treatment, p. 167.)

Calcium, magnesium and iron compounds can be precipitated with suitable chemicals at the same time as clarification is carried out. The chemicals can be selected so that the calcium salts etc. are precipitated together with the colloids (see softening and iron removal, below).

4.4 CHEMICAL SOFTENING AND IRON REMOVAL

4.4.1 Softening and iron removal by precipitation process

a. The lime or lime-soda process. If water contains bicarbonates, the addition of alkalis converts them into carbonates, which then precipitate the calcium ions in the form of calcium carbonate:

$$HCO_3^- + OH^- \rightarrow CO_3^{--} + H_2O$$
$$Ca^{++} + CO_3^{--} \rightarrow CaCO_3$$

The alkali used is generally slaked lime ($Ca(OH)_2$) so that the following reaction takes place:

$$Ca(HCO_3)_2 + Ca(OH)_2 \rightarrow 2\,CaCO_3 + 2\,H_2O$$

If more calcium ions than bicarbonate ions are present, additional CO_3^- ions must be added in order to remove the excess of calcium ions as follows:

$$Na_2CO_3 + CaCl_2 \rightarrow 2\,NaCl + CaCO_3$$

Fig. 4.4 Picture of the 'accelerator' clarifier shown in fig. 4.3.

or by the reaction:

$$Na_2CO_3 + CaSO_4 \rightarrow Na_2SO_4 + CaCO_3$$

Whether lime alone, or lime and soda, must be used in the softening process depends, therefore, on the composition of the water.

The lime or lime-soda process can be carried out either at room temperature or at some higher temperature. Hot lime softening has the advantage that silica is removed at the same time, while at lower temperatures, the formation of the precipitate is hindered by the colloids present to such an extent that the addition of aluminium salts as coagulants is necessary. Hot lime-soda softening gives, in addition, a lower residual hardness, without using excess of softening chemicals, while the water is also degassed to a large extent at the same time.

Magnesium ions in the water are precipitated as magnesium hydroxide by the action of the slaked lime:

$$Mg^{++} + 2\ OH^{--} = 2\ Mg(OH)_2$$

As the OH^- ions originate in the lime so added, this reaction means that an equivalent amount of Ca^{++} ions is formed in the solution. Although slight excess of lime may be used the precipitation of Ca^{++} and Mg^{++} ions is incomplete because both calcium carbonate and magnesium hydroxide are slightly soluble.

Water softened by the lime-soda process is sometimes further softened with sodium phosphates. These precipitate the dissolved calcium and magnesium salts as tricalcium phosphate $Ca_3(PO_4)_2$ or as hydroxy apatite $3Ca_3(PO_4)_2 . Ca(OH)_2$, depending on the alkalinity of the water and the phosphate used (mono-, di- or trisodium phosphate). These phosphates may also be used for the softening of water which has not previously been softened by the lime-soda process.

For waters containing relatively large amounts of magnesium, it may be useful to add, in addition to lime and soda, a calculated amount of sodium silicate, since magnesium is very effectively removed by silicates in the course of hot lime-soda softening. Sodium silicate also helps to precipitate colloidal silica (silicic acid).

Hot lime-soda softening may be performed continuously by spraying raw water, the required chemicals and exhaust steam in a reaction compartment of a vessel. The treated water flows in a second compartment of the same vessel in which the precipitates are allowed to settle.

The various precipitates formed may also be removed from the water by filtration (see ch. I) or together with other solid impurities in the clarification processes discussed in the preceding section.

In discontinuous lime-soda softening processes, use is made of two or more tanks, one supplying soft water which has been previously treated, while the others are being filled and treated with the softening chemicals. In the latter tanks the water is agitated to ensure thorough mixing and then the mixture is allowed to stand quietly to permit settling of the precipitated solids.

b. Removal of iron. In general, iron in solution in water is also removed in the course of precipitation softening. It is often necessary, however, to remove iron without softening the water at the same time, e.g. a high iron content in drinking water gives rise to an unpleasant taste. In other cases, as in paper and textile factories, the removal of iron from water is necessary in order to prevent the formation of spots of rust, while the removal of calcium and magnesium salts is not always required.

In such cases, iron present, for example, in the water from deep wells in the form of ferrous bicarbonate, $Fe(HCO_3)_2$, is oxidised and precipitated as ferric bicarbonate by introducing into the water oxygen from the air, after the water has first been neutralized, if necessary, with lime.

In the so-called 'open system' water is sprayed into large basins so as to facilitate absorption of oxygen from the air, when the following reaction takes place:

$$4 \text{ Fe(HCO}_3)_2 + 2\text{H}_2\text{O} + \text{O}_2 \rightarrow 4\text{Fe(OH)}_3 + 8\text{CO}_2$$

Ferric hydroxide is only slightly soluble in water which is neutral, and does not form soluble carbonates with carbon dioxide, since it is a much weaker base than ferrous hydroxide Fe(OH)_2. The water is then filtered through a layer of gravel or coke. The filters are back-washed at suitable intervals to remove the sludge, which also contains precipitated manganese dioxide.

A 'closed system' is often used in which water and compressed air are introduced into a vessel filled with gravel or hard porous slag, in order to increase the area of the air-water interface. The water is then filtered in order to remove the ferric hydroxide formed. Modern installations for iron removal often consist of a set of several oxidation compartments and filters in a single vessel, so that the filters, in which, for example, quartz may be used, are easily removed for cleaning with high-pressure water jets.

4.4.2 Softening and iron removal by complex formation

a. General. Complex ions are stable ions formed from several ions, or from ions and molecules, a process in which the properties of the constituents of the complex are wholly or partly lost. Neutral compounds formed from one or more complex ions are called complex compounds.

Complex ions may be formed by positive ions with polar or polarisable ions or molecules. A positive ion can often attract an electron pair from one of the atoms of a polar particle, and this electron pair then moves in an orbit around both the positive ion and the atom concerned. A so-called coordination compound is then formed. These coordination compounds can be very stable when the dipole moment of the polar particle is increased by the effect of the charge on the positive ion (The polar particle is then also polarisable.)

Complex ions are formed mainly from metal ions with polar ions or molecules. Divalent and tetravalent metal ions are capable, in general, of forming coordination compounds with 4 and 6 ions or molecules respectively; with trivalent metal ions, the number is usually 4 or 6, and with monovalent ions, 2. The alkali metals do not form any complex ions. Simple examples of complex ions are ferricyanide ions, $(\text{Fe(CN)}_6)^{++}$ formed from ferric ions and cyanide ions (see p. 355) and the complex ions formed from silver ions and ammonia, $\text{Ag(NH}_3)_2$.

Metal ions also form complexes with polyphosphate ions. All polyphosphates of multivalent metal ions are insoluble. They may be kept in solution, however, by an excess of sodium polyphosphate, since the metal ions form coordination compounds with the phosphorus atoms of this excess of phosphate. The most important poly-phosphates are sodium tripolyphosphate (crystalline) and the polyphosphates of higher molecular weight (glassy), such as calgon (see p. 376). Polyphosphates prevent precipitation in water also in another way, as shown by the following phenomenon. If a polyphosphate is added to an already formed precipitate of calcium salts, the amount which goes into solution is smaller than the amount of calcium salts kept in solution if the polyphosphate is added before the precipitate is formed. This is known as the 'threshold effect'. It can be explained on the assumption that the formation of a precipi-tate, e.g. of calcium carbonate, is prevented, not only by complex formation, but also by the adsorption of polyphosphate on to the crystal nuclei (crystallites) of calcium carbonate, so that further crystal growth is prevented.

Cyclic compounds can also be formed, with suitable polar substances, in the course of complex formation. Ring formation appears, in general, to stabilise complexes (chelate effect). Complexes of this type are often called chelate compounds (from the Greek chele, meaning claw). Well-known examples of chelate compounds are the intensely blue complexes of divalent copper ions with polyhydroxy compounds, such as tartaric acid (see Fehling's solution, p. 570). The acid probably combines with the copper as follows:

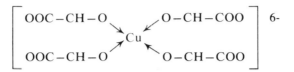

Coordinate bonds are usually shown by means of a broken line or an arrow, and the complex ion is indicated by means of square brackets.

A special type of cyclic complex is produced when a metal ion is incorporated in the ring by means of an ionic link on one side and a coordinate bond on the other. Such complexes are called internal complexes or internal chelate compounds. Various amino-acids are capable of forming such chelate compounds, and of these the most important are the sodium salts of ethylenediamine tetra-acetic acid (EDTA) (see organic acids, vol.   ). The salts of ethylenediamine tetra-acetic acid form chelate compounds with most metal ions. The reaction with calcium ions may be represented as follows:

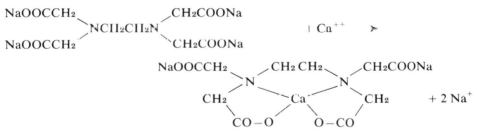

The complex formed by ethylenediamine tetra-acetic acid with ferric ions is shown in fig. 4.5. It is clear that any further reactions of the metal ion are impossible, not only as a result of complex formation, but also because the metal ion is surrounded by the substance which has formed the chelate compound. (Compare the formation of inclusions in which atoms or molecules are surrounded by other molecules without any compound being formed. Examples are the formation of clathrates by inert gases, p. 86 and the formation of adducts by crystals of urea and thiourea, p. 348). Although the use of complex formation is not restricted to water softening, it has been discussed in detail here because most of the important complexing agents are used to prevent the precipitation of hardness ions in water.

b. *Treatment of water with complexing agents (sequestration)*. The formation of soluble complexes of metal ions in the presence of chemical reagents which, in the absence of a complexing agent, would cause precipitation, is called sequestration. This is used, in the case of water, mainly for the removal of iron, calcium and magnesium

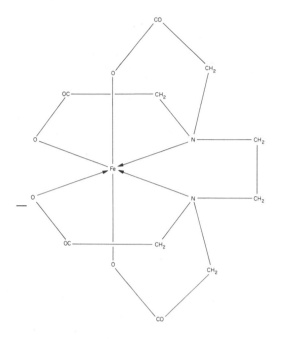

Fig. 4.5 Formula of the complex formed from ethylene diamine tetra-acetic acid and ferric ions.

ions. As is evident from the definition, soluble complexes are formed in sequestration. For this reason, complexing agents must, in general be soluble in water for use in it. (Oil-soluble complexing agents for combining with traces of metal ions in oils and petrol are also known and include compounds of aldehydes with amines. They prevent the oxidation of oil and petrol, which is catalysed by metal ions.)

For sequestration in water, the following complexing agents are the most important:

1. Sodium salts of ethylenediamine tetra-acetic acid. These compounds are known as Trilon B, Complexon III, Sequestrene and Versene.
   (The free acid is only slightly soluble in water and is therefore not used as such in this medium; it is also known as Complexon II).

2. Sodium salts of nitrilotriacetic acid, $N(CH_2COONa)_3$ (known as Trilon A, Complexon I and Versenol).

3. N-hydroxyethyl ethylenediamine triacetic acid (HEDTA or EDTA-OH), and its sodium salts.

4. Hydroxycarboxylic acids (and their sodium salts), such as gluconic acid, tartaric acid and citric acid. (See carboxylic acids, vol. IV).

5. Polyphosphates, such as tetrasodium pyrophosphate, sodium tripolyphosphate and polyphosphates of higher molecular weight, of formula:

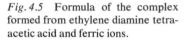

The most stable complexes are those formed by EDTA and the polyphosphates, and these are therefore most often used. The complexing ability of certain complexing agents, as a function of the acidity, is shown in fig. 4.6.

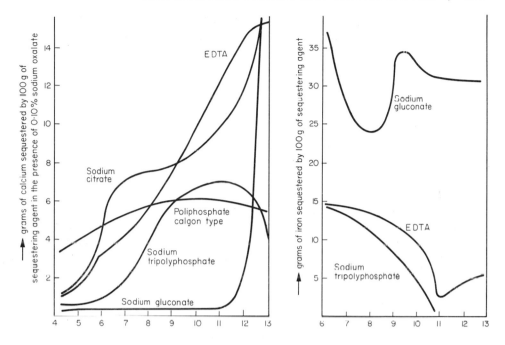

Fig. 4.6 Sequestration of calcium ions and ferric ions by various sequestering agents (sodium citrate can be used for sequestering calcium ions in sodium hydroxide solutions up to 10% strength, and sodium gluconate up to 15% strength).

A very important use of complexing agents is in the softening of water in laundries, in order to prevent the precipitation of calcium soaps (see p. 122). For the same reason, complexing agents are usually added to soap powders and other detergents and cleaners for domestic use. In liquid, strongly alkaline cleaners (corresponding to caustic soda solutions of strength greater than 1%), polyphosphates are less effective, since they undergo hydrolysis (see fig. 4.6 for pH values greater than 12). For this reason, EDTA is used in such cleaners. In other cases sodium tripolyphosphate and calgon are used, since they are much cheaper. Apart from their softening action, both the poly-phosphates and EDTA have other effects when used in detergents: polyphosphates increase the surface activity, while EDTA increases the stability of foam. For this reason, EDTA is often added to synthetic detergents, although they do not, in general, form precipitates with calcium and magnesium ions. Complexing agents are also important in laundering for the removal of ferric ions from water; such ions, particularly in an alkaline medium, can cause the formation of rust spots in and on various products, such as textiles. Apart from EDTA and polyphosphates, sodium gluconate can also be used for this purpose, since this compound forms highly stable complexes with ferric ions.

Removal of ions by complexing agents is also of great importance in textile dyeing since the dyes used may form undesirable precipitates or complexes with these ions, or adherence to the textile may be completely or partially lost.

In tanneries, complexing agents are added to the water to combine with ions which are liable to cause spots. In the paper industry, EDTA and EDTA-OH are added to the water or pulp, since ferric ions and copper ions, if these are present, can affect the colour of the paper. In the same way the colour of dyes and pigments intended for use in the paper industry can be improved. In the photographic industry and in film processing laboratories, complexing agents are added to water to prevent the formation of objectionable precipitates in the light-sensitive material.

4.5 SOFTENING AND PURIFICATION OF WATER WITH ION EXCHANGERS

4.5.1 Definition and history

Although ion exchange reactions can occur in a number of ways (for instance the distribution of ions between immiscible solutions in liquid-liquid extraction) the term ion exchange is usually used to mean the exchange of ions that occurs on contacting an insoluble ionic solid with an electrolyte solution. Since water purification is by far the major application of ion exchange reactions at the surface of insoluble ionic solids this type of ion-exchange reaction is discussed in this section.

For many centuries it has been known that sea water loses a part of its salt when it passes through and over a layer of any sand or rock. However, modern ion exchange technology is based on the work of the two English agricultural chemists, Thompson and Way, who recognized and studied the phenomenon of ion exchange in soils in 1848-54. Their experiments showed that a layer of soil, which contains sodium, can adsorb a certain quantity of calcium and magnesium from an aqueous solution which percolates through the soil, and that the soil releases at the same time a definite quantity of its sodium content into the solution. This ion exchange is important in soil treatment for agriculture since sodium-rich soils are dense and magnesium-rich or calcium-rich have a granular structure. In the latter crops grow better, since the roots obtain more water and air. In 1876 Lemberg discovered that the mineral leucite ($K_2O.Al_2O_3.4SiO_2$) can be converted into the mineral analcite ($Na_2O.Al_2O_3.4SiO_2$) by leaching the former with a solution of sodium chloride. He also discovered that the reaction can be reversed by leaching the analcite with a potassium chloride solution. Thus he showed the reversibility of ion exchange.

At the beginning of the twentieth century ion exchange was applied on an industrial basis for the first time for water softening. Natural clays and synthetic silicates were used for exchanging calcium and magnesium ions with sodium ions. After 1935 other synthetic ion exchange materials were discovered for various other applications and ion exchangers have since made considerable progress.

4.5.2 Mechanism of ion exchange

a. The mechanism of ion exchange may be explained as follows. All ionic solids may be considered as being composed of positively and negatively charged ions. For example, in a crystal each ion is surrounded by a number of ions of opposite charge and is therefore subject to strong attractive forces. However, an ion at the surface is subject to less attractive forces than a similar ion within the crystal owing to the fact that it is not completely surrounded by ions of opposite charge. If placed in a polar medium such as water, the attractive forces of the polar molecules diminish the net attractive binding of the surface ions to the crystal surface and an exchange of these ions for other ions of like charge is possible. In general the exchange of ions in ionic solids is common, but in many cases the structure of the ionic substance is so dense that ions cannot penetrate beneath the surface, hence the ion exchange is limited to the surface of the solid mass; this results in a very small exchange capacity. For this reason the ionic solid must have a microporous structure which allows ions to penetrate into the solid. It is clear that ion exchangers can be selective in this way since the exchange of certain ions may be limited owing to the fact that they cannot penetrate into the pores. The selectivity of ion exchange can also be caused by differences in attractive forces of different ions to the surface of the ionic solid.

b. Another theory for the mechanism of ion exchange is based on the double layer theory of colloids. Colloid particles do not precipitate, since agglomeration of the colloid particles to larger particles is prevented. In various colloids, agglomeration is prevented by two layers of electric charges. Each particle has a charged surface and from a liquid it attracts ions of opposite charge. Thus it is surrounded by a diffuse and mobile outer layer of charges. Such a double layer also occurs at the surface of granules of insoluble ionic substances in ionic liquids and the outer layer of adsorbed ions can be replaced by other ions. The ion exchange capacity increases with the porosity of the granules since the double layer extends in the pores.

c. The mechanism of ion exchange can also be explained by the phenomenon of osmosis. In this theory the interface between the solid ionic substance and the electrolyte solution is compared with the diffusion of ions through a membrane between different electrolyte solutions.

It is believed that in fact ion exchange is the result of all three mechanisms described. One or more of the reaction mechanisms can predominate depending on the kind of ion exchanger. The mechanism of ion exchange in non-crystalline ion exchange resins is analogous to the ion exchange of crystals (see also fig. 4.8 and p. 137).

The ion exchangers can be subdivided in two groups: cation exchangers and anion exchangers.

Cation exchangers contain exchangeable cations attached to a solid insoluble microporous structure which is negatively charged. The microporous structure behaves like a plurality of anions which are bonded together

Similarly anion exchangers contain exchangeable anions attached to a solid insoluble microporous structure which is positively charged. The microporous structure behaves like a plurality of cations which are bonded together.

4.5.3 Cation exchangers

The inorganic ion exchangers are usually cation exchangers. The commonest inorganic cation exchangers are natural and synthetic aluminosilicates such as glauconite (greensand, a potassium-iron aluminosilicate) and the zeolites (alkali aluminosilicates and alkali-calcium aluminosilicates). Synthetic resins may be cation or anion exchangers depending on their functional groups.

Gels of hydrated zirconium oxide, which are treated with phosphoric, tungstic or arsenic acid, contain both hydroxyl and, e.g. phosphoric acid groups. Thus depending

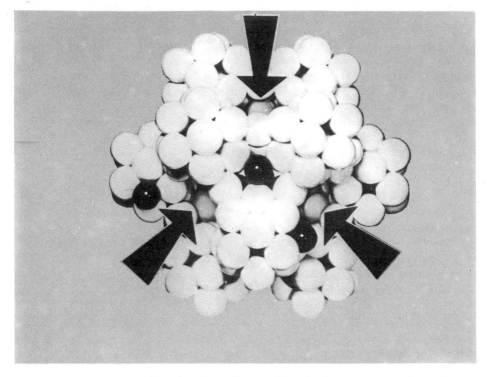

Fig. 4.7 A model of a small section of a zeolite crystal. Each sphere represents a tetrahedron of oxygen atoms with an aluminium or silicon atom. The tetrahedra enclose many tiny pores (see arrows) each measuring one sixteen-billionth of an inch in diameter.

on the pH of the leaching liquid, they can function as cation or anion exchangers. Synthetic resins with similar properties can also be prepared.

    a. Zeolites. If a zeolite is strongly heated the adsorbed water escapes, just as if the stone is boiling. Hence the name zeolite which is formed from Greek words meaning 'boiling stone'. Most natural zeolite crystals are found in volcanic rocks. They are rare. One of the commonest varieties is called chabazite which forms rhombohedral crystals. The structure of zeolite crystals can be represented as a plurality of tetrahedra each of which consists of four oxygen atoms surrounding a smaller silicon or aluminium atom. Each oxygen atom of a tetrahedron can combine with another silicon or aluminium atom, which, in turn forms a tetrahedron with four oxygen atoms. Thus a solid lattice is built up from a plurality of tetrahedra. In a zeolite the tetrahedra are arranged in such a way that they enclose empty spaces. The result is a solid insoluble microporous structure which is necessary for efficient ion exchange properties. See, for example, fig. 4.7. (Such a structure is not common. Felspars, for example, are built up of the same silicon-oxygen and aluminium-oxygen tetrahedra, but the tetrahedra are arranged in such a way that a uniform structure without pores results.) Since an aluminium atom in a zeolite is trivalent, it can satisfy only three negative charges of the four oxygen atoms which surround it. A neutral crystal is formed by sodium or potassium ions which make up the charge deficit of each aluminium atom. These sodium or potassium ions are loosely attached to the oxygen atoms at the corners of the tetrahedra and form the exchangeable ions.

The exchangeable ions in zeolites can be replaced by other ions by percolating a solution, containing the latter ions, through a layer of zeolite. The zeolite is regenerated by treating with a salt solution.

Zeolites can be prepared synthetically by mixing concentrated aqueous solution of sodium aluminate (obtained from bauxite and caustic soda, see p. 523) and sodium silicate to form a jelly-like mass of zeolite (compare silica gel, p. 553). After washing, the mass is dried and ground. In hot regions of the USA the gel is poured on to large concrete decks on which it dries in about 2-5 weeks. When about one-fourth of the free water has evaporated, the mass is sprayed with water to remove all soluble salts. (This cannot be done after complete drying since a zeolite dried in the presence of any soluble salt disintegrates to a fine powder.) After further drying the zeolite is collected with grabs and sieved to remove the dust, any lumps being broken up and sieved again.

b. Synthetic organic cation exchangers. The first cation exchangers of this group were produced by sulphonating porous coal and other organic substances such as lignite etc. A humus-like product is formed. If this is represented chemically by HR it can react as follows: $HR + NaCl \rightarrow NaR + HCl$. The exchanger can be regenerated with sulphuric acid, which replaces the adsorbed sodium ions again by hydrogen ions. These products are used only to a limited extent.

The most important group of organic cation exchangers comprises synthetic resins containing acid groups such as phenolic hydroxyl groups ($-OH$), carboxylic acid groups ($-COOH$), sulphonic acid groups ($-SO_3H$) and phosphoric acid groups ($-PO_3H$). Examples of such resins are sulphonated phenol-formaldehyde resins, carboxylic acid resins and phosphoric acid resins. These resins are known under trade names such as Permutite, Amberlite, Nalcite, Dowex, Duolite and Zeo-Rex.

Ion exchange resins consist of cross-linked long chain molecules which enclose a plurality of empty spaces (see fig. 4.8 for example). The result is a solid insoluble microporous structure similar to that formed by the tetrahedra in a zeolite crystal. The functional groups attached to the chains are responsible for the ion exchange capacity of the resins. If the functional groups are acid groups, they contain exchangeable hydrogen ions, hence the name *hydrogen-form cation exchangers*. These resins adsorb metal ions from a solution and release hydrogen ions into the solution. Hydrogen form exchangers can be regenerated by treatment with acids. It is also possible to replace the hydrogen ions by sodium ions (by treating with a solution of sodium chloride). The resulting exchanger is a *sodium-form cation exchanger* which can be used for exchange with other ions. It can be regenerated by treatment with a solution of sodium chloride.

4.5.4 Anion exchangers

The only inorganic anion exchanger of commercial importance is the naturally occuring 'apatite' (see calcium phosphate, p. 378). It is used to a limited extent for removing fluorine from water. The most important anion exchangers are synthetic resins which contain basic groups. Weakly alkaline anion exchangers contain groups such as amine ($-NH_2$) and imine groups ($=NH$). Strongly alkaline anion exchangers

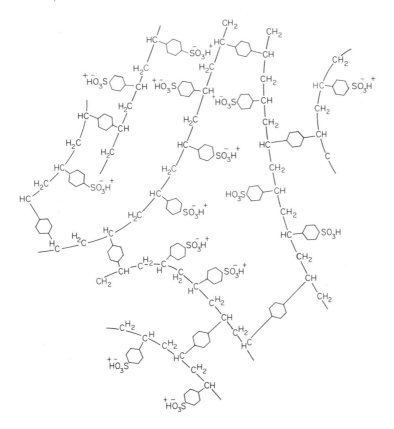

Fig. 4.8 Diagram of a cation-exchange resin. It consists of a sulphonated styrene-divinylbenzene polymer. The resin body is cross-linked and thus it is insoluble in water and porous. Sulphonic acid groups with exchangeable H^+ ions are introduced in the polymers by treating with sulphuric acid.

contain quaternary alkylammonium hydroxide groups $[-N^+ \equiv\equiv\equiv R_3] OH^-$ and

quaternary alkylalkanolammonium hydroxide groups $\left[-N^+ \begin{array}{c} \nearrow R_2 \\ \searrow ROH \end{array}\right] OH^-$.

These resins have trade names similar to those of the cation exchange resins but with different letters attached. The reaction of weakly basic exchangers is presumably different from that of the cation exchangers in that they take up entire acid molecules. If a weakly basic anion exchanger is stated as RNH_2, the reaction is $RNH_2 + HCl \rightarrow RNH_2.HCl$. The rule is that dibasic acids expel the combined monobasic acids and are in turn exchanged for tribasic acids. In the strongly basic anion exchangers the basic hydroxyl groups can be replaced by anions. It is remarkable that strongly basic anion exchangers also eliminate silica from water. After adsorption anion exchangers can be regenerated by treating them with an alkaline solution of e.g. caustic soda, ammonia and soda ash.

4.5.5 Water purification with ion exchangers

Ion exchange equipment usually consists of columns or other containers filled with a layer of ion exchanger in a granular form. The water to be purified is percolated through this layer. If the water contains colloids these must be removed beforehand (see clarification of water, p. 125), as they sometimes reduce the capacity of the ion exchanger, being often difficult to remove with the usual regenerators. There are some special cleansing solution formulae for removing colloids, but pre-clarification is usually more economical. It is also possible to eliminate colloidal substances beforehand using an ultrafiltration method with turbulent flow in tubes.

a. Water softening with cation exchangers (mono-bed installations). Water softening can be performed with sodium-form cation exchangers which react as follows:

$$\begin{array}{c} R - Na \\ | \\ R - Na \end{array} + Ca^{++} \quad \begin{array}{c} R \\ | \\ R \end{array} \!\!\!\!> Ca + 2Na^+$$

R-R represents the porous insoluble structure to which the exchangeable ions are attached. When the ion exchanger has been transformed into the 'calcium-form' it can be retransformed into the 'sodium-form' by flushing the ion exchanger bed with a sodium chloride solution.

Water softened in a sodium-form ion exchanger bed contains not only sodium ions but also the original quantity of bicarbonate and other ions. As bicarbonates decompose in boilers, where they may be a nuisance (see boiler feed water, p. 149), it is often advisable to use a 'split-stream system' for softening. A calculated fraction of the raw water is softened in a sodium-form cation exchanger and the other fraction in a hydrogen-form cation exchanger.

The following exchanges take place:

Sodium-form exchanger
$$\begin{array}{c} R - Na \\ | \\ R - Na \end{array} + Ca^{++} \rightarrow \begin{array}{c} R \\ | \\ R' \end{array} \!\!\!> Ca + 2Na^+$$

Hydrogen-form exchanger
$$\begin{array}{c} R - H \\ | \\ R - H \end{array} + Ca^{++} \rightarrow \begin{array}{c} R \\ | \\ R' \end{array} \!\!\!> Ca + 2H^+$$

If both currents are merged the H^+ ions convert the HCO_3^- ions present in the water into carbon dioxide:

$$HCO_3^- + H^+ \rightarrow H_2CO_3 \rightarrow H_2O + CO_2 \uparrow$$

When this mixture is passed through a de-aeration tower the carbon dioxide disappears.

Compared with the lime-soda softener, cation exchangers are simple to operate and give lower residual hardness, but do not eliminate silica. A very effective softening system comprises a hot lime softener followed by a sodium-form cation exchanger capable of withstanding high temperatures, e.g. Amberlite 120. With this system, the silica content can be reduced to ‹1 mg per litre, while the carbonate content is only 0.4 mg per litre. The dissolved gases are also eliminated.

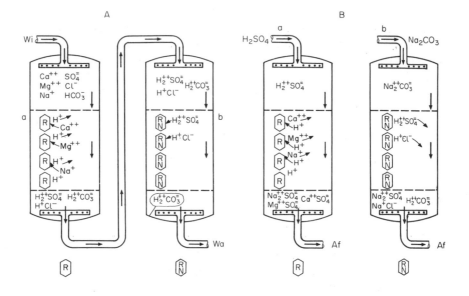

Fig. 4.9 Diagram showing the purification of water in a multi-bed ion exchange apparatus. In the purification section A, is shown which ions are carried along combined and which are allowed to pass with the water. In the regeneration section B, is shown how the cation exchanger is regenerated with sulphuric acid and the anion exchanger with a soda ash solution.

a. Cation exchange cell filled with cation exchanger represented by [R]

b. Anion exchange cell filled with anion exchanger represented by [R/N]

Wi. Inlet of raw water.
Wa. Outlet of deionized water.
Af. Outlet of spent regenerant.

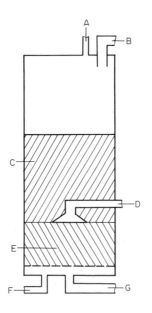

Fig. 4.10 Mixed bed ion exchanger.
A. Air outlet
B. Washing solution, washing water inlet
C. Anion exchanger
D. Sulphuric acid and washing water inlet
E. Cation exchanger
F. Air inlet
G. Outlet for purified liquid, etc.

b. Water purification with a cation and an anion exchanger (multi-bed installations). Hardness forming cations and bicarbonate ions can also be removed with a multi-bed installation regenerated with a sodium chloride solution. The following exchanges take place:

$$\text{Cation exchanger: } 2(R\text{-}Na) + Ca^{++} \rightarrow 2Na^{+} + R_2\text{-}Ca$$

$$\text{Anion exchanger: } R^1\text{-}Cl + HCO_3^{-} \rightarrow R^1\text{-}HCO_3 + Cl^{-}$$

(R^1 = the porous insoluble structure of the anion exchanger).

The reverse reaction takes place on regeneration. The effluent, i.e. the softened water, contains Na^{+} and Cl^{-} ions instead of the hardness forming cations and bicarbonate ions. The anion exchanger chosen for this system is a strongly alkaline anion exchanger. The anion exchanger also adsorbs silica but this is preferably removed by a pre-treatment since it is often difficult to remove with the aid of the sodium chloride regenerator.

All ions can be removed from water by passing the water through a hydrogen-form cation exchanger (regenerated with an acid) followed by passing through a weakly alkaline anion exchanger (regenerated with soda ash). Silica is not removed in this installation. A diagram of a multi-bed installation for the removal of all ions from water is shown in fig. 4.9.

c. Water purification with a mixed cation and anion exchanger (mixed-bed installations). Water can also be passed through a mixed-bed installation to produce pure water. In a mixed-bed, the cation and anion exchangers are mixed and put in a single shell. Once the exchanger is spent, the cation and anion exchangers are separated by back-washing (cation and anion exchangers having different specific gravities). The situation shown in fig. 4.10 then arises. The top phase is first regenerated and washed out and followed by the bottom phase. After regeneration both phases are pneumatically mixed again.

d. Other ion exchange methods for water purification. Many variations of the above-mentioned methods are of course possible. For example, part of the water can be fed through an acid-regenerated cation exchanger. This then merges with the main stream again, the carbon dioxide is vented and the water is then passed through a mixed-bed. How the process ultimately proceeds depends on what quality of water is required and on the composition of the raw water.

The equipment can also be modified. For instance, cylinders filled with ion exchanger are closed underneath with a strong elastic membrane. This membrane can be pressed up and down so that the cylinder contents pulsate so as to make the exchanger granules work more rapidly. The exchanger may also be mixed with the liquid to be purified. After a short time the purified liquid is separated from the exchanger with a cyclone and the exchanger is regenerated.

Packaged ion exchange resins are on sale in the form of briquettes for making sea water drinkable. These briquettes are contained in a plastic bag. After sea water is let in, the briquette adsorbs nearly all the salts. Drinking water can be squeezed out of the bag into the box in which the pack is contained.

The major portion of all exchangers is used for water purification, either for softening or for demineralization. The cost of demineralizing depends on the salt content. For lower salt contents, however, it is cheaper than evaporation. The purity of water can be measured by its electrical resistance. Water produced by industrial evaporators usually has a resistance of ‹100000 Ω per cm³ (approximately 5 mg per litre of carbon dioxide and salts). A multibed installation with a hydrogen-form cation exchanger and a weakly basic anion exchanger (as shown in fig. 4.9) will supply water of 100000 to 200000 Ω per cm³ and a mixed-bed installation with a hydrogen-form cation exchanger (regenerated with acid) and a strongly basic anion exchanger (regenerated with caustic soda or ammonia) can easily reach 2-5 million Ω per cm³. This is better than double-evaporated water.

The purest water is used for high pressure boilers, for photographic emulsions and for chemicals, pharmaceutical preparations and the like. In the USA, complete plants are built for water purification for high-pressure boilers. (For the use of ion exchangers in the form of membranes for water purification, see desalting water by electrodialysis, p. 162 and for purification of saline water with a silver zeolite see silver nitrate, p. 571.)

4.5.6 Additional applications of ion exchangers

Ion exchange is increasing in importance for concentrating metals in highly dilute solutions. The metals are adsorbed in ion exchangers and collected in the regenerated solution. Examples are the concentration of solutions of uranium and lanthanides obtained in the leaching of ores (see ch. 15 and p. 615) and the recovery of various valuable ions from effluents. A combination of ion exchangers and sequestering agents is used for the separation of the lanthanides. The acid effluents of viscose plants may contain 0.03% zinc, 0.06% sulphuric acid and 0.27% sodium sulphate. With certain cation exchangers, however, the zinc concentration can be cheaply increased to 6-8%. Effluents of plants making cuprammonium rayon contain extremely small quantities of copper. Some plants have over 10000 m³ of effluent a day, containing not more than 0.01% $CuSO_4$, from which a solution containing 8 to 10% copper sulphate is obtained by means of ion exchangers. This solution may be made to yield a ton of copper a day by electrolysis. Ion exchangers are also used to purify the chromate solutions used in anodizing of aluminium and chrome plating. The valuable chromates become polluted and converted into other compounds, so that a fresh bath is required. These expensive compounds are now recovered by first removing the cations with a cation exchanger and then the chromate ions with an anion exchanger. Part of an anodising bath can be drawn off in this way, the chromium compound recovered, re-prepared and added to the bath again. Other applications are the recovery of tin from tin plating baths, gold from cyanide waste, uranium from gold-winning waste. Metals can also be recovered from concentrated acid solutions. Thus metals (including iron) can be removed from 20 to 35% phosphoric acid pickling solutions.

Ion exchangers are also important in organic chemistry for eliminating salts from glycerol and sugar solutions, molasses, fruit juices, whey products, wine etc. (See under the various headings.) Antibiotics, such as penicillin, can also be purified in this way. Calcium ions in blood can be replaced by sodium ions and so prevent it from congealing for many days.

Ion exchangers can sometimes be used for purifying non-aqueous solutions.

Ammonia for instance, can be removed from acetone, vitamins from alcohol, formic acid from formaldehyde and traces of ammonia from water gas.

Special potassium- and ammonium-form ion exchangers are used in medicine. These ion exchangers can remove sodium ions from the intestinal tract. Thus the sodium content in the entire body is reduced. People with high blood pressure can thus take the normal amount of salt with their meals without increasing the blood pressure. A great drawback is the big daily dose required. These ion exchangers are also used in the treatment of oedema resulting from cardiac failure and kidney malfunctions. Weakly basic anion exchangers can be used in anti-acid stomach powders since they adsorb acids from the stomach.

Cation exchangers (such as polymers of methacrylic acid with divinyl benzene) can be mixed with cosmetic preparations to restore the pH of the skin after contact with soap or other alkaline materials.

Ion exchangers can also be used for the separation of non-ionic substances (including slightly ionizing materials such as weak acids and bases) from ionic substances (electrolytes). For example acetic acid can be separated from aqueous hydrochloric acid solutions and alcohol from aqueous solutions containing sodium chloride and alcohol. One separation method is based on the fact that non-ionic substances and slightly ionized materials are uniformly distributed on the surface of and within a resin if an aqueous solution of one of these materials is in contact with the resin. However, the concentration of a strong electrolyte is considerably smaller (perhaps even ten times smaller) in the solution within the resin particles than in the solution surrounding the resin particles. Thus a selective adsorption, of non-ionized and weakly ionized materials, takes place. This phenomenon is called *ion exclusion*. Before use the resin must be converted into the same ionic form as the ionic portion that is not adsorbed, otherwise common ion exchange would take place.

Resins containing both cation and anion exchange groups can also be used for the separation of non-ionic components from ionic components in aqueous solution. These resins adsorb both cations and anions from a solution, but the non-ionic substances are not adsorbed. This process is called *ion retardation*. The adsorbed ions are only weakly held and can easily be removed by washing with water, owing to the fact that the cation and anion exchange groups of the resins partially neutralize one another.

Another process, which can be used for the separation of strong acids from weak acids or non-ionic substances, is known as the *anion sulphate technique*. This method is based on the fact that the sulphate form of a strongly alkaline quaternary ammonium anion exchange resin possesses the acid-adsorbing properties of a weakly basic resin. It adsorbs strong acids from concentrated solutions (the exchange resin is converted into the bisulphate form if sulphuric acid is adsorbed). These acids are released again into solution when the resin is treated with water.

Ion exchangers are also used outside the ion exchange and adsorption fields. Thus a hydrogen-form cation exchange resin can be used, instead of acids, as a catalyst in epoxidation of olefins and in hydrolysis and esterification reactions. The advantage is that the acid resin can easily be separated from the reaction products.

Synthetic zeolites can be used for the separation of non-ionic substances. The diameter of the pores in zeolites is of the same order as the diameter of molecules and hence only smaller molecules can be adsorbed. Hence their name *molecular sieves*. Thus zeolites are used for the separation of various hydrocarbons (see also under adsorbents, vol. II) and for the separation of gases. For example straight-chain paraffins can be separated from branched-chain paraffins, hydrogen sulphide can be separated from natural gas and oxygen from argon (see purification of argon, p. 87).

4.5.7 Statistics

By far the major portion of ion exchange resins used in the USA consists of styrene-divinylbenzene resins which are modified with acids or basic groups. In the USA about 818000 ft³ of such resins were produced in 1961. The production of ion exchange resins other than styrene-divinylbenzene was about 20000 to 25000 ft³ in 1961.

An estimation of the consumption of styrene-divinylbenzene resins in the USA in 1961 for various uses was as follows:

		In '000 ft³
Cation exchange resins:	Industrial water treatment	175
	Household water treatment	375
	Epoxidation	8
	Pharmaceutical uses	9
	Sugar treatment	6
	Uranium extraction	5
	Other uses	27
Anion exchange resins:		55
Total		660

The resins for water treatment were sold in USA at $12 to $13 per ft³ in 1961. The prices of resins for non-water uses are usually much higher. Depending on the grade, the price ranged from $85 to $250 per ft³ in 1961.

4.6 POTABLE, INDUSTRIAL AND IRRIGATION WATER

4.6.1 Desirable purity and purification of potable water

About 60 to 70% by weight of the human body consists of water. We constantly lose water by respiration, as perspiration and in excreta. Replenishment is essential. Man can live longer without food than without water. The kidneys filter daily about 150 litres of blood in the glomeruli and extract 1-1½ litres of urine from it by counter-current extraction in the tubuli. Urine contains chiefly water and substances which, because of their relatively small molecular size pass the semi-permeable walls of the glomeruli with their ultra-filtering effect. A principal constituent is urea (see p. 344) which decomposes quickly, yielding ammonia. Hence, stale urine is alkaline and up to about two hundred years ago was the main source of alkali for many purposes (The many organic compounds in normal and abnormal urine are sometimes recovered with solvents. See Pharmaceutical products, vol. V.)

The kidneys cannot do their work if the salt content of the water consumed is too high. The total content of all salts must be below 1 g per litre. Absolutely pure water is unsuitable for drinking purposes. It has an unpleasant insipid taste. To taste fresh it must contain carbon dioxide, while a small quantity of hardness-forming ions (up to 500 p.p.m. in terms of $CaCO_3$) and of other ions is necessary if the taste is to be agreeable. It has been found that too little iodine in drinking water is harmful and can cause goitre, while too much may be injurious. Organic substances (e.g. phenol derivatives) must not be present since they give rise to colour and a bad taste. The iron and manganese contents must be low (below 0.1 mg and 0.05 mg per litre respectively), since their compounds cause an unpleasant taste. In particular, water must be free from harmful bacteria. Water from any source must be examined chemically and bacteriologically before consumption. Drinking water should be relatively soft, almost sterile, clear, uncoloured and preferably free from iron and manganese.

The major portion of all impurities can be removed from water in a natural or slow filtration process or by means of chemicals followed by rapid filtration (see catchment and clarification of water, p. 126). Iron and manganese are usually precipitated in the form of hydroxides by aeration (see p. 130) after neutralizing any acids in the water. Neutralization involves mainly reducing the carbon dioxide content, e.g. by adding lime or by filtering over pieces of marble or dolomite (the carbon dioxide content is also decreased by aeration). The neutralization of water is also necessary to reduce the corrosive action of acid water on pipes etc.

Very pure water is particularly important for soft drink manufacturers. It must be potable, odourless, tasteless and free from suspended and organic matter and colour. In the USA water for these purposes is sometimes prepared by passing the water through an electrolyser with an aluminium anode. This emits enough Al^{+++} ions to form a precipitate of aluminium hydroxide which absorbs all colloidal substances. The water then flows through a sand filter, the efficiency of which is improved by the remaining aluminium hydroxide and it retains nearly all undissolved matter. After the filter comes an ion-exchanger and then an activated carbon filter to remove all objectionable odours and tastes. This method is suitable for all large enterprises where water purity is important and flavours must be eliminated.

4.6.2 Disinfection of potable water

Water may contain numerous very harmful disease germs, making it unfit for drinking or for use in connection with food.

On a small scale disease germs may be destroyed by boiling the water for a relatively long time. However, on a large scale chlorination is the most common method for producing bacteriologically pure water. It is only comparatively recently that the mechanism of water chlorination has been properly understood. Chlorine mainly remains in a free state in water having an acidity higher than pH3. Between pH3 and pH6.5 the major portion of dissolved chlorine is converted into hypochlorous acid (HClO) which is responsible for the strong disinfecting action. At a pH value above 6.5 the hypochlorous acid concentration decreases owing to the formation of hypochlorite (ClO^-)ions, by dissociation of the hypochlorous acid. Since the disinfecting action of hypochlorite ions is lower than that of hypochlorous acid, the effect of chlorination decreases with increasing alkalinity. Hence the need for pH control of the water to be disinfected (compare hypochlorite bleaching, p. 236).

In the presence of phenols, which often occur in water containing wastes of chemical plants, any chlorine in the chlorinated water forms chlorophenols which cause an unpleasant smell and taste. The formation of chlorophenols is prevented if ammonia is also present in the water since ammonia diminishes the chlorine concentration by the formation of chloramine (NH_2Cl). The disinfecting action is not decreased in the presence of ammonia since chloramine decomposes slowly to form hypochlorous acid when the hypochlorous acid concentration of the water decreases:

$$NH_2Cl + H_2O \rightarrow NH_3 + HClO.$$

Usually the ammonia content of water is not sufficient to convert all the chlorine into chloramine. For this reason water is often disinfected by introducing both gases, ammonia and chlorine, into the water. Usually not more than 2 g of chlorine per m^3 of water is used. The residue must never exceed 3 p.p.m. to prevent an unpleasant smell and taste caused by the chlorine itself.

Owing to its strong oxidizing properties, hypochlorous acid also causes iron and manganese present to precipitate out as oxides or hydroxides.

As stated above, if water contains phenols, chlorophenols which taste and smell bad are often formed. This happens, for example, in the Rhine right down to the sea, particularly when the river is at low level, because both German and Dutch tar distilleries discharge their waste into the river. At high water levels little trouble is caused, but at low levels difficulties occur with drinking supplies, as in Rotterdam for instance. This can be prevented by eliminating phenols before chlorination. Activated carbon filters, which eliminate other unpleasant odours at the same time, are sometimes used for this purpose. In a French method the water (containing not more than 30 mg phenol per litre) is passed over trickling filters saturated for one month previously with sewer water. These filters then contain a flora which at about 25° C cleans the water down to a content of 2 mg phenol per litre.

Chlorination is also applied to industrial water supplies. Especially with the large volumes of cooling water needed for steam installations and other purposes there is a danger that slime-forming bacteria and algae will produce a thick coating on the heat exchange surfaces of the cooling equipment and so greatly reduce the heat exchange.

When sea water has to be passed (e.g., as the cooling medium) through large pipe systems, there is often a danger of mussels growing in such quantities that they reduce the inner diameter of the pipe and greatly increase the friction. Here again chlorination is the best remedy. In some cooling towers in large plants conditions for growth of microbes and algae are ideal. Chlorination is increasingly applied in such cases. Chlorination is also important in the disinfection of swimming pool water. In the summer, the swimming baths and pools need vast quantities of water which must be chlorinated. Chlorination is not sufficient for complete disinfection, because water in swimming baths is being constantly reinfected, for instance with athlete's foot fungus. It is estimated that a considerable percentage of the population of some big towns suffer from this. A contributory cause may be infection in domestic bathrooms.

In small waterworks plants, calcium hypochlorite, $Ca(ClO)_2$, is sometimes used for the disinfection of water.

In USA, France and UK water is sometimes disinfected by means of ozone. About 2 g of ozone per m^3 is necessary for water which is purified with chemicals and a rapid filtration process. Ozonisation is more expensive than chlorination, but ozone forms less compounds with obnoxious odours and tastes than chlorine in water containing organic substances (see ozone, p. 82).

Another disinfection method is irradiation with a quartz lamp. This emits ultraviolet rays which destroy nucleic acid and thus prevent normal growth and multiplication of microbes and may destroy them altogether. Water is passed in the form of a thin film along the lamps. The lamps are sometimes used to keep quantities of water sterile. Since ultraviolet light does not affect the taste, this disinfection method can be used for water in the food industry and for bottle washing etc. Quartz lamps are also used in pharmaceutical factories, although ultimate sterilization with heat or by fine filtration is essential. They are often cheap and easy for use in fermentation plants. Cloudy effluent can be greatly improved with them although the flow velocity must be much lower than with absolutely clear water. In some cases thin syrups are sterilised by this means. Complete equipment including all the regulators etc., suitable for many specialized purposes, is commercially available.

Micro-organisms can also be removed from water by filtration. Filters of dia-tomaceous earth, aloxite, sheets of cellulose, cellulose acetate or asbestos, layers of charcoal, activated carbon and bleaching earth are used. In general these filters are prepared in small units for the purification of small quantities of water and can often be regenerated by heating.

On a small scale water can also be disinfected by small quantities of metals or metal salts. This phenomenon is called the oligodynamic action of metals or metal salts. The word oligodynamic is derived from the Greek and means: action of only small quantities. Small quantities of copper, silver or mercury salts are dissolved in water (see also copper sulphate, p. 569). Metals (e.g. silver, copper or an alloy of silver and manganese) are used in the form of a finely divided precipitate on a porous or granular mass. The water to be disinfected is passed through filters made of the resulting mass. This method is known as the 'Katadyn method'. Silver can also be introduced into the water by electrolysis with silver electrodes. This process is named the 'Electro-Katadyn process'.

The US Army used to supply the troops with tablets for disinfecting drinking water by chlorine generation. Others are now used containing 'globaline' which is made from a solution of iodine in potassium iodide and glycine (amino acetic acid). Globaline (tetraglycine hydroperiodide) is precipitated, dried and mixed with acid sodium phosphate. This product acts as a strong disinfectant by discharging iodine into the water. Iodine in amounts of 5 to 10 p.p.m. makes even badly infected water absolutely safe to drink. The pH should be between 3 and 8. For disinfecting eating utensils for the troops the US Army also uses trichloromelamine (see also p. 362) which works better than the hypochlorite used in the past.

4.6.3 Distribution of potable water

Potable water is usually distributed in piping. Very large waterworks distribute their water with large pumping units which keep the pressure in the pipes as constant as possible.

Water towers (see fig. 4.11) are usually employed for applying pressure on water from smaller waterworks. Water is continuously pumped into a reservoir at the top of the water tower from which it flows into the main distribution pipes supplying the consumers. A booster pump may increase the pressure in part of the distribution system.

Underground mains are made of hot-tarred or bituminised cast iron, while domestic piping is made of lead or copper. The use of copper for this purpose is of growing impor-tance. As soft water corrodes lead, lead pipes must be tinned inside, though this is

Fig. 4.11 Modern water tower installed in the USA. This tower is an example of a design which is planned to avoid disfigurement of the landscape.

unnecessary with hard water. It is always advisable to run off the water in the pipes before use in the morning, lead compounds being very poisonous.

In the United Kingdom 95% of the population had piped water supplies in 1952. The percentages of some other countries were: Netherlands 82%, USA 72%, Belgium 60%, France 52%. The cost of mains connections in agricultural regions is usually high, but there too, piped supplies have the great advantage of better fire fighting, hygiene and farm management. It is estimated that when purified piped water is used the yield of a cow increases by £5 per year owing to a higher milk yield of better quality and saving in wages for watering, washing etc.

In many cases piped water is supplied at prices based on the size of the house. Industrial plants and business enterprises usually pay by volume. Water supplies as a whole are being increasingly regulated by special legislation and central water supply committees are being set up to examine every aspect of national water supply such as types of stocks, conservation, permissible consumption, etc.

In addition to domestic supplies, piped water is used for the food and beverages industry, for dairies, laundries and public baths. Most industrial areas need so much water that regeneration of used water is essential (see industrial water and waste water treatment, pp. 178 and 169).

4.6.4 Boiler water

A boiler consists basically of a vessel in which water is converted into steam by heating. Under the operating conditions of temperature and pressure, dissolved impurities undergo many complicated chemical changes and these can cause various troubles. Thus impurities are responsible for scale formation on the heating elements and can promote corrosion and discharge of water with steam from the boiler by frothing, splashing etc. Scale occurs not only in steam generators but also in many other installations using raw water.

a. Scale formation and prevention. The salts of calcium and magnesium are the major source of scale, primarily because of their low solubility. Some compounds of calcium and magnesium precipitate in the form of a sludge and are not harmful (e.g., the phosphates) but other salts such as calcium carbonate, calcium sulphate and magnesium sulphate cement themselves directly as scale on the boiler metal. For example calcium bicarbonate in the water decomposes above 62° C into carbonate and carbon dioxide:

$$Ca(HCO_3)_2 \xrightarrow{\text{heat}} CaCO_3 + CO_2 + H_2O.$$

The resulting calcium carbonate is less soluble in water than the bicarbonate and tends to deposit on the hottest parts of the boiler, i.e. on the heat transferring surfaces.

Owing to the heat insulating effect of the scale, the output of the boiler decreases and in addition the metal boiler wall may become overheated, leading to weakness of the metal and consequently to risk of explosion. For this reason scale must be removed periodically, e.g., by chipping off, by thermal shock or by chemical means such as treatment with dilute hydrochloric acid containing a suitable inhibitory material to prevent excessive attack of the metal. The prevention of explosions and the saving in maintenance costs fully warrant the cost of water softening. It is significant that, of the maintenance costs of steam locomotives (still important in many countries), between 9 and 38% represents the cost of servicing their boilers. The lowest figure applies to boilers fed with properly softened water. In many countries boilers are inspected at regular intervals by authorized experts.

To prevent scale formation a separate water-softening installation (see lime-soda softening process, p. 127; and softening by means of ion-exchangers, p. 134) is normally used, while the water is softened again in the boiler itself with phosphates (mono-, di-, or trisodium phosphate). Actually a separate softening installation is not necessary but phosphate softening in the boiler will suffice. In practice, however, a separate installation provides a much cheaper way because most of the hardness-forming ions can be eliminated with much cheaper chemicals in the separate installation. Additional phosphate treatment in the boiler itself is especially applied to water which has been partially softened in a separate lime-soda or soda process. The water is only partially softened in the latter process to avoid the risk of excess of soda which can decompose into corrosive alkali hydroxide and carbon dioxide at the high operating temperatures of the boiler.

Phosphates can be used in the boiler itself because they precipitate calcium ions as a calcium phosphate which does not encrust the heat transferring surface, but remains in suspension as a sludge and can be drained off with the boiler water. It is necessary to dose the water with sufficient phosphate (e.g. trisodium phosphate) to ensure that it always contains a slight excess of phosphate ions. Adequate alkalinity ensures that the calcium is precipitated by the phosphate as a hydroxy 'apatite' ($3 Ca_3(PO_4)_2 . Ca(OH)_2$) which remains in the water as a fine suspension. With the silica in the water, the magnesium ions form 'serpentine' ($3 MgO . 2SiO_2 . 2H_2O$) which can likewise be drained off. Where water contains an appreciable amount of magnesium compounds and little silica, a calculated amount of sodium silicate can be added to precipitate the magnesium ions (especially in low pressure boilers).

Silica (present in raw water or formed from sodium silicate) may be a nuisance, however, in very high-pressure boilers as it is volatile in very high-pressure steam and separates again as amorphous silica in turbines in which the high-pressure steam is reduced to lower pressure. For boilers operating at over 80 kg per cm^2 the silica content is thus kept below 5 mg per litre.

Remarkably enough, therefore, silicate is a nuisance with high-pressure boilers but acts as a water-treating agent in low-pressure boilers. A very useful method is to substitute potassium ions for sodium ions. Potassium silicates have much better solubility characteristics than sodium silicates (there is no deposition of amorphous silica). The replacement of sodium by potassium ions is moreover very effective against the concentrating film mechanism (see below).

With very heavy duty boilers, i.e. those where the number of heat units passing through per unit of surface (known as the heat flux) is very high, scale may still be formed, though the phosphate equilibrium is correctly adjusted. This scale is often composed of other constituents, e.g. 'analcite' (a sodium aluminium silicate) and 'acmite' (sodium ferrosilicate). The cause of this is that, when steam bubbles form, the salt concentration at the boiler wall bubble interface may reach as high as 100000 mg per litre, even though the salt content of the bulk of the boiler is only several hundred mg per litre. In boiler-water physics these phenomena, which are summarized as the 'concentrating film mechanism', provide one of the most difficult problems. The American pioneers in this field, R. E. Hall and E. Partridge, have done much to elucidate the concentrating film mechanism and have made practical suggestions for preventing complex silicate scale.

b. Prevention of corrosion. The most important constituents of boiler feed water which are responsible for corrosion are oxygen and carbon dioxide. Acidic and strongly alkaline waters are also corrosive.

Oxygen, dissolved in boiler water, promotes various forms of corrosion. For example, like all metals, iron tends to dissolve in water to a certain extent. The water quickly becomes saturated with dissolved iron as ferrous ions, Fe^{++}, which stops further dissolution. If oxygen is present the ferrous ions are oxidized to ferric ions (Fe^{+++}) and these, in turn, form the less soluble ferric hydroxide ($Fe(OH)_3$) with water. In this way ferrous ions are removed from the water and the concentration of ferrous ions becomes too low to stop the the dissolution of iron.

In alkaline water, a protective coating of ferrous oxide (FeO) or ferrosoferric oxide (Fe_3O_4) is formed on the metal surface. Reaction equations:

$$3\,Fe + 4\,H_2O \rightarrow Fe_3O_4 + 4H_2 \text{ (below } 570°\,C)$$
$$Fe + H_2O \rightarrow FeO + H_2 \text{ (above } 570°\,C).$$

The coating of these oxides is attacked by acidic water and by oxygen, even in alkaline water. (Oxygen oxidizes ferrous oxide to ferric oxide (Fe_2O_3) which does not form a protective coating).

Oxygen is removed by means of de-aerators in which water is heated (usually with steam). Residual oxygen can be combined with sodium sulphite (Na_2SO_3), to form sodium sulphate (Na_2SO_4). With very high-pressure boilers, where sodium sulphate may decompose to form hydrogen sulphide, H_2S, hydrazine hydrate or hydrazine sulphate is at present being used. In view of the small amount required, its high price is not a drawback. It is preferably used as a 5% solution in a slightly alkaline solution.

Bicarbonates and carbonates decompose in the boiler to form hydroxides and carbon dioxide which is entrained by the steam and acidifies the condensate. It can be combined with equivalent amounts of cyclohexylamine, benzylamine or morpholine. The amines are dosed into the boiler. They evaporate with the steam and bind the carbon dioxide, so that the condensate no longer gives an acidic reaction. A film-forming amine, such as octadecylamine acetate may alternatively be added. This is also carried along by the steam and where it condenses it forms a very thin anti-corrosive film on the metal. The nature of the complete water circuit ultimately determines which amine gives the best results.

The material of riveted boilers may become brittle by the action of alkali (caustic embrittlement), which is characterized by intercrystalline cracks along the grain boundaries of the metal. It is caused by a combination of high metal-stresses and very high alkali concentrations (e.g. 100 g per litre) which may occur when boiler water seeps through riveted joints. It can be prevented by adding nitrates to the feed water; sulphates, used in the past, have proved ineffective. This form of brittleness does not occur in high-pressure boilers because these are welded, not riveted, and no high local stresses occur.

Serious difficulties are sometimes experienced through brittleness due to hydrogen. Hydrogen is formed from iron and water and steam (see protective coating of ferrous oxides, above).

Sometimes the hydrogen (partially in atomic form) penetrates into the metal and forms methane with the carbides in the iron. This reaction reduces the amount of iron carbides, while the relatively large methane molecules tend to congregate along the grain boundaries and build up sufficient pressure to cause a type of intergranular rupture and damage. This type of brittleness can be prevented by providing a sufficient amount of neutral salts or by ensuring that the water is properly buffered.

Water to be used in 'once-through' boilers, i.e. those in which the water evaporates in one pass, must of course be very pure because all the salt present crystallises. Total solids must be less than 0.5 mg per litre. Adequate alkalinity is ensured by adding substances which leave no residue on evaporation, e.g. ammonium compounds (see also corrosion, vol. III).

c. Prevention of frothing. The composition of boiler feed water must be such that no frothing occurs whereby salts might be entrained by the steam and damage turbines, for instance. Since frothing can not be prevented completely, the total solids content of boiler water must not exceed a certain quantity. At a pressure below 20 atmospheres (300 p.s.i.) for instance, a residue after evaporation of about 3 500 mg per litre is permissible, but at 100 atmospheres (1 500 p.s.i.) only about 500 mg per litre.

Frothing increases with increasing alkalinity of the water and for this reason the alkalinity must be kept as low as possible; however the pH value in the boiler must not be lower than about 9.5 to prevent corrosion.

Suspended solids, organic matter and oils can also be responsible for frothing (oils are often present in the recovered condensate). All these substances can be removed by clarification with e.g. aluminium salts, activated silica or iron compounds if this has not been done already during the softening (see clarification of water, p. 125). Activated carbon is also used to remove oils.

An important improvement in the prevention of frothing is the development of anti-frothing agents (anti-foamants). Various anti-foamants such as polyesters, polyalcohols and polyamides are now available.

Outside the boiler water field, anti-foamants are particularly important in submerged coil evaporators (for the evaporation of solutions) which can then be used with a sufficiently high water level for full utilization of the heating surface without frothing, otherwise salt water may be carried by the steam. Without anti-foamants the water level often must be kept too low and the heating capacity is not fully utilised; in consequence the output of the submerged coil evaporators is considerably reduced.

If the evaporators, as is very often the case, operate at sub-atmospheric pressure, mixed preparations containing anti-foamants and sequestering agents (to prevent scale formation) are very effective. Examples are: (a) 'Hagevan LP evaporator compound' which is a mixture of polyethylene glycol ester and sulphonated lignine (anti-foamants) and a polyphosphate (to prevent scale formation); (b) 'Admiralty evaporator compound' (which is a mixture of the disodium salt of ethylenediamine tetra-acetic acid, sodium dinaphthylmethane disulphonic acid and a polyethyleneglycol ester) developed in England by Admiralty Materials Laboratories. The latter mixture does not reduce the formation of scale but reduces its adhesion to the metal, so that it is easy to remove (by thermal shock). It is said that with the use of this mixture and thermal shock there is practically no decline in the output of submerged coil evaporators even with protracted operation. In some cases the anti-foamants even increase their output by 50% over rated capacity.

It must be borne in mind that, in general, the mixtures of anti-foamants and anti-scaling agents are effective only as anti-foamant and not as anti-scaling agents.

The anti-scaling components in the mixtures (sequestering agents) are not effective in boilers since the soluble complexes, formed from the anti-scaling agents and the scale forming constituents decompose at the operating conditions of the boiler, which is operated at much higher temperature and pressure than an evaporator.

4.6.5 Cooling water and other industrial water

By far the major portion of industrial water is used as cooling water, e.g., for cooling coke, chemical reactors etc. Cooling water should be non-scaling, non-corrosive and non-sliming. It is usually cheapest to collect the water from the various plants and pass it in a single passage through the cooling equipment; this is known as the 'once-through' system. The water, which has a slightly higher temperature after use, is discharged into rivers.

In condensers and similar cooling installations of the once-through type there is usually no carbonate scale. This is because the cooling water does not boil, no carbon dioxide is produced and no CO_3 ions are formed. The temperature increase does shift the bicarbonate balance so that the pH rises with the temperature, but this is of little practical significance at the temperatures occurring in condensers. Only in a few cases, where the cooling water already contains carbonate or already has a relatively high pH value, is there any danger of scale.

Condensers and heat exchangers are often dirtied with sludge (clay, sand) and algae. Sludge is removed by brushing the condenser tubes periodically. Algae are counteracted by chlorination of the water (see chlorination of drinking water, p. 145). Chlorination about every four hours with a good excess of chlorine is usually more effective than continuous dosage with a relatively small amount.

An important point is that cooling water (especially in closed cooling systems under anaerobic conditions) may contain sulphate-reducing bacteria and the like. Steel and cast iron which are otherwise non-corrodible are then liable to corrode. There have been cases of microbes in water causing chemical decomposition of petroleum stored over it. Bacteria have sometimes multiplied so quickly in washing water at coke ovens that they have clogged the gas scrubbers.

The quantity of water which is available is often too small to meet the demand. In these cases there will be a saving of cooling water by allowing the warmed water to rain down on wooden grids in a very high concrete cooling tower which has often the form of a single walled hyperboloid (see fig. 4.12), the narrowing of which augments the chimney effect of the tower. Since wood is often attacked by microbes, the grids must be preserved with agents that cannot be washed out easily.

A low percentage of the water evaporates and provides sufficient cooling to allow the water collected in the reservoir to be used for cooling again. Such towers are usually not higher than 50 m, although some are over 100 m. Their height accounts for the fact that the draught caused by the difference between outside and inside temperatures disposes of a relatively large amount of water vapour and evaporates the freshly arriving water, giving considerable cooling.

If a natural draught in high cooling towers is impossible (for instance in the centre of big cities), a different kind of cooling tower which employs fans may be used. The fans drive air in from the outside via adjustable louvres and the water flows downward over the wooden frames. The air saturated with water vapour can escape at the top. In cooling towers carbon dioxide can escape from cooling water and thus carbonates, causing scale, are formed. Scale formation can be prevented by sequestration by means of polyphosphates.

Fig. 4.12 A part of the factory for the production of polyvinyl-chloride. In the middle a cooling tower, belonging to Shell Nederland Chemie N.V., Pernis, Holland.

Besides the boiler and cooling field, industrial water is used for various purposes, e.g. for chemical reactions, for washing chemicals and ores, for the production of food and beverages, as a solvent in various treating baths and as a dispersing agent for insoluble substances. For these purposes water of the same purity as drinking water is sometimes used. In many cases however (e.g. for the production of pharmaceuticals) the water must be further purified by distillation or by means of ion exchangers. In other cases only softening or removal of iron compounds (by means of ion exchangers or sequestering agents) is necessary. (See also uses of sequestering agents, p. 131). Water for industrial use should thus be properly tested from various aspects and purified to ensure its suitability. The water used in making dyes and in dyeing textiles may contain only very small amounts of iron, manganese and calcium as their presence may affect the resultant colour. Manganese in particular tends to 'yellow' fabrics. Water for the manufacture of some plastics and man-made fibres must be free from suspended matter and colour.

Special mention must be made of water in many food industries, when the water must be incorporated in delivered food, e.g., in beer, soft drinks and canned food or for washing meat, vegetables, fruits, etc. The water for these purposes can hardly be called industrial water. It must be very pure, practically sterile and of good taste especially controlled for the special kind of food.

4.6.6 Irrigation water

Irrigation means the artifical distribution of water to produce crops. Irrigation is particularly important in areas where there is a season of plentiful water followed by another of small supply and in areas (e.g. deserts) where rainfall is slight.

More simple forms of irrigation comprise the distribution of water from rivers by means of canal systems or the collection of water (either river or rain water) on large surfaces which are divided into compartments by means of banks. Great irrigation works usually comprise large dams which have been built across various rivers to store water.

The water from the large basins, formed by the rivers after the dams, is distributed by means of canals. Irrigation is also promoted by tapping large underground water supplies, for instance in Australia and the Sahara.

Usually the water for irrigation needs no purification. Sometimes harmful animal and vegetable life must be destroyed. Thus, in Sudan, cupric sulphate is distributed in irrigation water to combat bilharzia snails (see cupric sulphate, p. 569). Sea water and water from rivers containing much waste from chemical plants cannot be used for irrigation.

In Algeria, Israel and elsewhere water having a relatively high salt content is used succesfully for irrigating some crops. This is contrary to the old theory, which claimed that not more than about 1 000 p.p.m. of salt should be present in irrigation water. Nowadays it is believed that plants exposed to a solution containing ions thrive always if there is a physiologically correct balance between the ionic solution and the ions present in the plants. When a plant is endangered by an excessive quantity of sodium ions, the disturbance can be counteracted by adding potassium salts.

The difficulty in the irrigation of deserts is not usually due to the complete absence of water but to the inability of the soil to accept and hold water. The introduction of an inert cellular material in the top soil may improve the situation. For this reason large quantities of vermiculite are ploughed into the soil in some areas of Kuwait. One further advantage of vermiculite in soils such as those of Kuwait, which have a high salt content, is that the presence of the mineral reduces the amount of salt taken up by the roots of plants.

4.6.7 Statistics

Although the total quantity of fresh water available for use seems immense, it is often a great problem to meet the demand. For example, about 4 300 000 million gallons (1 US gallon = 3.78 litres) of water fall down on the USA on an average day. It is estimated that about 70% of this amount is recycled to the atmosphere by direct evaporation or by evaporation of water which is taken up by vegetation. Thus about 1 300 000 million gallons per day are available for use. As shown in the following table one-fourth was consumed in 1960 and it is estimated that in 1980 about 40% will be necessary to cover the demand.

The estimated water use from 1900 to 1960 and projection for 1980 in the USA in 1 000 million gallons daily average is shown in the table overleaf (source: Statistical Abstracts of the USA).

It is clear that there must be a shortage of water in various regions since the rain water is not uniformly distributed over the whole country. For this reason re-use of water is often necessary, especially for industrial water, although much water is

Water use in USA	In '000 million gallons per day				
	1900	1920	1940	1960	1980
Irrigation	20	56	71	135	178
Public water utilities	3	6	10	22	32
Self-supplied, uses					
Rural and domestic	2	2	3	6	7
Industrial miscellaneous	10	18	29	61	115
Steam electric utilities	5	9	23	99	162
Total	40	91	136	323	494

transported, even over long distances, and the water withdrawn for irrigation and cooling (the latter uses about 80% of the total industrial water) is not consumed but released after use again to become a part of the water which can be withdrawn from the sources and supplied. The extent of re-use of water by industry in the USA can be seen from the following table which shows the total use and intake of water by industry and the use and intake by the most important water using industries in million gallons per year (from Census of Manufacturing Establishments, 1959).

	In million gallons per year	
All industries	Total 25 065	Intake 12 177
Primary metal industries	5 255	3 702
Chemical industry	4 617	3 240
Paper and allied products	5 989	1 937
Petroleum and coal products	5 692	1 319
Food and allied products	1 192	624
Other industries	4 320	1 355

An estimate of the quantity of water required for the production of one ton of various products is as follows:

	In '000 gallons of water		
Alcohol (from grain)	4	Gasoline	3-4
Aluminium	2 000	Paper pulp	60-160
Ammonia (synthetic)	94	Soda ash	20
Butadiene (from alcohol)	380	Steel	65
Calcium carbide	30	Viscose rayon	350

Water supplied by public utilities must be potable in contradistinction to the enormous quantities used for irrigation and the major portion of the self-supplied industrial water. The public utilities in the USA purified and softened about 8 x 10^{12} gallons of water in 1960. An estimate of the consumption of the most important chemicals for this purpose is as follows:

	In short tons		
Lime (in terms of CaO)	710 000	Iron salts	40 000
Aluminium sulphate	260 000	Chlorine	45 000
Soda ash	170 000	Carbon	21 000

The total consumption of chlorine for the disinfection of water for various purposes (e.g. drinking, cooling, swimming pools and waste water) was close to 200000 tons in 1960 (in the USA). Much water is purified and softened by means of ion exchangers but the consumption of ion exchangers is relatively low since they can be regenerated many times.

Figures covering the complete water consumption in the UK are not available. Some figures covering an important portion of the consumption in England and Wales in 1955 are:

In million gallons per day

Water from public water undertakings	2 000
Self-supplied uses by some major industries	1 700

(The major industries include the electricity, coal, gas, transport, brewing, chemicals, iron and steel, leather, paper and textiles industries.)

4.7 SALINE WATER AND ITS DESALTING

4.7.1 Introduction

By far the major source of all water is the saline water of the oceans and the seas. The salt content of this water is usually about 1.5 to 4% (see common salt, p. 413). Many territories, especially those which lack supplies of fresh water, have considerable quantities of brackish water containing up to about 1.5% of salts (mainly common salt). The use of saline water as such is rather restricted. It is mainly used as cooling water by factories near the coasts, where supplies of good fresh water are not cheaply obtainable. Saline water is also used as a raw material for recovery of its constituents (see bromine, iodine, sodium chloride, potassium chloride and magnesium coumpounds).

In general the production of fresh water from saline water is far too expensive an operation. For this reason desalting of water is restricted to areas which have a shortage of fresh water and where transport of fresh water is still more expensive. Desalting plants are in operation in North America, North Africa, Kuwait and on some ships.

Distillation or evaporation, electrodialysis, ion-exchange and freezing are the four commercial methods for desalting of water. The commercial use of electrodialysis and ion-exchange (see p. 139) is restricted to brackish water. Sea-water is usually desalted by distillation.

The removal of salt may also be effected by pressing saline water through a membrane whereby the salt content of the filtrate is reduced. This method is called ultra-filtration or reversed osmosis and is now in the advanced pilot plant stage.

4.7.2 Distillation of saline water

On a small scale, e.g. for laboratory uses, fresh water is distilled to obtain very pure water. The water is usually boiled in a simple vessel and the resulting water vapour is condensed in a water-jacketed cooler. However for large scale production of fresh

Fig. 4.13 A Weir sea water distillation plant (of the flash evaporator type) producing 600 000 gallons of fresh water a day, supplied to the Kuwait Oil Company at Mina Al Ahmadi.

water from sea water, such a simple distilling apparatus is too expensive. In these cases use is made of multiple effect evaporators and flash evaporators.

Until recently multiple effect evaporators with submerged coils were practically exclusively used, especially on board ships. In multiple effect evaporators, the first evaporator (a so-called 'effect') is heated by passing waste steam through submerged coils. The subsequent heaters are heated by means of water vapour obtained in the preceding evaporator. (See also common salt, p. 418.) Formerly these evaporators had to be cleaned frequently owing to scale formation. Nowadays scale formation need no longer present a problem for some very effective 'evaporator compounds' are commercially available which keep the evaporators going for long periods without a perceptible falling off in the output (see under boiler water, p. 152).

More and more 'flash evaporators' are being used. This type of evaporator (see fig. 4.13 and 4.14) is much less prone to scale formation and is also cheaper to construct. The saline water is preheated by passing it through the coils of the condenser sections of a series of flash chambers.

The preheated saline water is heated further in a heater in which the pressure on the saline water is still such that no boiling can occur. The resulting hot saline water is then introduced into the first flash chamber where a vacuum is maintained. Since the saline water is now overheated with respect to the pressure in this flash chamber, the water immediately evaporates until the temperature of the liquid has fallen so as to bring about a state of equilibrium between the vapour pressure in the flash chamber and the saline water. The water vapour which has been formed condenses in the condenser

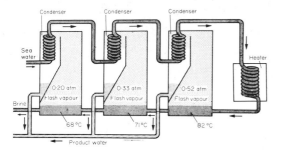

Fig. 4.14 Diagram of a three stage flash evaporator.

section of the flash chamber and transmits the heat of condensation to the coils conveying saline water which is preheated in this way. The remaining brine from the first flash chamber is introduced into the second flash chamber in which the evaporation of water is continued owing to the fact that in this chamber a higher vacuum is maintained than in the first flash chamber. In the third flash chamber the vacuum is higher again than in the second and so there also vapour is formed. The vapours condense in the condenser sections of the flash chambers and the resulting fresh water from each condenser section is collected.

Flash evaporators are preferably built with a large number of flash stages because the energy consumption per unit of fresh water decreases with increasing number of flash stages owing to the fact that the heat of condensation which is recovered in each stage is re-used more times with the increasing number of stages. Today it is possible to build flash evaporators having up to 50 stages. The complete system consumes the heat of about 0.12 kg water vapour of atmospheric pressure to produce one kg of fresh water from saline water.

The number of flash stages is limited by the capital cost. At a given pressure difference between the first and last stage the pressure difference between two succeeding stages, and thus the temperature difference available across the coils in the condenser section, decreases if the number of stages increases. Owing to the decreasing temperature difference across the heat exchange coils, a greater heat exchange surface is required in each evaporator stage if more stages are used. In this way the capital cost increases in addition to the increase of the capital cost caused by the increasing number of evaporators (compare multiple effect evaporators, under sodium chloride, p. 418).

The flash chambers can be arranged as shown in fig. 4.14 but installations having superposed flash chambers are also built. Recirculating flash evaporators are also known. In these part of the 'brine discharge' is recycled.

During the second world war an evaporator process was developed in the USA for distilling sea water for the Navy. This process, called 'forced circulation vapour compression distillation', uses a heat pump (see fig. 4.15). Water vapour originating from boiling saline water is drawn in, usually by a high-speed rotary compressor, and compressed to 3 p.s.i.; its temperature thereby rises. As it is now hotter than the boiling saline water, it acts as 'fresh' steam and evaporates more water. In this way the steam condenses to fresh water and the heat of condensation is used to evaporate saline water. The condensed fresh water and expended brine pass through a heat

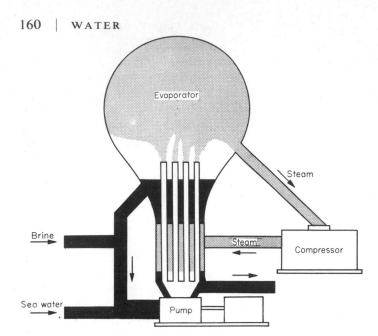

Fig. 4.15   Diagram of saline water conversion by means of forced circulation vapour compression distillation.

exchanger to heat the incoming feed of saline water as nearly as possible to boiling point. Owing to the continuous re-use of the heat capacity of the evaporated and condensed fresh water, only a small amount of additional energy is needed to compensate heat losses. This energy is added by means of the compressor. In this way one lb of water can be produced with only 15 Btu (1 Btu = 0.0003 kWh). This may be of great importance where fuel costs are high.

In 1935 the rated capacity of shore installations (all types) for sea water evaporation throughout the world was 0.3 million gallons a day, in 1940 0.5 m.g.d., in 1950 2.2 m.g.d., in 1955 5 m.g.d. and in 1960 12.5 m.g.d. The Aruba evaporators have a capacity of 2.5 m.g.d. and those at Kuwait have 2 m.g.d. but are to be greatly enlarged.

Distilling costs vary greatly. This is not only because of local differences in fuel costs and wages; it also depends on whether distilled water production is combined with electricity generation. The high pressure steam is allowed to expand in a turbine which drives an electricity generator and conducts the expanded (now low-pressure) steam to the evaporators. The steam for the evaporators thus costs: Steam raising cost – realised value of electricity.

In practice, such an 'ideal situation' is not always feasible and much water often has to be produced while there is no demand for electricity. Assuming that fuel costs $0.25 per 10^6 Btu (300 kWh) on a 'municipal basis', i.e. non-profit making but self-supporting (interest on capital about 4%), the cost of producing distilled water for very big installations (say 50000 m³ a day) and modern evaporators is said to be, without electricity generation, approximately $0.30 to 0.33 per m³ and with electricity generation approximately $0.11 to 0.15 per m³ (calculated in 1960).

Sometimes a cost of about $0.07 per m³ evaporated water is mentioned. This figure excludes cost of fuel and represents capital cost only.

Use of solar energy. In USA, North Africa and Australia the possibilities of evaporating brine by means of solar energy are being investigated. The solar distillation methods can be classified in two groups: (1) those methods in which absorption of solar heat and evaporation of the water is effected in one and the same apparatus (see fig. 4.16); and (2) those methods which produce steam, usually by means of a focusing collector, the steam being introduced into a conventional distillation plant (see fig. 4.17).

A large installation working along the lines of the first group was built at Las Salinas (Chile) as early as 1872, but the number of solar stills for the production of fresh water remains small. This is due to the facts that (a) solar stills require a large area for receiving the solar energy; and (b) they can produce water during part of the day only (about eight hours per normal day).

Attempts are being made to improve the economy of the solar stills by developing cheaper constructions, for instance by using transparent plastic materials instead of glass. Thus a solar still has been constructed by arranging black polyethylene sheets on

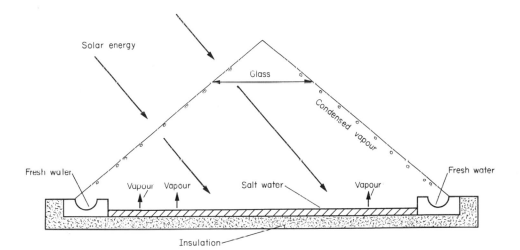

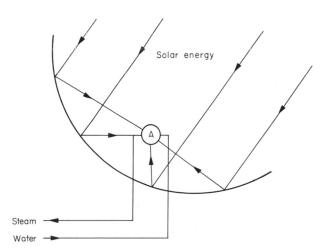

Fig. 4.16 Solar still of simple design. The solar energy is absorbed by the black bottom of a large container. Saline water evaporates slowly and the resulting vapour condenses on the transparent cover.

Fig. 4.17 Solar furnace. Tube A is heated by the solar energy which is concentrated on the tube by means of a reflector. Saline water contained in the tube evaporates and the resulting vapour is collected and condensed again.

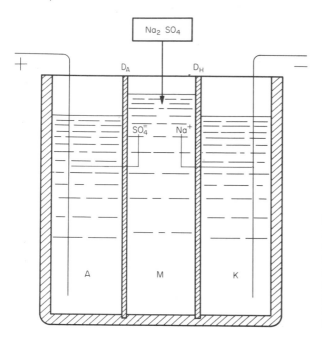

Fig. 4.18 Simplified diagram of an electrodialysis cell. A and K are the side compartments with the electrodes. M is the centre compartment which is regularly replenished from the centre compartment of a preceding cell. D_A and D_H are semi-permeable membranes.

cheap insulation material on the ground to form the evaporation pans. Transparent plastic films of Teflon, which are supported by a slight air pressure, form the 'cover' and the condensing surface. Special plastic films are being developed, which are sufficiently weather resistant to make plastic solar stills economically possible.

A multiple effect solar still has also been developed. In this, the multiple effect principle is unimportant as far as it improves the heat economy because no charge is made for solar energy, but it is important in so far as it permits a saving of ground area. With a 10 'effect' installation 4 to 6 times as much water may be produced per surface unit as with a single effect solar still.

It is expected that the costs of fresh water production by means of solar stills will eventually amount to less than $1.00 per 1000 gallons.

4.7.3 Desalting water by electrodialysis

Electrodialysis is based on the following fact: if an electric current is introduced into a solution of a salt by means of two electrodes, the positive ions (cations) move to the negative electrode (cathode) and the negative ions (anions) move to the positive electrode (anode).

Thus salts can be removed from water by an apparatus consisting basically of a vessel filled with saline water and provided with electrodes and two membranes (which are permeable for ions) between the electrodes (see fig. 4.18). With a sufficient voltage drop the negative and positive ions pass through the membranes and move to the positive and negative electrode respectively. Thus the salt content of the water in the space between the membranes (centre compartment) decreases and the salt content of the water around the electrodes increases. Colloids and even bacteria also move to these electrodes according to their charge. The centre compartment is constantly replenished to keep the water level a little higher than in the outer compartments, since water diffuses through the membranes from the centre compartment into the outer ones. The water of the centre compartment is purified in stages with a cascade system in which the water runs through all the centre compartments in succession. As charged ions and other particles from the centre compartments are eliminated at every stage, water with a lower salt content ultimately collects in a lower-level receptacle.

The drawback of the method described above is that salts diffuse back to the centre compartment when ordinary membranes such as cellophane foils are used. Consequently the efficiency is poor. Much better results are achieved by using membranes which show selective permeability ('permselective' membranes). These membranes allow passage of either cations or anions only and may be heterogeneous or homogeneous. The heterogeneous type may be envisaged as consisting of small particles of ion exchanger kept in membrane form by a binding agent; they are made by mixing a finely ground ion exchanger with a suitable binder and then calendering the mixture. Homogeneous membranes may be envisaged as an extended sheet of ion exchange material; they are made by passing large sheets of polythene, for instance, through chemical baths, in which reactions take place and so ionic groups are introduced into the membrane with the result that the membrane becomes permselective.

The ohmic resistance of good homogeneous membranes is relatively independent of

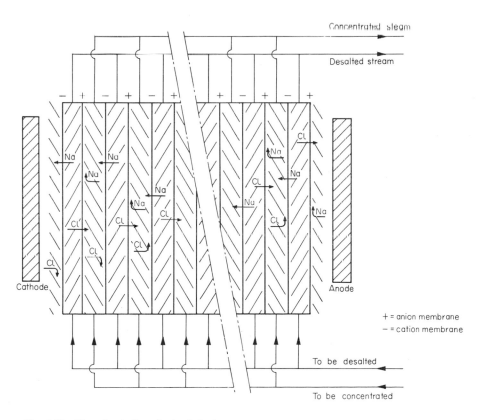

Fig. 4.19 Flowsheet of an electrodialysis process.

the salt concentrations of the solutions with which they come in contact, but this is not true for the heterogeneous membranes, in which the resistance increases at low salt concentrations. This is a drawback in demineralizing saline water for drinking purposes, where the final product should not contain more than 500 mg of salt per litre. For this reason homogeneous membranes are preferred, although they tend to be a little less selective than the heterogeneous type at very high salt concentrations.

Until recently, permselective membranes were very dear, but now they are being made in long lengths by simple methods. Their price is expected to fall very quickly to less than $10 per m².

The efficiency of electrodialysis equipment also increases when a plurality of desalting compartments is arranged between one pair of electrodes (see fig. 4.19).

If an electric current is applied to the electrodes, cations will tend to move towards the cathode and anions towards the anode. The cations cannot pass through an anion membrane but can pass through the cation membrane, and vice versa. The result is that chlorine ions, for instance, from cell No. 1 and sodium ions from cell No. 3 go to cell No. 2 and cannot leave it again. Hence the sodium ions from cell No. 5 and the chlorine ions from cell No. 3 go to cell No. 4. There is thus a concentration increase in the even numbered cells. From the odd numbered cells, both sodium and chlorine ions are eliminated, e.g. the sodium ions from cell No. 3 go to cell No. 2 and the chlorine ions to cell No. 4. Thus the odd numbered cells are desalted. Technical electrodialysis apparatus (see fig. 4.20) has been developed (in the Netherlands by the Netherlands Organization for Applied Scientific Research TNO and in the USA by American Machine and Foundry Company and by Ionics Co.) containing 800 compartments which have a breadth of 0.4 metres and a thickness of not more than 1 mm. This small thickness has been achieved by keeping the membranes separated by a thin sealing rim. In order to prevent the membranes touching each other, a thin separator is laid in the cells.

Several types of electrodialysis apparatus are already being exploited in North Africa and the Middle East.

The costs entailed by the desalting of saline water by means of electrodialysis are dependent on the salt content of the water. It is estimated that for a municipal (i.e. a non-profit making but self-supporting) works, the costs (for big plants) will amount to:

$0.08 per m³ for desalting from   3000 mg/l to 500 mg/l
$0.20 ,, ,, ,,   ,,   ,,   8000 ,, ,, 500 ,,
$0.55 ,, ,, ,,   ,,   ,,   35000 ,, ,, 500 ,, (sea water)
$0.40 ,, ,, ,,   ,,   ,,   35000 ,, ,, 500 ,, (sea water in very large plants)

Although it is in principle possible to obtain even lower salt contents, this is not economical owing to the rapid increase of the ohmic resistance of the desalted water. Moreover, in drinking water a lower salt content is not required. The processes quoted are more or less dependent on the composition of the water. Waters which contain chiefly hardness-forming ions involve much greater expense. The costs entailed by the evaporation of water on the other hand are substantially independent of the initial salt concentrations. It is even quite possible that the evaporation of brackish water will ultimately prove to be more expensive than the evaporation of sea water, because in evaporating seawater the formation of stony deposits can be prevented at small cost, but attempts at achieving this with hard brackish waters have so far been rather expensive.

Fig. 4.20 Commercial electrodialysis apparatus for desalting of saline water.

Although the cost of the preparation of fresh water from saline water by means of electrodialysis and evaporation techniques may be acceptable for the provision of drinking water in many places where fresh water is scanty, it is still too expensive for irrigation purposes. Many attempts are being made, especially in the USA, to develop new methods or to perfect older methods for converting salt water into fresh water at lower cost.

Thus use can be made of the fact that the reverse of the electrodialysis technique is also possible. If the compartments of an electrodialysis apparatus are alternately filled with concentrated and dilute liquids, this may start operating as a charged battery and supplying electrical energy. This energy is conducted towards a normal electrodialysis apparatus in which desalting is effected. The dilute liquid in the battery may be original brackish water and the concentrated liquid may be obtained by evaporating brackish water in open cisterns. It is as yet impossible to make any predictions as to whether this process will in the end prove less expensive than the dialysis technique.

In addition to its use for the desalting of saline water the technique of electrodialysis may be applied in industry. Thus in Japan a process has been developed for concentrating sea water by means of electrodialysis, for the purposes of winning salt therefrom. With the technique of electrodialysis it is also possible to carry out chemical reactions, for instance the conversion of soda ash (Na_2CO_3) and potassium chloride (KCl) into potassium carbonate (K_2CO_3) and common salt (NaCl).

4.7.4 Desalting water by freezing

Desalting by freezing is based on the fact that ice which has been formed on cooling saline water, consists of pure water. Although in general a cooling process is more expensive than a heating process, the former has attractive possibilities since the quantity of heat which must be withdrawn from a pound of water to freeze it, is much lower than the quantity of heat which must be supplied to heat and evaporate a pound of water.

Basically there are two methods of freezing water. In the first method sea water is evaporated by introducing it into a high-vacuum chamber. The heat of evaporation is withdrawn from the sea water itself and thus it cools to a temperature low enough to produce ice crystals. The ice-brine slurry is drawn off, filtered, washed with some fresh water and melted. The heat needed for melting can be withdrawn from the feed of saline water and the latter is pre-cooled in this way.

The second method comprises the cooling of sea water by means of refrigerants. (Cooling by common ice-producing refrigerators seems to be too expensive.) In this process, which is said to be attractive, use is made of hydrocarbons boiling at temperatures below 0° C, e.g. butane, isobutane and propane. The liquid hydrocarbon is mixed with saline water under pressure and allowed to evaporate by releasing the pressure. The heat of evaporation is withdrawn from the mixture which cools to form ice. The latter is recovered by filtration and the hydrocarbon can be recovered from the vapour by compression and used again.

When propane is used the brine needs no cooling below 0° C since propane forms an insoluble hydrate with water at temperatures slightly above 0° C. After filtration the hydrate is freed from propane by increasing the temperature.

All freezing processes encounter the most trouble in the ice-washing step. Elimination of the cold adhering brine without great loss of ice is not realizable economically without much difficulty.

4.7.5 Desalting by reversed osmosis or ultrafiltration

'Skinned' membranes of cellulose acetate have been developed, with an extremely thin dense upper skin, which is impermeable to salt ions, but permeable to water, forming the top layer of a much more porous membrane. With these membranes more than 99% of the salt in sea water can be retained, while ultrafiltering potable water is obtained at the rate of 250 litres per day per square metre of membrane under a pressure of 100 atmospheres. In Coalinga, California, a plant makes 7000 gallons per day potable water out of brackish water, using a tubular membrane system. The same system furnishes fresh water from sea water to San Diego's Gas and Electric Company's South Bay plant, California. The same system, with flat membranes, furnishes fresh water to Newport Beach, California. The major advantage of the reversed osmosis method is its extremely low energy consumption; in practice the energy needed for desalting 1000 gallons of sea water is 15 kWh, or even less.

4.8 EFFLUENTS AND EFFLUENT TREATMENT

4.8.1 General

In the first half of the last century, the consumption of water per head of the population was still low. The modern habit of taking baths and washing was far from widespread, especially when comparison is made with the high level of personal cleanliness current in Greek and Roman times. It is only about a century ago that the first attempts were made in various places to provide piped drinking water supplies, e.g. in London in 1830, Amsterdam in 1853, Brussels in 1855, Berlin in 1856 and Paris in 1865. With running water available for domestic purposes, water consumption increased and water also came into use for the flushing of toilets.

Arrangements for the disposal of wastes from urban centres, already unsatisfactory, became totally inadequate. After some time, the first sewerage systems were introduced, e.g. in London in 1848, Rio de Janeiro in 1857 and Berlin in 1874; these systems conveyed the domestic sewage to a river or other body of surface water. To an ever increasing extent large urban centres, and later smaller centres and, at the present time, even the smallest communities have been provided with piped water and a sewerage system. At the same time towns have been increasing in size, together with both the water consumption and the quantity of effluent discharged per head. In Western Europe the water consumption in small villages is still often only 40-80 litres per head per day, while in both large and small towns the figure is 100-200 litres. Water consumption per head has risen to 600-800 litres in Oslo, Stockholm and New York and even to 2200 litres in certain high-class residential districts of the USA.

Simultaneously with the development of what has been called a 'water civilization', enormous development has taken place in industry, as a result of which great quantities of heavily polluted effluents are produced. Streams, rivers, lakes and other bodies of surface water are being increasingly polluted by domestic and industrial effluents. At the same time, these waters must satisfy increasingly strict requirements from the point of view of the supply of drinking water for man and animals, for industrial purposes, agriculture and horticulture, and to meet the recreational needs of ever larger sections of the population.

It is clear that, unless the necessary steps are taken, this development can lead rapidly, particularly in densely populated countries, to a catastrophic situation. It can be said, without exaggeration, that the measures taken hitherto throughout the world are inadequate. This is the result of a failure to realize, particularly in the early stages, the true significance of the pollution of surface waters; as a result, there is a lack of suitable techniques for the treatment of effluents. More recently, shortsighted economic considerations have been an obstacle. At the present time, therefore, there is a great deal of leeway to make up.

Unpolluted surface water contains oxygen in amounts up to that corresponding to saturation at the temperature in question, as follows:

Temperature (°C)	Oxygen content (mg/litre)
0	14
10	11
20	9

The above data are for a pressure of 760 mm Hg.

When an effluent containing organic matter, such as domestic sewage, is introduced, a bacterial flora develops which, with the aid of the oxygen present in the surface water, converts the organic matter into carbon dioxide and water. The greater the amount of organic matter in the effluent, the greater the consumption of the oxygen present in the surface water. When the dilution of the effluent by the surface water is so great that the oxygen content of the water does not fall below about 5 mg/litre, no great damage is done, as a rule, to the fish population. The water picks up oxygen again downstream, and the oxygen content may once again reach the saturation value. The surface water has then been restored to its original condition by what is called 'self-purification' (see fig. 4.21). When the quantity of pollutants introduced is so great that the oxygen content of the surface water falls to 2-3 mg/litre, the fish population is greatly reduced, and can be restored only when the oxygen content rises again, downstream, to about 5 mg/litre.

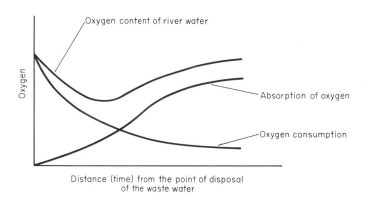

Fig. 4.21 Diagram showing the process of self-purification in a river.

With still greater pollution, all the oxygen dissolved in the water may be used up. If this happens the excess of organic matter, which has not been oxidised, is then decomposed by anaerobic bacteria. The fermentation or rotting which then takes place produces, not carbon dioxide and water, but methane, hydrogen and hydrogen sulphide. This last compound forms iron sulphide with any iron in the water, and the water becomes black. It has then become a malodorous open sewer and is no longer able to perform the functions of healthy watercourse.

It is clear from the above that the more an effluent is polluted, the more oxygen is removed from the receiving water. The various organic substances differ in the amounts of oxygen which they consume. In effluent technology and effluent treatment, the biochemical oxygen demand (BOD) is used as measure of the pollution of an effluent.

Domestic sewage is said to be weak when the BOD after primary sedimentation, i.e. after removal of the matter settling out during a period of one hour, does not exceed 100-150 mg/litre. For strong domestic sewage the BOD is in the range 350-450 mg/litre. In some industrial effluents the BOD may be 10 000 or even 20 000 mg/litre.

If the quantity and strength of the effluent are known, it is possible to calculate, e.g. for a particular town, how many kilograms of BOD are discharged daily into a river. This oxygen demand is often expressed in terms of the so-called population equivalent, which is defined in terms of the quantity of oxygen demand, measured in grams, discharged per head of population per day in the domestic sewage. In Western Europe, a figure of 54 g of BOD is taken for raw sewage which has not undergone primary sedimentation, corresponding to 19 g in the sludge which settles out during a period of one hour, and 35 g in the sewage remaining after the sludge has been removed.

If a town has a daily discharge of 1 000 kg of BOD, this corresponds to a population equivalent of (1 000 x 1 000)/54, i.e. about 18 500. In the same way, the quantity of pollutants discharged into an industrial effluent can also be expressed as a population equivalent, if the amount of the effluent and the BOD are known.

In the USA, the amount of BOD discharged per head is greater than in Europe, and a figure of 75 g is taken. It has recently been suggested that a higher value than 54 g should be used in Western Europe also, but this suggestion should be treated with caution, since it is probable that in a number of cases even the old figure of 54 g BOD is not reached.

Up to the present time, in many countries, as great a use as possible has been made, for economic reasons, of the self-purifying capacity of surface waters in the reception of domestic and industrial effluents, so that weak effluents are often discharged into rivers and streams.

It may be expected that, in the long run, the desire to see rivers and streams as pure and clear as possible will lead, at least in principle, to the treatment of all effluents before discharge.

4.8.2 Treatment of domestic sewage

A good example was set in this field by the United Kingdom, where as early as in 1880, i.e. several decades before this problem was even considered in other countries, the construction of sewage treatment plants began, and thus the UK took the lead. This development was, in part, the consequence of the geographical characteristics of the country, and in particular, of the fact that the rivers are short. In the UK it has been recommended by the Royal Commission on Sewage Disposal that effluents must be treated so that, on discharge, the BOD is less than 20 mg/litre and the suspended solids concentration less than 30 mg/litre. As a result, although many improvements could still be made, the UK in the field of effluent treatment is nevertheless the country in which a higher proportion of effluents is treated than in any other.

In some parts of the USA, where a great deal of leeway remains to be made up in the field of effluent treatment, a law has been introduced which requires that no untreated effluent may be discharged into a public water. A similar law recently came into force in Germany. In Ireland and Norway, countries which still remain largely unaffected by industrialization, great efforts are being made to keep the rivers and streams clean and pure, and to prevent them from becoming channels for weak effluents.

One of the oldest treatment methods, and one which is still often suggested, is that whereby agricultural land is irrigated or sprayed with sewage. The oxygen present in the soil oxidizes the organic matter present in the sewage and thus purifies it. Apart from this, the method has the advantage that a proportion of the potassium and phosphorus required as fertilizers (world reserves of these materials are being rapidly depleted) is provided by the sewage instead of being wasted. Every year, in fact, 3 kg of nitrogen, 0.75 kg of phosphorus and 2.2 kg of potassium are discharged, per head, in domestic sewage. The use of sewage in agriculture on a large scale would thus avoid the need for large amounts of synthetic fertilizers. Nevertheless, land treatment has been used in only a few cases, because of the associated disadvantages. It is usually impossible to find a sufficiently large area of suitable agricultural land close to a large town. In addition, it is also practically impossible to irrigate agricultural land with sewage the whole year round, so that during certain periods either untreated sewage must be discharged or the sewage must be treated in some other way. There are also serious difficulties from the hygienic point of view. In certain places in Germany, e.g. in Darmstadt, a widespread infection with roundworm eggs resulted from the irrigation of land used for horticultural purposes with sewage.

In India large amounts of untreated sewage, often diluted with river water, are used for the irrigation of agricultural land. The economic advantages and the consequent development of the country in many fields, including health, more than counterbalance in this case the disadvantages resulting from the spread of infectious diseases.

In the USA sewage may be used in agriculture and horticulture only after thorough treatment.

In some cases, irrigated meadows have been used. This method has the same disadvantages as land treatment, and has been abandoned because of hygienic difficulties.

In general, the treatment of domestic sewage is carried out as follows:

a. Preliminary treatment and primary sedimentation. The sewage is first passed through a screen, in which the largest particles, which might interfere with the operation of the pumps, are removed. At the present time, comminutors are sometimes used to grind down the large particles, and in this way, the need for screens is avoided. The next stage involves use of a sand trap, which removes most of the sand from the sewage. In winter, when roads in towns are sanded, large quantities of sand are carried away with the waste waters. If this sand was not removed, it would settle out in the treatment plant in places where this is not desirable.

The sewage then undergoes sedimentation in specially arranged circular or rectangular tanks (the primary sedimentation plant). The settleable coarse solids, the so-called 'primary sludge', are collected at the bottom of the tank by means of scrapers, and pumped to the sludge digestion tank.

The treated effluent, after primary sedimentation, passes out over the outlet weir, and in some cases is discharged directly into a river. The effluent is much less objectionable in character as a result of the removal of the coarse solids. From the point of view of the BOD, a reduction of only about one-third is achieved as a consequence of such removal. The results obtained by primary sedimentation can be improved somewhat by aerating the sewage for a short time before the sedimentation is carried out.

Fig. 4.22   Trickling filter with spray distribution of the sewage.

In most cases it is desirable for the effluent from primary sedimentation to undergo further treatment.

b. Trickling filters. A method for the treatment of sewage which was one of the earliest to be developed involves the use of trickling filters. In this process the sewage is passed through a bed of lumps of slag, for example, over which it flows in the form of a thin layer. In due course a gelatinous film is formed on the surface of the slag, consisting of bacteria and other micro-organisms. The bed is then ready for use. The impurities in the sewage are adsorbed on to the film and then oxidised by the bacteria. Oxygen is also necessary. The lumps of slag are about the size of a fist and are arranged in such a way that air can enter at the bottom and a natural draught is produced; oxygen can thus be absorbed by the thin film of liquid at all points in the bed. A distributor is provided for spraying the sewage on to the bed, e.g. a rotary sprinkler. The sewage leaving the orifices is thus distributed over the entire bed. Depending on the amount of pre-treated sewage handled by the filter, a degree of purification of 85-95% can be achieved. (See fig. 4.22.)

The film on the slag continuously increases in thickness. When a certain thickness is reached, however, the film becomes detached, and is carried away by the effluent. It is therefore necessary to pass the effluent through a settling tank again, in which the particles of humus sludge are retained. The humus is pumped to the sludge digestion tank.

In their original form trickling filters are very simple to use, but since the loading per cubic metre of contents is low, they are costly to construct. If the loading is increased,

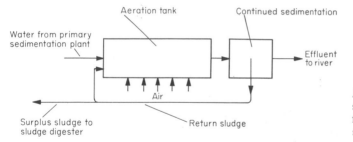

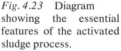

Fig. 4.23 Diagram showing the essential features of the activated sludge process.

the purification becomes less effective. In addition, the top layer then rapidly becomes choked, and as a result ponding occurs, and in consequence the efficiency decreases rapidly. The volumetric loading can be increased by diluting sewage with previously treated effluent: the risk of choking is then reduced and good purification can be achieved even at higher loadings. Another method is to use two filters in series; the film then grows rapidly in the first filter, and after one or two weeks the order is reversed. The second filter then receives partially purified effluent, so that the film disintegrates and is removed. In this way clogging can be avoided even at high loadings.

A nuisance associated with the operation of trickling filters in the summer is the presence of swarms of small flies, the larvae of which live in the filters. It is then sometimes necessary to cover them, a precaution which may also be required in winter in order to prevent freezing if severe frosts occur.

c. Activated sludge process. Another widely used method of treating domestic sewage after primary sedimentation is the activated sludge process, which was originally developed in the years just before the first World War. The essential features of the process are shown in fig. 4.23. The sewage is aerated in the aeration tank, where an aerobic bacterial flora develops which partly oxidises the impurities in the sewage to carbon dioxide and water; another part of the organic impurities is synthesized into bacterial substance. The bacterial flora grows in the form of a floc (the activated sludge), which is suspended in the effluent. The mixture of treated effluent and sludge is then allowed to settle and the purified effluent (free from sludge) is discharged. The sludge is then returned to the aeration tank (return sludge) to be used in the treatment process again. Since in this process the bacteria increase in number, the quantity of activated sludge increases and the surplus must be regularly removed. This surplus is digested, together with the primary sludge from the primary sedimentation, in the sludge digester (see sludge digestion, p. 175). With a correctly operated activated sludge plant, 92-95 % of the BOD of an effluent which has undergone primary sedimentation can be removed.

The activated sludge process has been widely adopted. Various types of apparatus have been used and various methods employed for the supply of air to the aeration tank. The most important systems are described below (see fig. 4.24).

(i) *Diffused air system.* Compressed air is passed in the form of fine bubbles into tanks of depth about 4 m by means of porous tiles or pipes, so as to produce a circulation of the liquid in the tank and thus prevent the settling out of the activated sludge. This method has been widely used. It has the disadvantage that the tiles tend to become clogged, but this can largely be avoided by passing the air through oil filters, by avoiding

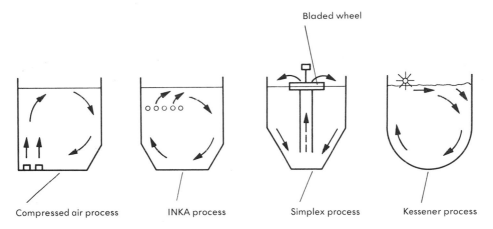

Bladed wheel

Compressed air process   INKA process   Simplex process   Kessener process

Fig. 4.24   Aeration systems.

the use of iron pipes for the air supply and thus avoiding rust formation, and by attaching the porous tiles or pipes to movable tubes or pipes, so that these can be lifted out of the tank when air is not passing through them, and sewage is thus prevented from penetrating into the pores.

(ii) *Swedish INKA process.* In this process the aim is to avoid fine bubble aeration. The air is introduced into the sewage at a depth of about 80 cm instead of 3 or 4 m. Much larger amounts of air are then needed, but the process has the advantage that fans can be used, instead of compressors, to force the air into the tank, as a result of the low back-pressure.

(iii) *Simplex process.* A cylindrical pipe, placed inside a tank, carries at the top a bladed wheel of special shape which rotates on a vertical axis. By this means the contents of the tank are drawn up through the vertical pipe and sprayed over the surface of the tank, whereby atmospheric oxygen is absorbed by the sewage.

(iv) *Aeration rotor process.* This is a development of the Kessener brush system (see fig. 4.24). A number of blades are attached to a horizontal shaft, and in this way air is introduced into the sewage, while this is circulated at the same time.

A number of other systems, used normally for the clarification of water, are also used in sewage treatment (for example modifications of the clarifiers discussed on p. 126).

The activated sludge process has been widely used during the last ten years for the following reason. Whereas it was originally believed that an aeration period of 6-10 hours was necessary in order to achieve complete purification of sewage, it is now realised that an aeration period of 1-2 hours is adequate, provided that sufficient oxygen is supplied. Where a degree of purification of 70% is considered satisfactory, the oxygen required, and thus the energy, are appreciably less than that needed for 'complete' (92-95%) purification.

The foam produced by synthetic detergents causes great difficulty in the treatment of sewage (see fig. 4.25). Some of these detergents (alkyl sulphates, esters and amides)

Fig. 4.25   Foam from detergents in an activated sludge plant.

are readily decomposed by bacteria, but others are much less easily broken down; these last include the alkylbenzenesulphonates and polyethyleneglycols. In the activated sludge process, in particular, where air is blown or drawn into the sewage, so much foam can be produced that the entire plant may be covered by it; this makes the operation of the plant both difficult and dangerous, while the plant itself becomes contaminated with pathogenic micro-organisms. Moreover the foam spread by the wind introduces the danger of contamination over an area outside the plant.

A solution to this problem is provided by the use of anti-foams or of other procedures. Non-foaming detergents, and detergents which are decomposed by bacteria, are now being marketed.

d. Chlorination. If a biological treatment plant is operating correctly, a high percentage of pathogens are either destroyed or removed from the sewage. It is sometimes desirable, however, to sterilize the sewage with chlorine, e.g. in the case of the sewage from a tuberculosis sanatorium, discharged into a stream used for the watering of cattle. Often too little attention is paid to such matters.

It may sometimes be necessary to chlorinate sewage which has undergone primary sedimentation; in this way, pathogens can be almost completely destroyed although pollution is not thereby prevented. The process is expensive, since large amounts of chlorine are required; much smaller quantities are needed for the chlorination of fully treated sewage. No worth-while result can be expected from the chlorination of raw sewage.

e. Sludge digestion. Sedimentation tank sludge (the so-called primary sludge) is digested by anaerobic bacteria, together with the humus sludge from the trickling filters or excess sludge from an activated sludge plant. This primary sludge is difficult to filter and contains a high proportion of water. The bacterial action, which takes place during sludge digestion, converts a large part of the organic constituents of the sludge into methane and carbon dioxide. In small plants, this process is always carried out in a simple open tank, in which the fermenting liquid is at the temperature of the ambient air (cold digestion). In large plants, fermentation takes place at higher temperatures in closed, heated and insulated tanks (see fig. 4.26). At these higher temperatures, which are generally in the range 30-35° C, digestion is accelerated, and can thus be carried out in tanks of smaller volume. In addition the gas formed during the process, which consists mainly of methane, can be collected and either used in the treatment plant itself for pre-heating the sludge, or supplied to other users, e.g. for mixing with town gas.

Fig. 4.26 Sludge digestion tank installed in Amsterdam-West (Holland).

The digestion, both of primary and excess sludge, is necessary because they cannot be dried as such; the associated water cannot be removed and objectionable odours are quickly produced. These difficulties are reduced by digestion, but the drying and disposal of sludge can nevertheless be extremely troublesome, especially in areas with moderate rainfall. In many parts of the world, in fact, sludge disposal is the most difficult part of sewage treatment. Attempts have been made, by washing the digested sludge and treating it with chemicals, such as ferric, calcium and aluminium salts, to condition it so that vacuum filtration can be carried out, followed by drying. This process, in most cases, is too costly. Tests have recently been carried out with centrifuges and with high frequency vibrating screens, but neither method has given results satisfactory for general application.

f. Other treatment methods. One method which constitutes a departure from the traditional treatment methods is the use of oxidation ponds, which have proved successful in semi-tropical areas. In these ponds, the diluted sewage is treated by means of the oxygen released by algae in the course of photosynthesis. It has been suggested that the algae should be harvested and used as a feeding stuff for cattle or in the production of alcohol, fats, etc. In more northern regions, fish ponds are used into which sewage diluted with river water is introduced. Such ponds require a large surface area.

Another method worthy of mention is the so-called Zimmermann process, in which sewage is heated to a temperature of 270-374° C, while at the same time oxygen under a pressure of 50-150 atm is introduced. The complete exothermic combustion of the organic matter then takes place, so that after the reaction has started, no further supply of energy is needed and in fact energy is released. In the Cederquist process incomplete combustion at lower temperatures and pressures takes place.

It will be clear from the foregoing that the treatment of domestic sewage can be effected in a number of different ways and that, with the exception of the sludge disposal problem, no technical difficulties are encountered. In addition treatment is not particularly costly. Although the construction of large treatment plants may cost several hundred thousand pounds, the total annual costs, including those for interest on capital, depreciation, and maintenance and operating costs, are relatively low, e.g. 10-12 shillings per head of population. Apart from the difficulty of obtaining the necessary capital, these costs should not prevent the construction of a treatment plant for a large town.

The position is quite different in the case of a small plant for the treatment of the sewage from a few hundred or even a few thousand inhabitants. The construction of the plant then becomes relatively far more expensive. As a result, throughout the world, the sewage from small communities (villages, military camps, hospitals) is only rarely treated, a state of affairs which constitutes a danger to public health.

A definite solution to this problem has been found in the Netherlands based on the idea that, by the use of prolonged aeration, the need for the digestion of the sludge by anaerobic bacteria might be avoided. Thus in this system not only is the sewage purified, but also the primary sludge present in it. The sludge is oxidized to such an extent that the excess sludge can be dried without having to undergo digestion by anaerobic bacteria. On the other hand more oxygen is needed, so that the power costs are higher than for traditional treatment methods. These increased power costs, however, are only a fraction of the saving in capital costs, since the primary sedimentation tank, aeration tank, final settlement tank and sludge digester, with all their associated installations, can be replaced by one large aeration tank of simple design, which may also act as a settlement tank. Such an 'oxidation ditch' can be operated both continuously and intermittently. Construction costs amount to £3-£7 per head of population, and operating and maintenance costs are very low. A diagram of an installation of this type for a population of 2 500 inhabitants is shown in figs. 4.27 and 4.28; it is capable of giving a degree of purification of 98% and an effluent of very low BOD. It is possible, by means of the oxidation ditch, for the sewage from small communities to be fully treated at a cost of only 10-12 shillings per head of population per year; costs as low as this were formerly attainable only with large installations. About a thousand installations of this type have already been constructed all over the world.

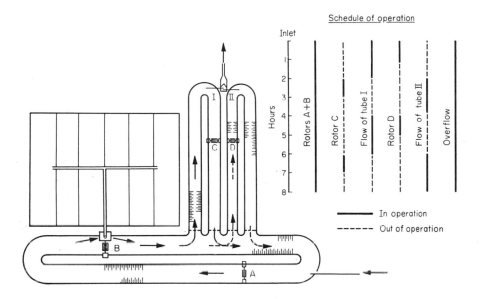

Fig. 4.27 Diagram of an oxidation ditch for 2500 inhabitants.

Fig. 4.28 An oxidation ditch for 2500 inhabitants for a mental hospital in Noordwijk, the Netherlands. (See also the diagram in fig. 4.27.)

4.8.3 Industrial effluents

Domestic sewage varies little in character from place to place. If water usage is high the sewage is weak, while a low water usage gives a strong sewage. In addition there are differences in sewerage systems. In a combined sewerage system surface water is also conveyed by the sewers; in a separate system there are separate sewers for domestic sewage. Furthermore, the location or the character of the land may be a decisive factor in the design of a treatment plant and in the choice of the method of treatment. Nevertheless, as long as domestic sewage alone is involved, there is no difficulty in obtaining a satisfactory result with the methods available.

When comparatively small amounts of industrial effluents are mixed with domestic sewage, they can be discharged as a rule without difficulty into the public sewerage system, and treated together with the sewage. This does not apply, however, to the discharge of effluents containing highly toxic substances or excessive amounts of mineral acids or alkali.

An acid effluent attacks the fabric of the sewers, while excessive amounts of alkaline effluent cause such a change in the pH value of the effluent as to interfere with the biological oxidation processes. In addition the discharge of highly acidic effluents, e.g., from the pickling baths used in the metal industry, may cause the evolution of harmful or poisonous gases when such effluents are mixed, in the sewerage system, with other industrial effluents. The bath liquors used in galvanizing contain, in addition to poisonous metal salts, cyanides which form the highly poisonous hydrogen cyanide by reaction with acids. It should therefore be made compulsory for a factory which discharges strongly alkaline or acid effluents, to neutralise these effluents before their discharge.

If an effluent containing toxic substances is discharged, it may be necessary for this to be done gradually, so that the bacterial flora in the treatment plant are not harmed by a sudden high concentration of toxic substances.

In large towns industrial plants of all kinds may discharge effluents into the sewerage system. Experience has shown, however, that although the character of the sewage may be changed as a result, it is usually possible for it to be treated in the normal manner already described for domestic sewage.

Sometimes, however, as when large amounts of substances resistant to bacterial decomposition are discharged, it may be necessary or advantageous to subject the effluent to a preliminary clarification in which, by the use of iron, aluminium or calcium compounds, or silicic acid, a precipitate is formed. Coarse or colloidal particles, which do not settle out readily, as well as some dissolved substances, such as colouring matters, are then adsorbed on to the floc produced, and can be removed by sedimentation.

An example of this technique is the so-called Niers process, developed by the Association for the Basin of the River Niers, in Germany; this technique is used for the preliminary treatment of domestic sewage containing large amounts of effluent from textile factories and tanneries. Iron hydroxide is used as the coagulant; it is obtained by contacting the effluent with waste waters containing iron and air. The iron is then dissolved, to be subsequently precipitated as iron hydroxide, and carrying down with it various substances present in the effluent.

Where, as in towns which are centres of the textile industry, the ratio of domestic sewage to industrial effluents is low (e.g. say 1:9) the choice of the treatment process is determined by the nature of the industrial effluents.

The problem of the treatment of industrial effluents varies with the industry concerned, and may also be different for different plants in the same industry. Every case must therefore be considered on its own merits. There are, nevertheless, a number of rules which are generally applicable.

In most cases, it is preferable to separate unpolluted, or only slightly polluted, effluents (e.g., cooling water) from the effluents as such. Cooling water is therefore discharged separately or recirculated, by the use of cooling towers (see p. 148). Even when cooling water is not polluted, or only slightly polluted, with organic substances, it may nevertheless have a harmful effect on the receiving water. If the temperature of the water is appreciably increased, as a result of the discharge of cooling water into it, the bacterial processes occur more rapidly, and the oxygen content of the water may decrease to a greater extent than would be the case at a lower temperature.

It may also sometimes be advisable to separate a weak effluent from one which is highly polluted and to treat them separately. In certain cases, on the other hand, it may be necessary to combine such effluents in order to reduce the concentration of the toxic substances present.

In the study of an industrial waste problem, an attempt should be made to modify the process used so as to reduce the amount of effluent produced. It is sometimes possible, for example, to change over from a 'wet' to a 'dry' production process. In other cases, the amount of effluent can be markedly reduced by recirculating a part of the water used. It is almost always worth while to track down losses due to leaks, etc., and reduce them as much as possible. This often results in a very marked reduction in the amount of impurities discharged.

Finely divided substances can be removed from effluents by screening and/or sedimentation or by chemical clarification. A flotation process is also sometimes used, in which fine bubble aeration is employed. The fine bubbles attach themselves to the particles present and cause them to rise; they can then be collected at the surface. This process is used in the paper industry for the removal of cellulose fibres from the effluent. A foaming agent or an adhesive, or sometimes also an oil, is often added in order to improve the adhesion of the bubbles to the particles. As far as possible, the material thus collected is re-used in the process.

It is impossible to give even a brief account here of each of the numerous types of industrial effluent. Reference should be made to the specialised literature on this subject. In the rest of this chapter a short general account is given of industrial effluents.

Industrial effluents can be divided into three groups as follow:

a. Effluents from industries based on natural products.
b. Effluents from the organic chemical industry.
c. Effluents containing inorganic pollutants.

a. Effluents from industries based on natural products. Such industries produce enormous quantities of highly polluted effluents, e.g. in the manufacture of dairy products, sugar, cellulose, paper and strawboard, potato flour and other starches, preserves, fermentation products, leather, fats and soap, as well as the effluents from slaughterhouses, breweries, tanneries, flax retting plants, etc. (See the appropriate chapters in vols. V to VIII inclusive.)

Effluents of these types can sometimes be satisfactorily treated by means of the processes used for domestic sewage. In a limited number of cases, an activated sludge plant or a trickling filter has been constructed for use by a dairy products factory, a slaughterhouse or a fermentation plant, while a number of dairy products and preserves factories, slaughterhouses, breweries, tanneries, and fats and soap factories discharge their effluents into municipal sewerage systems connected to treatment plants.

In other cases, a restricted form of effluent treatment is adopted. For example, soil particles brought in with the raw materials will usually be removed, together with coarse material produced in the manufacturing process, by means of sedimentation, frequently in simple ponds.

In a number of modern beet sugar factories, most of the highly polluted water from the diffusers is recirculated after chlorination. The whole of the equipment, including the diffusers, pipes, etc., must then be made of stainless steel.

In both the sugar and potato flour industries, the most highly polluted effluents are often collected in large digestion ponds, which occupy a large surface area and in which the effluent undergoes fermentation by anaerobic bacteria. After several months the BOD of the effluent is markedly reduced, and is then discharged gradually.

Good results have been obtained by some potato flour factories by the discharge of the effluent, which is rich in potassium, on to land.

In some industries in which strong effluents are produced, e.g. the fermentation industry, they are used, as far as possible, as a source of by-products, such as feeding stuffs for cattle; these can be produced by evaporating down the effluents.

In spite of all the above-mentioned treatment methods, by far the greater part of the pollutants produced by the industries based on natural products are discharged into rivers or other surface waters, with consequences which can be imagined. In the USA the Ohio River is so highly polluted with effluents of various kinds that the establishment of new factories on its banks has been prohibited. Other large rivers are in a similar condition. In one single area of a few hundred square kilometres in the north of the Netherlands, there are no less than 20 potato starch factories, the same number of strawboard and paper factories and two large sugar refineries. In this area a quantity of effluents is produced, the pollution of which corresponds to a population equivalent of 15 000 000. (The population of the Netherlands is 11 000 000). In the autumn, in particular, the condition of the surface waters in this area is disastrous.

As a general conclusion it may be said that surface waters are badly affected by pollution wherever industries based on natural products have been developed on a large scale. This is due to the fact that, for economic reasons, the undertakings concerned fail to take the measures necessary to prevent pollution. For the same reason governments have hesitated to make drastic treatment measures compulsory.

It is sometimes possible to discharge industrial effluents into the sea, although the construction of long pipelines may also be very costly. Before this procedure is adopted, care must be taken to ensure that the pollution is not transferred to a place where damage may be caused, in the future, to other interests. The effluent from certain factories is concentrated and carried out to sea in tankers.

It is clear from the foregoing that the future of the treatment of industrial effluents cannot be said to be bright. Some improvement may be expected from measures taken within the industries concerned by changing over to 'dry' processes or, where possible, the use of recirculation. Improvements may also be expected as a result of the manufacture of by-products from wastes. An example of this is the process, now under development, for obtaining albumen from potato juice, whereby the BOD is reduced from 14 000 to about 8 000 mg/litre.

Oxidation ditches, which can be constructed at a relatively low cost, are undoubtedly capable of treating the effluents, polluted with organic materials, discharged by small factories. A pilot plant installation of this type has been tried out in the Netherlands for the treatment of the wash water from potato flour factories. Complete purification was achieved, so that the re-use of the treated effluent as wash water might be possible.

A number of oxidation ditches are already in use for the purification of dairy waste, malting waste, and wastes from slaughterhouses, breweries, leather processing, textile processing and oil refineries.

b. Effluents from the organic chemical industry. Other industries giving rise to organic wastes produce effluents of a completely different kind. Among these industries may be included the oil industry, the rubber industry, the organic chemicals industry, coke ovens and gas works. (See the corresponding chapters in vols. II and IV.)

In oil production and refining large amounts of effluents containing oil are produced. As much oil as possible is removed in various ways, e.g. by centrifuging, flotation, the 'breaking' of oil/water emulsions by means of chemicals, etc. The effluent, after as much oil as possible has been removed, is then sprayed over adsorbent materials so as to remove the remaining oil as well as other substances. The partially treated effluent is also sometimes discharged into the ground at great depths (1 500 m).

The effluents from the synthetic and natural rubber industries are also treated by various mechanical methods; volatile substances are sometimes removed by distillation.

Coke ovens and gas works produce effluents containing large amounts of phenolic compounds, as well as many other substances. Phenol can be removed in a number of ways, e.g. by treating the effluent with a solvent in which phenol dissolves readily (see fig. 4.29); the solvent, e.g. benzene, is then recovered by distillation. In the Ruhr

Fig. 4.29 Installation for the recovery of phenols from the effluent from a coke oven.

Fig. 4.30   Oxidation ditch belonging to DSM Holland.

about 65% of the phenol is removed from the effluents from the coke ovens, but the remainder is discharged into the rivers.

It has become apparent, for all these effluents and for those from the organic chemicals industry, that, if the concentration of highly toxic substances is reduced so that a certain limiting value is not exceeded, they can be treated satisfactorily by biological methods. A substance such as phenol, in concentrations of hundreds of milligrams per litre or even in appreciably higher concentrations, can be decomposed by bacteria in the activated sludge process or in a trickling filter if an appropriate procedure is used.

Monsanto Chemicals Ltd, of Ruabon, Wales, has built a large and costly treatment plant, consisting of a combination of trickling filters, an activated sludge plant with Kessener brushes and filtration through sand filters. The effluent from this organic chemicals plant is so successfully treated by means of this installation that the trout in the River Dee, into which it is discharged, are not adversely affected by it.

An oxidation ditch has been constructed by the Netherlands State Mines in the Province of Limburg (see fig. 4.30) for the treatment of the effluent from two coke ovens and a number of chemical plants. This installation has given excellent results; thiocyanates are completely decomposed, and phenols are 99% decomposed, while cyanide compounds, added deliberately, were also completely decomposed. The installation can handle 30 000 m³ (6 600 000 gallons) of effluent daily, which is equivalent to the treatment of the domestic sewage from 250 000 people.

c. Effluents containing inorganic pollutants. Such effluents are produced mainly in the mining industry, the metal industry, the potassium, salt and soda industries, paint factories etc.

In the Ruhr the River Emscher is so highly polluted by the effluent from coal washeries that the entire river is passed through a sedimentation plant. A purification plant for biological treatment of the primary effluent will be in operation in the near future.

In the metal industry pickling baths are used, among other methods, for removing scale from the iron from rolling mills, since this is necessary before further work can be carried out. These pickling baths generally consist of acids, especially sulphuric acid. Attempts have been made to treat the spent pickle liquor so as to render it harmless, and to extract the metal salts dissolved in it. The choice of the process also depends on whether or not it is possible to dilute the liquor and the wash waters before discharge.

A number of rivers are severely polluted by the effluents from the potassium industry, e.g. the River Elbe in Germany. Potassium salts are poisonous to many forms of animal life at quite low concentrations (above 200 mg/litre).

Generally, in the case of industries producing inorganic wastes, if the pollutants cannot be removed by sedimentation or in some other way, the only remaining possibility is dilution of the effluents to such an extent that the dissolved salts do not have any harmful effect on the receiving water. The location of the plants concerned, in so far as it is not determined by the place where the raw materials are obtained, is therefore of great importance.

A problem which has become of increasing importance in recent years is that of the treatment of effluents polluted with radioactive substances; numerous processes have been developed or investigated for this purpose. One of these, which has been used in practice, is the treatment of the effluent with adsorbent materials (e.g. clay) or with ion exchange materials, in such a way that only harmless amounts of radioactive substances remain in it. The adsorbent material is then fired or made into a solid mass with cement; this can then readily be sunk to a great depth in the sea, or buried in some other place.

4.9 LITERATURE

DEGREMONT ACFI PARIS. *Water treatment handbook,* transl. from French by D. F. Long. Caxton Hill, Hertford, Austin and Sons, 1960.

K. DORFNER. *Ionen Austauscher.* Berlin, Walter de Gruyter, 1962.

R. FREIER. *Kesselspeisewasser, Kuhlwasser.* Berlin, Walter de Gruyter, 1963.

K. IMHOFF and G. M. FAIR. *Sewage treatment.* 2nd ed. London, Chapman & Hall, 1956.

INSTITUTION OF WATER ENGINEERS. *Manual of british water engineering practice.* 3rd ed. Cambridge, Heffer, 1961.

G. V. JAMES. *Water treatment.* 3rd ed. London, Technical Press, 1965.

O. JENTSCH. *Aufbereitung des Wassers.* Berlin, Veb. Verlag Technik, 1956.

F. C. NACHOD and J. SCHUBERT. *Ion-exchange technology.* New York, Academic Press, 1956.

L. I. PINCUS. *Practical boiler water treatment.* New York, McGraw-Hill, 1962.

W. RUDOLFS. *Industrial wastes, their disposal and treatment.* New York, Reinhold, 1953.

F. SIERP. *Gewerbliche und industrielle Abwässer - Entstehung, Schädlichkeit, Verwertung, Reinigung und Beseitigung.* Berlin, Springer, 1953.

B. A. SOUTHGATE. *Treatment and disposal of industrial waste waters.* London, HMSO, 1948.

K. S. SPIEGLER. *Salt water purification.* London, Wiley, 1962.

A. C. TWORT. *Water supply.* London, Arnold, 1963.

CHAPTER 5

Ice and

Refrigeration

5.1 HISTORY

As early as the Middle Ages ice was used as a cooling agent. Ice and snow were packed into the lower half of an underground room during winter and meat, fish, poultry and other food was stored in the upper half during the summer. Thus the food remained cool enough to prevent decay if the summer was not too hot.

Up to the second world war, natural ice from Scandinavian countries and Canada was a commercial product. It was stored and shipped in well insulated chambers and containers. Nowadays natural ice has been ousted from the market by synthetic ice. The first ice-making machine was developed in 1861 but the early commercial ice-making machines came into operation around the turn of the century. The demand for cooling means increased rapidly during the twentieth century, but the production of ice did not follow the increasing demand for 'cold' due to the development of non-transportable and transportable refrigerators in various sizes, which provide cold storage without the intermediate step of ice-making.

5.2 PRINCIPLES OF THE MODERN REFRIGERATION SYSTEMS

Today the most important refrigeration systems are the vapour compression, absorption and steam jet systems, of which the first is the most widespread.

All the systems are based on the fact that heat is required for the evaporation of a liquid (heat of evaporation) and the expansion of the resulting vapour to a larger volume (Joule-Thomson effect). This heat is withdrawn from the bulk of the liquid and the surrounding atmosphere and results in a temperature drop. The process is usually performed in a closed circuit containing a gas or a volatile liquid (the refrigerant). In one section (the cold section) the refrigerant is evaporated and absorbs heat; in the other section (the warm section), the refrigerant is liquefied again and releases the heat absorbed in the cold section. The various refrigeration systems differ in the method of repeated evaporation and liquefaction of the refrigerant.

5.2.1 The vapour compression system

In this system a gas (the refrigerant) is liquefied by compressing it outside the chamber to be cooled. The heat developed during the compression stage is removed by cooling in a heat exchanger (with a cooling medium such as water or air). The resulting liquefied refrigerant is evaporated again by releasing the pressure inside the chamber to be cooled. The energy (heat) which is required for the expansion and evaporation of the refrigerant is withdrawn from the refrigerant itself and from the surrounding chamber, and thus the temperature of the refrigerant and the chamber declines. The refrigerant which has absorbed heat is recycled and compressed again. A diagram of a simple vapour compression refrigeration system is shown in fig. 5.1.

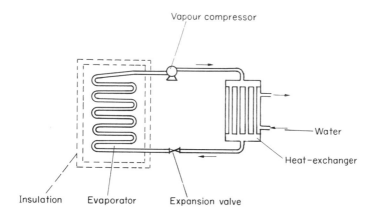

Fig. 5.1 Diagram of a vapour compression refrigeration cycle. The heat evolved during lique-faction of the gas by the compressor is removed in a water-cooled heat exchanger. The resulting cool liquid is expanded by passing through an expansion valve and evaporated in the evaporator. The heat of evaporation is withdrawn from the insulated evaporator chamber and thus the temperature in the latter declines.

A relatively low temperature can be reached in a two-stage vapour compression system (with one refrigerant) in which the refrigerant is compressed in two stages to a much higher pressure than in the one-stage system. Between the compression stages, the refrigerant (having an intermediate pressure) is cooled with water or by mixing with cold refrigerant obtained by expansion of a portion of the high pressure refrigerant from the second compressor to intermediate pressure. Cooling by means of water and by injection of a portion of the expanded refrigerant may be combined in one cycle (see fig. 5.2). Compression in three or more stages is also possible.

A very low temperature can be obtained in a cascade of two or more single vapour compression cycles (a split-stage vapour compression system with two or more refrigerants). In a cascade the expanded cold refrigerant in the evaporator of the first cycle is used to cool the compressed refrigerant in the second cycle and so on. A cascade of two single vapour compression cycles is shown in fig. 5.3.

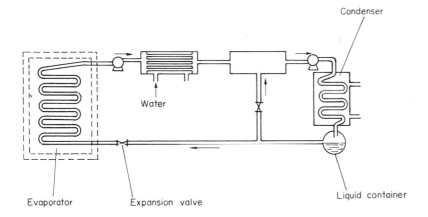

Fig. 5.2 Diagram of a two-stage vapour compression refrigeration cycle.

Some of the most important gases and liquids, used in vapour compression refrigeration systems, are shown in the table on p. 188.

The refrigerant used depends on the maximum pressure which can be tolerated in the system and the temperature range which is required. In cascade systems different refrigerants are used in the various cycles. It must be noted that the temperature of the cooling water must be lower than the critical temperature of the refrigerant. For this reason carbon dioxide and Freon 13 cannot be used in several regions of the USA, since the available cooling water temperature is too high in these regions. (Carbon dioxide and Freon 13 can be used in the second or third stage of a cascade.)

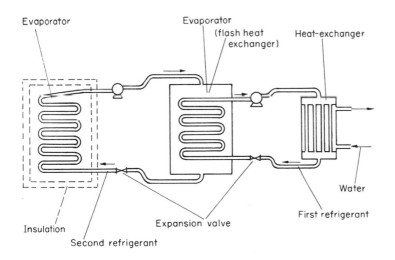

Fig. 5.3 Cascade vapour compression system.

Some gases and liquids used in vapour compression refrigeration systems

	Formula	M.P.	B.P.	Critical temp.	Minimum temp. reached
		°C	°C	°C	°C
Dichloromethane	CH_2Cl_2	−96.7	+40	216	−10
Monofluorotrichloromethane (Freon 11)	$CFCl_3$	−111	+23.7	198	−25
Sulphur dioxide	SO_2	−75.5	−10	157	−45
Carbon dioxide	CO_2	−56.6	−78.5	31	−50
Methyl chloride	CH_3Cl	−97.6	−23.7	143	−60
Ammonia	NH_3	−77.9	−33.4	132	−65
Difluorodichloromethane (Freon 12)	CF_2Cl_2	−155	−29.8	112	−65
Difluoromonochloromethane (Freon 22)	CHF_2Cl	−160	−40.8	96	−70
Trifluoromonochloromethane (Freon 13)	CF_3Cl	−181	−81.5	29	−110

The common non-ferrous and ferrous materials of construction can be used for refrigerator equipment operated with halogen compounds (and carbon dioxide and sulphur dioxide when dry). Ammonia can only be used with ferrous material (especially low-carbon steel). Since the heat exchange velocity of the halogenated hydrocarbons is relatively low, extended surface heat exchangers should be used in equipment operated with those compounds as refrigerant.

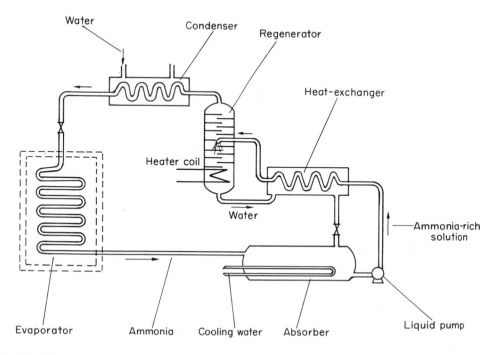

Fig. 5.4 Diagram of a one-stage ammonia absorption system.

The most important compressors used in refrigeration systems are the piston-type reciprocating compressor, the screw compressor and the centrifugal compressor.

Cold storage chambers in which the evaporator section of a refrigeration system is installed are usually double walled with an insulation material between the walls. Common insulation materials are: asbestos fibres, cork, cotton, wool, infusorial earth, silica aerogel, perlite, mineral wool and foamed plastics and rubber.

5.2.2 The absorption system

In this system (see fig. 5.4) the gaseous refrigerant (usually ammonia) is dissolved in water in an absorber and the heat evolved is removed by cooling with water. The resulting solution is pumped to a boiler (regenerator) which is operated at a higher pressure than in the absorber, and the gaseous refrigerant is separated from the water by heating. The pressure of the ammonia vapour is sufficiently high to liquefy the ammonia in a water-cooled condenser. The resulting liquid is evaporated by releasing the pressure by means of an expansion valve resulting in a lower temperature of the ammonia itself and the surrounding evaporator chamber. The evaporated ammonia is recycled to the absorber and absorbed in the water, which is recycled from the regenerator into the absorber.

The power requirements of the liquid pump are small compared to those of the compressor in the vapour compression system but much heat is needed to evaporate ammonia from the solution in the absorber; for this reason the absorption system can only be operated economically if cheap heat sources such as waste process steam are available. The heat requirements in the regenerator can be lowered by passing the solution of ammonia in water through a heat exchanger in which it is preheated by the hot water which is returned from the regenerator to the absorber.

A modification of the ammonia absorption system is the Platen-Munters absorption system, also known as the Electrolux household refrigerator system. This absorption system is characterized by the absence of a liquid pump and expansion valve, and the presence of hydrogen gas under a fairly high pressure (besides ammonia and water). Due to the high pressure caused by the hydrogen gas, ammonia can be liquefied by cooling with water. The evaporation of liquid ammonia can easily be understood by means of fig. 5.5 which shows a vessel containing a layer of liquid ammonia and a vessel containing water. The spaces over the liquids are connected by means of a pipe.

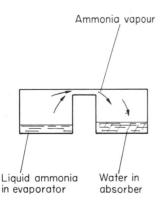

Ammonia vapour

Liquid ammonia
in evaporator

Water in
absorber

Fig. 5.5 A greatly simplified diagram showing the evaporation of liquid ammonia in the presence of water which absorbs the resulting ammonia vapour.

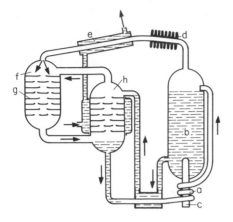

Fig. 5.6 Platen-Munters absorption refrigeration system. The heating element (c) causes evaporation of the ammonia from the ammonia-water mixture in the regenerator (b). Any water vapour in the ammonia vapour is condensed in (d) and flows back into (b). The ammonia vapour is condensed in the water-cooled condenser (e) and the resulting liquid ammonia is evaporated in the evaporator (f) provided with distributor plates (g). The ammonia vapour moves to the absorber (h), in which it is dissolved in water, which is withdrawn from the regenerator (b). The resulting ammonia solution is passed through coil (a), heated by the heating element (e) and the boiling solution obtained flows in regenerator (b).

Ammonia in one closed vessel evaporates spontaneously, but the evaporation comes to an end when the space over the liquid is saturated with ammonia vapour. However, the evaporation of ammonia in the system of fig. 5.5 is continued, since ammonia vapour is withdrawn from the space above the liquid by absorption in the water in the second vessel (until the water is saturated with ammonia). The result is a temperature drop in the vessel containing the liquid ammonia. The combination of evaporation vessel and absorption vessel is also used in the Platen-Munters absorption system shown in fig. 5.6.

The absorption of ammonia in the absorber (h) causes evaporation of the liquid ammonia in the evaporator (f). The evaporation of ammonia and the absorption in water is accelerated by a convection flow between the evaporator and the absorber, which is effected by the fact that the ammonia-rich hydrogen gas in the evaporator has a higher density than the ammonia-poor hydrogen gas in the absorber. The ammonia solution produced in the absorber passes through a heated coil (a) and the resulting boiling solution moves upwards into the regenerator (b) in which ammonia is separated from the water by evaporation. The resulting ammonia vapour is liquefied again in the water-cooled condenser (e).

In a modification of the Platen-Munters absorption system water is used as the refrigerant, and a solution of lithium bromide as the absorbent. Since the boiling point of water is much higher than that of ammonia the entire system is maintained at a fairly high vacuum to permit the evaporation of water at low temperatures (in contrast with the ammonia-hydrogen-water system which is maintained under a fairly high hydrogen pressure to permit the condensation of ammonia at cooling water temperatures). Like the Platen-Munters ammonia absorption system, the lithium bromide-water system does not contain expansion valves. A liquid pump is usually present to accelerate the circulation of the lithium bromide solution.

5.2.3 The steam jet system

In this system a liquid (usually water) is partially evaporated by spraying it in an evaporator in which a low pressure is maintained by means of steam jet ejectors. The vapour is removed from the system by the steam jet ejectors and the temperature of the remaining liquid declines since the latter supplies the heat of evaporation. The steam jet system is used for lowering the temperature of large quantities of cooling water.

(The latter serves simultaneously as the refrigerant in the steam jet refrigeration system.) Fresh water is usually supplied since the evaporated portion is continuously removed from the system, Fig. 5.7 shows a diagram of a steam jet cooling system in which the heat of condensation is recovered by condensation of the vapour. The heat of condensation is used for heating any desired medium.

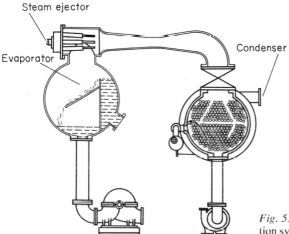

Steam ejector

Condenser

Evaporator

Fig. 5.7 Diagram of a steam jet refrigeration system.

5.2.4 Indirect refrigeration systems (brine cooling)

In many cases the low temperature obtained in one of the systems described above is used to cool a secondary liquid which is used as a heat transfer medium between the evaporator and the material to be cooled. A secondary heat transfer liquid has the great advantage that it can be used to cool objects of any desired form and shape by immersing them in the heat transfer liquid or by passing the latter through a jacket around the subject. In this way compact and uniform refrigeration systems can be used for various purposes.

For temperatures above 0° C the most common secondary heat transfer liquid is water. At temperatures between 0° C and −35° C aqueous solutions of sodium chloride, calcium chloride, ethylene glycol, glycerol and sugar are used. Organic liquids such as trichloroethylene, methylene chloride and some Freons are used at temperatures below −35° C. Since aqueous solutions of sodium chloride and calcium chloride are the most common secondary heat transfer liquids the term 'brine' is used to include all liquids used for this purpose, although it may give cause for much confusion.

5.2.5 Natural refrigeration processes

In these processes 'cold' is obtained by melting a solid or evaporating a liquid at atmospheric conditions without recovery of the refrigerant (as distinct from the refrigeration systems mentioned above, which are also named mechanical refrigeration processes). The most important natural refrigerant is ice. Other refrigerants which are used at lower temperatures are solid carbon dioxide and liquid butane and propane. The water and the gaseous carbon dioxide resulting from ice and solid carbon dioxide are wasted. The gaseous butane and propane resulting from the corresponding liquids are often used as a fuel. Liquid butane and propane are prepared by compressing the gases. (For the production of solid carbon dioxide see p. 535.)

Natural refrigeration systems are sometimes used to cool refrigerator cars.

5.3 PRODUCTION OF ICE

Ice is usually produced by means of a vapour compression refrigerator which may be used either directly or indirectly by means of a heat transfer liquid.

Ice blocks can be produced in various ways. In the oldest method a vessel filled with water is immersed in brine. To prevent enclosure of air bubbles and impurities the water is agitated with air. Freezing starts at the walls of the vessel and impurities concentrate in the remaining water at the centre of the vessel. Thus a core of impure water remains at the end of the freezing period. This impure water is removed and replaced with fresh water which is frozen by continued refrigeration. The resulting ice blocks are known as 'canned ice'. In this production method the freezing time is long due to the fact that the layer of ice is a thermal insulator which diminishes the refrigerator capacity. In addition much labour is involved in filling, loosening, etc. For this reason other ice-making methods were developed.

Another block ice-making machine comprises a vapour compression refrigerator in which the evaporator consists of a number of double-walled tubes. Evaporating ammonia enters each tube between the walls and leaves the tube through the centre. The evaporator tubes are immersed in water and a block of ice is formed around the tubes. The ice blocks are removed from the evaporator tubes by reversing the direction of the ammonia cycle in the refrigerator for a short time. Ammonia is then condensed in the evaporator and, due to the heat evolved, some ice around the evaporator tubes melts, and the blocks get free from the tubes. The ice blocks rise to the surface of the liquid and can easily be removed.

Flakes of ice (flake ice) can be produced by partly submerging a rotating drum in water and passing cold brine through the drum. Thus a layer of ice is formed on the drum wall which may be removed from it by scraping with a knife. In many ice-making machines of this type the method of discharge is typical. The rotating drum of these machines is flexible and inside the drum at the point of discharge a deflecting roller is mounted, which distorts the circular form of the drum. Due to this distortion the ice layer is loosened from the drum. The resulting flakes are sold as such or pressed into briquettes.

5.4 PROPERTIES OF ICE

Loose crystals of ice are colourless, but large masses of pure ice have a vivid blue colour when seen by transmitted light. Although the outward form of ice crystals varies greatly, they have the same lattice structure in which the water molecules are arranged in tetrahedra. The specific gravity of ice is 0.9 and thus it floats on water. Ice melts at 0° C and absorbs much heat during melting (about 80 kilocalories per kg, or 144 British thermal units, Btu, per lb). The absorption of the large quantities of heat is the basis of the use of melting ice for cooling purposes. Since the melting temperature of pure ice is still too high for many purposes, ice is often mixed with a salt. Such a mixture freezes and melts at a lower temperature, and for this reason it can withdraw heat from the surrounding atmosphere at a lower temperature during melting. Depending on the kind of salt and the quantity added, the freezing temperature can be lowered to $-50°$ C. The freezing temperatures of common salt and water are shown in fig. 5.8. When a solution of (for example) 10 g sodium chloride in 100 g water is cooled, pure ice separates and the salt concentrates in the remaining solution. Due to the increasing salt content the freezing point falls (see the declining line in fig. 5.8). On further cooling the solution becomes saturated with salt and then ice and salt will separate in the same ratio as they exist in solution, the temperature remaining constant until the solution is solidified completely. The minimum temperature, reached when the ice and the sodium chloride (the solvent and the solute respectively) separate together on cooling a solution, is called the eutectic temperature and the mixture separating is called a eutectic mixture. The eutectic mixture of sodium chloride and water freezes and melts at a temperature of $-21°$ C.

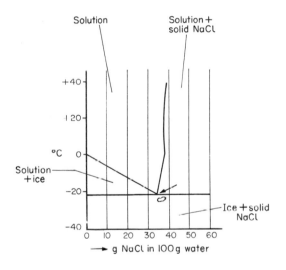

Fig. 5.8 Diagram showing the phases of various mixtures of water and sodium chloride (NaCl) at various temperatures. The arrow indicates the eutectic point.

5.5   USES OF ICE AND REFRIGERATION SYSTEMS

By far the most important quantities of ice are used for the conservation and transportation of fish and especially in Northern America also for the conservation of vegetables. Fish and crushed ice are usually stored in alternate layers in wood containers. Small quantities of chemicals such as nitrites are sometimes added to the ice to increase the keeping qualities of the fish.

Ice is also used in ice boxes which consist of well insulated cabinets with a special compartment for bars of ice, e.g. one or more smaller containers may be placed in the cabinets and the space around the containers is filled with ice. In general the ice must be mixed with common salt to obtain a temperature below 7° C in the ice boxes.

Formerly ice boxes were widely used for storing food, but nowadays they are mainly replaced by other refrigeration systems. Ice boxes are still used if no electric power is available for the operation of compressors and heating elements (e.g. for the refrigeration of ice-cream on the cars of ice-cream vendors, and for the refrigeration of railway cars on sections which are not electrified).

In the USA low freezing mixtures of water and other products are sold. These mixtures can be poured into small double walled containers and frozen in a home refrigerator. The resulting ice boxes are used as lunch box carriers etc. Frozen mixtures of ice and glycerol are used in hospitals for cooling purposes.

Mechanical refrigeration systems, especially the vapour compression refrigeration systems, are more widely used for the conservation, storage and transportation of food products. In these cases the food products are stored in deep-freeze cabinets, quick freezers, home refrigerators, etc., consisting of double-walled chambers, boxes, vessels, etc. with an insulation material between the walls and containing the evaporator section of a refrigeration system. The remainder of the refrigeration system is placed outside the insulated chamber.

The variety of uses of mechanical refrigerators outside the food conservation field is enormous. It is impossible to enumerate the individual applications. A survey of the most important types of applications is shown below.

Control of chemical reactions. The temperature of chemical reactions in which heat of reaction is evolved is often controlled by refrigerating process fluids prior to entrance to the reactor, or by cooling the reaction mixture by means of a refrigerator. Usually a secondary heat transfer fluid such as salt brine is used. The addition of flake ice to the reaction mixture is an effective cooling method when the dilution of the reactants with water can be tolerated. Rapid cooling by means of a refrigeration system is used to stop a chemical reaction. In the plastics industry monomers and partially polymerized resins are frequently cooled quickly to prevent further polymerization.

Cooling of products. Gaseous products such as chlorine and ammonia are often stored in the liquid form. Refrigerators are used for the liquefaction process and sometimes to prevent evaporation of the liquefied gas.

Recovery of materials from mixtures. Cooling by means of a refrigerator is often applied for the condensation of easily condensable vapours of valuable products in gas mixtures and for the separation of solids from a solution by crystallization.

Freeze-drying. This drying method comprises freezing a material by means of a refrigerator followed by drying in a high vacuum. Freeze-drying is used for materials which would decompose if dried at elevated temperatures (e.g. vitamins, insulin, liver extract and antibiotics), and also for food products, to prevent the decomposition of constituents which do not resist an elevated temperature (e.g. vitamins).

Air conditioning. In air conditioning use is made of vapour compression systems and steam jet systems to produce chilled water.

5.6 LITERATURE

INTERNATIONAL INSTITUTE OF REFRIGERATION. *Practical guide to refrigerated storage.* London, Pergamon, 1966.

W. R. WOOLRICH. *Handbook of refrigerating engineering.* 4th ed. 2 vols. Westport, Conn., A.V.I. Publishing CO., 1965.

CHAPTER 6

Hydrogen Peroxide

6.1 HISTORY

Hydrogen peroxide (H_2O_2) was discovered by Thenard in 1818. Even before 1900 hydrogen peroxide had become an article of commerce owing to the discovery of its bleaching and antiseptic properties. Its importance is still increasing, both in chemical processes and for military uses in rockets and missiles.

6.2 PRODUCTION

Before 1910 *barium peroxide* was the only source of hydrogen peroxide. Barium peroxide is produced by roasting barium oxide in air at 600 to 700° C. Under these conditions a second oxygen atom is taken up in the barium oxide molecule according to the equation:

$$2\ BaO + O_2 \rightarrow 2\ BaO_2$$

Hydrogen peroxide is obtained by treating barium peroxide with dilute sulphuric acid:

$$BaO_2 + H_2SO_4 \rightarrow H_2O_2 + BaSO_4$$

The solid barium sulphate formed is removed by filtration and a solution of 6-8% hydrogen peroxide in water is obtained.

In about 1910 the *electrolytic production* of hydrogen peroxide came into use. In this process a solution of sulphuric acid or ammonium acid sulphate in water is electrolysed with a potential drop of about 5.5 volt per cell. Persulphuric acid or ammonium persulphate is formed at the anode and hydrogen at the cathode. After electrolysis the solution is concentrated by evaporation under reduced pressure and with increasing concentration the persulphuric acid (or ammonium persulphate) is hydrolysed to give hydrogen peroxide and sulphuric acid (or ammonium sulphate).

Reaction equation: $H_2S_2O_8 + 2H_2O \rightarrow 2H_2SO_4 + H_2O_2$. During the concentration process, hydrogen peroxide is vaporized together with water. The vapours are collected and hydrogen peroxide of commercial strengths (30-40%) is obtained by fractional distillation under a pressure of 40 mm mercury (Hg).

When ammonium sulphate is electrolysed, potassium acid sulphate may be added after electrolysis and cooling. Potassium persulphate crystallizes out and can be separated from the mother liquor. Hydrogen peroxide solution can be obtained by treating a mixture of potassium persulphate and sulphuric acid with steam.

In 1954 about 10% of the world's hydrogen peroxide production was obtained from barium peroxide and over 80% was obtained by the electrolytic process. Nowadays the latter seems to be still predominant, but two new processes are of growing importance. The main expansion of hydrogen peroxide capacity since 1954 came from the *autoxidation process.*

The autoxidation process consists essentially of the reaction of 2-ethyl anthraquinone with hydrogen to give 2-ethyl anthraquinol (hydrogenation, reduction) followed by subsequent splitting off of the hydrogen with oxygen from the air (dehydrogenation, oxidation).

In this way 2-ethyl anthraquinone is reformed with the simultaneous formation of hydrogen peroxide, according to the equations:

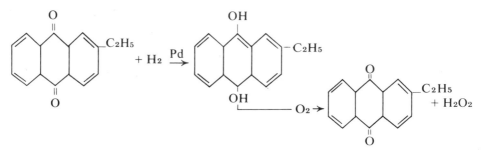

The process can be carried out by treating a solution of 2-ethylanthraquinone in a mixture of aromatic hydrocarbons and a higher alcohol or a cyclohexylester with pure hydrogen in the presence of a palladium catalyst, on a finely granulated support suspended in the solution. After separation from the catalyst, the hydrogenated solution is autoxidized with atmospheric oxygen by blowing air through the solution.

Hydrogen peroxide is separated from the organic solution by liquid-liquid extraction with de-ionized water i.e. water treated with base exchangers to remove ions. The organic solvent is recycled into the process, while the aqueous extract is collected and contains approximately 20% hydrogen peroxide.

The excess of hydrogen is continuously recycled in the hydrogenation stage. The oxygen content of the hydrogen recycled is recorded continuously in order to guard against the formation of explosive mixtures. Vapours of crganic solvents in waste gases are recovered by means of activated carbon and used again.

Fig. 6.1 is a picture of a modern British installation for the production of hydrogen peroxide by the autoxidation process. It is said to be Europe's biggest hydrogen peroxide plant. The plant cost was £2.5 million ($6 million). It is built almost entirely of aluminium and is installed in the open. The aluminium columns, piping etc. are separated from contact with steel structures, by the use of PVC sheet and roofing felt, to prevent corrosion.

The second new process is the partial oxidation of secondary alcohols with oxygen to ketones and hydrogen peroxide.

The process is performed by oxidizing isopropanol to acetone and hydrogen peroxide in the liquid phase at a temparature of 90-140° C and a pressure of 200 to 300

Fig. 6.1   An autoxidation hydrogen plant operated by Laporte Chemicals.

p.s.i. (14-20 atmosphere). (See also oxidation of alcohols, vol. IV). Reaction equation:

$$CH_3 - CH(OH) - CH_3 + O_2 \rightarrow CH_3 - \overset{\displaystyle O}{\overset{\|}{C}} - CH_3 + H_2O_2$$

The reaction is promoted by adding about 0.5 weight % hydrogen peroxide to the feedstock.

The reaction mixture is diluted with water, to avoid explosive conditions, and distilled to vaporize acetone and unconverted isopropanol. The remaining solution contains about 6-10% hydrogen peroxide. Unconverted isopropanol is recycled and acetone is sold as a by-product.

A plant for the production of hydrogen peroxide by this process, having a capacity of 30 million pounds a year has been built in the United States.

Oxidation of isopropanol may also be carried out in the vapour phase at a temperature of 350 to 500° C with air as an oxidizing agent.

Hydrogen peroxide solutions obtained by any of the processes described may be sold as such, but they are usually concentrated to standard commercial strengths. Hydrogen peroxide solutions are concentrated to 35 and 50% solutions by fractional distillation under a pressure of about 200 mm Hg.

High concentration hydrogen peroxide solutions (90-92%) are obtained by distillation in two stages under a pressure of 40-50 mm Hg. In the first stage about 70% and in the

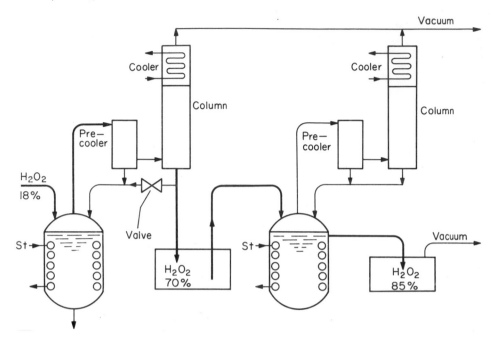

Fig. 6.2 A flow sheet of the concentration of diluted hydrogen peroxide by distillation in two stages.

second stage 90-92% hydrogen peroxide is obtained. Before distillation the pH is adjusted to lie between 3 and 5. The fractionating columns are constructed of aluminium and are either provided with ceramic Raschig rings or with plates. A flow sheet of the distillation of dilute hydrogen peroxide is given in fig. 6.2.

6.3 PROPERTIES AND STORAGE

Hydrogen peroxide is a colourless liquid miscible with water and glycerine in all proportions. The boiling point of pure hydrogen peroxide is 155.5° C, but since 100% hydrogen peroxide is not usually available, the physical constants of pure hydrogen peroxide are not of practical value.

Highly purified aqueous solutions of hydrogen peroxide are fairly stable. In the presence of impurities, such as traces of metal ions, hydrogen peroxide is decomposed into water and nascent oxygen. For this reason de-ionized water is used in hydrogen peroxide production. Decomposition of hydrogen peroxide is also catalysed by contact with various materials. Only a few such as aluminium, aluminium alloys, Pyrex glass, quartz and some plastics have no influence on the decomposition rate of hydrogen peroxide. On that account high purity aluminium is now used to manufacture equipment for production and containers for storage and transportation of hydrogen peroxide solutions, Hydroxyl ions cause rapid decomposition of hydrogen peroxide. Hence it cannot be stored in ordinary glass vessels for a long time, as alkali may dissolve from the glass.

The temperature of storage containers is recorded continuously as decomposition of hydrogen peroxide is accompanied by heat development, which in turn promotes the decomposition rate.

The stability of hydrogen peroxide may be increased by adding small quantities of one or more stabilizers. Sodium stannate, sodium pyrophosphate or mixtures of sodium pyrophosphate and 8-hydroxyquinoline stabilize hydrogen peroxide solutions when added in quantities of about 1 to 100 p.p.m.

Several other compounds having stabilizing properties are known, but they are not used commercially. Various stabilizing agents must not be used in hydrogen peroxide which is to be used in medicine.

Like water, hydrogen peroxide forms relatively stable crystalline addition compounds with several organic and inorganic compounds. For example, the dry urea addition compound can be stored for a long time (see also urea, p. 348).

6.4 USES

The greatest use of hydrogen peroxide is as a bleaching agent. The bleaching effect of hydrogen peroxide is due to its decomposition to water and nascent oxygen in the presence of hydroxyl ions and the oxidizing properties of the nascent oxygen obtained. Cellulose fibres such as cotton, linen, jute, rayon and wood pulp, and protein containing substances such as wool, hair and silk are bleached with 0.1 to 3% hydrogen peroxide solutions having a pH between 8 and 10.5 and a temperature between 40 and 75° C. These bleaching processes are used commercially in the textile and paper industries.

Wood may also be bleached with a hydrogen peroxide solution. The bleached wood is used for radio and television cabinets, baseball bats, etc.

Fats, oils, waxes and soaps may be decolourized by the oxidizing action of hydrogen peroxide but, in most cases, the coloured impurities are removed by absorption on activated carbon or silica gel.

Smaller quantities of hydrogen peroxide are used for bleaching tobacco, feathers, leather, bones and other animal and vegetable materials.

Although hydrogen peroxide is rather expensive, compared with other bleaching agents such as chlorine, it is preferred in some bleaching processes as it has a mild and specific action and its decomposition product is only water.

Considerable quantities of hydrogen peroxide are used as an energy source in aircraft jets, rockets and missiles. Concentrated hydrogen peroxide solutions (85-90%) are used for this purpose.

When hydrogen peroxide is decomposed in the presence of a catalyst the heat developed is more than sufficient to vaporize the water obtained. Hence a mixture of steam and oxygen, at high pressure, results. When used in rockets, jets or missiles this gas mixture is expanded by allowing it to escape through a cut-out with an enormous velocity. According to the fundamental law: 'action = reaction', the apparatus is propelled in the opposite direction.

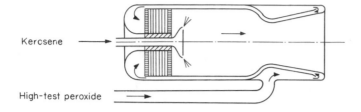

Kerosene

High-test peroxide

Fig. 6.3 Simplified diagram of a rocket motor propelled with kerosene and hydrogen peroxide –
(HTP).

The expansion of the steam oxygen mixture may be used as such for propulsion of
rockets etc., but is commonly combined with combustion of a fuel such as alcohol or
a hydrocarbon in the nascent oxygen obtained. Combustion with a fuel before expansion
of the steam oxygen mixture can approximately double the energy developed.

Fig. 6.3 shows a simplified diagram of a rocket motor propelled with kerosene and
hydrogen peroxide. HTP (= high test hydrogen peroxide = 85% hydrogen peroxide) is
preheated between the walls of the double-walled combustion chamber and decomposed
by passing through a catalyst chamber filled with silvered nickel wire-netting. The fuel
is sprayed into the steam oxygen mixture obtained, and combustion occurs. Hydrogen
peroxide and fuel are fed into the combustion chamber by pumps operated by the
exhaust gases.

In the United Kingdom, submarines which use hydrogen peroxide as an oxygen
source for combustion have been built.

In the United States lightweight helicopters have been produced in which propulsion
is obtained by hydrogen peroxide fuelled jets located in the rotors.

Considerable quantities of hydrogen peroxide are also used in the chemical industry.
An important application of hydrogen peroxide in chemical synthesis is the epoxidation
of ethylenically unsaturated oils and esters of fatty acids:

$$-C\overset{H_2}{=\!=}C\overset{H_2}{—} + H_2O_2 \rightarrow -C\overset{H_2}{\underset{\diagdown}{—}}C\overset{H_2}{\underset{\diagup}{—}} + H_2O$$
$$O$$

These reactions are performed in the presence of glacial acetic acid and an ion exchange
resin. Hydrogen peroxide forms peracetic acid from glacial acid in the presence of the
resin as a catalyst (see peracetic acid, vol. IV).

Peracetic acid reacts with the unsaturated compound to give an epoxide. The
epoxidized products are stabilizers and plasticizers for polyvinylchloride resins (see
vol. IV).

Hydrogen peroxide is also used for the oxidation of tertiary amines (see vol. IV)
according to the following equation:

$$\begin{matrix} R \\ R' \\ R'' \end{matrix}\!\!\!> N + H_2O_2 \rightarrow \begin{matrix} R \\ R' \\ R'' \end{matrix}\!\!\!> N \rightarrow O + H_2O$$

The resulting tertiary amine oxides are used in detergents and soap compositions.

The complete list of chemical uses of hydrogen peroxide is seemingly endless, but the quantities used are relatively small. Examples of the chemical uses are the production of organic and inorganic peroxides, peracids and insecticides. Some pharmaceuticals and several cosmetics contain hydrogen peroxide.

Hydrogen peroxide is also used as a blowing agent in the production of cellular and porous materials of rubber, plastics, concrete etc. Hydrogen peroxide is mixed with the materials to be foamed before hardening the latter. Oxygen obtained by decomposition of peroxide forms gas cells or pores in the material.

6.5 STATISTICS

The United States and Western Germany are the largest producers of hydrogen peroxide in the western world, producing each about 60 to 70 million pounds a year (on 100% basis). The United Kingdom is also a large producer of hydrogen peroxide but production data are not available. The installed capacity of the United States amounted to 115 million pounds a year in 1963. The excess capacity is due to the fact that the consumption for military uses in rockets etc. has not increased as much as expected during recent years.

New chemical processes which are potential consumers of hydrogen peroxide have been developed. In the United States a new process has been developed for the production of glycerine from allyl alcohol and hydrogen peroxide. The new German process for the production of caprolactam from cyclohexylamine and hydrogen peroxide may be introduced in the United States.

About 40% of the United States hydrogen peroxide is consumed for textile bleaching, and about 15% for bleaching of paper and paper pulp. The chemical industry consumes about 15-20% and another 15-20% is used as an energy source in the military field.

In the United States about 85-90% of all cotton bleaching is done with hydrogen peroxide. The amount of hydrogen peroxide consumed in the bleaching of wool and synthetic fibres seems to be small in the United States. The opposite is true in the United Kingdom.

The most important commercial grades of hydrogen peroxide are 3%, 6%, 35%, 50% and 90% hydrogen peroxide solutions. 90% hydrogen peroxide is mainly used as an energy source.

6.6 LITERATURE

'A new process for hydrogen peroxide', *The industrial chemist*. 1959, **35**, 9-15.

P. W. SHERWOOD. 'Hydrogen peroxide from petrochemical sources', *Chemical and process engineering*. 1960, **41**, 89-91, 97.

W. C. SCHUMB, C. N. SATTERFIELD and R. L. WENTWORTH. *Hydrogen peroxide*. New York, Reinhold, 1955. ACS monograph no. 128.

CHAPTER 7

The Halogens
and their Compounds

7.1 INTRODUCTION

The halogens form the seventh main group of the periodic system and comprise the non-metallic elements fluorine, chlorine, bromine, iodine and the very unstable radioactive element astatine. A comparision of the halogens among themselves shows that chlorine, bromine and iodine are allied but the first element (fluorine) occupies rather a special position as compared with the others (as is usual in the main groups of the periodic system).

Fluorine is invariably univalent in its compounds as distinct from the other halogens which can also exhibit valencies of three, five and seven (with the exception of bromine which is never heptavalent in its compounds). In addition chlorine forms chlorine dioxide (ClO_2) in which it is quadrivalent.

Fluorine corresponds in its behaviour with the other halogens in their unique property of forming strong oxygen-free acids and oxygen-free salts. The oxygen-free acids are hydrogen fluoride (HF), hydrogen chloride (HCl), hydrogen bromide (HBr) and hydrogen iodide (HI). The salts are fluorides, chlorides, bromides and iodides, corresponding with the oxygen-free acids in which the hydrogen atoms are replaced by metal atoms. The fluorides often differ from the other halides. The alkaline earth metal chlorides, bromides and iodides, for example, are very soluble in water but the alkaline earth metal fluorides are insoluble. Conversely silver halides are insoluble in water with the exception of silver fluoride.

Fluorine itself differs from the other halogens in respect of its inability to form acids which contain oxygen (oxyacids). Chlorine, bromine and iodine form various oxyacids.

They are monovalent in hypochlorous acid (HClO), hypobromous acid (HBrO) and hypoiodous acid (HIO). Chlorine, bromine and iodine are pentavalent in chloric acid ($HClO_3$), bromic acid ($HBrO_3$) and iodic acid (HIO_3). Chlorine and iodine can form perchloric acid ($HClO_4$) and periodic acid (HIO_4) wherein they are heptavalent. Chlorine also forms chlorous acid ($HClO_2$) in which it is trivalent. Many of these acids and salts derived from them are unstable, like the oxides from which the acids can be derived.

The tendency to form oxyacids increases from chlorine to iodine. This is shown by the fact that elementary iodine can liberate bromine and chlorine from their oxyacids, and bromine can liberate chlorine from its oxyacids. Conversely fluorine can liberate the other halogens from the salts of their oxygen free acids (chlorides, bromides and iodides). Chlorine displaces bromine and iodine in bromides and iodides, and bromine only displaces iodine in iodides.

7.2 F L U O R I N E (F$_2$, mole weight = 38.00)

7.2.1 History and occurrence

Although Scheele had obtained hydrogen fluoride (HF) in 1771 by treating fluorspar with sulphuric acid, the element was not isolated until 1886 by H. Moissan, who obtained it by electrolysis of a solution of potassium hydrogen fluoride in anhydrous hydrogen chloride at a temperature of $-23°$ C. The name fluorine is derived from the mineral calcium fluoride which is named 'fluorspar' because of its fluxing power (from the latin *fluere* meaning to flow).

Fluorine does not occur free in nature, with the exception of traces which are found as occlusions in some felspars. Many minerals such as cryolite, topaz, tourmaline and some species of mica contain fluorine. Cryolite (Na$_3$AlF$_6$) is an important fluorine mineral, which is used as a flux in electrolytic aluminium production (see vol. III, Aluminium). Fluorine is also a constituent of the calcareous parts of animal organisms (bones, teeth, marine shells etc.).

The main source for the production of fluorine and its compounds is the mineral fluorspar (CaF$_2$). Commercially important deposits of this mineral are widely distributed (see fluorspar in vol. II). Appreciable quantities of fluorine also occur in phosphate rocks which contain fluorapatite (see calcium phosphate, p. 378) so that fluorine compounds arise as by-product in the form of fluosilicic acid or fluorsilicates.

7.2.2 Production

Fluorine is produced by electrolysis of hydrogen fluoride. The various processes vary mainly in the composition of the electrolyte. (Liquid anhydrous hydrogen fluoride must be made electrically conductive by the addition of metal fluorides.) Usually the electrolyte is composed of one of the complex salts of potassium fluoride and hydrogen fluoride of the formula KF.(HF)n. The preferred electrolyte for most large cells is the bifluoride KF.2HF (which has a melting point of 71.7° C) to which an excess of hydrogen fluoride is added periodically as the source of the fluorine. The temperature of operation is a little below 100° C.

Various types of cells having a capacity of up to several thousand amperes are employed in the industrial production of the element. One industrial cell having a capacity of 4000-6000 amps is roughly 6 ft long by 3 ft wide and 2 ft 6 in deep (see fig. 7.1) and contains nearly a ton of electrolyte. It comprises a mild steel tank, a mild steel cathode, a 'skirt' or septum to keep the anodic gas (fluorine) and cathodic gas (hydrogen) separated, and a set of porous carbon anodes. (Under anodic condition in the electrolyte (KF.2HF) carbon in the form of natural graphite swells rapidly and disintegrates.) Provision is made for either heating or cooling the electrolyte by passing hot or cold water through cooling coils immersed in the electrolyte in the cathode space. The disposal of these components in a cell is best understood by reference to fig. 7.2

Fig. 7.1 A British fluorine cell room.

which shows the arrangement of a laboratory fluorine cell made available to university and industrial laboratories to facilitate research into fluorine chemistry. These cells are made in two sizes, 10 A and 60 A, producing 7 g and 40 g F_2 per hr respectively. These, unlike the commercial cells, do not require internal cooling arrangements. Notwithstanding the aggressive nature of fluorine, it is stated that cells of this type only require servicing about once every two years.

In the USA diffusion plants for the separation of uranium 235 from natural uranium have their own fluorine plants. These can produce 7600 lb F_2 per day (1200 short tons/year) from 40 cells each of 6000 A capacity. The feed is of high purity (99.95%) anhydrous hydrogen fluoride. The cells, made of Monel, hold 3000 lb of electrolyte, and each has 32 carbon anodes 2 in × 8 in × 20 in. A cylindrical jacket or 'skirt' of Monel sheet immersed 4 inches in the electrolyte separates the fluorine and hydrogen produced in the cell, and attached to the 'skirt' is an open mesh Monel screen or diaphragm. In this respect these cells differ from the laboratory cell described above. The anodic current density is nearly 0.2 A/cm² and the voltage lies in the range of 8-12 volts. In these cells appreciable voltage increases sometimes occur. This is referred to as polarization and to overcome the difficulty shock treatment such

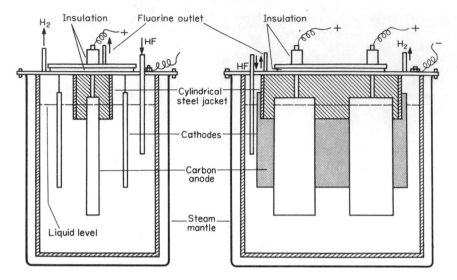

Fig. 7.2 Diagram showing the arrangement of components in a fluorine cell. The carbon anode is surrounded by a cylindrical steel jacket to prevent fluorine mixing with hydrogen evolved at the steel cathodes. The broken line shows the level of the molten hydrogen fluoride/potassium fluoride electrolyte.

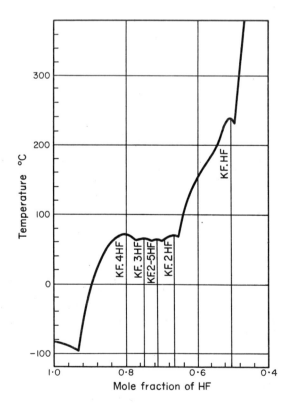

Fig. 7.3 Melting points of the KF/HF electrolyte systems.

as raising the applied voltage to 50 V is required. The addition of lithium fluoride is said to have a beneficial effect.

It is important that the temperature of the electrolyte should never fall below its freezing point since expansion and contraction during freezing and remelting puts a severe strain on the carbon anodes and causes them to crack. The changes in melting point with composition in the KF.2HF system are shown in fig. 7.3.

Cell life is stated to be limited by corrosion of the metal current leads (invariably of copper) at the point of attachment to the anodes.

The hydrogen evolved at the cathode and the fluorine evolved at the anode leave the cell and are collected separately. Both gases are charged with hydrogen fluoride vapour at a concentration determined by the temperature and composition of the electrolyte. Thus for a typical potassium bifluoride (KF.2HF) electrolyte at a temperature of 80° C the vapour pressure of hydrogen fluoride in the gases is 21 mm Hg, which corresponds to a mole percentage in the gases of about 3%. It is desirable that hydrogen fluoride should be scrubbed from the hydrogen before it is discharged to atmosphere, and from the fluorine before it is used. A convenient method is to pass the gases through separate scrubbers containing sodium fluoride. The HF which is present to the extent of 4-8% in the gases forms the double compound NaF.HF. In the USA the HF is removed in some plants by refrigeration at −15° C. Final traces can be removed from hydrogen by means of caustic potash solution; caustic soda is unsuitable because it forms a fluoride of low solubility.

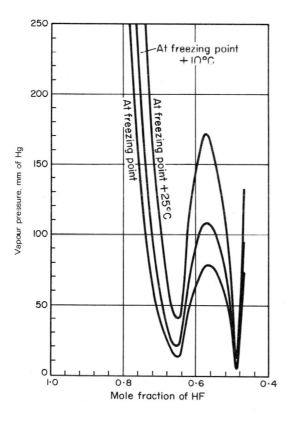

Fig. 7.4 Partial pressure of hydrogen fluoride over the KF/HF system.

The effect of composition on the vapour pressure of hydrogen fluoride over the KF/HF system is shown in fig. 7.4.

Fig. 7.5 shows the essential features of a fluorine plant. It is of vital importance that even traces of organic matter or reactive metal be excluded from contact with elementary fluorine. Very thin gasket material should be used and should not project beyond the inside edges of flanges. The preferred materials are polytetrafluoroethylene or a special grade of neoprene.

Fluorine cells operate at high current efficiencies (90-96%). The residual loss of current efficiency is attributed to recombination of hydrogen and fluorine and to the electrolysis of traces of water in the hydrogen fluoride feed. In this connection it is customary to employ rigorously dried hydrogen fluoride. Published information suggests that US cells require the water content to be as low as 0.001%-0.003%, but British cells are not so exacting and can tolerate up to 0.2% of water. Apart from causing a loss of current efficiency the presence of water in the electrolyte leads to the production of oxygen fluoride (F_2O) in the gas. This may be objectionable for some purposes (see below). The purity of fluorine will normally be better than 99.5%. Apart from the oxide the likely impurities are carbon tetrafluoride and sulphur hexafluoride which are stable towards fluorine.

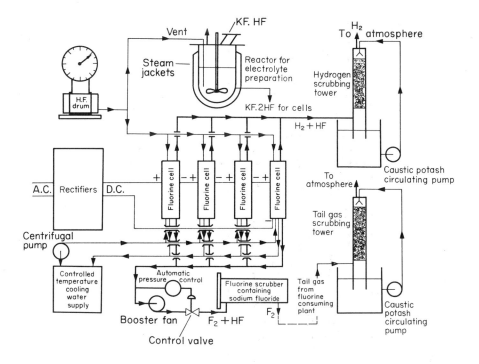

Fig. 7.5   Diagram showing the essential features of a fluorine plant.

7.2.3 Storage and transportation

Because of its high reactivity it is customary to use fluorine captively (i.e. directly near the plant producing it). In the USA it has been packed by compressing into cylinders, but the practice incurs an element of risk and elaborate precautions have to be taken by the user since it is possible for valves to ignite in the gas during use.

More recently in the USA and Britain liquid fluorine has been transported in tonnage quantities (compare chlorine storage). The fluorine is first liquefied in a condenser cooled in liquid nitrogen which has a boiling point 8° C lower than liquid fluorine. From the condenser it flows into the middle container of a triple-shell tanker. This container, which is made of Monel, is surrounded by a tank containing liquid nitrogen, which in turn is surrounded by the outer shell, the intermediate space being packed with an insulating powder in a vacuum. The fluorine in the inner compartment is maintained under its own vapour pressure, which is below atmospheric; any heat flow into the system is compensated for by a small evaporation of liquid nitrogen. In the USA a liquid fluorine container of this type weighs 2 tons and holds $2^{1}/_{4}$ tons of fluorine.

7.2.4 Properties

Fluorine is a yellow gas somewhat paler than chlorine. It has a melting point of $-219.6°$ C and a boiling point of $-188°$ C. It is a 'permanent gas', its critical temperature being $-129°$ C. It is the most electronegative of the elements and therefore the most powerful oxidizing agent. Reactions often need to be initiated but then proceed explosively or with detonation since the energy evolved leads to a sharp temperature rise. The energy of the reaction $H_2 + F_2 = 2HF$ is 128.4 kcal, which compares with the corresponding value of 115.6 kcal in the formation of two molecules of water. The reaction with water yields hydrogen fluoride, oxygen, hydrogen peroxide, fluorine monoxide and occasionally ozone.

Fluorine reacts vigorously with the other elements at room temperature, frequently with ignition. The resulting products are themselves usually highly reactive but some, such as sulphur hexafluoride and carbon tetrafluoride, are remarkably inert. Recent work has shown that reactivity with fluorine even extends to krypton and xenon, which were previously thought to be completely inert chemically.

Fluorine is potentially capable of reacting with all metals, but several in the massive form tend to form a protective layer which prevents further attack at temperatures below those at which the film is appreciably volatile. Metals which form volatile fluorides include uranium, tungsten, molybdenum, titanium and zirconium. The metals of low fluoride volatility include steel, copper, aluminium, nickel and magnesium, and alloys such as Monel and certain brasses; these can be employed for constructional purposes.

7.2.5 Uses and statistics

Most commercial fluorine-containing products stem from hydrogen fluoride rather than from elementary fluorine. Elementary fluorine so far has found its major application in the field of atomic energy and there is additionally a prospective large scale application in rocketry. Outside the atomic energy and rocketry fields there is little production of sulphur hexafluoride (see below).

In the atomic energy field natural uranium has to be converted to uranium hexafluoride (UF_6) so that it can be enriched in respect of the fissionable isotope [235]U in a diffusion plant (see uranium, ch. 15). Uranium hexafluoride is made by fluorinating the metal, its oxide or its tetrafluoride at a suitable temperature with either elementary fluorine or hydrogen fluoride.

Other uses for elementary fluorine in connection with nuclear power are in the production of the fluorinating agents chlorine trifluoride (ClF_3) and bromine trifluoride (BrF_3), and in the production of inert lubricants (fully fluorinated hydrocarbons or chlorofluoro hydrocarbons) for equipment handling fluorine, such as valves, fans and pumps.

Chlorine trifluoride and bromine trifluoride are almost as reactive as fluorine but they are easier to handle because they are liquids at room temperature. These products are prepared by mixing the elements in stoichiometric proportions.

Bromine trifluoride, for example, is used in recovery of uranium from radioactive waste. When the fissionable content of metal in a nuclear reactor has been partly spent, it is necessary to remove the fission products from the metal and either restore its ^{235}U concentration in a diffusion plant or fortify it with enriched material. One method under consideration for treating the spent fuel is to dissolve the metal rods in bromine trifluoride and thus convert the uranium, the fission products and plutonium into their fluorides. The radioactive fission products can then be eliminated by a suitable fractionation procedure which yields a radioactive-free uranium hexafluoride, suitable for transfer to a diffusion plant or to a plant for mixing with enriched uranium hexa-fluoride. The plutonium is recovered as the tetrafluoride. In this connection bromine trifluoride is more reactive than chlorine trifluoride presumably as a result of its ionic nature indicated by the equilibrium

$$2\,BrF_3 \longleftrightarrow BrF_2^+ + BrF_4^-.$$

In another process, applicable to partly spent fuel elements containing uranium within a cladding metal or alloyed with it, the fluorination is carried out in a fused fluoride medium using anhydrous HF and elementary fluorine. An example of such a medium is the low melting point bath of sodium fluoride/zirconium fluoride at 600-700° C.

In rocketry, liquid fluorine participates in bipropellant systems of the highest energy storage value. It has to be stored cryogenically (see above). It is considered that an immediate advance in rocket engine performance could be obtained through the use of fluorine with a conventional fuel such as hydrazine, since it would yield an increase in specific impulse of 46 sec over that obtained in a conventional hydrocarbon system. (The specific impulse I is the amount of thrust in pounds that can be obtained per pound of propellant consumed per second.)

The USA and the UK are the major producers of elementary fluorine in the free world since nearly all elementary fluorine produced goes into nuclear processing applications. The quantity produced is not disclosed, but the US production in 1963 may be up to 10000 short tons (up to 50% of the hydrogen fluoride consumption by the Atomic Energy Commission in the UK which was about 20000 short tons in 1963).

7.3 HYDROGEN FLUORIDE

7.3.1 History

Anhydrous hydrogen fluoride, although a relative newcomer to industry, ranks as a tonnage chemical. It is an essential intermediate for practically all the products in the newly developed fluorine technology. Until 1942 there was little demand for hydrogen fluoride in Britain, although in the USA a use had developed in the production of fluorinated organic chemicals and in the petrochemical industry in the early 1930s. In Britain the demand arose in connection with the production of uranium for the atomic bomb, for which purpose it was required both as a hydrofluorinating agent and as a source of fluorine in fluorine cells.

7.3.2 Production

Anhydrous hydrogen fluoride (HF) is manufactured in horizontal or near horizontal retorts by the action of sulphuric acid ($> 96\%$ H_2SO_4) on powdered fluorspar according to the reaction $CaF_2 + H_2SO_4 \rightarrow CaSO_4 + 2HF$.

The pre-heated and pre-mixed feeds (5-10% excess H_2SO_4) are passed into the retort at one end and moved progressively to the discharge at the opposite end. In some plants the retort itself rotates and the charge is moved by the action of helical flights attached to the inside of the retort. In others the shell of the retort is fixed and the charge is moved by rotating internal blades. The retort is heated in the range 200-350° C to drive off the HF gas which passes out to condensers after passing through scrubbers to remove sulphuric acid spray and dust. The condensed product may be purified by distillation: the initial pasty mix changes to a dry solid in its passage through the reactor and is discharged continuously. It is suitable for making building products.

An American retort of the type described is 40 ft long and 6 ft in diameter, and is constructed of $^3/_4$ inch thick steel; it rotates at 1 rev/min and is heated by means of gas or oil. Its capacity is 6 tons per day of 80% acid.

An important aspect of reactors is the form of the inlet and discharge connections to avoid escape of the noxious vapours, or to prevent the ingress of moist air which would impair the quality of the product and hinder the condensation of the product gas. Steel is not a satisfactory material of construction for acid of strength lower than 70% HF. Carbon, lead, bronze, copper, Monel or rubber-lined materials must be used for less concentrated acids. Lead is often used for solutions containing less than 60% HF.

The resistance of lead is sensitive to fluorosilicic acid contents of > 2 3%. Monel is adversely affected by aeration, while copper is widely used for distillation plants. The reaction of calcium fluoride and sulphuric acid is endothermic, and heat has to be applied to enable the reaction to proceed to near completion. Some idea of the rate of reaction is afforded by a statement that to effect the release of 98% of the fluorine from fluorspar the reaction time required is 30-60 minutes at 200-250° C with the HF leaving at 100-150° C. An excessive temperature leads to corrosion difficulties, and in practice a compromise has to be struck between efficient utilization of the fluorspar and the cost of corrosion.

Apart from the main reaction there are side reactions which are of economic importance. Thus commercial fluorspar contains silica which reacts to give silicon tetrafluoride:

$$4HF + SiO_2 \rightarrow SiF_4 + 2H_2O$$

The silicon tetrafluoride has little value. It leaves the system in the tail gas which is absorbed in water to give a 40% solution of HF containing 6-10% fluorosilicic acid. Calcium carbonate in the fluorspar leads to wasteful consumption of sulphuric acid and dilution of the product gas with CO_2. Sulphur impurities in the fluorspar give rise to sulphide and sulphur dioxide in the gas and the deposition of sulphur in the product lines, which can be troublesome.

Hydrofluoric acid (aqueous solution of HF) is made in the same way as anhydrous hydrogen fluoride, but the product is absorbed in water instead of being condensed.

7.3.3 Storage and transportation

In its anhydrous form hydrogen fluoride does not react with most of the common construction materials such as mild steel, nickel and nickel alloys, copper, etc. In the USA anhydrous hydrogen fluoride is supplied in two grades containing $<$ 99.5% and 99.9% HF (the remainder is water, sulphuric acid and fluorosilicic acid). Hydrogen fluoride is shipped in steel cylinders, drums and tank cars holding up to 40 tons. As with all easily liquefiable gases special attention must be paid to maximum allowable filling ratio (compare chlorine, p. 221).

Hydrofluoric acid is marketed in several concentrations. Acid of 60-70% strength can be shipped in the USA in steel drums of 20, 55 and 110 gallon capacity. The usual impurities are fluorosilicic acid and sulphuric acid but grades are supplied containing less than 0.1% of each. In small quantities, hydrofluoric acid was formerly shipped in lead, gutta percha or cerasin bottles only, but nowadays polyethylene is a more satisfactory material for small containers. Both anhydrous hydrogen fluoride and hydrofluoric acid rapidly attack glassware.

7.3.4 Properties

Hydrogen fluoride is a liquid (b.p. 19.4° C and m.p. $-83°$ C). At 88° C and 740 mm the density of the gas corresponds with the formula HF but between $28 - 38°$ C it corresponds to the dimer $(HF)_2$ at low pressure, and to more highly associated species at higher pressures. In this respect hydrogen fluoride differs from the other hydrogen halides. It is this tendency to associate which accounts for the high boiling point (compare HCl $-83°$ C, HBr $-68°$ C, HI $-36°$ C). There is evidence that in solution the ion HF_2 exists: the electrical conductivity of pure hydrogen fluoride is of the order of 10^{-5} Ω cm at $-15°$ C, but small amounts of dissolved material lead to large increases in conductivity. It is miscible in all proportions with water, the freezing point curve showing maxima corresponding to $H_2O.HF$, $H_2O(HF)_2$ and $H_2O(HF)_4$. The constant boiling mixture (azeotropic mixture) boils at 120° C and contains 36% of hydrogen fluoride.

Liquid hydrogen fluoride is outstanding as a solvent for both inorganic and organic compounds. Its uses are limited in many cases by its reactivity but it provides a medium for decomposition and precipitation reactions which parallel those which occur in water. For instance the following precipitation reaction can be carried out:

$$TlF + KClO_4 \rightarrow TlClO_4 + KF.$$

The hazards with dilute hydrofluoric acid are essentially those of any mineral acid, and with sensible precautions the acid can be handled safely. The stronger acids and anhydrous hydrogen fluoride are extremely corrosive to the skin, and danger from contact with them is heightened by the fact that the effects are not immediately apparent: very severe and painful burns develop only gradually after contact. Inhalation of the vapour can cause fatal oedema of the lungs. When working with the concentrated solutions and the anhydrous liquid full protective clothing comprising polyvinyl chloride aprons and gloves, face shields and head covering should be employed, and the working area should be well ventilated. In the event of accidental contact the skin or eyes should be irrigated with copious quantities of water and medical attention sought immediately. Penetration of the acid can be arrested by a timely subcutaneous injection of sodium gluconate around the affected parts.

7.3.5 Uses

Anhydrous hydrogen fluoride is mainly used for the production of fluorinated hydrocarbons, chlorofluorinated hydrocarbons (freons) and other organic fluorine compounds (see vol. IV) which may be used as refrigerants, solvents, lubricants, insecticides, etc. One of the freons (chlorodifluoromethane) is used for the production of tetrafluoroethylene ($CF_2=CF_2$) which polymerizes under pressure to yield the well known plastic 'Teflon'.

Hydrogen fluoride is also used in the electrochemical production of fluorinated chemicals in the Simons cell. In this process the electrolyte is either anhydrous hydrogen fluoride alone or in combination with a solute to render it electrically conducting. Such electrolytes have a strong solvent action. The Simons cell process has application to the production of specialized compounds.

Anhydrous hydrogen fluoride has the advantage of sometimes preserving functional groups in a compound intact whilst exhaustively replacing hydrogen atoms in skeletal positions.

In the petroleum industry anhydrous hydrogen fluoride is used for desulphurizing petroleum, and also in catalytic alkylation and isomerisation reactions to improve the anti-knock properties of gasoline, etc. Hydrogen fluoride is also used in the production of elementary fluorine (see above) and fluorosulphonic acid (see below).

The major portion of aqueous hydrofluoric acid is used for the production of aluminium fluoride and synthetic cryolite, which are starting materials in electrolytic aluminium production.

Hydrofluoric acid has also considerable use in metallurgical industries for the descaling of metals, in the glass industry for etching and in the production of a number of inorganic fluorides for use in fluxes, plating baths, catalysts, and in impregnating arc-carbons and in extractive metallurgy. The last application is important because the great affinity of fluorine for the alkali and alkaline earth metals can give rise to the 'thermite' type of reaction. An example is the production of uranium metal by the reduction of the tetrafluoride by reaction with calcium or magnesium. Another use which may develop is in fluoride electrolytes, e.g. potassium fluorzirconate, for the electrolytic extraction of metals such as zirconium and titanium.

7.3.6 Statistics

The world production of hydrogen fluoride and hydrofluoric acid is not precisely known, but the USA is the most important producer. In 1963 about 216 000 short tons were produced in the USA (including amounts which were converted into fluorine products without isolation of the acid). This corresponds with about 55% of the total fluorspar consumption of about 740 000 tons.

The USA consumption of hydrogen fluoride and hydrofluoric acid in 1963 by kind of use is shown in the following table:

	Percentage of total consumption
Aluminium production: aluminium fluoride	30
synthetic cryolite	10
Fluorocarbons production	30
Uranium production	10
Stainless steel pickling	5
Other metals and ore treatment	4
Petroleum alkylation	5
Inorganic fluorides (excluding aluminium compounds)	4
Etching and frosting	1
Miscellaneous	1

In 1965 the US prices of hydrogen fluoride were for aqueous 70% in tanks \$ 13.40 per 100 lb, in 55 gallon drums \$ 19.25 per 100 lb, anhydrous in tanks \$ 18 per 100 lb. In the UK 60% acid in ton lots was sold at £ 110 per long ton.

7.4 OTHER FLUORINE COMPOUNDS

Sodium fluoride (NaF) and *sodium bifluoride* (sodium hydrogen fluoride, $NaHF_2$) are white crystalline powders which are made by treating soda ash or caustic soda with aqueous hydrofluoric acid under controlled pH conditions. Sodium fluoride is used mainly as a flux for steel plating, for impregnating wood, for adding to drinking water to combat tooth decay and for frosting of glass. Sodium bifluoride is used in the process for tinning tin plate (i.e. thin steel sheet). It is also used for acidifying scouring baths in textile mills, for etching and frosting glass, for removing iron stains and for cleaning stone buildings.

In the USA, the production of sodium fluoride was about 5 900 short tons in 1964. The US price of sodium fluoride (95%) was \$ 0.14 to \$ 0.15 per lb in 1965. In the UK it was sold at £ 5 15s 6d per cwt in the same year.

Ammonium bifluoride (ammonium hydrogen fluoride NH_4HF_2) is obtained in the form of flakes by passing ammonia through an aqueous hydrochloric acid solution, followed by evaporating the resulting solution to allow ammonium bifluoride to crystallize. Ammonium bifluoride is extensively used in the frosting of decorative glass articles (e.g. lamp blanks). It is also used in cleaning stone buildings, in timber preservation, for acidifying water in oil wells, and for cleaning pipes used to convey beer. In the USA the price of ammonium bifluoride was $ 0.22 to $ 0.24 per lb in 1965.

Boron trifluoride (BF₃) is manufactured by first treating borax with hydrofluoric acid, or boric acid with ammonium fluoride or bifluoride, to form an intermediate compound $Na_2O(BF_3)_4$ or $(NH_4)_2 O (BF_3)_4$. The intermediate is then reacted with fuming sulphuric acid or oleum (20% SO_3). The gas evolved is passed through a cooling tower which also removes spray, and then compressed into steel cylinders at 1 800 lb/in² pressure. An alternative method is to react boric acid with fluorosulphonic acid. The commercial gas which usually contains 99% BF₃ can be handled in glass equipment provided that HF and water are absent.

Boron trifluoride is a colourless gas with a boiling point of − 100.3° C which fumes in air as a result of hydrolysis. It readily forms complexes with oxygen and nitrogen-containing organic compounds. Thus the complex with acetic acid which is a viscous liquid containing 40% BF₃ is commercially available.

Boron trifluoride is mainly used as a catalyst in numerous organic reactions, e.g. in decomposition reactions such as cracking of hydrocarbon oils, dehydration of alcohols, acids and ketones, polymerization of unsaturated compounds, and alkylation, halogenation, oxidation and hydrogenation reactions.

Fluoroboric acid (fluoboric acid, HBF₄) is prepared in the form of an aqueous solution by dissolving boron trifluoride in concentrated hydrofluoric acid. The commercial solutions usually contain about 42% fluoroboric acid. These solutions can be converted into *fluoroborates* (MBF₄, wherein M stands for a metal atom) by neutralizing with the appropriate hydroxide or carbonate. Ammonium, sodium, potassium, copper, silver, zinc, cadmium, tin, lead, chromium, iron and nickel fluoroborates are available commercially. Both fluoroboric acid and fluoroborates are used in electroplating (especially lead and tin plating). Fluoroboric acid is also used in electropolishing of aluminium and for cleaning metals preparatory to electroplating.

Aluminium fluoride (AlF₃) is made by adding hydrated alumina (aluminium hydroxide) to hydrofluoric acid, followed by crystallization, filtration and calcination. It may also be prepared by the reaction of hydrated alumina with gaseous HF at temperatures above 400° C.

Aluminium fluoride forms white or colourless crystals which sublime at temperatures of about 1 200-1 300° C. Aluminium fluoride is very slightly soluble in almost all inorganic and organic solvents (about 0.5 g dissolve in 100 g water at 25° C) and is relatively inert chemically. It decomposes slowly on melting with sodium carbonate, and on treatment with steam at elevated temperature.

Aluminium fluoride is mainly used for the electrolytic production of aluminium and for the production of synthetic cryolite (see below). Small quantities of aluminium fluoride are used as a flux and opacifier in the production of glass and enamels. In the USA about 81 500 short tons of aluminium fluoride were produced in 1963.

Cryolite (Na₃AlF₆) is prepared synthetically by reacting a mixture of hydrated alumina (or aluminium fluoride) and caustic soda with hydrofluoric acid at a temperature of 85-100° C.

$$Al_2O_3.3H_2O + 6NaOH + 12HF \rightarrow 2Na_3AlF_6 + 12H_2O$$

The resulting cryolite precipitates and is recovered by filtration.

Natural cryolite is obtained from deposits in Greenland from which it is extracted by open-pit mining methods. The impure mined product is purified by conventional methods such as screening, hand-picking, magnetic separation and flotation (see mining of ores, vol. III).

Cryolite is very slightly soluble in water. Its melting point is about $1000°$ C. In its molten form, cryolite is employed as the solvent for alumina in the electrolytic aluminium production cell. It is also used as a flux in metallurgy and as a filler in resin or rubber-bonded abrasive wheels.

Silicon tetrafluoride (SiF_4) occurs as a by-product in the phosphate fertilizer industry but is usually collected after it has reacted with water to form fluorosilicic acid or sodium fluorosilicate. It can be regenerated by heating the sodium fluorosilicate with sulphuric acid and diatomaceous earth in a jacketed lead tank at a maximum temperature of $70°$ C. It is a colourless fuming gas which is compressed into steel cylinders for distribution. One of its uses is to 'kill' the unreacted alkali in freshly made concrete to improve its resistance to weathering. It may also be used to seal oil boreholes.

Fluorosilicic acid (hydrofluorosilicic acid, silicofluoric acid, H_2SiF_6) and *sodium fluorosilicate* (sodium silicofluoride, Na_2SiF_6) are formed by dissolving silicon tetrafluoride in water and caustic soda solution respectively. Both the acid and the salt are recovered cheaply from the gases formed in superphosphate manufacture (see above and calcium phosphate, p. 378). Fluorosilic acid is commercially available in the form of a 30-35% aqueous solution. The sodium salt is a colourless crystalline solid. Fluorosilicic acid and its salts are very poisonous. They are used as constituents of disinfectants (in breweries), defoliators (mixed with cyanamide) especially for cotton crops to facilitate mechanical harvesting, rat poisons and insecticides. Mixed with sodium chlorate they are employed for removing magnesium from aluminium magnesium alloys. Fluorosilicic acid is also used for the production of various fluorosilicates (by neutralizing with the corresponding metal oxide or hydroxide). Zinc fluorosilicate and calcium fluorosilicate are used as wood preservatives and as insoluble insecticides. Ammonium fluorosilicate is used as a dry insecticide in combination with silica gel. Potassium fluorosilicate is being used more widely for producing frit. The production of synthetic mica may entail the use of large quantities.

In the USA about 40 000 short tons of sodium fluorosilicate were produced in 1963. This quantity is about two-thirds of the total fluorosilicic acid and fluorosilicate production in the USA. The US price of fluorosilicic acid in 1965 was around $ 0.06 per lb. Sodium fluorosilicate was sold at $ 0.08 to $ 0.09 per lb in the USA, and at £35 per long ton in the UK in 1965.

Hexafluorophosphates are salts of hexafluorophosphoric acid (HPF_6). An aqueous solution of the acid is prepared by treating phosphorous pentoxide with hydrogen fluoride $P_2O_5 + 12HF \rightarrow 2HPF_6 + 5H_2O$.

Salts of hexafluorophosphoric acid are prepared by neutralizing the acid with the corresponding metal oxide, hydroxide or carbonate. Fluorophosphates are claimed to have applications in electropolishing aluminium and stainless steel.

Antimony trifluoride (SbF_3) may be prepared by reacting hydrofluoric acid with antimony trioxide or trichloride. The resulting product is a white crystalline solid which is useful as a catalyst in fluorination and hydrofluorination reaction in organic chemistry.

Sulphur hexafluoride (SF_6) is manufactured by reacting sulphur with elementary fluorine. The crude gas contains the tetrafluoride (SF_4, b.p. $-37°$ C), and the decafluoride (S_2F_{10}, m.p. $-92°$ C, b.p. $29°$ C), which are toxic. The latter impurity can be removed from sulphur hexafluoride by pyrolysis at 400-600° C, which brings about disproportionation

$$S_2F_{10} \xrightarrow{\text{400-600° C}} SF_4 + SF_6.$$

The tetrafluoride is removable by caustic scrubbing. The purified gas is compressed into steel cylinders for distribution. Sulphur hexafluoride is a very dense, colourless gas (about five times heavier than air) which is notable for its high chemical stability. On cooling it forms a white solid at −63.7° C. It is inert and virtually non-toxic. The electrical breakdown voltage of SF_6 is some two-and-a-half times that of air, and it finds application, principally in the United States, as a spark extinguishing medium in high-voltage electrical equipment such as switchgear, cables (gas-filled), x-ray machines and van de Graaf generators. To prevent deterioration of the gas in any apparatus by repeated sparking it is advisable to include some KF as a scavenger for any breakdown products.

Fluorosulphonic acid (HSO_3F) is prepared commercially by treating hydrogen fluoride with sulphur trioxide under anhydrous conditions. The resulting product is a colourless liquid having an irritating odour and fuming in moist air. It is used as a catalyst in the alkylation of hydrocarbons and in the polymerization of olefins. It may also be used in the synthesis of various organic compounds such as alkylfluorosulphonates, arylsulphofluorides and sulphamic acid.

7.5 LITERATURE

A. K. BARBOUR. 'Industrial aspects of fluorine chemistry', *Chemistry and Industry* (July 1961), pp. 958-72.

J. F. GALL. 'Recent advances in fluorine chemistry and technology', *American Rocket Society Journal* (Feb. 1959), pp. 95-103.

V. GUTMANN, ed. *Halogen chemistry*. Vol. I. London, Academic Press, 1967.

R. N. HASZELDINE and A. G. SHARPE. *Fluorine and its compounds*. Methuen (Monographs on chemical subjects), 1951.

H. R. LEECK. 'Some aspects of inorganic fluoric compounds in chemical industry', *Chemistry and industry* (1960), pp. 242-50.

J. W. MELLOR. *Comprehensive treatise on inorganic chemistry*, vol. II, suppl. II, part 1. London, Longmans, 1956.

J. RUDGE. *The manufacture and use of fluorine and its compounds*. Oxford University Press, 1962.

7.6 CHLORINE (Cl_2, mole weight = 70.9)

7.6.1 History and occurrence

Chlorine (the name is derived from the Greek word *chloros,* meaning yellow-green), was discovered in 1774 by Scheele, the famous Swedish pharmacist and chemist. His method of producing chlorine from hydrochloric acid (obtained from common salt and sulphuric acid) and manganese dioxide continued to be used industrially for over a century until it was superseded by more economical methods. Chlorine quickly became of commercial importance since some years after its discovery it was found in France that chlorine had a bleaching effect.

Owing to its great affinity for most other elements chlorine occurs usually in the form of compounds. In a free state it is only found in some volcanic gases. Chlorine occurs mainly in the form of common salt (NaCl), potassium chloride (KCl), magnesium chloride ($MgCl_2$), and various double salts of the chlorides mentioned (see under the various headings). Small quantities of chlorine are found in the form of chlorates and perchlorates in Chile saltpetre. In the form of hydrochloric acid it occurs in living organisms (e.g. in gastric juice) and in some volcanic gases. By far the most common raw material used for the production of chlorine is common salt.

7.6.2 Production

Most of the chlorine manufactured today is made by electrolytic processes (see p. 429).

When an electric current (direct current) is passed through a strong solution of sodium or potassium chloride between non-corrodible electrodes, e.g. graphite or platinum anodes and iron or graphite cathodes, chlorine is liberated at the anode; the reaction is represented by the equation

$$2Cl^- \rightarrow Cl_2 + 2e$$

This accounts for approximately 97% of the current flowing through the cell. The remainder of the ionic current, is attributable to discharge of hydroxyl ions:

$$OH^- \rightarrow OH \text{ radicals} + e.$$

The OH radicals react to produce hypochlorous acid, oxygen, carbon oxides (by reaction with graphite anodes) or chlorate ions. The OH^- arises from the ionization of water or migrates from the area of the cathode.

At the cathode the primary reaction is the discharge of hydrogen ions (H^+)

$$a \quad H_2O \rightarrow H^+ + OH^- \qquad b \quad H^+ \rightarrow \tfrac{1}{2}H_2 - e$$

Thus the discharge of H^+ leaves an excess of OH^- so that the solution in the vicinity of the cathode becomes progressively more alkaline. It is interesting to note that the discharge of H^+ occurs even though the concentration may only be about 10^{-13}. This is due to the fact that the tendency of hydrogen ions to be discharged is much higher than that of the alternative sodium ions. If a cathode which is not inert, such as mercury, is used, Na^+ is discharged preferentially (see Amalgam cells and Diaphragm cells in the Alkali metal chapter).

In the electrolysis of fused sodium chloride to produce metallic sodium, and in the electrolysis of magnesium chloride to produce magnesium, chlorine is obtained in a quantity equivalent to that of the sodium and magnesium. In magnesium production, however, the chlorine is mostly re-used in the process.

Nowadays, with the marked increase in hydrocarbon chlorination processes, the by-product hydrogen chloride (HCl) is produced in large quantities. Thus although pure HCl is of necessity still manufactured by the reaction of hydrogen and chlorine to meet special requirements there is nevertheless overproduction of hydrogen chloride for which an outlet has to be found.

One way of dealing with this situation is to electrolyse hydrochloric acid (HCl dissolved in water). The process has been investigated on a semi-industrial scale and at least one commercial unit is operating (September 1958), but the process needs to be on a very large scale to be economic. It is claimed for one such process that the capital cost is only one-third that of a chlorine-alkali plant producing the same amount of chlorine. This helps to offset the disadvantage that only hydrogen and chlorine, without alkali by-product, are produced.

Formerly, hydrogen chloride was oxidized with air by passing it over a heated catalyst of copper salts deposited on a porous carrier. This is known as the Deacon process and was operated for many years as a method of utilizing by-product HCl from the old Leblanc process (see p. 225) to produce chlorine. The disadvantage of the process for chlorine production is that it yields a dilute chlorine gas which, although satisfactory when the chlorine was required to produce bleaching powder, is quite unsuitable for modern conditions where a concentrated gas is required which can be readily liquefied or used in 'captive' processes, i.e. processes operating on chlorine taken directly from its producing plant.

Several variants of the old Deacon process have been examined. Thus one process employs 'tonnage' oxygen to carry out the oxidation, while another (the so-called Grosvenor-Miller process) makes use of a molten salt mixture of ferric chloride and potassium chloride in two steps carried out alternately, represented by the equations

$$Fe_2O_3 + 6HCl \xrightarrow[+ KCl]{250\text{-}300°C} 2FeCl_3 + 3H_2O$$

$$2FeCl_3 + 1\tfrac{1}{2}O_2 \xrightarrow{275\text{-}500°C} Fe_2O_3 + 3Cl_2$$

About 1936, when the USA was short of chlorine, the Solvay Process Co set up a plant for producing chlorine from sodium chloride without obtaining caustic soda or metallic sodium (supplies of which were adequate at the time).

In this process nitric acid is reacted with sodium chloride under the action of applied heat. Chlorine and nitrosyl chloride are removed from the reaction mixture by steam stripping. The stripped liquor is neutralized with sodium carbonate and the sodium nitrate crystallized out. The stream of chlorine and nitrosyl chloride is fractionated to yield liquid chlorine and liquid nitrosyl chloride. The latter is oxidized to dinitrogen tetroxide (N_2O_4) and chlorine according to the equation

$$2NOCl + O_2 \rightarrow N_2O_4 + Cl_2$$

The dinitrogen tetroxide is reoxidized for re-use in the process. The principal products therefore are sodium nitrate (see Nitrogen compounds) and chlorine and the economics of the process as a method of chlorine production is greatly dependent on the market value of the sodium nitrate. Nowadays it accounts for only a minor proportion of chlorine produced.

7.6.3 Drying and liquefaction of chlorine

Moist chlorine, as for example from aqueous electrolysis cells, is usually treated by cooling (with cooling water and sometimes additionally with chilled water) to reduce the moisture content, and then finally dried by bringing it into contact with concentrated sulphuric acid in drying towers packed with Raschig rings or similar packing material. By this means chlorine can be dried to a moisture content of 3 g/100 kg after which it can be safely handled in metal equipment without risk of serious corrosion. A popular method of cooling the gas before drying is by direct contact with a counterflow of cold water. One American concern supplies a packaged chlorine drying unit which employs a titanium cooler which is claimed to reduce investment costs by 30% and operating costs by 20%. Efficient cooling is important since it effects the usage of sulphuric acid in the drying stage.

Dried chlorine can be transferred by means of blowers such as sulphuric acid sealed displacement pumps (Rash-Hytor pumps) or centrifugal fans either to the user plants directly or to the liquefaction plant for eventual conveyance to internal or external users.

Liquefaction can be carried out at a little above atmospheric pressure by cooling to about −34° C. Often the gas is compressed to much higher pressures by means of reciprocating pumps or turbo-compressors so that it can be liquefied by the use of cooling water followed by a refrigerant. Turbocompressors can only be used effectively in very large production units. In one American-designed plant a fluorinated hydro-carbon (e.g. one of the freons, see vol. IV) is used as the refrigerant. The liquid refrigerant is held in a tank containing numerous tubes through which the chlorine passes. The vapour of the refrigerant is drawn off by means of a centrifugal pumps from the bulk liquor in the tank. In this way it removes latent heat and the temperature of the evaporating liquid is reduced. Cooling brought about in this way causes the chlorine passing through the tubes to condense. The advantage of a unit of this type in which the chlorine is cooled by the refrigerant liquor rather than by using brine as an intermediate heat transfer medium is that the plant is small and refrigeration losses are kept low, while the chlorine can be more completely liquefied, with less escaping in the residual gas. Other factors which determine the efficiency of the liquefaction plant are the hydrogen and air contamination of the gas leaving the chlorine production units. If a part of the gas entering the liquefaction plant with a high content of hydrogen condenses to liquid, the remaining gas inside the liquefier quickly reaches a state in which it becomes an explosive mixture of hydrogen and chlorine.

The residual gas leaving the liquefaction plant, containing the non-condensibles and some chlorine, is often called in Great Britain the 'tail gas' or in the USA the 'sniff gas'. The amount leaving the plant is dependent on the content of non-condensibles in the impure chlorine gas entering the liquefier. Since the disposal of the 'tail gas' is a major problem in chlorine producing factories it is clearly important to keep the non-condensible content (particularly hydrogen) of the impure chlorine gas from the production plant as low as possible and to achieve the maximum liquefaction ratio of chlorine by raising the pressure and lowering the temperature.

Apart from the non-condensibles chlorine frequently contains other impurities such as carbon tetrachloride and other chlorinated organic materials. These may be removed from the gas by scrubbing it with pure liquid chlorine in a special vessel or tower or by a conventional distillation of the liquid. The scrubbing procedure if carried out before the liquefiers improves the performance of the liquefiers.

7.6.4 Storage and transportation of liquid chlorine

Dry liquid chlorine does not corrode steel and can be stored and transported in steel cylinders (for small scale users), drums holding about 1 ton, road tankers holding about 20-30 tons and rail tankers holding up to 55 tons. For waterborne traffic several tanks each holding up to 150 tons can be mounted in barges or ships. In the USA, because of the large distances between producing and consuming factories, the distribution of liquid chlorine presents special problems. The practice of manufacturers sending their supplies to central distributing depots where bulk supplies are broken down into smaller packaged quantities, is growing. In order to ensure continuity of supplies at least one US manufacturer has developed a system of cryogenic storage in special tanks approaching spherical in shape which can hold several thousand short tons. Cryogenic storage is storage at just below the boiling point of the liquid under its own vapour pressure of less than 1 atmosphere.

The handling and transport of liquid chlorine calls for very stringent regulations and the keeping of careful records to obviate the risk of accidental spillage from overfilled containers. In the USA regulations or codes of practice have been laid down by the Interstates Commerce Commission. Most chlorine manufacturers provide an efficient technical service to customers to guard against misuse of their product.

The modern tendency is to use chlorine in 'captive' plants, i.e. plants closely linked to the producing plant and preferably taking the chlorine continuously as a gas although some take liquid chlorine. Consequently the proportion of 'merchant' liquid chlorine, i.e. chlorine sold outside of the factory, is declining although it is still a large-scale business.

Liquid chlorine can be transferred from one vessel to another under its own vapour pressure if the receiving tank is first evacuated or is vented. However since transfer often has to be made when the liquid is at a low temperature with a low vapour pressure, compressed air is usually employed to blow the liquid over. This however has the disadvantage of producing air contaminated with chlorine which leaves the tanks as 'vent gas' and which, like tail gas, presents a disposal problem. To overcome this, long submerged centrifugal pumps fitted with special glands to prevent leakages are employed to transfer liquid chlorine from tanks. In this connection the 'filling ratio' is an important aspect of safety in storing liquid chlorine in containers. If the 'filling ratio', defined as

$$\frac{\text{weight of liquid chlorine}}{\text{water capacity (wt.) of the container}} \times 100$$

is exceeded, then a dangerous situation can arise owing to the development of a high liquid hydrostatic pressure which can rupture the tank. The pressure arises from excessive expansion of the liquid so that it fills the container completely. For this reason also liquid chlorine should never be trapped in a pipe between closed valves. A complication which might arise is that if a tank is filled at a low temperature and the vent-valve is closed, the pressure on warming may be several times the pressure of the saturated vapour.

The accepted maximum filling ratio for chlorine containers specified by the Interstate Commerce Commission is 125% at 65° F (18° C).

Chlorine is commonly discharged from cylinders by vaporization at room temperature, although liquid can be discharged by inverting the cylinder. In Britain many cylinders are fitted with dip pipes so that liquid can be discharged in the upright position.

Large tanks, required to supply chlorine gas, discharge liquid chlorine through a heated vaporizer. It is inadvisable to empty tanks by vaporization since it has been known for materials such as the explosive nitrogen trichloride, present in quite small concentrations in the original liquor, to concentrate in the final residue.

7.6.5 Properties

Chlorine a is heavy yellow-green gas which severely irritates the mucous membranes. It is therefore extremely important that leakages should not occur. For this reason it is common practice, particularly when dealing with the corrosive wet gas, to keep the transfer lines under suction so that the tendency is for air to leak inwards rather than for chlorine to leak out.

Chlorine liquefies at $-34.5°$ C (b.p. at 1 atm) and solidifies at $-101°$ C. Its critical temperature and pressure are 144° C and 76.1 atm respectively. Chlorine is about two-and-half times as heavy as air. Its specific gravity (density) is 3.04 g per litre at 15° C. About 1 g chlorine can be dissolved in 100 g water at 10° C (atmospheric pressure). The solubility in water at 100° C is close to zero at atmospheric pressure.

Chlorine has an exceptionally strong affinity for almost all elements, but it does not react with the rare gases and its affinity for oxygen, nitrogen and bromine is low. With nitrogen and oxygen it forms compounds which can explode spontaneously, and with bromine it forms the unstable BrCl.

A mixture of equal parts of chlorine and hydrogen will explode when exposed to light forming HCl. The mixture remains explosive down to a lower hydrogen limit of about 5%. Antimony, sheet copper, phosphorus, turpentine, etc. ignite in it. In water it dissolves to give the chlorine-water equilibrium

$$Cl_2 + H_2O \rightarrow HCl + HOCl$$

In the presence of light however, chlorine-water reacts irreversibly to yield oxygen

$$Cl_2 + H_2O \rightarrow 2HCl + \tfrac{1}{2}O_2.$$

The nascent oxygen gives rise to the bleaching action of moist chlorine which is not present with dry chlorine.

In plants using chlorine, the chlorine contamination of the atmosphere may be monitored by means of certain organic compounds which darken when exposed to the gas. Air is drawn constantly through a small container filled with filter paper soaked in one of these substances; a photoelectric cell keeps a constant check on the colour and sends out a signal when this indicates a dangerous level of chlorine. Recently high sensitivity instruments employing ultraviolet light have become available for this purpose.

7.6.6 Uses and statistics

The most significant quantities of chlorine are used for the production of organic chemicals including solvents, refrigerants, plastics, plasticizers, detergent intermediates, insecticides and dyes. Some important organic products which are produced by means of chlorine are:

carbon tetrachloride	ethylene glycol	perchloroethylene
chloral	glycerine (synthetic)	pentachlorophenol
chlorotoluene	hexachlorobenzene	propylene glycol
dichloroethylene	methyl chloride	trichloroethylene
dodecyl benzenes	monochlorobenzene	tetraethyl lead
DDT	monochloroacetic acid	vinyl chloride
ethyl chloride	ortho dichlorobenzene	vinylidene chloride
ethylene oxide	para dichlorobenzene	

Important quantities of chlorine are also used for the production of inorganic chemicals such as synthetic hydrochloric acid, bromine, bleaching powder, sodium hypochlorite and metal chlorides such as aluminium chloride (for metal chlorides see under the various metal compounds). Chlorine is also used as a bleaching agent for paper and pulp and as a disinfectant in the treatment of water and sewage. It is also used for the refining of metals e.g. titanium and zirconium (extractive metallurgy, see titanium in vol. III).

The world production of chlorine and the production in the leading countries is shown in the following table:

	In '000s metric tons							
	1938	1948	1952	1956	1960	1962	1963	1964
Canada (capacity)						390	390	
France	47	67	106	182	331	406	470	548
Germany, West	150	119	279	462	660	801	820	
Germany, East (capacity)						300	300	
Italy	32	45	81	126	292	390	350	
Netherlands				50	84	115	100	
Japan		113	200	300	685		720	
Sweden	10	45	62	90	158	168	150	
United Kingdom				460	560	581	600	650
USA	467	1488	2367	3445	4600	4666	4770	5300
USSR				227	500		620	
World total	700			6123		9900	10000	

In 1963 the USA produced 74% of its chlorine in diaphragm cells, 21% in mercury cells, 4% in molten salt cells and 1% in non-electrolytic processes.

Before world war II there was overproduction of chlorine, but after it there was a shortage, as a result of which capacity was increased, especially in the USA. At the same time there was moderate overproduction of caustic soda which is a co-product of chlorine in the electrolytic method of production (see chlorine alkali electrolysis, p. 429). At present it seems likely that the rate of increase of demand for chlorine will exceed that for caustic soda. As a consequence electrolytically produced caustic soda is likely gradually to supplant that produced from soda ash (see p. 444).

Many smaller countries are now setting up their own chlorine producing factories.

A breakdown of the consumption of chlorine by kind of use in the USA in 1963 is as follows in '000s short tons (Source: Oil, Paint and Drug Reporter, 22 April, 1963):

Organic chemicals (65% by weight of the total)	
oxides (e.g. propylene oxide and ethylene oxide)	780
C-1 compounds* (e.g. carbon tetrachloride)	600
C-2 compounds* (e.g. ethylene dichloride for vinyl-chloride and ethyl chloride for tetraethyl lead)	1130
C-3 compounds*	275
aromatic compounds	430
other organic chemicals	200
Inorganic chemicals (9% by weight of the total)	
metal chlorides	155
sodium hypochlorite	75
hydrochloric acid	175
other	80
Pulp and paper (17% by weight of the total)	900
Water and sewage treatment (4% by weight of the total)	200
Other uses	300

*i.e. compounds with one, two or three carbon atoms.

The consumption by kind of use in other countries is often quite different. For example in Canada about 60% of the consumption (4 200 tons in 1962) was used in the pulp and paper industry.

The price of chlorine has more than doubled since 1945. In 1965 in the USA tank load lots cost $3.00 to 7.00 per 100 lb according to quantity. Liquefied chlorine in cylinders cost $11 per 100 lb. In the UK liquid chlorine was sold at £36 10s 0d per long ton in 1965.

7.7 HYDROGEN CHLORIDE

7.7.1 History and occurrence

The solution of hydrogen chloride (HC1) in water is often known as hydro-chloric acid whilst the name hydrogen chloride refers to the gas. Hydrochloric acid was known to alchemists long ago (for example as one of the constituents of *aqua regia*); its preparation by the distillation of common salt with sulphates ('vitriol') was mentioned by Basilus Valentinus whilst Libavius has given several prescriptions for its manufacture using alums in the starting mixture. Glauber, a German, described (1648) its preparation from common salt and oil of vitriol or alum. In 1787 Lavoisier coined the name, *'acide muriatique'* (from the Latin *muria* = brine), from which the English name muriatic acid is also derived. Priestley in 1772 collected the gas hydrogen chloride over mercury and determined its properties.

Hydrogen chloride is found in volcanic gases. Dilute hydrochloric acid occurs in the stomach of mammals where it plays a part in the digestion of food.

7.7.2 Production

Important quantities of hydrogen chloride are still prepared by reacting sulphuric acid with common salt. The reaction may be represented by one of the following equations depending on the reaction circumstances:

$$a \qquad NaCl + H_2SO_4 \xrightarrow{\ 150\text{-}300°\,C\ } NaHSO_4 + HCl$$

$$b \qquad NaCl + NaHSO_4 \xrightarrow{\ 600°\,C\ } Na_2SO_4 + HCl$$

$$c \qquad 2NaCl + H_2SO_4 \xrightarrow{\ 600°\,C\ } Na_2SO_4 + 2HCl$$

When sodium hydrogen sulphate is required as a by-product the process is performed in retorts. Ordinary cast-iron equipment can be used where the gas is dry. Otherwise non-corrodable materials such as glass or ceramic ware are employed.

Usually common salt and sulphuric acid are converted into sodium sulphate (salt cake) and hydrogen chloride in one step (reaction c) in a Mannheim type furnace. A modern Mannheim furnace consists basically of a stationary circular muffle (see fig. 7.6) comprising a pan made of refractory brick and a cover made of silicon carbide or cast iron. The muffle is enclosed in a firebrick construction which is heated with combustion gases. Common salt and sulphuric acid are charged through a feed chute in the centre of the cover. The reaction mass in the pan is agitated by means of ploughs mounted on the rotating arms of a centrally located shaft. The ploughs move the reaction mass slowly towards the periphery of the pan where the resulting salt cake is removed. The hydrogen chloride gas is removed through an aperture in the cover.

The gas is usually dissolved in water to yield hydrochloric acid. Important developments have occurred in making the dissolution process more efficient. A major requirement is that the heat of solution (225 cal per kg of 30% w/w HCl) should be removed, since low temperatures are necessary to achieve the most concentrated solutions. Originally the gas was passed upwards through a cascade of earthenware vessels in the opposite direction to the flow of water and acid. This was inefficient because of the poor thermal conductivity of the earthenware and because of the lack of turbulence in the liquid and gas streams. Consequently the absorption (dissolution) plant occupied a considerable area.

More use is being made nowadays of borosilicate glass cooled with water as for instance in the Raschig ring filled column shown in figs. 7.7 and 7.8.

Other materials which are employed are tantalum, and expensive but non-corrodible metal, and 'Karbate' which is graphite impregnated to make it impervious to gases and liquids. Graphite has an excellent thermal conductivity and can be employed in vertical tubes water-jacketed and with an internal film of water to absorb the gas. The process of impregnating the graphite does not impair its conductivity.

The reaction of sulphuric acid with common salt is the first stage in the Leblanc process for the production of soda ash.

In the original Leblanc process for the manufacture of alkali (see p. 450, alkalis) no attempt was made to collect the HCl formed as a by-product ans it was discharged into the atmosphere causing severe atmospheric pollution. In 1860 as much as 1000 tons/wk were being discharged in this way. With the growth of the industry the problem became so serious in England that it became necessary in 1863 to introduce the Alkali

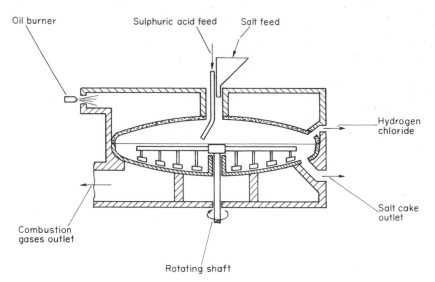

Fig. 7.6 Schematic diagram of a Mannheim-type furnace for the production of hydrogen chloride and sodium sulphate.

Act to control the nuisance. Later Weldon and Deacon developed their processes for making chlorine (and hence bleaching powder) from HCl, and this enabled the former Leblanc processes to remain in operation after the Leblanc process for making alkali had been superseded by the ammonia soda process (see p. 452, soda ash). After about 1900 these processes also were gradually superseded by the electrolytic processes for manufacturing chlorine.

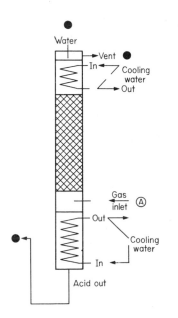

Fig. 7.7 Diagram of a 'Quickfit visible flow glass' plant for the conversion of a gas stream which is rich in hydrogen chloride, into strong hydrochloric acid. The gas stream is introduced to the column below the packed section (at A) and rises counter to a stream of water introduced at the top of the column above the condenser. The hot concentrated acid formed in the packed section of the column is passed through a cooler before being discharged at the bottom of the column.

Fig. 7.8 'Quickfit visible flow glass' column for the absorption of gaseous hydrogen chloride in water. The column is filled with Raschig rings made of glass.

Modifications of the Leblanc process such as the Hargreaves process for making HCl in which steam, SO_2 and O_2 are reacted with solid sodium chloride are now mainly of historical interest. In making HCl by the Leblanc process for use in the food industry it is necessary to use sulphuric acid of the highest quality to avoid the risk of contamination by arsenic, a common impurity in pyrites used in the manufacture of the sulphuric acid.

In one process for making hydrochloric acid from its elements, hydrogen and chlorine are burnt in a water-cooled steel vessel kept at a temperature above the dew-point of the burnt gases, and the product is passed to absorbers. An alternative process employs a water-cooled graphite combustion vessel (fig. 7.9).

Large quantities of hydrogen chloride, usually contaminated with organic compounds, are produced as a by-product of the chlorination of organic compounds. Many large-scale processes are integrated in such a way that HCl produced in one process can be

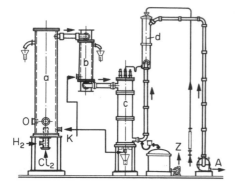

Fig. 7.9 Diagram showing the production of hydrogen chloride from its elements.
(a) Graphite combustion furnace with steel cooling jacket; (b) Condenser; (c) Graphite absorption tower; (d) Absorption of final HCl residues; (K) Cooling water; (A) Waste water; (Z) Hydrochloric acid outlet; (H₂) Hydrogen inlet; (Cl₂) Chlorine inlet; (O) Gas ignition-aperture.

utilized in another. Before by-product HCl can be used it may be necessary to scrub it with, for example, cold carbon tetrachloride or hexabutadiene to remove unwanted contaminants such as chlorine or organic matter before it is suitable for use in another process.

It is frequently necessary to recover hydrogen chloride from its concentrated aqueous solution. This can be done by trickling the acid down a tower packed with anhydrous calcium chloride. The dry gas passes out from the top of the tower whilst a strong solution of calcium chloride containing the water extracted from the acid runs off at the base of the tower. This liquor can be reconcentrated and dehydrated by the use of a submerged burner employing producer-gas. Hydrogen chloride can also be generated by mixing hydrochloric acid and strong sulphuric acid.

Pure hydrochloric acid is made in the course of igniting magnesium chloride in the presence of moisture. This operation is a step in the production of magnesia and magnesium oxychloride, a cement used for making terrazzo type floorings (see magnesium compounds p. 493, and Sorel cement in vol. II).

7.7.3 Storage and transportation

Hydrochloric acid is sold in small lots in glass or plastic carboys or demijohns. In some countries the railway authorities require the carboys to be encased in steel crates with rubber buffer supports to reduce the risk of breakage. Nowadays the containers are fitted with special plugs made of plastic materials which allow safe venting of the contents. In Great Britain carboys usually have a capacity of 10 gallons, a size which can be moved manually. In other countries other types of packages are employed. In France for example 'bonbonnes lint gommes' are employed. These are glass containers (there are four sizes from 10-28 litres) surrounded with an impregnated fabric sheath containing an intervening layer of shock-absorbent material such as cork powder. For special purposes (not HCl packaging) special carboy size containers are available in aluminium or stainless steel. These also are enclosed in cases to facilitate stacking.

A supporting cradle is used to enable the contents of the carboys to be poured easily: alternatively they can be emptied by employing a footpump to apply light pressure to force out the contents. It is, however, safest to employ a special syphon device which can be readily primed.

Large ebonite or plastic-lined steel tanks are employed for the transport of large bulk quantities of hydrochloric acid by road, rail and waterborne carrier. The use of bulk transport in this way has tended to equalize the cost of the acid over large areas of the USA. As a result it is not necessary to site manufacturing plant using HCl in areas of high population density.

Anhydrous hydrogen chloride gas is now also being shipped as a compressed gas in steel cylinders.

7.7.4 Properties

Hydrogen chloride is a colourless, pungent gas which fumes strongly in moist air and seriously affects both the skin and mucous membranes. Contact with the gas or solutions should be avoided (especially so far as the eyes are concerned). Most states in the USA accept 10 p.p.m. as the maximum level of hydrogen chloride gas that can be tolerated during an eight-hour period.

Hydrogen chloride condenses to a liquid under 1 atmosphere at a temperature of $-85°$ C and freezes at $-114°$ C.

At standard temperature and pressure (s.t.p.) water dissolves 450 times its own volume of HCl. If a bottle of the gas is opened under water the gas dissolves almost completely and creates a vacuum so that water rushes into the vessel and almost completely fills it. Whilst in the gaseous state HCl exists in a covalent state, but it largely dissociates into ions when dissolved in water and behaves as a strong acid. Even a low concentration of hydrogen chloride in the atmosphere is unpleasant.

Commercial grades of hydrochloric acid are sold at various strengths. The most common contains 36% HCl (w/w) which is the maximum which can be made with normal concentrations of hydrogen chloride gas.

Commercial grades of hydrochloric acid are classed as 16°, 18°, 20° and 22° Bé. The 16° Bé acid is a solution containing 24.5% by weight of HCl (specific gravity = 1.125). The 22° Bé acid contains 36% by weight of HCl (specific gravity = 1.180). The most concentrated hydrochloric acid which can be made by saturating water with the pure gas, corresponds to 24° Bé (40% by weight at 15° C; spec. gravity = 1.200). Pure hydrochloric acid is usually made by dissolving hydrogen chloride, produced from the elements, in pure water, and is usually sold at 22° Bé.

Hydrochloric acid on boiling *tends* to a constant boiling mixture containing 20.2% HCl (w/w) at 760 mm (azeotropic mixture). In these conditions the vapour has the same composition as the boiling liquor. Thus a weak solution of the acid cannot be concentrated above this value simply by evaporation at 760 mm pressure. It is for this reason that a dehydrating agent is used to obtain the gas from the solution.

7.7.5 Uses

The large demand for anhydrous hydrogen chloride is for the production of alkyl chlorides from alcohols and olefins, and for the production of vinyl chloride (by the reaction with acetylene in the presence of a catalyst). Hydrogen chloride is also used for the production of ethylene dichloride (EDC) by an oxychlorination process and for the production of neoprene. The various minor uses include the use as a catalyst in petroleum refining and organic synthesis.

The most significant quantities of hydrochloric acid are used in ore processing, in steel pickling (for which purposes it provides an alternative to sulphuric acid; inhibitors are added to allow the reaction with any oxide film on the metal without attack on the metal itself, see vol. III), in galvanizing and in solder fluxes, in gelatine manufacture, in sugar refining, in glucose and corn sugar production from starch (as a hydrolysing agent), and in rubber processing.

Important quantities of hydrochloric acid are also used in the Dowell process for reactivating oil wells. Hydrochloric acid removes obstructions in rocks (such as limestone) or improves the porosity to make the rocks penetrable by oil.

Smaller quantities of hydrochloric acid are widely used in industry, e.g. in dyestuffs manufacture for combining with basic intermediates, in reduction processes based on the use of nascent hydrogen (obtained from metals and hydrochloric acid), in the production of silica gel, in the removal of hair from skins and in the extraction of impurities from clay and sand.

7.7.6 Statistics

The production of hydrogen chloride and hydrochloric acid by some important producing countries is shown in the table below.

The production of hydrogen chloride and hydrochloric acid in the UK is not precisely known. The production in 1958 has been estimated at 200000 metric tons.

About 75% of the production in the USA is obtained as a by-product (mainly of the chlorination of organic compounds), about 15% is produced from chlorine and hydrogen and the remainder is produced from common salt and sulphuric acid.

The major portion of the US production is used in the production of various chemicals. About one-quarter of the production is used in metal and ore treatment, in oil well reactivation and in the food industry.

	1948	1954	1958	1960	1962	1963	1964
			In '000s metric tons of 100% HCl				
Canada		6	16	19	21	24	
France	46	73	87	102	112	114	123
Germany, East		80	68	75	80	82	
Germany, West		145	192	247	283	320	365
Italy	17	30	52	51	79	82	79
Japan	18	76	99	147	185	212	
Norway		4	9	13	–	–	
Poland	6	11	17	22	29	30	
Spain	6	9	15	21	27	32	
USA	416	693	749	880	959	970	1090

The US price for 20° Bé acid in ton lots on a freight equalized basis was $ 30 per short ton, and for 22° Bé acid $ 35 per short ton in 1965. Anhydrous hydrogen chloride was sold at $0.15 to $0.45 per lb, depending on the quantity delivered (see Baumé scale, p. 290).

In the UK the price for 18° Bé acid in ton lots was £ 14 to £ 15 per long ton in 1965.

7.8 CHLORINE BLEACHING AGENTS

7.8.1 History

Until towards the end of the eighteenth century the traditional method of bleaching textiles (linens) was by exposure to sunlight. For this purpose the goods were spread out on grass fields and the process was known as crofting.

Berthollet, the famous French scientist, discovered about 1784 that textiles could be bleached with chlorine water but the process gave uneven results and caused weakening of the fibre. He later dissolved chlorine in caustic potash to produce a bleach liquor called 'Eau de Javelle', a term which has since come to be applied to sodium hypochlorite made by reacting chlorine with soda ash solution. The patent for the production of solid bleaching powder by passing chlorine over slaked lime was granted to Tennant in 1799. The introduction of a solid transportable bleach was of tremendous importance to the textile industry.

The first commercial use of chlorine for bleaching cellulose appears to have been made in Russia in 1830, where it was used to bleach straw and esparto grass. By 1874 bleaching powder (also named chloride of lime or chlorinated lime) had been substituted for chlorine water for bleaching cellulose materials such as straw, pulp and paper.

7.8.2 Sodium hypochlorite

Sodium hypochlorite ($NaOCl$) is a salt of the unstable hypochlorous acid ($HClO$). The latter can only be prepared in the form of an aqueous solution. Solid hydrated and anhydrous forms of sodium hypochlorite are known but with the exception of the pentahydrate they are not stable and the pentahydrate itself cannot easily be handled because of its low melting point (27° C).

The sodium hypochlorite of commerce is usually an alkaline solution containing equimolar parts of common salt and sodium hypochlorite. The solutions are known as sodium hypochlorite bleach solution, Labarraque's solution and eau de Javelle.

Sodium hypochlorite solutions are prepared by introducing chlorine into a solution of caustic soda. Reaction equation:

$$2NaOH + Cl_2 \rightarrow NaCl + NaOCl + H_2O$$

Manufacture of sodium hypochlorite depends mainly on the need in many chlorine factories to use caustic soda solutions to absorb chlorine from dilute chlorine gas streams, e.g. liquid chlorine tail gas and various vent gases. Its cost depends on the locality since the trade will not bear heavy transport charges. For the same reason sodium hypochlorite bleach solutions for household uses are prepared locally in fairly simple plants from bulk chlorine and caustic soda transported from the large chlorine producing centres, and is then distributed in small packages.

Sodium hypochlorite can also be made by the low temperature electrolysis of brine in a simple cell containing an anode and cathode without a diaphragm.

Hydrogen is liberated at the cathode while the remaining anodic and cathodic products interact, leading to the overall equation $NaCl + H_2O \rightarrow NaOCl + H_2$.

The pH of the solution needs to be carefully controlled, otherwise the chief product becomes sodium chlorate which is ineffectual as a bleach.

Comparatively small electrolytic bleachers are only about half as efficient as the large chlorine manufacturing units. In many large bleaching works therefore it is still preferable to use the large electrolytic plants to produce elementary chlorine and caustic soda, which are then combined to form sodium hypochlorite liquid. A diagram of an electrolytic cell for the production of a sodium hypochlorite solution is shown in fig. 7.10.

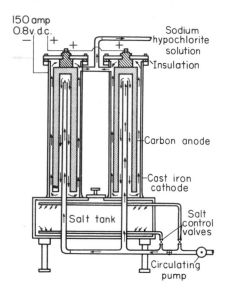

Fig. 7.10 An electrolytic cell for the production of sodium hypochlorite from saline water. Common salt is dissolved in fresh water by passing the latter through a container filled with crude salt. The resulting saline water is passed through the electrolysis cells. The cast iron wall functions as the cathode.

The sodium hypochlorite solutions for industrial purposes usually contain about 12-15% sodium hypochlorite. Solutions for household purposes usually have a sodium hypochlorite content of 3-5% but more concentrated solutions, which must be diluted before use, are coming to be used more widely.

Sodium hypochlorite solutions have a disagreeable, sweetish odour and a yellow colour. They are fairly stable at room temperature, due to the presence of excess sodium hydroxide (pH 9.5 or higher). In acid solutions, and even in neutral or weak alkaline solutions, the unstable hypochlorous acid is liberated by carbon dioxide from air.

Due to their high oxidizing power the hypochlorite solutions are widely used as a bleaching agent in the paper and pulp and textile industries. The solutions are also used as a bleach in laundries and in the home, and as a disinfectant for glass and ceramics and sometimes for water. For laundry applications liquors of low alkalinity are demanded. Sodium carbonate is used as a buffer to prevent the development of acidity in the bleaching process.

In power stations employing sea water for cooling purposes the water is sometimes passed through an electrolytic bleach cell to inhibit the growth of algae and shellfish which would otherwise impair heat transfer in the condensers or give rise to excessive pressure drop in pipelines (compare chlorination of water, p. 145).

7.8.3 Bleaching powder

Bleaching powder, chlorinated lime and chloride of lime (this name should not be confused with calcium chloride) are names for a product which is obtained by treating solid calcium hydroxide (slaked lime) with chlorine. The reaction may be represented by the following equation:

$$2Ca(OH)_2 + 2Cl_2 \rightarrow Ca(OCl)_2 + CaCl_2 + 2H_2O$$

For a long time the standard method of manufacture was to pass chlorine over beds of slaked lime contained in large chambers. These chambers were arranged in a continually changing sequence so that freshly charged chambers came into contact with weak gas whilst the strong gas passed over the final product. The so-called chamber method of manufacture has been superseded by more efficient methods based for example on the passage of chlorine in the opposite direction to slaked lime moving down large nearly horizontal rotating tubes which continually turn over partially chlorinated lime. In another type of reactor, lime is made to fall down a tower containing horizontal shelves (similar to the reactors used for roasting of pyrites, see p. 274) by means of paddles. Chlorine passes upwards through the tower. These processes are more efficient and require less labour.

Bleaching powder stabilized with quicklime (tropical bleach) is produced for export to hot climates. Its stability results from the readiness with which the quicklime reacts with humidity in the atmosphere.

Bleaching powder is a white product which is stable when kept dry. It may be regarded as containing very many compounds of calcium hypochlorite, calcium hydroxide, calcium chloride and water of crystallization. In addition free calcium hydroxide is usually present. The composition of the multiple compounds is not quite clear and probably it depends on the degree of chlorination. Usually, bleaching powder contains about 35-39% calcium hypochlorite (in terms of $Ca(OCl)_2$).

The traditional use of bleaching powder as a disinfectant and bleaching agent has now been largely supplanted by the use of elementary chlorine and liquid bleaches. In the textile industry and the paper and pulp industry it is still used for preliminary bleaching (the bleaching is completed with chlorine or other bleaching agents). For these purposes a clear solution of bleaching powder (bleach liquor) in water is prepared by dissolving and filtration. A bleach liquor for the pulp and paper industry is also prepared by chlorination of a slurry of slaked lime. A saturated solution of dibasic hypochlorite ($Ca(ClO)_2.2Ca(OH)_2$) is obtained. This solution contains about 8-9% of bleaching agent (calculated in terms of calcium hypochlorite).

Sometimes bleaching powder is converted into a solution of sodium hypochlorite by treating with soda ash or caustic soda. Reaction equation (for example):

$$Ca(OCl)_2 + Na_2CO_3 \rightarrow 2NaOCl + CaCO_3$$

the sludge of calcium carbonate is removed by filtration.

Before the second world war the world production of bleaching powder was about 800 000 long tons per annum. Since the war production has declined markedly in the face of competition from bleach solutions and from organic bleaches.

In the USA about 20 000 long tons of bleaching powder were sold in 1963. The UK is an important producer of bleaching powder and exported about 16 000 long tons in 1963.

In 1964 the US price of high purity bleaching powder was $39.50 per short ton; the UK price of bleaching powder (35%) £30 7s 6d per long ton.

7.8.4 Other chlorine bleaching agents

Apart from chlorine, sodium hypochlorite bleach solutions and bleaching powder, the following are of interest.

Chlorinated trisodium phosphate is obtained by chlorination of trisodium phosphate dodecahydrate. The resulting product is a solid solution of 3.5 to 5% sodium hypochlorite in the phosphate and is marketed under the trade name 'Diversol'. It has both bleaching and detergent properties and is used in dishwashing machines.

Lithium hypochlorite. Compared with sodium hypochlorite, lithium hypochlorite is fairly stable. In a pure anhydrous form it loses only a few percent of its activity per year. Its use is restricted by the high price of lithium compounds.

Chloramines are compounds containing chlorine, bonded to nitrogen, which is capable of being released in active form. Most chloramines are unstable. Perhaps the best known stable chloramine is chloramine T (sodium p-toluene sulphonchloramide; $CH_3 - \langle \hspace{1em} \rangle - SO_2NClNa$) which may be produced by treating toluene with chlorosulphonic acid producing a mixture of ortho- and paratoluene sulphonylchloride. The ortho compound is a starting material for the production of saccharin and the para compound is converted into chloramine T by treating with ammonia and sodium hypochlorite. Several related chloramine bleaches are manufactured including the chlorinated hydantoins of which the parent material is 1.3 dichloro 5.5 dimethyl hydantoin

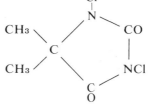

the chlorine is activated by the adjoining carbonyl groups.

Chlorinated cyanuric acid derivatives are also used in the field of package bleaches (e.g. in domestic detergent preparations) and water sanitizing (see cyanuric acids, p. 361).

Chlorine dioxide (ClO_2) has been used for bleaching and water treatment only fairly recently. It was first used in 1923 by a German chemist, E. Schmidt, to dissolve out lignin from wood. It was able to do this without impairing the bast fibres, but its general adoption was delayed by its hazardous nature and high cost. In 1930 the Mathieson Alkali Chemical Corporation developed a relatively cheap method for manufacturing chlorine dioxide. They converted it into sodium chlorite in which form it could be readily distributed for market research into chlorine dioxide uses. There are now more than sixty plants on the American continent manufacturing chlorine dioxide mainly for use in bleaching out pulp. Chlorine dioxide is made by reacting sodium chlorate with an acid together with a reducing agent which may be the acid itself in the case of HCl or for example sulphur dioxide or methanol. The Doy-Kesting process might be observed in which HCl is reacted with sodium chlorate always kept in excess. The reaction is

$$NaClO_3 + 2HCl \rightarrow ClO_2 + \tfrac{1}{2}Cl_2 + NaCl + H_2O$$

(If HCl is in excess the reaction gives only chlorine.)

The mixture of chlorine dioxide and chlorine is separated by air stripping followed by a countercurrent scrubbing with water to yield a chlorine dioxide-rich aqueous solution. The sodium chlorate concentration is maintained by continuous electrolysis of the recirculated liquors. The concentration of chlorine dioxide must be kept low ($< 5\%$) at all stages to eliminate the risk of spontaneous explosion.

Chlorine dioxide is a green gas which condenses to a red liquid at about $11°$ C. The liquid and gas mixtures or solutions having a high chlorine dioxide content are very explosive. For this reason chlorine dioxide is usually produced where it is to be used. Chlorine dioxide is about as hazardous for animal life as nitrogen dioxide. Its odour is detectable at a concentration of 14-17 p.p.m.

Due to its high oxidizing power, chlorine dioxide is a bleaching agent. The most important application of chlorine dioxide is the bleaching of cellulosic materials in the pulp and paper industry. Chlorine dioxide became an important chemical in the treatment of flour when the chemical previously used for the purpose, nitrogen trichloride, was shown to give rise to toxic derivatives (see flour, vol. VII). Other uses include bleaching of fats for soap-making and for disinfecting drinking water. For the latter purpose it has the advantage that it does not emit a smell of chlorine.

Chlorine dioxide is also used for the production of sodium chlorite (see below).

Sodium chlorite ($NaClO_2$) is a salt of the unstable chlorous acid ($HClO_2$). The chlorite is produced by reacting chlorine dioxide with sodium peroxide which functions as a reducing agent with elimination of oxygen: $2ClO_2 + Na_2O_2 \rightarrow 2NaClO_2 + O_2$.

Alternatively the reduction can be brought about by means of hydrogen peroxide and caustic soda, alkaline earth peroxides, carbonaceous materials and lime or by means of metal powders or metal oxides (e.g. MnO, Cu_2O).

Sodium chlorite is a white powder when pure. The commercial products are usually brownish flakes which are somewhat hygroscopic but do not cake. With suitable precautions sodium chlorite can be readily transported since it is much more stable than sodium hypochlorite. The bleaching powder of sodium chlorite is less than that of chlorine dioxide, but if necessary it can be rendered more effective by conversion into chlorine dioxide by means of acids or chlorine. For example, by passing a mixture of air and chlorine either over the dry powder or through a solution, chlorine dioxide is generated according to the following reaction equation

$$2NaClO_2 + Cl_2 \rightarrow 2ClO_2 + 2NaCl$$

The evolution of chlorine dioxide can be exactly controlled by regulating the chlorine feed. Thus a controlled bleaching action is possible. Since chlorine dioxide can be recovered from sodium chlorite, the latter is sometimes prepared as a transportable source of chlorine dioxide. Sodium chlorite as such is also used in bleaching of pulp and paper, textiles, oils, fats and flour.

7.8.5 The mode of action of chlorine bleaching agents in bleaching and disinfection

Various natural products are coloured due to the presence of minor quantities of coloured constituents. These natural products can be decolorized (bleached) by means of oxidizing and reducing agents (chemical bleaches). Chemical bleaches must be able to decompose coloured constituents into colourless decomposition products without damaging the main constituents of the natural products. Some oxidizing agents used in bleaching are hydrogen peroxide, metal peroxides (e.g. sodium peroxide), persalts (e.g. perborates, persulphates), dichromates, permanganates and the chlorine bleaching agents. Examples of reducing bleaches are dithionites, sulphur dioxide, sulphurous acid and sulphites. The reducing agents are also used as an 'antichlor' to remove traces of chlorine bleaching agents from natural products which are bleached with the latter.

Coloured liquids (e.g. oils and fats) are often decolourized by means of a physical process, e.g. by absorption of the coloured constituents on bleaching clays, active carbon etc. (see vol. II).

Bleaching effects are also obtained by neutralizing the colour present in a product without removing the coloured constituents of the products. Examples are the well-known starching blue which is used for neutralizing the yellow discolorations of laundry and the so-called optical bleaches, which transform ultraviolet light into visible light. In this way the products containing these optical bleaches look brighter. Although the expression 'optical bleaches' is used here, they are not actual 'bleaching agents', as the coloured constituents are not being removed.

The bleaching and disinfecting action of chlorine-type bleaching agents is based on the decomposition and destruction of coloured organic products and micro-organisms by means of nascent oxygen (oxidation), which is liberated from the chlorine bleaching agents in the presence of these organic products, etc.

Sodium chlorite and chlorine dioxide are most effective at pH6. The reaction mechanism of their bleaching action is not quite clear.

Chlorine and the hypochlorite type bleaching agents depend for their bleaching and disinfecting efficiency on the activity of the hypochlorous acid which they generate. The formation of hypochlorous acid in an aqueous solution of chlorine may be represented by the following equilibrium reaction:

$$a \qquad H_2O + Cl_2 \rightarrow HOCl + H^+ + Cl^-$$

The free hypochlorous acid formed is unstable (especially in the presence of organic matter) and decomposes to form nascent oxygen and hydrochloric acid.

This reaction may be represented by the following equation:

$$b \qquad HOCl \rightarrow H^+ + Cl^- + O$$

The position of the equilibrium of reaction (a) depends on the concentration of the reacting constituents and the reaction products. Due to the formation of hydrogen ions (H^+) in reaction (b) the hydrogen ion concentration in the reaction mixture increases and the position of the equilibrium of reaction (a) is moved to the left. Thus in the mixture the hypochlorous acid concentration decreases and the chlorine concentration increases. Hence it is necessary to keep the hydrogen ion concentration below a certain level (pH4 or higher) to minimize chlorination reactions and favour bleaching processes.*

---

* In this section the term 'chlorination' is used for processes comprising the production of chlorine compounds by treating any compound with elemental chlorine. Unfortunately the expression 'chlorination' is also used for bleaching processes using chlorine or chlorine compounds in which the formation of chlorine compounds must be prevented.

The presence of sufficient ammonia in water inhibits chlorination reactions. As already stated hypochlorous acid is formed from water and chlorine (see reaction (a)). Ammonia combines with hydrogen ions to form ammonium ions and combines with hypochlorous acid to form chloramines. For example:

$$c \qquad NH_3 + HClO \rightarrow NH_2Cl + H_2O$$

In this way the position of the equilibrium (a) moves to the right and the chlorine concentration in the water becomes too low to start chlorination reactions. For this reason, in disinfecting water with chlorine, ammonia is often added if the water contains phenol, to prevent the formation of pentachlorophenol which causes an unpleasant taste (see also Water chlorination, p. 145).

Hypochlorite bleaches such as sodium hypochlorite solutions are alkaline (i.e. pH 9.5 or higher) and the hydrogen ion concentration is low enough to minimize chlorination. The bleaching action of sodium hypochlorite may be represented by the following equations:

$$d \qquad NaOCl + H_2O \rightarrow Na^+ + OH^- + HOCl$$

$$b \qquad HOCl \rightarrow H^+ + Cl^- + O$$

The equations show that hydrogen ions produced in reaction (b) are neutralized by hydroxyl ions formed in reaction (d). Thus that sodium hypochlorite and bleaching powder are said to be internally buffered.

The bleaching effect of chloramines also depends on the action of hypochlorous acid which is slowly liberated in the presence of water. Reaction equation:

$$e \qquad RNHCl + H_2O \rightarrow RNH_2 + HOCl$$

The chloramines are also buffered internally since any acid resulting from decomposition of hypochlorous acid is neutralized (partially) by the amine which is present in the reaction mixture.

The bleaching agent content of chlorine solutions, hypochlorite preparations and chloramines is often expressed in terms of 'available chlorine'. This is the weight of chlorine from which the effective hypochlorite has been formed (or can be formed). According to equation (a), one mole chlorine (Cl_2) corresponds with one mole hypochlorous acid. In the case of sodium hypochlorite preparations, the available chlorine content is about equal to the sodium hypochlorite content, since one mole hypochlorous acid is equivalent to one mole sodium hypochlorite and the molecular weights of sodium hypochlorite and chlorine are about equal (71 and 74.5 respectively). Similarly, $\frac{1}{2}$ mole calcium hypochlorite (in bleaching powder) has been formed from 1 mole chlorine. The molecular weights are respectively 147 and 71 and thus the available chlorine content of bleaching powder is also about equal to its calcium hypochlorite content. However, the bleaching agent content of lithium hypochlorite in terms of available chlorine is much higher than the content of lithium hypochlorite since the molecular weight of lithium hypochlorite is considerably lower than that of chlorine. For this reason the available chlorine content of pure lithium hypochlorite is as high as 121%.

7.9 CHLORATES AND PERCHLORATES

7.9.1 Sodium chlorate

Sodium chlorate ($NaClO_3$) is a salt of chloric acid ($HClO_3$). The latter cannot be obtained in a pure form but aqueous solutions, up to 30%, are fairly stable when cold.

Sodium chlorate is prepared by electrolysis of a solution of sodium chloride in a cell which allows of complete mixing of anode and cathode products: the overall reaction is

$$NaCl + 3H_2O \rightarrow NaClO_3 + 3H_2$$

The reaction proceeds with good efficiency at a pH of about 5.5 and a temperature of 70° C or higher although in practice it may be advantageous because of reduced anode wear (see later) to sacrifice current and energy efficiencies by operating plant at lower temperatures.

Technical electrolysis is carried out in partitioned steel tanks which together form the cathode whilst the anode consists of graphite plates mounted in concrete covers and suspended between the partitions. Usually cells are operated with an almost saturated salt solution and the electrolyte is recycled until the sodium chlorate, which is very soluble, reaches a concentration of 750 g/l when it is removed, clarified and evaporated under vacuum (see Salt, Caustic Soda). During evaporation some salt precipitates and is filtered off on a Monel filter screen or on a rotary filter. When evaporation is complete the liquor is allowed to cool in a crystallization vessel. The crystals are washed, dried, ground and finally packed. Very stringent regulations govern the construction and operation of such a plant on account of the high explosive risk when carbonaceous material or dust comes into contact with chlorates.

Descriptions have been given of German cells which employed magnetite anodes. Platinum anodes were used in the USA in the early days of chlorate production. The life of graphite anodes is usually extended by impregnating them with an oil which blocks up the pores and prevents the absorption of brine. Cell voltages using graphite anodes are lower than cells based on platinum anodes.

The efficiency of chlorate formation is sensitive to the pH conditions. If the pH is too low chlorine is evolved in excessive amounts and could give rise to an explosive gas mixture. The system is self restoring in regard to low pH (high acidity) because the excess acid (HCl) is removed in the side reaction

$$2 HCl \rightarrow H_2 + Cl_2$$

If the pH is too high (high alkalinity) however one of the main products is oxygen resulting from the oxidation of the alkali

$$a \qquad 4 NaOH \rightarrow 4 Na + 2 H_2O + (O_2)$$

$$b \qquad 4 Na + 2 H_2O \rightarrow (2 H_2) + 4 NaOH$$

$$\overline{2 H_2O \rightarrow 2 H_2 + O_2}$$

Thus the products are hydrogen and oxygen from the decomposition of water. There is no removal of alkali in this side reaction and the system is not self correcting. A simultaneous reaction is

$$2 H_2O + C \rightarrow 2 H_2 + CO_2$$

the carbon deriving from the anode. This reaction is undesirable because it shortens the anode life. Owing to these reactions a too alkaline electrolyte tends to degenerate further. In practice the system is controlled in respect of pH by the addition of potassium chromate which acts as a pH buffer as a result of the equilibrium:

$$2\ Na_2CrO_4 + 2\ HCl \rightarrow Na_2Cr_2O_7 + 2\ NaCl + H_2O$$

The chromate is also claimed to passivate the cathode and thus to prevent cathodic reduction of the chlorate.

Cathodic current densities vary from 0.01 to 0.05 A/cm^2 and anodic current densities from 0.01 to 0.16 A/cm^2. The current efficiency for the production of $NaClO_3$ is about 80% and on the basis of a cell voltage of 3.6 the energy required is 7000 kWh/ton $NaClO_3$.

Sodium chlorate forms hygroscopic crystals which are readily soluble in water. About 100 g of sodium chlorate dissolve in 100 g water at 20° C and 209 g in 100 g water at 90° C. On heating, sodium chlorate decomposes into sodium chloride and oxygen. The reaction is catalysed by means of metal oxides (especially manganese oxide). Mixtures of sodium chlorate with any organic matter are very explosive, but the use of these mixtures as an explosive is not permitted in several countries (e.g. the USA) because of their extreme sensitivity to shock. Sodium chlorate solutions do not show oxidizing properties at room temperature, but in acid solutions chloric acid is liberated which has a strong oxidizing power.

Sodium chlorate is best packed and handled in nickel or aluminium alloy containers, which are least corroded by it.

The most significant quantity of sodium chlorate is used for the production of chlorine dioxide and sodium chlorite (bleaching agents in the pulp and paper industry). Considerably quantities are also used for the production of potassium chlorate and perchlorates and as a herbicide and defoliating agent (in cotton and soya bean defoliation). Solutions of strength 1-2% are sprayed along railway lines to prevent the growth of grass and hence to prevent grass fires; all plants are then killed. Stronger solutions are very inflammable in contact with clothes, skin, vegetable life etc.

Smaller quantities of sodium chlorate are used in uranium ore processing, dye manufacture and for the production of various chemical intermediates.

The production of sodium chlorate has increased rapidly, especially in the USA, from 20000 short tons in 1950 to 140000 short tons in 1964. A yearly production capacity of 170000 short tons was expected to be reached in 1964. The UK imports about 5000 long tons of sodium chlorate per year.

The usage of sodium chlorate for various purposes changed considerably during the 1950s and the 1960s, and it is reported that in the USA the distribution of the total production among various applications was as shown below.

	1952	1962
Herbicides	50%	20%
$KClO_3$ and perchlorates	30	26
Pulp and paper	4	40
Defoliating agents	5 ⎫	
Other	11 ⎭	14

In 1964 pulp and paper bleaching accounted for 65% of the US sodium chlorate sales. The price of sodium chlorate in the USA was $ 0.10 to $ 0.11 per lb in 1965. In the UK the price in 4 ton lots was £ 85 to £ 95 per long ton in 1965.

7.9.2 Other chlorates

Potassium chlorate ($KClO_3$) is produced by electrolysis of a solution of potassium chloride by virtually the same process as sodium chlorate. Potassium chlorate is also prepared by saturating a solution of sodium chlorate or calcium chlorate with potassium chloride. Potassium chlorate crystallizes since it is less soluble than calcium chlorate or sodium chlorate.

Potassium chlorate is a white crystalline product which is not hygroscopic. It is only moderately soluble in water. About 7 g dissolve in 100 g water at 20° C and about 47 g in 100 g water at 90° C. Just like sodium chlorate, potassium chlorate is explosive and very sensitive to shock in the presence of organic matter. Potassium chlorate is used mainly as an oxidizing agent in match heads. It also serves in the same way in pyrotechnics. Smaller quantities of potassium chlorate are used in pharmaceuticals and cosmetics and (mixed with sulphuric acid) in bleaching of mineral oils.

In the USA potassium chlorate was sold at $ 0.12-0.17 per lb in 1965.

Alkaline earth metal chlorates are usually made by treating a slurry of the corresponding hydroxide with chlorine. The resulting hypochlorite solution is slowly converted into a chlorate solution by acidifying (pH 6.5-7). Acidifying is usually performed by further absorption of chlorine.

Magnesium chlorate is used medicinally. Calcium chlorate is an explosive substance, used mainly in fireworks.

Basic calcium chlorate ($Ca(ClO_3)_2.Ca(OH)_2$), which is precipitated from a calcium chlorate solution by adding milk of lime, is used to destroy weeds. This basic chlorate is the least inflammable of all the metal chlorates.

Barium chlorate is used principally in fireworks and for the production of other chlorates. The price in the USA lay between $ 0.32 and $ 0.41 per lb in 1965.

7.9.3 Perchlorates and perchloric acid

Perchlorates are salts of perchloric acid ($HClO_4$). They can be obtained by thermal decomposition or oxidation (persulphate in acid solution) of chlorates but the predominant manufacturing process is by the electrolytic process using a saturated sodium chlorate solution as the electrolyte and electrolysing to the stage where only 5% of the chlorate remains unconverted. The process is carried out at a controlled pH 6.1-6.4 in the presence of a chromate buffer. (See sodium chlorate.)

Sodium perchlorate is not itself a commercial material but is used in the production of other perchlorates. The potassium salt is prepared by the addition of a hot saturated solution of potassium chloride in slightly above the stoichiometric amount. On cooling the perchlorate formed by double decomposition

$$NaClO_4 + KCl \rightarrow KClO_4 + NaCl$$

crystallizes to give a slurry which is then centrifuged and washed to remove adhering chloride. The solid, partly dried at the centrifuge, is discharged into continuous driers to give a moisture content of 0.05%. Ammonium perchlorate is made in a similar way starting with ammonium chloride. It is at its most explosive when it contains 0.2-0.5% water and it must therefore be quickly and thoroughly dried.

Perchlorates are shipped in regulation containers. Just like the chlorates, perchlorates decompose on heating, but at higher temperature than the corresponding chlorates. In general the perchlorates can be mixed with organic compounds to form explosives which are much more stable towards shock than the corresponding chlorates.

At present the most important perchlorate is potassium perchlorate, which is mainly used as an oxidizer in fuels for rockets and missiles. It is also used in explosives, flares and fireworks. Ammonium perchlorate is sometimes preferred in explosives since all the products of explosion are gaseous, whereas in the case of potassium perchlorate (or other perchlorates) a considerable quantity of the products of explosion is solid.

In 1965 the US price of potassium perchlorate was $ 0.14-0.20 per lb.

Perchloric acid may be prepared from sodium perchlorate by adding an excess of hydrochloric acid which precipitates most of the sodium ions in the form of sodium chloride. The resulting solution of perchloric acid is concentrated and purified by distillation.

Perchloric acid is a colourless fuming liquid which solidifies at $-122°$ C. It is the most stable and strongest acid of all oxygen acids of chlorine, and is usually sold as a 70-72% solution. Perchloric acid is used in analytical chemistry and together with acetic anhydride in the electrolytic polishing of metals.

7.10 LITERATURE

D. W. F. HARDIE. *Electrolytic manufacture of chemicals from salt.* Oxford University Press, 1959.

C. L. MANTELL. *Electrochemical engineering.* New York, McGraw-Hill, 1960.

J. W. MELLOR. *Comprehensive treatise on inorganic chemistry,* vol. II, suppl. 2. London, Longmans, 1956.

J. S. SCONCE. *Chlorine: its manufacture, properties and uses.* New York, Reinhold. ACS monograph no. 154.

J. D. SCHUMACKER. *Perchlorates, their properties manufacture and uses.* New York, Reinhold. ACS monograph no. 146.

7.11 BROMINE (Br₂, mole weight = 159.84)

7.11.1 History and occurrence

Bromine was discovered in France by Balard in 1826, Liebig probably obtained a small quantity earlier but mistook it for a compound of chlorine and iodine. It was named bromine (after the Greek *bromos* = a stench) at a later date.

Bromine does not occur in the free state and is usually found in the form of bromides accompanied by large quantities of chlorides in sea water, salt lakes and various deposits of solid sodium, potassium and magnesium salts (see occurrence of common salt, p. 412 and potassium chloride, p. 466). The bromide content of sea water (65 p.p.m.) and other deposits is about 0.2% of the chloride content. Small quantities of bromine occur in volcanic gases in the form of hydrogen bromide and in some silver deposits in the form of silver bromide, but these are not a commercial source of bromine.

Before 1930 the *Abraumsalze* of the potassium chloride deposits in Stassfurt (Germany) were the most important source of bromine, but nowadays sea water is the major raw material.

7.11.2 Production

Bromine is isolated from natural brines, mother liquors (bitterns) from the production of sodium and potassium salts, sea water and other saline waters by oxidation of the bromide by means of chlorine to form elemental bromine and removal of the bromine vapour from the resulting bromine solution. The process is basically the same for all raw materials.

The production of bromine from sea water is carried out in large plants located so as to ensure an intake of clear water and conveniently placed for discharge of the spent sea water again to sea at a point remote from the intake area.

Large volumes of water are pumped from the sea into lakes in which the temperature is raised to 32° C either by solar heating or by employing waste hot condensate water. From the lakes it is pumped through a filter and sulphuric acid is added to adjust the pH to 3.5. Chlorine in a 15% excess over the stoichiometric requirement is added, to oxidize the bromides to free bromine. The reaction mixture is sprayed in a wood packed air stripping tower and the free bromine (and excess chlorine) is driven out by a countercurrent stream of air. In one variation of the process, the halogen-laden air stream next passes through a series of towers in the opposite direction to a flow of soda-ash solution which fixes the bromine in the form of a bromide-bromate mixture and chlorine in the form of chloride. Reaction equations:

$$3\ Na_2CO_3 + 3\ Br_2 \rightarrow 5\ NaBr + NaBrO_3 + 3\ CO_2$$
$$6\ Na_2\text{-}CO_3 + Br_2 + 5\ Cl_2 \rightarrow 10\ NaCl + 2\ NaBrO_3 + 6\ CO_2$$

Bromine is liberated again from this solution by acidification, reaction equation:

$$5\ NaBr + NaBrO_3 + 3\ H_2SO_4 \rightarrow 3\ Br_2 + 3\ Na_2SO_4 + 3\ H_2O$$

and is recovered as a bromine solution by steam stripping (see also fig. 7.11).

More recently a modified process has come into use in which bromine in the air stream from the stripping tower is treated with SO_2 and steam to form a mixture of sulphuric acid and hydrobromic acid. Reaction equation:

$$SO_2 + Br_2 + 2\ H_2O \rightarrow 2\ HBr + H_2SO_4$$

The mixed acid solution is treated with chlorine which liberates bromine.

The released bromine is removed by stream stripping whilst the acid residue is returned to the beginning of the process to adjust the pH of the incoming sea water. The condensed bromine is freed of chlorine in a still fitted with a dephlegmator, the chlorine passing out as an overhead fraction and the bromine as an overflow from the boiler of the still.

7.11.3 Materials construction, storage and transportation

Ebonite or ebonite-lined pipes and vessels are extensively used for handling bromine. One large British plant is reported to contain 22 500 m² of such lined surfaces. The lining of large tanks and vessels is usually done on site. An uncured rubber sheet is applied to the surface and is vulcanized by filling the vessel with low pressure steam.

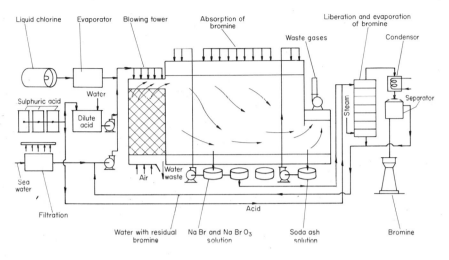

Fig. 7.11 Schematic flow sheet for the extraction of bromine from sea water.

Precautions have to be taken to avoid forming an explosive mixture with the solvent fumes displaced from the rubber. Tanks for the storage of acid are vulcanised with hot water. Lead (especially chemically pure lead) is particularly suited to use with bromine. Iron, steel or cast iron are attacked by both wet and dry bromine. Nickel is suitable for use with dry bromine. Bromine distillation columns are built of granite plates sealed with asbestos rope impregnated with sodium silicate and with oxychloride cement (see vol. II). White hard asbestos gaskets and bituminous tar are sufficiently resistant to make them suitable as jointing materials. Distillation columns are also made from Pyrex glass. Teflon and Kel-F are also bromine resistant.

This dangerous liquid is shipped in carboys or glass vessels embedded in boxes containing vermiculite powder (see vol. II) which is a relatively light and inert absorbent. Bromine containing even small traces of water is very corrosive. In America up to 100 kg quantities may be shipped in Monel or nickel drums of a specified wall thickness.

Sometimes bromine is dissolved in tetramethyl ammonium bromide with which it forms a low vapour pressure solid. From this the bromine is regenerated by heating and the quaternary salt can be reused for absorbing further quantities of bromine.

7.11.4 Properties

Bromine is a heavy dark red liquid, freezing at $-7°$ C (for extremely dry bromine $-4.5°$ C) and boiling at $58.8°$ C. The solubility of bromine is about 3.5 g per 100 g of water at temperatures between 6 and $54°$ C. At temperatures below $6°$ C and above $54°$ C the solubility in water decreases.

The vapour in air is an intense irritant at a concentration of only 0.001 % (10 p.p.m.) and can scarcely be tolerated for more than a few minutes. A concentration of 1 p.p.m. can be detected by odour. The American conference of Governmental Industrial Hygienists have adopted this level as the maximum concentration for eight hours' continuous exposure. A concentration of 100 p.p.m. is rapidly fatal. The liquid causes very severe burns on contact with the skin and should be used with the utmost caution.

Chemically bromine resembles chlorine except that it has a lower affinity for metals and a greater affinity for oxygen. It cannot be used for bleaching cellulose material because it forms a coloured insoluble compound with the traces of starch present in fibres as a result of processing; the corresponding compounds formed by chlorine are colourless.

In water it has strong anti-algal and disinfectant properties and in America it has been suggested that it can be used for disinfecting swimming pools because it does not affect the mucous membranes to the extent that chlorine does. A pool 60 ft × 407 ft is stated to require 4 lb/day.

7.11.5 Uses and statistics

By far the major portion of all bromine produced is used in the manufacture of ethylene dibromide. This product is usually made at the site of the bromine plant. Ethylene dibromide is added to petrol to increase the volatility of the lead breakdown products formed from the anti-knock additive tetraethyl lead (TEL, see vol. IV, Petrol) during combustion in the engine and thus assists in their removal from the engine.

Bromine is also used for the production of various other organic bromine compounds including methyl bromide (monobromomethane), tetrabromomethane, and flame retardants (for incorporating in textiles, paper, plastics). Methyl bromide is used as an insecticide and nematocide (soil and seed fumigant), as a fire extinguisher and as a methylating agent in organic synthesis. Tetrabromomethane, which is a liquid having the exceptionally high density of 3.42, is useful in ore dressing as for example in the recovery of tungsten oxides from ore concentrates. Compounds such as chlorobromomethane and trifluorobromomethane are used as fire extinguishers in aeroplanes.

Bromine is also used in dye manufacture (e.g. eosin, bromindigo) and in several pharmaceutical preparations such as certain vitamins. Where bromination under gentle conditions is required the brominating agent N-bromosuccinimide with or without a catalyst such as benzoyl peroxide is employed. The catalyst favours bromination in an aromatic side chain and increases the speed of reaction. It is effective at low temperatures and brominates without addition to double bonds.

The most important inorganic compounds produced from bromine are sodium bromide, potassium bromide and ammonium bromide. Smaller quantities of bromine are sold as such for laboratory uses, e.g. for the bromination of organic compounds and for the production of Grignard compounds.

The world production of bromine was estimated at about 150000 metric tons in 1962. The production in the major producing countries is shown in the following table:

| | In metric tons | | | |
	1958	1960	1962	1963
France	1610	5370	6110	6100
Germany (West)		2100	2150	2140
Italy	550	1280	1540	
Israel	770	2800	6400	
Japan	1500	2800	2900	3500
United States	80200	79600	86000	92000
United Kingdom (estimated)			20000	
USSR (estimated)			15000	

In the USA about 72% of the bromine consumed was used for the production of ethylene dibromide in 1963, 6% for the production of methyl bromide, and 9% for the production of all other bromine compounds. About 13% sold was the elemental form.

The uses to which bromine is put is similar in the case of many countries to that outlined above in respect of the USA. In West Germany, however, it is quite different since ethylene dibromide is only produced in very small quantities.

In the USA bromine was sold at $0.22-0.33 per lb in 1965. The price in the UK was 1s 3d per lb in 1964.

7.12 BROMINE COMPOUNDS

Potassium bromide (KBr) and *sodium bromide* (NaBr) are prepared by passing a bromine-water vapour mixture over iron turnings to form a dark red iron bromide ($Fe_3Br_8.xH_2O$). The latter is dissolved in a boiling solution of caustic potash, potassium carbonate, caustic soda or sodium carbonate to form a precipitate of iron hydroxide and a solution of potassium bromide or sodium bromide. The bromide is recovered from the solution by evaporation, and is purified by repeated crystallization. Alkali bromides may also be prepared by reacting alkali hydroxide or carbonate with hydrobromic acid (HBr).

Potassium bromide and sodium bromide form colourless crystals. At 20° C the solubility of potassium bromide is 65 g per 100 g water and the solubility of sodium bromide is 90 g per 100 g water. Both bromides are used in medicine and in photography for the production of light sensitive silver bromide and as a constituent of film and paper developers. Potassium bromide is also used as a reagent in the laboratory.

In 1965 the US price of sodium bromide and potassium bromide was $ 0.38-0.40 per lb; in the UK potassium bromide was sold at 2s 6d per lb.

Ammonium bromide (NH_4Br) is prepared from iron bromide, just like the alkali bromides, or by the reaction of bromine with excess ammonia solution. Reaction equation:

$$8 NH_3 + 3 Br_2 \rightarrow 6 NH_4Br + N_2$$

Pure colourless crystals of ammonium bromide are obtained from the solution by evaporation. Ammonium bromide is used in medicine, in photography, in acetate rayon production and in metal treatment.

Hydrogen bromide (HBr) is prepared by burning a mixture of hydrogen and bromine vapour in a heat resistant tube. The resulting vapour of hydrogen bromide is liquefied by cooling or dissolved in water to form the commercial 40% and 48% hydrobromic acid solutions.

Anhydrous hydrogen bromide is a colourless gas boiling at −67° C. Like hydrogen chloride, hydrogen bromide is irritating to the eyes and respiratory passages.

Hydrobromic acid is a very strong acid.

Hydrogen bromide and hydrobromic acid are used for the production of inorganic bromides and organic bromides (from olefins and alcohols), as a catalyst in the petroleum industry (for alkylation reactions) and in the controlled oxidation of hydrocarbons (e.g. to acids). Small quantities are also used in medicine. The US price of hydrobromic acid (48%) was $ 0.31-0.32 per lb in 1965.

Potassium bromate (KBrO₃) and *sodium bromate* (NaBrO₃) or salts of the unstable bromic acid (HBrO₃) are made by dripping bromine into a strong caustic alkali solution or by electrolysis of an alkali bromide solution in a cell without a diaphragm. Both bromates are colourless crystalline products which are soluble in water. They are used in combination with hydrochloric acid, wetting agents and colloids for shrink-proofing fabrics. Potassium bromate is also used as a bleaching agent in home hair-waving compositions.

Literature

Z. E. JOLLES. *Bromine and its compounds*. London, Benn, 1966.

7.13   IODINE (I₂, mole weight = 253.84)

7.13.1 History and occurrence

This element was discovered in 1811 by Courtois, an alert manufacturer of saltpetre, who was using a solution of kelp (ash of seaweed) for converting calcium nitrate from a nitre bed into saltpetre (KNO₃). He noticed the excessive corrosion of the copper vessels and traced the effect to a reaction between the copper and an unknown constituent of the liquid. On heating a residue obtained from the solution with sulphuric acid a beautiful violet vapour was formed, which condensed in a receiver in the form of crystalline plates. A year after the publication of this discovery, Gay Lussac published a paper on the subject in which he gave iodine its present name (from the Greek word *iodès* = violet).

As in the case of the other members of the halogen family, iodine does not occur free in nature. Usually it is found in the form of iodides, iodates or organic iodine compounds. The most important source of iodine are the iodates which occur in Chile saltpetre. Sea water contains traces of iodides which are absorbed by weed and sponges. Hence the ash from burning seaweed (kelp) was formerly an important source of iodine. Iodides also occur in water from springs and in saline water issuing with petroleum from oil wells which is now the source of several hundred tons of iodine annually.

Traces of iodine are essential to animal and vegetable life, hence its occurrence in many organic materials (see potassium iodide). Fish oil, shell fish and straw, for example, contain relatively large amounts of the order of 1 mg per kg.

7.13.2 Production

The solution used for the extraction of sodium nitrate from Chile saltpetre during about six months use accumulates iodine to the extent of 8-15 gm/litre and is sufficiently concentrated for efficient recovery of the iodine. This nitrate liquor is put in contact with anhydrous sulphur dioxide in an absorption tower to reduce iodates to sodium iodide (Sulphuric acid is formed at the same time by oxidation of the sulphur dioxide). The resulting solution is further blended with a small quantity of additional nitrate liquor to oxidise the sodium iodide to free iodine which precipitates in the form of a fine suspension. Reaction equations:

$$2\,NaIO_3 + 6\,SO_2 + 6\,H_2O \rightarrow 6\,H_2SO_4 + 2\,NaI.$$

$$5\,NaI + NaIO_3 + 5\,H_2SO_4 \rightarrow 3\,I_2 + 3\,Na_2SO_4 + 2\,H_2SO_4\ 3\,H_2O$$

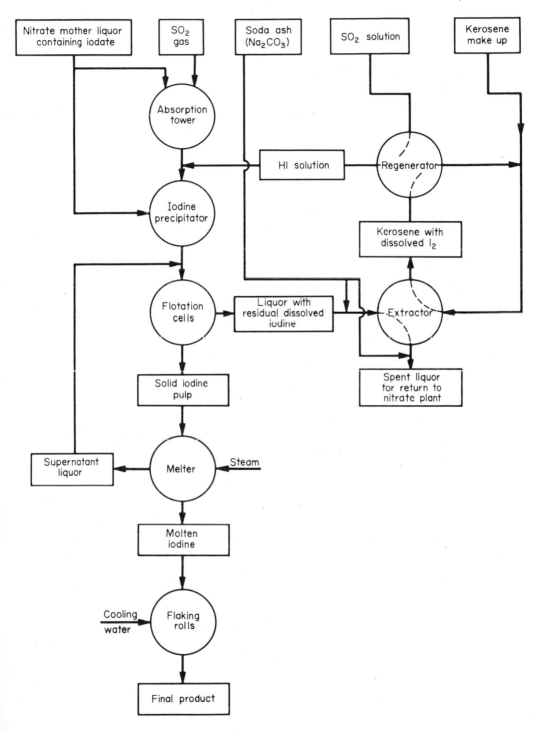

Fig. 7.12 Flow chart of iodine recovery from nitrate solutions.

The solid iodine is separated from the mother liquor by a flotation process (for flotation processes see volume III). The final product is obtained by melting followed by solidification in a rotating water cooled steel drum from which the iodine is scraped off in the form of thin flakes.

In California, brines containing iodide (e.g. from oil wells) are treated in one of three ways to recover iodine: (a) treatment with sulphuric acid and sodium nitrite; (b) treatment with chlorine and air (compare bromine recovery); and (c) with silver nitrate to precipitate insoluble silver iodide.

In France, Russia and Japan where alginic products are prepared from seaweed small quantities of iodine can be obtained at low cost as a by-product. There is a possibility that iodides may be recovered from solution more cheaply if a suitable ion-exchange can be developed.

7.13.3 Properties

Iodine forms blackish rhombic plates and has a melting point of 113.5° C and a boiling point of 184.5° C. Since its vapour pressure is relatively high at temperatures above room temperature iodine sublimes slowly (vaporizes slowly without passing through the intermediate liquid state) at normal pressure and temperatures below its melting point. Iodine vapour has a characteristic violet colour. Iodine is slightly soluble in water (about 0.03 g per 100 g water at 20° C) but it is very soluble in an aqueous potassium iodide solution (due to the formation of soluble compounds with potassium iodide) and in various organic solvents such as ethyl alcohol, toluene and ether. Like both chlorine and bromine, vapours of iodine irritate the mucous membranes. Vapour concentrations over 1 p.p.m. can not be inhaled for a long time without danger.

An important isotope of iodine is iodine 131 (I^{131}), a radioactive form of iodine which may be obtained by radiation of tellurium in a nuclear reactor (see isotopes and nuclear reactors, ch. 15). Iodine 131 is used as a source of radiation for biological research.

Iodine reacts with hydrogen to form hydrogen iodide (HI). It reacts also with various metals to form iodides. Iodine vapour combines with alkali metal vapours to produce a very luminous effect. With alkali metal hydroxides, iodine forms the corresponding hypoiodite (compare hypochlorites). Iodine reacts with concentrated ammonia to give nitrogen triiodide which is a detonating compound. Like chlorine and bromine, iodine is an oxidizing and disinfecting agent.

Iodine vapour is readily absorbed on many surfaces. Thus 100 g of charcoal can absorp up to 60 g of iodine and absorption from solution has been employed as a method for ascertaining specific surface areas of solids. When adsorbed on starch it gives a blue colour.

7.13.4 Uses

Iodine is the starting material for the production of all iodine compounds of which potassium iodide and sodium iodide are the most important. Iodine is also used for the production of non-toxic organic iodine compounds which can be injected into the bloodstream to assist in obtaining clear X-ray images of specific organs such as the kidneys. The iodine is effective in this respect owing to its ability to stop X-rays as a result of its high atomic weight. An example of such a compound is sodium 3-acetylamine 2.4.6. tri-iodo benzoate. Iodofluorescein and tetraiodofluorescein (erythrosin) are important dyes produced with iodine. Erythrosin is a sensitizer for photographic films. In organic chemistry iodine is used as a catalyst in the chlorination of aromatic compounds and in the alkylation of aromatic amines and in sulphation and sulphonation. In the form of 'tincture of iodine' (a solution of 2-5% of iodine in alcohol), iodine is widely used as a disinfectant and sterilizing agent.

Iodine is also used in iodine-quartz incandescent lamps which are used as a source of light in photography. These lamps can be used at a high over-voltage (resulting in a higher light yield), since the evaporation of the filament declines considerably when iodine is present in the lamp.

In analytical chemistry iodine is used for iodometric titrations. (Titration means the addition of small measured quantities of a liquid of known strength to a known quantity of another liquid of unknown strength until a certain chemical change is just completed. In this way the strength of the latter solution is measured.)

The concentration of iodine dissolved in an aqueous solution of potassium iodide can be accurately determined by means of arsenious oxide. Iodine oxidizes arsenious oxide to arsenic acid:

$$2I_2 + 5H_2O + As_2O_3 \rightarrow 4HI + 2H_3AsO_4$$

Thus a certain quantity of an iodine solution must be added to a known quantity of arsenious oxide (in solution) to convert the latter into arsenic acid. The end point is detected by the presence of a small amount of starch which gives a blue-coloured solution with any excess of iodine.

The standardized iodine solution can be titrated with an aqueous solution of sodium thiosulphate. The end point is also detected by the presence of a small amount of starch. Both standardized solutions are used in analytical chemistry to determine, in a mixture, the quantity of various constituents which can be oxidized or reduced with iodine or potassium iodide respectively.

The iodometric titrations are subject to several possible errors and a standard analytical methods reference book should be consulted if highly accurate titrations are required.

7.13.5 Statistics

The iodine production of some important producing countries is shown below:

| | In long tons | | | | |
	1956	1958	1960	1961	1963
Chile	691	1 308	1 653	2 413	2 140
Italy (from hot springs)	13	12			
Japan (mainly from oil wells)	587	710	930	1 102	1 400

The USA imported 1 500 long tons in 1963. About 38% of the US consumption (1 200 long tons in 1963) was used for the production of potassium iodide, 34% for other inorganic compounds, 23% for organic compounds and the remaining 5% was resublimed to get pure iodine into various uses (including medicine and fine chemicals).

The imports of elemental iodine into the UK were 365 long tons in 1963. In the same year, the exports (including some iodine produced in the UK) were about 20 long tons. In addition about 120 long tons of iodine were exported in the form of potassium iodide.

Chilean iodine (purity 99%) was sold at $1.18 per lb in the USA, and at 9s 0d per lb in the UK in 1965.

7.14 IODINE COMPOUNDS

Hydrogen iodide (HI) can be prepared from the elements at normal pressures in the presence of finely divided platinum heated to at least 300° C or under pressure at 150-200° C in the presence of chromic chloride. Hydrogen iodide can also be prepared by adding water to phosphorous iodides in the presence of excess iodine to avoid the formation of explosive phosphorous hydride (phosphorous iodides are formed from a mixture of red phosphorous and iodine). An aqueous solution of hydrogen iodide (hydriodic acid) is conveniently converted into the anhydrous form by dropping the solution on to phosphorous pentoxide and finally drying the resulting gas over phosphorous pentoxide.

Hydrogen iodide is a colourless gas boiling at $-35.4°$ C and freezing at $-50.9°$ C. Both the gas and the solutions are very corrosive and should be preserved in well stoppered dark bottles. Aqueous hydriodic acid is a strong acid which dissociates to at least 99% into its ions. Hydrogen iodide cannot be separated from a solution by distillation since at 127° C a constant boiling mixture of water and hydrogen iodide containing 57% (by weight) of the latter evaporates.

Hydriodic acid is used in pharmaceutical preparations and for the production of organic chemicals.

Potassium iodide (KI) is prepared by mixing iron filings and iodine with water to form a green solution of ferrous iodide. The latter solution is mixed with a boiling potassium carbonate solution to form a slurry of ferrous hydroxide in a solution of potassium iodide. Potassium iodide is crystallised by evaporating the solution after filtration. Potassium iodide is also prepared by treating iodine with potassium hydroxide to form a potassium iodide-iodate mixture. The mixture is evaporated to dryness and melted to convert the iodate into potassium iodide. The resulting melt is purified by recrystallization.

Potassium iodide is a white crystalline product melting at 686° C. Its solubility is 127 g per 100 g water at 0° C and 208 g at 100° C.

The purest grades of potassium iodide (and also of sodium iodide) are used in medical and photographic chemicals and for the production of light sensitive silver iodide for photographic emulsions. Silver iodide smoke has been used experimentally in nucleating clouds in artificial rain making (see also silver compounds, p. 572). Potassium iodide is also an effective catalyst in reactions involving aliphatic halogen compounds (e.g. the production of cyclopropane from 1.3-dichloropropane and zinc).

In view of the importance of iodine as a trace element in animal and vegetable life, potassium iodide is sometimes added to foodstuffs (e.g. for poultry), to table salt (iodized salt) and to fertilizers as an indirect method of addition to human diet. The absence of iodine in the alimentary intake of mammals leads to goitre, the enlarging of the thyroid gland. The iodine requirement for an adult is about 80-100 μ g per day.

The US production of potassium iodide was about 500 long tons in 1963. The UK is also an important producer and exports about 130-150 long tons annually. The US price of potassium iodide (in 250 lb drums) was $ 1.37 to 1.47 per lb in 1965. In the UK potassium iodide (in 50 kg lots) was sold at £ 1 1s 6d per kg in 1965.

Sodium iodide (NaI) may be prepared from iodine like potassium iodide. It is used for the same purposes as potassium iodide.

Alkali hypoiodite solutions are formed by the direct reaction between iodine and alkali metal hydroxides. The hypoiodites are salts of the weak and very unstable hypoiodic acid (HIO). The hypoiodite solutions are less unstable than the free acid but evolve oxygen readily. They are used in organic chemistry as an oxidizing agent.

Iodic acid (HIO$_3$) can be prepared by oxidizing iodine with nitric acid. Iodic acid forms colourless crystals which are very soluble in water (310 g dissolve in 100 g water at 16° C). It can be converted into the white crystalline iodine pentoxide (I$_2$O$_5$) by thermal dehydration. Both iodic acid and iodine pentoxide are used as an oxidizing agent in organic synthesis.

Potassium iodate (KIO$_3$) can be prepared (in moderate yield) by fusing potassium iodide with potassium chlorate, bromate or perchlorate. Potassium iodate can be isolated from the melt by recrystallization. The resulting white crystalline powder is moderately soluble in water (9 g per 100 g water at 25° C). Like the other iodates, potassium iodate is stable at room temperature but loses oxygen on heating. Potassium iodate is used in medicine and in analysis (e.g. iodate-iodide solutions release iodine for iodometric titrations).

Periodic acid (H$_5$IO$_6$) and *alkali metal periodates* are prepared by oxidation of an alkali iodate with a powerful oxidizing agent such as chlorine, bromine or potassium permanganate or by an electrolytic process. The resulting alkali periodate may be converted into the free acid by treating with a barium salt to form a barium periodate followed by treating the barium periodate with sulphuric acid to form a periodic acid solution and a precipitate of barium sulphate.

Periodic acid exists in three forms, meta-periodic acid HIO$_4$, dimeso-periodic acid (H$_4$I$_2$O$_9$) and paraperiodic acid (H$_5$IO$_6$) of which the latter is the only stable form. Paraperiodic acid forms colourless hygroscopic crystals which melt at 130° C and decompose slightly above this temperature.

The most important alkali periodates are, sodium para-periodate Na$_3$H$_2$IO$_6$, sodium meta-periodate (NaIO$_4$) and potassium meta-periodate (KIO$_4$) which are colourless crystalline products. Periodic acid and the periodates are powerful oxidizing agents. These products are used as oxidizing agents in analysis and organic synthesis. Solutions of periodic acid, for example, oxidize many organic compounds containing hydroxy, carbonyl and amino groups. This reaction is of importance in the elucidation of the structure of carbohydrates and other substances.

CHAPTER 8

Sulphur, Selenium, Tellurium and their Compounds

8.1 INTRODUCTION

Oxygen, sulphur, selenium, tellurium and polonium form the sixth main group of the periodic system. This group of elements is sometimes named 'the chalcogens' although the name, which means 'ore-forming elements' must be restricted to the first four of these which have a non-metallic character. Compounds of oxygen, sulphur, selenium and tellurium with metals are sometimes collectively called chalcogenides similar to the halides (see halogens, p. 203).

Polonium which has a metallic character is a short lived radioactive element which is only found as a trace element in products of radioactive decay.

Oxygen is frequently bivalent in its compounds (with the exception of some rare compounds in which it is univalent).

Sulphur, selenium, tellurium and polonium are tetra- and hexavalent in their compounds. In compounds with elements which have a low electron affinity (e.g. hydrogen and the metals), sulphur, selenium and tellurium are usually divalent, but in compounds with elements which have a strong electron affinity (e.g. oxygen, fluorine and chlorine) they are usually tetra- or hexavalent.

Sulphur, selenium and tellurium show a close analogy in their compounds as shown in the following table:

	Sulphur	Selenium	Tellurium
Acids	hydrogen sulphide (H_2S)	hydrogen selenide (H_2Se)	hydrogen telluride (H_2Te)
	sulphurous acid (H_2SO_3)	selenious acid (H_2SeO_3)	tellurous acid (H_2TeO_3)
	sulphuric acid (H_2SO_4)	selenic acid (H_2SeO_4)	telluric acid (H_2TeO_4)
Corresponding sodium salts	sodium sulphide (Na_2S)	sodium selenide (Na_2Se)	sodium telluride (Na_2Te)
	sodium suphite (Na_2SO_3)	sodium selenite (Na_2SeO_3)	sodium tellurite (Na_2TeO_3)
	sodium sulphate (Na_2SO_4)	sodium selenate (Na_2SeO_4)	sodium tellurate (Na_2TeO_4)

The analogous compounds of sulphur, selenium and tellurium also show a resemblance in their chemical properties, although, in general, the compounds of selenium and tellurium are less stable and, in addition, their acids are less strong than the corres-

Although the formulae of oxygen compounds show a close analogy with the compounds of the other elements of the sixth main group, the compounds themselves often show a different character.

8.2 ELEMENTAL SULPHUR (S, atomic weight = 32.07)

8.2.1 History

Sulphur in elemental form has been known for thousands of years. Twenty centuries before the birth of Christ it was used by priests in religious ceremonies. In very early times sulphur dioxide prepared by burning sulphur was used to bleach linen and cotton. The Chinese employed it as an ingredient of gunpowder about 500-600 B.C.

The sulphur deposits of Sicily have been worked since ancient times though it was not till about 1735, when manufacture of sulphuric acid from sulphur began, that exploitation on a large scale developed. For a hundred years thereafter a vigorous sulphur industry flourished in Sicily, virtually without competition. By the middle of the nineteenth century, however, demands of the rapidly developing chemical industry promoted a search for cheaper sources. Soon pyrites came into use as the raw material for sulphuric acid manufacture and sulphur recovered from chemical processes became available in considerable quantities; at the end of the 19th century about 40 000 tons of sulphur were being obtained annually in England by the method of Chance and Claus. (Reference 11, vol. V, p. 238 and reference 12, p. 126).

In this process (now obsolete) hydrogen sulphide was liberated from calcium sulphide by treating a paste of the latter with carbon dioxide. (The calcium sulphide was obtained as a by-product from a non-electrolytic caustic soda process which is also obsolete now.) The resulting hydrogen sulphide was converted into sulphur by the still commercial Claus Kiln process (see p. 270).

The discovery of the great American deposits of sulphur on the Gulf Coast occurred about this time and with the invention by Dr Herman Frasch of a cheap method of recovery by melting underground and pumping to the surface, this source became the most important for American industry and has remained so to the present time; vast quantities of American Frasch sulphur are exported all over the world. On the other hand sulphur from other sources, notably from natural gas and petroleum and from waste gases from chemical and metallurgical processes, is being produced in ever increasing quantities throughout the world and pyrites continues to play a major part as raw material in the manufacture of sulphuric acid which remains by far the largest product of sulphur.

8.2.2 Occurrence

Free sulphur occurs in extensive deposits in many areas. Deposits along the Gulf Coast of the USA, especially in Texas and Louisiana, and in Mexico are the most important on the American continent, and deposits in Venezuela and Colombia are also worked. Chile has large deposits, with a sulphur content of 45-75% but as these are situated at a height of 12 to 20000 ft in the Andes, exploitation has so far been slight.

In Europe native sulphur is found in Italy and Sicily. Poland has very large brimstone deposits and it is expected that these will be exploited commercially in the near future.

Russia has deposits in the Caracum desert permitting of very simple working. In Japan sulphur is found in large deposits in the volcanic region bordering the Pacific Ocean on the west and north.

China, Central Asia, the Middle East and elsewhere probably have very large resources of sulphur though information on their extent is lacking.

In most of the American deposits the sulphur has probably been formed from anhydrite ($CaSO_4$) and is present as a thick layer covering thick deposits of anhydrite which has been forced up in the course of time from deep layers under the influence of pressure, together with salt (see fig. 8.1). In Louisiana, Texas, Mexico and Venezuela, and also beneath the surface of the sea around these areas occur many hundreds of such deposits. Only the largest of these, containing sufficient quantities of sulphur can be worked, and then only when the subsoil lends itself to the exploitation. Up to now only sixteen such 'domes' have been worked, including two in Mexico, although the search for others is continuing.

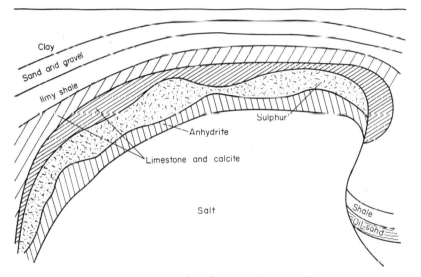

Fig. 8.1 Diagrammatic representation of the cap of a 'salt dome' in Texas. On top of the dome is a layer of anhydrite, on top of this a layer of sulphur which probably comes from the anhydrite by a process of reduction with petroleum-like substances.

Sulphur deposits probably result from compounds originating in deep high temperature zones. These are broken down into water and sulphur at some lower temperature. Free sulphur, and sulphide ores, can also result from chemical transformation under bacterial influence. In certain North African lakes, for instance, sulphur is produced from sulphates and suchlike by bacterial action. Hundreds of tons are washed out annually by local workers. Efforts are being made to grow bacteria in cultures and to improve the breeds in order to increase their productivity. The improved types of bacteria could then be used in various effluents which would simultaneously be purified and serve as a source of sulphur. It has been proposed in America to undertake large scale breeding of sulphate-reducing bacteria to inject into sulphur 'domes', not yet suitable for exploitation, in the expectation of accelerating sulphur formation. These domes might in due course become economic propositions for exploitation.

Sulphur is also found combined in many compounds such as sulphates, sulphides, albumins, etc. Many important minerals contain quantities of combined sulphur: examples are iron pyrites; FeS_2, copper glance (chalcocite); Cu_2S, galena; PbS, zinc blende; ZnS, and anhydrite; $CaSO_4$. These minerals, particularly iron pyrites (see section 8.3) are important sources of sulphur for the chemical industry. Many common gases, such as coal gas, petroleum refinery gas, flue gas and natural gas contain important quantities of sulphur compounds. Sulphur obtained from natural gas, especially in Canada and Lacq (France), is making an ever increasing contribution to world supplies.

8.2.3 Production from native deposits (mining)

a. Mechanical mining and concentration by melting. Native deposits in the island of Sicily and in some parts of Italy are worked by mining and the sulphur concentrated by melting. The rock containing sulphur is removed mechanically by drilling, with dynamite, or manually from mines. Rich ores contain 30-40% S, lean ores about 20-25% S. The ore is carried to the surface in baskets by manual labour, an expensive operation in spite of the low wages and poor social conditions of the workers.

In Sicily the sulphur rock is loosely piled in brick-lined trough-shaped pits, known as calcaroni. The piles are covered with a light layer of porous earth, then melted. The heat needed for melting is obtained by burning between half and a third of the sulphur, a wasteful process which results in a high cost price for the end product. Sulphur melted from the rock is tapped off from the bottom of the trough and cast, in wooden boxes, into rough blocks weighing about 65 lb.

Calcaroni of 7 000 ft³ capacity burn for about a month, whilst those of 25 000 ft³ run for some two months. The average yield is not more than 37.5% of the total sulphur content. In the months when there is blossom on the trees in Sicily, the use of these furnaces is prohibited, because the excessive quantities of SO_2 are deleterious to the blossom.

Nowadays use is made as a rule of Gill furnaces (forni) (see ref. 2, p. 2200). This design consists of a circular furnace having four chambers (see Brick Baking, vol. II). The air needed for combustion is preheated by passage through the hot finished product, while the hot waste gas preheats the ore to be melted. Such ovens have an efficiency approaching 90%. An even more economical process is to use vertical boilers in which steam is used to preheat the rock; the process also produces a better quality sulphur.

Installation costs for this type of furnace are high, however, while coal is expensive and water scarce. Such ovens are, therefore, only used for the richest ores and in the periods during which SO_2 may not be discharged into the atmosphere. The product of these furnaces is made available as calate in cakes of 130 lb weight.

A part of the raw sulphur production is purified by distillation in steel retorts. The vapours are condensed in large stone chambers in which the sulphur is deposited as finely divided flowers of sulphur on the walls. This continues until the temperature is high enough to melt the remainder. About a quarter of the contents of the retorts can be obtained as flowers of sulphur. This is very finely-divided and is considered better for dusting on plants than finely ground sulphur (see p. 263). The liquid sulphur is allowed to set into blocks in wooden moulds. Distillation is carried out in Marseilles as well as in Sicily.

  b. Concentration of mechanical mined ore by flotation. Where lean sulphur ore has to be worked the flotation system is applicable (see vol. III, Ores in general). This is the case in France, Central Asia (where everything except ore and water has to be brought in by air) and in Colombia in the Andes. In these places surface ores containing 20% sulphur are encountered, and in France even as low as 8%. These deposits are mined and broken down before wet-milling in a pebble or ball mill. The mud is heated, whereby the sulphur is melted and strong turbulence encourages the agglomeration of the small sulphur particles into larger units. After chilling with cold water the larger sulphur grains are sieved off. The remainder is obtained by flotation and after centrifuging is added to the larger grains for melting. In France the flotation has to be repeated before the melting process, since the ore has a lower sulphur content. Liquid sulphur, after the free acids have been neutralised with chalk, is filtered through stainless

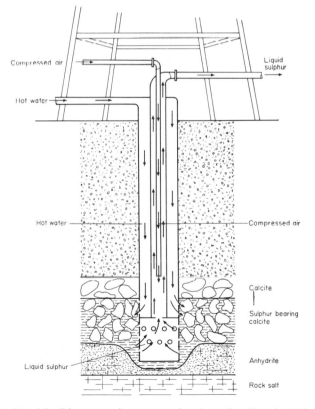

Fig. 8.2 Diagrammatic cross-section through a Frasch sulphur mining installation. Basically it comprises three coaxial tubes. Hot water is pumped downwards through the annular space formed by the outer and middle tubes to melt the sulphur in the deposit. Compressed air is passed through the inner tube in order to force the molten sulphur upwards through the annular space formed by the inner and middle tubes.

steel gauze to produce sulphur of up to 99.9% purity. Since such lean ores occur throughout the world a large increase in the number of such (American) installations is expected.

    c. Mining by the Frasch process. The Frasch process was developed to recover sulphur from the American Gulf Coast deposits. Mechanical mining is not practicable in these regions as quicksands cover the domes. Large quantities of sulphuretted hydrogen are also present, and the poisonous nature of this gas prohibits the usual sinking of mine shafts.

    Three coaxial tubes are inserted into the sulphur layer (see fig. 8.2). Water at 160° C is pumped through the outer tube to melt the sulphur; any solid matter present settles out of the molten sulphur. Compressed air at high pressure passed through the inner tube forces the liquid sulphur through the middle tube and out to the surface. In general the sulphur passes into a collective sump, together with sulphur from other sources. From there the sulphur is transported by compressed air to very large reservoirs containing 50 000 to 150 000 tons of sulphur. The walls of the reservoirs are built up gradually as they are filled (see fig. 8.3). Sulphur obtained in this way contains air. The light-coloured 'US Frasch bright sulphur' includes a maximum of 0.15% ash; dark Frasch sulphur contains minor quantities of bitumen in addition to the 0.15% ash. As a rule, many impurities have to be removed from the sulphur (ref. 4, p. 109), and this is done by allowing them to settle from the liquid sulphur after which filtration may be necessary. The filters are made of several layers of fine stainless steel gauze carrying infusorial earth as the actual filtration medium. Dark varieties are treated with fuller's

Fig. 8.3 View of a sulphur vat. The vat is filled with liquid sulphur and after solidification of the sulphur the walls of the vat are lifted and a further portion of liquid sulphur is poured on the top of the solidified layer. In this way enormous blocks of sulphur are formed.

Fig. 8.4 A vat of virtually pure sulphur is broken up by an electric shovel for loading into a conveyer belt at Port Sulphur, Louisiana, Freeport Sulphur Company's storage and shipping point on the Mississippi River.

earth and suchlike as adsorbers. After about four days the filters have to be cleaned. The filter cake has some value in the preparation of SO_2.

After solidification of the sulphur, explosives or electric shovels are used to break up the large blocks into lumps which are loaded by grabs into the waiting vehicles (see fig. 8.4). The local harbours have large storage, loading and unloading facilities.

A cheaper method of processing the sulphur, of more recent date, is to form the sulphur into flakes by allowing it to flow over slowly rotating chilled cylinders. Small additions of zinc stearate are made to prevent the formation of plastic sulphur; the setting up of dust is also eliminated by this means. The process is cheaper than that involving casting and then breaking down the massive sulphur blocks.

In large enterprises a very large boiler installation (see fig. 8.5) is needed for supplying the superheated steam. The water is led to the domes through heavily insulated pipelines. Several sources together deliver their sulphur to steam-heated tanks, for further transport by means of a distribution network to a reservoir in process of being built up. A layer of nearly 8 inches (10 cm) is added every fifteen minutes in this fashion. The pipelines and pumps used for this are heated, and are insulated to reduce loss of heat. Plastic sulphur, together with monoclinic sulphur is first formed, and finally passes to the rhombic form (see p. 264).

Fig. 8.5 View of a boiler installation which supplies the superheated steam for a Frasch sulphur mine in Mexico.

Much of the water used to melt the sulphur in the ground reappears, either by itself, or through installations of pipes, at the surface. This water is highly corrosive and contains a considerable amount of hydrogen sulphide. As a rule it is necessary to purify the water, which is done by passing it through washing towers having a flow of hot flue gases from underneath. The gases pick up and carry away the hydrogen sulphide. The waste gases are dispersed into the atmosphere through high chimneys. Sometimes the waste water is carried out to sea by long pipelines, and in other cases the hot waste water can be treated so that, after mixing with fresh water, it can be re-used for the 'subterranean sulphur-melting operation. Such treatment saves considerable heat.

In a few instances the towers and underground pipelines are built in swamps, and the rest of the installation is situated on solid ground or on boats. In 1960 a very large installation was put into operation, exploiting a dome a quarter of a mile out to sea. The installation cost $36 million. Special measures had to be taken to reduce corrosion. Also the process waste water required special treatment to prevent contamination of all the surrounding water. A pipeline consisting of three coaxial tubes carries the liquid sulphur in its inner tube. The second tube carries used hot water back from the dome and the outer tube consists of a thick insulation. The line is connected with two secondary pipes for recycling and reheating the water. Helicopters are used for transporting the personnel; extra safety precautions have to be applied since the mine is situated in the hurricane belt. Directional boring (see Petroleum, vol. IV) is used.

Many domes are of such small dimensions that the construction of a large plant for winning sulphur is not practicable. For such cases transportable installations have been developed, weighing 300 tons and capable of producing the same weight of sulphur daily. When one of the small domes is exhausted the entire installation is moved bodily to the next.

The largest installation has been built in America, in a swamp of large area; very long piles have been employed in this installation. The boiler house produces 460 000 ft^3 of water at 165° C daily. Since sufficiently fresh water can only be obtained in the period from June to February, artificial lakes have been built containing 140 000 000 ft^3. The lakes are filled during the period in which the water is least brackish. The plant has a capacity of 500 000 tons of sulphur per year, and cost $14 million. The molten sulphur produced is carried in insulated barges to Port Sulphur. Similar barges are also used for the transportation to the processing factories, in order to save the expensive melting. The temperature drops by 0.5° C in five minutes so that considerable fuel saving can be achieved by rapid transport over short distances.

8.2.4 Production from waste gases, industrial gases and natural gas

Considerable quantities of sulphur are obtained from the waste products of the chemical industry and gas, coke and petroleum processes.

In these gases, sulphur is often present in the form of hydrogen sulphide. Hydrogen sulphide can be separated from gases containing it by the use of alkaline solvents (ref. 5) such as an ethanolamine glycol mixture, or potassium phosphate, sodium carbonate, sodium phenolate, sodium hydroxide and sodium thioarsenate. The last named is used by blowing air through the solution after sufficient hydrogen sulphide has been taken up. Finely divided solid sulphur is then precipitated and separated. The solution can be repeatedly used. Increasing use is made of hydrogen fluoride to derive sulphur from petroleum gases (ref. 1). Iron and nickel oxides in alkaline solutions are also sometimes used for the same purpose. The resulting sulphides can easily be converted back to oxides with the formation of sulphur or sulphur dioxide (ref. 5, p. 286).

With ethanolamine-glycol the gas to be purified is compressed to about 60 atm and brought into contact with the liquid mixture. The liquid takes up the hydrogen sulphide and carbon dioxide present in the gas. When the absorbing liquid is saturated with impurities it is regenerated in a separate distillation column (see under alcohol and petroleum in vol. IV) in which the dissolved gases are liberated together with some water vapour. The liquid is recycled to the absorption stages whilst the gases from the distillation column containing mainly hydrogen sulphide and carbon dioxide may be treated by partial combustion to recover the sulphur content as free sulphur (see the Claus Kiln process under hydrogen sulphide, p. 270).

In the purification plants of gas works, hydrogen sulphide contained in coal gas, coke oven gas etc. is often absorbed in ferric oxide (dry absorption process). The latter is regenerated by exposing it to air which oxidises the sulphide formed to ferric oxide and free sulphur. The resulting mixture is used as absorbent several times until it loses its activity due to the accumulation of sulphur (see also coal gas and coke oven gas, vol. II). The exhausted mass (spent oxide) contains up to 50% elemental sulphur. This is recovered by solution in carbon disulphide. The solution is stirred with oleum (fuming sulphuric acid) which oxidises the tarry products. The sulphur can also be dissolved at high temperature in a hydrocarbon. Pure sulphur crystallizes on slow cooling. In England some 100 000 tons of sulphur are produced from this source annually. Spent oxide is sometimes burned to obtain sulphur dioxide for sulphuric acid manufacture and iron oxide.

The exhaust gases from the spinning baths in rayon production also contain hydrogen sulphide which is recovered by means of purifiers similar to those used in gas works (see gas production, vol. II). Hydrogen sulphide obtained in this way is purer than that from gas works, since there are no tarry components in the raw material.

Sour natural gas often contains a large amount of hydrogen sulphide, reaching 14% (in terms of sulphur) in the gas from Lacq (France). The recovery of this sulphur is increasing rapidly throughout the world so that the world sulphur production situation is being strongly influenced. In 1957, for instance, 28 000 tons of sulphur were produced in Lacq, a figure which had risen to 1 500 000 tons in 1964. The largest possible number of other components are of course simultaneously produced from the natural gas.

Raw petroleum always contains sulphur (in the form of mercaptans, hydrogen sulphide etc.) ranging from 0.4% (Pennsylvania) to 8% (Middle East). Large refineries can produce as much as 100 000 tons of sulphur a year. In these refineries mercaptans and various other sulphur compounds are converted into hydrogen sulphide by catalytic processes (see Petroleum refining, vol. IV) and the latter is recovered by means of alkaline solvents as mentioned above. A good deal of progress can be made in this field throughout the world. England, for example imported 50 million tons of crude petroleum in 1963, with an average sulphur content of 2%. It has been estimated that 10% of the total sulphur originally imported in oil can be recovered.

8.2.5 Production from sulphide ores

In Scandinavia and Iberia pyrites is processed by the Orkla-method (ref. 8, p. 82). Copper-rich pyrites is heated in a form of blast furnace together with coke, limestone and quartz. The resulting gas mixture contains sulphur, sulphur dioxide, carbon oxysulphide (COS), hydrogen sulphide, carbon dioxide and nitrogen from the air. Catalytic treatment of the mixture can produce 80% of elemental sulphur. In addition, a 'matte' is formed with 6-8% copper (see Copper, vol. III).

The resultant sulphur contains a large amount of arsenic. This is removed by melting the sulphur and stirring in milk of lime. Calcium arsenate is formed, which can be filtered off from the liquid sulphur.

Many metals occur as sulphides, and these are used as sources of the metals and also for the manufacture of sulphuric acid, sulphur and sulphur dioxide (see sulphuric acid, sulphur dioxide, iron, nickel, copper and zinc). In one process pyrites is ignited with small quantities of air, when part of the sulphur is obtained as the element. The fluid bed method is often used. Sulphur is condensed from the gas mixture formed, and sulphur dioxide is also recovered.

In Canada thousands of tons of pyrrhotite (magnetic pyrites) are won daily by flotation of valuable ores, such as those of copper. In current practice the waste is made into a mud and heated in an autoclave with oxygen to above 114° C. Liquid sulphur is then freed in the form of fine drops. The mixture is cooled and the sulphur sieved out. It still contains a small quantity of sulphides.

8.2.6 Commercial forms of sulphur, their storage and transportation

Sulphur is frequently transported as a liquid in heated tankers and even in barges which are specially insulated to avoid solidification.

Lump sulphur formed by crushing blocks is sold commercially as crude run-of-mine material in grades generally over 99.5% pure and material of similar purity is available in the form of flake or roll sulphur (see p. 259); it is transported loose in trucks and in the holds of ships and may be stored in piles in the open or with some protection from the weather.

Refined sulphur produced by distilling crude sulphur, generally sold to a specification in excess of 99.8%, is available in lumps and cast sticks.

Sublimed sulphur or flowers of sulphur and sulphur milled to very fine degrees of subdivision are available at a premium. Large quantities of sulphur are ground each year mainly for use as a fungicide (see uses of sulphur, p. 265).

The milling operation is done in grinding and pulverizing machines in an atmosphere of carbon dioxide or nitrogen (see Ores, vol. III). The milled material is sieved into various degrees of fineness; this operation is also carried out in an inert atmosphere, because of inflammability of the powder and the danger of explosions of the sulphur-air mixture. The finer the powder the more suitable it is for dusting on the plants and for this reason colloidally divided sulphur is preferred. Certain brands fetch a good price in vine-growing districts. Sometimes the powder is prevented from agglomerating by mixing with the finest type of silica-'aerosil'. In order to obtain extremely fine division the process referred to as 'micronizing' is being increasingly used in the United States. The grains to be treated are introduced into a stream of superheated steam, or an inert gas, which is tangentially discharged at high velocity into a steel cylinder which may be about 60 cm in diameter. The grains come into contact with one another and with the cylinder and gradually descend inside the cylinder. By this process they are so finely ground that sometimes particle sizes of 0.005 mm result. The smallest and lightest particles are driven towards the axis and are carried upwards with the gas and are led out through a tube to be passed through cyclones and filters to recover the fine material.

Micronizing is used not only on sulphur but also for insecticides, fungicides, pharmaceutical preparations, grinding and polishing powders, iron oxide, etc. Operation of the machine is relatively expensive as a high-powered fan is involved. The equipment is often combined with mixing and packaging devices.

The Szegvari mill is particularly useful for milling sulphur into dispersions suitable for use in rubber. This mill takes the form of a vertical drum of stainless steel with a double wall for heating or cooling, and containing steel balls. A vertical shaft carrying horizontal arms rotates inside and throws the steel balls (or sometimes hard stones) against the powder so violently that, for instance, in fifteen hours' operation it is dispersed in water to the same degree as was achieved in ten days by previous methods.

Premium grades of sulphur are prepared for the rubber trade in particular with special specifications for low acid, ash and moisture content. A grade sold as 'Insoluble Sulphur' and consisting largely of the allotropic 'mu'-form (see p. 264) is used especially in the rubber industry.

8.2.7 Properties

Sulphur forms rhombic crystals, sometimes of great beauty. The sulphur obtained by casting liquid sulphur in cylindrical moulds ('roll sulphur') consists of a mass of rhombic crystals. The melting point is 114° C, at which temperature a thin liquid forms, which first thickens with increasing temperature, and subsequently becomes thin again until evaporation takes place at about 450° C. The changes in viscosity can be explained by assuming that the atoms keep re-forming into different groups or molecules. A plasticine-like form, known as plastic sulphur, is produced by pouring liquid sulphur

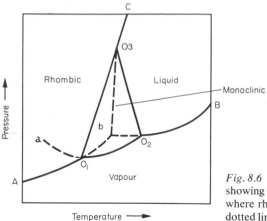

Fig. 8.6 Phase diagram of elemental sulphur, showing the regions of temperature and pressure where rhombic and monoclinic sulphur are stable: dotted lines indicate metastable conditions.

at about 200° C into water. Plastic sulphur has a specific gravity of 1.96, against that of 2.07 for the rhombic form; this again is a consequence of the molecular regrouping.

When an element occurs in different molecular groupings the phenomenon is known as allotropy and the different varieties of the element are called allotropic modifications. At low temperatures the rhombic modification of sulphur is the stable one, so that the other sorts – including the plastic form – return to this. Flowers of sulphur contains at least one-third part of an amorphous modification. It is supposed that the accelerators used in the vulcanization of rubber (see vol. V) transform the sulphur catalytically into a more rapidly reacting sulphur modification.

When melted sulphur is cooled until a solid crust covers the surface and the remaining liquid is poured off the sides of the vessel will be found covered with needle shaped (monoclinic) transparent crystals. The monoclinic allotropic form of sulphur melts at 119° C and has a specific gravity of 1.96; on exposure to air it reverts slowly to the rhombic form.

Fig. 8.6 illustrates the regions of temperature and pressure where rhombic and monoclinic sulphur are stable; dotted lines indicate metastable conditions; thus O_1A represents stable rhombic sulphur in equilibrium with vapour, O_1O_2 stable monoclinic sulphur in equilibrium with vapour and aO_1 a metastable monoclinic sulphur in equilibrium with vapour; O_1 is the transition temperature for change of rhombic into monoclinic sulphur (about 95° C) and O_2 the melting point of monoclinic (about 119° C) in equilibrium with sulphur vapour; O_1O_3 indicates the effect of pressure on the transition of rhombic to monoclinic and O_2O_3 the same effect on the melting point of monoclinic.

A further allotropic sulphur modification is the 'mu'-form, which has become important in the last twenty years. This is prepared by dissolving rhombic sulphur in carbon disulphide. The solution is rapidly chilled so that a polymerized variety of sulphur (with a molecular weight probably of several hundreds of thousands) is precipitated. This modification is insoluble in all solvents. By the application of heat the 'mu'-form is converted back to rhombic sulphur. It is used especially in the rubber industry, where ordinary sulphur would begin vulcanisation prematurely, giving rise to 'blooming'.

Sulphur is a good insulator of heat and electricity. It is insoluble in water and most acids. The solubility in carbon disulphide, sulphur chloride, and strongly heated oils is fairly high.

In many chemical compounds sulphur may take the place of oxygen and the prefix thio- to the corresponding oxygen compound denotes such replacement, e.g. phosgene or carbonyl chloride ($COCl_2$) and thiophosgene or thiocarbonyl chloride ($CSCl_2$): sodium sulphate (Na_2SO_4) and sodium thiosulphate ($Na_2S_2O_3$). For a more precise definition see ref. 7, p.

8.2.8 Uses

By far the greatest quantities of sulphur are used in the preparation of sulphuric acid (see p. 562). An important alternative for the preparation of sulphuric acid and sulphur dioxide is pyrites. The best material to use from an economic point of view depends on the geographical situation of the mines, transportation and similar considerations.

Much sulphur is also used for preparing the sulphur dioxide needed for ice machines, for purifying sugar juice, for sulphite-cellulose etc. In burning sulphur to sulphur dioxide special furnaces are used as described under Section 8.6.

An important use is for the manufacture of carbon disulphide. Sulphur is also used for vulcanizing rubber (see p. 264), as a constituent of gunpowder (for which purpose the very finest ground material is needed) and for the preparation of ultramarine, vermilion, sulphur chloride and polysulphides.

In pharmacy sulphur is used primarily for veterinary purposes, such as the treatment of skin diseases. This application is encountering increasing competition from organic compounds of many sorts (see vol. IV).

Large quantities of flowers of sulphur and milled sulphur are used each year in fighting the formation of fungus on plants; this use is specially important in the vine-growing industry.

Calcium polysulphide, sometimes known as 'lime sulphur', is obtained by boiling sulphur with an equal quantity of slaked lime in water, usually in the modern process, at high pressure. It is used as protective agent against fungus; formerly an emulsion in water was used for washing sheep. Its fungicidal effect is due to the polysulphides it contains which should amount to at least 20%.

The wine industry uses a relatively large amount of sulphur for making 'sulphur bandages'. For these, cotton bandage or cord is treated with molten sulphur. When such a bandage is burnt SO_2 is formed, and if the bandage is placed in a barrel or bottle, the sulphur dioxide disinfects the wet walls of the vessel. A large quantity of sulphur is also burnt for the bleaching of wool.

Liquid sulphur impregnates paper and wood readily to form a water and corrosion-proof material. Thin paper is sometimes impregnated with sulphur for use as a non-corrosive robust packaging material. Tubes are centrifugally cast from a mixture of ground coke, sand and sulphur (see Centrifugal casting, vol. III); steel tubes are also internally clad with the material to make them serviceable with corrosive media.

Good homogeneous mixtures of sulphur and finely ground sand together with carbon or similar fillers and thiokol (polymer prepared from an alkali polysulphide and an organic dihalide; see Synthetic rubbers, vol. V) are commonly used as cements for acid-proof floors and containers. They are also used for fixing metal in stone and for sealing large steel pipes. These cements are converted to other modifications at high temperatures and they are, therefore, not usable above about 95° C. They may be used for non-oxidizing acids and salts but not for alkalis, organic solvents, oils and suchlike. If protected by a covering of stone supported in a synthetic resin cement, they can be used at somewhat higher temperatures. They generally require a completely impervious undercoat. In each case the appropriate filler depends on the nature of the chemicals coming into contact with the floors and surfaces.

8.2.9 Statistics and trade

The world production of sulphur and the production in various important producing countries is shown in the following table:

	Elemental Sulphur			Sulphur content of other forms (not recovered as elemental sulphur)	
	In '000 long tons				
	1960	1964		1960	1964
*World total	10400	13800		8000	8000
Canada, mainly from natural gas	250	1440	smelter gas	260	390
			sulphides	390	150
*China, native	120	120	pyrites	400	500
from refinery gas and sulphides	120	120			
France, from natural gas	780	1490	pyrites	120	80
Germany (West), from various sources	80	80	pyrites	180	180
Germany (East)	110	120	pyrites	50	40
Italy, native	80	30	pyrites	690	630
Japan, native and from sulphides	240	240	pyrites and pyrrhotite	1000	1140
Mexico, native (mainly Frasch)	1270	1660			
from natural gas	45	36			
Netherlands, from sulphide ores	30	34			
Norway, from sulphide ores	70	—	pyrites	290	320
Poland, native	25	290	pyrites	80	85
Portugal, from sulphide ores	10	3	pyrites	290	280
Spain, mainly from sulphide ores	26	70	pyrites	1030	1030
United Kingdom, from spent oxide	100	90	anhydrite	160	200
other inc. petrol ref.	60	54	zinc concentr.	60	65
USA, native (mainly Frasch)	5030	5220	smelter gas	340	350
from natural gas etc.	760	1020	H_2S and SO_2	90	120
			pyrites	420	350
*USSR, native	800	950	pyrites	1460	1670
other	200	400			

(* estimated)

The most important sulphur exporting countries are Canada, France, Mexico and the USA which exported 1156000; 1028000; 1812000 and 1928000 long tons respectively in 1964. (In the USA however about 1500000 long tons were imported from Mexico and Canada in the same year).

The most substantial quantities of elemental sulphur for consumption are imported into the UK. The imports were 500000 and 708000 long tons in 1960 and 1964 respectively. The USA, France and Mexico are the major suppliers of the sulphur imports into the UK. Federal Germany imported 398000 long tons and Australia 377000 long tons in 1964.

In 1964 about 85% of the elemental sulphur consumed in the USA (about 7.5 million tons total) was burned to sulphur dioxide for the production of sulphuric acid. In many European countries pyrites is a more important raw material for sulphuric acid production and for this reason the percentage of elemental sulphur used for the production of sulphuric acid is considerably lower.

The price of crude sulphur in the USA was $27 to $31 per short ton in 1965. The price of various refined forms of sulphur (lumps, flowers, etc.) ranged from $2.25 to 5.75 per 100 lb depending on the grade. In the UK crude sulphur was sold at £13 to £18 per long ton in 1965.

8.3 PYRITES

8.3.1 Occurrence
Pyrite, more specifically iron pyrite or pyrites, is largely composed of iron sulphide (FeS_2); it is present in many parts of the world, occurring generally in lens-shaped deposits, sometimes enormous in size, containing varying amounts of FeS_2 and of numerous other substances. The richest deposits occur in Spain where the 'pyrites belt' is about 100 miles long and 18 miles wide, running through into Portugal. Other deposits in Europe of commercial importance are found in Cyprus, Norway, Yugoslavia, Greece, Sweden, Germany and Italy. The most important Norwegian deposits are expected to be exhausted in about twenty-five years' time. Deposits in Russia are widespread and extensive especially in the Ural districts. In Asia very large deposits occur in Japan and these have been worked extensively for many years. In the United States important deposits occur in the Appalachian mountains and in California.

Coal nearly always occurs in association with pyrites and the total quantities are very large although the major portion of sulphur in coal is present in the form of organic sulphur compounds.

Pyrites also occurs in ores which are mined for their non-ferrous value. Canadian mineral undertakings, for instance, turn out considerable quantities of pyrites as a by-product.

8.3.2 Mining, concentration and purification
Pyrites is mined in open cast mining or underground mining depending on the situation of the deposit.

The large Spanish deposits occur close to the surface and open cast mining has been extensively used. Spanish pyrites formerly contained as much as 2% of copper and even now the copper content may reach about 1%. This makes it desirable to treat the pyrites for copper production (see Copper, vol. III). Pyrites may be treated for copper removal by techniques of flotation and leaching after weathering; the ore after such treatment is traded as 'washed pyrites'.

Pyrites is sometimes recovered from coal dust and is separated by flotation. Up to the present time very large quantities of inferior coal, containing sometimes as much as 13% sulphur (as pyrites), have been stored in large dumps in the vicinity of the mines. This waste is now being examined with a view to recovering the pyrites content and in

America large installations have been designed to recover 500 tons pyrites daily. According to calculations this is being carried out on very attractive terms.

8.3.3 Properties

In the pure condition pyrites contains 53.4% S and 46.6% Fe. Common qualities generally contain less than 47% S and pyrites of still lower sulphur content is very common.

There is a chance of self-ignition, in particular with finely divided damp pyrites and because of this only small quantities are stored together. The introduction of cool chimney gases to the enclosed silos is desirable. Finely divided pyrites can also be one of the causes of self-ignition of coal.

Pure pyrites has a density of 5.0 and melts with decomposition when heated above 400° C.

8.3.4 Uses

The principal use of pyrites is in the production of sulphur dioxide for sulphuric acid manufacture (see Section 8.6). The pyrites is burned to form gaseous sulphur dioxide and the residual cinder consisting largely of ferric oxide is usually sold for iron manufacture. In some instances the cinder is worked up for small amounts of valuable metals e.g. silver and gold. Pyrites often contains much arsenic as well as traces of selenium and tellurium. The last two elements are often obtained as by-products in processes in which pyrites is burned.

Sulphur may be produced directly from pyrites and in Spain and Norway special methods are employed to do this (see p. 262).

8.3.5 Statistics

The world production of pyrites (including cuprous pyrites) and the production in some important producing countries is shown in the following table:

| | Gross weight | | Sulphur content | |
| | (in '000 long tons) | | | |
	1960	1964	1960	1964
World (estimated)	19 000	19 000	9 000	9 000
Cyprus	914	655	440	320
Finland	256	542	110	260
Italy	1 523	1 375	690	630
Japan (inc. pyrrhotite)	2 278	2 729	1 040	1 260
Norway	820	708	360	320
Portugal	644	598	300	270
Spain	2 217	2 303	1 050	1 100
USSR	2 756	3 149	1 460	1 670

The largest exporter of pyrites is Spain which exported close to 1.2 million long tons (gross weight) in 1964. The most substantial quantities of pyrites are imported by Western Germany which imported about 1.5 million long tons in 1964. The imports of pyrites into the UK were 270 000 and 284 000 long tons respectively in 1960 and 1964.

In the USA the price of pyrites (containing 48-50% sulphur) was about $5 per short ton in 1965.

8.4 HYDROGEN SULPHIDE

8.4.1 Occurrence

Hydrogen sulphide occurs widely in nature and industry. It is found in most natural gas and petroleum deposits. Very large amounts are liberated in production of coke and coal gas. Hydrogen sulphide is a by-product of carbon disulphide manufacture by the reaction of sulphur with hydrocarbons. It is also formed in substantial quantities in the process for manufacture of viscose rayon (see vol. VI).

8.4.2 Production

Hydrogen sulphide is generally found as an undesirable impurity in natural gas and crude coal gas. It may be separated from the contaminated gas by one of the methods described in Section 8.2.4 and as indicated its sulphur content can be recovered in the form of elemental sulphur or as sulphur dioxide.

Quantities of hydrogen sulphide are manufactured for cobalt and nickel ore treatment by reacting hydrogen and sulphur vapour over a catalyst at about 500° C. Suitable catalysts are bauxite and aluminium hydrosilicate.

In the small-scale preparation of hydrogen sulphide, for instance in the laboratory, the raw material is generally iron sulphide (FeS). This is treated with an acid and reaction takes place according to the equation:

$$FeS + H_2SO_4 \rightarrow FeSO_4 + H_2S$$

8.4.3 Properties

Hydrogen sulphide is a gas smelling like bad eggs (many albumins contain sulphur, and this is freed in the form of hydrogen sulphide during decomposition). It dissolves to some extent in water, forming a weak acid. Most of the salts of this acid with heavy metals (sulphides) are insoluble in water and many have a characteristic colour which leads to their extensive use in qualitative chemical analysis.

Hydrogen sulphide in the presence of water vapour is strongly corrosive to iron and steel and attacks copper and silver rapidly. Inhaled it is extremely poisonous. Because of its poisonous nature it must not be allowed to escape into the atmosphere: this has often been the cause of industrial accidents and for this reason the maintenance of ducting carrying the gas must be stringently carried out. In plants where large quantities are made or handled, the operators often wear gas masks containing active carbon, charged with an oxide of vanadium, copper, iron and/or chromium. In the presence of oxygen even the slightest traces of hydrogen sulphide are converted rapidly to sulphur and water. The catalyst can be easily regenerated. Leakage of hydrogen sulphide into an enclosed space can be easily detected electrically by the heating effect produced on a platinum filament coated with catalyst.

Even very small quantities of hydrogen sulphide (e.g. the amounts contained in insufficiently purified town gas) can be detected with filter paper saturated with lead acetate solution. If hydrogen sulphide is present the dark brown glittering lead sulphide forms immediately. The presence of hydrogen sulphide in town gas is undesirable since on combustion the irritant and poisonous sulphur dioxide is formed (see also Gases, vol. II).

8.4.4 Uses

Hydrogen sulphide is an important raw material in the preparation of thio-urea (see p. 350) and also of calcium or potassium hydro-sulphides ($Ca(HS)_2$ and $NaHS$ respectively). It is also used for the purification of arsenical sulphuric acid, as the arsenic contained is directly converted to the insoluble arsenic sulphide.

It is used in large quantities in Cuba and the United States and elsewhere for the precipitation of sulphides from solutions obtained in leaching ores; for instance in the preparation of nickel and cobalt sulphides from ores. Some factories use 60 tons hydrogen sulphide per day in this fashion.

Hydrogen sulphide may under suitable conditions be converted directly to sulphuric acid. This is done in places such as petroleum refineries, natural gas installations, etc. where sulphuric acid is required and where hydrogen sulphide is at the same time available. This is the case, for instance, at the large refinery at Pernis in Holland, where the hydrogen sulphide resulting from the refining is transported to a neighbouring superphosphate factory. The hydrogen sulphide is burnt in refractory-lined insulated cylindrical furnaces to produce sulphur dioxide and water. A waste-heat boiler completes the installation.

Hydrogen sulphide by-product from industrial processes is often converted to elemental sulphur by the Claus kiln process. This process consists in burning one third of the hydrogen sulphide

$$2H_2S + 3O_2 \rightarrow 2SO_2 + 2H_2O$$

and subsequently reacting the sulphur dioxide produced with the remaining hydrogen sulphide

$$2SO_2 + 4H_2S \rightarrow 6S + 4H_2O$$

In modern Claus kilns the heat of reaction of the first stage is utilised to generate steam and the second stage is carried out very efficiently with the aid of catalysts, of which bauxite is the most commonly used (ref. 2, p. 2281). Instead of bauxite, it is possible to use active carbon impregnated with oxides of vanadium, copper, iron and/or chromium; this catalyst is particularly valuable when the hydrogen sulphide content of a gas is lower than 2%.

8.5 CARBON DISULPHIDE

8.5.1 Production

Carbon disulphide is produced by reacting carbon or hydrocarbons with sulphur. One method is to heat charcoal or coke in a retort, or a fixed or rotary oven. The fuel is often generator gas, burnt with hot air; the temperature being between 800 and 900° C. Gaseous sulphur is passed over the light red glowing mass, which combines with the carbon to form carbon disulphide. Charcoal is fed continuously to the installation by means of an endless conveyor.

The product gases are cooled to condense unreacted sulphur, then further cooled to condense carbon disulphide. The gases may then be scrubbed with a suitable solvent to recover more carbon disulphide. The impure carbon disulphide is purified by lime washing and distillation. Volatile impurities from the distillation and residual gases consisting mainly of hydrogen sulphide may be further treated to recover the sulphur present.

Electrothermal furnaces are also employed for manufacture of carbon disulphide. The electrodes are kept cool by contact with boiling sulphur. The power consumption of such a furnace is about 0.5 kWh per lb carbon disulphide obtained. In these furnaces charcoal is heated by an electric current passing through the charcoal bed. The electrodes placed above each other are cooled externally with liquid sulphur or internally with water at a lower pressure than the contents of the reactor to avoid leakage into the reaction mixture. Liquid sulphur is introduced through an annular space near the wall of the reactor to cool the reactor wall before the reaction with the heated charcoal (ref. Swiss patents 578580, 578581 and 578929).

Experimental work has been carried out using three furnaces simultaneously heated by an electric current. The internal heating can be realized very cheaply by using three-phase current, with one oven operating on each phase; the difficulties involved relate to the current-regulating equipment, the transformers and the control.

Another method makes use of fluidized finely-pulverized coke, which is partially burnt in air until the mass is at a temperature of about 900° C. The fluidized mass is passed over a series of grilles with sulphur vapour introduced below. After this reaction a process of purification then takes place along the normal lines.

Carbon disulphide can also be prepared from pure methane at about 4.5 atm pressure. At about 650° C the methane reacts with gaseous sulphur to form both carbon disulphide and hydrogen sulphide, which are then separated by treating the mixture with a light oil in which the carbon disulphide dissolves. The hydrogen sulphide is converted to sulphur, generally by the Claus process (see p. 270). The complete purification of carbon disulphide obtained by this method is rather complicated.

In countries such as Spain, where the main use of carbon disulphide is in the extraction of olive oil from olive kernels, the manufacture is mainly seasonal. Here the residue of the kernels is used as fuel for the ovens (see vol. VIII).

Carbon disulphide also occurs in the waste gases of the rayon factories. It is recovered in this case in a fluid bed of active charcoal, in which the gases and vapours are adsorbed and liberated again by steam-heating. The disulphide is condensed by cooling and the residual gas is treated to absorb hydrogen sulphide. By this method the atmosphere in the factory is greatly improved.

8.5.2 Storage and transportation

Large quantities of carbon disulphide are preferably stored under water. Transport to the artificial silk factories is usually carried out by road or marine tanker.

8.5.3 Properties

Carbon disulphide is a heavy, highly refractive liquid of specific gravity 1.29. Its boiling point is 46° C and its vapours form highly explosive mixtures with air, as a consequence of which legal requirements have been laid down for its storage and transportation. The liquid is spontaneously inflammable at 100° C or even lower. It is an excellent solvent for fat, rubber, sulphur, phosphorus etc. When inhaled or applied to the skin it is poisonous. With castor oil, caustic soda, methylated spirits and water, an emulsion can be made which is useful as an insecticide and which is harmless to plants. The vapour itself has strongly insecticidal properties.

8.5.4 Uses

One of the most important uses is in the manufacture of viscose (see vol. VI), rayon and cellophane (see above for recovery). Further uses are as a solvent for olive oil from olive kernels and for the preparation of carbon tetrachloride (see vol. IV) for which considerable quantities are necessary. Carbon disulphide is also used in the extraction of sulphur from the exhausted cleaning media from coke and gas works.

With dimethylamine a compound is formed which, when oxidized, gives tetraethyl diuram-disulphide, a substance which makes the consumption of alcohol obnoxious (see alcohol, vol. IV).

Carbon disulphide vapours, sprayed into the nests under careful control, are used to kill rodents and ants. To counteract hair-worms and wire-worms it is applied to the surface of loosened ground through special hollow prongs on rakes.

Para-substituted aniline derivatives produce, with carbon disulphide, important inhibitors for oxidation of rubber (see vol. V). An ammoniacal solution of carbon disulphide and formaldehyde gives condensation products which are important as locust-enticing poisons. They are also used sometimes as fungicides. The fairly strongly reactive nature of carbon disulphide makes it important in many cases of synthesis in organic chemistry.

8.5.5 Statistics

The production of carbon disulphide in some important producing countries is shown in the following table:

	In '000s metric tons			
	1953	1958	1962	1964
France	29	37	58	66
Germany (West)	55	58	73	97
Germany (East)	36	46	46	50
Italy	35	38	61	70
Japan	81	97	118	140
Spain	10	20	20	20
United Kingdom (sales)		66		
USA	227	250	300	337

In the USA about 70% of the carbon disulphide is used in viscose rayon and cellophane production and 15% for the production of carbon tetrachloride.

The price of carbon disulphide in the USA in 1965 was $0.04 to 0.07 per lb, depending on the quantity delivered.

8.6 SULPHUR DIOXIDE

8.6.1 Roasting of sulphide ores

Considerable quantities of sulphur dioxide are produced by roasting sulphide ores. Roasting is accomplished at high temperatures in a closed furnace into which air is injected for combustion. The sulphur dioxide produced is generally converted into sulphuric acid. Pyrites is employed widely in this way in the sulphuric acid manufacturing industry. Ores of zinc and copper sulphides are roasted in a similar fashion but in remote places the resulting sulphur dioxide is frequently allowed to go to waste since it is not worthwhile to convert it into sulphuric acid when the cost of transport would lead to uneconomic prices.

Combustion of pyrites can be represented by the equation

$$4FeS_2 + 11O_2 = 2Fe_2O_3 + 8SO_2$$

One of the advantages of pyrites over sulphur (see section 8.3.6) in the production of sulphur dioxide for sulphuric acid manufacture is that the heat of combustion of pyrites is considerably more than that of sulphur, on the basis of similar amounts of sulphur dioxide produced. The heat can be recovered in the form of steam by the use of a waste heat boiler.

The burned ore or cinder in the case of pyrites is often disposed of for iron manufacture and occasionally worked for traces of precious metals. The burned ore is the main product of roasting of zinc and copper sulphides and the process is controlled to obtain a quality suitable for metal extraction; as a consequence the sulphur dioxide produced is often of low strength.

8.6.2 Various roasting furnaces

One of the several types of roasting furnaces is the rotary stage or multiple hearth furnace of Herreshof for handling pyrites and suchlike. This comprises a large cylindrical steel vessel lined with blocks of refractory material and divided into seven or more internal hearths by means of horizontal brick-lined partitions. The vessel is provided with a central hollow shaft which is made from steel or cast iron and which is sometimes externally clad with refractory material. The shaft is mounted so as to permit rotation and is fitted with a number of hollow radial arms carrying fingers. The hollow shaft and arms are cooled by passing air through them.

Pyrites is introduced at the top of the furnace and is raked by the fingers along the partitions of the hearths. The fingers are arranged in such a way as gradually to shift the pyrites inwards in one hearth and outwards in the next hearth. The partitions are provided with openings alternately near the central shaft and near the walls of the vessel to allow the pyrites to pass from one hearth to the one situated under the first. The arrangement is illustrated in fig. 8.7.

The multi-stage furnace produces a combustion gas with relatively little dust and for this and certain other reasons it was much used for many years. Meanwhile, however, the technique of removing dust from gases has developed enormously, so that this advantage has become less significant.

Another type of roasting furnace is the rotary kiln developed by the German Badische Anilin und Soda Fabrik. This is a rotary furnace 100 ft long, of about 10-13 ft diameter in which the pyrites is burnt in a countercurrent stream of air. Relatively crude pyrites can be roasted in such furnaces and their main advantage is that roasting can be carried out down to a very low sulphur content, making the process very efficient. However, operation of these furnaces requires considerable skill.

The multi-stage furnace and the rotary kiln are becoming less popular, one of the reasons being that the heat developed is lost; this does not occur with the flash and fluid bed types of furnace. Modern designs aimed at recovering the lost heat have not met with much success, and furthermore, as mentioned earlier, the technique of dust

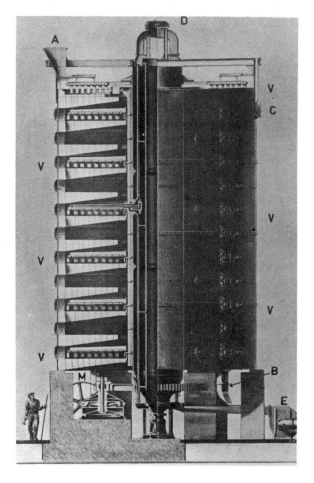

Fig. 8.7 A partly sectioned multi-stage furnace, designed by Herreshof. The man depicted at the bottom indicates the size of the unit. The oven is internally lined with refractory material. The large-diameter central hollow shaft supports hollow arms, which move slowly across the different stages, and shift the solid materials up to the opening of the next stage. The capacity of such a unit is often 100 tons per day. In the diagram: V – individual stages of the furnace; A – feed chute for pyrites; B – extraction of exhausted pyrites; C – extraction of gas; D – removal of air; E – fan supplying cooling air for the rotating shaft and radial arms; M – operating motor for turning the shaft.

separation has developed sufficiently for other systems to have become viable. In particular it has become important to develop furnaces in which fine pyrites (flotation pyrites) could be treated. One such modern furnace is the Nichols-Freeman flash furnace (ref. 3, p. 73) in which finely divided pyrites is sprayed in a stream of air through a hot, vertical, cylindrical chamber. The pyrites – preferably flotation pyrites – is previously reduced in a mill to a suitable particle size. Oxidation takes place very rapidly in comparison with the previously mentioned type of furnace and because of this relatively little combustion space is necessary and, therefore, the flash furnace offers a large capacity together with small dimensions. The costs of construction are also relatively low. Part of the pyrites ash is separated in the combustion compartment itself; hot gas, charged with the rest of the ash, is passed through a waste-heat boiler and then to a battery of cyclones and finally to an electrostatic precipitator. Of increasing importance is the fluid bed furnace, of which two types are most significant; the 'Fluo Solid' design of Dorr (see fig. 8.8) and the Wirbelschicht (a turbulent layer burner, see ref. 8, p. 25) furnace of the Badische Anilin und Soda Fabrik. Basically the fluid bed furnace is suitable for both flotation pyrites and coarse pyrites, although for the latter a certain maximum size is prescribed. 'Fluidisation' is the process by which a body of

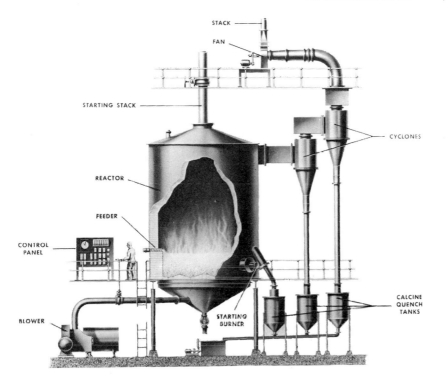

STACK

FAN

STARTING STACK

CYCLONES

REACTOR

FEEDER

CONTROL PANEL

CALCINE QUENCH TANKS

BLOWER

STARTING BURNER

Fig. 8.8   Furnace for roasting of sulphur bearing ores in a fluidized bed.

solid material is suspended in a vertically moving stream of gas, so that the suspended matter then behaves as an intensively stirred liquid. In the same manner as a liquid such a fluidized body sets up hydrostatic pressure and can be conducted through pipes. Because of the strong turbulence in the mass, both temperature and concentration are very uniformly distributed and the rapid movements of the solid particles in a stream of gas prevent over-heating of the ash particles, coagulation and sintering. The fluid bed furnace comprises a cylindrical compartment lined with refractory material into which air is introduced through a perforated grid to support the combustion. Pyrites is fed in at the side, and the ash is removed at a diametrically opposite point. Part of the pyrites ash is also carried away by the hot gas. A disadvantage of this type of pyrites furnace is that the ash contains large quantities of arsenic, which is objectionable in subsequent handling, because the rapid combustion causes the arsenic to be converted to non-volatile pentavalent compounds. At slower rates of burning the arsenic escapes in the gas as trivalent volatile As_2O_3. The gas-ash mixture is passed through a battery of cyclones to remove the bulk of the ash and it is then fed to a waste-heat boiler and finally to an electrostatic precipitator. At the beginning of 1959 there were sixty such furnaces in use in the USA. In Europe at the end of 1958 there were about seventy, varying in capacity from 20 to 500 tons a day. The furnaces produce gases with about 12-14% sulphur dioxide as against 7-8% in a multi-stage furnace. In spite of their relatively small volume they have a large capacity which can be as much as 4-6 times that of a multi-stage furnace.

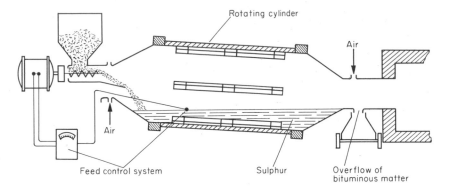

Rotating cylinder

Air

Air

Feed control system

Sulphur

Overflow of
bituminous matter

Fig. 8.9   Diagram of a rotary sulphur combustion furnace.

8.6.3 Production from elemental sulphur

The combustion of sulphur comprises melting, vaporization and conversion into sulphur dioxide. In early equipment all this was carried out in a single piece of apparatus, but in modern processes separate equipment is used for melting and, possibly after purification, a second item of equipment is used for vaporization and combustion.

Among the older types of equipment the rotary combustion furnace shown in fig. 8.9 may be mentioned. A further type is the cascade furnace, in which molten sulphur is allowed to flow downwards over stacked plates. Part of the sulphur burns with dry air on the first plate and the remainder flows on and is burnt on subsequent plates.

In newer equipment a separate section is available in which the sulphur is melted by means of tubes or plates, heated by high-pressure steam; care being taken that the sulphur is not too strongly heated, in order to avoid excessive viscosity of the melt.

Molten sulphur, after purification to remove bituminous hydrocarbons, e.g. by filtration after treatment with adsorption agents such as Fuller's earth, may be burned in a spray burner in suitable furnaces. The burner is similar in principle to a burner for heavy oil, and dry air is generally used. The furnaces consist of horizontal cylindrical steel vessels, refractory-lined and externally insulated to minimize heat loss. The vessel contains two or more transverse internal baffles and combustion takes place very uniformly. When the furnace is hot, the atomised sulphur is vaporized by the radiant heat and burns rapidly and completely. All pipelines, pumps and other parts of the installation carrying the molten sulphur are jacketed so that the temperature may be maintained by steam. The gas from a modern sulphur burner contains 8-11% SO_2. The furnaces are followed by waste-gas boilers, in which steam is produced.

The sulphur dioxide made by burning sulphur with air is diluted with nitrogen from the air and is mostly used directly for sulphuric acid manufacture. Some, however, because of its high purity is used to manufacture pure sulphur dioxide. In this case the burned gas is passed through a waste-heat boiler, where the heat value is recovered as steam, and into a battery of absorption towers where the sulphur dioxide is scrubbed out of the gas with a countercurrent flow of water. A battery containing as many as five towers may be used, the towers being packed with Raschig rings. The solution of sulphur dioxide in water is heated, giving off sulphur dioxide and some water vapour, and the water remaining is returned into circulation for further use as solvent.

The wet gaseous sulphur dioxide is compressed and fed into another tower packed with Raschig rings; the passage of a stream of sulphuric acid takes up the water vapour, and the dried sulphur dioxide is condensed by cooling and further compression. Extensive use is made throughout all stages of the process of corrosion-resistant metals in order to keep replacement costs as low as possible. Corrosion is sometimes set up because during the formation of sulphur dioxide a small amount of sulphur trioxide is also formed, and this latter produces sulphuric acid in combination with moisture from the air. As long as the temperature is high enough the acid evaporates and cannot corrode the steel piping, and because of this the piping is very heavily insulated. The acid is condensed by cooling in parts of the installation, where anti-corrosive materials are installed.

8.6.4 Production from waste gases

Very large quantities of sulphur dioxide are discharged into the atmosphere through chimneys. To a large extent this is due to the sulphur content of the ash from coal. The content can be reduced but it increases the price of coal by 5 to 7 shillings per ton. In the future it is certain that the high sulphur content of coal will be a further reason for treating the waste gases (see ref. 5, p. 197 *et seq.* and Gas purification, vol. II).

In England it is thought that the cheapest method of treating the chimney gases is with aqueous ammonia. The liquid is fed in drops into a coke-filled tower through which the chimney gases are forced. The liquid also contains an amount of manganese dioxide and considerable air, which is introduced by forcing it through a filter pack. In this way 90% of the sulphur dioxide present is recovered in the form of ammonium sulphate and free sulphur. At present these methods are only economical with gases containing more than 9% sulphur dioxide. Leaner gases can be economically treated by washing out the SO_2 with solvents such as xylidine, dimethylaniline, aluminium sulphate, concentrated water gas, etc. (see ref. 5, p. 197 *et seq.*). One of the first requirements in using basic aluminium sulphate is to remove all dust from the reducing gases.

In the xylidine process xylidine is prepared by reduction of nitroxylene (see Nitroxylene, vol. IV) and is mixed with water and some sodium carbonate or sodium sulphite in order to form xylidine sulphite but not sulphate. Even strongly diluted sulphur dioxide-containing gases can be advantageously treated in this way. Dimethylaniline with sodium carbonate solution has the advantage of improved solubility in water, but requires equipment made of lead in order to prevent corrosion.

One large electric power station, which was causing a good deal of trouble with its chimney gases, containing large amounts of sulphur dioxide, has gone over to washing by a sprinkling process. This takes place in a large concrete chamber in which more than 1 000 tons of water per hour (see ref. 5, p. 197 *et seq.*) containing milk of lime are sprayed in countercurrent to the stream of chimney gases. The concrete chamber is completely lined with nearly 95 000 acid-resistant tiles, which are secured to the concrete by means of a rubber cement, which remains elastic enough to carry the repeated expansion and contraction set up by the hot gases and cold water. Even the constructional beams employed are clad with the tiles. It is probable that this arrangement would be too expensive to be used generally and because of this other power stations will be equipped with chimneys of more than 360 ft, with forced flow set up by large fans to disperse the hot gases into the atmosphere in an attempt to minimize their deleterious effects.

Sulphur dioxide is sometimes washed from gas mixtures by water sprays, and in that case sulphur dioxide is removed from the solution by blowing in large quantities of air and by dissolving it in a small quantity of very cold water. The scrubbed air is recirculated into the process in order to avoid loss of sulphur dioxide.

In Leverkusen in Germany a different method is used. Solvents are not used, but the dried and compressed waste gases are chilled in successive stages. Heat exchangers are employed using cold water, liquid sulphur dioxide, cold exhaust gases and evaporating ammonia successively as refrigerant. By this means part of the sulphur dioxide in the gases is liquefied and drained off. The remaining gas is further chilled in three stages to $-68°$ C. Sulphur dioxide during this process is liquefied, and the waste gases are then used to cool fresh gas in a heat exchanger.

8.6.5 Production from other raw materials

Sulphur dioxide can be prepared from the waste sulphuric acid from oil refineries known as refinery sludge. The sludge is an emulsion of hydrocarbons, sulphuric acid and sulphonated compounds, of composition varying from one installation to another. In treating this sludge the sulphuric acid is not recovered directly but is reduced to sulphur dioxide, which is then reconverted to sulphuric acid. The waste acid is sprayed on a coke bed at about $200°$ C; the organic compounds then carbonize and sulphur dioxide is liberated, to be subsequently purified.

Sulphur dioxide is often conveniently made from hydrogen sulphide and this method is becoming more important as larger quantities of hydrogen sulphide become available from gas cleaning, and especially from petroleum refineries. The hydrogen sulphide is burned to give sulphur dioxide which needs little if any further treatment prior to feeding with air to a contact converter for the production of sulphuric acid (see p. 286).

Sulphur dioxide is also prepared from anhydrite (anhydrous calcium sulphate $CaSO_4$).

Anhydrite occurs in natural deposits of relatively high purity in England, Europe and elsewhere. In England the anhydrite for this process is obtained from mines with the aid of heavy electrically operated machinery which is readily movable (see fig. 8.10). This operates with several drills simultaneously and bores the holes for the explosives needed to break up the rock.

The process of converting anhydrite to sulphuric acid consists essentially in the reduction of the dry sulphate with coke breeze at high temperature; clay is added to the reaction mixture so that the solid end product or clinker is suitable for cement manufacture; sale of the clinker is essential for the economics of the process which, in consequence, is referred to as the cement-sulphuric acid process.

The reaction kilns, large horizontal revolving fire-brick lined drums, are fed continuously with the carefully proportioned mixture of anhydrite, coke and clay and are internally fired with powdered fuel. Gaseous products from the kilns are led into the sulphuric acid production plant and the solid clinker (Portland clinker) is discharged continuously into the cement manufacturing plant (see cement, vol. II).

In England the process is operated in a few very large factories, so that the amount of sulphur which has to be imported for acid production is very much reduced; in this way a large amount of foreign currency is saved.

Germany had a factory of this type as early as 1939, and other countries also have factories under construction.

Fig. 8.10 Electrically operated machinery for anhydrite mining (used in British anhydrite mines).

By heating magnesium sulphate with finely ground coke, sulphur dioxide, carbon dioxide and magnesium oxide are produced; this process is employed especially in Germany where large quantities of waste magnesium sulphate are available.

Pure sulphur dioxide may be obtained at a low cost by igniting finely ground nickel sulphate with oxygen (see Nickel, vol. III). Since nitrogen is not present the equipment used in purification can be made smaller and operate more cheaply than previously when the ores were oxidized in air. In Canada some 19 000 tons per year of sulphur dioxide are produced in a factory which is able to produce and deliver in tanks at a price considerably lower than sulphur dioxide produced from imported sulphur.

Very pure sulphur dioxide is obtained by reacting sulphur trioxide with molten sulphur; this process has the great advantage that further purification is unnecessary. In Germany the method is used on a large scale for the preparation of hydrosulphites.

8.6.6 Storage and transportation

Much of the sulphur dioxide produced is converted into sulphuric acid on site. Sulphur dioxide to be transported is usually liquefied by compressing and is marketed in strong glass bottles or steel cylinders; the latter in particular are used for the purest anhydrous quality of sulphur dioxide for use in refrigeration. Liquid sulphur dioxide is also transported in tank wagons.

8.6.7 Properties

Sulphur dioxide is a colourless gas of pungent odour which condenses at atmospheric pressure to a liquid at $-10°$ C; it is toxic to animals and plants. Gaseous sulphur dioxide is readily soluble in water, as can be demonstrated in the same way as the high solubility of hydrogen chloride (see p. 229). Sulphur dioxide is a reducing agent, and in consequence can be oxidised readily itself, for instance, by passing fine streams of air through the dioxide-water solution, mixed with a solution of ferrous sulphate. Sulphuric acid is then formed from the sulphur dioxide and water, while the ferrous sulphate ($FeSO_4$) is converted to ferric sulphate ($Fe_2(SO_4)_3$).

Sulphur dioxide is corrosive and in addition it absorbs oxygen and water vapour from air to form sulphuric acid and it is because of this that the stone of buildings decay in large towns where the many chimneys feed sulphur dioxide into the air.

Dissolved in water sulphur dioxide forms sulphurous acid (H_2SO_3) which can only exist in solution. Sulphurous acid is a weak acid, which has a strongly disinfecting effect and can be used to bleach many dyes. The colourless compound of the dye formed by the reducing action of the sulphur dioxide can be transformed back to a coloured compound by oxidation. This explains the necessity for thorough rinsing of goods in water after bleaching with sulphur dioxide.

Sulphur dioxide reacts with aqueous solutions of the hydroxides of alkali and alkaline earth metals to form sulphites or bisulphites; these compounds like sulphur dioxide have good bleaching, reducing and disinfecting properties. Sulphur dioxide or sulphites are oxidized by hydrogen peroxide to sulphuric acid which can be detected in the normal way with barium chloride; this reaction is employed in the analysis of sulphites.

8.6.8 Uses

Gaseous sulphur dioxide is the base material used in the production of sulphur trioxide, and therefore of sulphuric acid. The major consumers of sulphur dioxide prepare it on site.

Further important applications are in the preparation of sulphite cellulose (see Paper, vol. VI), in the production and conservation of gelatin, casein, soybean protein etc., in the purification of raw sugar and in the production of chemicals such as sodium hydrosulphite, thiosulphates and sulphites of sodium, potassium and ammonium (see Alkali metals, ch. 10).

Sulphur dioxide is used increasingly in the irrigation water used for alkaline soils. It is also introduced into the annealing furnaces used in the manufacture of glass in order that it may combine with alkaline material on the surface of the glass; in this way after rinsing, bottles and ampoules are made more suitable for use with liquids which must not absorb alkalis, e.g., penicillin.

Large quantities of liquid sulphur dioxide are used by the petroleum industry in the purification of oil by the Edeleanu process (see vol. IV).

A highly purified and practically anhydrous quality with a moisture content less than 0.01% is used in refrigeration circuits. It can be prepared by dissolving the impure gas in cold dimethylaniline after careful filtration. On heating, the solution gives off its sulphur dioxide. The remaining traces of water are then removed from the gas by washing with concentrated sulphuric acid; when liquefied the purity is of the order of 99.9975%.

In a number of wool and silk factories the wet textiles are bleached by hanging them in stone enclosures in which sulphur is burned. Straw hats are also bleached in this fashion. It is essential to rinse the material thoroughly after bleaching, as explained previously.

Frequently the bisulphites and sulphites of sodium, potassium and ammonium may be used instead of sulphur dioxide as a bleaching agent, disinfectant, reducing agent, and as chlorine antidote etc.

The high toxicity of sulphur dioxide is exploited in such applications as the destruction of rats. The toxicity is indicated by the fact that its presence in any amounts higher than 0.04% completely prevents respiration. Rats on ships are the cause of much damage to the cargo and their fleas can communicate disease to humans: because of this rats in ships are sometimes exterminated by burning sulphur in large pans and allowing the fumes to penetrate into all corners of the ship. Fresh infestation by rats is prevented by fitting rat catchers to the cables mooring the ship.

Sulphur dioxide is also used to prevent contamination by vermin: horse scabies, for example; is treated by shutting the horse in an enclosed space with its head left outside, and then filling the space with sulphur dioxide fumes. Plants are attacked by sulphur dioxide, and in the vicinity of boiler houses account should be taken of this, as coal always contains sulphur. The disinfecting effect is particularly valuable for the decontamination of wine barrels and bottles (see sulphur, p. 265). In wine the sulphur dioxide content may not exceed 0.125%, nor may this percentage be exceeded in the case of gelatine. Sick rooms are also disinfected by burning sulphur and simultaneously boiling water to moisten the air in them. Sand filters are also purified with sulphur dioxide.

In the USA liquid sulphur dioxide is sometimes 'fed' to freshly mown grass which is to be stored in silos. The grass absorbs the sulphur dioxide rapidly and can then be stored for long periods. Sometimes the siloed material is mixed with about 0.5% of sodium bisulphite.

8.6.9 Statistics

The enormous quantity of sulphur dioxide produced for use in sulphuric acid manufacture is evident from the production figures for sulphuric acid. In the USA, for example, about 15 million short tons of sulphur dioxide were consumed for the production of sulphuric acid in 1964. Outside the sulphuric acid field, production in the USA was about 100000 tons in 1964. 48% was used in the paper industry, 16% for the production of sodium hydrosulphite, 16% in processing of soybean protein and 8% in oil refining.

The price of liquid sulphur dioxide in the USA was about $0.05 to $0.13 per lb in 1965 depending on the quantity delivered. Refrigeration grade was sold at $0.33 per lb.

8.7 SULPHUR TRIOXIDE

Sulphur trioxide (SO_3) was known as early as the seventeenth century. It was obtained in small quantities from impure pyrites which had been partly transformed to ferrous sulphate. This was converted by oxidation into ferric sulphate. After crystallization solid ferric oxide and sulphur trioxide vapour were obtained by heating in refractory retorts. The sulphur trioxide was then dissolved in water or sulphuric acid to form the fuming or 'Nordhausen' sulphuric acid (the latter named after the place where the first acid was made). This 'fuming' sulphuric acid was at that time extremely costly. Scheele had recognized that sulphur trioxide was in fact the anhydride of sulphuric acid. Nowadays the raw materials for making it are pure dry sulphur dioxide and clean dried air. For the production process see p. 286. Pure sulphur trioxide is an unstable substance which rapidly changes to a rather intractable polymer and because of this it has usually been converted directly to sulphuric acid. Recently, however, it has been discovered that polymerization can be avoided by treating dry sulphur trioxide with a mixture of sodium silicofluoride and carbon tetrachloride (or compounds of titanium, antimony or boron). One or two percent in the mixture is sufficient. It is necessary then to keep the sulphur trioxide below 30° C to retain the stable alpha modification. It is possible to use this material for sulphonation where formerly a special oleum had to be used.

Sulphur trioxide is used in the preparation of saccharin.

8.8 SULPHURIC ACID

8.8.1 History

Sulphuric acid (H_2SO_4) is still one of the most important 'heavy chemicals'. These are the chemicals which are generally marketed by the ton, in distinction to those which are sold in smaller quantities, and known as 'fine chemicals'. The heavy chemicals of purest quality are generally classified under the fine chemical group.

Originally sulphuric acid and especially that won by the Nordhausen process was a very expensive product (see above). Because of this it was not widely used for technical purposes but mostly by medical charlatans or by alchemists. During the seventeenth century it became cheaper as chemists began to produce it by combustion of sulphur, which was a common, well-known and cheap substance. Sulphur dioxide was obtained, which was dissolved in water. In the early stages this was converted naturally into sulphuric acid, but it was later accidentally discovered that by the addition of saltpetre to the sulphur the formation of sulphuric acid was considerably accelerated. Although the quantities made were at first a mere few tons a year, this increased gradually in the course of time. The development took place especially in the German states.

The well-known quack doctor Joshua Ward, in about 1730, improved the production process by using glass bulbs in the preparation instead of earthen vats. Up to that time the so-called oil of vitriol had cost about 2s 6d an ounce, but through the use of the glass bulbs this was cut to the same amount a pound. In about 1749 the process was further improved by Roebuck (1718-94), who replaced the glass with lead, which enabled large quantity production of the order of hundreds of pounds and later even of tons. The lead tanks, measuring about 4 x 6 x 6 ft, were gradually enlarged until at the end of the eighteenth century these had dimensions of 10 x 10 x 12 ft. Moreover the introduction of numerous technical improvements – e.g. the introduction of steam under pressure and the use of oxides of nitrogen (see later) – lowered the production costs considerably. The fields of application were enlarged and the production increased notably due to the fact that in England the strongly diluted acid came into use in the cotton bleaching industry and similar applications.

Around 1800 the leading factories making sulphuric acid in England had a total capacity of more than 130 000 ft³ of lead chambers. Factories were also set up in France, once the joining of lead plates without the use of solder had been learnt. However total production amounted still only to a few hundred tons per annum, but at least the price of diluted acid had meanwhile fallen to about 0.4 pence a pound.

Nowadays two methods are commonly used in the preparation of sulphuric acid. The first, known as the lead chamber process, is a development from the eighteenth century process, converting sulphur dioxide into sulphuric acid by water and air under the catalytic influence of oxides of nitrogen. The second, known as the contact process, involves oxidation of sulphur dioxide with air at high temperature by means of a solid catalyst followed by a stage in which the SO_3 produced is taken up in water.

8.8.2 Production in the lead chamber process

The raw materials for this process are sulphur dioxide, oxygen and water. (For the preparation of sulphur dioxide see p. 273.) In the lead chamber (see below) H_2SO_3 is formed from SO_2 and H_2O; the H_2SO_3 is oxidized by nitrogen dioxide (NO_2) through 'Nitrosyl' sulphuric acid to H_2SO_4, while NO_2 is converted to NO and a part is simultaneously reduced further to N_2O and so made unusable for the preparation process. Formerly NO_2 was obtained from nitric acid, but to-day it is more usual to use oxidized ammonia (see p. 327). The above description is of course only superficial as in practice many other processes simultaneously take place (ref. 3).

a. *Various lead chamber processes.* In a typical plant the oxidation of sulphurous to sulphuric acid takes place in large chambers, made of lead plates, autogenously welded without solder, from which the name of the process derives. The plates are

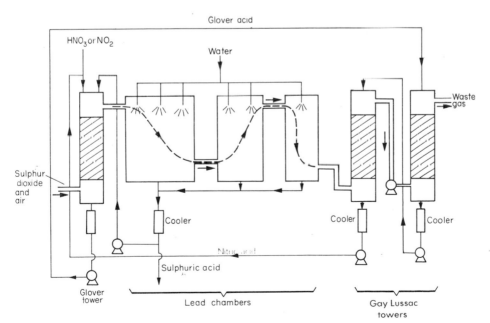

Fig. 8.11 Flowsheet of a lead chamber sulphuric acid plant.

attached to one another with lead strips on a framework. Soft lead is used because this is practically the only metal which is sufficiently resistant to dilute sulphuric acid. A three-chamber factory, which has a volume of at least 100000 ft^3 requires something like 220 tons of lead.

The hot gases, leaving the roasting furnace, consist in the main of sulphur dioxide and nitrogen. Nitrogen oxides and air are added and the mixed gases passed upwards through a Glover tower (see fig. 8.11) in which they are cooled to the correct temperature and allowed to take up nitrogen dioxide and water vapour, from a mixture of 'chamber acid' and 'nitrated acid' (see below) flowing downwards through the tower. The Glover tower is usually constructed of lead sheets internally lined with acid and heat resisting brick (ref. 3, p. 121) and is packed with similar brickwork or Raschig rings. Gases and vapours leaving the Glover tower are led to the first and largest lead chamber, where they are sprayed with droplets of water. The quantity of water sprayed is accurately regulated in order to control the process so as to avoid the necessity later of having to remove excessive water from the acid by evaporation. By using sulphur dioxide containing water vapour, it is possible to hold the quantity of sprayed water to a minimum. Acid of 60% is possible by this method. In the first lead chamber the temperature is above 100° C. The processes described take place in these chambers, of which three are generally used in series to ensure good conversion of the sulphur dioxide. Two chambers would not permit complete conversion. Excess nitrogen dioxide is always present in the chambers and from the last chamber a gas mixture is removed comprising the costly NO_2, which must be recovered, as well as a number of valueless gases. Recovery of the nitrogen peroxide takes place in the Gay-Lussac towers which are lead-lined and packed with rings. Concentrated sulphuric acid flows downwards and dissolves the nitrogen dioxide flowing upwards to form a solution known as 'nitrated acid'. This is mixed with chamber acid, that is to say, acid tapped from the lead chambers, and is then introduced into the top of the Glover tower in which it gives up its nitrogen peroxide and cools the roasting gases. A strong impure sulphuric acid, known as Glover acid, is removed from the bottom of the Glover tower.

The old chamber process is sometimes modified, for instance in England, to the system of Mills-Packard, in which use is made of conically shaped chambers, sprayed externally with water, for cooling. It is said that they are slightly more economical to operate than chambers in small factories.

Packed towers may also be used instead of lead chambers, with the advantage that the expensive lead is saved. Moreover the volumetric efficiency is higher. Such towers are built of refractory stone or in some cases of steel frames. Such constructions were made possible by the development of reliable acid pumps of high mechanical efficiency. Due to the good contact between gas and acid in a tower, the reaction can take place very quickly. Intensive cooling is necessary, because, amongst other reasons, heat is not carried away through the walls of the tower as is the case with the chamber. The tower system of Peterson is well known and consists of a battery of six towers including a Glover tower, three towers replacing the chambers, and two Gay-Lussac towers. The course of the reaction in the system is rather complicated. The system has the reputation of being suitable for handling gases from copper smelting, which vary considerably in volume and concentration.

An interesting new development of the old lead chamber process is the Kachkaroff process which is operated in factories in France, Italy and Great Britain (ref. 9). The method of operation is based on the theory that sulphuric acid formation takes place in the liquid phase and that the rate of formation is increased markedly at high concentrations of nitrogen oxides. The process is carried out by passing gases containing sulphur dioxide and air into packed towers through which a concentrated solution of nitrogen dioxides in sulphuric acid is circulated. A typical plant consists of a concentration tower followed by a denitrating tower and then usually by four Kachkaroff reaction towers and finally by a filter tower for recovering nitrogen oxides from the exit gases. The concentration and denitration tower act in a similar way to the Glover tower in the old lead chamber process and the filter tower serves as the Gay-Lussac tower. Nitrogen oxides, to make up for losses in the process, are generally supplied from an ammonia oxidation unit and are fed into the first reaction tower. The gas inlet temperature to the concentration tower is 600-650° C and the acid from the base of this tower is generally about 78% H_2SO_4 and is nitre free. This is the product acid but proportions are recirculated round the concentration tower and used to irrigate the filter tower. The construction of the concentration tower is similar to conventional Glover towers. Denitrating, reaction and filter towers are constructed of acid-resistant brickwork with packing of similar material. Acid is circulated round the tower using modern vertical glandless centrifugal pumps and the heat of reaction is removed by passing the acid through external coolers. Coolers are of lead construction for acid from the concentration and denitrating towers and may be of borosilicate glass (e.g. Pyrex glass) for reaction tower acid. The acid circulating round the reaction towers enters the towers at about 25-30° C and leaves at about 40-45° C; the acid strength is about 80% H_2SO_4 and the nitre content is usually in the range 8-10% N_2O_3. Most of the water required in the process is added to the denitrating tower where, by dilution of the acid, it assists in nitre removal.

The efficiency of the Kachkaroff process is high; the sulphur dioxide content in the exit gas is satisfactorily low and the cost of ammonia for nitrogen oxide production is less than in the conventional lead chamber process.

The Kachkaroff process can be operated for combined production of nitric acid and sulphuric acid. The production of nitric acid may be achieved by withdrawing a stream of sulphuric acid of high nitrogen oxide content into a separate denitrating tower where steam is injected for denitration. The product gases from this tower contain nearly 100% nitrogen oxides with only traces of water and are led off and converted into concentrated nitric acid. The denitrated sulphuric acid is fed back into the sulphuric acid synthesis section of the process. Since it incorporates technical features favourable to the synthesis of both products the integrated production of nitric acid and sulphuric acid by the Kachkaroff process has important commercial potential (ref. 10).

   b. Concentration of sulphuric acid. Chamber acid usually contains less than 70% acid. The acid was formerly concentrated in lead tanks; at the present time, copper coils, clad externally with lead (duplex metal; see Rolling, vol. III) are used as heating elements. These can withstand a higher steam pressure, so that they can be heated to a higher temperature than lead pipes. Lead would be attacked at a certain concentration, so that the evaporation is continued in apparatus made of Volvic stone (*pierre de Volvic;* a type of lava found in France). Apparatus made of stainless steel is also used.

8.8.3 Production in the contact process

A large proportion of high strength sulphuric acid nowadays is manufactured in contact plants. These plants are generally of large capacity and consequently economic to operate; a modern unit may have a capacity of upwards of 250 tons of acid per day. It is most important in the contact process that the feed gases (sulphur dioxide and air) to the converters should be completely dust free to avoid contamination of the catalytic mass used to convert the mixture to SO_3.

a. Purification of sulphur dioxide. In early installations dust was removed from the sulphur dioxide gas in very long settling channels fitted with numerous baffles but this method is inadequate for purifying gas for use with the contact method. In recent years cyclones have become more and more common because of the high costs of electrostatic precipitation as well as the large dust production in modern furnaces. In the cyclones, water is sprayed to ensure that the dust is made into mud, which is then thrown against the wall of the cyclone.

Gas from pyrites contains arsenic in the form of arsenic trioxide (As_2O_3). This must be removed before use in the contact process in order to avoid catalyst poisoning, although arsenical gas is not unsuitable for a chamber factory making a crude commercial acid. The arsenic trioxide is removed by cooling the gases, either indirectly in an air cooler, with water as a coolant or directly by spraying the gas with water or by streaming the gas through a coke-filled sprayed cooling tower, in which the gas is washed as well as cooled. Direct cooling is generally used nowadays. Mist formed is removed by passing the gas through a coke-filled tower or by means of electrostatic precipitation. The gas is finally dried with strong sulphuric acid. It is not always necessary to dry the gas before the catalytic process, and the combustion products of hydrogen sulphide in particular are often further treated without dehydration.

After oxidation of sulphur dioxide into trioxide the water is present for forming H_2SO_4. If wet hydrogen sulphide is burnt with moist air, acid of 80% is produced, which is suitable for a number of purposes, and the installation of the factory is then simplified. One necessary requirement is, however, that no sulphuric acid may condense in the converter.

When the sulphur dioxide is produced by burning sulphur little if any purification of the gas is needed. Factories handling pyrites require three times the capital investment involved in sulphur-based factories, largely because of the extensive purification needed in the preparation of the sulphur dioxide in the former case.

b. Oxidation of sulphur dioxide to sulphur trioxide. Purified sulphur dioxide is fed together with large quantities of dry air through the catalyst, which is usable for long periods when the gas is dust-free. The catalyst is specially sensitive to fluorine, so that special precautions have to be taken against the waste gases of any neighbouring superphosphate factory. Originally platinum was used as catalyst; this, although expensive, ensured efficient conversion. It was later discovered that iron oxide was also active, but resulted in lower efficiencies. In the Mannheim-process iron oxide was used as a first catalyst, followed by platinum to complete the oxidation. At the present time iron oxide is obsolete and platinum is also practically no longer used because of its very high price and susceptibility to poisoning. The currently used catalyst consists of vanadium in the form of oxide to which various agents (alkali compounds) are added as promoters. Porous substances such as silica, kieselguhr and artificial zeolites, derived from sodium or potassium silicate, are used as carriers for the catalysts. The catalyst mass contains a small percentage of vanadium oxide. Modern converters consist of a vertical cylinder in which the catalyst mass is spread out on horizontal shelves.

The reaction $2SO_2 + O_2 \rightleftharpoons 2SO_3$ is exothermic and reversible. Consequently as the temperature of reaction increases the equilibrium concentration of SO_3 tends to diminish. To obtain a high degree of conversion it is therefore essential to cool the gases in the course of the reaction. Generally reaction is carried out in a series of converters, the gases being cooled in heat exchangers between the converters (or in one converter containing several catalyst layers). The last converter or catalyst layer would require

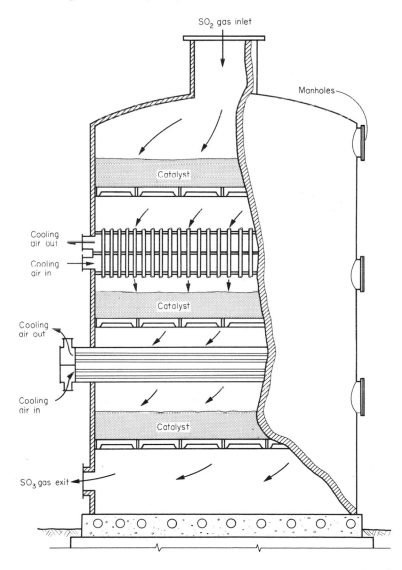

Fig. 8.12 Schematic drawing of a contact process converter with internal cooling elements.

to be run at a temperature not exceeding about 440° C to obtain conversion efficiencies higher than 98% (ref. 3, p. 274). The cooling can be carried out in a number of ways, such as by having cooling elements in the converters (see fig. 8.12) or, where sulphur dioxide containing more than 10% SO_2 is the starting material, by introduction of cold air at various places in the converter, which is then known as a quench converter (see fig. 8.13). A combination of several types may also be employed. The reaction temperature is frequently around 500° C at the inlet and 415° C at the end of the process. In most contact plants the cold incoming gases are heated up by passage through the heat exchangers before entering the first converter. Some contact factories have changed

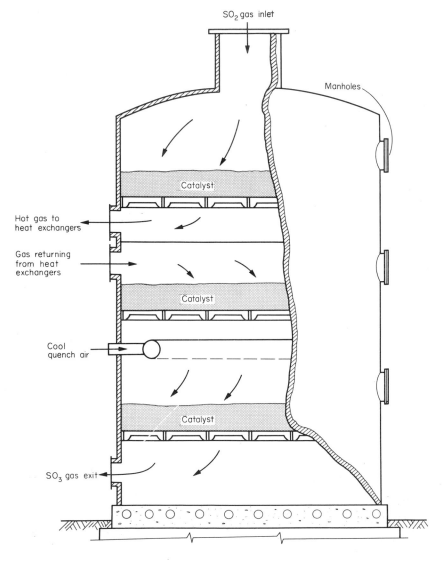

Fig. 8.13 Schematic drawing of a contact process converter cooled by introduction of cold air (quench converter).

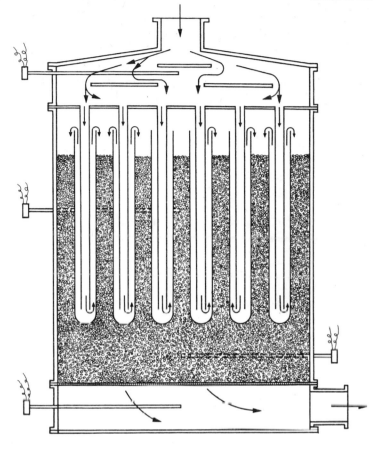

Fig. 8.14 Contact process converter in which the catalyst mass is cooled by means of the cold sulphur dioxide-air mixture before the latter passes through the catalyst layer. (The gas flow is shown by the arrows.)

over to oxidation of the sulphur dioxide with oxygen instead of with air. One old factory was able to increase its nominal 35 ton capacity to 200 tons of 100% acid a day by this means. This was, however, only possible because cheap oxygen could be used. (See also fig. 8.14.)

  c. Conversion of sulphur trioxide into sulphuric acid. The reaction of sulphur trioxide with water cannot conveniently be carried out with the pure substances, owing to the formation of non-settling mists. For this reason the sulphur trioxide is brought into contact with sulphuric acid of 97.5-99% strength: the trioxide then reacts smoothly with the small amount of water present in the acid, so avoiding the formation of mist. The absorption of sulphur trioxide is carried out in a series of cast iron absorption vessels, some of which take the form of tall cylinders, packed with quartz. Depending on the quantity of absorbed sulphur trioxide, very strong sulphuric acid or the even stronger oleum is produced.

8.8.4 Storage and transportation

Quantities of up to 100 kg are transported in glass carboys or in steel drums. Large quantities are transported (and stored) in tanks which may be loaded on ships, heavy vehicles, etc. For dilute acid (up to 78% sulphuric acid) the tanks are lined with lead or acid-resistant bitumen or materials such as butyl rubber and ebonite; acid in the strength range 78-85% sulphuric acid attacks both lead and cast iron; the 85-98% acid on the other hand does not attack iron at normal temperatures and can be stored in iron vessels.

For the very pure acid used in accumulators, containers made of polyethylene are coming into use. Such containers of capacity about 1.7 quarts are obtainable in fibre cases holding three firmly placed together; the whole can then be handled easily and safely. It is advisable, after emptying, to rinse with water and only then to throw them away.

Account must be taken of the affinity for water of sulphuric acid (see section 8.8.5), especially when tanks or drums are returned 'empty'; washing out such containers must be done with great care.

8.8.5 Properties and classification

At ordinary temperatures, sulphuric acid is one of the strongest of all acids. It has a very strong affinity for water, and presumably forms compounds with it, since large amounts of heat are liberated on mixing. The affinity is so strong that sulphuric acid can remove hydrogen and oxygen in the proportions in which they form water from all kinds of compound. Removal of water vapour from the air is considerably reduced when the acid strength falls below about 85%.

The chemical analysis of sulphuric acid is usually effected by means of the formation of $BaSO_4$, which is insoluble; $CaSO_4$ is soluble to a small extent.

For those types of acid containing water, the acid strength is still often expressed in degrees Baumé (abbreviated to Bé). This and also other* methods for dividing up the scale on hydrometers is, in fact, quite arbitrary. Thus Baumé made his scale divisions by marking a hydrometer for liquids heavier than water with O at the upper end at the point to which it sank in water, and with 15 at the point to which it sank in a 15% solution of common salt in water at 10° Rëaumur (12.5° C). The distance on the stem was divided up into 15 equal parts, and the divisions continued on the stem. Tables are available from which the strength of the acid can be read off from the number of degrees Bé (ref. 3, p. 411).

Acid of strength 98-100% H_2SO_4 is called monohydrate (i.e. $SO_3.H_2O$) and the 85% acid, dihydrate. The following types are usually distinguished: chamber acid, of strength 50° Bé, with a specific gravity of 1.53 and containing 62.5% acid, though chamber acid containing 57% is also available; Glover acid, of strength 60° Bé, specific gravity of 1.7, containing 78% acid; English sulphuric acid or vitriol, of strength 66° Bé, specific gravity 1.83-1.84, containing 93-97% acid; oleum, with 45%

---

* Hydrometers calibrated in the same arbitrary way are used for the determination of the strength of other liquids of various types, and are sometimes suitable only for the determination of the strength of a given type of liquid. Tables also exist for these so that corrections can be made for determinations carried out at different temperatures. Almost all the different hydrometers are made of glass (see under the appropriate heading) and they are often officially calibrated.

free SO$_3$, has a specific gravity of 1.97. The specific gravity falls off again at higher SO$_3$ contents.

8.8.6 Uses

Dilute acid for the preparation of foodstuffs and luxury goods, and for accumulators, must be very pure. The impure acid is used for metal pickling, in tanning, in the carbonisation of wool, in metal plating, dyeing, cotton printing, in the production of citric, tartaric and lactic acids, and of many sulphates, etc.

The 60° Bé acid, and also chamber acid, are used mainly in the production of superphosphate and ammonium sulphate, for parchment paper, in the manufacture of fatty acids, and sometimes even as a fertiliser, since it converts phosphate into a soluble form and destroys many weeds. The 66° Bé acid was formerly used mainly for the production of nitric acid, for petroleum purification, and in organic chemistry, and is still used extensively in these industries. It is also one of the best drying agents for gases. It is used further in the refining of gold and silver, and for the production of many ethers and esters.

The consumption of sulphuric acid can still be taken, in general, as a barometer of industrial health, since it is indispensable in many industries.

In addition to the applications mentioned above sulphuric acid is used in large tonnages in the rayon and transparent paper industries, in production of lithopone and titanium dioxide pigments, in the manufacture of hydrochloric and hydrofluoric acids, in the production of soap, glycerine and detergents etc. Demand is, however, diminishing somewhat, since there is competition from hydrochloric acid, from gypsum (for the production of ammonium sulphate), from the use of naturally occurring sodium sulphate etc.

8.8.7 Statistics

The world production of sulphuric acid and the production by the major producing countries is shown below:

| | In '000 metric tons of 100% H$_2$SO$_4$ | | | | | |
	1920	1938	1948	1958	1962	1964
World	9490		21300	41800	52000	56000
Australia	60	503	493	1008	1150	1450
Belgium	280	650	829	1087	1159	1348
Canada	60	343	616	1356	1539	1778
France	1250	1100	1275	1786	2271	2700
Germany, West	680	2050	—	2917	3100	3600
Germany, East			190	650	860	937
Italy	330	1150	975	2016	2550	2870
Japan	310	2500	1217	3802	4910	5370
Netherlands	200	525	370	747	818	976
Spain	200	150	353	1072	1500	1680
United Kingdom	1070	995	1577	2277	2775	3185
USA	3750	3629	10393	14470	17870	20800
USSR	100	—	—	4800	6130	7650

It is estimated that about 85% of sulphuric acid production in the USA in 1964 was obtained from elemental sulphur. In the UK about 55% of the sulphuric acid was produced from elemental sulphur, 17% from anhydrite, 12% from pyrites, 9% from spent oxide, 6% from zinc concentrate and 1% from other sources.

The percentage of sulphuric acid (and even the absolute quantity) made in the chamber and tower process is decreasing slowly. This may be illustrated by the following production figures in the USA and the UK:

		Contact process In '000 long tons	%	Chamber and tower process In '000 long tons	%
USA	1959	14 000	89	1 800	11
	1964	19 300	93.5	1 330	6.5
UK	1959	2 010	84.5	370	15.5
	1964	2 800	89	340	11

The estimated consumption of sulphuric acid for various purposes in the USA and the UK was as follows in 1964 (expressed as a percentage).

	USA	UK
Phosphatic fertilizers	32	26
Inorganic pigments	8	16
Chemicals (not included below)	9	15 inc. rare earths
Iron and steel pickling	5	4
Ammonium sulphate	7	9
Other sulphates	2	3
Oil refining and petroleum products	3	3
Rayon and film	2	10 inc. transparent paper
Non-ferrous metal treatment	3	0.2
Other uses and unclassified	29	14

In 1965 the price of sulphuric acid in the USA was $19 to $26 per short ton depending on the concentration and purity. In the UK sulphuric acid was sold at prices between £8 13s and £13 6s.

8.9 OLEUM

8.9.1 Production

Oleum (Nordhausen or fuming sulphuric acid) is produced by absorbing sulphur trioxide in anhydrous sulphuric acid. The absorption is accompanied by considerable development of heat suggesting that chemical combination takes place. Strengths of oleum up to 60% extra SO_3 are manufactured. The oleum containing 45% extra SO_3 in fact has the composition $H_2S_2O_7$ and is called pyro-sulphuric acid. The preparation of this acid involves rather large vessels because of the cooling which is necessary. In a new method gas containing sulphur trioxide is passed under pressure through stainless steel tubes into which the sulphuric acid is sprayed. Cooling water is sprayed on the outside of the tubes. This particular equipment requires only a quarter of the steel plate work and tubing used in the earlier models.

8.9.2 Properties

Oleum is a very powerful dehydrating and sulphonating agent. It reacts violently with water and must be handled with great care. The physical properties such as vapour pressure and freezing point vary with the percentage of free sulphur trioxide.

8.9.3 Uses

Mixtures of oleum and nitric acid are often used for nitration of explosives and to form nitro-cellulose for plastics, as well as in the preparation of many dyes. Oleum is also sometimes used in the preparation of chlorosulphonic acid (see section 8.10). Oleums containing 20% or 60% of extra SO_3 are used for purifying ceresine and for other applications in petroleum refining. Oleum is used as a convenient method of transporting sulphur trioxide which may be obtained in the gaseous form by heating the oleum; the residual sulphuric acid may be returned for further absorption of sulphur trioxide gas from a contact sulphuric acid plant.

8.10 HALOGEN AND NITROGEN COMPOUNDS OF SULPHUR

8.10.1 Chlorosulphonic acid

Chlorosulphonic acid (SO_2ClOH) is generally prepared by reacting dry hydrochloric acid with sulphur trioxide; the reaction is rapid and is accompanied by considerable evolution of heat. Oleum may be used in place of sulphur trioxide.

Chlorosulphonic acid may be transported in carboys or in steel drums and great care must be taken in handling it because of its powerful acidity and violent reaction with water. Use of rubber gloves, rubber apron and acid-proof goggles is recommended for handling the acid. Fumes from chlorosulphonic acid are irritating to the skin and good ventilation should be provided in areas where personnel may be exposed.

Chlorosulphonic acid is a liquid boiling at about 152° C with some decomposition. It is a vigorous dehydrating agent and in its violent reaction with water forms hydrochloric and sulphuric acid. It is widely used, principally in the field of organic chemistry, as a sulphating, sulphonating and chlorosulphonating agent. It is preferred in many applications because it gives good yields of desired isomers. It makes possible the one-step preparation of sulphonyl chlorides. In particular it is used – as is sulphur trioxide – in the preparation of saccharin. It can also be used in the preparation of sulphamic acid by reaction with ammonia.

8.10.2 Sulphuryl chloride

Sulphuryl chloride (SO_2Cl_2) is generally prepared by the reaction of dry sulphur dioxide with chlorine in presence of a charcoal catalyst. The reaction is carried out in steel vessels, water-cooled to remove the heat of reaction. The product, when dry, only slightly corrodes steel and lead and is conveniently handled in iron or steel equipment though lead, glass or nickel are preferred because of their greater resistance to corrosion. Storage containers for sulphuryl chloride must be vented frequently to release hydrogen chloride which is formed by the reaction of sulphuryl chloride with moisture.

Sulphuryl chloride is a colourless liquid with an extremely pungent odour. It melts at −46° C and boils at 69.1° C. It is hydrolysed slowly to form a mixture of sulphuric and hydrochloric acids. Sulphuryl chloride is a hazardous chemical; its vapour is highly toxic and the liquid attacks the skin. In organic chemistry it is both a chlorinating and a sulphonating reagent; by careful control of conditions and by the use of catalysts it is often possible to obtain highly selective chlorination.

Sulphuryl chloride finds its main use as a chlorinating and chlorosulphonating agent; it is used as a selective chlorinating agent in the production of the disinfectants chloro-phenol and chlorothymol. It is also used in synthesis of various pharmaceuticals, dyestuffs and surface active agents.

8.10.3 Sulphur monochloride

Sulphur monochloride (S_2Cl_2) is prepared by reacting chlorine with molten sulphur. On the manufacturing scale steel vessels are used for the reaction. The heat of reaction is sufficient to volatilise the sulphur monochloride, and suspended sulphur in the vapour may be removed by the incoming chlorine. Commercial sulphur monochloride is available in a variety of grades depending on the chlorine content. Dry sulphur monochloride does not corrode steel at ordinary temperatures and it is stored and shipped in steel containers.

Sulphur monochloride is a yellow oily liquid of pungent odour. It freezes at $-82°$ C and boils at $138°$ C. It is hydrolysed with water, slowly at room temperature but rapidly at higher temperatures. It is a strong dehydrating agent and reacts with organic acids to produce the corresponding acid anhydride or acid chloride. When treated with dry ammonia in a suitable solvent, at low temperatures, it yields sulphur nitrides. Sulphur monochloride reacts with ethylene to produce mustard gas ($CH_2Cl.CH_2)_2S$.

Sulphur monochloride, generally freshly prepared, is used for cold-vulcanizing rubber. It is also an important intermediate in the manufacture of carbon tetrachloride by chlorinating carbon disulphide (see vol. IV). Sulphur monochloride is absorbed rapidly by oil-based dyes, printers' ink, linoleum etc. and has a drying and vulcanising effect; the remaining traces must, however, be removed in order to avoid the risk of rotting the printed or dyed material.

If liquid sulphur monochloride is cooled to about $10°$ C further chlorine can be introduced, forming sulphur dichloride (SCl_2). This substance is strongly irritant and is not stable; it dissolves sulphur and is used for cold-vulcanizing rubber-based adhesive substances.

8.10.4 Sulphamic acid

Sulphamic acid (HSO_3NH_2) is produced in large quantities, especially in the USA, by passing sulphur trioxide into ammonia; it can also be obtained from oleum with urea, or from chlorosulphonic acid and ammonia.

Sulphamic acid is a non-hygroscopic, crystalline material. Although a very strong acid in aqueous solution it is handled as an easily transportable stable solid; cardboard drums are used as packages. It has a melting point of $205°$ C. Aqueous solutions are stable at room temperatures but at higher temperatures the acid hydrolyses to give ammonium hydrogen sulphate. Nitrous acid reacts rapidly with sulphamic acid forming nitrogen quantitatively according to the equation:

$$HSO_3NH_2 + HNO_2 \rightarrow N_2 + H_2SO_4 + H_2O$$

This reaction is used to destroy nitrites in the manufacture of dyes. Sulphamic acid is used in place of sulphuric acid in tanning where it gives a more attractive grain and a less porous leather. It is also used for the removal of boiler scale and other types of deposit (scale) in milk and sugar factories. It is specially recommended for the preparation of boiler water of optimum composition and is also used in cooling towers to prevent deposition and slime formation. It finds use also in swimming baths and paper factories for the control of all types of bacteria.

8.10.5 Sulphamates

The inorganic sulphamates are readily produced by reaction of sulphamic acid with oxides, carbonates or active metals. Most sulphamates are very soluble in water especially the lead salt.

Sulphamates are highly compatible with cellulose and are extensively used in the textile and paper industries as fire inhibitors.

Sulphamates are very poisonous to weeds, but are quickly converted into sulphates. They are used mainly with amines to make paper and textiles non-inflammable and soft, provided that the material does not have to be wetted. Methylol-sulphamates (especially that of calcium) are also highly soluble and can be used for the production of formaldehyde, e.g. for making casein and other proteins insoluble. The condensation products of methylol-sulphamates are also of importance for the improvement of casein in synthetic horn, for textile finishing etc.

Sodium sulphamate has a solubility of about 80 g in 100 g water at 0° C. It is very sweet, and can be used as a synthetic sweetening agent. For this purpose the sodium salt of cyclohexyl sulphamic acid (obtained by reacting cyclohexylamine with sulphamic acid) is more frequently used at the present time; it has a pleasantly sweet taste and is also very soluble in water; it has been much advertised in America as 'Cyclamate' and 'Sucaryl'.

Ammonium sulphamate is very highly soluble, and also strongly hygroscopic. It is used mainly for making textiles non-inflammable, as a weedkiller, and for killing tree stumps. Strong solutions can hydrolyse spontaneously at high temperatures with a marked evolution of heat, and for this reason must be heated in open vessels.

Ammonium sulphamate is unique among ordinary fire-inhibitors as it does not cause stiffening or otherwise adversely affect the hang and feel of paper and fabrics.

8.11 SELENIUM AND TELLURIUM

8.11.1 Selenium (Se, atomic weight = 78.96)

This element was discovered by Berzelius in 1817. He named it 'selene' (the Greek name for the moon goddess) since it accompanies tellurium in many ores. (About 20 years before, tellurium was named by Klaproth who derived its name from the Latin word 'tellus' meaning earth.)

Selenium is usually found in nature in the form of selenides (see p. 253) of metals such as copper, iron, lead, silver and zinc. These selenides are fairly widely distributed but usually the concentration is too low to work selenium ores solely for their selenium content. From the chemical point of view selenium resembles sulphur and tellurium closely and the selenides occur usually associated with metal sulphides and with tellurides. Swedish pyrites for example contains important quantities of selenides.

In some regions of the USA and Canada the upper soil contains appreciable quantities of selenium, and certain plants growing in these areas may contain as much as 1.5% selenium. Cattle feeding on these plants may be poisoned (mainly damage to liver and lungs).

Selenium is mainly produced as a by-product from electrolytic copper refinery slimes. Smaller quantities are obtained as a by-product from pyrites roasting and lead chamber sulphuric acid production.

The recovery of selenium from copper refinery slimes is based on the fact that selenium (and also tellurium) has a great affinity for copper, and for this reason practically the whole of the selenium in the ore passes to the crude copper (see Blister copper, vol. III) in copper production processes. After electrolytic refining of crude copper, selenium (together with tellurium, gold and silver) is found in the anode slimes which collect at the bottom of the electrolysis cell. The slimes which consist mainly of copper compounds, contain 3-28% selenium corresponding with up to 30 lb of selenium per 100 tons of crude copper treated.

Various processes are used to recover selenium from the slimes. In one process used in Canada, the slimes are treated with sulphuric acid at a temperature of about 180 to 200° C to convert copper compounds into copper sulphate. The resulting slurry is roasted. Selenium volatilizes as the dioxide which is collected in the form of a dust in a wet scrubber and a Cottrell precipitator. Tellurium dioxide remains in the slimes since the roasting temperature is kept relatively low to prevent decomposition of the copper sulphate. The selenium oxide dust is dissolved in hot water. The resulting solution is acidified with hydrochloric acid and treated with sulphur dioxide gas to reduce the selenium oxide to elemental selenium which precipitates. The resulting selenium has a purity of 99.85% after repeated washing with acidification water.

Selenium is also recovered from the flue dust from pyrites roasters in which it is present in the form of elemental selenium and selenium dioxide. In one of the recovery processes the gases from the pyrites roaster are passed through hot carbon in which selenium remains in the elemental form. On leaching the carbon with a sodium sulphite solution, a solution of sodium selenosulphate (Na_2SeSO_3) is obtained from which elemental selenium is precipitated by acidification.

Solid selenium exists in various allotropic modifications (compare sulphur). The grey hexagonal crystal form, which melts at 217° C, is the stable form at ordinary temperatures and is the only form of industrial use. Grey selenium is photosensitive; it has a low electrical conductivity in the dark and relatively high conductivity on exposure to light. More important is the asymmetric conductivity of grey selenium crystals. Asymmetric conductivity means that the electrical conductivity is much higher in one direction (the forward direction) than in the reverse direction. Silicon and germanium show the same phenomenon (see p. 544 and vol. III respectively).

Massive grey selenium is a stable and water-insoluble product which is not very poisonous. However very fine dust of selenium and many selenium compounds are very poisonous. These products cause lung and liver damage when inhaled, ingested or absorbed through the skin hydrogen selenide, H_2Se, especially is very dangerous).

Other less important modifications of selenium are a crystalline red modification, melting at 144° C, and amorphous selenium which is observed as a black vitreous product or a red powder. When heated all these modifications are transformed to grey selenium.

The major consumer of selenium is the electronic industry which uses selenium for the production of rectifiers, and photoconductive cells. Because of its photosensitive properties selenium is also used in xerography (see Photography, vol. VI).

The second largest consumers of selenium are the glass and ceramics industries which use elemental selenium for colorizing and decolorizing glass and for colouring enamels. Selenium ruby glass, for example, is prepared by incorporating a mixture of selenium and cadmium sulphide in the glass. The decolorization of glass is usually based on the fact that the colour of selenium compounds formed in the glass neutralizes the colour of iron compounds.

Less important quantities of selenium are used in metal alloys to improve machinability and in rubber to improve the mechanical properties and the rate of vulcanization.

The world production of selenium and the statistics for various countries are shown in the following table:

| | | In short tons | |
	1956	1960	1964
World	960	835	1050
Canada	165	260	225
Belgium, Lux. (exports)	41	36	47
Japan	81	140	165
Peru	2	6	8
Sweden	85	89	99
USA	464	270	470
Zambia	16	25	29

About 96, 154 and 129 short tons of selenium were imported into the UK in 1956, 1960 and 1964 respectively.

In 1965 price of elemental selenium (99.5% powder) in the USA was $4.50 per lb.

8.11.2 Selenium compounds

Selenium dioxide (SeO_2) is prepared by oxidation of elemental selenium with air at relatively high temperatures or with nitric acid. Selenium dioxide is a white hygroscopic product which is soluble in water and alcohols. Because of its oxidizing power it is used as an oxidizing agent in organic chemistry, e.g. for the oxidation of methyl and methylene groups to aldehyde and ketone groups respectively.

Cadmium sulphide-selenide (cadmium red) may be prepared by treating a cadmium carbonate solution with a solution of a mixture of water-soluble sulphides and selenides. The resulting product is an orange to deep red pigment depending on the combined selenium content. It is used in various fadeproof paints e.g. motorcar paints and artists' paints.

Selenium disulphide is used in medicinal soap for diseases of the scalp.

Sodium selenate (Na_2SeO_4) has been used in the USA as a systemic insecticide, but this insect combating method is obsolete now because selenium can accumulate in some crops in the form of poisonous selenium compounds. It has been proposed to use sodium selenate as an additive in chromium-plating solutions to improve the quality of chromium coatings.

8.11.3 Tellurium (Te, atomic weight = 127.6)

Tellurium was discovered by Müller von Richenstein in 1782 and named by Klaproth who derived the name from the Latin word 'tellus' meaning earth. Tellurium occurs in the form of tellurides (see p. 253) associated with sulphides and selenides in ores of copper, lead, iron, silver and other metals. Native tellurium is also known.

Like selenium and the precious metals, tellurium accumulates in the anode slimes of electrolytic metal refining processes (especially in refinery slimes of blister copper and crude lead). Tellurium is often present in the slimes to the extent of about one-fifth of the selenium. Various processes have been developed to recover tellurium from the slimes. In the sulphating roast process (described under selenium) tellurium dioxide remains in the slime residue, which may be leached with boiling sodium hydroxide solution to form a sodium tellurite solution from which tellurous acid is precipitated by acidifying. Tellurous acid may be converted into elemental tellurium by reducing a solution in strong mineral acid with sulphur dioxide.

Tellurium is a silvery white crystalline product and has a metallic look. A grey amorphous modification is also known. Tellurium melts at 450° C. Chemically it closely resembles sulphur and selenium. Like selenium, large amounts of tellurium are not very poisonous, but fine dust and tellurium compounds are very harmful.

The most substantial quantities of tellurium are used as an additive to rubber to increase the resistance of the latter against abrasion and heat. Tellurium rubber is used as an extremely tough and heat resisting jacket for portable cables used in mining and welding.

Tellurium is used in metallurgy. Lead containing 0.07 to 0.1% tellurium, which is known as tellurium lead, has a greater resistance to attack by sulphuric acid and has better mechanical properties than pure lead. Tellurium is also an excellent degasifier for stainless steel, which it makes easier to machine, but it is not used on a large scale since poisonous tellurium fumes are formed at the processing temperatures. About 0.5% tellurium will also make copper considerably easier to machine.

Since tellurium is volatile at the melting temperatures of the metals mentioned above it is recommended that a master alloy is first made with the desired metal before adding it to the bulk of the molten metal.

Small quantities of tellurium are used in the glass and enamel industries to produce blue to brown colours. It is also used as a semi-conductor material in thermocouple elements. In the form of the chloride tellurium is used to produce a permanent black finish to silverware.

The world production of tellurium is declining slowly. The total output was close to 200 short tons in 1960 and about 140 short tons in 1964. The major quantity is produced in the USA. Other producing countries are Canada, Japan and Peru.

8.12 LITERATURE

1. *Reports on the progress of applied chemistry.* Society of Chemical Industry, p. 336. London, 1951.
2. *A half century of the American sulphur industry,* Industrial and Engineering Chemistry **42** (Nov. 1950), pp. 2 186-2 302.

3. W. W. DUECKER and J. R. WEST. *The manufacture of sulphuric acid.* ACS monograph series no. 144. New York, Reinholt Publishing Company, 1959.

4. *Freeport sulphur handbook.* Freeport Sulphur Company, USA, 1959.

5. A. L. KOHL and F. C. RIESENFELD. *Gas purification.* New York, McGraw-Hill, 1960.

6. TEXAS GULF SULPHUR COMPANY. *Sulphur manual.* Texas Gulf Sulphur Company, 1959. Appendix A: Physico-chemical properties of sulphur.

7. F. EPHRAIM. *Inorganic chemistry,* 6th English ed., P. C. L. Thorne and E. R. Roberts. Edinburgh, Oliver & Boyd, 1954.

8. *Reports on the progress of applied chemistry* 39. Society of Chemical Industry. London, 1954.

9. F. C. SNELLING. *'Chemistry and industry'.* Journal of the Society of Chemical Industry, p. 300. London, 1958.

10. Industrial chemist **33,** p. 44, 1957.

11. C. SINGER *et al. A history of technology,* 8 volumes. Oxford University Press, 1954-58.

12. D. W. F. HARDIE. *A history of the chemical industry in Widnes.* ICI Ltd., General Chemicals Division, 1950.

13. H. GUERIN. *Chimie industrielle I: Industries du soufre.* Paris, Presses Universitaires de France, 1962.

14. K. W. BAGNALL. *Chemistry of selenium, tellurium and polonium.* London, Elsevier, 1966.

15. B. MEYER, ed. *Elemental sulphur.* London, Interscience, 1965.

16. L. C. SCHROETER. *Sulphur dioxide: applications in foods, beverages and pharmaceuticals.* London, Pergamon, 1966.

17. W. N. TULLER, ed. *The sulphur data book.* Freeport Sulphur Co. London, McGraw-Hill, 1959.

CHAPTER 9

The Nitrogen-Phosphorus Group of the Periodic System

9.1 INTRODUCTION

The elements of the fifth main group of the periodic system are nitrogen, phosphorus, arsenic, antimony and bismuth. These elements have several chemical properties in common. Towards hydrogen they are trivalent and their valency towards oxygen and several other elements such as halogens and sulphur is three or five. Nitrogen and phosphorus can also be mono-, di-, or tetravalent towards oxygen. Thus the elements of the nitrogen-phosphorus group form many corresponding compounds as shown by the following examples. Trioxides, pentoxides and trichlorides of each of these elements are known. The hydroxides formed from the pentoxides all have the character of acids, but the acid properties decrease in the order given above. Ammonia, phosphine, arsine, stibine and bismuth hydride are also known (having the formulae NH_3, PH_3, AsH_3, SbH_3 and BiH_3 respectively). If one or more hydrogen atoms of the hydrides are replaced by hydrocarbon radicals such as alkyl groups they form amines and organic phosphines, arsines, stibines and bismuthines respectively. With the exception of bismuth a fourth hydrocarbon group can be introduced, thus forming organic ammonium, phosphonium, arsonium and stibonium compounds. The formation of an ammonium ion from NH_3 by adding on another hydrogen ion persists also as a property of PH_3 but to a much smaller degree.

Elemental nitrogen and phosphorus have a non-metallic character (metalloids). The ordinary modification of elemental arsenic, antimony and bismuth is metallic, but with the exception of bismuth they have dominant non-metallic properties in chemical reactions.

(See for elemental nitrogen chapter 3, p. 83, and for metallic antimony and bismuth, vol. III).

9.2 AMMONIA

9.2.1 History and occurrence

As ammonia (NH_3) is a component of putrescent urine, its penetrating odour was known even in prehistoric times. Its name is derived from salt of Ammon or sal Ammoniac (ammonium chloride).

Many alchemists and chemists worked on urine and ammonia solutions in the early days of chemistry. In those days ammonia was practically the only known soluble base. Hence it was used for fulling wool, in the dyeing of woollen goods and for tanning (the Eskimos still use it for this purpose), etc. In England urine was collected for these purposes and fetched fairly high prices.

In his experiments with urine Priestley collected ammonia gas over mercury in 1774. He spoke of 'alkaline air'. Berthollet discovered its chemical composition in 1785.

From the introduction of coal gas in the early part of the nineteenth century up to the end of the first quarter of the twentieth century, the chief source of ammonia was the gas liquor from gasworks. Nowadays ammonia is still produced in this way but is chiefly made synthetically from nitrogen and hydrogen. During and shortly after the first world war ammonia was also obtained from calcium cyanamide by treating the latter with steam (see also calcium cyanamide, p. 357).

Immense quantities of ammonia are constantly formed in nature by the putrefaction of the protein of dead plants, animals and micro-organisms. Part of this is rapidly absorbed from the earth by living plants to build up new protein. Much is washed away by the rain and is recycled for the building of protein by micro-organisms and plants in rivers and oceans. (See also recycling of phosphorus in the sea, p. 363). Ammonia and ammonium compounds are recycled in a similar way.

9.2.2 Production of ammonia as a by-product from gas liquor

Gas liquor is obtained from coal gas works, coke ovens and producer gas plants. The ultimate source of the ammonia in this case is, of course, protein derived from fossil plants. To be suitable for use in ammonia by-product coke ovens, coal must contain on average about 1.5% nitrogen (in the form of organic compounds). About 6 lb of ammonia per ton of coal is recoverable. This is a yield of about 15-20% of the original nitrogen in the coal. Recovery of ammonia from coal containing less than about 1.5% nitrogen is relatively unprofitable, due to the existence of high capacity synthetic ammonia plants.

A mixture of tar, ammonia, ammonium compounds and water is obtained by washing the gases of the coke ovens with water. Tar is allowed to settle and is then removed. The remaining solution is distilled with milk of lime. Ammonium compounds such as ammonium carbonate and ammonium sulphide are decomposed by milk of lime, and ammonia gas evaporates.

For example: $(NH_4)_2CO_3 + Ca(OH)_2 \rightarrow CaCO_3 + 2H_2O + 2NH_3$

The ammonia gas is cooled to remove most of the water vapour and collected either in water to form by-product ammonia (ammonia liquor) or in sulphuric acid to form ammonium sulphate. (See also production of ammonium sulphate, p. 313).

9.2.3 Production of anhydrous ammonia from hydrogen and nitrogen

a. Principles. The basis of the very important synthetic production of ammonia from hydrogen and nitrogen is the following equilibrium reaction:

$$N_2 + 3H_2 \rightleftharpoons 2NH_3 + heat.$$

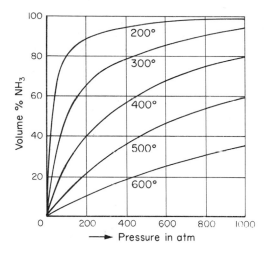

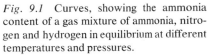

Fig. 9.1 Curves, showing the ammonia content of a gas mixture of ammonia, nitrogen and hydrogen in equilibrium at different temperatures and pressures.

In an equilibrium reaction the starting materials react until an equilibrium between these materials and the resulting product is formed. When this equilibrium is achieved the reaction seems to come to a stop, since at this point as much resulting product is formed as is decomposed again. The position of the equilibrium depends on the reaction conditions such as the temperature and the concentration of the components that are present. An equilibrium can only be achieved when the starting materials react with sufficient speed. The reaction velocity can be increased by increasing the temperature or by adding a catalyst to the mixture. In the reaction of nitrogen with hydrogen both a catalyst and a high temperature are needed.

Unfortunately increases in temperature reduce the equilibrium concentration of ammonia and for maximum efficiency it is therefore necessary to keep the temperature as low as may be consistent with a reasonable rate of reaction. For this reason a high pressure is applied to increase the equilibrium concentration of ammonia. The percentages of ammonia in equilibrium with a mixture of three volumes hydrogen and one volume nitrogen are given in fig. 9.1.

These effects are special cases of Le Chatelier's principle: 'If a constraint is applied to a system in equilibrium, then the system will tend to adjust the equilibrium in order to nullify the effect of the constraint'.

According to this principle, increases in pressure on a system favour such change as results in a decrease of volume. (Four parts of nitrogen and hydrogen form two parts of ammonia.) Also according to this principle, when the temperature of the system is lowered, a change occurs which emits heat, and when the temperature is raised change occurs which absorbs heat (heat is emitted during formation of ammonia and heat is absorbed during decomposition of ammonia).

F. Haber developed the first process for commercial production of synthetic ammonia according to the principles already mentioned. His work was based on his own scientific findings and on the investigations of Nernst and Jost who confirmed the ammonia equilibrium at various temperatures and pressures between 1903 and 1907. In 1908 Haber made an agreement with the Badische Anilin und Soda Fabrik who financed large-scale manufacture and instructed a team with Carl Bosch as the chief chemist to work with him. In Sept. 1913 the first factory came into operation

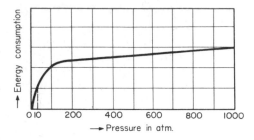

Fig. 9.2 Relation between the pressure and power needed for compressing gases.

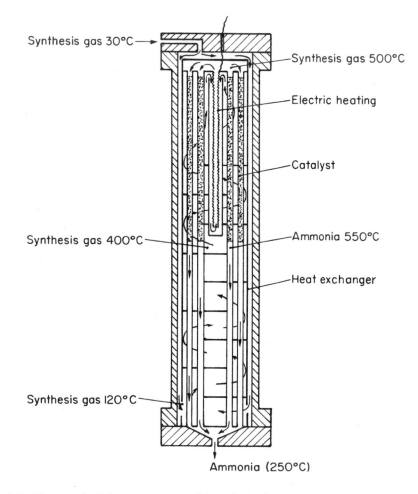

Fig. 9.3 Diagram of a high pressure reactor for synthesis of ammonia.

with an output of 10 tons ammonia per day. Production was soon increased to 30 tons a day. About 750 tons of ammonia were produced in that year.

b. Starting materials. The reaction requires a mixture of three parts (by volume) hydrogen to one part nitrogen. This gas mixture is called synthesis gas. Nitrogen is usually obtained by liquefaction and distillation of air (see liquefaction of gases, p. 43). The major portion of hydrogen for ammonia synthesis is produced *in situ* and may come from various materials, including water (electrolysis), natural gas, refinery gas, water gas, fuel oil and coal gas (see hydrogen production, p. 62 and statistics of hydrogen, p. 72).

Since hydrogen usually contains nitrogen only additional nitrogen from air liquefaction plants is needed to obtain synthesis gas. When very cold or liquid nitrogen is added, impurities such as methane liquefy and are removed at the same time (see separation of hydrogen from gas mixtures, p. 64).

c. The Haber-Bosch process. All modern plants are modifications of the Haber-Bosch process. The modern process of the Badische Anilin und Soda Fabrik is most like the original Haber-Bosch process and is still the most important process for producing synthetic ammonia.

In the process, temperatures between 500 and 550° C and pressures between 200 and 350 atm are applied. Thus synthesis gas must be compressed to about 200-350 atmospheres. The cost of the process is largely determined by the power required for compression (see fig. 9.2). Hence considerable attention has been paid to economic power utilization and efficient design. Compression takes place in stages, the gas being cooled after each stage. This reduces the power consumption, which is about 25% higher for hot gas than for cold. Both piston and turbo compressors are used. Hydrogen gas at a pressure of 100-150 atm is often available, as removing carbon monoxide with ammoniacal cupro salts is performed at high pressures. When liquid nitrogen is injected to the compressed hydrogen, only supplementary compression is needed.

Ammonia synthesis is performed in a high pressure reactor (called a converter), as shown in figs. 9.3 and 9.4. The length of such a converter is about 15 m and its bore about 1 m. It may weigh 100 tons or more. The converter is often constructed of low carbon steel containing small quantities of chromium and vanadium. This material loses little of its original tensile strength, even when carbon is removed by the action of hydrogen. In the very first experiments ordinary carbon steel was used. This kind of steel becomes very brittle since under operating conditions rapid decarbonization occurs.

The converter consists of two parts. The lower part is a heat exchanger in which the synthesis gas is preheated to about 400° C by heat exchange with the reaction product, containing ammonia. The upper part of the converter consists of reaction chambers filled with catalyst in pieces the size of a pea. One converter may contain 4-8 tons of catalyst. Since heat is evolved during the reaction, the reaction chambers are cooled with preheated synthesis gas, which is thus further heated to about 500° C at the same time.

Converters containing several catalyst layers alternated with heat exchange parts are also used.

The catalyst is a 'promoted iron catalyst'. This consists of a finely divided iron

Fig. 9.4 Forged steel vessel, threaded ring and end cover for a chemical synthesis column 68 ft long, 57 inches in diameter and weighing 75 tons manufactured by English Steel Forge and Engineering Corporation Ltd., Sheffield.

catalyst in a mixture of an alkali oxide and an amphoteric oxide such as alumina or silica. Without iron the oxides can not be used as catalyst, but they can promote the catalytic action of the iron catalyst. For this reason they are called 'promoters'. The catalyst is prepared *in situ* by bringing an iron oxide and the other oxides into contact with synthesis gas. Hydrogen in the latter reduces iron oxide to iron metal. The promoted iron catalyst is basically the same as that developed by Haber at the beginning of the century. Some modern catalysts contain, in addition, a third promoter based on an alkaline earth element.

About 8% by volume of the synthesis gas is converted into ammonia. (The conversion is lower than shown in fig. 9.1 as the gas mixture leaves the converter before the reaction equilibrium is achieved.) The gas mixture still being at high pressure and having a temperature of 550° C is cooled to about 250° C by the feed gas in the lower part of the reactor and is further cooled by water to about 25° C. Some ammonia liquefies. The remaining ammonia liquefies in a cold exchanger cooled with expanded cold ammonia. The liquid ammonia obtained and the remaining gas enter a separator in which liquid ammonia collects at the bottom and can be drawn off; the gas mixture leaving the top of the separator is returned into the converter. As synthesis gas also contains some argon and methane, the concentrations of these gases would increase and would thus decrease the ammonia output. For this reason a part of the remaining gas is not recycled but withdrawn from the system (see fig. 9.5).

The production capacity of one converter is about 150-250 tons of ammonia per day.

d. Other processes. There are many modifications of the Haber-Bosch process. All of them are fundamentally the same, but different pressures, gas velocities, temperatures and catalysts are applied. The most important of these processes are those of the Nitrogen Engineering Corporation, Mont Cenis, Fauser-Montecatini, Claude, and Casale processes.

The Claude and Casale processes depart most from the Haber-Bosch process as much higher pressures are used. The operating pressures and temperatures of the Claude process are 900-1000 atm and 500-650° C respectively. The converters used in this process are made of alloys containing much less iron than those used in the Haber-Bosch process. An alloy containing about 60% nickel, 9% chromium, 25% iron and small quantities of tungsten and manganese is often used. The unconverted gas of the reaction in the Claude converter is not recycled after removal of the ammonia formed, but it is passed through a set of converters and ammonia condensers in series.

The very high pressure processes are advantageous in that the increased cost of applying the higher pressures is relatively small as compared with the reduced cost resulting from the improved conversion rate. At 200 atm there is a maximum conversion of 20%, at 600 atm, 40% and at 1000 atm, over 50% at the same temperature (500° C) (see fig. 9.1). Other advantages of the very high pressure processes are their greater compactness (the gases occupy smaller volumes) and simplified construction of the heat exchangers. Owing to the higher pressures the exchange capacity of the gases is increased and ammonia can be liquefied at higher temperatures.

Disadvantages of the very high pressure processes are the shorter life of the equipment and the increased danger owing to the higher pressures.

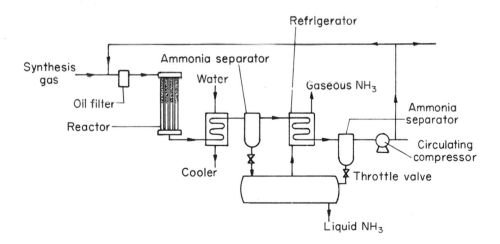

Fig. 9.5 A simplified diagram of liquid ammonia production.

Fig. 9.6   Picture of a Horton sphere for storage of liquid ammonia at a pressure between 40 and 55 p.s.i. The sphere is heavily insulated (double walled) and often painted with white paint to decrease heat absorption.

9.2.4 Storage of anhydrous ammonia

There are three normal methods of storing anhydrous ammonia. Most ammonia is still stored at a pressure of 40-55 p.s.i. (3-4 atm). Ammonia, which is collected in the condensers of the synthesis process, is allowed to expand. The cold liquid ammonia obtained is stored in large insulated steel tanks. Double-walled Horton spheres having a diameter up to 60 ft are often used (see fig. 9.6). These spheres may contain up to 2000 tons of ammonia. The liquid ammonia in such tanks absorbs heat and thus it partially vaporizes as the boiling point of ammonia is around 0° C at pressures between 40 and 55 psi. To prevent rupturing storage tanks, each tank is provided with relief valves. Ammonia gas that escapes continuously is collected, liquefied in a refrigerating unit and returned into the tank. This gas may also be absorbed in water to make by-product ammonia or it may be used directly if an ammonia consuming plant, for instance a nitric acid plant, is operated at the same location.

Storage of liquid ammonia at atmospheric pressure (at a temperature of $-33°$ C) is becoming more important. Large tanks containing 7000 to 15000 tons of liquid ammonia have been built. The tanks are vertical cylinders with conical tops. They have double walls with a $2\frac{1}{2}$ foot insulation (of perlite) between the walls. Vaporizing ammonia is liquefied in a refrigerating unit and returned into the tank. Storage of large quantities of ammonia is necessary, especially in the USA, since about one-third of the ammonia produced there is used as fertilizer in the form of liquid ammonia or ammonia solution. This causes a peak season in the demand for ammonia.

Ammonia which has to be transported is stored at a pressure of 225-250 p.s.i. (about 16 atm) either in cylinders containing up to 150 lb or in rail tank-wagons.

9.2.5 Properties

Ammonia is a gas, having a strong pungent smell even if it is present only in very small quantities in the air (50 p.p.m. by volume). Ammonia at a concentration of 500 p.p.m. or more causes irritation to the surface tissues of the eyes, nose, throat and lungs. Concentrations of 0.2% in air are very dangerous and liquid ammonia produces burns on the skin within a few seconds.

The boiling point of ammonia is $-33.35°$ C and its freezing point is $-77.70°$ C. Gaseous ammonia does not support ordinary combustion but it is inflammable when mixed in proportions of 16-27% with air. It burns with a yellowish flame and may explode to form nitrogen and water.

The solubility of ammonia in water is high, one part of water dissolving over 1100 parts of NH_3 at $0°$ C and normal pressure; and at $20°$ C the solubility is 700 parts. The stronger the solution the lower its specific gravity. Industrial ammonia of $26°$ Bé has a specific gravity of 0.90 and contains 29.4% ammonia.

Solutions of ammonia are often called *ammonia liquor* (not to be confused with *liquid ammonia*). People usually speak of ammonia (an old name is 'spirits of hartshorn' because the alchemists prepared small quantities by dry distilling horn).

Ammonia combines directly with several acids. The compounds must be considered as true salts containing the positive NH_4^+ ion, which is known as the *ammonium ion:*

$$2NH_3 + H_2SO_4 \rightarrow (NH_4)_2SO_4$$
$$NH_3 + HCl \rightarrow (NH_4)_2Cl.$$

For this reason ammonium salts are often compared with the alkali metal salts. Ammonium ions are also formed from ammonia in aqueous solutions. Reaction equation:

$$NH_3 + H_2O \rightarrow NH_4^+ + OH^-$$

Due to the formation of hydroxyl ions at the same time, aqueous solutions of ammonia act as a base. Ammonia reacts with many organic compounds to form amines, imines etc. (see vol. IV). The general term *ammonolysis* refers to the occurrence of this characteristic in numerous reactions. Reactions of this kind can take place with several organic compounds containing one or more halogen atoms or hydroxyl, keto or sulphonic acid groups ($-OH$, $= O$ or $-SO_3H$). Such compounds are alcohols, phenols, aldehydes, ketones, chlorinated aliphatic or aromatic hydrocarbons and several others.

Liquid ammonia is a good solvent for alkali metals and alkaline earth metals.

Solutions of these metals in ammonia are powerful reducing agents in the synthesis of organic compounds.

9.2.6 Applications

The largest quantities of ammonia are used in the manufacture of ammonium sulphate, ammonium nitrate, ammonium phosphate, nitric acid, sodium nitrate, calcium nitrate and urea. Many of these compounds are used as fertilizers. Large quantities of nitric acid and ammonium nitrate are also used in the explosives industry. In the USA important quantities of ammonia solutions and anhydrous ammonia are used as fertilizers without conversion to other compounds. Ammonia is also known to kill fungi and nematodes, especially if a fairly large amount is applied to the soil.

Ammonia is also used for the production of other compounds such as Solvay soda (ammonia-soda process, see p. 452), ammonium carbonate, hydrazine, sodium cyanide, ammonia soap etc.

Ammonia gas dried with potassium hydroxide is the most commonly used refrigerant. A very low water content is essential in order to avoid choking the refrigerating plant with ice. Ammonia is used in refrigerators for ice production, cold storage depots, air conditioning etc.

In the textiles industry ammonia is used for manufacturing hexamethylene diamine $NH_2(CH_2)_6NH_2$ and other amines used as intermediates in nylon production. Cuprammonium-rayon is produced by spinning a solution of cotton linters in ammoniacal copper hydroxide. Acetate rayons can be delustred by immersing the material in a 2% ammonia solution. The textiles industry also uses ammonia for cleaning cotton, wool, rayon and silk fabrics. Before dyeing, fabrics are thoroughly cleaned in a soap solution made alkaline with ammonia.

Ammonia is useful as a cleaner. It removes fats and other dirt from surfaces. For this reason it is used for priming surfaces which have to be painted.

The synthetic resin industry may also rank as a major consumer of ammonia which it needs for producing urea in urea-formaldehyde resins. In addition this industry uses ammonia for the production of hexamethylene tetramine by treating formaldehyde with ammonia. Hexamethylene tetramine is used as a catalyst during polymerization of synthetic resins such as urea-formaldehyde and phenol-formaldehyde. Ammonia is also used for the production of melamine-formaldehyde resins (see resins and plastics, vol. IV).

The chemical industry uses very large quantities of ammonia for the production of several inorganic and organic chemicals and pharmaceuticals etc.

Smaller quantities of ammonia are used for various purposes. Combined with chlorine, ammonia purifies water (see p. 146). Ammonia is also a nutrient for yeast. For this reason it is added to molasses etc. for yeast and alcohol production (see industrial alcohol production, vol. IV). Ammonia is added to raw rubber latex to prevent coagulation. It is also used in a number of processes to neutralize acids that could attack the equipment.

Various new applications of ammonia and its compounds are still being discovered. For example in the USA, di-ammonium succinate has been used in packing fruit. In humid atmospheres this compound continuously evolves gaseous ammonia which kills mould spores. Similar results can be obtained with a relatively cheap mixture of ammonium sulphate and dry soda ash.

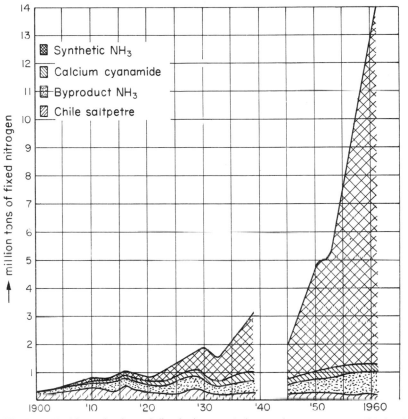

Fig. 9.7 World production of fixed nitrogen (primary nitrogen compounds) in the twentieth century.

9.2.7 Statistics

The world production of ammonia is still increasing. In 1962 it was estimated at about 16.5 million tons (calculated on dry ammonia). This corresponds with about 13.5 million tons of fixed nitrogen. In that year the world's total fixed nitrogen production was 14 million tons (in terms of nitrogen). Thus, both synthetic and by-product ammonia accounted for 97% of the total production of fixed nitrogen (synthetic ammonia 90-92%); the 3% being accounted for by calcium cyanamide and Chile saltpetre. The enormous expansion of ammonia production in the twentieth century is shown in fig. 9.7 and the rate is likely to continue to increase as potential consumers of ammonia are the caprolactam plants, of which a number are in course of construction in Great Britain, USA and several other countries (see vol. IV).

Ammonia is the starting material for almost all nitrogen compounds. The world production of nitrogen compounds (including USSR) is shown in the table on p. 312.

About 83% of the world production of ammonia is used in fertilizers. In highly industrialized countries, for instance the USA, about 75% of the ammonia produced is consumed as fertilizer. The figure approaches 100% in agricultural countries.

The production of synthetic ammonia in some countries is shown in the following table:

	In '000s metric tons of nitrogen	
	1958/59	1961/62
From ammonia	years from 1 July-30 June	
Ammonium sulphate	3089	3084
Calcium nitrate	415	467
Ammonium nitrate as such for use as fertilizer	1144	2124
Lime ammonium nitrate types	1639	1885
Ammonia and solutions for use as fertilizer	1301	1760
Urea for use as fertilizer	519	979
Other forms of nitrogen (including urea, ammonia and ammonium nitrate for industrial use)	2615	3722
Calcium cyanamide	322	290
Chile saltpetre	240	214
Total	11284	14525

	In '000s metric tons of nitrogen				
	1958	1959	1960	1961	1963
Belgium	275	304	319	276	309
Canada		290	348		
France	593	664	724	863	936
Germany (West)	1121	1093	1242	1277	1300
Italy	502	612	680	772	850
Japan	870	1000	1070		
Netherlands	395	408	410	420	
Norway	240	247	266	293	330
United Kingdom	440	470	490	550	700
United States	2900	3380	3900	4300	4900

The following is an estimate of the production and end uses of ammonia in the United Kingdom in 1962:

In '000s long tons of nitrogen

		Production:	
		Synthetic ammonia	590
		By-product ammonia	72
		Total	662
Used for production of:			
Ammonium sulphate	237	Ammonium carbonates, chlorides, etc.	25
Nitric acid (excl. nitric acid for ammonium nitrate)	50	Metallic cyanides	16
		Alkylamines, hexamine Alkanolamines	9
Ammonium nitrate	160	Losses in production	15
Ammonium phosphate	75	Miscellaneous*	26
Urea	45	Exports of ammonia	4

* Miscellaneous includes: metallurgical purposes, ammonia soda process, dyestuffs, hydrogen cyanide, water treatment, refrigeration etc.

About 70% of the nitrogen compounds mentioned above is used as fertilizer, 6% is used in explosives and 5% for synthetic fibre production (nylon etc.). The corresponding figures for the United States are about 76%, 5% and 3% respectively.

The difference in use of ammonia as such for fertilizer purposes in the United Kingdom and the USA is remarkable. In the United Kingdom only small quantities of ammonia solution are used for this purpose (about 6000 tons of N per year). However in the USA about one-third of the total anhydrous ammonia production is applied as such to the soil as fertilizer.

In 1965 the USA prices of ammonia were: anhydrous, fertilizer grade delivered in tanks, $92.00 per ton; aqueous 30%, fertilizer grade delivered in tanks, $95.00 per ton (dry basis); anhydrous refrigeration grade delivered in tanks, $94.50 per ton; solutions (40-45%) pure industrial grade, $0.21 per lb.

Corresponding prices for the UK are not available. Apparently ammonia is not sold in very large quantities in the United Kingdom; prices would be higher than in the USA as the hydrogen prices are higher. In the USA hydrogen is cheaper since it is mainly obtained from natural gas (Hydrogen facilities represent nearly two thirds of the big ammonia plants which require more than 80000 ft^3 per ton of NH$_3$).

In the UK the prices of smaller quantities of ammonia were in 1965: anhydrous: 11d to 2s 2½d per lb, solutions 1½d to 3½d per lb.

9.2.8 Literature

A. J. HARDING. *Ammonia, manufacture and uses.* Oxford University Press, 1959.

J. W. MELLOR. *Comprehensive treatise on inorganic chemistry.* Vol. VIII, Suppl. I, Part 1. London, Longmans, 1964.

V. SAUCHELLI. *Fertilizer nitrogen: its chemistry and technology.* New York, Reinhold, 1964. ACS monograph no. 61.

C. A. VANCINI. *La Sintesi dell'ammoniaca.* Milan, Ubrico Hoepli, 1961.

9.3   AMMONIUM SULPHATE

9.3.1 Production

a. *The saturator process.* Ammonium sulphate (NH$_4$)$_2$SO$_4$ is produced by introducing a mix of ammonia gas and water vapour into a reactor (called a 'saturator'). The saturator contains a saturated solution of ammonium sulphate and about 2-4% free sulphuric acid at a temperature of about 60° C. The reaction is represented by the following equation:

$$2NH_3 + H_2SO_4 \rightarrow (NH_4)_2SO_4 + heat.$$

The ammonia gas may be by-product or synthetic ammonia. Concentrated sulphuric acid (containing 60-80% by weight of H$_2$SO$_4$) is added continuously to keep the solution at the acidity of about 2-4% sulphuric acid. The heat evolved during the reaction is sufficient to maintain the temperature of the saturator at about 60° C.

Ammonium sulphate crystallizes out, since the solution is saturated with the salt.

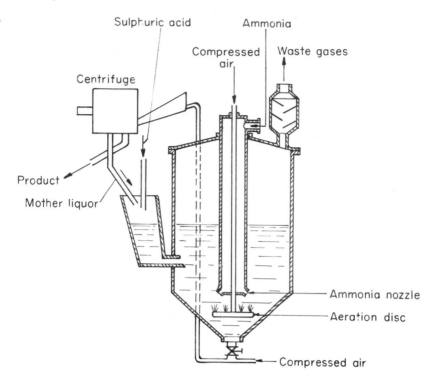

Fig. 9.8 Diagram of a saturator for the production of ammonium sulphate. The crystal slurry is pumped to the centrifuge by compressed air. Several modifications of this saturator are in use.

The crystals collect at the bottom of the saturator and are continuously removed from the bottom which is often conical (see fig. 9.8). The crystal slurry is pumped to centrifuges or vacuum filters which separate the crystals from the mother liquor. The latter is returned to the saturator and the crystals are washed and dried. The crystals are often washed with water containing ammonia since the solubility of ammonium sulphate in water decreases in the presence of ammonia. At the same time the last traces of acid are removed. Acid would corrode storage bins and destroy sacks in which ammonium sulphate is packaged. Free sulphuric acid also causes caking of ammonium sulphate as it makes it hygroscopic.

Semicontinuous centrifuges are often used for separating ammonium sulphate from the mother liquor. A typical centrifuge in ammonium sulphate plants is the horizontal automatic short-cycle filtering centrifuge (see fig. 9.9). The centrifuge is fed with liquid and crystals. When the layer of crystals is thick enough, the feed is stopped and the layer is washed. The crystal layer is partially dried by leaving it for some time in the still rotating centrifuge. The crystals are removed from the rotating centrifuge with a scraper. The loosened crystals emerge through a chute. After removal of the crystal layer, the centrifuge is fed again with crystal slurry from the saturator.

New plants often use continuous centrifuges, the crystal slurry being fed to the centrifuge continuously. A continuous centrifuge which is suited for filtering ammonium sulphate is the reciprocating conveyer continuous filtering centrifuge (see fig. 9.10).

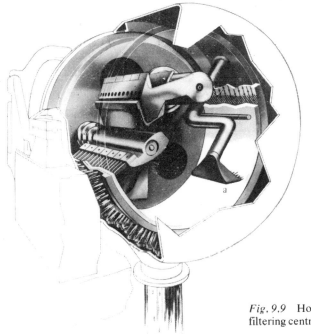

Fig. 9.9 Horizontal automatic short-cycle filtering centrifuge. Loading at *a*; unloading at *b*.

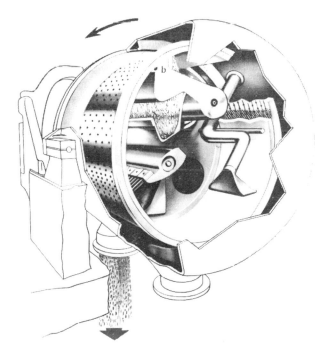

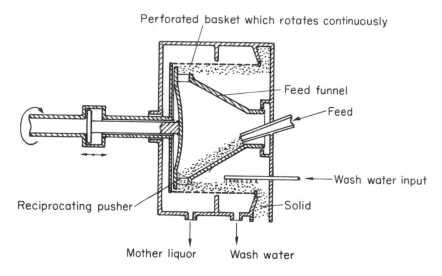

Fig. 9.10 Reciprocating-conveyer continuous filtering centrifuge. The solid on the walls of the basket is moved to the right by the reciprocating pusher. The feed funnel is fixed to the pusher, and moves with it.

Formerly all equipment was made of mild steel, lined with lead, to prevent corrosion. Nowadays Monel metal is used increasingly for building the saturator, centrifuges, pumps and other parts in contact with the mother liquor.

The process for producing ammonium sulphate is very simple, but particular attention has to be paid to prevent the caking of stored ammonium sulphate. Long thin crystals are formed in a mother liquor containing trivalent ions. Much dust is formed from these crystals and they also show a tendency to cake. For this reason trivalent ions, especially ferric ions (Fe^{+++}) have to be removed. Ferric ions occur in sulphuric acid, and the concentration of these ions in the mother liquor would increase without removal. Ferric ions may removed in several ways. For instance by precipitation with hydrogen sulphide containing gases or with oxalates, by reduction to bivalent ions (ferrous ions) with sodium thiosulphate or by complex formation with phosphoric acid. In the absence of ferric ions, crystals shaped like grains of rice are formed.

The tendency to cake also decreases with increasing grain diameter. Larger crystals are obtained by decreasing the acidity of the solution in the saturator, by diluting the feed ammonia with water vapour, and by agitating the contents of the saturator. This may be performed by blowing air through the solution or by injecting the ammonia gas into the solution through small nozzles at high velocity (see fig. 9.8).

b. Other routes to ammonium sulphate. Due to the heat development during formation, ammonium sulphate can also be produced in a dry form by spraying sulphuric acid into a reaction chamber filled with ammonia gas (Fauser process). A powder of ammonium sulphate is formed as the heat evolved during the reaction causes evaporation of all water present. Ammonium sulphate collects at the bottom of the reactor and can be withdrawn. Water vapour and excess ammonia are separated by cooling the gas mixture below 100° C in a fractionation column. Ammonia is returned to the reactor. The powder of ammonium sulphate has a tendency to cake; for this reason it is caked by pressing and broken to small pieces.

A process which is fairly widely employed in the USA is the evaporation process. Ammonium sulphate is obtained by washing gases containing ammonia in a counter-current flow with an acid solution of ammonium sulphate in a column. The liquor leaving the scrubber is partially evaporated to cause crystallization of ammonium sulphate.

Instead of sulphuric acid, finely ground gypsum or anhydrite can be used to produce ammonium sulphate. A saturated solution of ammonium carbonate is continuously prepared by passing ammonia, carbon dioxide and water into a saturator:

$$2\ NH_3 + CO_2 + H_2O \rightarrow (NH_4)_2CO_3$$

(Carbon dioxide is often available from hydrogen plants which produce hydrogen for synthetic ammonia.) The ammonium carbonate solution obtained at temperature of 45° C, is drawn off and mixed with gypsum powder in vessels provided with stirrers. The following reaction takes place:

$$(NH_4)_2CO_3 + CaSO_4 \rightarrow CaCO_3 + (NH_4)_2SO_4$$

The temperature increases to 60° C as heat is evolved during the reaction, which takes ten hours. The conversion is 95%.

The ammonium sulphate solution obtained is separated from the precipitated calcium carbonate by filtration, and for this reason the carbonate precipitate should not be too fine. As a small excess of ammonia is present, impurities such as iron are removed at the same time. The excess of ammonia is needed to keep the solution of ammonium sulphate free from calcium sulphate which would promote scale formation in evaporators.

A crystal slurry of ammonium sulphate is obtained by evaporating the filtered solution in multiple effect crystallizers (ch. 1). Large crystals are obtained by keeping the slurry in motion. Ammonium sulphate is separated from the mother liquor in the same manner as described in the saturator process. Calcium carbonate is recovered as a by-product and is used as a lime fertilizer or in composite fertilizers.

Ammonium sulphate is commercially produced from gypsum or anhydrite in some countries having large sources of the latter (United Kingdom, France, India).

9.3.2 Properties and uses

Ammonium sulphate is a white crystalline compound. Its solubility in water is relatively high (about 73 g in 100 cm^3 of water at 10° C). Its solubility decreases when ammonia is added (36 g dissolve in 100 cm^3 water containing 15% NH_3). Ammonium sulphate is extensively used as a nitrogenous fertilizer. In combination with a phosphate or borate it is used for fireproofing timber, plastics and insulating materials. Ammonium sulphate is also a nutrient in yeast production from molasses. In combination with chlorine, ammonium sulphate disinfects water. (The sulphate furnishes ammonium ions which in turn react with chlorine and water to form chloro amines.)

Ammonium sulphate is also used in treatment of hides for leather production. It dissolves the lime in the hides and is a buffer which activates the pancreas enzymes used in leather production (see leather, vol. V).

9.3.3 Statistics

The world production of ammonium sulphate was estimated at about 15 million tons in 1961. The production of several countries is given in the following table:

Production of ammonium sulphate in '000s long tons (estimated)

	1955	1957	1959	1961	1963
Australia	78	111	105	104	87
Canada	275	280	290	269	247
France	320	340	350	350	340
Germany, East	780	790	820	810	820
Germany, West			2020	2080	2000
Israel		38	64	30	70
Italy	730	760	1150	1340	1310
Japan	2100	2440	2590	2470	2220
India	390	380	380	390	440
Netherlands			320	350	330
Poland	100	110	120	145	
Portugal	80	60	190	180	245
Spain	140	140	210	400	
United Kingdom	1010	1110	1020	1080	1150
USA	1980	1840	1540	1380	1590

Most ammonium sulphate is obtained from synthetic ammonia. In the UK about three-quarters and in the USA about two-thirds of total ammonium sulphate comes from synthetic ammonia.

The UK production is more than enough for home demand and considerable amounts are exported as shown below.

	1955	1958	1960	1962
Long tons	204000	304000	178000	360000
Value £	3892000	4903000	2447000	

The price of ammonium sulphate in 1965 was $ 32-$ 56 per short ton. In the UK ammonium sulphate was sold at £ 18 11s per long ton.

9.3.4 Literature

V. SAUCHELLI. *Fertilizer nitrogen: its chemistry and technology.* New York, Reinhold, 1964. ACS monograph no. 161.

9.4 AMMONIUM NITRATE

9.4.1 Production

Ammonium nitrate (NH_4NO_3) is manufactured in three stages: production of a solution of ammonium nitrate in water, concentration of the solution by evaporating the water, and production of a ground solid from the concentrated solution.

The most important method for producing a solution of ammonium nitrate is the neutralization of nitric acid (at a concentration of 50-60%) with ammonia gas. A solution containing about 70% ammonium nitrate is obtained according to the following reaction equation:

$$NH_3 + HNO_3 \rightarrow NH_4NO_3 + heat.$$

This process is basically the same as the saturator process for the production of ammonium sulphate. Unfortunately there are several difficulties in the way since ammonium nitrate is explosive, its solubility in water is extremely high, and both the original materials are volatile. For these reasons the saturator process must be modified. Because of its high solubility ammonium nitrate must be concentrated in the solution to get a solid product. The heat developed during the process would be sufficient for simple evaporation of the water, but the temperature of the reactor must be controlled by cooling to avoid hazard and loss of volatile original materials. Thus only a part of the heat developed can be used economically.

The second and third stages of the process can be combined in a crystallization process. Water is partially removed from the solution by heating at a temperature of about 75° C in a crystallizer. This is often a long narrow vessel in which the crystallizing slurry is kept in motion by a helical stirrer. Water is evaporated by heating with steam coils or by evacuation (vacuum crystallizers). A concentrated solution of ammonium nitrate containing crystals is produced. This slurry is drawn off, the crystals are centrifuged off and dried. The mother liquor is returned to the crystallizer for further evaporation.

There are several other methods for concentrating and solidifying ammonium nitrate solutions.

a. Graining. In this process the solution of ammonium nitrate is evaporated almost to dryness (98%) at a temperature of 150-155° C in an open pan provided with steam coils, and the molten mass of ammonium nitrate is then slowly cooled in a graining vessel while stirring with rake-stirrers (or ploughs). In this way ammonium nitrate solidifies in the form of small pellets.

b. Prilling. In this process the solution of ammonium nitrate is concentrated to a concentration of 95% at a temperature of 125-135° C in a vacuum evaporator. The hot liquid obtained is sprayed into the top of a tower 50 to 200 feet high. In this tower (prilling tower) the sprayed mass is cooled, and it solidifies to porous particles of ammonium nitrate (prills). A part of the remaining water is removed in the prilling tower. Further drying of the prills is needed. This drying process is performed in rotary dryers by treating with heated and dehumidified air. A similar prilling process is used in urea plants (see also fig. 9.23).

c. In a modification of the prilling process the solution is concentrated to over 99% in steam heated evaporators and the molten ammonium nitrate obtained is introduced into a short prilling tower or into a spray chamber. In the latter, ammonium nitrate is sprayed by running it on to the surface of a rotating disc. A part of the ammonium nitrate is solidified as a fine dust. This dust is not collected at the bottom of the spray chamber but is blown to another stage of the process by air.

Nowadays the processes described above are widely used. Several new processes have been developed but these do not differ fundamentally. There is a tendency to recover a greater part of the heat of reaction and to eliminate the evaporation stage of the process. A more concentrated solution of ammonium nitrate may be obtained by introducing a fresh feed of ammonia and nitric acid into the mother liquor which is withdrawn from the crystallizer.

The evaporation stage is also eliminated in the Stengel process which is used to some extent in the USA and the United Kingdom. By this process molten ammonium nitrate containing 2% water can be obtained in one stage by feeding hot nitric acid and ammonia into a stainless steel tube filled with Raschig rings or glass beads. Most of the water is converted into steam and removed by passing the hot reaction mixture in the opposite direction to a hot air stream through a separator which also contains packing (see fig. 9.11). The feed air is heated by steam withdrawn from the system. The temperature of the reactor is controlled by the temperature to which the nitric acid is preheated. Explosions are prevented by the packing.

The ammonium nitrate obtained is solidified by one of the methods mentioned before.

9.4.2 Properties

Ammonium nitrate is a white crystalline solid.

The melting point of water-free ammonium nitrate is 169° C. The solubility of

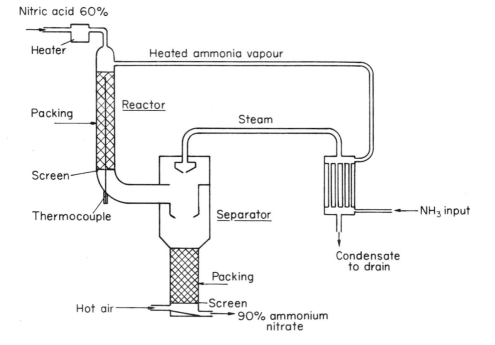

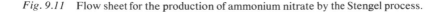

Fig. 9.11 Flow sheet for the production of ammonium nitrate by the Stengel process.

ammonium nitrate in water is extremely high; 100 g water dissolve about 150 g ammonium nitrate at 10° C, producing a 60% solution of ammonium nitrate.

Since solid ammonium nitrate is hygroscopic, it will cake when it is stored as such. The tendency to cake is decreased by coating the particles with a finely powdered material. For this purpose the particles are often treated with finely divided diatomaceous earth or kaolin in rotating drums. Caking can also be prevented by spraying a 0.01% to 0.03% solution of the dye 'acid magenta' on freshly prepared ammonium nitrate particles and drying them. Other comparable dyes have been discovered, but acid magenta is preferred as it is commercially available. Some ammonium nitrate dissolves from the surface of the particles. The dissolved ammonium nitrate recrystallizes on the surface of the particles during drying, but a change of crystal habit occurs in the presence of acid magenta. The particles thus modified can be stored in paper bags for a year or more without caking.

Ammonium nitrate decomposes on heating at temperatures above 200° C. At temperatures between 200 and 260° C nitrous oxide is formed and the decomposition can be controlled. At higher temperatures ammonium nitrate decomposes to nitrogen, water and oxygen. Reaction equation: $2NH_4NO_3 \rightarrow 2N_2 + 4H_2O + O_2$.

This reaction is very violent and explosions can occur in caked or molten masses. Since oxygen is formed ammonium nitrate supports combustion of organic matter. In 1947 an explosion occurred in some thousand tons of ammonium nitrate, some time after a fire had broken out on a ship in which the nitrate was stored. The ammonium nitrate particles were coated with a mixture of kaolin and paraffin to prevent caking and the product was stored in paper bags. Undoubtedly the explosion was caused by the organic matter present. For this reason organic materials are no longer used for prevention of caking in large quantities of ammonium nitrate.

9.4.3 Uses

Ammonium nitrate has been a very important nitrogen fertilizer since the first world war. The NO_3^- ions are assimilated by plants very quickly, while the NH_4^+ ions are absorbed slowly. The nitrate thus promotes rapid growth, while its effect continues to be felt through the entire growth period. In the USA much ammonium nitrate is used in pure form. It is also used in mixed fertilizers, especially in Europe. Mixed fertilizers with calcium carbonate, dicalcium phosphate or other fertilizers are often produced. These mixed fertilizers do not cake and there is also far less danger of explosion (see fertilizer chapter).

In its pure state ammonium nitrate will explode at temperatures above 230° C and pressures of 170 atm (2500 lb/m²) and more and large quantities of ammonium nitrate are therefore used in the manufacture of explosives (see explosives). The explosiveness increases in the presence of carbonaceous matter. It is said that ammonium nitrate containing about 1.5% carbonaceous matter can explode at a temperature of about 150° C and a pressure of 17 atm (250 lb/m²).

Explosions occur at high temperatures because ammonium nitrate decomposes with the formation of gases. As the pressure of the gases increases, more heat is developed. This heat promotes more violent decomposition. In this way the decomposition reaction moves through the solid with a velocity of about 3000 metres per second and a vigorous explosion occurs.

9.4.4 Statistics

The world production of ammonium nitrate was nearly 10 million tons (in terms of NH_4NO_3) in 1960. The production of some countries was as follows:

	1955	1957	In '000s long tons 1959	1961	1963
United States	1 860	2 300	2 600	2 900	3 500
France	770	1 060	1 060	1 140	1 400
Italy	260	370	680	790	700
Netherlands			680	660	600
United Kingdom	260		380		460

The production of the United Kingdom was large enough to cover home demand. Small quantities are exported (6 000 tons in 1955 and 500 tons in 1960). In the United States and United Kingdom about 80-85% was produced as fertilizer grade in 1960. Most of the remaining part was explosive grade. In the USA the price of ammonium nitrate, fertilizer grade was $ 70 per short ton in 1965; the price in the United Kingdom was £ 39 per long ton.

9.5 OTHER AMMONIUM COMPOUNDS

9.5.1 Ammonium chloride

Ammonium chloride (NH_4Cl) was known to the Egyptians about 400 years before the Christian era. They recovered it from the smoke of dry camel or donkey dung which was used as a fuel. Ammonium chloride occurs in several plants which are consumed by camels. Their dung usually contained a good deal of this salt and several others. That ammonium chloride occurs in the smoke is due to the fact that this salt sublimes, i.e. forms a vapour, without melting or decomposing, which at once forms a solid again when cooled. Thus ammonium chloride settled on the walls and the chimneys of the huts, from which it was scraped off. The salt got the name salt of Ammon or sal ammoniac. This is probably due to the fact that much camels' dung was collected near the temples of Jupiter Ammon.

Ammonium chloride is obtained as a by-product in synthesis of sodium carbonate (see p. 452). Ammonium chloride is also produced in a saturator process by introducing gaseous ammonia and gaseous hydrochloric acid (or an aqueous solution) in a saturated solution of ammonium chloride. This process resembles the saturator process for the production of ammonium sulphate.

Ammonium chloride can also be obtained by dissolving common salt in a solution of ammonium sulphate at boiling temperature. The following double decomposition reaction takes place:

$$(NH_4)_2SO_4 + NaCl \rightarrow Na_2SO_4 + 2NH_4Cl.$$

Much sodium sulphate precipitates at this temperature. After filtering, the filtrate is cooled and ammonium chloride crystallizes out.

Crude ammonium chloride can be purified by cooling hot saturated solutions (recrystallization) or by sublimation of the solid.

Ammonium chloride is a white crystalline compound. It sublimes at a temperature of 338° C and a pressure of 1 atm. Just as liquids slowly evaporate at temperatures below their boiling points, so ammonium chloride sublimes slowly at temperatures below 338° C. Ammonium chloride is soluble in water. About 29 g dissolve in 100 g water at 20° C and about 77 g in 100 g water at 100° C.

The most significant amounts of ammonium chloride are used in dry cells which are produced in various sizes and shapes. A paste of ammonium chloride and manganese oxide fills the space between a graphite rod (positive electrode) and a zinc container (negative electrode). (See dry cells, vol. II) Ammonium chloride is also used as a flux material in soldering and in tinning and galvanizing iron.

Some ammonium chloride is used in pharmaceuticals such as cough syrups. It has also diuretic properties.

The most important producer of ammonium chloride is Japan. In 1951 its production was 14000 tons; in 1961: 380000 tons. This large expansion of the production is caused by the enormous demand for fertilizer purposes. The consumption of ammonium chloride for industrial purposes was nearly constant at 7000 tons per year during the nineteen fifties and sixties.

Only small quantities of ammonium chloride as such and of mixtures with calcium carbonate are used as fertilizer in the USA and Western Europe, but this application is of growing importance. The production of ammonium chloride in the USA was nearly 23000 short tons in 1963. The exports from the United Kingdom are shown in the following table:

	1955	1957	1959	1961	1963
In tons	12800	9900	11000	16000	11000
In £	437000	314000	343000	529000	367000

In 1965 the price of ammonium chloride in the USA was $ 0.06 per lb for technical grade and $ 0.20 per lb for pharmaceutical grade; in the United Kingdom a pure grade was sold at £ 30 2s 6d per long ton.

9.5.2 Ammonium carbonates

Ammonium bicarbonate (NH_4HCO_3) can be obtained in a saturator process (see also ammonium sulphate and ammonium chloride). Carbon dioxide is fed into a saturated solution of ammonium bicarbonate containing a large excess of ammonia. Ammonium bicarbonate crystallizes out and is separated from the mother liquor which is used again. Alternatively ammonium bicarbonate can be prepared by the reaction of a strong ammonia solution with carbon dioxide gas in an absorption column. In both processes a pure product containing 21.6% nitrogen is obtained from synthetic ammonia and pure carbon dioxide. Impure products obtained from by-product ammonia are purified by sublimation.

Ammonium bicarbonate decomposes below its melting point into the components ammonia, carbon dioxide and water. Even when stored at atmospheric temperature a considerable loss of weight occurs.

A considerable amount of ammonium bicarbonate is used as baking powder. It gives off gaseous products in raising dough and leaves no solid residue. For the same reason it is used as a 'blowing agent' for the production of cellular or sponge rubber and plastics and for the production of light-weight bricks. Small quantities of ammonium bicarbonate are used as a fertilizer. It has a fertilizing value but it cannot compete with other fertilizers because of its loss of weight when stored. Ammonium bicarbonate is also used as 'smelling salts' (usually mixed with oil of lavender).

Ammonium carbonate ($(NH_4)_2 CO_3$) is not available in a pure form. Crystalline products consisting of double salts of ammonium carbonate, ammonium bicarbonate and ammonium carbamate ($NH_4CO_2NH_2$), are prepared by reacting mixtures of water, ammonia and carbon dioxide. The mixture is distilled and condensed to a solid crystalline mass. By suitably varying the composition double salts containing any desired proportion of nitrogen from 22% to nearly 33% can be obtained.

These products are more volatile than ammonium bicarbonate and they are used for the same purposes as the latter.

In ancient times the Arabs prepared such ammonium carbonate mixtures by destructive distillation of the antlers of the hart. For this reason the resulting product was called 'hartshorn'. The name 'salts of hartshorn' is still used for both ammonium bicarbonate and the double salts of carbonates and carbamates.

The United Kingdom is an important producer of ammonium carbonate and bicarbonate. About 3000 tons per year (value £ 120000) have been exported from this country during the decade 1950-1960. The price of ammonium bicarbonate in the USA in 1965 was $ 7.50 per 100 lb.

9.5.3 Ammonium sulphides

Ammonium hydrosulphide (NH_4HS) is made by passing hydrogen sulphide into an ammonia solution. Ammonium sulphide ($(NH_4)_2S$) is not formed since it is not stable at temperatures above $18°$ C.

Ammonium hydrosulphide solutions are of importance in chemical analysis, to precipitate sulphides of the heavy metals which are insoluble. The solutions are also used for the denitration of nitro artificial silk. The 40-50% solution sold at $160 per short ton (dry basis) in 1965.

By dissolving sulphur in an ammonium hydrosulphide solution, the so called 'yellow ammonium sulphide' (ammonium polysulphide) is obtained. This product is more extensively used as an analytical reagent than the colourless ammonium hydrosulphide.

The solutions and the vapours of both ammonium sulphides are very poisonous.

9.6 OXIDES OF NITROGEN

Of the five oxides of nitrogen only three, the gases nitrous oxide (N_2O), nitric oxide (NO) and nitrogen peroxide (NO_2) are of interest.

Nitrous oxide (N_2O) is prepared by heating ammonium nitrate

$$NH_4NO_3 \rightarrow N_2O + 2H_2O.$$

The gas liquefies at $-89.5°$ C, or at a pressure of about 70 atm (critical temperature is $+ 36.5°$ C). It is stored and transported in steel cylinders. Nitrous oxide is used as an anaesthetic for minor operations. During early stages of inhalation it produces a kind of intoxication or hysteria, from which the name 'laughing gas' is derived.

Nitric oxide (NO) may be produced by dissolving metals in nitric acid. Immediately NO comes into contact with air, each molecule combines with one atom of oxygen and the brown nitrogen peroxide is formed (see also nitric acid, p. 326).

Nitrogen peroxide (NO_2) can also be obtained by decomposing nitric acid. It is also formed from air in an electric arc or by oxidizing ammonia with air. It is very poisonous even in great dilution and the more dangerous as symptoms do not show themselves immediately. The gas can cause fatal pneumonia. With water it forms nitric acid (HNO_3) and nitric oxide. It has the following unusual property. It changes into a brown liquid at a temperature below 22° C. This liquid turns paler on cooling and becomes colourless at temperatures below zero. When heated, this colourless liquid becomes brown and evaporates to a dark brown gas. This phenomenon is due to the fact that colourless N_2O_4 is formed at lower temperatures and NO_2 at higher temperatures.

Nitrogen peroxide is a powerful oxidant. It contains over 70% oxygen. Potassium, phosphorus, charcoal and sulphur will burn in it. Nitrogen peroxide is important as an oxygen carrier in the lead chamber process for making sulphuric acid. Nitrogen peroxide is a common waste gas in many factories using nitric acid.

9.7 NITRIC ACID

9.7.1 History

This acid (HNO_3) is believed to have been known in ancient times. It was probably obtained from the widely known mineral potassium nitrate. It was mainly used for refining and assaying precious metals. In 1776 Lavoisier discovered that it contains oxygen. The complete chemical composition was established by Gay-Lussac and Berthollet in 1816.

Before and during the first world war nitric acid was chiefly produced by treating Chile saltpetre with concentrated sulphuric acid. Sodium bisulphate (nitre cake) was obtained as a by-product. Reaction equation: $NaNO_3 + H_2SO_4 \rightarrow NaHSO_4 + HNO_3$. Nitric acid (92% solution in water) was obtained by distilling the reaction mixture.

During the first world war other processes became increasingly important since production from Chile saltpetre depended on imports. One of these processes is the electric arc process which came into use for the first time in Norway in 1905.

Successful plants were among others the Birkeland and Eyde and the Nitrum A.G. plants. A gas containing about 2% nitric oxide can be obtained from nitrogen and oxygen in air by passing air rapidly through an electric arc. As an excess of oxygen is present, nitric acid is converted to nitrogen peroxide and nitric acid is formed from the latter by dissolving in water. Nowadays the very expensive electric arc processes are replaced by the processes described below.

The Wisconsin thermal process is another process for producing nitric acid from air. It was used on a small scale during the first years after the second world war. A gas containing 2% nitric oxide can be obtained by blowing preheated air into a fuel gas flame and rapidly cooling the combustion gas obtained (at 2 540° C) by passing it through magnesia pebbles. The difficulty of lining the furnaces which could resist the very

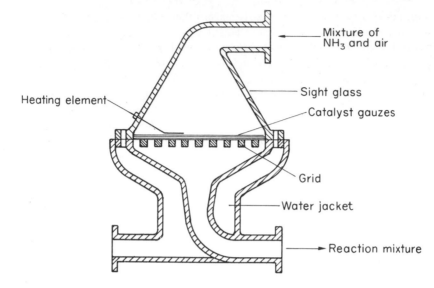

Mixture of
NH_3 and air

Heating element

Sight glass

Catalyst gauzes

Grid

Water jacket

Reaction mixture

Fig. 9.12 Sectional view of a reactor for the production of nitric acid.

high temperatures for a sufficiently long time apparently diminished the value of this process.

The second process which was of growing importance during the first world war is the ammonia oxidation process. The principles of this process had been known for some time, but technical application of ammonia oxidation was not started until it was investigated by Wilhelm Ostwald in the early days of the twentieth century. Nowadays ammonia oxidation is the only commercial process.

9.7.2 Production

a. Principles. Modern methods of nitric acid manufacture are based on three reactions. First, nitric oxide is obtained by oxidizing (burning) ammonia with oxygen from air in the presence of a catalyst:

$$4\,NH_3 + 5\,O_2 \rightarrow 4\,NO + 6\,H_2O$$

This quick reaction is followed by oxidation of the nitric oxide obtained to nitrogen peroxide and absorption of the nitrogen peroxide in water to form nitric acid. These reactions are relatively slow:

$$2\,NO + O_2 \rightarrow 2\,NO_2 \quad 3\,NO_2 + H_2O \rightarrow 2\,HNO_3 + NO.$$

The process can be carried out in two stages. Ammonia oxidation in a relatively small equipment and conversion of the nitric oxide obtained into nitric acid in a larger apparatus (absorption stage).

The equipment for the absorption stage must be much larger than that for the first stage and demands careful design if considerable quantities of unconverted nitric oxide are not to remain. This is due to the fact that the second and third reactions are relatively slow as compared with the first reaction and the nitric oxide reformed during the third reaction has to be absorbed once more.

The third reaction is an equilibrium reaction and the equilibrium concentration of nitrogen peroxide decreases if the pressure increases (see Le Chatelier principle, p. 303). Consequently the absorption efficiency increases when pressures greater than atmospheric pressure are used enabling a smaller equipment at lower capital cost to be employed. However, there is no single optimum way to manufacture nitric acid since a higher pressure causes a lower oxidation yield, a greater power consumption and higher catalyst losses. The number of modified nitric acid plants in use indicates this.

b. Ammonia oxidation. The oxidation of ammonia is performed in conical converters (see figs. 9.12 and 9.13). The converter is provided with a catalyst which consists of a horizontally disposed composite of gauzes made from an alloy of platinum and rhodium (90% and 10% respectively). A typical gauze is woven from wire of 0.003 inch diameter with a mesh of 80 to the inch. From twenty to forty-five gauzes are laid together to form a composite. This composite has a low mechanical strength and is therefore supported by a heavy stainless steel grid. There is a definite loss of catalyst during operation (see fig. 9.14) owing to disintegration of the surface of the metal by the stream of hot reaction gases. This loss of material may be 80 mg per ton HNO_3 and

Fig. 9.13 Characteristic conical reactors for nitric acid production. The remaining part of the plant is installed in the open air. See fig. 9.15.

Fig. 9.14 Photomicrographs (x 100) of platinum rhodium catalyst gauzes. Left, a fairly new catalyst: right, a well-used catalyst.

amounts to about 4% of the total cost of acid production at atmospheric pressure. The loss increases with increasing pressure. The catalyst dust can be recovered by means of fibreglass filters, or may be collected from the inside walls of the apparatus. Filters have not been universally adopted as they cause a pressure drop in the plant.

The converter and the other equipment are built from chromium-nickel steel containing small quantities of 'stabilizer metal' (for instance 1% titanium and 1% tungsten). The lower and hotter part of the converter is cooled by a water jacket.

An ammonia-air gas mixture containing 9.5 to 11 volume per cent ammonia is fed to the upper part of the converter and is blown through the gauze composite. The reaction is started by bringing an electrically heated nichrome wire near the gauze composite. The combustion of ammonia starts at the heated spot and spreads over the whole catalyst surface. Much heat is developed during this process. The reaction temperature remains at 850-920° C since the heat of reaction is partially removed together with the reaction gases and is partially used to heat the cold feed gas.

The yield of the reaction is 96% or more (ammonia is burnt completely but small quantities are converted to nitrogen and water vapour). A mixture of nitric oxide, water vapour, excess of oxygen and nitrogen (the inert constituent of air) is obtained. This gas mixture is cooled and most of the nitric oxide is oxidized to nitrogen peroxide by the excess of oxygen at the same time.

c. Conversion of nitrogen peroxide to nitric acid of moderate strength. The oxidation process described before is basically the same for the different plants using different pressures, but the absorption systems differ considerably.

The oldest nitric acid plants are operated at atmospheric pressure. In these plants the products of combustion leave the converter and are cooled by passing through a waste heat boiler and a series of coolers. (The waste heat boiler produces cheap steam which is supplied to other plants.) In the coolers weak nitric acid is formed from a part of the nitrogen peroxide and condensed water vapour. The remaining nitrogen peroxide with excess air is passed through a series of seven to ten absorption towers. Typical

Fig. 9.15 Picture of the absorption towers of a nitric acid plant with plate coolers. See also fig. 9.13.

towers are about 6 feet in diameter by 56 feet high. They are built of chrome-nickel steel and filled with earthenware or metal rings.

Water is passed in the opposite direction through the towers moving from the last tower to the first. Thus nitrogen peroxide is brought in contact with increasingly more dilute solutions of nitric acid. The weak acid formed in the coolers is introduced to the appropriate absorption tower. As heat is developed during absorption, the liquid is cooled between the towers (see absorption towers with plate coolers, fig. 9.15). Nitric acid of about 60% strength is withdrawn from the first tower. The acid containing some NO_2 is bleached with air. The residual gas which leaves the last tower contains about 0.3% NO. (This oxidizes immediately to NO_2 in the atmosphere.) The concentration of nitrogen oxides is still too high. For this reason the gas is passed through one or more additional towers in which it is contacted in countercurrent with a lime suspension or a sodium carbonate solution. By-product calcium nitrate or sodium nitrate is obtained from these towers. The waste gas still contains 0.05 to 0.1% nitrogen peroxide which cannot be recovered economically. Nitrogen oxides can also be removed from the residual gases by catalytic reduction to nitrogen. The waste gases are strictly controlled by the health authorities owing to their toxic properties even in small quantities.

Such gases also encourage the formation of smog. In Great Britain discharge of waste gases has been forbidden since 1958.

A modification of the atmospheric pressure absorption process is the complete pressure process. In this, ammonia is oxidized at about 8 atm (100-120 p.s.i.) and a pressure of about 7 atm is employed in the absorption system. Only one tower is needed for absorption. This tower may be about 40 feet high, 6 feet in diameter and is provided with 30 to 40 bubble cap trays (see bubble cap fractionation columns, vol. IV). Cooling coils are fixed on the surface of the bubble cap trays to remove the heat of reaction. Water enters at the top of the column and nitrogen peroxide at the bottom. Weak acid from the coolers is introduced at the appropriate place between top and bottom.

This process is most widely used in the United States. The power consumption is much higher in this process but about 65% of the power used in compression can be recovered by heating the waste gases with the hot gases leaving the ammonia converter and then expanding by passing through a gas turbine coupled to the feed gas compressor.

Another modification of the absorption plant is the intermediate pressure process, in which pressures of about 4 atmospheres are applied either before or after the ammonia oxidation stage. Six absorption towers are used in this process which was developed in Europe.

d. Concentration of moderate strength acid. Much nitric acid of 60% strength is used as such, but for some purposes important quantities of 95-100% nitric acid are required.

Nitric acid cannot be separated from water by simple fractional distillation because an azeotropic mixture of water and nitric acid containing 68.5% of the latter is always formed. An azeotropic mixture is a mixture which distils unchanged. When a mixture containing less than 68.5% nitric acid is distilled, a mixture containing relatively more water is evaporated until the remaining mixture contains 68.5% nitric acid. Then a mixture of unchanged composition distils at 122° C. In the same way a vapour containing relatively more nitric acid is obtained from a mixture containing more than 68.5% nitric acid until the remaining mixture contains 68.5% nitric acid. Further concentration by distillation is possible if dehydrating agents are added.

The oldest dehydrating agent is sulphuric acid. The concentration with sulphuric acid is performed by introducing this acid (containing 93-96% H_2SO_4) and nitric acid (60%) in the top of a steel tower having a lining of acid proof cement and bricks. The tower is packed with silicon-iron rings or with lumps of quartz. The sulphuric acid withdraws water from the nitric acid and the temperature becomes so high that nitric acid evaporates. Additional heat is supplied by steam injection at the bottom of the tower. A vapour containing 95% nitric acid leaves the top of the tower and is condensed by cooling. Sulphuric acid of about 65% strength collects at the bottom of the tower and can be concentrated again by evaporation of the water.

Another concentration process is based on the dehydrating properties of magnesium nitrate. This process is basically the same as the concentration process for sulphuric acid. Molten magnesium nitrate (containing 70% anhydrous Mg $(NO_3)_2$ and 30% water) and nitric acid (60%) are contacted by introducing into the top of a dehydration tower lined with acid resisting tiles. A vapour containing 90-95% nitric acid is withdrawn from the top of the tower and molten magnesium nitrate containing 40% water is collected at the bottom. The nitric acid is distilled in a rectifying column provided with bubble cap trays. One fraction containing 99% nitric acid is stored. The other fraction containing 80-90% nitric acid is recycled to the dehydrating tower. The magnesium nitrate is concentrated again by evaporating a part of the water in a reboiler. Thus steam is obtained which is used to heat the dehydration tower indirectly. (The steam is not injected but passed through steam coils.)

Since molten magnesium nitrate containing 30% water has a freezing point near to 100° C, the whole equipment must be kept above this temperature. Pipes are heated by electrical heating elements wound on them. The equipment is made of stainless steel or silicon iron. The pipes of the strong nitric acid condensers are often made of aluminium. Although the concentration equipment is expensive to construct, the concentration of nitric acid by this process is cheaper than concentration with sulphuric acid since the cost of operation, which can be practically automatic, is relatively low.

e. Direct production of high strength nitric acid. A process for producing high strength nitric acid without a concentration stage has been developed by Fauser. This process was modified to a commercial process by the German firm Bamag Mequin. In the Bamag process ammonia is oxidized with a mixture of steam and oxygen instead of air. The reaction products are cooled and further oxidized to nitrogen peroxide. The water vapour condenses with a part of the nitrogen peroxide. The remaining gas is compressed to 8 atm and further cooled in a condensation tower. Nitrogen peroxide liquefies as dinitrogen tetroxide. Liquid dinitrogen tetroxide and the weak acid from the coolers are mixed and treated with oxygen at a pressure of 50 atm in an autoclave. A 98% acid is produced in the autoclave which is discharged by means of compressed oxygen. This process is used in Europe and Japan (see also fig. 9.16).

9.7.3 Properties and storage

Pure nitric acid is a colourless liquid having a boiling point of 83° C and a melting point of −41.6° C. Nitric acid is commonly available as a solution in water

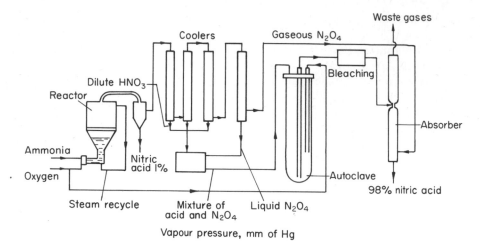

Fig. 9.16 Flow sheet of the Bamag process for the production of 98% nitric acid. The feed mixture is passed upwards through the catalyst gauze of the reactor via a water layer. This is necessary since explosions can occur in hot gas mixtures of oxygen and ammonia accidentally containing 30% NH_3 or less.

containing 50 to 65% of the acid (sp. gr. 1.3 to 1.4). Acid solutions containing 90-99% HNO_3 usually have a yellowish or even red colour, due to the decomposition of a small quantity of the acid, according to the following equation:

$$4 HNO_3 \rightarrow 4 NO_2 + 2H_2O + O_2.$$

This acid fumes strongly in moist air. Large quantities of nitrogen peroxide can be dissolved in high strength nitric acid to produce a red liquid known as 'fuming nitric acid'.

The more concentrated acid very rapidly destroys organic tissues producing a yellow discoloration. Continued contact may result in smarting and burning. As strong nitric acid contains the very poisonous nitrogen peroxide, respiration of fumes even in great dilution is very dangerous.

Nitric acid has three important chemical properties:

1. It is strong monobasic acid and forms salts (nitrates) with basic materials

2. It is a nitrating agent. Nitro compounds and nitric acid esters are formed with organic compounds (see vol. IV).

3. It is a strong oxidizing agent, especially the red fuming type. Recently the (green) solution of nitric oxide (NO) in 68% HNO_3 has come into use as a strong and specific oxidizing agent.

Most metals are dissolved by nitric acid of moderate strength with formation of nitrates. Some metals (arsenic, antimony and tin) are converted to insoluble oxides. The noble metals platinum, rhodium, iridium and gold are not attacked by nitric acid. Noble metals can only be dissolved in a mixture of nitric acid and strong hydrochloric acid. For this reason this mixture (usually used in the proportions of one part nitric acid to three parts hydrochloric acid) is known as *aqua regia*. This mixture also contains

Fig. 9.17 Carboys of acid, resisting earthenware for storage of nitric acid. In the foreground, glass bottles for transporting nitric acid.

nitrosyl chloride (NOCl), chlorine and water. Its strong action is caused mainly by the nitrosyl chloride.

Some metals such as silicon iron, stainless steel and aluminium resist high strength nitric acid (95-100%). This acid can therefore be stored in tanks or drums made of these materials. Moderate strength acid must be stored in glass bottles and carboys of glass or earthenware (see fig. 9.17). When transported in carboys particular care is needed because nitric acid can produce self-igniting compounds, and poisonous fumes with straw, paper, wood, etc.

9.7.4 Uses

Nitric acid is used for the production of nitrates, for instance sodium nitrate (fertilizer), potassium nitrate (fertilizer and gunpowder), barium and strontium nitrate (for fireworks), calcium nitrate (fertilizer) and ammonium nitrate (fertilizer and explosive). See alkali metal compounds, alkaline earth metal compounds, fertilizers, explosives, and ammonium nitrate.

Nitric acid is also used for the production of esters from alcohols. An important ester is nitroglycerine (glycerol trinitrate), which is an important explosive. Cellulose can also be esterified with nitric acid to nitrocellulose. The maximum possible nitrogen content of nitrocellulose is 14.1%. For explosives a nitrogen content of 12.2 to 13.5% is needed. Nitro cellulose containing 10.8 to 12.2% is used in plastics, varnishes and lacquers (see explosives, vol. IV and nitrocellulose lacquers, vol. V).

Nitric acid is sometimes used instead of sulphuric acid or mixed with sulphuric acid for treating phosphate rock. The resulting reaction mixture is treated with ammonia to give a composite fertilizer containing ammonium nitrate and dicalcium acid phosphate (either mixed with calcium sulphate or not). Such composite fertilizers are called nitro-phosphate fertilizers (see fertilizer chapter).

By treating sodium chloride (common salt) with nitric acid, a mixture of sodium nitrate, chlorine and nitrosyl chloride (NOCl) is obtained. The latter is used in the production of the synthetic detergent mixture 'Nytron'. This detergent is prepared by treating an olefin mixture with nitrosyl chloride and reacting the product obtained with a sulphide solution.

Some 100% nitric acid and fuming nitric acid is used as an oxidant in rocket propellants. Liquid N_2O_4 can also be used for this purpose.

Nitric acid is also used in other chemical syntheses. For instance nitric acid is an essential reactant in the production of diazo dyes.

9.7.5 Statistics

In most cases, large plants needing the acid for industrial purposes produce their own requirements. Thus trade in nitric acid is relatively small. The world production data of nitric acid are not available. Production of the main producing countries is given in the following table:

| | In '000s metric tons, on 100% basis | | | | | |
	1954	1957	1959	1961	1962	1963
Canada	211	—	—	248	264	310
France	711	1052	1296	1634	1737	1753
Germany (West)	24*	—	30*	43*	470	510
Hungary	40	49	130	168	175	191
Italy	390	440	516	813	865	900
Japan	87	91	108	149	155	183
Poland	201	413	540	631	698	750
Sweden	51	87	94	148	143	—
Spain	33	56	59	77	95	83
United Kingdom	300	360	470	—	580	—
United States	2076	—	2579	3066	3310	3800

* For industrial purposes only

The uses of nitric acid changed considerably during a period of twenty years. In 1937, 65% of the nitric acid produced in the USA was used in the manufacture of explosives. By 1957 only 15% of the total was used for the manufacture of explosives but 75% was used for the production of fertilizers.

In 1962 nitric acid was used for the following purposes in the United Kingdom:

Production of ammonium nitrate	61%
Direct use for explosives	12%
Production of synthetic fibres	21%
Chemical synthesis and other uses	6%

In 1965 the prices of nitric acid in the USA were:

58%-68% acid delivered in tanks $3.90 per 100 lb (on 100% basis);

94%-95% acid delivered in tanks $4.90 per 100 lb (on 100% basis);

technical acid in carboys 36°-42° Bé $5.75-$7.25 per 100 lb;

chemical pure acid $0.18-$0.20 per lb.

The price of nitric acid 70° Tw in the United Kingdom was £33 to £37 per long ton.

9.7.6 Literature

F. D. MILES. *Nitric acid.* Oxford University Press, 1961.

9.8 SODIUM NITRATE

9.8.1 History and occurrence

Sodium nitrate ($NaNO_3$) is usually known as Chile saltpetre because the most important deposits are still found in Chile. The nitrate was probably obtained from these deposits in small amounts as early as the eighteenth century. The Czech Haenke described in a publication in 1809 how he prepared saltpetre from the deposits. Production was however restricted to small amounts. For example in 1820 it was only 1000 metric tons, but it increased to 25000 tons in 1850 because more was known about artificial fertilizers by that date. The work of Justus von Liebig in particular was important. In the second half of the nineteenth century Chile saltpetre supplied about 70% of the world's requirements of nitrogen fertilizers and production increased to nearly 3 million tons in 1913. After this year production declined because of the increasing production of synthetic fertilizers. At present, total production is about 1 million tons and supplies only a small fraction of the total demand of fixed nitrogen (see ammonia, p. 311).

Natural deposits containing large quantities of sodium nitrate are uncommon. Relatively small deposits are found in Argentina, Bolivia, Peru, Mexico and California. Nitrate bearing shale occurs also to some extent in Egypt and the Union of South Africa.

The enormous deposits of sodium nitrate in the completely barren soil of Chile (pampa salitreta), between the nineteenth and twentieth South parallels of latitude, are unique. Numerous explanations have been put forward to account for the origin of Chile saltpetre but none is quite satisfactory. It has been suggested that Chile saltpetre is a deposit from sea water like other salt deposits, but sea water does not contain sodium nitrate. A natural conversion of excrement of birds and other animals, by nitrifying bacteria, is not plausible since the deposits do not contain phosphates (phosphates are present in excrement). The formation of nitrogen oxides from air by electric discharges, radioactivity and/or ultraviolet rays, needs rainfall to form nitric acid and to deposit the acid formed. The latter could form sodium nitrate with sodium salts present in the soil. However sodium nitrate is very soluble and would have been washed away by the rainfall which is needed to deposit nitric acid.

More plausible are the suggestions that sodium nitrate might be of volcanic origin, or that nitrates might be conversion products of seaweed. Enormous quantities of seaweed may be isolated from the sea when the coast rises. Ammonia is formed from putrescent seaweed and this can be converted to nitric acid by nitrifying bacteria. The seaweed theory also gives an explanation for the presence of iodates and borates in the

Fig. 9.18 The Chilean saltpetre district.

deposits (see also the iodine chapter). It is also possible that sodium nitrate was formed elsewhere according to one of the theories mentioned above, dissolved in rain water, and was carried in rivers to an inland sea, which has since evaporated.

In every case a very dry climate is necessary for the formation of sodium nitrate deposits and the Chilean saltpetre district belongs to the dryest regions of the world. This district in northern Chile is shown in fig. 9.18. A mixture of sodium nitrate with other salts is found in a layer which varies in thickness from 6 inches up to 14 ft and which occurs a short distance below the surface. The layer is named Caliche. It is covered with two relatively thin layers of other minerals. The uppermost layer *(chuca)*

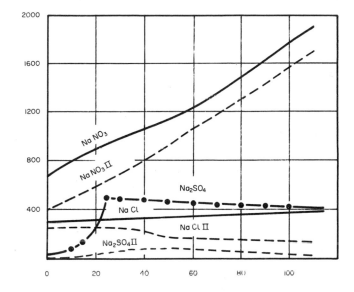

Fig. 9.19 Solubility curves of sodium nitrate, sodium sulphate and common salt. The solubility of the salts is lower in mixed solutions (see dotted curves). The solubilities are given in grams per litre (vertical) and the temperatures in °C (horizontal).

consists of gypsum, sodium sulphate, sand, clay and some other minerals. The second layer *(costra)* is a rocky one containing clay, gravel, felspar and other minerals which are caked with common salt and some sodium nitrate. Below the caliche are further layers with a large amount of common salt, sodium sulphate, sand, gravel and clay.

The caliche which is the raw material for Chile saltpetre contains sodium nitrate, some potassium nitrate, chlorides and sulphates of sodium, calcium and magnesium, small quantities of sodium borate, perchlorate, iodate, iodide, chromates etc., and insoluble substances such as clay, sand and gravel. The saltpetre content of the caliche varies from a small percentage up to 70%. High percentages now occur very seldom since the richer deposits have been exhausted. In early days sodium nitrate was only recovered from caliches containing 50% and more sodium nitrate. Nowadays low grade caliche can be mined due to the development of modern mining methods.

The length of the area is 800 km, and its width is, on an average, 40 km. The relatively long distance to the sea (between 50 and 150 km) often makes transport rather expensive.

9.8.2 Mining and refining

At first the overburden is removed by large drag lines as far as possible. The rocky costra is removed by drilling holes and blasting with explosives. These products are transported to exhausted fields. The caliche is loosened in the same way and the pieces are selected *in situ* by means of sieving into a number of pieces of various sizes. It is known from experience that material that has passed through sieves of 6 × 6 mm has a low saltpetre content and does not warrant processing. (The saltpetre content of the caliche was previously estimated by holding a piece in a burning match.) This size is therefore rejected whilst the remainder is transported by railway to the preliminary breaking point. For a long time the crude caliche was transported by means of cars drawn by mules. These are still used for some purposes.

The caliche is treated in various breakers according to size, each breaking process

Fig. 9.20 View of a long series of large leaching tanks. To their left runs a long conveyor belt which delivers the broken caliche.

being followed by sieving. The pieces of 9 × 9 mm and somewhat less go to the fine breaking plant after which they are carefully sieved. In each case, the mass passes magnets in order to remove pieces of iron which may be present. The finest particles are removed by passing through a filtering device as otherwise they could silt up the tanks. For the same reason breaking is preferred to grinding. Sodium nitrate is recovered from the caliche by leaching out and crystallization. The dust which passes the filtering device is leached out separately. The remaining silt is filtered off and the solution is used for leaching out the small pieces.

Use is made of the fact that the solubility of the three main constituents which can dissolve in the liquid is considerably lower when mixed than in the pure state (see fig. 9.19). (The solubility of common salt and sodium sulphate in particular diminishs). Two refining methods are in use.

According to the oldest method *(Shanks)* only caliche containing more then 12% saltpetre can be refined. This process has been in use since 1876. The broken caliche is deposited, in layers, in eight tanks (see fig. 9.20) which are traversed successively by the same liquid. Using steam pipes, these tanks are slowly brought to the boil (138° C). Mother liquor from which saltpetre has already been obtained serves as the solvent. This solution is saturated with sodium chloride and sodium sulphate. Thus only sodium nitrate and some other salts which are present in small quantities can dissolve. The liquid is fed in each case after a few hours to the next tank, while the former one is drained. The solid settled parts are allowed to dry in the sun and are taken away as worthless waste. After settling the last insoluble substances in a settling tank, the solution is cooled to 22° C in crystallizing tanks. This takes about four days. Sodium nitrate crystallizes out. The surface layer is stirred repeatedly and sinks to the bottom so that evaporation will not be hindered by a layer of crystals. After cooling, the mother liquor is removed and the wet salt goes to drying platforms where it is dried by the heat of the sun. The salt obtained contains 96-98% saltpetre (including some potassium nitrate). It is often packed in sacks weighing 80 kg. The mother liquor is used again for leaching out, until it becomes saturated with other salts. Potassium nitrate, sodium iodate (see iodine chapter, p. 246) and perchlorates are than recovered from this liquor.

The second refining method is the *Guggenheim* method, which is basically the same as the Shanks method. It was developed in 1923. In this process the leaching temperature is 50° C. The heat is obtained from the cooling water of the diesel engines which serve the electric power station, and also from the waste heat of the ammonia cooling machines. The saturated solution is first cooled to 15° C in heat exchangers. In the crystallizing section the brine is cooled to 5° C by boiling liquid ammonia from an ammonia liquefaction plant. Sodium nitrate is separated from the resulting crystal slurry and is dried in centrifuges. Further drying takes place by melting and spraying into granules (see fig. 9.21). In the granule form sodium nitrate is less hygroscopic than in the crystalline form. The product obtained in this process has a purity of about 98-99%.

About 70% of the Chilean nitrate is produced according to the Guggenheim method. This method is not much cheaper than the method of Shanks because of the higher initial costs, but is has the big advantage that caliches having a saltpetre content of 7% can be processed economically. However, if the Guggenheim method is used, about 25% of the saltpetre present in the caliche remains in the residues. This, and also the fact

Fig. 9.21   Shed into which molten nitrate is sprayed to obtain granules with low water content.

that the saltpetre content of the ores has declined to an average of about 8%, has led to attempts to recover more nitrate from these residues (called *ripio*). Solar evaporation plants have been built for this purpose. The ripio is treated with water to dissolve the salts and the solution obtained is evaporated in large shallow reservoirs using the heat of the sun (see also common salt, p. 415). Sodium chloride and a double salt of sodium sulphate and magnesium sulphate crystallize first and are removed by filtering. When the concentration of nitrates in the solution is sufficiently high, the latter is cooled to about 0° C and a mixture of potassium and sodium nitrate crystallizes. Many millions of metric tons of saltpetre are also still heaped up on the old waste so that the solar evaporation process is very important for Chile. It is expected that the ripio-extraction process can also be used for the processing of caliche containing only 4% sodium nitrate.

9.8.3 Production of synthetic sodium nitrate

Sodium nitrate is produced synthetically by reacting sodium carbonate with weak nitric acid and evaporating the solvent. A saturator process can be used for this purpose (see also ammonium sulphate, p. 314). Much sodium nitrate is prepared as a by-product in nitric acid plants by absorption of waste nitrogen peroxide in a sodium carbonate solution (see nitric acid, p. 330). The crystalline product, obtained after evaporating the solution, is often melted and sprayed in a cooling chamber to reduce its hygroscopic properties.

9.8.4 Properties and uses

Pure sodium nitrate is a colourless crystalline product which is somewhat hygroscopic. Its melting point is 308° C and its solubility in water is 88 g per 100 g water at 20° C.

Chile saltpetre is an excellent nitrogen fertilizer. It is possible however that it may contain more than the maximum permissible content of 0.04% perchlorates (calculated as $KClO_4$). Above this content perchlorates have a destructive effect on plants (see also herbicides, vol. VII and perchlorates, p. 239), and agricultural testing stations therefore carry out regular tests. The sacks must all bear the trade mark of the producer so that rapid action can be taken in cases of too high a perchlorate content. It is sometimes considered that Chile saltpetre works better than artificial nitrates, this being ascribed to the presence of small quantities of iodates and other salts. The minimum nitrogen content of ground saltpetre is set at 15%, including nitrogen which is present in the form of potassium nitrate. (Chile saltpetre can contain up to 3% potassium nitrate.)

Sodium nitrate is also used in the chemical industry for the production of potassium nitrate, sodium nitrite, sulphuric acid, dyes etc. It is also used for curing meat and in the production of explosives. However, potassium nitrate is often preferred for the latter purpose, since sodium nitrate is hygroscopic.

9.8.5 Statistics

Natural sodium nitrate is mainly produced in Chile. Only very small quantities are produced in Peru, Mexico and Egypt. The Chilean saltpetre production during the last century is shown in the following table:

In '000s metric tons							
1850	25	1922	1600	1952	1400
1870	132	1932	700	1954	1580
1890	670	1933	433	1958	1260
1902	1300	1942	1300	1962	1080
1913	2800	1944	990	1963	1110

As stated before (see history, p. 335) Chile saltpetre was at one time the most important source of fixed nitrogen. Nowadays it supplies only 1-2% of the world production of fixed nitrogen.

The state of Chile has for a long time had a financial interest in the saltpetre industry. In 1913 this brought in 57% of the state income, and in 1929 the figure was 30%. The state became involved in the many crises which the industry underwent particularly when synthetic nitrogen started to become an important competitor.

On several occasions trusts, voluntary or otherwise, were set up for production and sale, in which the Chilean state acquired increasing influence and interest. Finally, after many failures the Corporation de Ventas de Salitre y de Yodo de Chile was founded. This takes care of sales and distributes 65% of the profits obtained to the producers. The Chilean state receives about 24% of the profits as well as the interest on loans which were advanced in the past. In the very difficult postwar years the government also often had to render help, in order to maintain the position of the sales organisation against foreign competition.

In 1965 the price of Chile saltpetre in the USA was $ 44.00 per short ton; in the UK the price was £ 29 per long ton. The price is closely calculated since competition with artificial nitrogen fertilizers depressed the selling price. In addition transport costs account for a great part of the price.

Important quantities of synthetic sodium nitrate are prepared in Western Germany and the USA. The production of Western Germany in 1962 was about 360000 tons (including calcium nitrate). Small quantities of synthetic sodium nitrate are produced in several countries, e.g. Norway, Italy, France. In 1965 synthetic sodium nitrate was sold for about the same price as Chile saltpetre.

The imports of sodium nitrate in the USA and the UK were as follows:

	1955	1957	1959	1961	1963
UK Long tons	18900	20500	9300	19800	13400
Value £	383000	438000	189000	371000	244000
USA Long tons	560000	540000	440000	441000	107000

9.8.6 Literature

J. J. LEHR and J. HUDIG. *Chilisaltpeter.* 's-Gravenhage, Uitg. Inlichtingenbureau voor chilisaltpeter, 1947.

F. A. HENGLEIN. 'Chilisaltpeter heute', *Chemiker-Zeitung,* **82** (May 5, 1958), pp. 287-94.

9.9 CALCIUM NITRATE

Calcium nitrate (nitrate of lime, $Ca(NO_3)_2 . 2H_2O$) is prepared by treating crushed limestone with nitric acid (50% solution). The solution obtained is neutralized with a slight excess of crushed limestone and the excess is removed by filtering or by settling in settling tanks. Excess of nitric acid can also be neutralized by adding ammonia. The clear solution, containing about 40% calcium nitrate, is concentrated in a multiple effect evaporator (see p. 418) to about 85% calcium nitrate. The resulting molten calcium nitrate is mixed with about 5% molten ammonium nitrate and converted into a granular product by spray-drying in a large prilling tower. The melt can be sprayed in this tower by dropping on a rotating disc. Since the granules have a tendency to agglomerate before solidifying, the product obtained is screened and the large pieces are crushed.

The product can also be solidified on a cooling drum. The solid mass is scraped off and the resulting flakes are crushed.

A few modifications of this process have been developed. By using a Dutch continuous evaporation process the concentration of a solution containing 80% calcium nitrate can be increased to about 95%. The solution is heated in a high pressure double-effect system, the pressure being sufficient to prevent boiling. Rapid evaporation occurs in a flash evaporator by expansion to a lower pressure. Because of the lower water content, the product solidifies more easily on a drum cooler or in a prilling tower. When the resulting calcium nitrate is made for fertilizer purposes, the molten nitrate is often mixed with 20% ammonium nitrate to make processing and handling of the granular product easier.

Calcium nitrate must be packed in waterproof bags as it is very hygroscopic. When bulk stored it becomes wet and dissolves in the water absorbed from the air and in its water of crystallization. The presence of ammonium nitrate reduces its hygroscopicity. 100 g water at 0° C dissolve 73 g calcium nitrate. At a temperature of 100° C about 180 g of calcium nitrate can be dissolved in 100 g water.

Calcium nitrate is an important fertilizer. Smaller quantities are used for the production of explosives and pyrotechnics. It can also be used as a coagulant for rubber.

Calcium nitrate is mainly produced in Europe. The major producing country is Norway which produced 1 160 thousand tons in 1963. Italy produced 330 thousand tons, France 190 thousand tons and the Netherlands 140 thousand tons in the same year. Calcium nitrate is also manufactured in Germany and Switzerland.

9.10 HYDRAZINE

Hydrazine (H_2N-NH_2) was prepared for the first time in 1887 but it was a laboratory curiosity until the second world war when Germany used it as a fuel for rockets in conjunction with the oxidizing agent hydrogen peroxide.

9.10.1 Production

There are two commercial processes for the production of hydrazine. These processes, the Raschig process and the urea process, were developed in the first years of the twentieth century and improved during the last twenty years.

The Raschig process is based on the oxidation of ammonia by sodium hypochlorite according to the following equation:

$$2NH_3 + NaOCl \rightarrow H_2N-NH_2 + NaCl + H_2O.$$

Inhibitors such as gelatin or starch must be added to avoid undesirable side reactions.

The urea process is essentially a modification of the Raschig process. It is based on the oxidation of urea by hypochlorites in the presence of sodium hydroxide and an inhibitor. Reaction equation:

$$(NH_2)_2CO + NaOCl + 2\,NaOH \rightarrow H_2N-NH_2 + NaCl + Na_2CO_3 + H_2O$$

9.10.2 Properties

Hydrazine is a colourless liquid having a boiling point of $113.5°$ C and a melting point of $2°$ C. It is commercially available in the form of the monohydrate ($H_2NNH_2.H_2O$) and as anhydrous hydrazine (95%). As hydrazine forms an azeotropic mixture with water, anhydrous hydrazine can only be obtained by distilling hydrazine-water mixtures in the presence of dehydrating agents such as solid sodium hydroxide. Hydrazine is toxic. It has a particularly irritant action on skin, eyes and respiratory system.

In its chemical reactions hydrazine is very reactive. It is a powerful reducing agent. Anhydrous hydrazine must be stored in glass-lined or stainless steel containers. With acids it forms salts by addition (hydrazine hydrosalts or hydrazinium salts: the last name is chosen because of the analogy with ammonium salts).

9.10.3 Uses

Since hydrazine combines readily with oxygen, it can be used for eliminating oxygen from boiler water to prevent corrosion (see p. 151).

Hydrazine also combines readily with free chlorine and for this reason it can be used for removing free chlorine from hydrochloric acid gas.

Because of their reducing properties, hydrazine hydrohalides may be used as fluxes for welding and soldering metals. These fluxes decompose completely and no corrosive residue remains. Care must be taken in bringing hydrazine into contact with strongly oxidized surfaces, as several oxides are readily reduced with flaming decomposition of hydrazine.

Hydrazine precipitates metals such as silver and nickel from their solutions. Thus it can be used in production of mirrors, metal coatings on plastics, finely divided metal catalysts etc.

Hydrazine is also used as a reducing agent in several organic syntheses. For example: reduction of nitro and nitroso compounds to amines and reduction of carboxylic acids to aldehydes etc. (see also vol. IV).

Hydrazine is a starting material for the production of several organic hydrazine derivatives. Some of them, such as phenylsulphonyl hydrazide, generate gaseous nitrogen when heated. For this reason these hydrazine derivatives are used as blowing agents for the production of rubber and plastic foams (see vol. IV). Some acyl derivatives of hydrazine have therapeutic or herbicidal properties. Maleic hydrazide is a plant growth suppressant and isonicotinic acid hydrazide is used in treatment of tuberculosis.

Hydrazine mixed with an oxidant such as hydrogen peroxide releases a large amount of energy (16300 calories per gram mole) when burnt. At the same time it is converted to low-molecular gases. Hence it is used as a jet fuel for guided missiles. Hydrazine has the disadvantage that it solidifies at the low temperatures prevailing in the upper layers of the air. For this reason derivatives, such as dimethyl-hydrazine, solidifying at much lower temperatures are sometimes used.

Amino-triazol polymers can be prepared from hydrazine and sebacic acid. Synthetic fibres can be prepared from this polymer which might be valuable if the starting materials could be made sufficiently cheaply.

In 1939 the price of hydrazine was about $ 50.00 per lb. In 1952 the price had fallen to $ 3.00. In 1965 the hydrate (85%) was noted at $ 1.00 to 1.05 per lb.

9.11 HYDROXYLAMINE

Hydroxylamine (H_2NOH) is produced in the form of hydroxylammonium salts (formula: $(H_3NOH)^+ x^-$) especially hydroxylammonium chloride (also named hydroxylamine hydrochloride), hydroxylammonium acid sulphate and hydroxylammonium sulphate. In the USA hydroxylammonium salts are mainly produced by treating nitroparaffins with water and a strong acid. Reaction equation:

$$RCH_2NO_3 + H_2O + H^+ \rightarrow (NH_3OH)^+ + RCOOH.$$

In other countries hydroxylammonium acid sulphate is produced by reducing sodium nitrite with sodium bisulphite and sulphur dioxide. The hydroxylammonium disulphonate, obtained as an intermediate, is hydrolysed to give hydroxylammonium acid sulphate:

$$NaNO_2 + NaHSO_3 + SO_2 \rightarrow N(SO_3Na)_2OH$$
$$\longrightarrow + 2 H_2O \rightarrow (NH_3OH)HSO_4 + Na_2SO_4$$

Hydroxylamine and its salts are strong reducing agents. For this reason the salts are used as stabilizers in photographic developers for developing colour films and colour prints.

Hydroxylammonium salts can also be used to arrest the polymerization processes which are catalysed by peroxides. The hydroxylammonium salt destroys the catalyst and thus the polymerization process is stopped. It is used in the production of butadiene-acrylonitrile rubber (see vol. V).

An important potential consumer of hydroxylamine is the synthetic fibres industry, as hydroxylamine can be used in the production of cyclohexanone oxime from cyclohexanone. The latter can be converted into caprolactam which is an intermediate in production of polyamides (nylon-6 etc.).

9.12 UREA

9.12.1 History and occurrence

Urea (H_2NCONH_2) was known as long ago as 1773 as a compound which is always present in urine. Urea is an important product of the metabolism of mammals.

In mammals, proteins of food are decomposed to amino-acids, carbon dioxide and ammonia. In the liver these decomposition products are converted into urea which is excreted into the blood. The latter is ultrafiltered by the kidneys and urea is excreted again into the urine.

In 1821 pure urea was isolated from urine by Prout. Urea was synthesized by Wöhler in 1828. This synthesis was of great scientific importance because previously it had been generally accepted that carbon compounds could only be formed by some mysterious life force. After Wöhler's synthesis this idea was gradually abandoned and it became possible to construct a system of organic chemistry as an important part of the general science of chemistry.

9.12.2 Production of urea solutions
All commercial urea processes are based on the two following reactions.

a. *The reaction of ammonia and carbon dioxide at high temperature and pressure to form ammonium carbamate:*

$$2 NH_3 + CO_2 \rightarrow NH_2COONH_4$$

b. *The dehydration of the latter to produce urea and water:*

$$NH_2COONH_4 \rightarrow NH_2CONH_2 + H_2O$$

The reactions, which are equilibrium reactions, are performed in the same autoclave in one step. At any given temperature ammonium carbamate has a definite decomposition pressure. Below this pressure ammonium carbamate decomposes to ammonia and carbon dioxide. Thus at any given temperature ammonium carbamate can only be formed as long as the partial pressure of ammonia plus carbon dioxide exceeds the decomposition pressure of ammonium carbamate. At lower pressure the reverse reaction takes place. At 60° C the decomposition pressure is about one atmosphere. Hence ammonium carbamate can be formed at atmospheric pressures and temperatures below 60° C.

However the reaction velocity of the second reaction is too low at these temperatures. This reaction velocity increases on raising the temperature, but the decomposition pressure of ammonium carbamate increases at the same time and for this reason a higher pressure must be applied to avoid decomposition. Reaction temperatures of 160 to 210° C and pressures between 170 and 400 atmospheres are commonly used.

The first reaction is readily completed under the given conditions. When a large excess of ammonia is used, practically all the carbon dioxide is converted to ammonium carbamate. It is remarkable that a much larger excess of carbon dioxide might be necessary to cause a complete conversion of ammonia. For this reason the reaction is performed with excess ammonia.

The second reaction is incomplete under all practical conditions. This is due to the water which is formed during the reaction; about 40-70% of the ammonium carbamate can be converted to urea in one step. Thus a reaction mixture of urea, ammonium carbamate, water, ammonia and some carbon dioxide is obtained in the autoclave. This reaction mixture is withdrawn from the autoclave and expanded in a carbamate separator. The unconverted ammonium carbamate decomposes into ammonia and

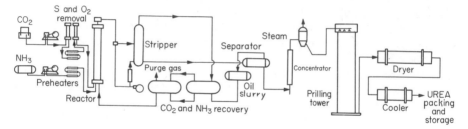

Fig. 9.22 Flow sheet for urea production by the oil slurry process.

carbon dioxide. In this way a hot gas mixture containing water vapour, ammonia and carbon dioxide and an aqueous solution containing 80-90% by weight of urea are obtained.

Urea can only be produced economically when the unconverted gases can be used again. Sometimes ammonia is converted into nitric acid, ammonium sulphate, etc. (for example, in the process used by the Dutch state mines), but this is not possible if no other plants are available on the site.

In most cases the gases must be compressed and recycled to the autoclave. Several methods have been developed to avoid deposition of solid ammonium carbamate in the compression system. Only a few processes are mentioned below.

a. The solution recycle process, developed by E. J. du Pont de Nemours and Co. and modified by Montecatini (Italy). A mixture of ammonia, carbon dioxide and copious water vapour is compressed to a solution of ammonium carbamate which is recycled. To obtain sufficient vapour, the reaction in the autoclave is performed with a large quantity of water. For this reason, a high yield can only be obtained at high temperatures and high pressures (200-210° C and 400 atm respectively).

b. The oil slurry recycle process developed by Pechiny (France). The gas mixture is mixed with mineral oil at a pressure of a few atmospheres. The mixed system is cooled and ammonia and carbon dioxide condense to solid carbamate which is dispersed in the oil. The slurry obtained is recycled to the autoclave. After the reaction the aqueous solution of urea is separated from the oil layer. The latter is used again (see figs. 9.22 and 9.23).

c. The hot gas recycle process of the Badische Anilin und Soda Fabrik (Germany). The mixture of carbon dioxide and ammonia is compressed by means of heated compressors having a temperature which is high enough to prevent formation of ammonium carbamate. The hot compressed gas is recycled to the autoclave.

d. The absorption processes of Inventa (Switzerland) and Chemical Construction Corporation (USA). Ammonia and carbon dioxide are separated by selective absorption of one of the components and the separated gases are compressed and recycled separately. (Ammonia is selectively absorbed in urea nitrate or carbon dioxide is absorbed in monoethanol amine. The gases can be desorbed by heating the absorbents.)

Fig. 9.23 W. R. Grace's urea plant at Memphis. Tennessee. The prilling tower is on the left. The urea converter and the carbonate decomposer are on the right. The plant is based on a modified oil slurry process and has a capacity of 100 000 tons per year.

Formerly, the largest problem in all urea processes was the prevention of corrosion in equipment. At atmospheric pressure and temperatures up to 60° C ammonia, carbon dioxide and ammonium carbamate do not attack steel but compressed mixtures at higher temperatures are extremely corrosive. Nowadays stainless steel or ordinary steel lined with lead or silver are used for the equipment. Monel metal may also be used. These materials resist the reaction mixture but it is necessary to keep the equipment free from oxygen and sulphur. For this reason the equipment must be washed with nitrogen before it comes into operation and the starting materials must be purified.

9.12.3 Recovery of urea from solutions

The urea solutions obtained by the processes described before contain 80-90% by weight of urea and are sometimes used as such as fertilizer solution.

Solid urea is obtained by concentration in a vacuum evaporator. The molten urea obtained is solidified by spraying in a prilling tower (see also ammonium nitrate and fig. 9.19). The solid urea which contains 3-5% water is dried in rotary dryers. This urea is not pure as it contains 0.5% to 5% biuret. This product is formed in molten urea according to the following equation:

$$2 \; H_2NCONH_2 \rightarrow H_2NCONHCONH_2 + NH_3$$

The greater part of biuret is formed during the concentration process. The lower the concentration temperature, the lower is the biuret content of urea. For this reason vacuum evaporators are used.

Urea, having a low biuret content (about 0.05%), can be obtained by crystallization from a solution and centrifuging. An impure mother liquor remains. Crystallization is performed in the presence of 0.2% to 0.5% cyanuric acid to prevent the formation of long small crystals which have the tendency to pulverize.

9.12.4 Properties

Pure urea is a colourless crystalline solid having a melting point of 132.7° C. At this temperature it decomposes. Urea dissolves readily in water forming a neutral solution. It also dissolves in alcohol and ammonia but not in hydrocarbons. Neutral solutions in water decompose very slowly to ammonia and carbon dioxide. Chemically urea acts as a monobasic compound. It forms salts with hydrochloric acid, sulphuric acid, acetic acid and several other acids.

9.12.5 Uses

Large quantities of urea are used as fertilizers, especially in the USA. For some fertilizer purposes urea must not contain more than about 2% biuret, because some crops such as pineapples and citrus trees are affected by biuret. Several other plants are relatively insensitive to biuret damage. When urea is used as a foliar spray on plants it must not contain more than about 0.5% biuret.

Important quantities of urea are also used in the resin and plastics industries. With formaldehyde and other aldehydes, and with or without catalysts, urea forms synthetic resinous condensation products.

The urea-formaldehyde resins are widely used in adhesives, as additives for textiles, and in the form of moulding powders (see urea-formaldehyde resins, vol. IV).

About 1-2% urea may be mixed with feeding stuffs for ruminants, especially with cattle feeds, when these are low in protein but contain sufficient starch. Urea is converted into proteins by the micro-organisms present in the rumen. Urea is slightly poisonous to animals other than ruminants.

Urea reduces the viscosity of aqueous solutions of animal glue, gelatin, starch and casein, thus enabling solutions of higher concentration to be made. For this reason urea is used in adhesives and size for paper products.

Urea forms crystalline inclusion complexes (adducts) with several inorganic salts and with straight chain aliphatic organic compounds. Urea does not form adducts with branched chain hydrocarbons. This phenomenon is used in the petroleum industry for the separation of straight chain aliphatic hydrocarbons from a hydrocarbon mixture. The straight chain hydrocarbons are extracted with saturated aqueous solutions of urea. They can be released by diluting the saturated urea solution with water (compare chelates in the water chapter, p. 131). It is remarkable that thiourea only forms complexes with branched chain and cyclo-aliphatic hydrocarbons and not with straight-chain and aromatic compounds.

Urea also stabilizes hydrogen peroxide solutions (see hydrogen peroxide, p. 199).

Urea is also used in the chemical industry for the production of hydrazine, several pharmaceuticals such as veronal and other barbituric acid derivatives and several other compounds (see also barbituric acid and veronal, vol. V).

9.12.6 Statistics

Because of its growing importance for fertilizer purposes, the expansion of urea capacity in recent years has been enormous. This is shown by the following estimates of world capacity and the capacity of the leading producing countries:

	In tons			
	1950	1959	1963	1966
World	250 000	2 000 000	3 900 000	8 500 000
USA	100 000	800 000	1 100 000	1 500 000
Japan	14 000	550 000	750 000	1 240 000

Especially in many eastern countries large factories are under construction. It is estimated that in Asia nearly 3 million tons of urea per year will be produced around 1966. In that year India will be the second producing country of Asia (625 000 tons).

It is estimated that the production capacity of Western Europe will increase from 450 000 tons in 1959 to 1 500 000 tons in 1966 with Italy as leading producing country (270 000 tons in 1966). The production of the UK increased from 85 000 tons in 1959 to 100 000 tons in 1966.

In the USA about 80% of the production in 1963 was used as fertilizer, 12% in ruminant feeds and 8% for industrial purposes (mainly urea-formaldehyde resins).

In the United Kingdom only small quantities of urea are used as fertilizer. A breakdown of the end uses of urea in that country (in 1962) is as follows:

Resins for chipboard production	7%	Cellophane	3%
Urea-formaldehyde moulding powders	20%	Pharmaceuticals	1%
Resins and glues for other purposes	18%	Detergents	0.5%
Fertilizers	9%	Exports	37.5%

In the USA the price of urea has greatly declined during the last decade. In 1952 the price of fertilizer grade (containing 45-46% nitrogen) was $ 142.00 per short ton and in 1965 only $ 90.00 to $ 96.00 per short ton. In 1963 the price of feed grade urea (containing 42% nitrogen) was $ 100.00 per ton and industrial grade (over 46% nitrogen content) cost $ 104.00 per short ton. In the UK, urea technical grade was sold at £41 5s per long ton.

9.12.7 Literature

v. SAUCHELLI. *Fertilizer nitrogen: its chemistry and technology.* New York, Reinhold, 1964. ACS Monograph No. 161.

9.13 THIOUREA

Formerly thiourea (also known as thiocarbamide, H_2NCSNH_2) was an important product for the production of thiourea-formaldehyde resins as it was cheaper than urea. Nowadays this situation is reversed. Thiourea-formaldehyde resins have several disadvantages as compared with urea-formaldehyde resins. For this reason thiourea became less important in this field.

Some thiourea is produced by heating ammonium thiocyanate. The latter is a by-product of coke-oven gas production. Reaction equation:

$$NH_4SCN \rightarrow NH_2CSNH_2.$$

Thiourea is also produced from calcium cyanamide by treatment with sulphuric acid. After removal of the precipitated gypsum, the remaining cyanamide solution is made alkaline and treated with hydrogen sulphide. Reaction equations:

$$CaCH_2 + H_2SO_4 \rightarrow CaSO_4 + CN.NH_2;$$
$$CN.NH_2 + H_2S \rightarrow H_2N\ CSNH_2.$$

Thiourea is a colourless crystalline compound. It has a low solubility in water (14.2 g per 100 g water at 25° C), and it melts at 178-180° C when heated rapidly. When heated slowly thiourea is partially reversed to ammonium thiocyanate (see the equilibrium reaction mentioned above). In its chemical behaviour thiourea resembles urea. Like urea it forms salts with several acids and it forms inclusion complexes (adducts) with several metal salts and with some organic compounds (see uses of urea, p. 348). Thiourea cannot be used as a fertilizer since it is more toxic to plant life than is urea.

· As stated thiourea is still used for producing synthetic resins. As a sulphide solvent, thiourea is an ingredient of some silver polishes. Thiourea has fungicidal properties, but its use on oranges has been prohibited because its poisonous residues may be dangerous. Thiourea is also used as a sepia toner in photography. It is also an accelerator of rubber vulcanization. In the chemical industry it is used for the production of fumaric acid, thioglycollic acid, sulphathiazole and several other organic chemicals. In the USA thiourea cost $0.33 per lb in 1965.

9.14   CYANIDES AND OTHER CYANOGEN COMPOUNDS

9.14.1 Introduction
Cyanogen compounds are compounds containing the CN group (which is also sometimes written 'Cy'). The name is an old one dating back to 1704, when the blue substance Prussian Blue was prepared from animal remains as the first cyanogen compound; the colour is connected with the presence of iron. The word cyanogen is derived from a Greek word meaning 'blue'.

9.14.2 Hydrogen cyanide
a. Occurrence. Hydrogen cyanide (hydrocyanic acid, prussic acid, HCN) occurs naturally in several glycosides. The best known glycoside is amygdalin which is present in bitter almonds. Glycosides containing hydrogen cyanide are often poisonous. In a free state, hydrogen cyanide is found in the seeds of the Java tree Pangium edule. Hydrogen cyanide is formed during carbonization of coal. Thus it occurs in coal gas and coke-oven gas.

b. Production. In the laboratory, the usual method for production of hydrogen cyanide is to treat sodium or calcium cyanides with acids. On a large scale, hydrogen cyanide may be prepared by any one of several methods.

Hydrogen cyanide is recovered as a by-product from coal gas or coke-oven gas, hydrogen sulphide being obtained from this at the same time. After tar, naphthaline, benzol, ammonia etc. have been separated off, coke-oven gas is brought into close contact with a 6-7% soda solution at a pressure slightly above atmospheric pressure. Hydrogen sulphide, hydrogen cyanide and some carbon dioxide go into solution. This solution is sprayed into a desorption tower, in which the pressure is reduced to 0.2 atmospheres. The dissolved gases are driven off by water vapour. The water vapour is obtained by heating the desorbed soda solution at the bottom of the tower to 53° C. The resulting gas mixture contains about 60% hydrogen sulphide, 20% hydrogen cyanide and 20% carbon dioxide (besides water vapour). The gases cannot be driven off by aeration since most of the hydrogen cyanide would be converted into thiocyanates. The desorbed gas mixture is brought into contact with water slightly acidified with sulphuric acid. Hydrogen cyanide is dissolved and the other gases pass on and are burned to produce sulphur dioxide. Hydrogen cyanide is driven out of the solution by heating and is liquefied in a condenser, or is used for the production of sodium cyanide.

Hydrogen cyanide is also produced synthetically from methane, ammonia and air according to the following equation:

$$2\,CH_4 + 2\,NH_3 + 3\,O_2 \rightarrow 2\,HCN + 6\,H_2O + 144\,Kcal.$$

The source of methane may be natural gas (in USA) and coke-oven gas (in Germany) carefully freed from sulphur compounds.

In Germany a process has been developed for enriching coke-oven gas in methane. Coke-oven gas is contacted with a nickel catalyst at a temperature of 250 to 400° C. Methane is formed from carbon monoxide, carbon dioxide and hydrogen, which are present in coke-oven gas. This process is based on the following reactions which were discovered by Sabatier and Senderens:

$$CO + 3\,H_2 \rightarrow CH_4 + H_2O \qquad CO_2 + 4\,H_2 \rightarrow CH_4 + 2\,H_2O.$$

Sometimes the coke-oven gas is first enriched in carbon monoxide by mixing it with water gas from which all the sulphur has previously been removed.

The ammonia required for hydrogen cyanide production is dissolved in water and then stripped out with air, which is also needed in the process. In this way ammonia is freed from traces of oil and at the same time air is freed from dust.

A homogeneous mixture is made, containing 12-13% methane, 11-12% ammonia and the rest air. The mixture also contains some hydrogen since this is contained in the methane. Nitrogen contained in the air must be present as a diluent to avoid explosion risks. Hydrogen cyanide is formed from this gas mixture by passing through fine mesh gauzes of platinum/rhodium at a temperature of 950 to 1250° C. Several gauzes are laid above each other and the bottom gauze is supported on a ceramic grid (see also nitric acid production, p. 326). A layer of a granular catalyst may also be used. The granular catalyst consists of inert silica grains which are coated with platinum/rhodium.

A yield of 65% based on methane is possible in this process. Unchanged ammonia is recovered by washing with a solution of ammonium sulphate, containing a large excess of sulphuric acid (ammonium sulphate production). Hydrogen cyanide can be recovered by absorption in water, followed by evaporation.

By utilizing a new process hydrogen cyanide can be obtained from methane and ammonia in the absence of air. Reaction equation: $NH_3 + CH_4 \rightarrow HCN + 3\,H_2$. In this process, ammonia and methane in correct proportions are heated to 1200° C in alumina tubes, lined internally with a platinum catalyst. Hydrogen is produced at the same time as a useful by-product. As soon as the gas mixture leaves the tubes, it is cooled down to below 300° C so as to avoid decomposition of the hydrogen cyanide. In this process the reactor must be heated since heat is absorbed during the reaction (endothermic reaction). In Germany a plant producing 100 tons of hydrogen cyanide per month is in operation. The yield is 85-90% based on methane. A modified process using a fluidized bed of coke at a temperature of 1 400-1 600° C has been developed in the USA. Besides methane, propane can be used as the original material.

Another commercial process for the production of hydrogen cyanide is based on the decomposition of formamide by heating, according to the following equation:

$$HCONH_2 \rightarrow HCN + H_2O.$$

Formamide is produced in two stages. In the first stage methyl formate is produced from methanol and carbon monoxide. In the second stage methyl formate is treated with ammonia. Reaction equations:

$$CH_3OH + CO \rightarrow HCOOCH_3$$
$$HCOOCH_3 + NH_3 \rightarrow HCONH_2 + CH_3OH.$$

Methanol is recovered. Thus hydrogen cyanide is indirectly produced from carbon monoxide and ammonia.

c. Properties, handling and grades. Hydrogen cyanide is a colourless mobile liquid having a boiling point of 25.7° C. It possesses the characteristic odour of bitter almonds and is very poisonous. Hydrogen cyanide is fatal on inhalation in amounts as low as 300 p.p.m.

Hydrogen cyanide is usually transported as a liquid in steel cylinders that can resist 100 atmospheres (the vapour pressure of hydrogen cyanide at 50° C is 2.5 atmospheres). In the USA large-scale producers use tanker shipments, and provide all the necessary help in the safe handling, storage and use of bulk liquid hydrogen cyanide. Commercial hydrogen cyanide usually contains about 2% water and 0.05% free mineral or organic acid (as stabilizer). Nowadays hydrogen cyanide containing less than 0.5% water is also available. The liquid can also be adsorbed on infusorial earth in tin boxes to produce an easily handled material sold under the trade name of Cyklon.

d. Uses and statistics. Large quantities of hydrogen cyanide are used in the production of acrylonitrile, which is a starting material in the production of acrylic fibres, nitrile rubber and other plastics (see vol. IV). Another important end use of hydrogen cyanide is nylon-66 which can be obtained from hydrogen cyanide via adiponitrile (see vol. IV). Hydrogen cyanide is also used for the production of methyl methacrylate. Polymers of the latter are used in latex paints and for the production of transparent sheet (Perspex, Plexiglass). On account of its poisonous effect on practically all animal life, hydrogen cyanide is used for disinfecting trees and buildings (flour mills, dairies, etc.) by fumigation. Care and experience are obviously needed in handling it. Buildings or rooms to be fumigated must be sealed around doors, windows etc. to prevent leakage of the gas to the outside. When trees (e.g. citrus trees) are fumigated with hydrogen cyanide, large tents are pulled over them and hydrogen cyanide is applied beneath the tents (see also vol. VII, grains, fruits). For this purpose

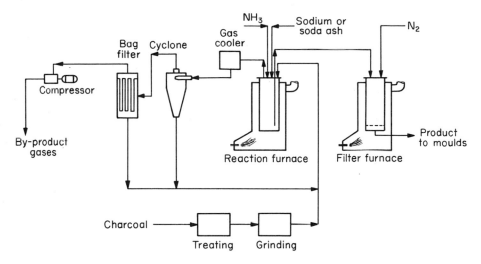

Fig. 9.24   Flow sheet for production of sodium cyanide.

calcium cyanide is also used (see calcium cyanide, p. 355). In the United States 60 tons of hydrogen cyanide are used annually for the protection of citrus trees against insects.

The USA production of hydrogen cyanide in 1963 was estimated to be 140000 short tons. The breakdown of the consumption in the USA in the same year was as follows:

Acrylonitrile	72000 tons	Sodium cyanide	10000 tons
Methyl methacrylate	25000 tons	Other	13000 tons
Adiponitrile	20000 tons		

Sodium cyanide (see above) is obtained by absorption of hydrogen cyanide in caustic soda. Hydrogen cyanide for this purpose is mainly obtained by decomposing formamide and by purification of coke-oven gas (by-product). In the USA the price of 98% hydrogen cyanide was $ 0.12 per lb in 1963.

9.14.3 Sodium cyanide

a. Production. Sodium cyanide (NaCN) is obtainable by several methods. The most important method is the Castner process. In this process sodium cyanide is produced from sodium, ammonia and charcoal, according to the following overall equation:

$$2\,NH_3 + 2\,Na + 2\,C \rightarrow 2\,NaCN + 3\,H_2.$$

In fact the reaction takes place in three stages with sodamide (NaNH$_2$) and sodium cyanamide NaCN$_2$ as intermediates respectively. In modern processes these stages are combined as follows:

Red-hot charcoal is slowly added to an equivalent proportion of molten sodium in a steel vessel. The mixture is heated at a temperature of about 750° C and ammonia is introduced gradually until the reaction is complete. The fused reaction product is pumped to a filter furnace which is kept at about 650° C in which the molten sodium cyanide is filtered from solid residues in a protective atmosphere of nitrogen (see also fig. 9.24). In this process pure sodium cyanide is obtained with a yield of 94%. Sodium cyanide is made in batches up to 9 tons. Eight to twelve hours are needed for each batch. The process is widely used, e.g. in the USA, the United Kingdom, Germany and France.

Sodium cyanide is also obtained by absorption of hydrogen cyanide in a solution of 50% sodium hydroxide; the gas stream is passed up a cooled absorber filled with Raschig rings. A solution containing 28 to 30% sodium cyanide can be obtained. Crystalline sodium cyanide is recovered by means of a vacuum evaporator.

b. Properties and grades. Sodium cyanide is a very poisonous white crystalline product. The melting point of sodium cyanide is 563° C. Sodium cyanide must be melted in a protective atmosphere of nitrogen since it is oxidized in air at temperatures above 370° C. About 58 g sodium cyanide dissolve in 100 g water at 20° C.

Sodium cyanide is available in flake form or in the form of spheres or 'eggs' having a weight of 10 to 30 g. These products are obtained by moulding molten sodium cyanide. Sodium cyanide is also available as a crystalline product. The cyanide content is sometimes calculated in terms of potassium cyanide. Since the atomic weight of potassium is higher than that of sodium, pure sodium cyanide can have a purity of 125% (in terms of potassium cyanide).

c. Uses and statistics. Sodium cyanide solutions are used for the extraction of gold and silver from their ores. Many finely divided metals dissolve in sodium cyanide solutions in the presence of oxygen, due to the formation of complex salts. In the case of silver this can be represented by the following reaction equation:

$$8\,NaCN + 4\,Ag + 2\,H_2O + O_2 \rightarrow 4\,Na(Ag(CN)_2) + 4\,NaOH$$

These complex salts contain a complex anion of the metal and a number of CN groups.

Large amounts of sodium cyanide are used in electroplating. In this process, metals are coated with a thin layer of gold, silver, copper, zinc or cadmium by electrolysis of solutions containing sodium cyanide and a gold, silver, copper, zinc or cadmium salt respectively. When the metal to be coated is used as anode, a layer of the dissolved metal is deposited on its surface.

Fused mixtures of sodium cyanide, sodium carbonate and sodium chloride are used for hardening steel (case hardening).

A solution of sodium cyanide and sodium carbonate containing 0.15% sodium cyanide, is effective in washing off adherent impurities and rust from steel and iron and is therefore also used in cleaning materials.

Sodium cyanide is a 'retarder' for zinc sulphide and pyrites during flotation of lead sulphide or copper sulphide containing sulphides of iron or zinc. Retarders inhibit the floation of certain substances (see flotation of ores, vol. III).

Sodium cyanide is also used for producing Prussian blue pigments (see complex cyanides) and as intermediate in the production of several organic compounds.

In almost all its applications, a little sodium or potassium cyanide remains behind in the effluents, which makes them extremely dangerous. The most common method for cyanide regeneration involves the acidifying of the waste cyanide solution with volatilization of the hydrogen cyanide. The latter is absorbed in a caustic soda solution. Cyanides in effluents can be destroyed by treating with chlorine or hypochlorite in alkaline solution, thus oxidizing them to products which are not dangerous. Cyanides can also be converted into insoluble salt complexes such as Prussian blue (see p. 356) which can be recovered. Cyanides can also be removed and recovered from very dilute solutions with strongly basic anion exchangers. These are used for the effluents from gold processing in South Africa.

In the USA the production of sodium cyanide was about 20000 tons in 1963. About 8000 tons were imported. In 1965 the USA market price of sodium cyanide was $18.00 to $20.00 per 100 lb; in the UK it was sold at £6 18s per 100 lb.

9.14.4 Potassium cyanide

Potassium cyanide (KCN) can be prepared in the same way as sodium cyanide but in practice it is mainly produced by absorbing hydrogen cyanide in a potassium hydroxide solution.

Potassium hydroxide is a white crystalline hygroscopic solid. Its melting point is 634° C. Like sodium cyanide it is very poisonous. The chemical properties of potassium cyanide are analogous to those of sodium cyanide. Hence potassium cyanide is used for the same purposes. Although potassium cyanide is more expensive than sodium cyanide, it is preferred for electroplating silver and copper. There are several reasons for this preference, e.g. the current density range is less critical and a higher carbonate concentration can be used in the solution, because potassium carbonate is more soluble than sodium carbonate.

The price of potassium cyanide in the USA was $42.50 to $43.50 per 100 lb in 1965.

9.14.5 Calcium cyanide

Calcium cyanide ($Ca(CN)_2$) is produced by heating calcium cyanamide in the presence of common salt in an electric furnace at a temperature of about 1000° C. The following reaction takes place:

$$Ca\ CN_2 + C \rightarrow Ca(CN)_2$$

Sufficient carbon for this reaction is contained in impure calcium cyanamide (see p. 358). The reaction mixture is cooled rapidly by tapping the melt on to a flaking wheel. Thus reversion to cyanamide is prevented. Impure dark grey flakes (black cyanide) are obtained. The colour is caused by the presence of carbon.

This product decomposes in the presence of air to form hydrogen cyanide and calcium hydroxide, hence its use as fumigant (see hydrogen cyanide). It is also used for the same purposes as sodium cyanide with the exception of electroplating. In addition it is used for the production of ferrocyanides (see below).

9.14.6 Complex cyanide compounds

The cyanides have a strong tendency towards complex salt formation. The complex cyanides of gold and silver have already been mentioned before (see sodium cyanide, p. 354). Complexes are also present in solutions for electroplating. In general cyanide complexes can be formed by mixing two salts, possessing the common cyanide ions, in a solution. The best known complex cyanide salts are potassium and sodium ferrocyanide and potassium ferricyanide. These complexes are very stable.

a. Sodium and potassium ferrocyanide. These compounds are yellow crystalline products and are also called: yellow prussiate of potash ($K_4Fe(CN)_6.3H_2O$) and yellow prussiate of sodium ($Na_4Fe(CN)_6.10 H_2O$).

Potassium and sodium ferrocyanide were formerly obtained exclusively from spent oxides used for coal gas purification. This method is still used at the present time. The spent oxide is freed from sulphur and sulphur compounds by extraction with various solvents and then the ammonium compounds are removed with water. The cyanide compounds are finally extracted by mixing the material with a calculated quantity of slaked lime. Calcium ferrocyanide is formed. The latter is extracted with water. The resulting solution is treated with potassium carbonate or sodium carbonate. Calcium carbonate is precipitated and removed. After clarification, the remaining solution containing potassium or sodium ferrocyanide, is concentrated by vacuum evaporation to give crystalline products.

Potassium and sodium ferrocyanide are also produced from calcium cyanide, ferrous sulphate (copperas) and potassium carbonate or sodium carbonate. These products are mixed with water and well stirred. A solution of mixed alkali and calcium ferrocyanide is obtained. The solution is filtered and the filtrate is freed from calcium by dissolving more alkali carbonate in it, the calcium being precipitated as the carbonate, which settles out. The liquid is siphoned off and evaporated. The crystals pass directly to filters and thence to rotary dryers.

Sodium and potassium ferrocyanide are used mainly in the preparation of Prussian blue (see below). They are also used in the textile industry as oxygen carriers or developers in certain dyeing processes. In the wine industry, they are used to precipitate heavy metals. They are also used to free various metal salt solutions from iron and other heavy metals. Thus stannic chloride is used in tin plating, in the production of tin-plate; if a small amount of sodium ferrocyanide is added, impurities are precipitated, which would otherwise give rise to an objectionable sludge. This method of purification is also used to purify water which is to be used for fermentation purposes, for the removal of copper from hydrocarbons after desulphurization, etc.

b. Potassium ferricyanide. Potassium ferricyanide (red prussiate of potash, $K_3Fe(CN)_6$) is a red-brown crystalline product. It is prepared by oxidizing sodium or potassium ferrocyanide with an aqueous solution of chlorine. Then the solution is evaporated to the crystallizing point and made alkaline with potash. (When sodium ferrocyanide is used as starting material, the solution is saturated with potash.) Potassium ferricyanide crystallizes and is purified by repeated recrystallization.

Crystalline potassium ferricyanide is also formed in the anode compartment of a diaphragm cell in which potassium ferrocyanide is electrolysed with nickel electrodes.

If a ferric salt is added to a solution of potassium ferrocyanide, the beautiful Prussian blue, a pigment insoluble in water, is produced (the finest grade is called Paris blue). If ferrous salts are added to a solution of potassium ferricyanide, Turnbull's blue is produced. For this reason both alkali ferrocyanides and alkali ferricyanides are used in cotton printing. The best grades of Prussian blue are used in artists' colours, the lower grades in ordinary paint. The reactions mentioned above also provide the basis for blueprints (see vol. VI). Potassium ferricyanide is also used for bleaching silver images on photographic films and prints, e.g. in colour photography.

The prices of complex ferro- and ferricyanides in the USA were in 1965 as follows:

potassium ferricyanide $ 0.50 per lb; potassium ferrocyanide $ 0.25 per lb; sodium ferrocyanide $ 0.13-$ 0.15 per lb.

9.14.7 Calcium cyanamide

Calcium cyanamide (lime nitrogen, nitrolim, $CaCN_2$) was first prepared in 1876 by Drechsel. The first commercial calcium cyanamide plant came into operation in 1906 and 12 years later the world production was about 600000 tons. This expansion was caused by the fact that Europe was cut off from Chile during the first world war. During this period calcium cyanamide was the starting material for the production of ammonia by treatment with steam ($CaCN_2 + 3H_2O \rightarrow CaO + 2NH_3$). After the first world war the synthetic ammonia process replaced the cyanamide process for the production of fixed nitrogen. Nowadays the conversion of calcium cyanamide to ammonia is not economical.

a. Production. The starting materials are nitrogen and finely divided calcium carbide (CaC_2) mixed with about 2% calcium chloride or calcium fluoride which reduces the reaction temperature greatly without reducing the speed of reaction.

The reactors consist of cylindrical steel boxes lined with refractory tile or firebrick. Sometimes a perforated steel basket is places in the reactor (see fig. 9.25). The reactors have a capacity of 1 to 10 metric tons. Graphite rods are used as resistances in order to start off the reaction. A large steel tube is lowered into the centre of the furnace before it is filled with calcium carbide and is afterwards removed. There is then a space in the centre in which the graphite rod can be placed. The furnace is closed by a cover after loading and the edges of the latter are sealed in a sand trough. Nitrogen is introduced into the reactor at a pressure slightly above atmospheric pressure. An electric current is passed through the graphite rod for 1 to 3 hours to heat the reactor to the initiation temperature of the reaction (700-800° C; without the addition of a calcium halide, a temperature of 1 100° C is necessary). Once initiated the reaction is self sustaining since sufficient heat is developed during the reaction (exothermic reaction). The reaction proceeds as follows:

$$CaC_2 + N_2 \rightarrow CaCN_2 + C + 72 \text{ Kcal.}$$

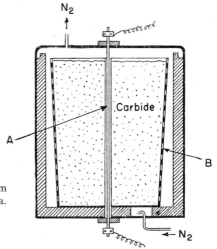

Fig. 9.25 Cell for the preparation of calcium cyanamide. The carbide is shown by the dotted area. (A = graphite rod; B = perforated basket.)

After about six days the reaction is complete, and after cooling for one day the sintered ingot of calcium cyanamide is removed from the furnace by a crane to be conveyed to a cooling chamber. This ingot contains about 70% calcium cyanamide, 12% calcium oxide, $\frac{1}{2}$% unreacted carbide and 12% free graphite formed in the reaction.

After cooling to room temperature the ingot is broken into large pieces by means of a pneumatic hammer which is dropped from a permanent crane. The diameter of the pieces is reduced to a particle size of about 1/8 inch by grinding and passing through a series of sieves. Bar mills may be used for this purpose. About 10% of water is added to react with the remaining carbide and to slake the calcium oxide. Often 2-4% oil is mixed with the material to prevent it becoming dusty.

Tunnel ovens, which are very expensive, have also been built to prepare calcium cyanamide, especially in Germany. The feed of calcium carbide (and calcium chloride or fluoride) is placed in boxes constructed of perforated steel plates. These boxes are placed on flat trucks which move through the tunnel along railroad tracks against a current of nitrogen.

A more recent continuous method operates more cheaply. It uses rotating cylindrical furnaces. Into these furnaces there is placed granulated calcium carbide containing 2% fluorspar, while a stream of nitrogen passes in against it. When the reaction has begun (by firing) virtually no further addition of heat is needed. The temperature is kept up to 1 100° C. The product remains in the reactor for about 24 hours. Calcium carbide leaves the reactor in a granular form. Finely divided calcium carbide (less than 0.3 mm particle size) cannot be used in this process since this tends to cake.

A modification of this process has been developed in Germany. In this process a suspension of finely divided calcium carbide, fluorspar and calcium cyanamide in nitrogen is blown in into a preheated rotating furnace. The nitrogen is also preheated. Throughout a third of the length of the furnace, the diameter is twice as large as that of the remaining two-thirds. The reaction takes place in the first section. The product moves out of the end of the furnace and is led to a cooling drum. A finely divided calcium cyanamide is obtained. The particle size can be controlled by controlling the quantity of calcium cyanamide in the feed. Since even the primary raw materials can vary considerably in composition, continuous control is necessary in order to obtain a good yield. A product which is as fine as dust requires the addition of oil to render it dustless. Furnaces of this type with capacity of 48 tons per day have been built.

b. Properties and uses. Calcium cyanamide in the pure state is a white solid. As a result of the presence of about 12% graphitic carbon, however, the commercial product has a dark colour. Crude calcium cyanamide absorbs moisture and carbon dioxide from air. Commercial cyanamide which has been treated with water and/or oil does not change when it is stored under normal conditions of temperature and humidity. The material is often packed in waterproof paper bags.

About 70% of the calcium cyanamide produced is used for agricultural purposes. Calcium cyanamide is somewhat more expensive than other forms of nitrogen. It is, however, fairly strongly basic and consequently suitable for acid soils. With water, air and carbon dioxide in the soil it forms successively: urea, ammonium carbonate and calcium nitrate. In this way it continues to act as a nitrogen fertilizer for a long period. This is particularly advantageous in the case of cereals and root plants.

Calcium cyanamide acts as a defoliant when spread dry on cotton, soya, tomatoes etc. It is sprayed on cotton about one month after the last bolls that make cotton are set, and causes the leaf to drop off the plant. In this way the bolls are exposed to sunshine and open quickly so that harvesting can take place mechanically and rapidly. When used as a defoliant on tomatoes and soya beans, ripening of the crops is accelerated. When spread on potatoes, calcium cyanamide has a lethal effect on the larvae of the Colorado beetle.

Calcium cyanamide is also a weedkiller. For this reason, about 1 to 2 lb per square yard are sometimes mixed with the soil about two months before seeding.

The remaining 30% of the world's calcium cyanamide production is used for chemical purposes. It is used for the production of calcium cyanide (see p. 355) and for the production of dicyandiamide. The latter can be obtained by heating calcium cyanamide with steam and carbon dioxide. Cyanamide ($H_2N.CN$) and calcium carbonate are formed. Cyanamide can be converted to dicyandiamide ($H_2N.C:NH.NH.CN$). The latter is the starting material for the production of melamine (see p. 362). Acrylonitrile, ethyl acrylate, cyanogen chloride and guanidine salts can also be produced from dicyandiamide. The guanidine salts can be converted to important derivatives such as sulphaguanidine (a pharmaceutical) and nitroguanidine (a propellant).

The world production of calcium cyanamide was about 1.4 million tons in 1960 and 1.34 million tons in 1961 (containing about 22% nitrogen). The production of the most important producing countries is shown in the following table:

| | In long tons | | | | | |
	1953	1955	1957	1959	1961	1963
Formosa	73 000	73 000	74 000	64 000	63 000	63 000
France	–	40 000	11 000	8 000	13 000	13 000
Germany, West	80 000	–	–	102 000	102 000	–
Germany, East	–	63 000	63 000	80 000	71 000	72 000
Italy	–	227 000	121 000	167 000	78 000	112 000
Japan	496 000	503 000	398 000	405 000	329 000	314 000
Poland	168 000	174 000	144 000	170 000	178 000	–

The USA market price of calcium cyanamide in 1965 was $ 120 to $ 140 per short ton.

The imports of calcium cyanamide by the UK have declined slowly as is shown by the following figures:

	1955	1957	1958
Cwt	29 600	27 400	21 500
£	44 400	45 100	32 900

Import figures of the UK in more recent years have not been published.

c. Literature

M. L. KASTENS and W. G. MC. BURNEY. 'Calcium Cyanamide', *Industrial and engineering chemistry* **43** (May 1951), pp. 1020-33.

KAESS. 'Fortschritte auf dem Gebiet der Kalkstickstoff Fabrikation', *Chemie-Ingenieur-Technik* **31** (Feb. 1959), p. 80.

9.14.8 Thiocyanates

Thiocyanates (sulphocyanates, rhodanides) are compounds containing the group SCN.

Ammonium thiocyanate (NH_4SCN) is the most important compound of this group. Ammonium thiocyanate is present in impure coal gas. Thus it can be recovered from gas liquor obtained during the purification of coal gas. It can also be prepared by boiling a solution of ammonium cyanide (NH_4CN) with sulphur or polysulphide. Ammonium thiocyanate is also formed by reacting ammonia with carbon disulphide (CS_2).

Ammonium thiocyanate is a colourless, hygroscopic and crystalline solid. It becomes red when it is exposed to light. It melts at a temperature of 149-150° C. At this temperature it is partially converted into thiourea (see p. 350). 122 g of ammonium thiocyanate can be dissolved in 100 g water at 0° C.

Ammonium thiocyanate is a starting material for producing thiourea and thiocyanates such as calcium and barium thiocyanate. The barium and calcium salts act in solution as powerfull dispersing agents for cellulose. Ammonium thiocyanate is a rust inhibitor. For this reason it is used in paint undercoats. Ammonium thiocyanate is also used as a defoliant for cotton (see vol. VII). Small quantities of this ammonium salt are used in printing pastes for textiles, in photography for dissolving silver, for pickling iron and steel, as a weedkiller and as a catalyst for the polymerization of resins. It cost $ 0.17-0.26 per lb in 1965.

Potassium and sodium thiocyanates are produced by boiling an alkali cyanide solution with sulphur. Sodium thiocyanate is a hygroscopic white crystalline substance. Its melting point is 287° C. Like ammonium thiocyanate it is very soluble in water. It is used in dyeing and printing of textiles, as a weed-killer, for producing other thiocyanates and in processing of colour films and paper.

Potassium thiocyanate is an anhydrous colourless crystalline product. Its melting point is 172° C. 177 g potassium thiocyanate can be dissolved in 100 g water at 0° C and 239 g in 100 g water at 25° C. It is used for the same purposes as sodium thiocyanate.

Mercury thiocyanate, on ignition and combustion, produces a remarkable voluminous ash (Pharaoh's serpents); this is a poisonous toy, which is being replaced by p.p.[1]-oxy-dibenzylsulphonyl-hydrazide (see foamed rubber, vol. V) in indoor fireworks.

Thiocyanates form deep red coloured complexes with trivalent iron ions (ferric ions). For this reason they are used in analytical chemistry as a reagent for ferric salts. (Of course thiocyanate ions can also be detected with ferric ions.)

9.14.9 Cyanates and isocyanates

Potassium and sodium cyanates (KOCN and NaOCN) can be obtained by oxidizing cyanides, e.g. with oxygen in the presence of nickel or Monel.

These cyanates, and potassium salt in particular, are used as a weedkiller. Potassium salt is preferred as it is more soluble in water than the sodium salt.

Organic cyanates are not known. Organic isocyanates are formed when organic groups are introduced into inorganic cyanates, e.g. by reacting potassium cyanate with diethyl sulphate, an ethyl isocyanate (C_2H_5NCO) is formed. The organic isocyanates have become of great importance. They are widely used in adhesives, paints, plastics and textiles industry (see adhesives, plastics, foamed plastics, synthetic rubber, vol. V and organic chemistry, vol. IV).

9.14.10 Cyanuric compounds

Cyanuric chloride (2, 4, 6-trichloro-1, 3, 5-triazine) is prepared in two stages. Hydrogen cyanide is reacted with chlorine to produce cyanogen chloride and the latter is passed through a bed of carbon catalyst where it is converted into cyanuric chloride. Reaction equations:

$$3 \text{ HCN} + 1\tfrac{1}{2} \text{ Cl}_2 \rightarrow 3 \text{ CNCl} \rightarrow$$

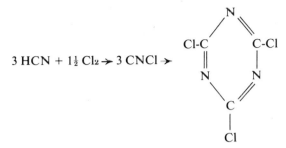

Cyanuric chloride is a polymer (trimer) of cyanogen chloride. The CN groups form a ring of 6 atoms of which three are nitrogen atoms (a triazine, see heterocyclic compounds, vol. IV).

Cyanuric chloride must be produced in well-sealed apparatus to prevent hydrolysis with moisture from air. With water it is hydrolysed to cyanuric acid and hydrochloric acid according to the following reaction equation:

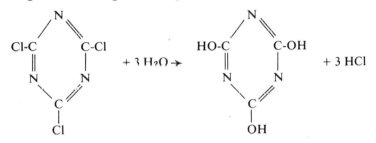

$$+ 3 \text{ H}_2\text{O} \rightarrow \qquad\qquad + 3 \text{ HCl}$$

For this reason all the effluents from the production process are scrubbed with caustic soda before release.

Pure cyanuric chloride is a colourless crystalline product with a pungent odour. The chlorine atoms of cyanuric chloride are easily replaceable in chemical reactions Hence cyanuric chloride is an intermediate in the production of dyes, optical bleaches, pharmaceuticals, explosives, insecticides, plastics, etc. For example: with ethylene amine, cyanuric chloride forms the important medical product triethylene melamine which is used for treating leukaemia and lymphoma. Triallyl cyanurate is a starting material for the production of clear, heat-stable plastics. The chlorine atoms of cyanuric chloride can also react with sodium azide, to form cyanuric triazine. This is a very efficient detonating agent.

Chlorinated cyanuric acids and their salts ($Cl_3(NC)_3O$; $Cl_2H(NC)_3O_3$; $Cl_2Na(NC)_3O_3$ etc.) are also of importance, since they can liberate free chlorine for bleaching and disinfecting. They act as if they contain 60-90% of loosely bound chlorine, e.g. as follows:

$$2Cl_3(NC)_3O_3 + NaCl + 12H_2O \rightarrow 6Cl_2 + 3(NH_4)CO_3 + 3Na_2CO_3$$

They are dry, stable, powders, which are prepared by the reaction of phosgene with urea.

Melamine (2, 4, 6-triamino-1, 3, 5-triazine) is produced from calcium cyanamide by treating a solution of the latter in water with carbon dioxide or sulphuric acid. Calcium carbonate or sulphate is precipitated and a solution of cyanamide (the free acid of calcium cyanamide, H_2NCN) is obtained. Cyanamide is polymerized to dicyandiamide by heating the solution. Dicyandiamide crystallizes when the mixture is cooled. Dicyandiamide can be converted, by heating under pressure with ammonia, into melamine. This process may be represented by the following reaction equations:

$$CaCN_2 + H_2SO_4 \rightarrow CaSO_4 \downarrow + H_2NCN$$

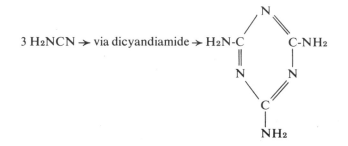

$$3\ H_2NCN \rightarrow \text{via dicyandiamide} \rightarrow$$

In a new process melamine is produced by condensation of urea to melamine in the presence of ammonia. The first large-scale plants have been built in the USA. The total melamine production capacity in the USA was 75 000 short tons in 1963.

Melamine may be considered to be the trimer of cyanamide. It is a colourless crystalline solid, melts at a temperature of about 350° C and is only slightly soluble in water.

Melamine is an important raw material for the production of plastics (see melamine formaldehyde resins, vol. IV). These resins are used as laminating, moulding and coating resins. The resins are also used as adhesives and in the production of paper with good wet strength. The price of melamine was $ 0.26-0.28 per lb in 1965.

Chlorinated melamines have a sterilizing and bactericidal action. Due to this property, trichlormelamine mixed with a detergent and a buffer has been introduced in the American army as a disinfectant for kitchen equipment and washing materials. It seems to be able to prevent even the dreaded amoebic dysentery, and is effective against cholera and streptococcal throat infections. It can also be used for cleansing green vegetables, which have come into contact with infected materials. Its general application in restaurants for cleaning plates and dishes and glassware may be expected.

9.15 PHOSPHORUS (P, atomic weight = 31.0)

9.15.1 History

Phosphorus was probably discovered in 1669 in Hamburg by Brand, who produced it from urine. Keeping it closely guarded, he sold his secret to others until at last Boyle learned about it and obtained it himself in 1681. It was called phosphorus from its property of emitting light, many other substances being given the same name (phosphorus, from the Greek, 'light bearer'). The name was later reserved for the element and the word phosphor has been used as a generic term for all phosphorescent substances (see p. 671).

Scheele discovered that phosphorus (in the form of calcium phosphate) is a constituent of animal bones. Lavoisier in 1777 proved that it was an element. In 1840 Liebig perceived its importance to all plants and animals and recommended using phosphates as fertilizers.

We know that, besides being a constituent of bones, phosphorus is contained in many proteins essential to animals and plants. About twenty years after Liebig's principal work, when phosphorus was also found to be indispensable for brain substance, much importance was attached to the statement of Moleschott (a Dutch chemist working in Italy) 'No thought without phosphorus'.

9.15.2 Occurrence

Because of its great affinity for oxygen, phosphorus never occurs free in nature. Its compounds are very widely distributed, almost exclusively in the form of salts of phosphoric acid. It is estimated that about 0.5% of the earth's crust consists of phosphorus. Phosphorus is an essential constituent of both animal and vegetable organisms which may contain up to 0.1%. It occurs in meat, brains, tissue fluids, egg yolk and faeces. Animal bones contain large quantities of calcium phosphate and are an important source of phosphorus compounds.

Ordinary soil contains about 0.1% of phosphorus in the form of calcium phosphate. Much calcium phosphate is washed out of the soil every year, and must be replaced in the form of fertilizers. It is remarkable that in regions where hygiene is virtually unknown, phosphorus is more economically conserved, since much excrement is put back into the soil. With our hygienic water-closets it is nearly all carried out to sea.

The phosphates in sea water (corresponding to 0.001% phosphorus) form an indispensable basis of life for countless chlorophyll-containing organisms. In the presence of light these organisms form numerous vital compounds with the carbon dioxide in the water. In this way vast quantities of food are produced for the widespread micro and macro fauna of the sea. In the summer, all the supplies of phosphorus are consumed, being largely accumulated in the fats and proteins essential for life and reproduction. In the winter the surface zone of the sea cools. It becomes denser and sinks, being replaced by deep sea water which brings fresh supplies of phosphorus compounds with it. With the approach of spring, the surface zones are again rich enough in phosphorus compounds for the life cycle to proceed intensively again.

The main source of phosphorus and its compounds is phosphate rock (see calcium phosphates). This mineral frequently contains only 13% of phosphorus. Consequently it is not economic to transport it over great distances for phosphorus manufacture; this can only be carried out economically in the neighbourhood of the place of occurrence, where cheap electricity must also be available. The case is different when the mineral is to be used for making superphosphate, since this has in any event to be transported over long distances.

The main constituents of phosphate rock are apatite, a calcium phosphate containing fluorine and/or chlorine, which is a double compound of tertiary calcium phosphate and calcium hydroxide. Phosphate rock occurs in large quantities in North Africa, the USA

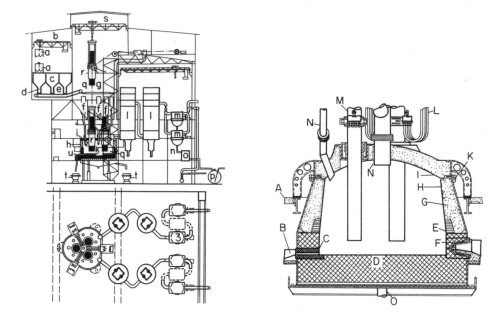

Fig. 9.26 (left) Cross-section of an electrical phosphorus plant. The upper figure is a vertical cross-section. a. Grabs which convey the phosphate rock; b. Crane for manipulating the grabs; c. Bunkers (with scales underneath) which carry the mixture of phosphate rocks on to a conveyor belt (e); f. Bunkers of the furnace in which the phosphate rock mixture is distributed by a rotating hopper (g); h. Phosphate furnace having Söderberg electrodes (q) in holders (r); i. Side feed chutes with slides; k. Centre feed chute; l. Cottrell separators; m. Washers; o. Measuring apparatus for production control; p. Storage container; s. Crane for manipulating the electrodes (r) and (g); t. Containers for slag and ferrophosphorus drainage; u. Slag.

Fig. 9.27 (right) Vertical cross-section through a rotating phosphorus furnace. (The outlet for vapours and gases in the upper part and one electrode are not shown.)
A. Charging floor; B. Ferrophosphorus tap hole; C. Graphite; D. Carbon; E. Firebricks; F. Water cooled slag tapping device; G. Refractory cement; H. Large rotatable crucible; I. Stationary roof; K. Gas seal with molten lead; L. Water cooled electricity supply; M. Graphite electrode; N. Side feed shute; O. Shaft on which the furnace rotates.

and the Pacific islands. The major part of phosphate rock is used for the production of fertilizers (see p. 381 and the fertilizer chapter). Only relatively small quantities are used for the production of phosphorus.

9.15.3 Production of elemental phosphorus

Phosphorus is produced from phosphate rock. The crude phosphate rock is tipped into heaps (arranged according to phosphorus content). These heaps are usually located over a central chute, making underground transportation possible with conveyor belts moving in a tunnel. Among other things, this allows a uniform mixture (with about 13% phosphorus) to be obtained very cheaply. Lumps are preferred. If there is a lot of dust, this is made into pellets, sintering furnaces, which are heated with waste furnace gases usually being used for this purpose (see iron ore, vol. III).

The phosphate mixture is at the same time mixed with coke and silica sand (SiO_2). The equations, shown below, and the analysis of the raw materials enable the required quantities of crude impure materials to be ascertained. The resulting mixture is heated to about 1 500° C in an electric arc furnace. The equations for the reactions in the furnace are:

$$Ca_3(PO_4)_2 + 3\ SiO_2 \rightarrow 3\ CaSiO_3 + P_2O_5$$
$$P_2O_5 + 5\ C \rightarrow 5\ CO + 2\ P.$$

At this high temperature silica sand acts as an acid and can expel phosphoric acid (or phosphorus pentoxide) from its compounds. The phosphorus pentoxide is vaporized and is then reduced to elemental phosphorus by the carbon. Calcium silicate is formed as a slag. (The reaction is shown above in simplified form; actually phosphate rock also contains calcium fluoride, which remains in the slag.)

Fig. 9.26 shows a diagram of an electric arc furnace plant which uses three-phase current with potentials of 200-300 volts between the electrodes. Three electrodes are arranged in a symmetrical triangle. Other arrangements of the electrodes, such as a linear arrangement are used less often. The electrodes may be Soderberg electrodes (see vol. II), baked carbon electrodes, or graphite electrodes. The electrode openings and the discharge points can be cooled.

The furnace is a large steel tank. The bottom and lower parts of the side walls have an inner lining of carbon, which protects the furnace against the slag. The upper parts of the walls and the roof are lined with high-grade firebrick and refractory cement.

An improved electric arc furnace (see figs. 9.27 and 9.28) is a rotating furnace which was developed from Norwegian furnaces for the production of ferro-alloys and carbides. This furnace rotates on a shaft with a rate of one revolution in 24 to 120 hours but its roof and the electrodes are stationary. The rotating part is sealed off with a molten lead gas seal. The whole of the reaction mixture comes into contact with the parts that have the highest temperature. Consequently this furnace works with greater regularity and has a lower power consumption. There is no other essential difference from the stationary furnace, first mentioned.

About 90% of phosphorus is recovered with both types of furnaces. The phosphorus is collected as a gas from a tap hole in the roof. The remaining 10% phosphorus goes into the slag. A part of the latter is recovered by adding iron fillings to the mixture of starting materials. The iron melts and forms ferrophosphorus with phosphorus in the slag. The resulting alloy and the slag sink to the bottom and form two separate liquid layers. The slag being lighter floats on the heavy ferrophosphorus. The latter protects the bottom of the furnace against the slag. These products are removed from the furnace, in liquid form, by two tap holes; a lower one for ferrophosphorus and an upper one for the slag. The slag is run into water forming a grit that is usable for road surfacing or for mixing with clay. The ferrophosphorus is quite valuable (see iron and steel, vol. III).

The phosphorus vapour collected at the top of the furnace contains considerable carbon monoxide (see the equations) and compounds of iron, sodium, potassium and silicon, which form a fine dust. The dust is removed by passing the gas mixture through Cottrell precipitators (see p. 103) which are operated at a temperature above the boiling point of phosphorus. The dust-free vapour is condensed with water sprays in a tower. The phosphorus obtained is stored under a water layer.

Fig. 9.28 Picture of a part of a rotating phosphorus furnace from which the dimensions can be assessed. The supports which fasten the roof to the charging floor are clearly distinguishable (see also the supports shown in fig. 9.27 to the right of A and under K). The dimensions of the diameter of the electrodes (see at the top of the roof) can also be judged by comparison with the figure of the workman. Around the electrodes (which are water cooled) are the flexible tube systems for the electricity supply.

The waste water, which contains some phosphorus, is neutralized with sodium carbonate as a small quantity of phosphorus oxidizes to phosphorus pentoxide (forming corrosive phosphoric acid with the water). The neutralized water is recycled a few times and may only be disposed after thorough oxidation of the traces of phosphorus with chlorine.

The carbon monoxide gas which is obtained from the phosphorus condenser is burned with sufficient air to convert phosphorus to phosphorus pentoxide (compare p. 369) or well washed in order to remove traces of phosphorus. The purified gas may be used as fuel.

9.15.4 Properties and handling of elemental phosphorus

The phosphorus obtained by the process mentioned above is a yellow waxy solid (white phosphorus). It has a purity of 99.9%, a melting point of 44.1° C, a boiling point of 282° C and a specific gravity of 1.813. It is soluble in carbon disulphide. At the melting point it burns when exposed to air with a vivid blinding light. Even at ordinary temperature it oxidizes slightly in air, producing a weak phosphorescence which is visible in the dark. On friction it burns spontaneously and it is very active in chemical reactions. In the stomach or in wounds even minute quantities of white phosphorus are very poisonous. The workmen handling this dangerous substance wear asbestos clothing, gloves and rubber boots etc., in order to avoid the severe cases of phosphorus poisoning that arose before these precautions were adopted.

The properties of phosphorus demand a special transportation method. Phosphorus is kept fluid with water at about 50° C for easy automatic transportation. Tanks and pipelines are jacketed so that hot water can be passed through and the jackets are covered with insulation. Important consumers receive their supplies in double-walled tank trucks under a water seal. The greatest care is required in drawing it off to avoid fire and poisoning. For use in small quantities sticks of phosphorus are made which are kept under water in tins or glass containers.

On account of its toxicity and inflammability by friction, many countries have prohibited the use of white phosphorus for matches. Up to about 1890 large amounts were still incorporated in match heads, causing many fatal cases of poisoning, fire etc.

By heating white phosphorus at a temperature of about 260° C in a closed steel or cast-iron vessel (batch process), a red powder is formed. This is red phosphorus, another modification of phosphorus (see also modifications of sulphur). Red phosphorus has a specific gravity between 2.1 and 2.2. It melts at a temperature of 590° C under a pressure of 43 atm, and it is insoluble in carbon disulphide. On heating at atmospheric pressure it is converted directly into vapour at a temperature of about 450° C. White phosphorus is obtained by cooling this vapour.

Red phosphorus does not glow, ignites only above 400° C, is not poisonous and is not active in chemical reactions. Probably red phosphorus is a mixture of scarlet amorphous phosphorus (sp. gr. 1.88) and crystalline violet phosphorus (sp. gr. 2.34). It contains also some white phosphorus and phosphorus pentoxide. The white phosphorus and phosphorus pentoxide are removed by extraction with carbon disulphide and washing with a boiling caustic soda solution.

Pure crystalline violet phosphorus may be prepared by heating ordinary red phosphorus in a sealed vessel at a temperature of about 530° C. The crystalline product sublimes in a cooler part of the vessel.

Scarlet phosphorus may be obtained by boiling a solution of white phosphorus in phosphorus tribromide (PBr₃) for ten hours. The scarlet phosphorus (Schenck's scarlet phosphorus) is separated from the solvent by distilling the latter. It is more active than red phosphorus and violet phosphorus.

The high melting point, the low volatility and the insolubility in solvents suggest that red, scarlet and violet phosphorus are polymers of many phosphorus atoms. This may be an explanation for the difference in properties of white and red phosphorus.

White phosphorus may also be converted into red phosphorus by a continuous process as follows. White phosphorus is heated for six hours under an inert gas (nitrogen or carbon monoxide) at a temperature of 276-278° C (slightly below its boiling point), until about 30-50% is converted into the red form.

The mixture is passed through a tube at a higher temperature (up to 295° C), in a countercurrent inert gas stream. In this tube, the mixture is vigorously agitated and pounded to crush any lumps. The white phosphorus is evaporated and the vapour is carried along with the stream of inert gas. The white phosphorus is condensed and treated again in a second unit. The red phosphorus that remains is washed with water, filtered and dried. This method yields a product of better quality than the discontinuous batch process mentioned before.

9.15.5 Uses of elemental phosphorus

Only a very small quantity of white phosphorus is used as such because of its poisonous properties. Some of its uses are for rat poisons, pharmaceuticals, munitions and pyrotechnics. It is estimated that about 90% of white phosphorus production is burned to phosphoric pentoxide, which is a starting material for the production of phosphoric acid, phosphates and other phosphorus compounds.

The main part of the rest is converted to phosphorus chlorides and sulphides and smaller quantities to red phosphorus. Red phosphorus is used mainly in the match industry. It is included in the striking surface on boxes of safety matches. When the head of a match is rubbed on it, a minute quantity of red phosphorus is transformed into white. This ignites in air and produces sufficient heat to ignite the head of the match. The burning white phosphorus is visible as a luminous streak (see matches, vol. IV). Red phosphorus is also used for the production of phosphorus compounds and in the manufacture of fireworks.

Exposed to radiation in a nuclear reactor, sulphur yields the radioactive isotope P^{32}. This is used for the recording of the electron rays from a histological section which has absorbed it (see photography, vol. VI and radioactive isotopes, p. 643).

Fig. 9.29 shows a list of the most important uses of phosphorus and its compounds.

9.15.6 Statistics

The world production of elemental phosphorus, which was some 1000 metric tons in 1900, rose to 100000 tons in 1940 and was close to 550000 tons in 1962. About 410000 metric tons were produced in the USA, 45000 tons in Western Germany, 35000 tons in the United Kingdom, 12000 tons in France and 11000 tons in Italy. Phosphorus is also made in Eastern Germany, Japan, Sweden and the USSR.

The great bulk of the phosphorus manufactured is yellow phosphorus, only limited amounts are converted into red phosphorus for matches and pyrotechnics.

The end uses in the USA in 1963 are shown in the following table (the total consumption was 440000 metric tons in 1963):

Sodium tripolyphosphate	38%	Fertilizers and miscellaneous	25%
Tetrasodium pyrophosphate	5%	Direct chemical use red phos-	
Sodium metaphosphate	4%	phorus, phosphor copper, phos-	
Other sodium phosphates	9%	phorus halides, oxyhalide and	
Calcium phosphates	9%	sulphides)	10%

In 1965 white phosphorus was sold in the USA at $ 0.20 per lb, and red phosphorus at $ 0.55 per lb.

9.16 PHOSPHORUS PENTOXIDE AND ACIDS OF PHOSPHORUS

9.16.1 Phosphorus pentoxide

Phosphorus pentoxide (P_2O_5) is prepared by melting white phosphorus and atomizing the liquid with dry air with a special (cooled tip) burner. Secondary air is supplied round the tip for complete combustion. A tall tower of high heat conductivity graphite firebrick and with a firebrick top is used. The outside is cooled continuously with water to keep the temperature low enough to protect the graphite. In order to prevent serious losses by corrosion, the air used for combustion of the atomized phosphorus, has to be extremely dry. This air is dried with aluminium oxide. The phosphorus pentoxide obtained is condensed by mixing with cool dry air in a large room (called a 'barn').

Another production method is to burn the mixture of phosphorus vapour and carbon monoxide (which is obtained in the production of elemental phosphorus) with sufficient air to convert the phosphorus into pentoxide; 95% of the CO remains unchanged. After separation of P_2O_5 it can be used for fuel. The resulting production is a snow white powder subliming at 160° C. Phosphorus pentoxide is hygroscopic and dissolves in water with a violent heat evolution. For this reason it must be packed in tightly sealed steel drums. Most of the P_2O_5 is immediately converted into phosphoric acid (see also fig. 9.29).

Being hygroscopic it is used as a drying agent for gases and liquids and as a dehydrating agent in organic chemical reactions, e.g. polymerization and condensation processes. It is also used in the production of phosphoric acid esters and polyphosphoric acids.

It is also employed as a catalyst for making blown asphalt for road surfacing (see asphalt, vol. IV) and as a drying agent in the manufacture of methyl methacrylate.

Phosphorus pentoxide itself is increasing in importance in industrial applications.

In the USA about 10000 short tons of phosphorus pentoxide for non-acid uses were produced in 1963. Its price in 1965 was $ 0.14 to $ 0.15 per lb.

9.16.2 Production of (ortho)phosphoric acid

a. From elemental phosphorus. Phosphoric acid (H_3PO_4) is prepared by burning elemental phosphorus to P_2O_5 (see above). The gas obtained from the combustion chamber is passed through a graphite lined gas cooler. The cooled air – P_2O_5 vapour

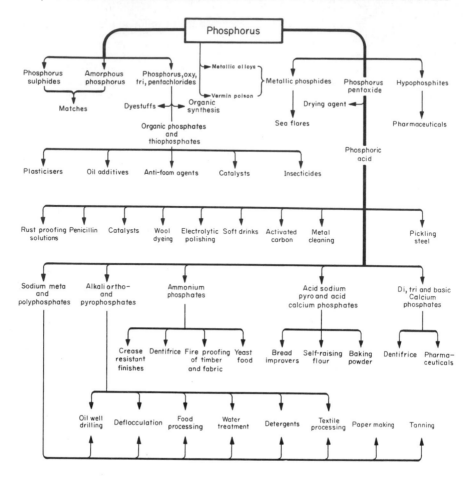

Fig. 9.29 Survey of the most important compounds derived from phosphorus, and their most important uses.

mixture is passed through an acid resistant hydrating tower (also graphite lined) into which water is sprayed. Phosphorus pentoxide forms phosphoric acid with water according to the following equation:

$$P_2O_5 + 3\ H_2O \rightarrow 2\ H_3PO_4$$

In a Cottrel separator (see electrostatic separators, p. 103) the waste gases are freed of all the residual P_2O_5 which is likewise converted into acid. With this process a 95% acid can be obtained.

   b. From phosphate rock. Phosphoric acid is also prepared from phosphate rock (the wet process). Finely ground crude phosphate rock is stirred in 90% sulphuric acid solution. A precipitate of calcium sulphate and a solution of phosphoric acid in water is obtained.

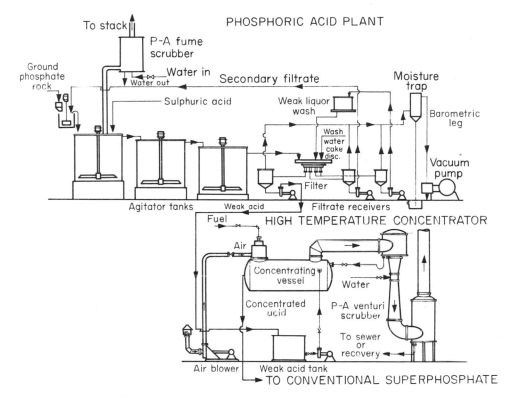

Fig. 9.30 Diagrammatic representation of phosphoric acid production according to the wet process from rock phosphate, with filtering and concentrating sections.

The reaction may be represented by the following equation:

$$Ca_5(PO_4)_3F + 5\ H_2SO_4 \rightarrow 5\ CaSO_4 + 3\ H_3PO_4 + HF$$

Usually the reaction mixture passes through several baths in succession (see fig. 9.30) because care has to be taken that the calcium sulphate does not cake but forms large individual crystals. The mass is filtered and the filter cake is carefully washed to prevent losses of phosphoric acid. Fig 9.31 shows a rotating filter with several filter plates. The solid calcium sulphate is separated from the phosphoric acid solution and washed on the filter plates. The washed filter cake is dumped by turning the filter plates.

The phosphoric acid solution, containing about 40% phosphoric acid, is mainly concentrated by evaporation with hot combustion gases which are blown through the acid. These gases are often obtained by combustion of oil or natural gas with air and are introduced immediately into the phosphoric acid below liquid level. Hence the name submerged burners (see fig. 9.32). Graphite lined apparatus is used for this purpose. This method has several advantages. It has a high fuel efficiency; the apparatus is comparatively small; scale formation and corrosion are prevented.

Usually an impure phosphoric acid solution containing 70-80% phosphoric acid is obtained by the wet process followed by concentrating with the submerged flame method.

In all stages of the wet process, gaseous fluorine compounds are liberated. These gases are treated as with superphosphate production (see superphosphate, p. 382).

Very diluted phosphoric acid solutions, being unprofitable to concentrate by evaporation, may be concentrated by adding PCl_5. The hydrochloric acid, which is produced at the same time, is recovered.

The strength of phosphoric acid can also be increased by putting P_2O_5 in the solution.

The wet process is the most economical and oldest method for manufacturing phosphoric acid. A new development in this process in the USA is the recovery of uranium. Several phosphate rocks contain 0.01 to 0.02% uranium. This uranium is dissolved by the sulphuric acid and remains in the crude phosphoric acid from which it is recovered (see uranium compounds).

Other impurities in wet process phosphoric acid are hydrofluoric acid (HF), arsenic, several metal ions, etc. The hydrofluoric acid content may be reduced to less than 50 p.p.m. by blowing superheated steam into concentrated phosphoric acid, containing not less than 75% H_3PO_4. Arsenic is removed by treating the acid with sodium sulphide. The excess of hydrogen sulphide gas, which is formed from the sodium sulphide is removed by aeration.

9.16.3 Properties and uses of phosphoric acid

There are many grades and purities of phosphoric acid. In Great Britain phosphoric acid is marketed in grades defined by density, for example 1 500 and 1 750 containing 67 and 90 weight % of H_3PO_4 respectively. Anhydrous phosphoric acid (a moderately strong tribasic acid) is a crystalline solid having a melting point of 42.3° C. It may be diluted to any desired strength with water. Mixing with water must be performed by pouring phosphoric acid into the water. If water is poured into the acid the heat generated may cause dangerous splashing of the acid.

The impure acid, manufactured by the wet process, is mainly used for making fertilizers (double and triple superphosphate and ammonium phosphate). Very concentrated phosphate fertilizers are sometimes made from the stronger acid obtained from elemental phosphorus. Significant quantities of phosphoric acid are consumed in water softeners (sodium pyrophosphates, sodium tripolyphosphates etc.). Phosphoric acid is also used for phosphating and pickling steel and other metal and for the production of several phosphates (calcium phosphate, sodium phosphate etc.). Very pure acid is used in many beverages, in food, for pharmaceutical preparations and in bacteriology etc. (see fig. 9.29).

Consumption may be increased by the use of phosphoric acid to stabilize clay soils, used in road construction. Phosphoric acid forms complexes with the clay minerals. Clay containing 2% acid resists the disintegrating effect of water.

9.16.4 Statistics

The USA, with a total output of 2 600 000 metric tons (calculated as P_2O_5) in 1963, is by far the biggest producer of phosphoric acid. About 67% was wet process phosphoric acid and the remainder was produced from elemental phosphorus. The expansion of phosphoric acid production in the USA is enormous. In 1929 only a few thousand tons were produced and the production in 1950 was 539 000 tons.

Fig. 9.31 Prayton rotating, pan-type filter for the wet-phosphoric acid process. On it, calcium sulphate as gypsum is filtered from dissolved phosphate, washed three times, and dumped. Filtrate (32% P_2O_5) goes to concentrating tower; washes (20 to 24% P_2O_5) recycle to the dissolving system for further enrichment up to about 32% P_2O_5.

The production of phosphoric acid in Italy, Western Germany and France in 1963 was 120000, 130000 and 90000 metric tons respectively (in terms of P_2O_5). In these countries by far the major portion is produced in the wet process from phosphate rock. Only small quantities are obtained from elemental phosphorus.

In the USA phosphoric acid 85% was sold at $ 7.00 per 100 lb in 1965. The price of 80% food grade was $ 6.00 per 100 lb. In the United Kingdom phosphoric acid (spec. gravity 1.750) was 1s 4d per lb, and phosphoric acid technical grade (spec. gravity 1.70) was sold at £ 104 per long ton.

9.16.5 Other acids of phosphorus

Pyrophosphoric acid ($H_4P_2O_7$) is obtained by adding P_2O_5 to a concentrated phosphoric acid solution. This acid can be transformed by heating into *metaphosphoric acid* (HPO_3). The salts of these acids are important (see sodium phosphates).

Fluorophosphoric acids are receiving more attention especially the salts of mono-, di- and hexafluorophosphoric acid. The acids are of particular importance as catalysts and sometimes for pickling metals and in electrolysis. Hexafluorophosphoric acid is produced in silver or aluminium apparatus, with facilities for cooling it, from concen-

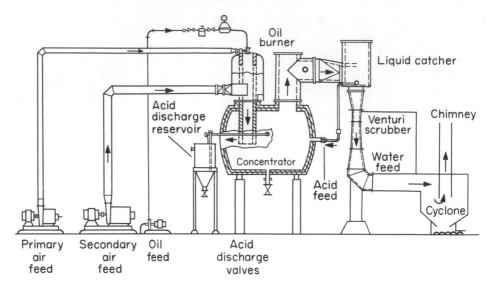

Fig. 9.32 Diagram for concentrating a phosphoric acid solution with the aid of the submerged flame.

trated orthophosphoric acid solution and hydrogen fluoride gas according to the following equation:

$$6 \text{ HF} + \text{H}_3\text{PO}_4 + 2 \text{ H}_2\text{O} \rightarrow \text{HPF}_6. \text{ 6 H}_2\text{O}.$$

The hexahydrate of hexafluorophosphoric acid crystallizes by cooling. Ammonium hexafluorophosphate is excellent for etching glass, being easier to handle than HF itself.

Phosphorous acid (H_3PO_3, a strong dibasic acid) is prepared from phosphorus trichloride with water or hydrochloric acid solution according to the following equation:

$$\text{PCl}_3 + 3 \text{ H}_2\text{O} \rightarrow \text{H}_3\text{PO}_3 + 3 \text{ HCl}.$$

The resulting phosphorous acid solution is purified and concentrated by evaporation below 180° C and above 76° C (the boiling point of PCl_3) so that the residual PCl_3 and hydrochloric acid are expelled. Phosphorous acid and its compounds have reducing properties. Hence salts of phosphorous acid (phosphites) are used as reducing agents.

Hypophosphorus acid (H_3PO_2, a monobasic acid) is prepared by treating white phosphorus with a boiling slurry of calcium hydroxide (see also production of phosphine). Crystals of calcium hypophosphite are obtained by evaporating the resulting solution. A hypophosphorus acid solution and a precipitate of calcium sulphate are obtained by treating a solution of calcium hypophosphite with sulphuric acid. Hypophosphorus acid and its salts (hypophosphites) are powerful reducing agents, precipitating metals from metal salt solutions. Sodium hypophosphite is used as reducing agent for nickel chloride and cobalt chloride in electrodeless nickel and cobalt plating of steel (see vol. III).

9.17 ALKALI AND AMMONIUM PHOSPHATES

9.17.1 Sodium (ortho) phosphates

Monosodium phosphate (NaH_2PO_4) and *disodium phosphate* (Na_2HPO_4) may be produced by adding the correct quantity of phosphoric acid to a sodium carbonate solution and evaporating the solution. Anhydrous and hydrated forms of both phosphates are known. Monosodium phosphate is very soluble in water. About 80 g (in terms of anhydrous phosphate) dissolve in 100 g water at 20° C. The solubility of disodium phosphate is about 9 g at 20° C.

Mono- and disodium phosphate are mainly used for the production of polyphosphates. Mixtures of mono- and disodium phosphate are used in buffer solutions in order to control the pH in the range from 4 to 9. Both phosphates are employed in baking powder. If made from phosphoric acid obtained direct from crude phosphate, the sodium phosphates may contain fluorine, but not if made from phosphoric acid obtained from white phosphorus. Many countries prescribe a maximum fluorine content of 0.0003 % for use in food. Disodium phosphate is also used in water treatment as a precipitant for metal ions. It is also used as an emulsifier in processed cheese (a cheese which remains soft and easy to spread). Its emulsifying property depends on the ability of orthophosphates to adsorb at water-fat interfaces. Disodium phosphate is also added to milk to prevent it from curdling when heated.

In the USA about 15000 short tons of monosodium phosphate and 24000 tons of disodium phosphate were produced in 1963 (excluding amounts used for the production of polyphosphates). In the USA monosodium and disodium phosphate were sold at $ 170 to $ 200 per short ton (anhydrous basis) in 1965. The price of disodium phosphate in the UK was £ 40 per long ton.

Trisodium phosphate (Na_3PO_4) is obtained by adding a slight excess of sodium hydroxide to a solution of disodium phosphate and evaporating the solvent. By cooling on a drum dryer the melt, resulting from evaporation, solidifies to flakes of trisodium phosphate containing about 45 % (by weight) of water and some sodium hydroxide. This product which is the commercial 'dodecahydrate' can be converted into anhydrous trisodium phosphate by spray-drying.

Trisodium phosphate is used in cleaning compositions and in water treatment just like disodium phosphate. It is also employed as an anti-caking agent in many powdered materials. Trisodium phosphate can crystallize with sodium hypochlorite (it forms a double salt). In solution this double salt acts as a disinfectant cleaner. It contains 3 % active chlorine. Production of trisodium phosphate has decreased during the last fifteen years because synthetic detergents and polyphosphates (see below) suitable for use in hard water are making much progress. In the USA the production of trisodium phosphate was about 56000 short tons in 1963. (In 1947 the production was 89000 short tons). Anhydrous trisodium phosphate was sold at $180 to $200 per short ton in the USA; in the UK the price of the anhydrous product in 1965 was £87 per long ton.

9.17.2 Sodium polyphosphates

Sodium acid pyrophosphate ($Na_2H_2P_2O_7$) is prepared by heating monosodium phosphate at a temperature of 250° C. In equation:

$$2\ NaH_2PO_4 \rightarrow Na_2H_2P_2O_7 + H_2O.$$

The resulting solid is used as a leavening agent in baking powders.

Tetrasodium pyrophosphate ($Na_4P_2O_7$) is prepared by calcining disodium phosphate in a rotary kiln at temperatures between 350 and 500° C. The resulting product is used in cleaning compositions and in processed cheese (see below).

Sodium tripolyphosphate (pentasodium triphosphate, $Na_5P_3O_{10}$) is produced by heating a mixture of monosodium and disodium phosphate at temperatures above 250° C in a rotary kiln or spray tower. Reaction equation:

$$NaH_2PO_4 + 2Na_2HPO_4 \rightarrow Na_5P_3O_{10} + 2H_2O.$$

The resulting product is an anhydrous solid which forms a hexahydrate by mixing with water. The solubility of the anhydrous product in water at 20° C is about 15 g per 100 g water.

Sodium tripolyphosphate (and also the other polyphosphates) have the very important practical property of softening water by taking metal ions (Ca^{++}, Mg^{++} and Fe^{+++}) into their molecules. Hence their use in water treatment (see complex formation, p. 133). Due to its ability to form complexes with various metal ions tripolyphosphate is also used in cleaning compositions. Mixtures of the tripolyphosphate with alkaline substances, such as sodium silicate and soda, are used as a dishwashing agent for domestic and restaurant use. Sodium tripolyphosphate is also added to surface active detergents. The polyphosphate eliminates the influence of water hardness and promotes the surface active properties of the detergent although the tripolyphosphate itself is not surface active.

Sodium tripolyphosphate is also used in foodstuffs. It is added to sausage fillings and cheese to impart greater consistency. The presence of small amounts of tripolyphosphate in orthophosphate used in processed cheese causes stabilizing and hardening of the cheese.

Other sodium polyphosphates and *sodium metaphosphates* are prepared by heating monosodium orthophosphate at temperatures between 350 and 900° C. With the evaporation of water a glassy mass is obtained. Depending on the heating temperature glassy polyphosphates having various compositions and properties are obtained. These products are known under various names. Some polyphosphate glasses are named after the first producer for instance: Graham's salt or Maddrell's salt and Kurrol's salt. These products are polymers in which phosphorus and oxygen atoms alternate in ring systems or in short to very long chains. Formerly these polyphosphates were named condensed phosphates or metaphosphates. Now the chain polymers (having the general formula $Na_{n+2} P_n O_{3n+1}$) are named polyphosphates and the ring polymers (having the formula $(NaPO_3)_n$) are called metaphosphates.

The metaphosphates are much less important than the polyphosphates. Sodium tetrametaphosphate is a tannic acid saver in tanneries due to its ability to precipitate proteins at pH 2 to 3.

The most important glassy polyphosphates are sodium tetraphosphate and calgon (Graham's salt). Sodium tetrapolyphosphate is a mixture of lower polyphosphates having 4 to 6 phosphorus atoms in the molecule. Calgon is a glassy mixture of higher polyphosphates having 13 to 25 phosphorus atoms in the molecule. Calgon is also called 'hexametaphosphate' but this is a misnomer as the product does not contain important quantities of a phosphate polymer which has 6 phosphorus atoms in the molecule.

The glassy polyphosphates are turned immediately into a fine powder by spraying solutions of them into a heated spraying tower. These powders form a sticky mass in moist atmosphere, are water soluble and (like sodium tripolyphosphate) they have the property of taking metal ions into their molecules. Hence they are used for the same purposes as sodium tripolyphosphate although the latter is preferred since it does not form a sticky mass in moist atmosphere.

Solutions of glassy sodium polyphosphates are also used in medical treatment of skin diseases. Metal surfaces are protected against oxidation when a polyphosphate solution is dried on it. (The polyphosphate forms a hard protective coating.)

The polyphosphates occur mixed with other industrial products under various proprietary names such as Calgonite which is a dishwashing agent consisting of calgon, sodium metasilicate and soda. (For further uses see fig. 9.29.)

Statistics

The production of various polyphosphates in the USA is shown in the following table:

| | In '000s short tons | | | |
	1951	1956	1961	1964
Sodium acid pyrophosphate	11	15	18	23
Tetrasodium pyrophosphate	86	102	86	114
Sodium tripolyphosphate	331	587	756	885
Other polyphosphates	52	59	65	78

In the USA sodium tripolyphosphate was sold at $ 6.50 to $ 7.80 per 100 lb in 1965.

9.17.3 Potassium phosphates

Potassium phosphates have similar properties to those of the corresponding sodium phosphates. They are used as water softeners, emulsifiers etc. The ortho-phosphates are often used as a nutrient in yeast production and wine fermentation. Microbes require phosphorus, ammonium and potassium compounds in order to multiply.

Very concentrated solutions of tetrapotassium pyrophosphate may be prepared as 1 lb of water is sufficient to dissolve 1 kg of the salt at a temperature of 25° C. This pyrophosphate is used in liquid detergent compositions. The US production of tetra-potassium pyrophosphate was about 50000 short tons in 1964.

9.17.4 Ammonium orthophosphates

Mono- and diammonium phosphate can be made by mixing phosphoric acid and ammonia in a vacuum crystallizer or saturator. These processes are similar to those for ammonium sulphate (see p. 314). Diammonium phosphate crystallizes when the pH of the mother liquor is maintained at approximately 6.5 (ratio of ammonia to phosphoric acid in the liquor is about 1.75). Monoammonium phosphate crystallizes at pH 4.5 to 5.0. The crystals of ammonium phosphate are separated from the mother liquor with centrifuges and dried.

The ammonium phosphates are white crystalline products which are soluble in water. The largest quantities of both ammonium phosphates are used as fertilizer (see fertilizers, vol. VII). These phosphates are also used as nutrients for yeast and in fireproofing plastics, wood and paper. Afterglow of matches is prevented by impregnating the wood of the matches with small amounts of monoammonium phosphate.

Monoammonium phosphate can crystallize in large beautiful crystals having piezoelectric properties like Rochelle salt, quartz etc. These crystals are utilized in electronic apparatus.

The USA imported about 130000 long tons of ammonium phosphates in 1963, mainly from Canada. The imports of the UK were 15000 long tons in the same year. The largest quantity was imported from Belgium. The UK is an important producer of ammonium phosphates. The production was estimated at 400000 tons in 1961. This is about five times the production of 1952. In the USA diammonium phosphate was sold at $ 192 per ton (in 1965). The price in the UK was £ 97 10s per ton and that of monoammonium phosphate was £ 106 per ton.

9.18   CALCIUM PHOSPHATES

9.18.1 Occurrence

Calcium phosphates are widely distributed in the earth's crust in the form of crystalline minerals of the apatite group. Apatite is a double salt having the formula $3 Ca_3(PO_4)_2 . Ca(ClF)_2$. As such it occurs in granite and basic rocks from magmatic origin. Commonly the phosphate content is too low for economical mining. Some rich igneous deposits are found in the Kola peninsula in the USSR, in South Africa and Brazil. Apatite also occurs as veins associated with minerals such as nepheline (a sodium aluminium silicate). More important is the occurrence of apatite in magmatic deposits of magnetite (iron ore) in Kiruna in Sweden. This ore contains up to 9% phosphates in terms of $Ca_3(PO_4)_2$. These phosphates are obtained as basic slag in the iron industry (see iron production, vol. III, and fertilizers, vol. VII).

The most important rich deposits are of sedimentary origin. Guano and phosphate rock are two forms of sedimentary deposits. Sedimentary deposits of iron ore and phosphates are also known. Guano is formed by accumulation of bird excrement. It occurs on islands in the southern latitudes and besides phosphates it contains also nitrogen compounds (see fertilizers, vol. VII).

Phosphate rock (also named phosphorite) consists of apatite, hydroxy apatite (containing calcium hydroxide) and carbonate apatite (containing calcium carbonate). The composition is not always the same. Phosphate rock often occurs in the form of small pebbles or pellets in beds of sand, clay, mica, calcium carbonate and other materials (see fig. 9.33). The crude mineral varies, from a hard flintlike mass to soft products resembling kaolin, depending on the kind of impurities. Commonly the pebbles are in the size range of 0.1 to 1 mm. The phosphate often contains organic matter. All types of plant and animal remains, such as sharks' teeth, are found in crude phosphate. For this reason it has been suggested that phosphate rock deposits are formed on the bottom of the seas from organic remains. In later periods these deposits are elevated

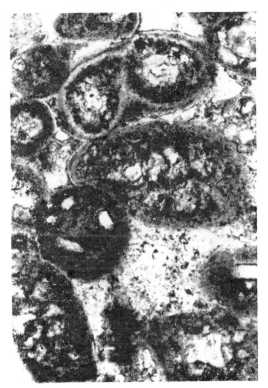

Fig. 9.33 Cross-section through a deposit of phosphate rock pellets (greatly enlarged).

above sea level or can be moved by water to other places and be settled again (primary deposits). More soluble substances can be leached out from primary deposits and phosphates remain (secondary deposits). The phosphate rock deposits of the Pacific islands are guano deposits which have been leached with water. In general it is said that the phosphates occurring in the earth's crust are concentrated in regions where there was a concentrated animal life in former ages (and now). (See also phosphorus in animal life, p. 363.)

The phosphate content of phosphate rock is expressed in terms of phosphorus pentoxide, or in terms of tertiary calcium phosphate ($Ca_3(PO_4)_2$). The latter is often known in the trade as BPL (bone phosphate of lime).

The main places where phosphate rock is found are in the USA, in North Africa and certain islands in the Pacific. The BPL content of the ores which are mined at present ranges from about 25% to 75%. In Florida, phosphate rock containing 60-75% BPL occurs in an area of aproximately 15 by 30 miles. The thickness of the layer is 6-25 ft.

New deposits have been found all over the world, e.g. in North Transvaal, where they are to be exploited by the government and will meet a large part of local requirements, if not all. Exploitation and export have begun in Jordan and Israel. New deposits have also been discovered in Peru, India, Spitsbergen and Spain. Some of these beds also contain potash and nitrates.

9.18.2 Mining and concentrating of phosphate rock

Phosphate rock is usually mined by surface mining. The raw material is removed first by means of draglines. The valuable phosphate (matrix) is dumped into a sump by means of the same dragline. In the sump, streams of high pressure water are used to disintegrate the phosphate rock and the slurry obtained is pumped in 14 to 16 inch pipelines to the refining plant. This typical mining process via a sump is used to release clay, etc., from the phosphate rock pebbles. Mining is worth while only in the case of large deposits, particularly since an extensive purification and concentration process is necessary if freights are not to become too high.

The slurry from the mine is agitated strongly in water to release the remaining clay. The solids are sieved. Pieces larger than 1 mm form the 'pebble'. The pebble contains 65 to 75% BPL and needs no further purification.

The smaller pieces are freed from finely divided clay and other colloidal products by means of hydroseparators or Dutch cones (see classification of ores, vol. III). The purified product is sieved into two sizes, one size from 16 to about 35 mesh (per inch) and the other from 35 to 200 mesh. The particles which pass the 200 mesh sieve are dumped in mined-out areas together with the slime of the hydroseparators. These wastes contain sometimes about 20% BPL, but an economical method for processing these finely divided phosphates has not yet been found. Consequently up to about one-third of the phosphate mined is sometimes wasted.

The fraction from 35 to 200 mesh is subjected to flotation. This fraction is mixed with fatty acids, sodium hydroxide and fuel oil. In the flotation cells the oil-coated phosphate particles rise to the surface with the air bubbles (see flotation, vol. III), and the uncoated sand remains at the bottom. The phosphate particles are freed from oil with dilute sulphuric acid. Sometimes this fraction is subjected to a second flotation process with amines as flotation agent. In this process, sand and clay particles rise and the phosphate sinks. The resulting product has a BPL content of 75-77%.

The fraction from 16 to 35 mesh is purified by various processes. In these processes the phosphate particles are agglomerated by adding a mixture of fatty acid, kerosene, fuel oil and caustic soda to a slurry containing this fraction. The agglomerated particles can be separated by means of sieves placed under liquid level. The agglomerated phosphate particles can also be separated from the ore mixture by classification methods which depend upon differences in specific gravity. Shaker tables, spray belts and Humphrey spiral classifiers may be used (see ores, vol. III). The Humphrey spiral is a gutter in the form of a spiral. The slurry travels down in the spiral; the heavy particles concentrate on the inner rim and the lightest particles concentrate on the outer rim. Phosphate rock concentrates on the outer rim due to its lower specific gravity. Phosphate concentrates containing 75% BPL can be obtained by means of the spiral. Various classifiers and screens are used in cascade depending on the kind of phosphate to be purified.

The amounts of water necessary in the purification processes are enormous. The water is passed into large vessels so that as much as possible can be recovered. Everything is separated as far as possible into slurries. These slimy masses have to be dried out slowly and can sometimes be used in the dry state for making concrete. The pebble phosphate, flotation phosphate and agglomeration phosphate are stored wet. Before shipping to the consumer, the phosphates are dried, using direct-fired rotary kilns. These are slowly rotating horizontal cylinders. The phosphate flows in against the flames, and is raised again and again by baffles and then falls back through the flames. The dry powder is finely ground.

The mining and concentrating method described before is most commonly used in the United States. Underground mines are also in operation in that country. Sometimes the concentration process is simplified since much low grade phosphate sand can be introduced as such in electric furnaces to produce elemental phosphorus.

The American mining methods are used more and more in North Africa, but manual labour is still used in mines outside the United States. There are also phosphate mines in North Africa on the edge of the desert where, in some cases, no water is available for concentrating the ore. Pneumatic concentration is then used, the material being separated by currents of air according to particle size and specific gravity.

9.18.3 Uses of phosphate rock

Phosphate rock is the most important material for the production of elemental phosphorus, phosphoric acid and other phosphorus compounds. It is mainly used for the production of fertilizers. The majority of phosphate rock is processed into super-phosphate for this purpose. Phosphate rock, as such, cannot be used as fertilizer since tertiary calcium phosphate in apatite minerals is not sufficiently soluble in water to be absorbed by plants. In the production of superphosphate and triple superphosphate (see p. 385), tertiary calcium phosphate is converted into primary calcium phosphate, which is much more soluble in water. (See also mixed fertilizers, vol. VII.)

During World War II there was a shortage of bone meal in America, and it was desired to supplement this by using crude phosphate. This nevertheless contains 4.2% fluorine which can be very harmful in cattle fodder. A method was therefore sought to defluorinate the phosphate and at the same time to obtain HF. This can be achieved by heating crude ground phosphate with sand and steam. In some cases the heating is so intense that the mass melts. A rotating furnace is used with oil heating. The product is quenched with water after removal from the furnace. It then contains about 28% P_2O_5 and still about 0.4% fluorine. The gases given off are carefully washed in order to obtain all the fluorine.

It is estimated that the United States have about 600 years' supply of fluorine in phosphates. It is, however, somewhat more expensive to obtain than from fluorspar, unless it is desired to obtain fluorsilanes. With the exhaustion of supplies of fluorspar, the production of fluorine compounds from phosphates can be of great importance.

Phosphate which has been defluorinated is much more valuable than the ordinary type. Nowadays defluorinated phosphate rock is prepared to some extent for fertilizer purposes (in USA). Since the apatite structure is destroyed as a result of this treatment, the product is more easily absorbed by plants.

9.18.4 Production of normal superphosphate

a. Principles. Normal (or single) superphosphate is produced from phosphate rock and sulphuric acid. A constant composition of the crude phosphate is one require-ment for the easy preparation of superphosphate. It is, therefore, desirable always to buy from the same pit or with a guarantee regarding composition. Admixtures can have a harmful effect by opposing the formation of superphosphate when combined with acids. Phosphate rock is finely ground (95% should pass a sieve with 100 mesh per inch; see also grinding, vol. III) and is then mixed intensively with sulphuric acid. Care is taken that both the acid and the phosphate are added in a constant weight ratio. The reaction is as follows (it may vary depending on the kind of phosphate rock):

$$2 Ca_5(PO_4)_3F + 7H_2SO_4 \rightarrow 7 CaSO_4 + 3 Ca(H_2PO_4)_2 + 2HF.$$

The resulting mixture of primary calcium phosphate and gypsum is called super-phosphate.

In all processes the precise amounts of phosphate and sulphuric acid are intro-duced into a mixing device. The initially thin slurry tends to harden, but before this happens, the still liquid mass is released into a closed chamber (known as a 'den') in which it hardens to superphosphate. The hardening of superphosphate is due to the hydration of the monocalcium phosphate ($CaH_4(PO_4)_2$) which is first formed, to $CaH_4(PO_4)_2.H_2O$. The product which has hardened in the den is excavated and powdered by shredding machines within 1 to 24 hours and is transported to storage piles. The excavated superphosphate has a temperature of between 110° and 120° C and the reaction has not yet reached equilibrium. For this reason the superphosphate is allowed to 'ripen' for a few weeks. During this period the chemical reaction continues as does also the formation of primary phosphate. Ripening is followed by grinding, sieving and packing in bags.

The superphosphate (also called 'super') contains 10-15% water, depending on the strength of the sulphuric acid used. The water content should not be too high because of caking and ease of spreading. For this reason the superphosphate is often dried in rotating drum dryers before curing. Direct current drying is used, the super and com-bustion gases flowing in the same direction. Heating is carried out to 80-95° C. In this way superphosphate with up to 20% P_2O_5 content can be made with better caking properties than undried super.

b. Treating of waste gases. According to the above equation hydrogen fluoride is liberated in making superphosphate. However this cannot be recovered completely as such since it partly reacts with silica which is present in phosphate rock. Reaction equation:

$$4 HF + SiO_2 \rightarrow Si F_4 + 2 H_2O.$$

Thus a mixture of hydrogen fluoride and silicon tetrafluoride is formed. About one-third of the fluorine present in phosphate rock is evaporated in these forms at the curing temperature. For this reason the dens for curing superphosphate must be closed chambers equipped with means to collect the vapours. These vapours are usually absorbed in water in spray towers or in vapour condensers. In the latter the gases are caused to pass through a number of chambers with transverse partitions while rotating plates placed under the partitions allow water which has been admitted to splash up in a fairly thick mist. The fluorine compounds dissolve in this. Most of the solution goes to waste since recovery of fluorine compounds is often too expensive. Sometimes the fluorine is recovered in the form of sodium fluorosilicate (Na_2SiF_6) by means of soda ash.

c. Characteristic equipment. The reaction of phosphate with sulphuric acid is carried out continuously or by a batch process. Modern plants all work continuously, but there are nevertheless a fairly large number of batch plants.

The mixing devices of a batch plant are usually cast-iron vessels provided with one

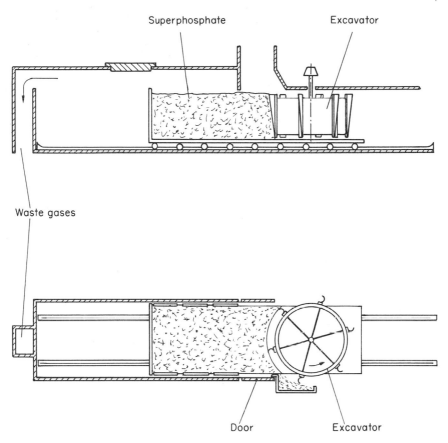

Fig. 9.34 Simplified diagram of the Beskov den.

or more stirrers (see mixers, vol. VII). The main differences between the batch plants refer to the form of the dens and the method of excavation.

For example, the *Beskov den* (see fig. 9.34) is a car from which the sides can be removed when the superphosphate contained has been hardened. The solidified mass on the car is excavated and pulverized by moving the car to the excavator. The latter consists of a cylindrical steel framework rotating on a vertical shaft. The framework is provided with a series of cutting knives arranged in staggered relation to one another. The *Sturtevant den* is basically the same, but in this an excavator moves into the fixed den. Such dens usually have a capacity of 20-50 tons, but large concrete dens having a capacity up to 400 tons have also been built. These dens are discharged by means of large shredding machines. The production capacity is relatively low since several hours (up to eight) are needed for filling the den.

In the modern continuous plants the powdered phosphate rock and sulphuric acid are fed simultaneously and continuously into a mixer. The mixer is a horizontal cast-steel trough. Through the entire length of the trough runs a horizontal shaft which is equipped with several mixing blades. These mixing blades mix and transport the slurry of phosphate and acid at the same time. The mixed material is discharged into a den. Two quite different kinds of dens which operate continuously are in use.

The *Broadfield den* consists of three slowly moving conveyors, one of which forms the floor and the other two the side walls. There are also fixed end walls and a fixed roof. The superphosphate hardens into a block on the conveyers, which feed it on to an excavator which cuts it off. These plants are made with capacities of between 10 and 35 metric tons per hour. The *Nordengren den* (see fig. 9.35) and *Kuhlmann den* are basically the same as the Broadfield den but consist of one conveyor in a closed chamber. A similar conveyor den is used in the newer *Sackett process*. However, in this process the reaction between the pulverized phosphate rock and sulphuric acid is accelerated by spraying the starting materials in reaction towers. The reaction product is passed through a mixer and then discharged into the den. The capacity is 20 to 50 tons per hour.

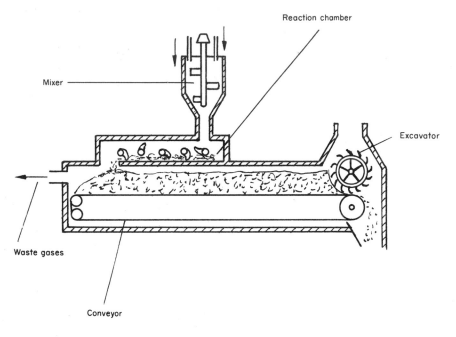

Fig. 9.35   Diagram of a continuous conveyor superphosphate den.

A quite different continuous den is used in the *Moritz Standaert process* (see fig. 9.36). The den consists of a concrete-lined circular construction rotating slowly around a vertical shaft. The den is covered by a fixed roof. A curved cast-iron plate, which is attached to the roof, is placed in the den near the wall. The superphosphate slurry is fed continuously into the space between the plate and the wall of the den. The superphosphate hardens during the very slow rotation of the den and an annular cake is formed. This cake is excavated at the other side of the curved plate by means of a rotating scraping device. The Moritz Standaert dens have a capacity of 7 to 20 tons per hour.

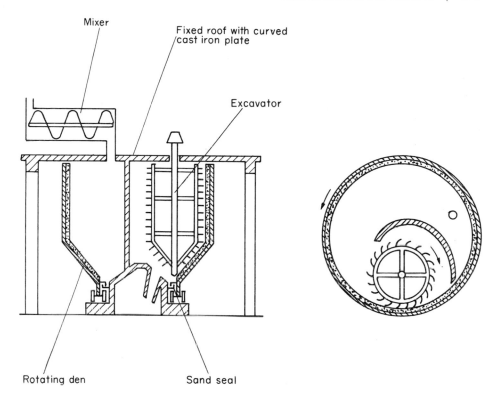

Mixer

Fixed roof with curved
cast iron plate

Excavator

Rotating den

Sand seal

Fig. 9.36 Diagram of the Moritz Standaert den and horizontal cross-section.

9.18.5 Production of triple superhphosphate

This is obtained by treating phosphate rock with phosphoric acid instead of sulphuric acid, the reaction being (for example):

$$Ca_5(PO_4)_3 F + 7H_3PO_4 \rightarrow 5 Ca (H_2PO_4)_2 + HF$$

Phosphoric acid of 70-78% strength is commonly used.

As a result of this, the superphosphate is not diluted with any less active material (such as calcium sulphate). The more valuable 'triple' thus involves relatively lower freight costs.

The equipment is basically the same as for continuous production of normal superphosphate. Since the setting time of the slurry obtained is only three to four minutes, the processes are slightly modified. The dens for normal superphosphate such as the Broadfield den can be used when triple superphosphate is prepared with phosphoric acid of less strength such as wet process phosphoric acid. A simple one-step continuous process for the production of granular triple superphosphate has been developed in the United States. Finely divided phosphate rock (including recycled dust) is introduced into a rotating drum. Concentrated phosphoric acid (or preheated wet process phosphoric acid) and steam are fed through perforated pipe distributors under the bed of tumbling solids in the drum. The product obtained passes through a rotating cooler and is then screened. Large pieces are crushed and recycled along with the dust to the rotating reactor. No drying is required.

9.18.6 Properties and use of normal and triple superphosphate

The superphosphates are grey in colour and are obtained as a powder or as a granular product. The main constituent of the superphosphates is monocalcium (ortho) phosphate. The minor constituents are dicalcium phosphate and tricalcium phosphate (besides the gypsum content of normal super).

Monocalcium phosphate (primary calcium phosphate, $Ca (H_2PO_4)_2$), the effective constituent of normal and triple superphosphate, is soluble in water. Dicalcium phosphate ($CaHPO_4$) is very much less soluble in water but dissolves in a neutral ammonium citrate solution.

The superphosphates are only used as fertilizers. The water-soluble types are more effective for direct use than those which are insoluble in water. This is important in the case of granular fertilizers which are intended to be quick acting. The nature of the plant, the pH of the soil and many other factors influence the estimation of their value.

Superphosphate is marketed according to its content of water-soluble P_2O_5. It comes on the market with contents between 16 and 22% P_2O_5 as normal (or single) superphosphate, and with contents from 40 to 46% P_2O_5 as triple (or double) super-phosphate.

9.18.7 Statistics

As already stated, the starting material for almost all phosphorus compounds (including fertilizers) is phosphate rock. Relatively small quantities of products containing phosphorus are produced from bones, tankage, fishmeal and basic slag (see fertilizers, vol. VII). The production of concentrated phosphate rock by the major producers and the world production are as follows:

| | In '000s metric tons (including guano) | | | | | |
	1938	1948	1953	1958	1961	1963
World (excl. USSR)	—	17 100	26 700	35 300	43 300	50 000
Algeria	584	671	619	565	426	340
Christmas Island	162	178	285	350	789	730
France	87	105	83	69	35	44
French Polynesia	113	187	276	368	425	330
Gilbert and Ellis Isl.	304	127	287	329	306	350
Israel	—	—	23	210	226	295
Jordan	—	—	40	294	423	605
Morocco	1487	3226	4097	6538	7950	8400
Nauru (Oceania)	855	268	1247	1186	1360	1550
Netherlands Antilles	99	59	96	87	152	126
Peru	—	—	261	166	159	189
South Africa	2034	1864	1719	2280	1982	2330
Tunisia	458	300	443	558	627	602
UAR (Egypt)	—	40	80	217	297	450
USA	3922	9539	12704	15118	18857	19840
USSR (estimated)	—	—	4030	6000	8600	10900

The figures relate to concentrated phosphate rock containing from 68-78% BPL (bone phosphate of lime) in most cases. Although world production of phosphate rock is about 50 million tons and is still increasing, world reserves are large enough to cover world demand for thousand of years. In 1953 the world reserves were estimated at 100000 million tons of BPL excluding reserves of several South American and Asian countries. Phosphate rock is imported by almost all European countries. The imports of the United Kingdom were:

	1955	1957	1959	1961	1963
In 1000 tons	1132	1102	1056	1356	1414
In 1000 £	7603	7476	6446	7985	8422

Since most phosphate rock is used for the production of superphosphates, the imports of the most important countries can roughly be estimated from the production of superphosphates. The production of superphosphates (normal and triple) by the major producing countries is shown in the following table:

	P_2O_5 content %	1938	1948	1953	1958	1961	1963
				In '000s metric tons			
Australia	—	1253	1205	1606	2256	2572	2900
France	17	1370	1651	1018	1273	1365	1550
Italy	19	1406	1225	1864	1787	1560	1475
Japan	16	1234	993	1427	1917	1879	1660
Netherlands	18	570	882	733	1056	1083	970
New Zealand	20	—	567	691	805	1067	1220
Poland	15-18	—	—	425	581	823	1010
Spain	18	190	708	1282	1789	1627	1990
United Kingdom	19 ⎰	432	1121	1028	773	665	525
	46 ⎱			67	116	169	70
USA	18	3443	9511	10763	10724	11446	11790
USSR	19	—	—	—	—	6800	7860

Source: *Statistical yearbook of the UN.*

About 12-15% of the total superphosphate production in Western Europe is triple superphosphate (calculated in terms of P_2O_5). It is mainly produced in the United Kingdom and the Netherlands.

In the United States about 25% of the phosphate rock produced is used for the production of normal superphosphates; 16% for triple superphosphate, 2% for de-fluorinated rock etc., 21% for wet process phosphoric acid, and 16% for the production of elemental phosphorus. The remaining 20% is exported.

In other countries relatively more phosphate rock is used for the production of superphosphates. The technical and pure calcium phosphates which are produced from phosphoric acid (see below) demand only 2% of the original phosphate in the USA. Prices of phosphate rock and superphosphate in the USA were: In 1965 normal superphosphate, $ 15 to $ 20 per ton depending on the P_2O_5 content; triple superphosphate, $ 40 to $ 46 per ton depending on the P_2O_5 content; phosphate rock, $ 6 to $ 10 per ton depending on the BPL content.

9.18.8 Technical and pure calcium (ortho) phosphates

The commercial pure calcium phosphates are not prepared directly from phosphate rock and superphosphates by purification, but from phosphoric acid and lime.

Monocalcium orthophosphate, $Ca(H_2PO_4)_2$, is prepared by reacting concentrated phosphoric acid with a lime slurry at a temperature of about 80° C. A crystalline hydrated salt having the formula $Ca(H_2PO_4)_2 \cdot H_2O$ is obtained. It is a fertilizer, and it is also a common baking powder ingredient which prevents 'rope' when added to bread.

In view of the requirement that phosphates for food may not contain fluorine, it must be prepared from fluorine-free materials, which makes it dearer than the grade of phosphate used as fertilizer.

The price of monocalcium phosphate was $ 7.45 per 100 lb in 1965.

Dicalcium orthophosphate, $CaHPO_4 \cdot 2H_2O$ is manufactured by reacting phosphoric acid (30-40%) with a lime slurry at a temperature of about 25° C. It is employed in dental polishing agents.

Anhydrous dicalcium phosphate is used in animal feeding stuffs. For this reason it is prepared from wet process phosphoric acid having a low fluorine content. Dicalcium phosphate is the most important of the commercial pure calcium phosphates. The USA produced 240 000 tons in 1963. In the USA the pure grade was sold at $ 8.25 per 100 lb and the feed-grade at $ 4.20 to $ 4.80 per 100 lb in 1965.

Tricalcium orthophosphate, $Ca_3(PO_4)_2$ exhibits the unusual property of improving the flowability of dry powders when mixed in amounts of about 1%. Hence it is employed in sugar and salt. It has also anti-caking properties in powders which are somewhat hygroscopic, such as table salt.

Important quantities of tricalcium phosphate are added to tooth pastes.

Tricalcium phosphate was sold at $ 9.25 per 100 lb in 1965.

9.19 OTHER PHOSPHORUS COMPOUNDS

9.19.1 Phosphine and metal phosphides

Phosphine (hydrogen phosphide, PH_3) is a colourless, very poisonous gas which may be prepared by dissolving white phosphorus in warm caustic potash and collecting the gas evolved:

$$4 P + 3 KOH + 3H_2O \rightarrow PH_3 + 3 KH_2PO_2$$

Large quantities of very pure phosphine are obtained by treating a mixture of magnesium phosphide and aluminium phosphide with water. Simultaneously magnesium hydroxide and aluminium hydroxide are formed:

$$Mg_3P_2 + 2 AlP + 12H_2O \rightarrow 4 PH_3 + 3 Mg(OH)_2 + 2 Al(OH)_3.$$

Phosphine forms salts (phosphonium salts) like ammonia. By mixing phosphine gas with hydriodic acid gas, white crystals of phosphonium iodide are obtained:

$$PH_3 + HI \rightarrow PH_4I.$$

Tetrakishydroxymethyl phosphonium chloride is obtained by reacting phosphine with formaldehyde and hydrochloric acid:

$$4\,CH_2O + HCl + PH_3 \rightarrow (HOCH_2)_4\,PCl.$$

Metal phosphides may be produced by heating red phosphorus with the appropriate metal in atomized form (in a protective atmosphere).

Phosphides of the alkali metals and alkaline earth metals react vigorously with water, with the formation of phosphine. Aluminium phosphide and zinc phosphide react slowly with water and phosphides of other metals either do not react or else show a very slow reaction with water. The phosphine obtained from alkali phosphides or calcium phosphide contains small quantities of the spontaneously inflammable di-phosphine (P_2H_4) and for this reason it burns spontaneously in air to give phosphorus pentoxide and water, according to the following equation:

$$2\,PH_3 + 4\,O_2 \rightarrow P_2O_5 + 3\,H_2O.$$

The smoke of phosphorus pentoxide and phosphoric acid formed therefrom is visible by day and the highly luminous flame is visible by night. The phosphine obtained from aluminium phosphide and magnesium phosphide does not contain diphosphine and for this reason it does not ignite spontaneously in air unless about 0.1-1% of nitric oxide is mixed with it. Because of these properties some phosphides are used in sea-flares.

The slow evolution of pure phosphine from aluminium phosphide with moisture may be used in fumigation of grain containing weevil. Packets of aluminium phosphide may be placed in the grain for about one day.

Fatal poisoning has occurred by phosphine which penetrated common walls between granaries and dwelling houses.

Zinc phosphide is used as a rat and mole poison. Some phosphides are used in preparing phosphorus-containing metal alloys, e.g. phosphor bronze (see vol. III).

Ferrophosphorus which contains iron phosphide is used as an auxiliary material in the manufacture of steel. (Ferrophosphorus is obtained as a by-product in the production of phosphorus; see p. 365.)

9.19.2 Phosphorus sulphides

There are several sulphur compounds of phosphorus, containing different quantities of sulphur. These compounds are manufactured technically by passing molten white phosphorus into molten sulphur in a cast iron vessel under a carbon dioxide atmosphere. The white phosphorus is added in small quantities, as it reacts very violently with sulphur at temperatures above 200° C.

The reaction mixture, containing calculated quantities of sulphur and phosphorus, is heated for some time at 320-380° C if *phosphorus sesquisulphide,* the most important sulphide, is to be prepared. Phosphorus sesquisulphide (P_4S_3) is purified by vacuum distillation or by washing, using either water or dilute sodium bicarbonate solution. The resulting product is a yellow crystalline powder melting at 172° C. It has very low toxicity. Hence it is used in the manufacture of 'strike anywhere' matches. These matches are fairly dangerous as they can ignite spontaneously by accidental friction.

Phosphorus pentasulphide (P_2S_5) is prepared by heating a mixture of precise quantities of phosphorus and sulphur at a temperature of 300-400° C. Phosphorus pentasulphide is purified by washing with carbon disulphide. It may not be washed with water, which decomposes it slowly. The resulting sulphide is a yellow crystalline product melting at 286-290° C. It is a starting material in the preparation of several organic compounds, for example mercaptans, thiophosphate esters and several insecticides (see organic compounds, vol. IV and insecticides, vol. V). It is also used as a lubricant additive.

The phosphorus sulphides may also be prepared from red phosphorus and sulphur. This reaction is not violent.

9.19.3 Phosphorus chlorides

Phosphorus trichloride (PCl_3) is manufactured by burning molten white phosphorus in dry chlorine gas. White phosphorus and chlorine gas are continuously introduced into the reaction mixture. The phosphorus trichloride vapour obtained is condensed and purified by fractional distillation. The reaction is started in the presence of a phosphorus trichloride 'precharge' which moderates the reaction heat by evaporation. During the reaction a part of the PCl_3 obtained is refluxed in order to cool the reaction mixture.

Phosphorus trichloride is a colourless fuming liquid boiling at 76° C and decomposing in the presence of water. The liquid as well as the vapour is corrosive and dangerous. They cause damage to living tissue especially of the eyes, mouth and lungs. Phosphorus trichloride is used in the production of di- and trialkyl phosphites, phosphorus oxychloride, phosphorus pentachloride and phosphorous acid. It is also used in the production of dyes, pharmaceuticals, insecticides and lubricant additives.

In the USA about 37000 short tons of phosphorus trichloride were produced in 1963. Its price was $ 0.10 to $ 0.12 per lb in 1965.

Phosphorus pentachloride (PCl_5) may be prepared by spraying molten trichloride into a chlorine atmosphere or by introducing chlorine into a solution of PCl_3 in carbon tetrachloride. The crystalline phosphorus pentachloride is separated by filtration.

Phosphorus pentachloride is a colourless-to-pale yellow solid which sublimes at about 100° C and decomposes with water. Like phosphorus trichloride it is a dangerous product. It is used in organic synthesis, e.g. for converting alcohols and organic acids to halogen containing hydrocarbons and acid chlorides respectively (see organic compounds, vol. IV).

On a small scale the phosphorus chlorides are also prepared from red phosphorus and chlorine.

Phosphorus oxychloride ($POCl_3$) is prepared by oxidation of phosphorus trichloride by gaseous oxygen. The gas is passed through the phosphorus trichloride in small bubbles. The heat of reaction is removed by cooling. The yield is about 98% of a colourless fuming liquid which solidifies at 1° C and boils at 107° C. Like phosphorus trichloride and pentachloride, phosphorus oxychloride causes damage to living tissue and is unstable in the presence of water.

Nickel and lead-lined metal equipment is used for production and transport of the phosphorus chlorides and oxychloride. Vacuum equipment is widely used in manufacture and it must be kept absolutely dry. Those using phosphorus chlorides and oxychloride must wear gas masks with some air pressure to avoid inhaling the very dangerous vapours of these substances.

Phosphorus oxychloride is important in forming esters of phosphoric acid which are used as insecticides, plasticizers, gasoline additives, etc.

The production of phosphorus oxychloride was about 24000 short tons in the USA in 1963. In 1965 the US price of phosphorus oxychloride was $ 0.12 to $ 0.14 per lb; the price in the United Kingdom was 1s 1d.

9.19.4 Phosphonitrilic polymers

A mixture of polyphosphonitrilic chlorides may be prepared by reacting phosphorus pentachloride with ammonium chloride (NH_4Cl) in an inert solvent such as tetrachloroethane at a temperature of 135° C and distilling off the solvent in vacuo.

$$n PCl_5 + n\,NH_4Cl \rightarrow (NPCl_2)n + 4\,n\,HCl.\ n = 1, 2, 3, 4, 5, \text{etc.}$$

A solid trimer and tetramer are separated from the resulting buttery mixture by extracting with low boiling petroleum ether.

The basis of these polymers is the $- PCl_2 = N -$ group, the shortest having three such groups combined in a ring:

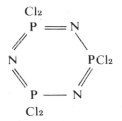

The other polymers for which $n = 4, 5, 6$ and 7 also exhibit ring structures.

When heated at 300° C the trimeric phosphonitrilic chloride is converted into a rubbery polymer which is said to be built up from very long chains having the following structure:

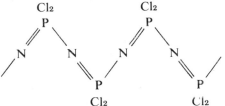

This polymer is an example of a truly inorganic polymer.

Some polymers can be used for fireproofing fabrics and plastics. Materials produced from asbestos and a mixture of polyphosphonitrilic chlorides, having 3-6 $NPCl_2$ groups, are suitable for gaskets, insulators and packings for use at temperatures up to 500° C.

The chlorine atoms in phosphonitrilic chlorides are replaceable by monovalent groups. Hence many other compounds can be prepared from them. Polymeric phosphonitrilic esters are prepared by reacting a solution of the trimer or tetramer in pyridine with alcohols.

The compounds obtained are useful plasticisers for the plastics industry (see plastics, vol. IV).

9.19.5 Organic phosphorus compounds

Esters of phosphoric acid may be prepared by reacting phosphorus pentoxide, phosphorus oxychloride or phosphorus pentachloride with alcohols or phenols (see also esters in organic compounds chapter, vol. IV).

Several triaryl phosphates and trialkyl phosphates (neutral esters) are used as flame retardant plasticizers in plastics. The most important neutral ester is tricresyl phosphate. Some esters are also used as gasoline or lubricant additives and as insecticides.

Tributyl phosphate is used as an anti-foaming agent in water-based paints and inks.

Liquid trialkyl phosphates (and dialkyl acid phosphates), being immiscible with water, are used in liquid-liquid extraction processes for the separation of uranium ions from other metal ions in acidic aqueous solutions (having a pH of about 1). Uranium carbonate can be precipitated by adding sodium carbonate to the solution in trialkyl phosphate.

Vanadium ions may be extracted from an aqueous solution at a pH of about 2-3. Thus uranium and vanadium ions can be extracted selectively from a solution containing both ions.

Monoalkyl acid phosphates such as monobutyl phosphate are acidic catalysts for the polymerisation (hardening) of urea- and phenol-formaldehyde resins at low temperatures. Hence they can be mixed with the resins in enamels so that objects can be enamelled and baked without any risk of damage owing to a high temperature.

Phosphorous acid esters act as stabilizers in synthetic rubber, oils and plastics such as low pressure polyethylene. Triphenyl phosphite stabilizes the colour of alkyl resins.

Thiophosphate esters are used as flotation agents and insecticides.

Tributyl phosphine is used as a gasoline additive. Other phosphine derivatives (phosphonium compounds) may be employed in flameproofing plastics and textiles (see vol. IV).

Combating insects, nematodes, etc. is a very important application of several organic phosphorus compounds (see insecticides, vol. VII). Various organic phosphorus compounds are nerve gases which are similar in physiological properties to the insecticides.

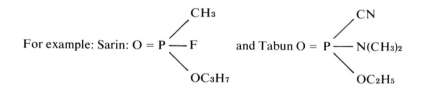

For example: Sarin: O = P⟨CH₃, —F, OC₃H₇   and Tabun O = P⟨CN, —N(CH₃)₂, OC₂H₅

9.19.6 Literature

W. H. WAGGAMAN. *Phosphoric acid, phosphates and phosphatic fertilizers,* 2nd edn. New York, Reinhold, 1952. ACS monograph no. 34.

J. R. V. WAZER. *Phosphorus and its compounds:* volume I, *Chemistry:* volume II, *Technology: biological functions and applications.* New York, Interscience Publishers, 1955, 1961.

V. SAUCHELLI. *Chemistry and technology of fertilizers.* New York, Reinhold, 1960. ACS monograph, no. 148.

9.20 ARSENIC AND ITS COMPOUNDS (As, atomic weight = 74.91)

9.20.1 History and occurrence

Both naturally occurring sulphides, realgar and orpiment (derived from *auri-pigmentum,* which refers to the yellow colour) were known to the philosopher Aristotle. The roasting of arsenic sulphides to white arsenic was described for the first time by Dioscorides in the first century A. D. The element was probably first prepared as such by Albertus Magnus (about 1 250). From the age of the alchemists white arsenic has often been used as a poison. It was also taken in minute amounts as a means of improving the skin and hair. Paracelsus introduced the use of arsenic compounds in medicine.

Native arsenic is only found in very small quantities, mainly in ores of silver and cobalt. Several minerals containing arsenic are known but only a few are of commercial importance. The most important minerals are arsenopyrites (a mixture of iron sulphide (FeS_2) and iron arsenide ($FeAs_2$), containing 46% arsenic), arsenical pyrites or löllingite (iron arsenide, containing 73% arsenic), and the arsenic sulphides: realgar AsS and orpiment As_2S_3 (see also paints, vol. V).

The major quantities of arsenic compounds are obtained as a by-product of the treatment of other metal ores. Arsenic, in the form of the sulphide or of a metal arsenide, accompanies various other ores, particularly those of gold, silver, lead, copper, nickel and cobalt, e.g. enargite ($3 Cu_2S.As_2S_5$) and smaltite ($CoAs_2$). In general arsenic is so widely distributed that metals produced from sulphide ores are almost invariably arsenical. The complete removal of arsenic from metals is often very difficult. As a result of the presence of arsenic in iron pyrites, a certain amount of this element is always present in cast iron. The cumulative effect of this can lead, in the long run, to a general deterioration in the quality of cast iron, when scrap iron is re-used. In high quality steel, an arsenic content higher than 0.03-0.04% is not permitted, since quantities in excess of this adversely affect the properties.

9.20.2 Elemental arsenic

Elemental arsenic is only produced in small quantities. It can be prepared by heating arsenical pyrites or arsenopyrites in a cast-iron vessel. Elemental arsenic sublimes and can be collected in a water-cooled condenser. Arsenic is mostly produced by reduction of arsenic trioxide by heating with charcoal and collecting the sublimed arsenic. Since impurities are carried over, resublimation is often required to get a pure product (for example by distillation *in vacuo* with the aid of a stream of hydrogen). For very pure arsenic purified starting materials are used.

Like phosphorus, arsenic exists in several modifications. The ordinary form is grey arsenic. This is a steel-grey crystalline mass which sublimes without melting at 604° C, under normal pressure. This metallic product is brittle, rather soft and not very poisonous. It must be noted that very poisonous yellow arsenic is formed when arsenic vapour is suddenly cooled. Yellow arsenic consists of crystals which are plastic and soft as wax. Other modifications are black and brown arsenic (compare modifications of phosphorus and sulphur, pp. 367 and 264).

Elemental arsenic is used for alloying with lead. Lead containing 0.5% of arsenic is particularly suitable for shot. Rounder shot is obtained since arsenic increases the surface tension of molten lead. Alloys containing up to 0.5% arsenic are prepared with copper, brass and bearing metals. Copper which contains small quantities of arsenic is used in seamless copper boilers, condenser tubes and in locomotive staybolts. Arsenic increases the strength of copper at higher temperatures (up to about 200° C). Only small quantities of arsenic can be used in alloys since the alloys become brittle when larger amounts are used. Thin coatings of arsenic are sometimes applied to copper or iron by dipping polished copper or iron in a solution of arsenic trioxide (As_2O_3) in hydrochloric acid. This method is used to give the appearance of steel plating on copper or iron ornaments, umbrella knobs, etc. Small quantities of high purity arsenic (up to 99.999% purity) are used in the production of the raw materials for transistors.

The production of metallic arsenic is very low as compared with arsenic trioxide production. The world production is not known, but it may be a few hundreds of tons per year. Sweden exported 150 tons of metallic arsenic to the United States in 1963. It was sold at $ 0.50 per lb.

Fig. 9.37 Filter section of an arsenic trioxide factory. The exhaust equipment is clearly visible.

9.20.3 Arsenic trioxide

Most arsenic trioxide (arsenious oxide, white arsenic, As_2O_3) is obtained as a by-product from the roasting (i.e. heating in the presence of air) of other ores at temperatures between 550 and 1 000°C depending on the kind of ore (see occurrence, p. 393). The most important quantities are obtained from the gold mines in Boliden (Sweden) and from the copper-lead ores and copper ores in Montana, USA. It occurs in the flue dust from the roasting plants (see also fig. 9.37). Hence the production is restricted to the collection of these dusts from fly-ash channels, Cottrell separators, bag filters, etc. and the recovery and purification of the white arsenic contained in them (see also the roasting processes and furnaces in the sulphur chapter, p. 273).

The flue dust (containing about 30% As_2O_3) is roasted again at a temperature of about 550° C and the gases pass a dust separator which is kept at a temperature above the condensation point of white arsenic. The dust-free gas is cooled in a series of condensing chambers. The temperature ranges from about 200° C in the first to 100° C in the last chamber. An impure grey mass, containing up to 95% As_2O_3 is obtained in the first and a white crystalline product of 99 to 99.9% purity in the last chambers. The impure particles can be purified by repeated evaporation and condensation.

Arsenopyrites can be treated in a similar way. However lead-lined condensers sprayed with water to flush out the condensed arsenic trioxide are necessary since the gases contain much corrosive sulphur dioxide.

Arsenic trioxide is a dense material (spec. gr. 3.71) which vaporizes readily when heated. Its melting point is 310° C and its boiling point 465° C. On condenser walls having a temperature above 310° C it condenses in the form of a glass (arsenic glass). Below this temperature a crystalline product is obtained. Arsenic trioxide has weakly acidic properties and dissolves in alkaline solutions to form arsenites (salts of the tribasic arsenious acid, H_3AsO_3, or the monobasic meta-arsenious acid, $HAsO_2$). Arsenic trioxide is slightly soluble in water.

Both arsenic trioxide and arsenic compounds of other types are deadly poisons to the higher and lower animals. The highly poisonous effect is so that the ore-roasting process of the ore from Boliden is carried out on an isolated island, the off-gases being removed by means of a chimney 145 metres high; strict watch must nevertheless be kept for As_2O_3 in the gases evolved as with an east wind the population on the mainland would be in danger. It can also happen, particularly as the result of using impure mineral acids, that arsenic compounds are present in beverages and foodstuffs. For example, an epidemic of arsenic poisoning once occurred in England. It was caused by beer containing glucose which was prepared with sulphuric acid containing traces of arsenic. In general the tolerated maximum arsenic content is around 0.1 p.p.m. for beverages and up to 1 p.p.m. for solid foodstuffs. In dyes for foodstuffs, not more than 5 p.p.m. may be present, and in dry extract of liquorice 2 p.p.m. is the maximum.

It appears that, in the healthy human hair at the most 0.03 mg of arsenic per 100 g is present; in cases of arsenic poisoning, this can rise, especially in the hair roots, to 2.2 mg per 100 g of hair (even when arsenic compounds are consumed in small portions over a relatively long period arsenic poisoning can occur since arsenic is cumulative). In the finger nails, after administration for a month, 13 mg per 100 g and in the toe nails up to 6 mg per 100 g, have been found.

Arsenic trioxide is the starting material for all arsenic compounds (e.g. arsenic trichloride, arsenites and arsenates) which are used in insecticides, weedkillers, cattle and sheep dips, wood preservatives, pharmaceuticals, etc. Calcium arsenate and lead arsenate (see p. 398) are the most important compounds. Fruits and other vegetables sprayed with arsenic compounds must be carefully washed and peeled to avoid dangerous poisoning, since arsenic compounds remain on the surface of fruit, etc., for a very long time.

Arsenic trioxide as such is used as rodent poison and in the East in particular, it is used for the preservation of skins and furs. Arsenic trioxide is also used in glass manufacture. It forms colourless complexes with ferrous iron and with manganese, thus removing the green colour caused by the former and the violet colour caused by the latter.

The production of arsenic trioxide by the most important producers and the world production are shown in the following table:

	1936	1950	1956	In short tons 1958	1960	1962	1963
Belgium (exports)	3000	2100	3060	540	—	—	—
Canada	680		900	1160	860	80	90
France	11000	3100	9460	8350	9200	10300	11000
Italy	—	700	1170	930	650	140	—
Japan	3000	—	1830	1430	1250	1100	1100
Mexico	10000	9700	2910	3410	13400	12000	12000
Portugal	190	660	1660	1170	800	630	700
Sweden	34000	3200	13440	11190	13000	12000	12000
United States	15000	13000	12200	11510	—	—	—
World (estim.)	90000	46000	48000	41000	57000	54000	54000

The United Kingdom imports of arsenic trioxide are set out below:

	1955	1957	1959	1961	1963
In long tons	6100	3300	4600	8600	8800
In £			139000	259000	269000

The major proportion is exported in the form of arsenic compounds of which the value, per ton, is twice the value of arsenic trioxide.

Sweden (Boliden) alone would easily be able to meet the demand of the whole world. Enormous quantities of arsenic were stored in that country in prewar years since excess arsenic trioxide was obtained in the processing of gold ore. Because of its toxicity it could not be disposed of. After the second world war the stock was about 350000 tons, which was stored in three large storehouses. The stored quantity has probably not much increased in the last fifteen years.

The sudden decrease in the US production and the increased production in Mexico is remarkable. The Mexican arsenic trioxide is obtained from several ores and is processed by US companies, who export the whole output to the United States.

The decline of the world production before 1958 was caused by the decreasing use of arsenic trioxide for the production of insecticides (due to the development of various other insecticides such as DDT and organic phosphorus compounds). The decrease in the use for insecticides has probably stopped now since arsenic compounds are used for combating insects which have become immune to organic insecticides.

In the years after the second world war several new uses for arsenic compounds which were developed, e.g. leaf desiccant and wood preservation, increased output. About 50% of the world production of arsenic trioxide is consumed in the United States. Weed killers and leaf desiccants accounted for 49%, insecticides (including cattle dips) for 28% and the glass industry for 17% of the consumption in 1959. Before the second world war 70% was used as insecticide.

In 1965 the price of crude arsenic trioxide (95%) in the USA was $ 0.032 to $0.048 per lb; arsenic trioxide (99%) was sold at $0.041-0.059 per lb and pharmaceutical grade at 0.48 lb.

9.20.4 Arsenites

Arsenites are salts of ortho-arsenious acid (H_3AsO_3) or meta-arsenious acid ($HAsO_2$). These acids are not known in a free state. Arsenic trioxide is obtained at once if these acids are liberated by adding acids to arsenites.

Sodium arsenite ($NaAsO_2$) is produced by mixing arsenic trioxide with solid sodium hydroxide. The reaction is started by adding a small quantity of water. A water-soluble powder is obtained after grinding the resulting solid mass. Sodium arsenite absorbs carbon dioxide from air and is very poisonous. In contrast with insoluble arsenic compounds which are less poisonous for vegetable life, water-soluble arsenic compounds such as sodium arsenite are very poisonous to both vegetable and animal life. Hence they cannot be used as insecticides on commercial crops or for killing weeds growing with commercial crops.

Sodium arsenite is used in insecticides, especially for destroying locusts and mosquito larvae in regions without commercial crops. In the United States it is also used in washes for cattle and sheep (dips) to combat the usually fatal Texas fever. This dangerous infection could be stamped out by the use of sodium arsenite and the introduction of barbed wire, which prevents cattle from approaching the bushes containing the ticks, which transmit the infection. Sodium arsenite is still used as a weedkiller though newer products are coming increasingly to the fore here. It is used for killing crab grass and weeds on paths, road verges etc. In the United States, sodium arsenite is used as a cotton desiccant (to dry up the leaves on cotton plants so that mechanical pickers can do more efficient jobs). In Great Britain the use of sodium arsenite as a potato haulm killer has not been permitted since 1960. Small quantities of sodium arsenite are used for the preservation of skins and furs and in arsenical soaps for taxidermists.

Sodium arsenite was sold at $ 0.18 to $ 0.19 per lb in 1965.

Copper arsenite (Scheele's green, $Cu(AsO_2)_2$) and a double salt of copper arsenite and copper acetate (Schweinfurt green or Paris green) are precipitated by mixing a solution of sodium arsenite with a solution of a copper salt. Small quantities of these compounds are used as insecticides and as fungicides for wood preservation. Ammoniacal solutions are used for impregnating wood.

These compounds were used about a century ago as beautiful green pigments for printing expensive wallpapers and clothes. Owing to the danger of dust particles given off by them these pigments were replaced by aniline dyes. However arsenic acid was formerly used as oxidizing agent in the production of these dyes in which traces of arsenic then remained. This contributed to the bad reputation of certain wallpapers. Improved techniques and stricter control have meant the end of this danger.

Zinc arsenite sometimes mixed with copper sulphate is also used for wood preservation and in some insecticides.

9.20.5 Arsenic acid and arsenates

Arsenic acid (H_3AsO_4) is prepared by oxidizing arsenic trioxide with nitric acid. Arsenic trioxide is added to an equivalent quantity of a 38% solution of nitric acid. The fumes of nitrogen oxides are recovered and converted into nitric acid again. The equipment is made of stainless steel. Unlike arsenious acid, arsenic acid can be obtained as a crystalline solid. Arsenic acid is hygroscopic and its solubility in water is enormous. 630 g in terms of As_2O_5 can be dissolved in 100 g water of 20° C. When heated at 500°C it can be converted into arsenic pentoxide As_2O_5. However this is very hygroscopic and forms arsenic acid again with moisture. Arsenic acid is an oxidizing agent, hence it is used in the synthesis of organic chemicals (see also arsenites). Arsenic acid is also of importance for the production of certain important pharmaceuticals such as Salvarsan and Neosalvarsan. The major portion of arsenic acid is used for the production of arsenates.

Sodium arsenates are prepared by mixing arsenic acid with a solution of sodium hydroxide in appropriate proportions. Disodium arsenate (Na_2HAsO_4) is the most important. It is mainly used for the production of other arsenates. Smaller quantities are used as mordant in the dyeing and printing of textiles. In the United States it is also used in Wolman salt. This is a wood preservative consisting of sodium fluoride, sodium bichromate, sodium arsenate (25%) and dinitrophenol. In Sweden a mixture of arsenic acid (20%), sodium arsenate (21%), sodium bichromate and zinc sulphate, named 'Boliden salt' is used for the preservation of wood. It appears that it is especially effective against the extremely destructive teredo (ship- or pile-worm).

Monopotassium arsenate is obtained from arsenic acid and potassium hydroxide. It is used as insecticide in flypaper.

Calcium arsenate ($Ca_3(AsO_4)_2.3H_2O$) is prepared by adding a solution of arsenic acid to milk of lime. The flow rate, temperature, velocity of stirring and the mixing proportions are carefully controlled to obtain a precipitate which contains some free lime. The precipitate is dried and finely ground. Precautions must be taken in handling dust of calcium arsenate since it is very poisonous. Calcium arsenate is mainly used as insecticide, especially for combating boll weevil on cotton. It is also used for the protection of potato plants against the Colorado beetle. A product containing free lime is preferred for these purposes, since calcium arsenate itself shows a tendency to decompose to calcium carbonate and acid calcium arsenate in the presence of carbon dioxide from air. Acid calcium arsenate is more soluble in water than the neutral arsenate and thus it is more harmful for the plants sprayed with it. But when free lime is present in calcium arsenate, the decomposition is delayed until all free lime is converted into the carbonate, the lime acting as an absorbent for the carbon dioxide.

The USA is an important producing country. However the production (and also exports) have declined during recent years. The production and the exports of the USA were:

	In short tons			
	1957	*1959*	*1961*	*1963*
Production 70% $Ca_3(AsO_4)_2$	9 700	3 200	4 000	1 650
Exports	1 400	60	330	

In 1965 the price was $ 0.09 to $ 0.10 per lb (in drums).

Lead arsenate is prepared by reacting a suspension of lead oxide (litharge) with arsenic acid or a solution of a lead salt (e.g. lead nitrate) with disodium arsenate. Acid lead arsenate $PbHAsO_4$ precipitates. This is filtered off, dried and packed, after having been ground to a fine powder. As is the case with calcium arsenate, strict precautions must be taken, in the manufacture and especially in the grinding and packing, against the inhalation or absorption in any other way of the very poisonous substance.

Acid lead arsenate is known as 'standard arsenate' and contains 33% of As_2O_5. A neutral lead arsenate can be produced containing only 25% As_2O_5. Lead arsenate is used mainly as an insecticidal dust for the protection of cotton, fruit trees, tobacco etc. It can be used in combating codling moth, plum curculios, cabbage worm, potato bug, tobacco hornworm etc.

The production of the USA declined slowly from 6 000 short tons in 1959 to 4 000 short tons in 1963. In 1965 the price of lead arsenate in the USA was $ 0.26-$ 0.36 per lb.

9.20.6 Detection of arsenic compounds

Methods for the detection of arsenic compounds, even in traces, are very important because of their very poisonous character and their widely distributed occurrence in several products and even in food (see arsenic trioxide and occurrence of arsenic compounds). In the USA, food control is a growing necessity since in that country arsenic compounds have been used during the last ten years as a food additive, e.g. in poultry feed for stimulation of growth and disease control, and in swine feed for a better feed efficiency. In 1960 about 500 to 1 000 tons of arsenic compounds were used for this purpose in the USA.

Very minute quantities of arsenic can be detected by means of the Marsh test. Arsenic-free zinc and sulphuric acid are added to a small flask (see fig. 9.38) together with the material to be investigated, e.g. stomach contents, suspected foodstuffs, etc.

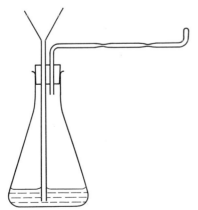

Fig. 9.38 Apparatus for Marsh test.

Nascent hydrogen is then formed which reduces any arsenic (or antimony) compounds present to arsine (AsH_3) and stibine (SbH_3) respectively.

The gas is passed through a narrow tube having a constriction in the middle and drawn out at the end to a jet at which the issuing gas is lighted. In the presence of arsine the flame is of a greyish colour and, if a cold porcelain dish is lowered into it, a black stain of arsenic is deposited. Antimony behaves in a similar manner owing to the formation of stibine (SbH_3), but in this case the black stain, unlike that of arsenic, is insoluble in calcium hypochlorite.

Another method of depositing the arsenic is to heat the tube by means of a small flame close to the constriction, on the side nearest the flask. Arsenic is then deposited as a 'mirror' at or near the constriction. By making tests with known amounts of arsenic a set of standard mirrors can be prepared from which the arsenic present in an unknown sample can be estimated with a reasonable degree of accuracy.

Antimony produces similar mirrors, but these are deposited at a point nearer to the heating flame than in the case of arsenic, owing to the fact that stibine is more readily decomposed by heat than arsine.

In an automatic method for monitoring the amount of arsenic present in factory atmospheres, samples of the air are passed at intervals into an apparatus generating hydrogen from sulphuric acid and zinc. The gas stream is freed from hydrogen sulphide, if present, by passing through lead acetate solution and is then passed into a vessel containing a solution of diethyldithiocarbamate. This substance, originally yellow, is turned red by arsine. This colour change can be easily detected by means of a photo-electric cell arranged to give an automatic warning if the safe limits are exceeded.

9.21 ANTIMONY COMPOUNDS (Sb, atomic weight = 120.2)
(for the metal see vol. III)

9.21.1 History and occurrence

Metallic antimony seems to have been known in China about 4000 B.C. The early Egyptians made articles of copper coated with a thin layer of antimony. At the same time, the natural sulphide of antimony was used as a paint for eyebrows. Formerly the Greek name 'Stibium' was generally used, the name 'antimony' coming into use much later. Both names were used for the sulphide, in particular, up to the time of Lavoisier.

Antimony occurs in several minerals, but only a few of them are of commercial importance. The most important is stibnite (antimony glance, Sb_2S_3) which often occurs in a relatively pure form. China is considered to have the largest ore reserves. Antimony trisulphide occurs in smaller quantities in iron pyrites and in lead, mercury, copper and gold ores (e.g. in the gold ores of South Africa). In these metal ores arsenic compounds are also often present. In some silver veins, native antimony has been found. Antimony also occurs in the form of oxides. The mineral valentinite (Sb_2O_3) is the most important oxide. In Bolivia it is found in a fairly pure state.

9.21.2 Antimony trioxide

Antimony trioxide (Sb_2O_3) is mainly obtained by volatilization-roasting, either as principal product from stibnite ores or as a by-product from other ores containing stibnite. The principles of the process are similar to those for the production of arsenic trioxide but modified equipment, with carefully controlled temperature and air feed, is used to suppress the formation of antimony tetroxide (Sb_2O_4). Antimony trioxide is easily separated from any arsenic trioxide (if it is present due to impurities in the ore) since the latter is much more volatile than the former.

The second source of antimony trioxide is the mineral valentinite. The very pure ores are mined and sold as such and the impure ores are purified by volatilization and condensation of the antimony trioxide. The finest grade of antimony trioxide is obtained by burning antimony metal in air and collecting the volatilizing antimony trioxide.

Pure antimony trioxide is a snow-white crystalline product. Its melting point is 656° C and it is only slightly soluble in water. It is much less poisonous than arsenic trioxide. Antimony trioxide has an amphoteric character. Thus it dissolves in strong acids with the formation of antimony salts and in strong bases to form antimonites. Like the corresponding oxide of arsenic, antimony trioxide can be oxidized to antimony pentoxide (Sb_2O_5) by means of nitric acid. Similarly to the formation of arsenates, antimonates are formed by reacting antimony pentoxide with alkali metal hydroxides.

Important quantities of antimony trioxide are used for the production of metallic antimony (see vol. III). Antimony trioxide is also used as a white pigment in paints. Its covering power is greater than that of lithophone. Porcelain enamels and glass are made non-transparent by adding antimony trioxide. Antimony trioxide is also used in fireproofing compositions. Canvas and other fabrics are fireproofed by impregnating with a composition containing antimony trioxide, chlorinated paraffin and several other products. It has also a flame extinguishing effect in chlorine containing polymers, e.g. polyvinyl compounds.

Antimony trioxide is also used for the production of potassium antimony tartrate (tartar emitic, $KSb(OH)_2.C_4H_2O_6$). The latter is prepared by heating acid potassium tartrate with antimony trioxide. The product obtained is important for medicinal purposes. Antimony trioxide is also the starting material for the production of organic antimony compounds for medicinal purposes.

In 1965 antimony trioxide was sold in the USA at $0.50 to $0.51 per lb and antimony potassium tartrate at $0.84 to $0.88 per lb.

9.21.3 Antimony sulphides

Antimony trisulphide (stibnite, Sb_2S_3) is obtained from ores. If necessary it is separated from other ores and concentrated by grinding and flotation (see flotation, vol. III). Due to its relatively low melting point, pure antimony trisulphide can be obtained from concentrated sulphide ore (or directly from rich ores) by heating them to 550-600°C in a perforated vessel. The molten sulphide is collected in a lower container. This process is named 'liquation'.

Antimony trisulphide is a black crystalline product. A dark red or brown modification is obtained by precipitation of antimony trisulphide from solutions of antimony compounds. The major quantity of antimony trisulphide is used for the production of metallic antimony and antimony trioxide. Antimony trisulphide is also used in safety matches and in fireworks. In the second world war precipitated antimony trisulphide was used in camouflage paints. It has about the same infrared reflection characteristics as leaves of plants and thus objects painted with it are difficult to distinguish when photographed with infrared rays. In 1964 antimony trisulphide (65%) was sold in the USA at $ 0.23 to $ 0.26 per lb.

Antimony pentasulphide (golden antimony sulphide, Sb_2S_5) can be prepared by boiling antimony trisulphide with a solution of sodium polysulphide. Sodium thioantimonate (Schlippe's salt, Na_3SbS_4) is formed. The latter can be decomposed with hydrochloric acid into antimony pentasulphide, which precipitates.

Antimony pentasulphide is available in several colours ranging from yellow, via orange, to dark red, depending on the method of preparation and the composition (it can contain antimony trisulphide and sulphur). These products are used in oil and water paints. Formerly much antimony pentasulphide was used in the rubber industry for colouring rubber red. Nowadays it is largely replaced by organic pigments for this purpose.

9.21.4 Antimony halides

Antimony trichloride (SbCl₃) is prepared by dissolving antimony trisulphide in , concentrated hydrochloric acid. The excess of acid is distilled off and the chloride is purified by volatilization and condensation. A colourless hygroscopic crystalline solid is obtained. The melting point is 73° C and the boiling point is 223° C. Antimony trichloride picks up moisture from the air and then forms a butter-like mass (antimony oxychloride, SbOCl), known from the Middle Ages as 'butter of antimony'. Other oxychlorides such as $Sb_4O_5Cl_2$ (powder of algaroth) are also formed.

Antimony trichloride is used for the production of other antimony compounds, especially pharmaceuticals. In the dry state antimony trichloride is used as a catalyst in the petroleum industry. Mixed with oil it is still used for the burnishing of steel, e.g. for rifle barrels. When used in solution in hydrochloric acid, it covers several metals with a corrosion-resistant layer. In 1965 the price of antimony trichloride was $0.59 to $ 0.61 per lb.

Antimony pentachloride (SbCl₅), which is obtained by treating the molten trichloride with chlorine, is used as a catalyst in the production of organic halogen compounds.

Antimony trifluoride (SbF₃) is prepared by dissolving antimony trioxide in a solution of hydrofluoric acid in water and evaporation of the water. Antimony trifluoride is used for the production of inorganic and organic fluorine compounds, from corresponding chlorine or bromine compounds, by substitution reactions. It is also used for making double salts with chlorides, fluorides or sulphates of sodium or ammonia. They are of the type $SbF_3.NaCl$ or $SbF_3.Na_2SO_4$ and are used as a mordant with tannin in the dyeing of cotton (see dyeing, vol. VI).

9.21.5 Statistics

The production of antimony ores by the major producing countries, and the world production are shown in the table on p. 403.

	1937	1953	1957	1961	1963
		In short tons of antimony content			
Algeria	1090	1900	1550	720	—
Austria	240	490	430	670	550
Bolivia (exports)	7130	5780	7030	7430	8300
Canada	20	320	680	650	760
China (estimated)	—	11000	15400	16500	16500
Czechoslovakia	—	1800	1800	1800	1800
Italy	660	410	220	280	270
Mexico	10640	4290	5730	3980	5300
Peru	1420	1040	920	790	800
South Africa	10	2730	11020	11800	12400
Turkey	640	690	1230	1510	2000
USSR (estimated)		5500	5500	6600	6700
USA	1150	340	710	690	650
Yugoslavia	1510	1860	1950	2720	2900
World	43000	22000	56000	58000	61000

The end uses of antimony ores in the USA by class of materials produced were as follows in 1963:

In short tons of antimony content	
Metal products	8800
Flame proofing chemicals and compounds	1600
Ceramics and glass	1500
Pigments	1000
Plastics	1350
Rubber products	600
Other, including matches and fireworks	1650
Total	16500

The real consumption of antimony in metal products is much greater in the USA, but this is mainly recovered from scrap metal.

The USA imported in 1963 10000 short tons of antimony ore (in terms of antimony) and Great Britain 5700 short tons (about 5100 long tons).

In the UK antimony was used for the following purposes:

	1961	1962
	In long tons	
Metal products	2995	2770
Oxides for white pigments	1298	1007
Oxides for other uses	1133	1070
Sulphides (incl. crude)	64	71
	5090	4918

9.22 BISMUTH COMPOUNDS (Bi atomic weight = 209.0)
(for metallic bismuth, see vol. III)

Bismuth as a metal has been known since the Middle Ages but it was often confused with antimony, tin and zinc until it was identified as a metallic element in the eighteenth century.

Bismuth occurs in the earth's crust as native metal, as the sulphide (Bi_2S_3, *bismuth glance,* as oxide (Bi_2O_3, bismite) and in some other forms. Small quantities are found in several lead, copper and tin ores and it is mainly obtained as a by-product in the concentration of these ores.

The starting material for the production of bismuth compounds is metallic bismuth. Bismuth is dissolved in nitric acid and the solution is partially evaporated. *Bismuth nitrate* ($Bi(NO_3)_3.5H_2O$) crystallizes after cooling. If the solution is given a predetermined acidity a basic bismuth nitrate, *bismuth subnitrate* can be obtained. This product is used in medicine and in cosmetic preparations. *Bismuth subcarbonate* (a basic carbonate) is obtained by treating a solution of bismuth nitrate with an excess of alkali carbonate. Like the subnitrate, it is used in medicine and in cosmetic preparations. *Bismuth oxychloride* (BiOCl) is precipitated from a solution of bismuth nitrate by adding a common salt solution. The white precipitate is used as a pigment, for the polishing of synthetic pearls and in cosmetics. *Bismuth oxide* (Bi_2O_3) is precipitated from a bismuth nitrate solution by adding an alkali hydroxide solution. It is used in the painting of porcelain, for the production of enamels and also for the production of *bismuth subgallate* by treating with gallic acid. Bismuth subgallate is a bright yellow powder which is sold as 'Dermatol' for the treatment of skin diseases such as eczema.

The world production of metallic bismuth was 3 200 short tons in 1963, 1 000 short tons of which were consumed in the USA. About 35% was used for pharmaceutical and chemical purposes. Most of the remainder is used in alloys, etc.

CHAPTER 10

The Alkali Metals
and their Compounds

10.1 INTRODUCTION

The alkali metals are lithium, sodium, potassium, rubidium, caesium and francium. These elements form the first main group of the periodic system (see p. 620). Francium occurs only in minimal quantities as a product of radioactive decay (for radioactive decay see p. 633). The alkali metals are very soft. They are extremely reactive chemically and for this reason they are not found in a free state. In their chemical compounds all the alkali metals are monovalent, and they have corresponding properties. The alkali metals form oxides with oxygen. These oxides form strong bases with water. The bases (hydroxides) are known as caustic alkalis since they have a strongly corrosive action on the skin. The bases form salts with almost all known acids.

It is remarkable that ammonia forms salts with several acids which correspond strikingly with the alkali metal salts of the same acids. Ammonium hydroxide reacts like a less strong base than the alkali metal hydroxides (for ammonia see p. 309).

The word 'alkali' is of Arabic origin (al-quali), but the precise meaning is not known. It refers mostly to substances having properties similar to those of the ash obtained from plants. This ash yielded what was known at the time as 'soft alkali', which comprised substances called soda ash and potash and now known as sodium and potassium carbonates. What we now call 'caustic alkali' was well known at the beginning of the Christian era; the term referred to both caustic soda (sodium hydroxide) and caustic potash (potassium hydroxide). These were obtained from soft alkali by the use of slaked lime, and used for soap manufacture. Ideas about basic and acid substances became clear only towards the end of the eighteenth century, with the advance of chemical knowledge.

10.2 SODIUM AND ITS COMPOUNDS

10.2.1 Metallic sodium (Na, atomic weight = 22.99)

History and occurrence. The continentals use the name 'natrium' in chemical context, but English speaking people use the word 'sodium'. Both words came into use when it was realized that the same metal formed the principal constituent of various sorts of 'soda', some of which were referred to as 'natron'. It was Davy who in 1807 isolated it for the first time as a metal by the electrolysis of molten common salt. This method could not be used for large-scale manufacture until the end of the nineteenth century, when it became possible to construct improved sources of electricity.

Metallic sodium was first prepared commercially by heating NaOH with a mixture of carbon and iron. This was carried out with the aim of using metallic sodium in the production of aluminium. After 1890 this method was superseded when the electrolytic method for producing aluminium was developed. New uses were then created for sodium, as for example in the production of sodium cyanide (NaCN) and sodium peroxide (Na_2O_2).

Sodium never occurs in the free state in nature because of the excessive ease with which it is oxidized. In the form of compounds, sodium is widely distributed in the earth's crust, which contains about 2.7% sodium. Sodium occurs most commonly in sodium aluminium silicates such as sodium potash felspar and soda felspar. Commercially important are deposits of rock salt, Chile saltpetre, sodium carbonate, sodium sulphate and the dissolved salt in the sea and in salt lakes (see the sodium compounds in this chapter).

10.2.2 Production

Some sodium is still prepared from sodium hydroxide (NaOH), molten NaOH being decomposed electrolytically, using very large currents, according to the equation:

$$4NaOH \rightarrow 4Na + 2H_2O + O_2$$

Molten sodium metal is liberated at the cathode, the metal floating on the molten sodium hydroxide. Since the metal burns instantly on coming into contact with the air, it must be prepared and stored in an inert gas atmosphere. Above all, contact with water, which is liberated at the anode, must be avoided. Molten NaOH is therefore continuously fed in at the cathode so that the water-containing liquid flows regularly away from the anode. The electrolyte usually contains 10% sodium chloride and 5-10% sodium carbonate, and operates in the temperature range 300-310° C.

Molten sodamide ($NaNH_2$) may be added to the molten sodium hydroxide to improve the operation of the cell. This is said to act in two ways; in the first place it lowers the cell operating temperature, and in the second place it reacts with water according to the equation:

$$NaNH_2 + H_2O \rightarrow NaOH + NH_3$$

and thus removes water from the melt by direct chemical reaction and by carrying away water vapour in the ammonia which is evolved. By these means the risk of explosion of hydrogen formed by reaction of the liberated sodium and water in the melt is eliminated (see properties of sodium, p. 410), and the current yield is greatly increased.

The cells used for the electrolysis of sodium hydroxide are constructed of steel, and have nickel anodes and copper cathodes. They are built for currents of between 8 500 and 9 500 A at a cathode current density of 7 A/m². The current efficiency is 40%. The yields of sodium are 0.4 g/ A h and 90.0 g/kWh.

The preparation of sodium from sodium hydroxide has now been largely replaced by the method using the electrolysis of common salt. Salt in its natural state is nearly always impure and needs to be purified before it can be used in an electrolytic cell.

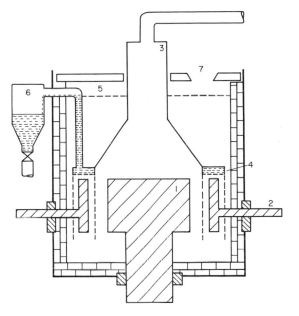

Fig. 10.1 Downs cell for production of sodium metal.

1. Anode; 2. Cathodes; 3. Hood for chlorine removal; 4. Ring-shaped trough with open side facing downwards for collection of liberated metal; 5. Level of molten salts; 6. Collecting tank for sodium, which passes upwards from the trough into a pipe, and is removed above the salt level; 7. Inlet openings for mixture of raw materials.
(For the sake of simplicity, the drawing has been made on the assumption that two cathodes pass through the wall.)

The electrolysis of molten salt is now usually carried out in the Downs cell (see fig. 10.1). The Downs cell consists of a well-insulated steel tank lined with firebrick or heat resisting cement. The anode (1) is a massive circular graphite rod which projects vertically upward through the centre of the bottom of the cell to about half the height of the container. An iron cathode (2), which is cylindrical, is arranged coaxially with the anode. This cathode is suspended by means of steel arms which rest on firebrick set in the vertical wall, the supporting arm providing a convenient connection to the current lead. A steel hood (3) supported on a steel frame resting across the top of the steel container is fitted above the anode. A diaphragm made of iron gauze supported from this steel hood is held in the annular space between anode and cathode. The steel hood is also provided with an annular trough (4) placed upside down above the annular cathode.

The melt in the cell consists of common salt (NaCl) and calcium chloride (CaCl$_2$). The melting point of this mixture is 505° C and is considerably lower than that of pure NaCl (800° C). Consequently the cell can operate at a relatively low temperature, thus making the operation easier and reducing the maintenance required. The molten sodium chloride dissociates into positively charged sodium ions and negatively charged chlorine ions, and these move to the cathode (negative electrode) and anode (positive electrode) respectively. At the anode the chlorine ions are discharged and converted into chlorine gas, which is collected in the hood above the anode. The chlorine gas can give rise to serious corrosion at the high operating temperature, and special resistant materials are required. At the cathode the sodium ions are discharged and converted into metallic sodium. The latter rises up through the melt and is collected above the cathode in the annular trough from which it is passed into the outlet pipe. Because of its low specific gravity the level of sodium in this pipe is higher than that of the heavy fused salt mixture, and it can readily flow out of the cell at the top.

The cell is fed with common salt in such a manner that the fresh salt is first heated by the molten salt. All the water which it may contain is then driven off and only comes into contact with the molten mass at the surface. An explosion due to the sudden evolution of steam is thus made impossible.

Currents between 28 000-35 000 A (or even higher) are employed in the Downs cell. The passage of the current heats the mixture greatly and maintains it in a molten state. About 15 000 kWh are necessary per ton sodium. The average operating voltage of a cell is about 6 V.

As the melt also contains calcium chloride, calcium is deposited at the cathode in small amounts along with the sodium. Calcium crystallizes on cooling and can be removed from the liquid sodium by filtering. The filter sludge is returned to one of the cells adapted for this purpose, in which the calcium from the sludge exchanges with sodium in the fresh melt. Thus the loss of calcium from the cells is much reduced. There are several references in the literature to other methods of dealing with the calcium sludge problem. Thus for example the sludge can be reacted with ethanol, or with ethanol from the corresponding sodium alkoxide, which leaves the calcium as a fine crystalline powder for which there are special applications.

The energy efficiency of the Downs cell process from salt to sodium is about three times that of the composite process for producing sodium hydroxide by electrolysis of brine (e.g. mercury cell process, see p. 437) followed by electrolysis of the fused hydroxide, so that the latter will quickly become obsolete.

A typical layout of a complete sodium production plant, shown diagrammatically in fig. 10.2, comprises a salt dissolver, purification plant, evaporation plant and dryer, an electrolysis plant, sodium filtration and finally a chlorine liquefaction plant with a bleaching powder production unit as an alternative method of utilizing the chlorine.

10.2.3 Handling

The molten sodium obtained by electrolysis is allowed to solidify, always in the complete absence of oxygen and water vapour, in enclosed iron moulds, in which blocks of weight 1, 2, 5, 12 or 24 lb are formed. It can also be pumped through steel pipes into tank wagons filled with dry nitrogen, in which it solidifies. The block formed can be melted before the wagon is unloaded, by means of the metal pipes with which it was cooled in the first place.

The soft metal may also be pressed in the cold state to form wire or ribbon, and is stored under paraffin oil.

Blocks are usually shipped in air-tight containers in preference to the older method of shipping under naphtha oil.

Great care is required in the handling of sodium at a plant or in the laboratory. It forms detonating mixtures with organic halogen compounds; on this account carbon tetrachloride must not be used to put out sodium fires, and water may also not be used because of the violence of the reaction and the risk of spreading the fire by spattering molten sodium. Fires are best dealt with by smothering with *dry* sand and soda ash (N.B. not bicarbonate). For removing sodium from equipment ethanol or methanol can be used but oxygen must be excluded. Large vessels can be decontaminated by heating the vessel to a uniformly high temperature to burn off any residual sodium. Before starting work with sodium the precautions given in several authoritative publications should be consulted (see the end of this section).

Sometimes traces of oxygen and nitrogen, even in minute quantities, are objectionable

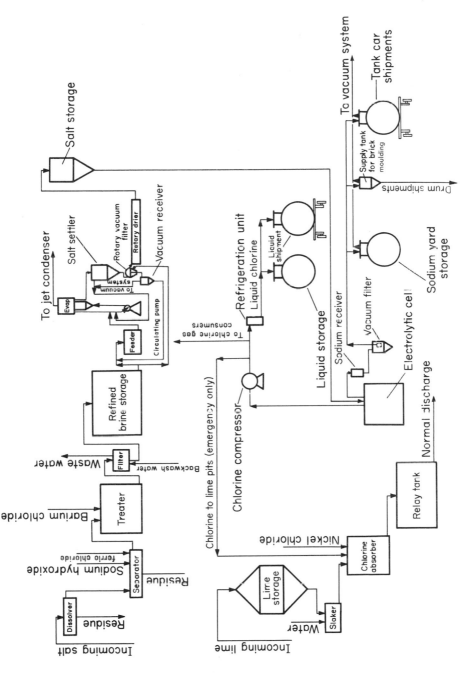

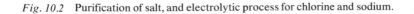

Fig. 10.2 Purification of salt, and electrolytic process for chlorine and sodium.

in sodium metal. For this reason, in the United States, the practice of filtration and packing of molten metal in an argon atmosphere is coming into use. This very pure grade is sold as argon grade material.

Sodium can be converted into a form which is easier to handle and which possesses greater reactivity by making it into an emulsion in an inert liquid.

The molten sodium is mixed with kerosene, xylene or any similar liquid and heated to 110° C under a nitrogen atmosphere (the melting point is 97.6° C). The whole is vigorously agitated and then passed through a colloid mill. A little oleic acid or an amine derivative of a fatty acid is added to make the operation easier. The extraordinarily finely divided sodium emulsion obtained in this way has a greatly increased reactivity as a result of the greatly increased surface. In the latest process the sodium is melted under a liquid of the type mentioned (under nitrogen), and then submitted to ultrasonic vibrations. This gives an even finer subdivision than can be obtained with mechanical agitation.

Another form of dispersed sodium is made by melting sodium in a jacketed vessel under nitrogen and vigorously stirring it with crystalline materials such as common salt, calcined soda, aluminium oxide or carbon. In this way it is possible to divide up, for example, 10% of sodium as a surface layer on the 90% of the particles of the other substance. The quantity of sodium to be used can thus be controlled much more accurately, even if it is to be used in the dry state. This 'high surface sodium' reacts with salts and oxides in solid form, so as to release the metal from them. It can also be used for the purification of gases, hydrocarbons and ethers. Apart from this, it is also better than other forms of sodium as a catalyst, e.g. for polymerization. It can also be used to prepare sodium hydride or sodamide.

10.2.4 Properties

Sodium is a very soft silvery white metal which very quickly oxidizes and becomes dull when exposed to air. The specific gravity is 0.97, the melting point 97.6° C and the boiling point 880° C. It is a good conductor of heat and electricity.

It reacts readily with water as follows:

$$2Na + 2H_2O \rightarrow 2NaOH + H_2$$

Sodium is a powerful reducing agent, and combines readily with oxygen and chlorine.

It forms alloys with potassium, lead and mercury, and it attacks many metals, so it must be used in apparatus made of steel, nickel or glass. The alloy of lead with 10-30% of sodium does not react nearly as strongly as the pure metallic sodium, and is therefore used, e.g. in the preparation of tetraethyl-lead. Even an alloy of this type, however, must be handled carefully and kept away from water, oxygen, chlorine, etc.

Sodium and also sodium compounds which are not too non-volatile emit yellow light (wavelength 5 890 Å) when heated at high temperatures, for example in a flame or in an electric arc. When this light is examined in a spectroscope, two sharp yellow lines, having a characteristic position are observed.

10.2.5 Uses

The largest use of sodium is for the production of tetraethyl-lead (see production of tetraethyl-lead, vol. IV). Other applications of importance are the production of metals by reduction of their chlorides, e.g. titanium, tantalum, zirconium, hafnium, the deoxidation of stainless steel and non-ferrous alloys such as brass; the filling of copper tubes for light electrical conductors; and the filling of the stem of the valves of internal combustion engines to assist heat transfer and thus promote cooling of the valve heads. (For reduction of metal chlorides see the specified metals in vol. III.)

It also seems probable that sodium will become of very great importance for heat transfer in nuclear reactors since the small nucleus of the sodium atom is not seriously modified by neutrons. One reactor designed for 150 000 kW, for example, requires an initial charge of 2 250 000 kg of sodium.

If sodium is used in heat applications, pumps of the centrifugal type can be used for conveying liquid sodium. Special arrangements are necessary to prevent contact with air. Considerable attention has also been given to various types of electromagnetic pumps for this purpose. These pumps developed pressure on the sodium by electromagnetic interaction and no moving mechanical parts are used.

Sodium metal is also used for filling sodium vapour lamps. In order to ensure a correct charge the required amount is introduced into the lamp bulb in a sealed capsule, which is then broken.

Various sodium-potassium alloys are made in America, especially for use as reducing agents. They are obtained by passing sodium vapour countercurrently to fused potassium chloride under vacuum in a packed column, the fused potassium chloride having a temperature of 850° C; the packing material is Raschig rings made of stainless steel. The sodium exchanges with the potassium ions so that the vapour of potassium and sodium leaves the top of the column, while at the bottom fused common salt and some sodium flow out; these are easily separated by taking advantage of their different specific gravities. Alloys of this type, which have a lower melting point than their constituents, are used as coolants or heat transfer fluids.

Sodium was at one time used a great deal in organic chemistry for the reduction of fats or esters of fatty acids to fatty alcohols (see vol. IV), though it is being less used now as a result of the introduction of hydrogenation; and there are important outlets in the production of dyestuffs, e.g. indigo, pyrazole and the Hanza group of dyes, of drugs such as the sulpha drugs and barbiturates and of synthetic perfumes such as phenylethyl alcohol. It can be used in the preparation of sebacic and isosebacic acids. together with other dibasic acids, for the production of plasticizers. It may also be used for the preparation of alcohols from aldehydes, of amides from nitriles, and for the polymerization of butadiene to form synthetic rubber.

10.2.6 Statistics

The world production of sodium metal reached only 25 000 tons in 1930, but by 1939 had risen to 120 000 tons. In the period between 1955 and 1960 the world production fluctuated between 160 000 and 180 000 tons per year, of which two-thirds was produced in the USA. Most of the remaining sodium was produced in France, Germany, Japan and the United Kingdom, each producing 5 000-10 000 tons per year.

In 1930 about 50% of the world production was obtained from sodium chloride and the remaining 50% from sodium hydroxide. Nowadays less than 5% of the world production is obtained from sodium hydroxide.

Between 1950 and 1960, the estimated output of the USA and UK was as shown in the following table.

Product	UK (average)	USA	
	%	1950 %	1960 %
Tetraethyl lead	35	50	72
Sodium cyanide ⎱		18	11
Sodium peroxide ⎰	60	4	7
Metal production	1	—	5
Ester reduction	2	18	0.2
Miscellaneous	2	10	5

In the USA the price of sodium was $0.17-0.21 per lb in 1965.

10.2.7 Literature

J. W. MELLOR. *Comprehensive treatise on inorganic chemistry,* vol. II suppl. 2. London, Longmans, 1961.

M. SITTIG. *Sodium, its manufacture, properties and uses.* New York, Reinhold, 1956. ACS monograph No. 133.

D. W. F. HARDIE. *The electrolytic manufacture of chemicals from salt.* Oxford University Press, 1959.

C. L. MANTELL. *Electrochemical engineering.* 4th edn. New York, McGraw-Hill, 1960.

10.3 SODIUM CHLORIDE

10.3.1 History

Sodium chloride (common salt, NaCl) is one of the oldest articles of commerce in the world. It is mentioned even by the earliest writers, both of the west and of the east, and the earliest known roads were often 'saltways'. Those routes were used to transport salt which was only obtainable in a sufficiently pure form for condiment purposes in a few places before purification methods were developed. It was very valuable and as can be seen from the word 'salary' both the officers and the men of the Roman legions were paid in salt. This form of payment was replaced by money only in the later period of the Roman empire. Salt in the form of large tablets served as money in Asia and in Africa, and it played a part in the religious rites of many peoples, and in the relationships with inferiors, as in the right to hospitality.

10.3.2 Occurrence

Sea water can be mentioned first, since about three-quarters of the salts dissolved in the sea consist of common salt. The salt content of the sea varies from place to place, a content of 0.1-1.5% being found in the Baltic, for example, while the salt content

Fig. 10.3 Schematic section through the Straits of Gibraltar. The arrows show the direction of the two currents leaving and entering the Atlantic Ocean. The amount of water brought in keeps the salt content of the Mediterranean relatively low.

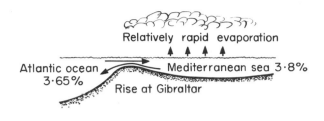

Relatively rapid evaporation

Atlantic ocean 3·65% Mediterranean sea 3·8%

Rise at Gibraltar

of the Atlantic Ocean is 3.44% on the average, but can attain 3.65%. The salt content of the Mediterranean reaches 3.8% and that of the Black Sea is 1.75%. The differences are explained by variations in the influx of fresh water from rivers and of less salt water from other seas, together with different rates of evaporation.

An illustration of this process is given in fig. 10.3 which shows schematically the straits of Gibraltar. Far more water evaporates (relatively) from the Mediterranean as a result of the subtropical climate than from the Atlantic Ocean to the west of Europe. For this reason, water flows in on the surface from the Atlantic Ocean to the Mediterranean. Due to the evaporation and the fresh salt supplied by the inflow of water, the salt concentration of the Mediterranean is higher than that of the Atlantic Ocean. However, the surface current (and also rivers) carry more water into the Mediterranean than is needed to restore the water level, which tends to decline by evaporation, and under the surface current a current of water moves in the opposite direction. For this reason the water in the Mediterranean contains less salt than would be the case if it were an enclosed sea. The relatively low salt content of the Black Sea can be explained by the influx of river water and the loss of salt water to the Aegean.

Many lakes which do not have large outflows of water contain very large amounts of salt. Thus, for example, the Utah Lake (Salt Lake) has more than 19%, of which 15% is common salt. The Dead Sea contains about 24% of salts of which 7% is common salt, 12% magnesium chloride, 3% calcium chloride and 1% potassium chloride. In the Atlantic Ocean, for every 100 parts of salt there are 8.4 parts of magnesium chloride ($MgCl_2$), 5.2 parts of magnesium sulphate ($MgSO_4$), 4.6 parts of calcium sulphate ($CaSO_4$), 4 parts potassium chloride (KCl) and 1 part magnesium bromide (MgBr).

In several places salt deposits are found beneath the surface of the earth (see mining of salt). These salt deposits are sometimes very thick and extensive. They have probably originated from earlier salt seas or lakes, followed by the washing out of the other substances contained in them. They sometimes also take the form of 'salt domes' (see p. 255).

Natural concentrated solutions of salt are also known, that at Reichenbach, for example, containing 22.5% NaCl. Salt also occurs in almost all the body fluids (see properties of sodium chloride).

10.3.3 Mining of salt

a. Dry mining. Large amounts of pure salt (rock salt) are obtained in the solid state from some salt mines, the material being excavated by the use of explosives. Pillars of salt are allowed to remain as a support for the roof, so that no wooden props are needed. The salt, when brought to the surface, is passed through sieves, and then

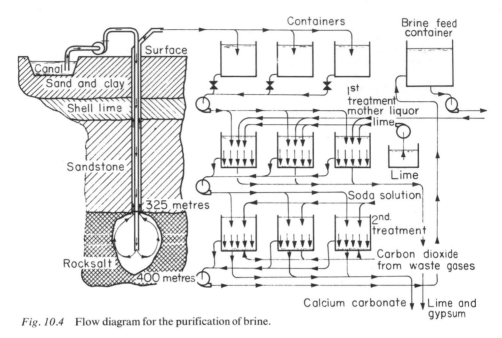

Fig. 10.4 Flow diagram for the purification of brine.

goes to crushers. The large pieces pass on to sorting belts, where the easily recognisable impurities such as anhydrite (calcium sulphate) are removed. After the crushers and grinders, the material is again passed through sieves, which sort the salt out according to fineness. Pure rock salt is sold as such. Impure rock salt must be dissolved before it can be purified. For a new infrared method of purification of rock salt containing at the most 2.5% of impurities and of coarsely crystalline type see p. 424.

b. Wet mining or brine well mining. In very large deposits of rock salt, which sometimes contain milliards of tons of salt, a water pumping method is employed for extracting the salt. Essentially, this is a simplified version of the Frasch method for extracting sulphur. Wells are bored deep into the deposit, and are clad with steel pipes of, e.g. 8 inch internal diameter. A somewhat narrower pipe is let down inside this, which carries water deep into the salt layer. The salt dissolves, and the brine is transported to the storage tanks at the surface by compressed air (see figs. 10.4 and 10.5). Here the quantity of brine is measured, and the brine is then passed to the first purification stage, in which it is mixed with mother liquor from the refining plant and with lime. By this means appreciable quantities of magnesium compounds and some calcium sulphate are precipitated.

After the first purification, the brine passes a second set of storage tanks for further purification. This is effected by means of a soda solution, while flue gases, rich in carbon dioxide, are passed through at the same time. This treatment results in the precipitation of calcium carbonate and magnesium and iron hydroxides. The brine thus obtained, after settling, is evaporated to recover the salt. There are variations on this method of purification depending on the type of brine and the local circumstances. Thus albumin or blood may be added to assist flocculation and to carry down some of

Fig. 10.5   Derricks and brine tanks.

the impurities. The precipitate obtained in the course of purification is sometimes used in road construction, or it can be returned to the bore holes.

Iron and steel are corroded by brine; for this reason wood, concrete or plastics (sometimes reinforced with glass fibre) are also used as construction materials.

10.3.4 Production of solar salt

Solar salt is salt produced by solar evaporation of sea water and water from salt lakes. Very large flat tanks lined with clay have been constructed on the flat coasts of hot countries (1 500 hectares in size in Europe and 12 000 hectares in California) and near salt lakes (see fig. 10.6), and these are divided by low walls into rectangular sections. They are either allowed to fill at high tide, or are pumped full. Operations begin in April in the northern hemisphere, and the water is allowed to evaporate by the action of sun and wind until the solution reaches a concentration of 25° Bé, at which calcium sulphate and other substances are precipitated (see fig. 10.7). The solution then passes to another group of tanks, in which the concentration reaches 27° Bé, and in which very pure salt, suitable for use as table salt, is precipitated. In a further group of tanks the evaporation is continued until a concentration of 29° Bé is reached, and industrial salt crystallizes. In the final group, the concentration is 32.5° Bé and an impure salt is obtained, containing a large number of impurities (among others, a good deal of magnesium chloride); this is specially suitable for the salting of fish.

The crystalline masses in each group of tanks are raked into little heaps on a space specially arranged for this purpose on the low walls (in August in Europe) (see fig. 10.6), and then piled into large heaps. Rain then dissolves out a certain amount of magnesium chloride from the salt, which makes it less hygroscopic.

The quantity produced depends on the climate and on the weather; thus 45 to 178

Fig. 10.6 Salt park in California. The harvesting machine in operation.

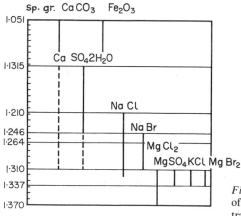

Fig. 10.7 Concentrations at which the constituents of sea water crystallise out. The broken lines indicate traces of the salts.

tons per hectare are obtained in the south of France, but only 4 to 28 tons on the western shores of France. Very little labour is required to collect the salt from the salt pans.

The mother liquor (bittern), which remains behind after the salt and other substances have crystallized out, contains per 100 000 tons of salt obtained:

27 300 tons magnesium chloride (MgCl₂ .6H₂O)
16 000 tons magnesium sulphate (MgSO₄ .7H₂O)
 2 800 tons potassium chloride (KCl)
  240 tons bromine, combined in bromides.

Only in a few of the large salt pans is the mother liquor worked for its valuable constituents. Bromine, magnesia and calcium sulphate (see the appropriate chapters) are principally obtained.

English scientists have effected an improvement in the solar evaporation process which makes it possible to use the solar energy more efficiently, since in operations according to the usual method only 60-70% of the sun's heat is absorbed by the solution, while the rest is reflected. Far more than this proportion can be taken if the dyestuff naphthol green is added to the salt solution to increase the heat absorption, and it is then possible to crystallize out 20% more salt in the same time. The salt layer thus becomes thicker and it is relatively less expensive to obtain salt from it (see also potassium chloride and saltpetre). The dyestuff mentioned is not decomposed by light.

In California and elsewhere the European method described above has been extensively improved by mechanization, although the basic procedure is virtually unchanged. The crop of salt crystals is harvested by special dredging machines, transferred into narrow gauge trucks and conveyed to a washing unit where the crystals are washed with pure brine. The washed crystals, after being centrifuged, are transferred to a large stockpile. From here the salt goes to be refined, and in this process a purity of 99.95% can be achieved, though a purity of 99.4% is usually satisfactory. The large surface area used and the high degree of mechanization make the price of the salt relatively low.

In the far north, sea water is allowed to freeze so that the ice, which contains no salt, can be removed. The stronger salt solution thus obtained can then be concentrated in vacuum apparatus with a heat pump, and made to crystallize.

Crude sea salt forms roof-shaped crystals, built up from the characteristic cubic salt crystals. It is used mainly for the salting of fish and in industry, since it is completely free from iron compounds, which is often not the case with rock salt. The Portuguese varieties are considered specially suitable for the salting of herring.

It has been observed that sea salt is often the cause of reddening and decomposition of fish. This is due to the presence of two kinds of bacteria with which salting works are often infected, and which can live and grow in strong salt solutions in sunlight and even at temperatures of 55° C. Sea salt in general contains so many bacteria, that its use is best avoided in, e.g. the preparation of tinned foods. The moisture content is often high (greater than 10%).

10.3.5 Production of salt from brine

Crystalline salt is obtained from brine by evaporation. Brine is an impure salt solution made from crude sea or rock salt. Such brine is first purified. This can be done by the methods already outlined. Evaporation is performed in two ways. The open pan evaporation (grainer salt or open pan salt) and the vacuum pan evaporation (vacuum pan salt, sometimes named granular salt). The concentration of natural brine can be increased by throwing in raw, impure salt before evaporation or by using it to wash raw salt.

a. Open pan evaporation. This is the oldest process, but it is still used. Large flat pans, heated by steam pipes, are used for evaporation of brine. When heated at temperatures slightly above atmospheric temperatures, the same roof-shaped crystals as in the solar process are obtained. Usually the brine is heated to temperatures above 100° C to promote rapid evaporation, so that a special kind of salt with not too large crystals is obtained. The heating is taken to the point, as in solar evaporation, at which calcium sulphate crystallizes out, but not salt (see fig. 10.7). The calcium sulphate is removed with wooden shovels or mechanically, so that it is not deposited as a scale on the heating surfaces. The temperature at which the subsequent evaporation is carried out is reduced accordingly as coarse or fine salt is required. The salt which is crystallized out is removed from the bottom of the pans with rakes and is placed on wooden covers so that the liquor drains off. It is then centrifuged and dried in drum dryers or on a continuous belt.

The mother liquor contains, besides common salt, a number of other salts. These are sometimes obtained separately by means of careful fractional crystallization, but in the main the mother liquor is cooled and the crystals which deposit are sold for use as bath salts for medical baths.

The advantage of the open pan process is the formation of larger salt crystals. For this reason this process is still used although it is less economical than the newer vacuum pan processes (see below).

A modification of the open pan process is the Alberger method which is used in the United States for making pure salt from impure solutions. The process is designed to produce salt of high quality with a distinctive grain. The solution passes through preheaters under pressure to raise the temperature to 143° C and then into cylindrical vessels filled with gravel, on which the calcium sulphate is deposited, then through three flash-vessels in succession and finally through an open figure-of-eight shaped evaporating pan. The first two of the flash vessels are maintained at progressively lower pressures, so that steam flashes off and is led away for further use. The third flash vessel is at atmospheric pressure, and the salt begins to crystallize out here, the liquor then passing to the open pan, which is fitted with mechanical rakes. The steam evolved is drawn off through a dome hood and the salt is raked into a well or salt leg from which a salt slurry passes via a valve to the centrifuges. These do not dry the salt completely, the drying being completed in rotating drums. The first of these is heated with dust-free air, heated by flue gases, while in the second the drying is taken further and the salt cooled at the same time with cold air. The fine dust formed in the drums is fed to cyclones (see p. 105), so that the salt can be recovered.

The Alberger process is costly, but produces a salt of high purity (99.95% pure).

b. Vacuum pan evaporation. Modern salt works use multiple-effect evaporation crystallisation (see fig. 10.8).

A multiple effect evaporator consists of a number of so-called 'effects' (i.e. single evaporators), which are arranged in vacuum and steam cascade. Process steam at above atmospheric pressure is fed to the heater section (calandria) of one effect, and the vapour from the liquor in that effect is fed to the calandria of the second effect, and similarly vapour from the second effect to the calandria of the third. The pressure decreases from the first to the last effect. The vapour from the last effect passes to a water-cooled condenser which may be of the direct sparge type or an indirect type

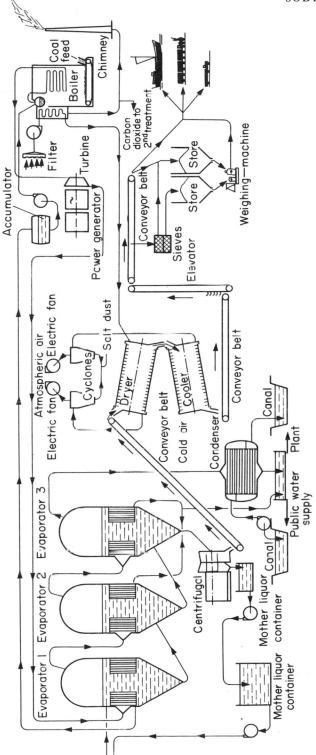

Fig. 10.8 Flow diagram for the production of usable salt from the purified salt solution. The diagram shows how the first evaporator of the system is supplied with heating steam from a bleed-off turbine (which is returned to the boiler via a storage vessel), while the other evaporators receive steam from the preceding unit (the heat pump is omitted), which is finally condensed. It also shows how the purified brine passes through the three evaporators, so that the final salt crystals with the mother liquor pass to continuously operating centrifuges, where they are separated. The centrifuged salt passes through two cylindrical dryers, one operating with hot air, and the other with cold; it is then sent on conveyors to the sieves, packed and despatched: the fine salt dust is recovered by means of cyclones. In The Netherlands, where water transport is good. 60% is carried by ships.

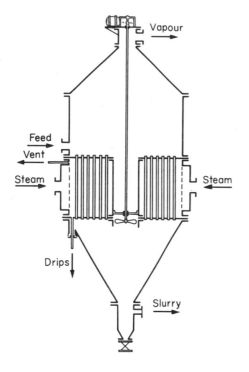

Fig. 10.9 Calandria evaporator of the natural circulation type.

condenser. The direct type is sealed by means of a barometric leg, i.e. a vertical pipe sealed by a water lute at its lower end and having a height greater than the equivalent barometric height of the vacuum on the system.

It must be realized that only in the final effect is latent heat lost from the system. In the intervening effects water is merely transferred from solution in one effect to condensate in the next, so that the only heat quantity required is heat of solution. Increasing the number of effects for a given steam pressure decreases the temperature difference available across the calandria tubes and hence increases their area and capital cost. Savings in steam usage must therefore be balanced against extra capital cost.

The effects may be of the natural circulation or the forced circulation types. In the natural circulation types (see fig. 10.9) the evaporating liquor is circulated through the vertical tubes of the calandria by the gas-lift action of the vapour bubbles. The tube bundle is provided with one or more wider tubes, the downcomers, for the return of liquor to below the calandria. Sometimes natural circulation is assisted by means of a large propeller suspended on a shaft attached to the top of the calandria. Steam for evaporation is fed to the chest of the calandria so that heat flows from the outside to the inside of the heating tubes. Condensate from the steam chest is removed through special steam-traps which allows water to flow freely while preventing the passage of steam. These operate either by gravity action, when a bucket fills with condensate and opens the release valve, or by thermal expansion due to the higher temperature of the steam relative to the condensate, which thus closes the valve immediately steam appears but allows cold condensate to pass.

In the forced circulation effects the calandria is relatively long and has fewer and narrower tubes than the natural circulation type. The calandria is usually placed outside the main body of the effect, and liquor and slurry are recycled continuously through the calandria and effect by means of a pump. The action of forcing the liquor through the pipes at a high velocity is to improve the heat transfer coefficient greatly, with the result that a smaller heating surface is required; it is thereby possible to operate with a lower temperature gradient across the tube wall and hence with lower pressure steam. The circulation also helps to keep the insides of the tubes free of deposit so that the frequent shutting down of the evaporator for cleaning purposes is avoided.

In the design of the effects attention has to be paid to the efficient separation of vapour and liquor. For this reason ample vapour-liquor disengagement space is provided. Since spray from one effect would enter the steam chest of the next and cause contamination of the condensate, it is usual to provide tangential separators in the vapour removal system. These separators (by means of deflector plates) cause the vapour to change direction sharply, and in consequence of the swirling action spray droplets are thrown out by centrifugal action.

The condensate from the next effect is thus often pure enough to be used as process or boiler feed water. Inerts (permanent gases) in the effects are removed by reciprocating pumps or by steam ejectors. The latter operate in the same way as the familiar water pump used in laboratories, except that high velocity steam entrains the inert gases.

In the salt industry multiple-effect evaporators are made of Monel metal or stainless steel. The temperatures and the flow rates are so controlled that at the most only a thin deposit of calcium carbonate is formed on the heating surfaces. The fourth vessel is very large and rubber-lined. Sometimes everything is so controlled that no preliminary purification of the brine is necessary, and the calcium and magnesium salts which precipitate during evaporation are kept in suspension with extremely fine salt. The suspended particles can then be separated by means of cyclones, the liquid subsequently being evaporated and salt crystals obtained of any desired size, up to a millimetre.

Pure water obtained from the steam from the last evaporator (effect) can be usefully employed in the factory, and in a town's water system.

The crystal slurry of the effects is drawn off and de-watered prior to drying. Centrifuges are often used. The salt crystals are commonly dried in continuous rotary dryers (see open pan evaporation, Alberger method). The mother liquor is returned to the effects.

A fluidized-bed dryer designed to reduce the moisture content of moist salt from 3% to 0.03% has been introduced in the USA. The moist salt passes into the top of a cylinder divided into three sections by means of perforated aluminium plates, which are provided with rotating valves to allow the passage of a central pipe. The air, preheated by being passed first through the cooler for the hot salt and then heated in an oven, passes up through the holes and keeps the salt in suspension, so that it gives off its water on all sides. After a fixed period of time, it passes through the valve into the section below, passing finally through an endless screw conveyor to be fed to the sieves (see also dryers, p. 31). In the vacuum pan process, small cubic crystals are obtained. In general these crystals are much smaller than the crystals obtained by the open pan process.

Vacuum pan plants can be built for the production of 60 tons of salt per hour, and can also be employed for the production of other salts (sodium sulphate, bisulphite etc.).

Such large plants, which operate more economically, are slowly displacing those older plants which still make use of open pans and require a large amount of labour. As an example it may be mentioned that about twenty years ago the salt industry at Winsford, Cheshire, UK, employed about 1000 workers. As a result of the closing down of the open pans and the production of vacuum salt, the number of workers is now only about 450, while the production has greatly increased both in quantity and value.

Modern plants are particularly complicated, being designed for large outputs of various crystal sizes, and are provided with expensive equipment to ensure as much heat economy as possible. The large salt works often operate with purified salt solutions which they work up in part to give open pan salt (large crystals). Another part is converted into fine salt with vacuum pan evaporators. Sometimes the brine is first partially crystallized in vacuum pan evaporators and the crystals are then allowed to grow in open pan evaporators.

A fluidization technique is sometimes employed to obtain crystalline salt from pure salt solutions which have been evaporated down until saturation has been reached. In this process the solution is taken to supersaturation and then passed through an Oslo fluidized crystallizer (see fig. 10.10). A pump is provided to pass the overflow liquor together with fresh liquor through a heater again to remove more water as vapour. The crystallizer can be controlled in such a way that crystals of the required size are obtained. (Compare the cooled crystallizer for Glauber's salt in fig. 10.20.)

10.3.6 Properties of salt and its transportation

Pure common salt forms cubic crystals of specific gravity 2.2, it melts at 800.4° C and boils at about 1413° C. A litre of water at 0° C dissolves 356 g and a litre of boiling water 398 g.

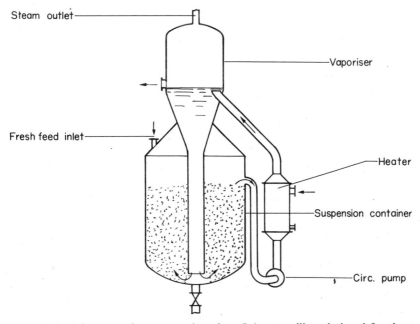

Fig. 10.10 Diagrammatic cross-section of an Oslo crystalliser designed for the production of crystals of salt, ammonium sulphate, etc. of the desired size.

Salt has important physiological functions. It is an important constituent of blood and it also serves to regulate the potassium content of the body. The human body contains 2.5 g of salt per kg weight. It needs to be continuously replaced since the kidneys regularly excrete salt as a 2% solution, from which it follows that man cannot drink sea water because its salt content (3.5%) is higher than this. The high salt content of sea water would force the body to withdraw too much water from the tissues in order to allow the kidneys to work normally. With excessive sweating, as occurs in workers in deep mines or in furnace men, a great deal of salt is lost in the sweat, and it is therefore necessary to add salt to their drinking water. Workers in the deep mines of South Africa are said to require as much as 10 litres per day of water treated in this way.

Like other salts from strong bases and strong acids, more concentrated salt solutions coagulate many albumins and flocculate colloidal solutions.

Solutions of salt are highly corrosive. For this reason tanks and pipes of Inconel or Monel metal must be used for transporting the solutions. Polyethylene is coming into use for pipe lines. Large diameter pipes, in 9 metre lengths, are joined together with polyethylene flanges or butt welded by using a hot air torch. These pipes may be bent.

Solid salt is often transported in paper, jute or linen bags. For large users, solid salt is transported in large metal tanks, mounted on lorries with equipment for pneumatic discharge.

Bunkers of concrete are often used for storing solid salt.

10.3.7 Salt grades and their uses

Salt is produced in several different forms for specific purposes.

Crude open pan salt is being slowly replaced by *vacuum salt* for all purposes since the latter can be produced as regular crystals which do not easily adhere to one another. The large coarse crystals of open pan salt are preferred for some purposes, e.g. for the production of hydrochloric acid and for salting high-grade hides, and some food products such as fish.

Compressed salt. Vacuum, solar, grainer and rock salt are often compressed into blocks by the same procedure as for briquetting of coal or for making drug tablets. For this purpose very dry salt is needed. Such briquettes dissolve much more slowly than fine salt, and are therefore used to keep the concentration of a salt solution (e.g. for cooling purposes) constant. This is effected by throwing in an excess of the tablets. The UK and France, in particular, export appreciable amounts of salt briquettes to desert countries. Salt briquettes have partially replaced bulk salt for canning and bottling of foods since they can be distributed more easily by automatic equipment. Salt briquettes are also used as salt licks for cattle. Sometimes an iodide and traces of other metal salts are incorporated to provide the trace metals required to maintain health.

Dendritic salt, which consists of hollow conglomerations of loose crystals does not absorb water easily and is used in hot, moist regions. It has, in bulk, only half the density of ordinary vacuum salt.

Table salt. Vacuum salt is commonly produced in a size range of 20-70 mesh. Table salt represents a cut between approximately 40 and 60 mesh (rock salt having the same size range is also used for this purpose). The finer sizes of vacuum salt are used in industry. In some cases, table salt (also baking powder and the like) is mixed with 15-30 parts of iodine per million parts of salt (iodized salt). An iodide is usually diluted with one hundred times the quantity of salt, the diluted mixture then being mixed, either dry or in solution, with the bulk of the salt. In some countries (e.g. the UK) this procedure is used only for package salt. The packing must then be chosen so as to be damp-proof and proof against loss of iodine. It has been proposed in the United States also to add a little soluble fluoride, since this is supposed to have a beneficial effect in preventing dental decay, especially with children. This is thought to be better than adding fluorides to drinking water since fluorides are not then automatically consumed and the individual is thus free to determine whether he will take any fluoride and, if so, how much.

Table salt is kept free flowing by adding 0.5 to 1% of a free-flowing agent such as calcium silicate, calcium carbonate, calcium phosphate or magnesium carbonate. These compounds attract moisture to a greater extent than the salt, so that the latter does not. become wet and flows more easily from a sprinkler. The term, 'free flowing' must not be confused with 'non-caking'. For example, fine grained salt containing magnesium chloride becomes wet in atmospheric conditions. The wet salt is not free flowing but it does not cake. (Of course, when salt is caked, it is not free flowing.)

Salt for bakeries, mixed with anti-oxidants for fat, is available commercially in the United States.

Brine. Purified brine is often supplied as such by a producer for various industrial uses (e.g. for electrolytic chlorine and caustic soda production).

Large single crystals. Pure salt crystals readily transmit infrared and ultraviolet light. For this reason pieces of rock salt which are as clear as glass and which are found in salt mines are made into prisms and lenses for use in optical instruments. Large single crystals of sodium chloride are also made synthetically by slow crystallization under carefully controlled conditions. Crystals have been made synthetically weighing up to 11 kg. Prisms are made from such pieces by sawing them with warm, wet wires. These prisms are used mainly in infrared spectrometers, instruments which have become of great importance, especially since World War II, for the study of organic compounds. Prisms of potassium chloride, iodide and bromide for use in optical instruments are also made in the same way.

It may be possible to take advantage of the capability of sodium chloride to transmit infrared light for further purification of rock salt containing 2.5% impurities or less. This is usually purified by manual sorting on a moving belt, but this is not always satisfactory for separating the various kinds of salt specially suited for, e.g. the electrolysis of alkali chlorides, the tanning of hides, or for use in dyeing textiles.

In the method using infrared light, coarsely crystalline rock salt is conveyed on a moving belt and treated in such a way with infrared light that the impurities, but not the pure salt crystals, are heated. When the temperature has been increased sufficiently, the salt falls on another conveyor belt, which has been treated with certain vinyl plastics which easily become sticky. The heated impurities then stick to the belt, while the purer salt does not, and is carried away, the impurities being removed from the belt later.

10.3.8 Uses of salt

Large quantities are required as a condiment. It is estimated that 7-9.5 kg are needed per person per year for physiological reasons. The requirement sometimes reaches 15 kg. Demand rose markedly in Europe during the second world war, the lack of meat and milk causing a larger consumption of vegetables, and hence an excess of potassium, which had to be counteracted.

Salt is also used for the preserving of meat, fish, hides, vegetables, offal etc. There are various theories to explain the preservative action of salt. In general it can be said that bacterial growth is prevented by dehydrating the bacterial cells by plasmolysis or by destroying the bacterial protoplasm. Pure salt passes quickly into the material to be preserved, but the presence of magnesium chloride and calcium chloride delays the penetration. Small amounts of magnesium chloride make the scales of fish attractively shiny, while small amounts of calcium chloride make the flesh harder and whiter. 'Salt machines' are used in large plants for the salting of fish and other foodstuffs. These machines require very dry salt, which falls from a storage tank on to a rotating disc, punctured with holes. In turning, the disc brings a known amount of salt above an opening in a closure plate under it, so that the desired amount of salt falls into a tank.

Large quantities of salt are still needed for the salting out of hard soap and for the production of sodium compounds such as soda, caustic soda, sodium metal and for the production of chlorine.

Salt is also used in acid dyeing of wool. The reaction velocity of acid dyes with the basic wool is too rapid to give a uniformly dyed product. Salt promotes uniform dyeing. This can be readily understood by the fact that dyed wool loses more colour in a boiling salt solution than in boiling water. Thus the salt promotes uniformity by holding dye off the wool.

The increasing application of ion-exchange means that here too more and more salt is required to regenerate the spent exchanger (see p. 139).

For use in fused salt baths, salt is often mixed with aluminium chloride and ferric chloride, because such a mixture melts easily at a much lower temperature and then forms a readily flowing mass. This is often especially suitable as a heat transfer fluid in plant where a constant temperature is needed. Plant using such salt mixtures and constructed of non-corroding metals are already being mass produced and are thus obtainable at a relatively low price.

Crude salt is used in large quantities (e.g. at a cost of about $10 million per year in the USA) for keeping roads open after moderate or heavy snow falls in winter time; it is spread over the road after the way has been cleared by a snow plough. There are more effective materials for this purpose, but they are much dearer. Calcium chloride is also suitable for this purpose. In both cases, corrosion of motor vehicles is greatly increased.

Many centuries ago, in the Middle East, flat plates of crude salt (e.g. from the Dead Sea) were used to form the bottom of baking ovens. This salt contains potassium salts which act as catalysts in the combustion of the dry dung used as fuel. In the long run, the upper layer becomes exhausted, while all the pores of the plates are closed up by the phosphates which remain behind, the salt plate then having become inactive. In the Gospel of St Matthew and in other books of the New Testament this phenomenon gave rise to the passage (incorrectly translated) in which the question is asked: If the salt has lost his savour wherewith shall it be salted? The expression 'lost his savour' is incorrect and should be translated by 'become inactive'.

The following table shows some important chemical products and classes of products derived directly or indirectly from salt.

Products derived from salt

Acetphenetidin	Insecticides	Sodium bisulphate
Acetylchloride	(BHC, DDT, etc.)	Sodium chlorate
Bleaches	Methylchloride	Sodium cyanide
Carbon tetrachloride	Monochlorobenzene	Sodium sulphate
Chlorine	Refrigerants	Sodium phosphate
Chloroform	Soaps and detergents	Sodium metal
Disinfectants, fumigants	Sodium bicarbonate	Tetraethyl lead
Explosives	Sodium carbonate	Vinyl chloride
Hydrochloric acid	Sodium hydroxide	

10.3.9 Statistics

The world production of common salt rose in the nineteenth century to 11 million tons, and was 18 million tons in 1914 and 28 million tons in 1930. After this it decreased by 2 million tons, but reached the level of 1930 again after the economic depression. It was 36 million tons in 1945 and about 102 million tons in 1963.

The production of common salt in the major producing countries is as follows:

	In '000s short tons (1 short ton = 0.9 metric tons)				
	1953	1956	1959	1961	1963
Brazil	840	880	940	1000	1200
Canada	960	1600	3300	3200	3600
China	5500	7300	12000	13000	11000
Egypt (UAR)	–	580	420	580	420
France	3300	2800	3800	4200	4000
Germany, West	3900	4000	4000	5200	6000
Germany, East	–	1900	1900	2000	2200
India	3500	3500	3500	3800	4900
Italy	1800	2100	2200	2900	3200
Japan	500	700	1300	900	850
Mexico	–	217	512	1100	1300
Netherlands	500	700	1100	1200	1600
Poland	1300	1400	2000	2300	2300
Spain	1500	1300	1500	1500	1800
United Kingdom	4600	5600	6200	6400	7000
United States	20800	24200	25200	25700	30000
USSR	6800	7200	7200	9000	9400
World (estimated)	65400	75300	88000	96400	102000

The exports of the most important exporting countries were in 1963:

	In '000s metric tons		*In '000s metric tons*
Canada	3600*	Mexico	990
Egypt	300*	Netherlands	850
Formosa	280	Spain	460
Germany, West	880	United Kingdom	360
India	190	USA	250

* estimated

Imports in 1963 by the chief importers were:

In '000s metric tons			In '000s metric tons
Belgium-Luxembourg	640	Norway	260
Canada	300	Sweden	630
Italy	55	USA	1200
Japan	2900	Finland	260
		Malaya	80

Since salt is cheap, freight charges sometimes play a large part in determining the selling price and it can happen that a particular country can both export and import salt for use in different localities. Many countries both export and import salt of different grades for different application, e.g. the UK exported 360 thousand tons of salt in 1963, consisting mainly of vacuum salt. In the same year 170 thousand tons of salt for fish preservation were imported.

The distribution of salt consumption among its various applications is shown by the following figures for the USA in 1963:

Salt consumption (USA) in 1963	'000s short tons
Chorine	11985
Soda ash	6513
Textile and dyeing	260
Soap (including detergents)	35
All other chemicals	1418
Meat packers, tanners and casing manufacturers	747
Fishing	26
Dairy	63
Canning	239
Baking	115
Flour processing	68
Other food processing	138
Ice manufacturers and cold storage companies	38
Feed dealers	1030
Feed mixers	383
Metals	128
Ceramics and glass	15
Rubber	107
Oil	169
Paper and pulp	135
Water softener manufacturers	507
Grocery stores	862
Railroads	51
Bus and transit companies	33
Other (inc. state, countries and other subdivisions: exc. federal)	5579
Total	30644

Source: US Dept. of Interior, Bureau of Mines.

The consumption in the USA of different kinds of salt was in 1963:

Evaporated	4 774
Rock salt	8 345
Brine	17 525
Total	30 644

Brine was mainly consumed in the production of chlorine, soda ash and other chemicals. Evaporated and rock salt were used for all purposes.

Since the raw material cost is low, the cost of salt is greatly dependent on the amount of labour used. As has already been indicated, mechanization is being introduced extensively in production (mining or solar evaporation), purification, crystallization and packaging. As a result the cost relative to the cost of living index has decreased. Thus in the Netherlands the price is 18 c per kg compared with the prewar price of 7 c, i.e. a multiple of 2.6, whereas the cost of living in the same time has increased by a multiple 5 or more.

The USA prices of different grades of salt were in 1965:
table salt in paper bags, $ 1.34 per 100 lb; rock salt in paper bags $ 1.09 per 100 lb; pure sodium chloride (USP grade) $ 0.05 per lb.

In the UK pure vacuum dried salt was sold at £6 15s per ton.

10.3.10 Literature

H. BORCHERT and R. D. MUIR. *Salt deposits*. London, Van Nostrand, 1964.

D. W. KAUFMANN. *Sodium chloride*. New York, Reinhold, 1960. ACS monograph No. 145.

10.4 SODIUM HYDROXIDE

10.4.1 History

Sodium hydroxide (caustic soda, NaOH) is the most important alkali. It was prepared even in ancient times in those countries where soda (sodium carbonate) was found naturally, by the action of slaked lime on a solution. The method of production was very primitive.

A mixture of the raw materials was exposed to rain and the impure solution of alkali produced was collected and used in the manufacture of soap. Only when sodium carbonate could be obtained on a large scale (see p. 450) was it also possible to produce the hydroxide on a large scale. The development of the electrolytic method of production subsequently made an even larger output possible. The old lime-soda process is still used, but in the USA surplus output of electrolytically prepared alkali is sometimes converted into sodium carbonate with carbon dioxide.

10.4.2 The lime-soda process for production of caustic liquor

In the lime-soda process a hot sodium carbonate solution is mixed with slaked lime, the reaction being represented by:

$$Na_2CO_3 + Ca(OH)_2 \rightarrow 2\,NaOH + CaCO_3.$$

About 90% of the carbonate is converted, the process being shown schematically in fig. 10.11. It is worth using only if care is taken to preserve all the effluents for use again. It was this industry, with its strongly corrosive substances, which was mainly responsible for the development of the modern rotary filter (see p. 25). The concentration of the liquor follows closely on the lines described later for concentrating electrolytically-produced caustic soda.

10.4.3 Electrolytic production of caustic liquor

a. Principles. Large quantities of sodium hydroxide (and also potassium hydroxide, chlorine, hydrogen, hypochlorites and chlorates) are obtained by the electrolysis of NaCl or KCl.

When sodium chloride crystals are dissolved in water the individual sodium and chlorine atoms retain the respective positive and negative charges which they possess in the crystal lattice and on the supermolecular scale the system still remains neutral.

If direct current (d.c.) is passed through such a solution using inert electrodes (e.g. Pt or graphite) the positive sodium ions (Na^+) move towards the cathode where they are discharged and similarly the chloride (Cl^-) ions are discharged at the anode. The discharged sodium reacts with water to yield caustic soda (NaOH) and hydrogen whilst gaseous chlorine is released at the anode. The overalreaction is

$$2\,NaCl + 2\,H_2O \rightarrow Cl_2 + 2\,NaOH + H_2$$

anodic   cathodic
product   products

Potassium chloride solutions behave in the same way.

This reaction is the starting point in the production of important electrolytic products as shown schematically in fig. 10.12.

The chlorine and caustic alkali set free in the above reaction would quickly react if

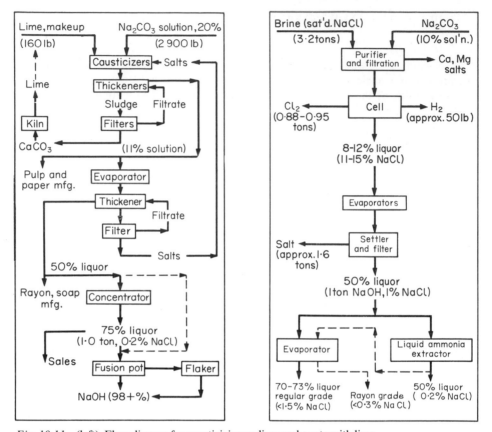

Fig. 10.11 (left). Flow diagram for causticizing sodium carbonate with lime.

Fig. 10.12 (right). Flow diagram for electrolytic plant for caustic soda and chlorine. The diagram shows that the salt must be purified, and that a further purification must follow the preparation and concentration. This is effected with liquid ammonia, in which the greater part of the salt and chlorate present dissolves; all the ammonia is, of course, subsequently recovered.

allowed to come together in a simple cell containing only an anode and cathode. Moreover an explosive mixture of hydrogen and chlorine would be evolved.

Commercial cells for the electrolysis of brine therefore are of highly specialized design to achieve the separation in safety with the minimum expenditure of electrical energy. They fall into two principal classes in one of which a porous diaphragm is used to isolate the reaction products whilst in the other a cell with a flowing mercury cathode is used to achieve the separation in two steps in separate compartments (see p. 437).

b. Diaphragm cells. Theoretically the decomposition represented by the equation on p. 429 can be brought about at a voltage of about 2.2 which is termed the decomposition voltage. In practice a higher applied voltage is required to overcome resistance in the cell such as the ohmic resistance in the electrodes and connections, in the diaphragm and in the electrolyte, and also excess voltage at the electrodes, called overvoltage, arising from so-called concentration polarization and other factors. Consequently the applied voltage of a working cell is usually in the range 3.5–4.5. Many subtle design and economic factors determine the voltage at which a cell operates. Since the energy consumption of the process is directly proportional to the voltage it is clearly advantageous to maintain as low an operating voltage as possible for a given operating load. The other important parameter in the cell performance is the current efficiency which expresses the amount of product actually produced by a given amount of current as a percentage of the theoretical quantity which the current should produce on the basis of Faraday's Law. Commercial cells usually work at current efficiencies above 95%. Loss of current efficiency results from the occurrence of side reactions and, as it is usually regarded, from recombination of the products formed at the electrodes.

Numerous types of diaphragm cells have been reported to have been in operation at various times, but most have been eliminated in the face of strong competition. Undoubtedly the most successful has been the Hooker cell, or variants of it, which

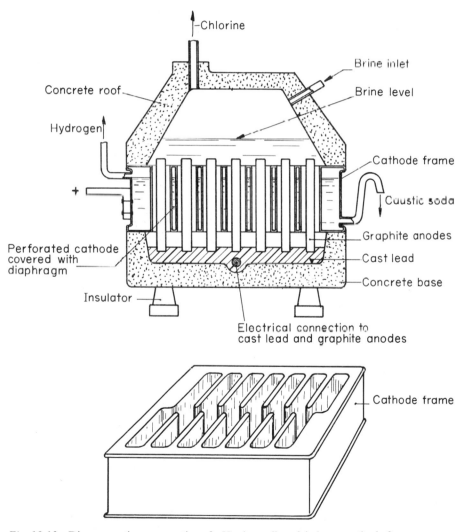

Fig. 10.13   Diagrammatic cross-section of a Hooker cell; and, below, a cathode frame.

accounts for a very big proportion of US chlorine and caustic alkali output and is also extensively operated in Europe and in many countries throughout the world. The cell owes its success to its compactness, relative ease of construction and its reliability and efficiency in operation.

The Hooker cell roughly a 1.5 m cube in size is built up of three main rectangular sections (fig. 10.13) comprising:

1. The base, which is a concrete mould into which are fixed vertical parallel rows of graphite plates supported in cast lead. The lead serves to seal the ends of the graphite plates and provides electrical contact to a copper current lead. The surface of the lead is protected from corrosion by a thick bitumastic layer.

2. The cathode block, which is of fabricated mild steel construction and rests on the concrete base and is sealed to it by means of a putty type material. The cathode block has an inner lining of woven steel gauze into which are joined transverse fingers or compartments also of gauze. When the cathode block is in position the transverse fingers or compartments interleave with the rows of graphite plates which extend to approximately the height of the block. The gauze of the inner lining with transverse compartments forms the effective cathode of the cell. Before the block is placed in position it is immersed in a tank of asbestos slurry and vacuum is applied to the inner space of the compartments by which means an adherent layer of asbestos is deposited on the outside surfaces of the gauze by suction. This asbestos deposit serves as the diaphragm. The cathode block has provision for the removal of hydrogen and causticized brine formed at the cathode surface. The negative current lead is joined to the cathode block.

3. The lid or cell top which is again of concrete construction; this rests on top of the cathode block and is sealed to it with a putty-type composition. The lid has connections for the offtake of chlorine and for feeding brine from a header pipe.

In operation nearly saturated purified brine is fed in, as stated, through the lid, and percolates through the asbestos and the steel gauze into the cathode compartment at such a rate that the tops of the anode plates and cathode/diaphragm fingers are kept submerged. The adjustable run-off from the cathode compartment is kept at a level which maintains the cathode partly flooded. (In some diaphragm cells the cathode is merely irrigated by the brine percolating through the diaphragm.)

Cells of the type described can be built to operate at currents of up to 30 000 A. They operate in electrical series in which the applied voltage may be as high as 700 V (350 V to earth) so that in electrical series there may be as many as 180 cells. Such a series requires 21 000 kW electrical energy at the above current.

In another type of cell, the Dow cell, the electrodes and diaphragms are arranged like the plates of a filter press and the electrodes are of the bipolar type in which one face acts as the anode of one cell and the reverse face the cathode of the adjoining cell in the pack. (See also electrolytic production of hydrogen p. 66.) In Germany some cells of the Siemens-Billiter type operate with a fluted horizontal diaphragm and cathode using wedge-shaped horizontal graphite anodes. Small units of the Gibbs or Vorce type of cylindrical cell are still in operation but are becoming obsolete (see fig. 10.14). These cells have vertical graphite stick anodes suspended from a chlorine

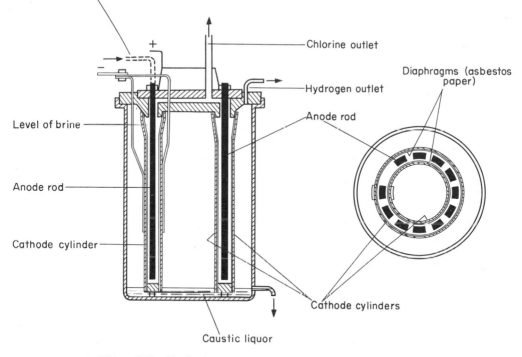

Brine feed pipe

+

−

Chlorine outlet

Hydrogen outlet

Diaphragms (asbestos paper)

Level of brine

Anode rod

Anode rod

Cathode cylinder

Cathode cylinders

Caustic liquor

Fig. 10.14 A Gibbs cell (double diaphragm cell).

resistant cover inside an annular space made of a woven gauze or perforated metal covered on the inside with a deposited asbestos diaphragm. Small cells of this type which operate at about 1 000 A are declining in importance because they require almost as much labour as the same number of larger cells.

The electrical energy requirements of diaphragm cells are significantly reduced by operating at a high temperature. Thus the brine fed to the Hooker cells is usually heated to above 95° C. The asbestos diaphragm is very effective in preventing the intermixing of the hydrogen and chlorine evolved and as a result the chlorine is obtained with a hydrogen content of less than 0.2% by volume. The chlorine also contains some oxygen (0.2-0.6%) produced electrolytically at the graphite anode, some carbon dioxide (about 1.0%) due to oxidation of the graphite anodes by discharge of hydroxyl ions and some miscellaneous organic materials (known in the USA as 'gunk') together with some air from the feed brine and from the atmosphere.

The operating procedure with diaphragm cells differs for the different cells and operators. In the Hooker cell for instance the brine is fed at a constant and predetermined rate so that for a given current on the cell the alkalinity of the brine leaving the cathode compartment is fixed at a value which lies in the range of 10-12% NaOH. The alkalinity concentration chosen is dependent on economic factors. Thus a high value leads to a high cell voltage and rapid attack of the graphite anode owing to back diffusion of hydroxyl ions, whilst a low value leads to excessive evaporation charges and considerable handling of salt (see below). During the life of a cell the resistance to flow of the diaphragm increases due to detritus from the anode, from the cell walls, and from the brine, depositing in the diaphragm. Thus to maintain the brine flow at a required rate the pressure drop across the diaphragm increases; an excessive pressure drop is one of the factors determining the life of the diaphragm.

In other cells, particularly the smaller cells, the brine head across the diaphragm is kept constant and the flow rate decreases steadily with result that the alkalinity of the electrolysed brine increases with time although the average of all the cells is maintained at a steady level.

In a representative case the composition of the cell liquid, i.e. electrolysed brine, is NaOH 11%, NaCl 15%, Na_2SO_4 0.5% (impurity from feed brine) and about 0.1-0.2% sodium chlorate (product of side reaction in the cell). The amount of sodium chlorate present is an indication of one source of current efficiency loss.

Owing to the gradual oxidation of the graphite anodes diaphragm cells have a limited life and need to be replaced periodically. The effect of wear is to cause the gap between the anode and cathode to become enlarged and thus the current path in the electrolyte is increased. As a result the cell resistance increases with time and either the voltage increases or the current decreases, and hence cell output, falls.

The current for the cells may be specially generated in a power station attached to a works by means of water or steam turbines, or may come from a public utility for which it can supply a useful base load and assist in smoothing demand by utilizing off-peak power. In such cases special tariffs operate to make the method of operating attractive to cell operators.

Usually the current is taken near the cells as high voltage alternating current (a.c.) and is then reduced in voltage to that required by the cells series in a step-down transformer and rectified to give direct current (d.c.). The rectifier types in common use are motor generators, synchronous convertors, mechanical contact rectifiers, mercury arc rectifiers and semi-conductor (silicon or germanium) rectifiers. The modern tendency is to move away from heavy rotating equipment in favour of the lighter static rectifiers. The efficiency of the mercury arc rectifier is high (*ca.* 98%) at high d.c. output voltages (*ca.* 500-600 V) but falls rather sharply at lower voltages. Mechanical and semi-conductor rectifiers operate at high efficiency at d.c. line voltages of practical interest.

A summary of the main construction and operating features of the Hooker 3B cell is given below:

Particulars of Hooker 3B Cell

Current capacity (max)	30 000 A
(rated)	27 000 A
Cathodic current density A/m² (rated)	1 330
Average overall voltage (rated)	3.83
Current efficiency (%)	96
Cell dimensions (without aisles) m	1.52 × 1.48 × 1.6 (high)
Cell construction (bottom, sides, top)	concrete
Total weight (lb)	16 000
Anode life (months)	10
Graphite consumption lb/ton NaOH	4.7
Cell gas H_2 %	0.2

The electrolysis of KCl in general is similar to that of NaCl.

Caustic liquor obtained in both the lime-soda process and in the diaphragm cell process requires to be concentrated for sale purposes and to remove salt.

For the evaporation of caustic liquor it is usual to employ double-effect evaporators to raise the concentration to 30% NaOH and to follow this with a single stage evaporator which raises the concentration to 50% NaOH. Sometimes triple-effect evaporators are used (for multiple-effect evaporators, see p. 418). As evaporation proceeds the concentration of salt in the liquor builds up to the point where it begins to crystallize out. This continues until the sodium hydroxide reaches a concentration of 30% NaOH when approximately 90% of the salt has crystallized out.

An important difference between caustic liquor evaporation and evaporation of brine or sugar is that the boiling point rise with increased concentration in the former case is much more pronounced. On this account the number of effects which can be operated in series for a given steam supply pressure is less.

Salt is removed from the effects by a bleed off of slurry from the delivery side of the liquor circulation pump, from which it is fed as a slurry either to a rotary filter or to a continuous centrifuge of the horizontal bowl or other automatic type, in which the salt can be simultaneously removed from the slurry, washed, and de-watered adequately to pass to a drier.

A rotary filter as used for this purpose consists of a cylinder of fine metal gauze supported on a cylinder divided radially into as many as twenty compartments (see figs. 10.15 and 10.16). The cylinder is supported on a horizontal shaft and rotates in a trough. Vacuum and air connections are made through the axle to the compartments in a given sequence. The liquid to be filtered containing suspended solid (a slurry) is fed to the trough where it is well stirred to prevent the solids settling out. The compartments when immersed in the slurry are automatically put into communication with an evacuated receiver. Liquor is thus drawn from the slurry through the gauze screen into the receiver and leaves a layer of solid on its surface which is termed the filter cake. As the cylinder rotates and the compartments emerge from the trough the surplus liquor is sucked off the filter cake. This draining stage is followed by a wash stage in which a spray of the wash liquor (water, purified brine or plant brine) is fed on to the surface of the filter cake (whilst still subjected to vacuum) which thus removes the last traces of the mother liquor clinging to the particles of the filter cake. The automatic arrangements divert the

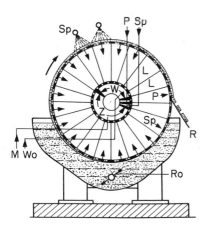

Fig. 10.15 Rotary filter divided into cells. W. Wash section; Z. Suction section; Sp. Sprays; R. Removal of material filtered off; Ro. Rotary equipment; P. Compressed air inlet; L. Cells into which air has been admitted; M. Suction opening; Wo. Opening for removal of warm water.

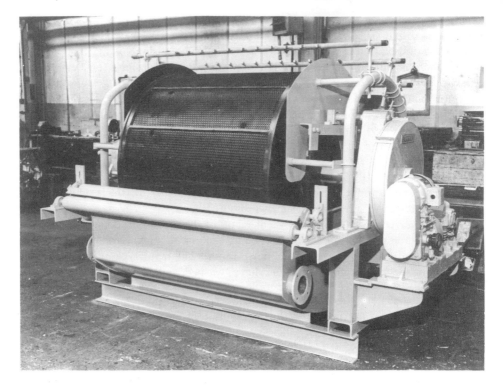

Fig. 10.16 Complete installation with rotary filter for a pilot plant. The picture shows the filter drum, various vacuum and other pumps, the vacuum vessel and various transmission devices, which ensure that the various operations take place at the right time.

wash liquor leaving the filter to a separate receiver from that used for the original alkali solution.

After the wash stage the vacuum on the compartments is released by admitting a little air and this has the effect of making the filter cake a little looser. When the compartment advances to the next stage air is blown in to dislodge the filter cake which is then easily removed and collected by a rake. In the final stage in the cycle water is sprayed on the gauze to clean it.

A photograph of a pilot scale rotary filter is shown in fig. 10.16 complete with motors and pumps for suction and for air blowing. Filters of this type are extensively used where slurries have to be de-watered.

During the evaporation procedure the sodium sulphate present in the feed brine, which it may be recalled is formed during the purification procedure by double decomposition between dissolved gypsum and added sodium carbonate

$$CaSO_4 + Na_2CO_3 \rightarrow CaCO_3 \downarrow + Na_2SO_4$$

is concentrated along with the salt and is precipitated with it. The procedure for washing the salt at the filter or centrifuge is therefore arranged in such a way that as much as possible of the alkali is recovered with the minimum of dilution whilst the sodium sulphate is concentrated in another fraction in which it can be discarded or if necessary treated for the recovery of Glauber's salt. The washed salt is dried and sold for industrial purposes, or, as is more frequently the case, redissolved and returned to the cells in the feed brine. It is important in the latter case to reduce the residual sodium hydroxide content and also the sodium sulphate to the minimum. Both impurities can lead to excessive electrolytic oxidation of the anodes.

The caustic soda liquor containing approximately 50% NaOH still contains about 2% NaCl, a little sodium sulphate (0.2% Na_2SO_4) and sodium chlorate (0.1% $NaClO_3$). This liquor is not pure enough for use in the rayon industry which is one of the major outlets for 50% liquor. It is therefore necessary to introduce a purification step to prepare diaphragm cell liquor for sale to rayon producers. This is mainly done in the USA where the bulk of caustic soda production is by means of diaphragm cells. The main process is the PPG (Pittsburgh Plate Glass) process which is based on the partition of the main impurities (NaCl + $NaClO_3$) between liquid ammonia and caustic liquor. This is done in a countercurrent extraction process in a spray column in which liquid ammonia rises in fine droplets through the caustic liquor and becomes progressively more concentrated in NaCl + $NaClO_3$.

The purified caustic liquor is run off at the bottom of the tower whilst the impurities leave at the top in the ammonia stream. The process operates under pressure (ca. 28 atm) to maintain the ammonia in the liquid form. Dissolved ammonia is removed from the purified caustic liquor under vacuum. In this way 'rayon grade' caustic liquor containing only 0.08% NaCl and 0.002% sodium chlorate is obtained. Typical analytical data for 50% caustic soda liquor before and after purification are shown in a later table in comparison with liquor made in mercury cells (see p. 442).

c. Mercury cells. The amazing growth of electrolytic processes dates from about the last decade of the nineteenth century when both the diaphragm and mercury cells came into being. The mercury cell had its origins in a patent of H.Y. Castner of 1892 which led to the first commercial process in 1894. The cell employed was the celebrated rocking cell which has since been featured in many standard textbooks and which clearly demonstrates the essential principles of the process.

An improved form of the Castner cell, now virtually obsolete, comprised a shallow horizontal tank mounted on a pivot along one edge of the base and supported on a rotating eccentric at the opposite edge (see also fig. 10.17). The tank was divided into

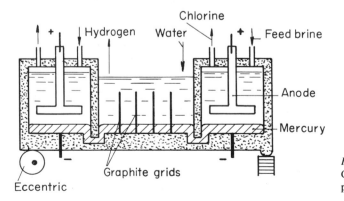

Fig. 10.17 Diagram of a Castner cell for chlorinealkali production.

three compartments by means of two partitions placed across the cell and almost reaching down to the base of the cell. The cell tank was made of a suitable chlorine resistant material such as concrete or hard rubber and the base was covered with a thin layer of mercury which was however sufficient to seal the undersides of the partition. The outer compartments were fed with purified brine and contained graphite anodes* held just above the mercury surface by means of suitable graphite supports protruding through the covers of the compartments. These supports also provided the electrical current leads to the anodes. The mercury served as the cathode in these compartments electrical contact being made by metal strips laid in the base of the compartments. The covers of these compartments were fitted with chlorine exit pipes.

The centre compartment was fed with water. This contained iron grids connected to the mercury (amalgam) either through an external circuit or by dipping directly into the mercury as shown in fig. 10.17. This compartment could, if required, be fitted with a lid and connection to a hydrogen collecting main.

When a current was passed through the outer compartments (which were in electrical parallel) chlorine was discharged at the anode whilst the sodium ions were discharged at the mercury cathode where they formed a fluid sodium amalgam with the mercury (and not hydrogen and caustic soda as occurs at the iron cathode in the diaphragm cell process).

The act of rocking the cell on the eccentric transferred the amalgam from the end compartments into the middle compartment. Here in the presence of the iron grids reaction takes place with water to yield hydrogen and caustic soda according to the reaction:

$$2 \text{ NaHg} + 2 \text{ H}_2\text{O} \rightarrow 2 \text{ NaOH} + \text{H}_2 + 2\text{Hg}$$

the hydrogen being discharged on the surface of the grid.

The mercury denuded of sodium returned under the rocking action to the electrolyser compartments. If the amalgam is connected through an external circuit to the iron grids instead of being shorted to them it is possible to draw energy from the system but at the expense of a slowing-down of the reaction rate. Considerable thought has been given by cell operators to means for recovering energy from this reaction in order to reduce the overall energy requirements of the electrolysis process but there is no authenticated instance of this being achieved on a commercial scale. The basic problem is discussed in one of the original patents of H.Y. Castner.

The Castner cell continued in operation in the USA and possibly elsewhere until after the 1939-45 war, but then quickly became obsolete when revelations by allied investigators of German industry drew attention to the revolution in design in mercury cells in Europe. These modern cells have load capacities of up to 180 k A and many are of the horizontal trough type comprising a shallow electrolyser and a shallow amalgam decomposer with interconnecting mercury flow system by which the mercury can be pumped continuously through the two compartments. Only the brine electrolyser carries current since the decomposer, as in the middle compartment of the Castner cell, operates as an electrically shorted primary cell.

The brine electrolyser and amalgam decomposer troughs are slightly inclined to the

---

* The electrothermal process for making the artifical graphite required for the anodes was developed at about the same time as the electrolytic cells were being developed.

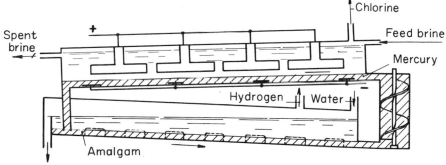

Fig. 10.18 Diagrammatic cross-section of a mercury cell for chlorine-alkali electrolysis with an amalgam decomposer (below).

horizontal and are arranged alongside each other or one above the other in the form of a Vee (fig. 10.18) with the amalgam transfer channels between them at the apex and the mercury pump at the opening of the Vee. The mercury pumps are of various types such as archimedian screw, vertical helix, centrifugal and bucket wheel. The brine electrolyser baseplate is usually constructed of mild steel or of an inert material with mild steel embedded in it to provide electrical contact to the mercury whilst the sides are of chlorine resistant material such as concrete, ebonite lined steel or tile lined. In the more advanced designs provision is made for adjustment of the anodes to compensate for wear due to anodic oxidation of the graphite. The mercury flows as a thin sheet over the baseplate and gradually becomes enriched in sodium as it progresses along the cell. The anodes are arranged to be as close as possible to the mercury surface without actually touching it in order to minimise the resistance of the current path in the electrolyte (see fig. 10.19). Provision is made for brine feed and exit connec-

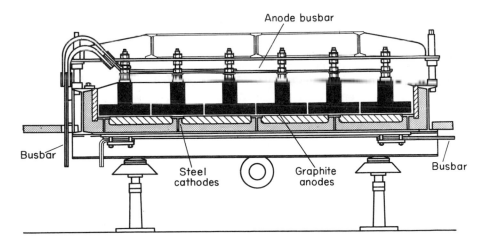

Fig. 10.19 Cross-section of a De Nora mercury cell. The decomposer (not shown) consists of a graphite lined tower in which mercury and water are contacted countercurrently.

tions and similarly for the mercury and amalgam and to take out the chlorine. The decomposer operates with a water feed at one end – the choice of end appearing to vary with the operators, and caustic liquor is taken off at the other end. The trough is of enclosed construction being luted at either end and always operates under a slight pressure to obviate the risk of ingress of atmospheric air. It is then able to deliver almost 100% hydrogen via the gas exit.

The practice of various operators differs in detail, owing, among other reasons, to different economic circumstances. Brine may be fed as an almost saturated solution and discarded as waste when the sodium chloride content has been reduced to the point where it becomes increasingly difficult to operate the cells efficiently. This reduction may be from about 25% NaCl to about 15% NaCl. This mode of operation is practised where brine can easily be won from underground deposits by water mining (see p. 414). In other cases where solid salt is employed the brine is recycled and continuously fortified with salt in the cycle so that the cells operate at high average salt content of 23-24% NaCl with consequent advantage in reduced operating voltage and less wear and tear of the anodes.

Generally the electrolysers operate at a high temperature (50-80° C) and in some instances, especially where high currents are employed, it may be necessary to provide some cooling. The electrolyser is usually operated under a slight suction to prevent the escape of asphyxiating chlorine gas and this results in some ingress of air. The chlorine content of the gas is in the range 95-98% the balance being made up of hydrogen (1%), carbon dioxide (from the brine and from oxidation of the graphite), oxygen (electrolytic) and air. The hydrogen comes from some decomposition of amalgam in the brine electrolyser compartment. The extent of this is a vital concern of mercury cell operation since it can give rise to explosions if the hydrogen is allowed to form to the extent of about 4% of the chlorine. The rate at which hydrogen is evolved is dependent upon a number of factors including the presence in minute amounts (0.1 p.p.m.) of trace impurities, e.g. vanadium, in the brine. The quality of the brine and of the cell components is therefore important.

In the caustic soda compartment the water feed is adjusted to give a caustic soda content at the exit of 50% NaOH by weight whilst the mercury is normally denuded of sodium. Considerable heat is evolved in the decomposition reaction and the caustic flows from the cell at a high temperature.

In Germany a rotary type of electrolyser has been extensively employed. This is based on the fact that amalgam is able to 'wet' steel. It comprises a set of parallel vertical discs which rotate on a horizontal shaft with the lower halves of the discs immersed in mercury and with graphite plates suspended between their upper halves. The discs, during rotation, carry a film of mercury which acts as the cathode, into the upper part where it becomes enriched in sodium whilst the graphite plates act as the anode for the release of chlorine. In this way the mercury in the tank is converted to amalgam. This amalgam is transferred to a tower-type amalgam decomposer in which amalgam is trickled over packed graphite which is flooded in caustic liquor. Water is fed to the tower to maintain the required caustic liquor strength.

In recent years several references have been made to the Szechtmann cell which embodies features of both the horizontal mercury cell and the Downs cell (see sodium). It employs a flowing lead cathode in a trough type of electrolyser and a fused electrolyte of sodium chloride. Lead sodium alloy is obtained as the cathodic product and may be used either to make tetraethyl lead or caustic soda. There is as yet no report of its having achieved commercial success.

As already stated the anodes used in brine electrolysers are graphite. In the early days platinum anodes were used but there have process disadvantages and the present day cost is prohibitive. Magnetite (an iron oxide) has also been mentioned as an anode material but has probably not been used extensively. Recently there have been references to the use of platinized titanium in which a very thin layer of platinum is deposited on the base of cheaper titanium metal which is exceptionally resistant to attack by chlorine. In this way a mechanically sounder anode can be constructed in which the platinum provides the effective anode surface but the titanium satisfies the mechanical requirement. Without a layer of platinum the titanium is unable to conduct current because when made anodic it forms a non-conducting oxide film. There are reports that several chlorine producers are evaluating the anodes under commercial conditions, but there have been no indications yet that it has been adopted for commercial operations.

An important difference between the diaphragm and mercury cell processes lies in the theoretical energy requirements for the respective processes and hence in the decomposition voltage. In the mercury cell process the reaction in the electrolyser is

$$2 \text{ Hg} + 2 \text{ NaCl} \xrightarrow{\text{2 Faradays}} 2 \text{ NaHg} + \text{Cl}_2$$

for which the decomposition voltage is 3.1 as compared with 2.2 V for the reaction

$$2 \text{ NaCl} + 2 \text{ H}_2\text{O} \longrightarrow \text{Cl}_2 + 2 \text{ NaOH} + \text{H}_2$$

of the diaphragm cells. This inherent disadvantage of the mercury cell process is offset by greater precision in the setting of anodes which is possible and which leads to reduced ohmic losses in the cell, and by the elimination of the need for evaporation of the caustic liquor and by higher purity of the product (see table p. 442).

Consideration has been given to alternative uses of sodium amalgam for the production of a number of chemicals other than caustic soda. It is reported to have been used in Germany for the reduction of nitrobenzene to hydrazobenzene (a precursor of the dyestuffs intermediate benzidine) and for the reduction of sulphur dioxide to yield sodium dithionite (see p. 462), and for reaction with alcohols to form sodium alkoxides.

The caustic liquor obtained from mercury cells is of very high purity and is suitable for rayon manufacture. After filtration to remove suspended graphite and mercury it is of analytical quality. Typical analyses of 50% caustic soda from diaphragm cells with and without purification and from mercury cells are given in the table on p. 442, showing composition of 50% caustic soda liquor from a diaphragm and/or mercury cell (per cent on 100% NaOH):

	Diaphragm cell		Mercury cell
Constituent	Direct from cell	Purified with liquor NH_3	
Na_2CO_3	0.10-0.30	0.15	0.10
NaCl	1.00-1.5	0.08	0.006
Na_2SO_4	0.013-0.020	0.01	0.0002
SiO_2	0.018-0.025	0.009	0.006
$NaClO_3$	0.05-0.10	0.0002	—
CaO	0.0017	0.0010	0.001
MgO	0.0010-0.0020	0.0010	0.0001
Al_2O_3	0.0013-0.0030	0.0015	0.0002
NH_3	—	0.00015	—
Fe	0.0005*	0.00025	0.0002
Ni	0.00003	0.00001	—
Cu	0.00003	0.00002	0.00003
Mn	0.00001-0.00006	0.00003	0.00002

* From nickel evaporators 0.007 from iron plant 0.0007 after treatment for iron removal.
Source Karl Hass, 'Chlor-alkali electrolysis', *Chemie ingenieur technik* **27**, 1955, 234.

The major items of cost in the joint production of caustic soda/chlorine have been reported as follows:

Costs of production of caustic soda and chlorine by electrolysis in diaphragm and mercury cells (dollars)
(Basis 0.53 tons NaOH 100% + 0.47 tons Cl_2, i.e. 1 mixed ton)

Cost item	Diaphragm cells		Mercury cell	
Materials		21.61		22.57
Utilities				
Power	22.80		26.25	
Steam	7.58		0.80	
Water	0.93		0.10	
	31.31	*31.31*	*27.15*	*27.15*
Labour		7.40		9.60
Maintenance		6.68		7.28
Overheads etc.				
Royalty	0.25		1.50	
Administration	2.60		2.60	
Depreciation (6% of plant cost)	20.00		21.82	
Taxes	6.68		7.28	
	29.53	*29.53*	*33.20*	*33.20*
Purification		9.50		
Total (dollars per short ton of mixed product)		106.03		99.80

Source: W. L. Hardy, *Ind. Eng. Chem;* **50** (5), 1958, 87a.

The figures given are by way of example. The actual costs will depend on local circumstances, e.g. cost of energy.

Solutions of potassium chloride (muriate of potash) can be electrolysed in much the same way as brine. The starting material is usually the solid salt (see p. 477).

10.4.4 Solid caustic soda from caustic liquor

The conventional process for concentrating caustic soda liquor to yield the anhydrous solid makes use of large cast iron pots directly fired by solid, liquid or gaseous fuels. The process does not give a very pure product and chemical treatment is employed to improve or 'shade' the final molten liquor to obtain a nearly white solid product. In recent years there has been a trend towards use of more sophisticated means for concentrating the liquor. In one process a nickel tube bundle heat exchanger employing Dowtherm (i.e. a mixture of diphenyl and diphenyloxide) in forced circulation as a heat transfer medium has been described. In this process temperatures as high as 405° C are employed. The evaporation is done under vacuum in all-nickel plant. The nickel is liable to corrode in the presence of compounds such as chlorate capable of evolving oxygen under the evaporation conditions. It is therefore necessary to reduce the active oxygen content by means of sugar (which is itself oxidized to CO_2 and H_2O) or iron. Iron is the more efficient but gives rise to iron contamination of the caustic. It is therefore only applied in plant equipped with means for the removal of iron as a ferrate absorbate on a carrier such as strontium sulphate or carbonate.

It is claimed that if forced circulation is employed Dowtherm decomposition amounts to 10% (or less) of the charge in one year.

Anhydrous caustic soda concentrated in this way does not usually require the settling and shading treatment which are features of the old iron pot method of concentration or 'caustic finishing' as it is sometimes called.

10.4.5 Properties and handling of sodium hydroxide

Sodium hydroxide is a white hygroscopic solid. Its melting point is 318° C and its boiling point 1390° C. Sodium hydroxide is often named caustic soda because it is corrosive to the skin. 109 g caustic soda dissolve in 100 g water.

Caustic liquor is sold to major users in very large road and rail tankers as 50% or even 73% NaOH. In the latter case owing to the high freezing point 60° C (it is a eutectic of the anhydrous and the monohydrate) it is necessary to make provision for heating the tank contents. It is however economic to do this in many cases to reduce the transport costs since a greater quantity of NaOH (100%) can be packed into a tank of given size.

Caustic soda may be transported in the solid state. Fused caustic liquor is poured into a steel drum in which it is allowed to solidify in a solid block; the drums are then hermetically sealed by soldering on the lids. The drums are usually expendable and are cut away from the solid block when it is required for use. Alternatively they may be pierced and the caustic soda removed by blowing in live steam. Special precautions are necessary to protect the operator from splashes of strong caustic liquor. High grade caustic is usually flaked by spreading on a cooled rotating drum. It may also be cast into sticks or into the more convenient form of pellets.

10.4.6 Uses

The following table showing US usage gives the most important users of caustic soda. The total quantities consumed are given in 1 000 short tons (one short ton = 907 kg).

	1929 %	1939 %	1945 %	1955 %	1959 %	1963 %
Chemicals	17.9	18.2	21.5	26.9	32.4	43.0
Artifical silk and cellulose film	14.6	19.1	20.9	17.8	14.9	13.0
Pulp and paper	5.8	4.6	5.9	6.6	11.4	10.0
Petroleum refining	17.8	9.7	7.2	5.5	5.4	5.0
Lye and cleansers	3.3	4.3	5.5	4.1	6.0	5.0
Soap	14.2	9.7	6.0	2.1		
Textiles	5.3	4.3	5.4	3.5	5.4	6.0
Rubber regeneration	5.1	1.8	1.3	0.7		
Vegetable oils refining	1.5	1.7	1.0	0.6	19.2	13.0
Other uses	6.4	13.9	19.9	26.3		
Exports	8.0	12.7	5.4	5.9	5.3	5.0
Total in 1 000 short tons	760	1 020	1 800	3 500	4 200	5 600

The uses are too numerous to describe in detail. For example under chemicals is included its use as absorbent for acids, promotor of catalytic reactions, regenerating agent for catalysts, dehydrating agent, neutralizing agent in several reactions, reagent for separating gas mixtures and process material for making inorganic and organic chemicals. The list of organic chemicals which are produced with sodium hydroxide is seemingly endless. It includes several dyestuffs.

Under 'other uses' is included consumption for metallurgical purposes, for mining etc.

A large amount of very dilute caustic alkali solution is used for washing and peeling fruit which is to be dried or preserved, especially in North America.

10.4.7 Statistics

Production has increased markedly since the last war. World production of both caustic soda (and chlorine) set new records in 1963 at 13 million tons (and 10 million tons). The constant demand for more chlorine has led to great changes in the caustic soda industry. While 50% of the world's caustic soda in 1950 was made by the lime-soda process (causticization of soda ash), only about 25% came from this process in 1963. In the USA the trend in favour of the electrolytic process was even more pronounced than in the world as a whole. About 20% of the caustic soda output came from the lime-soda process in 1950. This percentage declined to 7% in 1963.

The worldwide distribution of production is given on p. 445.

Production figures of the UK, although a major producer, are not available. The estimates range from 800 000 to 980 000 tons per year between 1960 and 1963. The United Kingdom is an important exporter as shown in the table on p. 445.

UK exports (caustic soda)	1955	1957	1959	1961	1963
In 1 000 metric tons	198	209	250	236	191
1 000 £	5 347	5 295	6 293	3 938	4 594

World production (caustic soda)	1938	1948	1963	1958	1961	1963
Australia	–	15	18	40	49	50
Austria	–	14	36	53	–	60
Canada	–	–	174	285	375	400
Czechoslovakia	–	37	61	93	133	140
France	190	290	420	360	420	540
Germany (East)	–	118	221	296	335	300
Germany (West)	–	–	442	636	811	1 200
India	–	5	23	58	120	140
Italy	165	211	206	254	483	500
Japan	117	106	372	592	843	1 200
Norway	–	–	24	40	49	45
Poland	30	47	82	151	186	230
Romania	–	14	21	41	129	180
Spain	–	58	87	140	139	140
Sweden	16	58	86	129	–	200
USA	800	2 200	3 250	4 000	4 900	5 200
USSR	177	244	448	700	–	1 000

The prices of caustic soda in the USA were in 1965:

flakes 7.6%: $ 5.20 per 100 lb

solid in drums 76%: $ 4.80 per 100 lb

liquid 50% and 73%: $ 2.90-$ 3.00 per 100 lb (dry basis)

pellets USP grade: $ 0.24-$ 0.28 per lb.

In the UK solid caustic soda (98-99%) was sold at £ 35 6s 6d per ton in 1965.

10.4.8 Literature

D. W. F. HARDIE. *Electrolytic manufacture of chemicals from salt.* Oxford University Press, 1959.

C. L. MANTELL. *Electrochemical engineering.* New York, McGraw-Hill, 1960.

J. W. MELLOR. *Comprehensive treatise on inorganic chemistry,* vol. II suppl. 2. London, Longmans, 1961.

H. A. SOMMERS. 'Chlorine-caustic cell development in Europe and United States', *Chem. Eng. Progr.* **53,** Sept. 1957, 409-17; **53,** Oct. 1957, 506-10.

10.5 SODIUM SULPHATES

10.5.1 Occurrence

Sodium sulphate (Na_2SO_4) occurs as an anhydrous salt (thenardite) in Spain, Asia and Africa. The deposits contain salt of a purity up to 99.9%. In the form of the decahydrate (Glauber's salt, $Na_2 SO_4.10H_2O$), it is found in Saskatchewan (Canada) and the USA. The Canadian deposits are estimated to contain 200 million tons. The water of some salt lakes in Wyoming and Saskatchewan in Canada and in the USSR consists of a rather pure sodium sulphate solution. Various other lakes, wells, seas and solid salt deposits contain sodium sulphate together with other salts, e.g. the salt lakes in the USA, the mineral springs in Germany, the potassium salt deposits in Germany, and the saltpetre deposits in Chile.

10.5.2 Production of sodium sulphate

a. *From natural sources.* The pure deposits of anhydrous sodium sulphate and Glauber's salt are easily mined. The crude product is crushed, washed and then dried in rotary driers.

The sodium sulphate solutions from the Canadian salt lakes, containing 50% Na_2SO_4 are pumped in summer into large ponds where some water evaporates. As the weather turns colder (in November), the sulphate crystallizes out in the form of Glauber's salt. About 600 kg Glauber's salt is obtained per m^3 solution. The remaining mother liquor is removed as waste. The still wet Glauber's salt is taken from the ponds with scrapers and dried in the factory. In a similar way Glauber's salt is crystallized from solutions of Russian salt lakes containing sodium sulphate and magnesium sulphate.

In Texas (USA) sodium sulphate is obtained from salt lakes containing sodium chloride, magnesium sulphate and 7-11% sodium sulphate. Sodium chloride is added until the solution is saturated with it, making the sodium sulphate far less soluble (see fig. 9.19 and production of Chile saltpetre, p. 338). Upon cooling to about $-10°$ C by means of cold waste and evaporating ammonia, Glauber's salt crystallizes out. The production of sodium sulphate from the salt lakes of California (e.g. Searles lake brine) is less simple since they contain several other salts. In the most economical process, the brine of Searles lake is treated with carbon dioxide. Sodium carbonate is converted into sodium bicarbonate and precipitates (see production of sodium carbonate). The remaining mother liquor is cooled in stages. Borax precipitates first and at a temperature of 5-6° C Glauber's salt precipitates. The remaining solution is evaporated to produce potassium chloride. In another process the brine of Searles lake is evaporated in vacuum evaporators. A crystalline mass of sodium chloride and burkeite (a double salt of sodium carbonate and sodium sulphate) is obtained. Glauber's salt can be recovered from this crystal mixture.

Fairly large amounts of Glauber's salt are obtained from Stassfurt salts (see wastes of the production of potassium chloride, p. 472).

b. *Synthetic sodium sulphate.* Large quantities of sodium sulphate are still obtained from common salt and sulphuric acid or in the Hargreaves process as a by-product in the production of hydrochloric acid (see p. 225). Anhydrous sodium sulphate (salt cake), which contains the impurities from sulphuric acid and common salt, is obtained. This product is often sold as such. It can be purified as follows: salt cake is

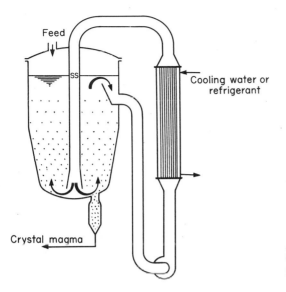

Feed

SS

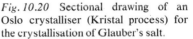

Cooling water or refrigerant

Crystal magma

Fig. 10.20 Sectional drawing of an Oslo crystalliser (Kristal process) for the crystallisation of Glauber's salt.

dissolved in hot water to a strong solution of 32° Bé. The solution is neutralised by adding sodium carbonate. At the same time, aluminium hydroxide and iron hydroxide are precipitated.

The solution is cleared and sodium sulphate crystallizes in the form of Glauber's salt in a vacuum crystallizer, e.g. an Oslo crystallizer provided with cooling means (see fig. 10.20 and compare fig. 10.11 and the heated Oslo crystallizer for common salt, p. 422). Sodium sulphate is also obtained as a by-product in the production of copper from roasted copper pyrites ($Cu\,FeS_2$) and other roasted pyrites containing valuable by-products such as copper, zinc and lead. Copper pyrites often contains zinc (up to 11%) which is recovered at the same time. Roasted pyrites, still containing about 3% sulphur, is mixed with about 12% common salt and roasted once more in a multiple hearth mechanical roaster (see roasting of pyrites, p. 273). The roasted product is leached with a mixture of sulphuric acid and hydrochloric acid. Iron oxides remain in the residue. The resulting solution mainly contains copper and zinc salts and Glauber's salt. Copper is precipitated by reduction with iron (cementation). Glauber's salt is precipitated from the remaining solution by cooling to $-10°$ C in vacuum crystallizers or by cooling to 0° C after adding a lot of sodium chloride (to decrease the solubility of Glauber's salt, see fig. 9.19). This cooling process is rather cheap since the cold mother liquor is used for cooling purposes. Only little additional refrigeration by means of vacuum evaporation is needed. The remaining mother liquor containing zinc and other compounds goes to a zinc factory (see also fig. 10.21). Sodium sulphate is also obtained as by-product in the manufacture of sodium dichromate (see p. 596) and in the manufacture of viscose rayon where it is formed in the spinning bath during spinning of viscose (see also viscose rayon production, vol. VI).

10.5.3 Properties of sodium sulphate and its dehydration

Glauber's salt, a colourless crystalline product, is usually obtained by crystallization from solutions in water since it is the stable modification of sodium sulphate at temperatures below 32.4° C. Glauber's salt melts at 32.4° C as at this temperature, the

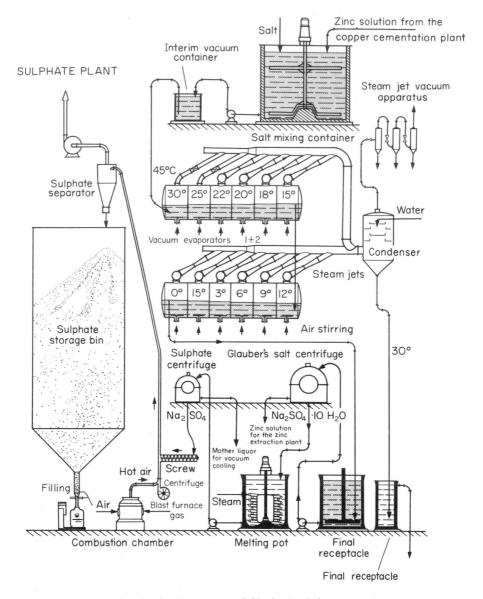

Fig. 10.21 Diagram of a plant for the recovery of Glauber's salt from roasted pyrite leaches.

anhydrous modification is formed which dissolves in the water of crystallization. Anhydrous sodium sulphate (thenardite) is a white crystalline solid having a melting point of 884° C. The solubility of both Glauber's salt and anhydrous sodium sulphate in water is shown in fig. 9.19.

Owing to the heavy freight costs, Glauber's salt is often freed from its water of crystallization. Glauber's salt is difficult to dehydrate to a crystalline product by simple evaporation due to its low melting point and the tendency of the anhydrous form to cake on to the equipment. Glauber's salt can partially be freed from water by spraying in a tower countercurrently with hot gases. The remaining water may be removed in a rotary drum drier. Dehydration may also be performed by means of submerged flame burners (see phosphoric acid, p. 374). A slurry of anhydrous sodium sulphate in a saturated solution is obtained. The anhydrous salt is separated from the mother liquor and the latter is treated again. In another drying process, Glauber's salt with 60% water is flung by paddle arms into a stream of hot combustion gases yielding a slurry containing 24% water, which is kept in vigorous motion. The slurry is dried in a long rotary drum drier in counterflow with hot gases.

10.5.4 Uses and statistics

Large quantities of sulphate are used in the sulphate process for the manufacture of kraft pulp (see paper, vol. VI). Important quantities of sodium sulphate are used in mixed washing preparations. The latter often contain 50 to 80% sodium sulphate. Sodium sulphate is also used in the manufacture of glass, in nickel refining, for salting of hides and for increasing the conductivity of galvanic baths. In acid wool-baths it is a dye leveller and guarantees moderate absorption (see also salt p. 425). Sodium sulphate is also the starting material for the production of various sodium compounds, e.g. water-glass (sodium silicate), ultramarine (a sodium aluminium silicate) and sodium sulphide.

Due to its latent heat of crystallization, Glauber's salt can be packed in tin con-tainers, placed in well insulated boxes and so be used to keep living tissues within a narrow temperature range (around 32.4° C) during transportation. (When the tempera-ture increases above 32.4° C, Glauber's salt is converted into anhydrous sodium sulphate and heat is absorbed. The opposite is true when the temperature decreases below 32.4° C.)

The production of sodium sulphate in some important producing countries is shown in the following table:

	In '000s metric tons			
	1957	1959	1961	1963
USA: Salt cake, technical	650	660	690	—
Anhydrous refined	250	260	280	1 100
Glauber's salt	115	100	63	—
Germany West:				
total in terms of Na_2SO_4	260	300	330	315
Canada: natural, in terms of Na_2SO_4	160	170	220	230
Japan	600	660	—	—

The United Kingdom is also an important producer of sodium sulphate. The sales in 1958 were 104 000 tons. The exports of sodium sulphate from the United Kingdom were about 40 000 long tons in 1962.

In the United States salt cake was sold at $ 28 per short ton and Glauber's salt at $ 36 per short ton in 1965. The prices of the corresponding products in the United Kingdom were £ 19 10s to £20 10s and £ 17 per long ton respectively in the same year.

10.5.5 Sodium bisulphate

Formerly most sodium bisulphate (nitre cake, $NaHSO_4$) was obtained as a by-product in the now obsolete process for the production of nitric acid from sodium nitrate and sulphuric acid. Nowadays it is obtained as a by-product in the production of hydrochloric acid (see p. 225), and by treating sodium sulphate with sulphuric acid.

Sodium bisulphate is a colourless crystalline product. Its melting point is 315° C. It is used as a safe sulphuric acid substitute in acid dyeing and bleaching baths for wool and cotton. It is also used as a flux in metallurgical processes and for cleaning automobile radiators and sanitary ware.

In the USA sodium bisulphate was sold at $ 40 to $ 70 per short ton in 1965. The price in the UK was £45 17s 6d per long ton in the same year.

10.6 SODIUM CARBONATE

10.6.1 History

Sodium carbonate (soda ash, Na_2CO_3) was in use even in ancient times. It was also found in salt lakes from which it could be obtained in a relatively pure form but was expensive because of its localized availability and the consequent high cost of transport. Its main use was in glass-making and in washing applications and, from Roman times, in soap manufacture. An alternative source was wood ash from which it could be leached. Later an important source was the plant 'Solsola sativa', related to the goosefoot family, which was extensively grown in Spain. In the eighteenth century kelp obtained by burning seaweed developed as an important source of soda ash especially in Scotland.

With the greatly increased growth of cotton, the production of textiles increased and there arose a correspondingly increased demand for soda for soap manufacture. In 1775, when because of her wars France had difficulty in importing soda ash in the required quantities, the French Academy of Science offered a 100000 franc prize for a solution to the problem of manufacturing soda ash industrially. The belief that an industrial process was possible had been inspired by Duhamel de Monceau who had demonstrated that the base of natural salt and of 'mineral (soda) ash' were identical.

The prize was won by Leblanc in 1789. His method was based on earlier known processes, but included the novel process of heating acid sodium sulphate with chalk and carbon to give what came to be known as 'black ash'. Water extraction gave sodium carbonate leaving behind an offensive waste of calcium sulphide.

The process was established in France in 1790, and by 1800 soda ash made by this process cost 20 francs per 100 kg as compared with 200 francs for the traditional product. There is evidence that the process was introduced into England in a small way at the beginning of the nineteenth century, but it was established as a major industrial process by James Muspratt (senior) in Liverpool in 1823. By 1867 there were 67 Leblanc factories in operation and the production of soda, after that of sulphuric acid, had become the basis of a developing chemical industry. The process came into disrepute because the intermediate process for making the acid sodium sulphate, by the reaction $NaCl + HSO_4 \rightarrow NaHSO_4 + HCl$, gave rise to large quantities of HCl which could not be efficiently absorbed and therefore gave rise to air pollution. The problem was largely overcome by Gossage, who developed an effective water scrubbing tower and incidentally created the foundation for the chlorine industry.

The Leblanc process for soda ash rapidly declined in importance in the face of competition by the Solvay process (see below). This latter process is still the principal method for the manufacture of soda ash although the recovery of natural soda ash from salt lakes is increasingly becoming an important source again.

10.6.2 Soda ash from natural sources

Sodium carbonate combined with varying amounts of water of crystallization, occurs in enormous quantities naturally; it is usually present as a mixture of trona (Na_2CO_3, $NaHCO_3$, H_2O) with various impurities such as borax, sodium sulphate, etc. There are important deposits in Africa (Egypt, Lake Magadi), Hungary, the USA, Canada, Mexico, Central Asia, etc. Thus Lake Magadi (Kenya) contains about 200 000 000 tons of soda as trona, forming a thick mass of needle-shaped crystals, which are found to a depth of three metres in the water. A dredger brings up the mass, grinds it and forces the semi-fluid material towards the solid bank, where it is washed to remove salt and mud, the rest being piled into large heaps to drain. After this, the mass is so fiercely heated in a rotary kiln (by means of generator gas from wood) that the trona is converted into soda with a sodium carbonate content of 97%. Salt is obtained as a by-product from the solution in Lake Magadi by means of solar evaporation and recrystallization. Japan used to be the largest consumer of Magadi soda, until Japanese production of Solvay soda became sufficient for local needs. At that time, Africa was only able to consume a little of the output, so that operations had to be suspended, and only after the last war was it possible to restart operations to supply soda for export; the output amounted to 126 000 tons in 1960. During the manufacture small amounts of sodium fluoride are obtained as by-product.

The well-known Searles Lake in California (see p. 446) produces annually about 320 000 tons of soda ash and appreciable amounts of borax (see p. 509). The naturally occurring solution is pumped away from beneath the hard salt crust on the surface by means of steel pipes protected by cement both inside and outside. The solution contains 6% soda, 2% borax and much salt, sodium sulphate, potassium chloride etc. It is sent to tall steel carbonators into which carbon dioxide is pumped; the gas is obtained partly from the process itself (see below) and partly from flue gases. Sodium bicarbonate is formed here; this is of low solubility and therefore quickly crystallizes out. It is allowed to settle in Dorr thickeners (see ch. 1, p. 16) to form a thick paste which is freed from water in rotary filters (see p. 23), and then passed through a long system of rotary dryers. The water first evaporates, and the material passes to a well insulated cylinder which is heated to 215° C. At this temperature the bicarbonate is completely converted into soda ash, while the carbon dioxide liberated is used again as described above. The soda passes to cooling cylinders and sieves, and then to the mechanical packing machines.

The effluent liquor from the bicarbonate is used for the preparation of impure borax (see p. 509) and potassium chloride.

10.6.3 Production by the Solvay process

The reactions on which the Solvay method depends had been known for many years before Ernst Solvay could utilize them to provide a practical and economic process. He, independently of previous inventors, discovered the essentials of the whole process. Plants were erected in Belgium in 1865, in France in 1872, in England in 1874, and in America in 1882. The process is now in operation in many countries throughout the world.

The raw materials of the process are limestone and brine which take part in the overall double decomposition

$$CaCO_3 + 2NaCl \rightarrow CaCl_2 + Na_2CO_3 \tag{1}$$

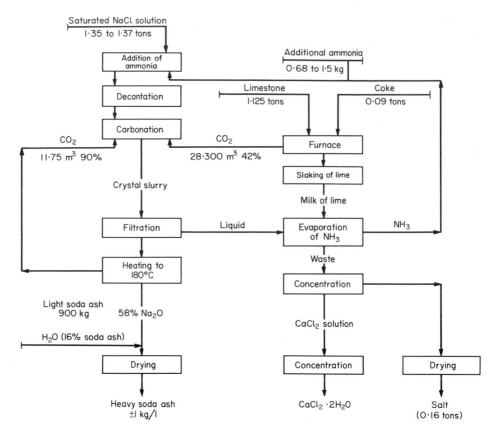

Fig. 10.22 Flow diagram of the Solvay process for soda.

the result of a series of separate stages. Ammonia is an important intermediate which however is not consumed in the process apart from small adventitious losses.

The essential reactions in the process are:

Lime kiln reactions

$$(CaCO_3 \xrightarrow{\text{heat}} CaO + CO_2) \quad \text{(2a) (see production of lime, vol. II)}$$

$$(C + O_2 \xrightarrow{\text{burn}} CO_2) \tag{2b}$$

Lime slaking

$$CaO + H_2O \rightarrow Ca(OH)_2 \text{ (Milk of lime)} \tag{3}$$

Ammoniation and carbonation

$$NaCl \text{ (brine)} + NH_3 + CO_2 + H_2O \rightarrow NaHCO_3 + NH_4Cl \tag{4}$$

Bicarbonate calcination

$$2\,NaHCO_3 \xrightarrow{\text{heat}} Na_2CO_3 + CO_2 + H_2O \tag{5}$$

Ammonia recovery

$$2\,NH_4Cl + Ca(OH)_2 \rightarrow 2\,NH_3 + 2\,H_2O + CaCl_2 \tag{6}$$

The steps are interrelated for example by the recovery of ammonia in reaction (6) and its return to reaction (4) and the return of CO_2 from the reaction (5) to reaction (4); the interrelationship of the various steps in the industrial process is shown in fig. 10.22.

The brine for the process is obtained usually by the water mining technique (see p. 414) and is purified with lime and soda. The brine saturated in salt is saturated first with gaseous ammonia in countercurrent operated ammoniating towers with stages suitably arranged to absorb ammonia from gas streams at high and low concentrations. The aim is to achieve maximum solution in the treated brine at the lowest temperature and highest ammonia partial pressure. This gives about 85 g NH_3 per litre of ammoniated solution. Since the solution of NH_3 occurs with evolution of heat it is necessary to cool the liquors in the towers.

In the next stage carbon dioxide is introduced into the ammoniated liquor. The first stage of carbonation occurs in towers under pressure employing kiln-gas CO_2 (obtained by decomposition of limestone according to equations 2a and 2b) which of course contains nitrogen. This stage proceeds with little evolution of heat and is termed the 'cleaning' stage. The partially carbonated liquor is then treated with carbon dioxide at a high concentration in separate towers which have to be cooled to remove the heat of reaction. The CO_2 for this step is mainly derived from the calcination of sodium bicarbonate (eqn. 5). Bicarbonate is precipitated in these towers which are called the 'making' towers. Because of the deposition of complex solids on the cooling surfaces the functions of the 'making' and 'cleaning' towers are changed on rotation to enable the deposits to be eliminated.

The slurry of bicarbonate taken from the 'making' towers is filtered on rotary vacuum filters (see also sodium bicarbonate, p. 457). The filter cake which contains physically and chemically combined ammonia is dried and calcined in large horizontal cylindrical calciners in which the mechanically entrained water is first driven off followed by the elimination of chemical water and the whole of the ammonia. The exit temperature of the calcined product which is the required soda ash is about 200° C. The calciner operates near to atmospheric pressure to avoid contamination with air since it is necessary to avoid inert gases in the CO_2 which would reduce the efficiency in the 'making' carbonation towers. Calcination of sodium bicarbonate in a fluidised bed has been claimed as a possible technique but it is not known whether it has been adopted for commercial application.

The calcined soda ash is transferred, after cooling, to large silos either for transfer to further operations or for sale.

The ash obtained by the above process is termed light ash and is in the form of a fine powder. For many uses however it is required in a coarse-grained form. This applies particularly to its use in glass manufacture where it can be more readily and uniformly mixed with the sand and lime charges to the glass furnaces.

The crystal size is increased by converting the anhydrous light ash to the monohydrate and allowing crystal growth to occur under specially controlled conditions at about 100° C. The monohydrate is then recalcined usually in an indirect fired drum and fine powders are removed in an air stream. The final step of removing fine powders gives a product which is not objectionable to handle in the consumer's works.

A process has recently been developed for making a new product which is granular light soda ash having the particle density of dense soda ash and the pour density of light soda ash, 30-36 lb/ft^3 (0.48-0.58 kg/dm^2).

The economical operation of the Solvay process requires that ammonia losses be kept very low. All effluent gas streams are therefore carefully scrubbed whilst the ammonia recovery still needs careful design and operation to avoid the ammonia loss in the 'distiller blow-off', the effluent from the still boiler. The overall loss amounts to about 2 lb per ton of output. The conversion of salt in the feed brine is about 75% so that about 25% of the original salt is discharged in the effluent together with the calcium chloride by-product.

The limestone required for the process is usually obtained by quarrying operations. However in some places such as on the Gulf Coast of America sea shells dredged up in coastal waters are used. These require the use of a special form of kiln usually of the horizontal type. The lime burning operation whether in the vertical or horizontal kiln needs to be controlled to obtain soft burnt lime which slakes quickly rather than 'dead burnt' lime which is more suited to building or agricultural purposes.

Some of the distiller blow-off liquors are treated for the recovery of the calcium chloride as liquor, or hexahydrate or anhydrous flake calcium chloride.

Ammonium chloride to some extent is recovered for sale by cooling the filtrate liquors from the bicarbonate filters. Make up ammonia gas is added to the system to compensate for this.

10.6.4 Properties and modifications

The solubility of sodium carbonate at different temperatures is shown in fig. 10.23. The discontinuities in the solubility curve are caused by the transition of sodium carbonate into other modifications. This transition occurs in both solid sodium carbonate and dissolved sodium carbonate. At room temperature crystalline sodium carbonate contains 10 molecules of water (water of crystallization) per molecule of Na_2CO_3. Sodium carbonate loses its water of crystallization when heated and this corresponds with the discontinuities in the solubility curves. Under some conditions the modifications can occur in a temperature range wherein they are metastable. The metastable forms have greater solubilities than the stable forms (see dotted lines in fig. 2.3).

On account of the lower freight charges, sodium carbonate is usually sold and despatched in the calcined form (soda ash), even the naturally occurring trona being calcined for this reason. These materials attract water if exposed to the air and form crystal carbonate ($Na_2CO_3.H_2O$). Calcined soda, together with an organic binder is pressed into briquettes the size of nuts for use in the removal of sulphur from crude iron; it is very convenient to measure out and handle in this form.

Soda crystals (washing soda, $Na_2CO_3.10H_2O$) can be made by treating the calcined soda ash, while still hot, with water or steam; the solution formed is allowed to crystallize out at temperatures below 30° C to give soda crystals containing 60% of water. In some cases soda ash is transported for conversion into crystals in small factories catering for local needs.

Large stationary tanks were formerly used for the crystallization and in these large crystals could be obtained; this method is relatively expensive in terms of labour costs.

Soda ash is being sold increasingly in America mixed with water to form a slurry, which occupies 30% less volume than the dry salt, i.e. 56 lb/ft³ (0.9 kg/dm³) as against 35 lb/ft³ (0.56 kg/dm³) for ordinary light ash.

The saturated soda solution passes in countercurrent flow to the cooling water, while the cylinder rotates, and cold air can also be passed through it. Large quantities of

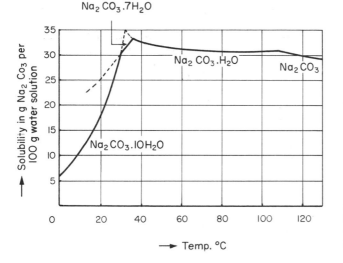

Fig. 10.23 Solubility curves for the various forms of sodium carbonate dissolved in water.

small crystals are then obtained, which are easily withdrawn and centrifuged and can eventually be further dried. This method is not particularly expensive so far as manpower is concerned and can also be used for a number of other crystallizable materials.

Soda crystals weather rapidly in the air. The aqueous solution is basic, and has a cleansing action in laundering since it emulsifies the fats and thus loosens all kinds of dirt.

10.6.5 Transport

Large consumers are increasingly transporting soda ash in covered wagons consisting, in some cases, of four pyramidal connected vessels, which are sealed at the bottom with flaps. Each vessel is easily filled with precisely weighed quantities (depending on the density of the soda). Unloading can be effected by allowing the soda to flow into a tank, which is then mechanically or pneumatically emptied so as to transfer the content to silos. Emptying can also be carried out by fitting a pneumatic connection underneath the wagon, which then draws its air through filter; this air fluidises the soda and makes it easier to unload. Large consumers also transport soda ash as a slurry in water, so that all loading and unloading can be effected by means of pumps.

In the transport of solid soda ash it is necessary to make the wagon vibrate by fitting a vibrator to the wall (see agitated sieves, vol. II). So soda ash must be allowed to remain adhering to the steel walls, because of the danger of corrosion.

10.6.6 Uses

The largest single user of sodium carbonate is the glass industry. The remainder is consumed by the same kind of industries as use caustic soda. These applications are also too numerous to describe in detail. The uses in the USA are illustrated by the table on p. 456; the relative importance of the various applications in other countries is not necessarily the same.

Uses to which sodium carbonate pur in USA	1931	1939/49 average	1959	1962
	%	%	%	%
Glass	22	27	38	44
Caustic soda and bicarbonate	30	24	34	26
Chemicals	17	22	—	—
Soap	7	4	—	—
Cleaning materials	5	3	6	5
Cellulose and paper	4	4	7	9
Water softening	3	3	3	3
Aluminium production	1	5	4	4
Textiles	1	2	—	—
Petroleum refining	—	1	5	6
Remainder	10	5	—	—
Exports	—	—	3	3
	100	100	100	100

Among the 'chemicals' are also included dyestuffs and their intermediates. Under 'remainder' is also included the use of soda solution for extracting petroleum from rocks, which cannot be done by water alone. Appreciable quantities, sometimes more than 250 000 short tons, are further used for the improvement of clay and this is included under 'chemicals'. The table shows clearly the enormous development of the American industry as a result of the last war and, e.g., of the replacement by synthetic products of part of the soap formerly used.

10.6.7 Statistics

The world production of soda ash in 1880 was 700 000 tons, and 2 million tons in 1910. After this, the marked development of the chemical industry brought about an increase to 11 million tons per annum in 1951 and to near 15 million tons in 1959. The production of the most important producers of soda ash is shown in the following table:

| | In '000s metric tons | | | | | |
	1939	1948	1953	1958	1961	1963
Bulgaria	—	—	—	104	129	208
Czechoslavakia	—	99	84	89	76	57
France	483	715	653	736	848	927
Germany, East	1258	—	297	553	599	653
Germany, West		—	794	902	1063	1055
India	—	30	58	91	177	267
Italy	405	385	430	480	—	—
Japan	655	221	784	1049	1400	—
Kenya (natural)	42	65	74	113	147	106
Poland	—	—	108	369	493	543
Romania	—	27	55	82	235	327
Spain	—	77	98	130	157	186
USA (synthetic)	2564	4150	4427	3923	4097	4247
(natural)	—	248	—	562	720	1000
USSR	—	489	1194	1600	—	2545
Yugoslavia	27	35	34	77	90	91
UK	—	—	—	1300	1500	—

The production of the United Kingdom is estimated. The production capacity in 1962 was estimated at 1 600 thousand tons. Formerly continental Europe was supplied chiefly by France and Germany, while the United Kingdom supplied mainly the Far East and South America, but the second world war brought about great changes in this trade.

The United Kingdom is an important exporter. Its exports are shown in the following table:

	1955	1957	1959	1961	1963
In 1 000 long tons	229	213	200	232	159
In 1 000 £	2 769	2 918	2 513	2 541	1 741

In early centuries soda ash was very expensive. This is shown by the following French prices. In 1780 the price of a fairly impure kind was about 1 500 francs per ton. It decreased to about 360 francs in 1824 and to 160 francs in 1866. After this, the Solvay process brought the price down markedly to 40-50 francs per ton.

In the USA several grades of soda ash are available. Distinction is also made according to the apparent specific gravity of the various types: we thus have 'light' and 'dense' ash, the last-named being preferable for dispatch over long distances and for special industrial applications like glass making. In 1965 the prices were as follows: light ash (58% Na_2O) and dense ash (58%) in bags $ 1.85-1.90 per 100 lb; bulk $ 1.55-1.60 per 100 lb; soda ash (58% Na_2O) is sodium carbonate monohydrate having a purity of about 99%.

The prices in the United Kingdom in 1965 were in the range of £ 15 0s 6d to £ 17 0s 6d per 100 lb according to the purity.

10.6.8 Literature

T. P. HOU. Manufacture of soda. New York, Reinhold, 1947. ACS monograph No. 65.
J. W. MELLOR. Comprehensive treatise on inorganic chemistry, vol. II, suppl. 2. London, Longmans, 1961.

10.7 SODIUM BICARBONATE

Sodium bicarbonate (baking powder, $NaHCO_3$) is produced in the Solvay process (see p. 452). Sodium bicarbonate must be purified by recrystallization below 125° C since it decomposes above this temperature to give sodium carbonate and carbon dioxide according to the equation:

$$2 NaHCO_3 \rightarrow Na_2CO_3 + CO_2 + H_2O$$

Very pure sodium bicarbonate can be obtained by allowing carbon dioxide to react with sodium carbonate in solution below 31° C. Sodium bicarbonate precipitates from the solution as it is slightly soluble in water (6.9 g dissolve in 100 g water at 0° C and 16.4 at 60° C).

Sodium bicarbonate is used as baking powder since it decomposes above 125° C to liberate carbon dioxide which makes dough porous (raising of dough). Chemical raising is used in particular for the heavy types of dough which contain, besides flour and water or milk, important quantities of other ingredients; if yeast were used, the time for such a dough to rise would be much too long.

The action of baking powder is accelerated in the presence of an acid compound. For this reason baking powder is often mixed with tartaric acid, monocalcium phosphate, acid pyrophosphate ($Na_2H_2P_2O_7$), sodium alum ($NaAl(SO_4)_2.12H_2O$) or potassium alum. In various countries including Australia, Denmark, Switzerland and the UK, the addition of alum is prohibited by law. Acid phosphate 'self-raising baking powders' are limited in use in many countries because they may contain too much fluorine. Compounds such as starch, sugar or glucose deltalactone are often mixed with baking powder, together with the acidic compound, since they moderate the action of the latter. Thus the evolution of carbon dioxide can be controlled by means of additives.

Ammonium bicarbonate with pyrophosphate can also be used as baking powder, but the self-raising flour of commerce never contains ammonium carbonate (or bicarbonate) because this smells of ammonia; confectioners use a great deal.

Much baking powder is used, especially in North America and England, and in 1952 it was estimated that the value of the baking powders and yeast for the whole world was about $ 400 million.

As a stomach powder, sodium bicarbonate is used in 'health salts', and, mixed with tartaric acid, in 'lemonade powder'. It is also used in washing wool for removing the fats and emulsifiable substances from the raw wool, and also for the removal of gum from silk.

A very dry, finely ground type of bicarbonate is used in powder type fire extinguishers. For this purpose it is stored in a strong container and as soon as the protection system comes into action, nitrogen, automatically admitted under pressure, blows the powder out. When used for extremely dangerous fires caused by easily oxidisable metals (magnesium, sodium, aluminium powder, etc.) it melts and completely excludes all oxygen. Mobile installations pressurized with nitrogen are also available.

When materials containing cellulose are impregnated with sodium bicarbonate solution the sodium hydroxide formed at high temperatures acts as a fire extinguisher. Dusting with solid bicarbonate is less effective, on account of poorer contact.

Use of bicarbonate in the dry distillation of wood ensures that no exothermic compounds are formed, and for this reason more charcoal is formed and less tar.

In the USA the production and sale of sodium bicarbonate is in the hands of a few large companies. The output in 1951 was about 110000 metric tons and the output in 1963 was estimated at 160000 tons. The French output is about 25000 tons per year. The United Kingdom is also an important producer of sodium bicarbonate. The exports from this country were as follows:

	1955	1957	1959	1961	1963
In tons	37000	36000	39000	37000	40000
In £	639000	667000	701000	653000	715000

The prices of sodium bicarbonate in the USA were in 1965: USP grade granular, $ 2.95-3.85 per 100 lb; USP grade powder, $ 2.55-3.45 per 100 lb.

In the United Kingdom refined sodium bicarbonate cost 18s per 100 lb.

10.8 OTHER SODIUM COMPOUNDS

10.8.1 Sodium percarbonate

Sodium percarbonate $((Na_2CO_3)_2.3H_2O_2)$ is, like the perborate (see p. 516), an addition product and not a true chemical compound. It contains about 12.5% of available oxygen, dissolves somewhat more easily than perborate, but is less stable. It is used mainly for bleaching purposes, and sometimes in foods. This is permitted in Great Britain, whereas the use of perborates is forbidden on account of the supposed harmfulness of boron when taken into the body.

10.8.2 Sodium hydride

Sodium hydride (NaH) may be obtained by the action of hydrogen on a layer of molten sodium, floating on molten sodium hydride, at a temperature of 250-300° C, the hydride passing into the bottom layer. Commercially it is probably more satisfactory to have the sodium in a finely divided or vapour form.

At the present time for laboratory use the hydride is prepared as an emulsion in mineral oil by first emulsifying liquid sodium in a mineral oil of high boiling point, and then introducing hydrogen. The hydride can eventually be extracted by means of a strong solution of caustic soda, but the emulsion is often used as being easier to handle. Sodium hydride is stable at temperatures up to 230° C in a dry atmosphere. In moist air it decomposes even at ordinary temperatures. It is used mainly in the molten state as a reducing agent, for de-scaling metals, e.g. to remove oxides in non-ferrous metals, stainless steel, and the like. For this purpose a solution of NaH in molten NaOH is used.

10.8.3 Sodium peroxide

Sodium peroxide (Na_2O_2) is obtained by the oxidation of sodium metal in long rotating steel cylinders by means of air free from carbon dioxide and water vapour, when sodium monoxide (Na_2O) and a little peroxide are formed. The product then passes to a long cylinder of large diameter, lined internally with nickel, which slowly rotates inside an oven, while oxygen is passed over the oxide so that peroxide is formed. For efficient conversion it is important to ensure that the peroxide does not melt. In Germany much of the product is used, in the factory in which it is produced, for the manufacture of perborate.

Sodium peroxide is a yellow powder which, in dilute solution in cold water hydro lyses to give caustic soda and hydrogen peroxide. It is used for this reason as a bleaching agent for many materials; it may advantageously be mixed with a little sodium sulphate, which acts as a stabilizer.

Since the caustic soda produced can damage many textile fibres, a certain amount of magnesium sulphate is added to the bleaching solution when used for bleaching textiles. This reacts as follows:

$$2NaOH + MgSO_4 \rightarrow Na_2SO_4 + Mg(OH)_2$$

Since magnesium hydroxide is insoluble the alkalinity of the solution decreases and the latter becomes less harmful. The sodium sulphate has no effect on the fibres.

Because of its powerful oxidizing action, sodium peroxide may be used for burning away paraffins, which sometimes cause blockages in oil wells. For the same reason also it constitutes a serious fire risk and therefore needs to be kept from contact with combustible materials. It sells for $0.22 per lb.

(Potassium peroxide behaves in a completely analogous way, and is used mainly as a source of oxygen in the canisters of certain types of breathing apparatus.)

10.8.4 Sodium sulphides

Sodium sulphide (Na_2S) is obtained by the reduction of sodium sulphate with carbon or hydrogen in a refractory oven and at high temperature. (Compare soda ash Leblanc process.) A shaft oven, for example, can be used, filled with coke, which can be brought to the correct temperature by blowing in air for some time so that the coke can act as a reducing agent. At the top, a mixture of sodium sulphate and finely ground carbon is fed in, to which is added a little potassium sulphate to lower the melting point.

The mixture melts, and in flowing downwards is reduced by the coke so that molten, impure sodium sulphide passes out at the bottom. Alternatively a horizontal revolving furnace can be employed.

For purification the sulphide is dissolved in water and $Na_2S.9H_2O$ is obtained by crystallization. Mild steel equipment was formerly used for the concentration of the solution, and this had to be replaced, because of corrosion, after a year, but at the present time steam heating pipes of Monel metal or Inconel are used, which survive more than five years. Nickel is widely used for agitators and pumps for the solution.

Since sodium sulphide is readily oxidized, the whole process must be carried out in a reducing atmosphere.

The product is called 30% sulphide (i.e. it contains 30% Na_2S) from which, by driving off a part of the water of crystallization, 60% sulphide can be obtained. Sulphide in the form of flakes can be obtained from it by melting it and allowing it to flow over cooled cylinders on which the sulphide solidifies; it can then be scraped off by means of a rake.

Sodium sulphide can also be obtained from water gas and from raw town or coke-oven gas, by washing the gas with caustic soda solution.

By utilizing a German method, sodium amalgam produced by the amalgam process for alkali electrolysis can be used in the production of sodium sulphide (see p. 406). The sodium amalgam is reacted with sodium polysulphide. Finally, the solution is passed into tanks lined with rubber. For other polysulphides, see below.

Sodium sulphide is a white crystalline powder, and its solution has a strongly basic reaction. On heating with sulphur to 125° C polysulphides are formed. Exposed to the air, it oxidizes quickly to form thiosulphate, and in fact is used for the production of this substance.

Sodium sulphide is used in appreciable amounts for the production of sulphur dyes, for the reduction of nitro compounds, in the dyeing of textiles, as a depilatory for skins, and in the extraction of silver and gold, since it readily forms the insoluble sulphides of these and other metals. It is also used in flotation processes involving sulphide ores.

About 27 000 short tons of sodium sulphide were produced in the USA in 1963 (containing 60-62% Na_2S). Its price was $ 0.06 to $ 0.07 per lb in 1965 (in the USA). The UK price was £ 43 per long ton in 1965.

Sodium hydrosulphide (NaHS) is prepared by treating calcium sulphide with sodium bisulphate in the cold. It is used in the preparation of sulphur dyes, for removing hair from hides, and (like sodium sulphide) for the desulphurization of artificial silk after spinning. It may also be used in the preparation of various thio-amides (e.g. thio-urea) and thio-acids.

The total output in the USA was about 25000 short tons in 1963. Its price was $0.07 to $0.08 per lb in 1965.

Sodium tetrasulphide (Na_2S_4), the most stable polysulphide, is prepared as an impure 40% solution by dissolving sulphur in a solution of NaOH, Na_2S or NaHS. The solution, which is highly irritant, is particularly recommended for softening hides before hair removal, since it makes the proteins much softer. Apart from this, it can be used in the reduction of nitrated organic compounds, in the preparation of sulphur dyes, and in flotation of ores. Its use in the preparation of thiokol (see vol. IV) makes it of increasing importance.

10.8.5 Sodium sulphites

Sodium bisulphite ($NaHSO_3$) is obtained by passing sulphur dioxide into a solution of sodium carbonate or bicarbonate. If the sulphur dioxide is allowed to react with soda crystals, sodium bisulphite is produced which dissolves in the water of crystallization.

Sodium sulphite (Na_2SO_3) can be obtained from this solution by saturating with sodium carbonate.

Commercial sodium bisulphite and solutions of sodium bisulphite usually contain sodium pyrosulphite ($Na_2S_2O_5$, a dehydrated form of sodium bisulphite).

Because of their reducing power, sodium bisulphite and sodium sulphite are used as bleaching agents in place of SO_2 (or sulphurous acid, H_2SO_3), also as a dechlorinator in the textile industry, for the decalcification of hides, and as a preservative in drinks, e.g. in beer. If a small bag of polyethylene filled with potassium bisulphite is suspended in wine or other drinks, water penetrates to the inside and dissolves the bisulphite: sodium bisulphite then diffuses very slowly through the wall of the bag, which acts as an ultrafilter, and this sodium bisulphite then acts as a disinfectant, without danger of excess being present. Sodium bisulphite and sulphite are also used in the preservation of food, for bleaching feathers, sponges, straw, cereals, starch, etc., and for help in the removal of dyes from textiles which are to be dyed again (stripping).

Important quantities of sodium bisulphite are used for the production of crêpe rubber. Sodium bisulphite is added to latex before coagulation to prevent it from colouring. For the same reason sodium sulphite is added to raw sugar solutions before evaporation.

Sodium sulphite is also used as stabilizer in photographic developers. In butchers' shops sodium sulphite is used to preserve the colour of minced meat: the effect is noticeable if 0.03% (calculated as SO_2) is added, especially if the mince is kept cool. The effect depends on the marked decrease of oxidation by atmospheric oxygen. It has been found, in tests on animals, that this quantity has no harmful effect on man, though the use of sulphite in this way is prohibited in many countries.

(Sulphited glucose, obtained from glucose and sulphur dioxide, can be added to the extent of 0.1% to fruit pulp, to improve the colour of the pulp without the introduction of any objectionable taste, which may be the case if SO_2 is used.)

The output of sodium sulphite in the USA was about 200000 tons in 1963. The United Kingdom is also an important producer. This country exported about 5000 tons (value £ 140000) in 1962.

In 1965 sodium sulphite sold at $3.50 to $8.00 per 100 lb and sodium bisulphite at $ 5.70 to $ 6.15 per 100 lb in the USA. In the UK the price of sodium sulphite was 27s per 100 lb.

10.8.6 Sodium dithionite

Sodium dithionite ($Na_2S_2O_4$ or $Na_2S_2O_4.2H_2O$) is also known as sodium sulphoxylate or sodium hydrosulphite. It is prepared via zinc hydrosulphite by stirring a suspension of zinc dust in agitated lead vessels, and introducing SO_2 at the correct rate, the zinc thus being slowly dissolved, a fact which is indicated by the change in colour. On adding soda ash zinc carbonate is precipitated, while the sodium salt goes into solution; this is filtered, and on addition of common salt, the dihydrate of sodium hydrosulphite ($Na_2S_2O_4.2H_2O$) crystallizes out. On heating the dihydrate to 52° C the anhydrous salt separates out and can be filtered in a nutsch or rotary filter, but to remove all the water it is washed a few times with methylated spirit, freed from the alcohol *in vacuo* and packed in well-sealed watertight containers.

The need for the containers to be well sealed and watertight must be emphasized, since dithionite is rapidly decomposed by moisture, and so much heat is then evolved that fires can be started. Large amounts of SO_2 are liberated, which hinder greatly the extinction of the fire.

In Europe it has been produced by the reduction of bisulphite ($NaHSO_3$) with sodium amalgam. The process has been so much improved that it is replacing the older method, although the latter has the advantage that zinc oxide can be prepared from the by-product zinc carbonate. Prepared in this way, the product contains usually 90% of hydrosulphite, with a little soda or sulphite as stabilizer although more efficient stabilizers such as salts of carboxylic acids have recently been claimed in patents. It is also known as blankite.

Sodium dithionite is used mainly in dyeing and printing with vat dyes (as a reducing agent) and in the bleaching of textiles; also for bleaching soap, oils and fats, glue and gelatin, and china clay, and in the sugar industry. Dithionites are also used for bleaching wood cellulose and wood pulp.

Sodium dithionite may be mixed with half its weight of anhydrous sodium pyrophosphate, and so be used for bleaching silk and wool, and for the cleaning of cotton thread in fabrics which have been dyed by means of vat dyes.

Mixed with sodium carbonate it is used for removing spots of dirt from washing. Too much sodium carbonate must not be used, otherwise there is the possibility that sodium sulphide will be formed. Dithionite is also used for removing the last traces of oxygen from the feed water for high-pressure boilers (see p. 151).

The dithionites of potassium, calcium and zinc are also commercially available.

The production of the USA was about 30000 tons in 1963; the price was $ 0.24 to $ 0.26 in 1965.

10.8.7 Sodium sulphoxylate

Although this name has also been given to the dithionites, it is usually intended to indicate that these are combined with formaldehyde or acetaldehyde. The compounds are easily soluble and resistant to alkalis, but not to acids. They are used mainly for removing the colour from dyed fabrics (stripping).

Sodium formaldehyde sulphoxylate ($NaHSO_2.CH_2O.2H_2O$) is also called rongalit, or formosul, with various capital letters after the name. The zinc compounds under various trade names for various applications are used for the redyeing of silk and for woollen goods and rags.

10.8.8 Sodium thiosulphate

Sodium thiosulphate (hypo), is incorrectly called hyposulphite; the formula is $Na_2S_2O_3.5H_2O$. It can be prepared from the sulphide, but is usually obtained as a by-product in dyestuffs manufacture, when organic nitro compounds are reduced with sodium polysulphides. There are several other alternative methods of manufacture available.

Its chief use is as a fixing agent in photography, since it converts unchanged silver chloride into a soluble compound; it also finds application in the extraction of silver. It is used as a dechlorinator in bleaching to ensure that the last traces of chlorine have been destroyed. It is also used in the manufacture of chrome leather as a reducing agent for dichromate.

End use distribution (USA)	
Photography	60 %
Leather	18 %
Tetraethyl lead	7 %
Thioglycollic acid	3.5%
Others	11.5%
	100 %

The output of sodium thiosulphate in the USA was nearly 31000 short tons in 1963 (in terms of $Na_2S_2O_3.5H_2O$). The West German output was about 6200 short tons in the same year. The price of anhydrous sodium thiosulphate was $ 7.75 to $ 8.15 per 100 lb in 1965 (technical and photographic grades). The pentahydrate cost $ 4.95 to $ 5.20 in 1965.

A competitive product for use in photography prepared in America is ammonium thiosulphate, which acts twelve times as quickly, is more easily soluble and relatively lighter.

10.8.9 Sodium nitrite

Sodium nitrite ($NaNO_2$) is made from the nitrogen gases of the nitrogen fixation industry, which contain NO and NO_2 (in an equimolecular mixture), and are added to caustic soda solution at 300° C, so that they react as follows:

$$NO + NO_2 + 2NaOH \rightarrow 2NaNO_2 + H_2O$$

The nitrite is allowed to crystallise out. Potassium nitrite is prepared and used in a similar way.

Sodium nitrite is mainly used in the dyestuffs industry for diazotization and for the preparation of nitroso compounds (see dyestuffs). It is also used in appreciable quantities for the preparation of hydroxylamine (see p. 344).

It is also used in the production of bacon, since it gives an attractive red colour with the traces of blood which remain. It is used, in amounts up to 0.1%, in the ice used for preserving fish, but when used thus can have a decidedly poisonous effect, especially for children, so that attempts have been made to have this application banned. It is formed in meat to which saltpetre has been added. In the USA, in particular, solutions of strength 0.01-0.1% are pumped through oil pipelines, so that oxides are formed on the inside wall of the pipe, and these prevent further corrosion.

The corrosion inhibiting effect can be nullified if a large amount of sodium sulphate is present in the water; the reason for this is not known.

Sodium nitrite is being increasingly used as an inhibitor to prevent rust formation in steel vessels, and if a 3-5% solution is sprayed on to steel objects (or if these are dipped into the solution) corrosion can be prevented for a period of months; it is used, for this reason, in the empty tanks of tankers.

It sells at \$9 to 11 per 100 lb, irrespective of the quality.

10.8.10 Organic acid salts

Sodium forms many important salts with organic acids, such as those of tartaric, citric and benzoic acids (see under these acids). The formic salt (sodium formate) is becoming increasingly important since it is suitable for use as a buffer (at pH4, approximately) in galvanizing, tanning, textile dyeing etc.

10.8.11 Organosodium compounds

Organosodium compounds can be prepared from an emulsion of metallic sodium with alkyl or aryl chlorides, for example as follows:

$$RCl + 2Na \rightarrow RNa + NaCl$$

in which R represents any alkyl or aryl group.

Organic sodium compounds are prepared on a large scale to replace the earlier reagents used in the Grignard reaction, for which they are more stable than those formerly used, which always had to be freshly prepared.

Disodium octadiene is of special importance as a catalyst for the preparation of isosebacic acid. It is estimated that at the present time, in regard to sodium usage, this catalyst follows in importance the preparation of tellurium (see vol. IV). The amount used as catalyst in 1959 had already reached more than 5000 tons in the USA.

It is believed that disodium octadiene is prepared by reacting finely dispersed metallic sodium in the presence of a catalyst with butadiene

$$2CH_2 = CH.CH.CH_2 + 2Na \rightarrow Na (CH.CH = CH.CH_2.CH_2.CH = CH.CH_2) Na$$

The disodium octadiene is treated with carbon dioxide to yield the sodium salt of the corresponding unsaturated carboxylic acid. This is hydrogenated to the saturated isosebacic acid. The product is required for use in the plasticizer and polyamide fields.

For *sodium bromide, iodide, fluoride, chlorate, perchlorate*, etc., see halogens.

10.9 METALLIC POTASSIUM (K, atomic weight = 39.1)

10.9.1 History and occurrence

Potassium metal was first isolated by Davy (as in the case of the other alkali and alkaline earth metals) in 1807, by electrolysis of molten potassium hydroxide. The name potassium is derived from the word 'potash'. In Europe it is also named 'kalium' which is derived from the Arabic term 'qali'.

Like sodium, potassium does not occur naturally in the free state. In the form of compounds it is widely distributed. The earth's crust contains about 2.5% potassium in several potassium aluminium silicates (felspars, orthoclase, mica, etc.), in volcanic minerals such as leucite and phonolite, in granite and several others. Very important sources of potassium are the large deposits in Germany and France and the salt lakes in the USA. These deposits contain potassium chloride (sylvite) and double salts of potassium and magnesium (see potassium chloride, p. 466). Potassium also occurs in seaweed and in the bodies of animals mainly inside the cells (e.g. in the blood corpuscles), while the sodium compounds are found mainly in the liquid around them (see sodium chloride, p. 423). It has been found that, in man, the potassium content decreases systematically after the twentieth year. Since the radioactive potassium isotope can be determined with great accuracy, it has been suggested that the potassium content of the body could be used as an objective measure of human age.

The raw materials for making potassium compounds were formerly the ashes of various types of land plant; those of marine plants contain relatively more sodium. Both groups of salts play an important rôle in the plant cells. The potassium salts are found much more in the cells (as in animals) while those of sodium are mainly present in large amounts in the liquid outside the cells. This is ascribed mainly to the effect of the ions on protein, and to the fact that the sodium ion, as a result of hydration, becomes much larger than the potassium ion, which does not attract water molecules so strongly. The enzyme system is also an important factor.

Potassium is also necessary for transmitting stimulation from nerves to muscles, and for the contraction of the latter. In the liver it plays a part in the synthesis of glycogen from sugar (glucose); when the glycogen is decomposed, potassium is liberated again.

The relatively high content of the weakly radioactive K^{40} is often thought to be of great importance in various reactions taking place in the animal body.

After death, potassium diffuses away through the cell walls.

When too much potassium is taken up, the excess is quickly excreted again; 90% is excreted via the kidneys while the rest passes out with the faeces.

It is estimated that a man weighing 70 kg contains 160 g of potassium, of which 157 g is present in the cells.

10.9.2 Production

Potassium can be produced by electrolytic processes, similar to sodium (see p. 406), but the electrolysis of molten potassium chloride (mixed with potassium carbonate) is limited since molten potassium chloride is very corrosive. Potassium can also be produced by passing the vapour of sodium through a molten potassium compound. The potassium compound is reduced to metallic potassium and a mixture of the vapours of potassium and sodium is obtained, so that the alloy K.Na is collected. Potassium can be separated from the mixture by fractional distillation.

A more important process for the production of potassium is the reduction of potassium fluoride by calcium carbide, according to the following reaction equation:

$$2 \, KF + CaC_2 \rightarrow 2 \, K + CaF_2 + 2 \, C.$$

10.9.3 Properties and uses

Potassium is a soft silvery-white metal. Its melting point is 63° C. Potassium has a specific gravity of 0.86. Its chemical properties are similar to those of sodium; however, the reactivity of potassium is greater. Metallic potassium can form explosive mixtures with some halogen substituted hydrocarbons, such as carbon tetrachloride, $C \, Cl_4$.

Potassium is often stored (as is sodium) under paraffin oil or in sealed cans.

Potassium is used in the synthesis of potassium oxide, peroxide and cyanide. Only relatively small amounts of potassium are produced, since sodium can often be used instead just as effectively, and this, because much cheaper raw materials are used in its production, is lower in price. In turn the high price of potassium is partially caused by the fact that it is only produced on a small scale. In 1963 sodium sold at about $0.20 per lb, while potassium then cost $3.60 per lb.

10.10 POTASSIUM CHLORIDE

10.10.1 History

Before the middle of the last century potassium salts were produced by leaching wood ash and ash from other plants. Another source of potassium salts was the mother liquor obtained in common salt production from sea water. In the fifteenth century the preparation of potassium salts from the ash from seaweed wood was an important industry in Scotland and New England (see also potassium carbonate).

Up to the middle of the last century, insufficient attention was paid to potash, large natural resources, particularly in Germany, being neglected. It was only through the efforts of Liebig in Germany and Dumas in France that this position was rectified. In Germany, large quantities of an apparently worthless material (*Abraumsalze* = waste salts) had to be removed from the upper layers in order to work deeper deposits of common salt required for the manufacture of soda. This so-called waste material was, however, rich in potassium salts, and in 1857 the value of this was at last realised, both as a material for direct agricultural use and also as a source of raw material for the preparation of potassium nitrate by the double decomposition method.

10.10.2 Occurrence

The most important potassium minerals are sylvite (KCl), carnallite (KCl. $MgCl_2.6H_2O$), kainite (KCl.$MgSO_4.3H_2O$), langbeinite ($K_2SO_4.2MgSO_4$), and polyhalite ($K_2SO_4.MgSO_4.2CaSO_4.2H_2O$). A naturally occurring mixture of sylvite and common salt (halite) is called sylvinite. Another mineral mixture consisting of sylvite, halite, kieserite ($MgSO_4.H_2O$) and/or anhydrite ($CaSO_4$) is known as *Hartsalz*. Of these minerals, sylvinite, sylvite and carnallite account for most of the world production of potassium chloride.

Rich deposits of potassium salts are found in the Stassfurt district (Germany), Alsace (France), Urals (USSR), Carlsbad (New Mexico, USA), Searles Lake (Califor-

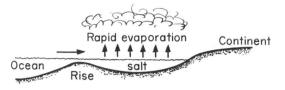

Fig. 10.24 Schematic representation of the cutting off of an arm of the sea by a bar. The left hand arrow indicates that new sea water always replenishes the water lost by evaporation (vertical arrows).

nia, USA), Poland, and Spain. Potassium salt deposits also occur in the UK, Canada and Italy (Sicily).

The waters of the salt lakes (Dead Sea, Searles Lake, etc.) and ordinary sea water can also provide large amounts of potassium chloride.

In 1958 the world reserves of potassium salts were estimated as follows:

In million tons of potassium oxide content			
Canada	18000	France	200
Israel (Dead Sea)	8500	Spain	200
Germany, East	14000	USA	300
Germany, West	9500	USSR	700

The ash of marine and land plants, numerous rocks, dirt from roads, etc. are sometimes important sources of potassium salts, or may become so.

The most generally accepted hypothesis concerning the origin of the potassium deposits assumes that a large inlet of the sea was cut off by a bar (see fig. 10.24) and then dried out, accompanied by continuous replenishment by sea water.

According to the theory of the famous chemist van 't Hoff, carbonates were first deposited and then other salts in the order gypsum ($CaSO_4.H_2O$), rock salt ($NaCl$) with gypsum, rock salt with anhydrite ($CaSO_4$), rock salt with polyhalite ($K_2SO_4.MgSO_4.CaSO_4.2H_2O$), magnesium sulphate ($MgSO_4$), potassium, magnesium sulphate ($K_2SO_4.MgSO_4.6H_2O$), kainite ($KCl.MgSO_4.3H_2O$), carnallite ($KCl.MgCl_2.6H_2O$), langbeinite ($K_2SO_4.2MgSO_4$), bisschoffite ($MgCl_2.6H_2O$); the last five always contain magnesium sulphate (kieserite) (see also fig. 10.25).

The potassium salt solution had already assumed a much smaller area than the original lake. Probably this had separated into smaller sections, some of which had dried up quickly and were covered with desert dust, and were later flooded by liquid from the lakes which had not dried out, so that crystallization began again. This sometimes took place many times. As a result of geological changes, the deposited layers were deep under the surface of the earth and acquired various foldings, as can be seen from fig. 10.26. The enormous pressures caused different plastic masses of salt to be pushed between others. Moreover many chemical reactions took place at the elevated temperatures and pressures. Thus, at about $100°$ C anhydrite was formed from gypsum and at $83°$ C sylvite-kieserite was formed from kainite. Since bisschoffite melts at $117°$ C, this explains the penetration of $MgCl_2$ into most layers.

The physico-chemical investigations of van 't Hoff, supplemented by those of others, gave a complete picture of the origin of the Stassfurt salts on the basis of the geological data. The Alsace deposits were probably formed much later. Deposits of salts resembling those of Stassfurt were dissolved in water and carried as a solution over great distances,

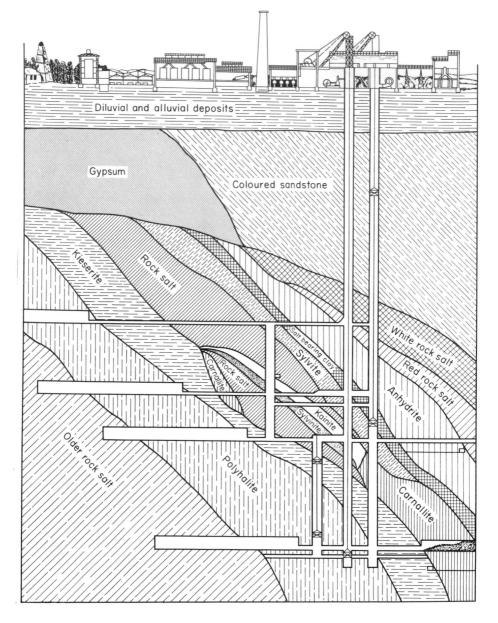

Fig. 10.25 Diagrammatic cross-section of a European mine, showing the various potassium salt deposits.

Fig. 10.26 Deposit of potash salts, showing how the deposited layers are covered by sand and other materials. The tremendous pressures and slow shifts have deformed the layers in various ways

crystallizing out again in Alsace. This explains why there are in Alsace other salts and deposits with far fewer by-products than have to be removed in Stassfurt.

10.10.3 Mining and refining of potassium minerals containing potassium chloride

a. Mining. Subterranean deposits of sylvite, carnallite, etc. are mined as underground mines. Some mines having nearly horizontal deposits of potassium minerals (e.g. in Carlsbad) can be exploited in the same way as modern coal mines. Shafts have therefore to be built for ventilation as well (see coal, vol. II). Work in mines is carried

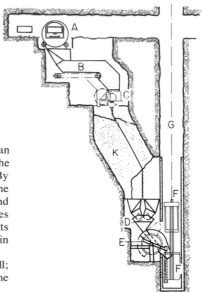

Fig. 10.27 Sketch of an underground installation in an American potash mine. Large bunkers are formed in the rocks, separated from each other by concrete walls. By means of special release valves in the mill one of the bunkers can be filled at will, e.g. one with potash salt and another with common salt. By opening the release valves it is possible to fill a release drum with one of the salts and from it, in turn, a transporting vessel which hangs in the shaft.
A. Rotatable truck emptier; B. Conveyer belt; C. Mill; D. Slide valves; E. Sluice; F. Transporting tanks; G. Mine shaft; K. Potash salts.

Fig. 10.28   Modern milling machine in a potash mine.

out with mechanical borers and cutting or scraping machines (see fig. 10.28), after which the layers of salt are broken up by explosives. The most modern shovelling and transporting installations are used for bringing the loosened mixture of salts to the transporting shafts (see fig. 10.27), so that they can be processed on the surface.

Fairly pure potassium minerals are ground and sold as such for fertilizer purposes. The large pieces fall on screens and then pass through magnetic separators and stamping machines before being broken in special mills to the required size of 3 mm.

In early days many potash mines were flooded with water, causing enormous damage, so that a careful watch for water seepage must be kept.

Brine well mining (wet mining, the Frasch method, see sodium chloride, p. 414) is not used for subterranean deposits, as it is less economical for potassium minerals.

The largest quantity of potassium minerals is refined to get pure potassium chloride (muriate of potash) or carnallite by dissolving and recrystallization or by flotation.

b. Refining by the solution and recrystallization process. In this process use is made of the property that potassium chloride is, at the boiling point of water, much more highly soluble than at ordinary temperatures, whereas magnesium chloride is very highly soluble even at low temperatures, and the solubility of common salt varies only slightly with temperature. Various modifications of the solution and recrystallization process are in use, depending on the kind of potassium mineral which has to be purified. Carnallite and sylvinite are processed as follows.

Potassium ores are crushed to permit efficient leaching and then a saturated solution in hot water is prepared. A variety of vessels has been developed for this purpose. The most common dissolving vessels are long troughs provided with heating tubes and a screw to mix and to advance the ore with the solvent. The still undissolved salts are carried away at the end of the trough to be leached out again in a second trough. The solids remaining after the second leaching go (in most cases) to the kieserite washing plant to be worked up into magnesium sulphate (see magnesium sulphate, p. 494).

The hot solution from the first trough contains a much greater amount of magnesium salts than that from the last. This solution is evaporated and cooled in vacuum crystallizers. A crystalline product consisting mainly of carnallite is obtained. Pure potassium chloride can be obtained from this product by dissolving and recrystallization. The solution from the second trough is cleared in large, well-insulated tanks, which are divided into several partitions, through which the liquid passes very slowly so that the suspended particles can sink or rise. The insulation ensures that no potassium chloride can crystallize out, since the temperature can only fall to a slight extent. The clarified solution is cooled. Potassium chloride and some carnallite crystallize and sodium chloride remains in the solution. At one time the cooling was carried out in very large tanks containing cooling tubes, through which cold brine flowed. Nowadays vacuum coolers are used. The use of vacuum coolers reduced the cooling time from days to a few minutes. The modern apparatus is much more compact than that previously used. The vapour which is drawn off is used again for a heat pump.

From each metric ton of crude salt about 850 m³ mother liquor are obtained in which 20% of the potassium ore is still present. This amount is further decreased by evaporation in vacuum (possibly together with the solution from the first trough). A crystalline product consisting of carnallite is obtained. Pure potassium chloride can be produced from this product by dissolving and recrystallization.

Sylvite and carnallite of several purities, obtained in several stages of the refining process are often withdrawn from the process and sold as such.

The crystalline products from each stage can easily be separated out by centrifuging or by filtering in rotating filters (for example a rotating disc filter, as shown in fig. 9.30). The crystal mass is dried in rotating drum dryers in which it is treated with hot gases, after which it is screened and mechanically packed, possibly after the coarser pieces have been finely ground.

Remaining mother liquors are recycled if the magnesium content of the treated ores is low.

c. Refining by flotation. Separation of potassium salts from their ores by flotation is now being used increasingly. Various modifications of this process are being developed, depending on the kind of mineral to be treated.

Potassium chloride can be separated from sylvinite (a mixture of sylvite and halite) by aeration of a slurry of finely divided sylvinite in water, saturated with potassium chloride and sodium chloride and containing a mixture of fatty acid amines. Sylvite floats and halite sinks to the bottom (see also flotation in volume III). It is necessary to keep the particle size within narrow limits. These limits differ for each particular salt. Here too it is in most cases necessary to process the salt in order for it to flow through several cells successively. The floating product from the last cell is filtered and dried. The residual liquid is often used again. Part of the treatment can be carried out in the potash mines underground. Use in the mines themselves saves much of the transport costs.

A product of 97% purity can be obtained. The halite still contains some potassium chloride which is recovered by a solution and recrystallization process. The waste salts are often used for filling up the mine shafts. The flotation process requires much lower initial costs than the older recrystallization processes which are also expensive to run because of repeated heating.

d. Waste liquors. Various compounds, such as magnesium chloride, magnesium sulphate (Epsom salts), sodium sulphate, sodium chloride and bromine, are obtained in a manner similar to that of potassium salts. Thus sodium sulphate is obtained from the waste liquors as follows: sodium chloride and magnesium sulphate present in them react with one another to form sodium sulphate and magnesium chloride. The solution is sharply cooled in large freezing plants. As a result, sodium sulphate ($Na_2SO_4.10H_2O$, Glauber's salt) crystallizes out, while the highly soluble magnesium chloride remains in solution. The resulting impure sodium sulphate is calcined and then covered with a pure solution to wash out the impurities. The pure salt is then dried in drying drums and is sold as anhydrous salt.

Magnesium chloride can also be obtained from waste liquors (see magnesium chloride, p. 493).

The remaining waste liquors have little value. Enormous quantities are tipped into rivers (whose water is then unsuitable for drinking, for industrial use or for the survival of fish). The waste liquors are only partially worked up to produce magnesium chloride and sulphate because the quantity available is much greater than the quantity which can be sold. By this the water of the 'Nieder-Elbe' is salted. The effluent of the Alsace potash mines is very noticeable even in the waters of the river Rhine in the Netherlands.

10.10.4 Extraction of potassium chloride from salt lakes or sea water

As an example we will look at the installation at the Dead Sea. The water contains about 24% of dissolved salts. At a depth of 50 m there is one-and-a-half times more potassium chloride (about 1.5%) and bromine salts than at the surface. Pipes with dimensions of 750 m long and 75 cm diameter are used to pump the solution from this depth to open tanks which are arranged in the form of a cascade. These decrease in size from 12 to $1\frac{1}{2}$ hectares (see fig. 10.29). The heat of the sun and the dry atmosphere cause water to evaporate quickly in the tanks and the concentrated solution is run off repeatedly to lower tanks. Naphthol green is added to the solution to increase the absorption of infrared rays and thus to increase the evaporation rate (see also solar salt, p. 415).

About 90% of the sodium chloride crystallizes out first and is taken away by suction dredges. After this, carnallite with some sodium chloride crystallizes out. When the layer is about 10 cm thick it is removed. This product can be refined by the methods described previously. The remaining mother liquor contains magnesium chloride and bromides. Bromine is recovered by boiling this mother liquor with steam and chlorine (see also bromine, p. 242). The waste liquor is passed into tanks and evaporated during the very hot summer (the liquid reaches a temperature of 70° C). Magnesium chloride crystallizes out in the form of long needles. Magnesium chloride is separated from the solution and slaked lime is stirred into the liquor so that calcium chloride is formed, this is then further evaporated so as to yield solids.

Fig. 10.29 Giant tanks in which the salts crystallise out, after evaporation of water by solar radiation.

The process for the production of potassium salts from Searles Lake brine is similar to that for Dead Sea salt. However, triple-effect evaporators are used for concentration of the brine. Other modifications are necessary since the composition of the brine is not the same as that from the Dead Sea (see also mining of boron minerals, p. 509).

Various processes have been developed for the production of potassium salts from sea water but none of them seems to be in commercial operation.

10.10.5 Properties, storage and uses

Potassium chloride (KCl) is a colourless crystalline product. Its melting point is 790° C. About 34 g potassium chloride dissolve in 100 g water at 20° C. Potassium chloride easily forms a hygroscopic double salt with magnesium chloride $MgCl_2$. $KCl.6H_2O$. The large deposits of carnallite show this.

In Germany potassium salts are stored in large storage sheds which can often contain up to 100 000 tons. These storage sheds are mainly built near waterways. By their extensive and first class mechanical apparatus these make rapid and cheap storage and loading in vessels possible.

Such storage sheds also often have well-heated high bunkers so that hygroscopic salts can be easily stored and transported. Potassium chloride is also transported in paper bags.

More than 90% of the world's potassium chloride is used as fertilizer. The remaining potassium chloride is used in the manufacture of potassium hydroxide, potassium salts and other chemicals.

10.10.6 Statistics

The production of potassium salts by the major producing countries is as follows:

Production of potassium salts			*In '000s tons metric* K_2O				
	1938	*1948*	*1953*	*1958*	*1960*	*1963*	*1964*
Canada	—	—	—	—	—	570	780
Chile	10	1	—	10	15	20	20
France	560	770	1030	1660	1740	1670	1750
Germany, East	1860	940	1380	1650	1700	1850	1860
Germany, West		?	1580	2020	2300	1950	2200
Italy	—	—	—	10	50	110	130
Israel	24	—	3	70	100	100	150
Spain	15	150	220	240	290	260	290
USA	290	1030	1730	1950	2380	2600	2700
USSR (estimated)	?	?	?	1000	1090	1400	1700
World total (estimated)	2800*	3500*	6000*	8300	9900	10600	11600

*exc. USSR

The quantities are given in terms of K_2O (the K_2O content of the potassium salts) since most is used as fertilizer. These quantities consist mainly of the K_2O content of pure and impure potassium chloride. About 90% of the production in West Germany and France and about 95% of the production in the USA is potassium chloride. Most of the remainder is potassium sulphate.

The United Kingdom imports large quantities of potassium chloride as shown in the following table:

	1955	*1957*	*1959*	*1961*	*1963*
In long tons KCl	510000	537000	610000	694000	680000
In £	8060000	8914000	9860000	10465000	10015000

Two other large importers of potassium chloride are Japan and Belgium, importing 950000 tons and 1100000 tons KCl respectively in 1963. However the major proportion of the Belgian imports is exported again (769000 tons in 1963).

In general the countries of Western Europe are the most important importers of potassium chloride since more than 90% of the world's production is used as fertilizer and the comsumption per hectacre of agricultural land is highest in these countries (see fertilizer chapter, vol. VII).

The output of potassium salts in the USA for use in the chemical industry increased from about 70000 short tons in 1945 to 110000 short tons as K_2O in 1963. In this period the output for fertilizer purposes increased from 540000 tons to over 2.5 million short tons (in terms of K_2O).

Large mining and purification plants are under construction in Canada. It is estimated that Canada will produce about 1.5 million tons of potassium salts (in terms of K_2O) in 1968.

The prices of potassium chloride were as follows in 1965 (in USA). Potassium muriate, min. 60% K_2O: $ 27.00 to $ 30.00 per ton (fertilizer grade). Potassium chloride 99.3-99.9% KCl: $ 33.00 to $ 38.00 per ton (industrial grade). Potassium chloride USP grades $ 0.17-0.26 per lb.

In the United Kingdom potassium chloride (96%) was sold at £ 27 to £ 30 per long ton in 1965.

10.11 OTHER POTASSIUM COMPOUNDS

10.11.1 Potassium sulphate

Potassium sulphate (K_2SO_4) occurs naturally as langbeinite and polyhalite (see potassium chloride, p. 466). Langbeinite is recovered as such (in Carlsbad, USA) and sold as fertilizer.

Potassium sulphate can be prepared from potassium chloride and magnesium sulphate (kieserite $MgSO_4.H_2O$). This process is especially used in Germany since much kieserite is available in that country. Kieserite is treated with a liquid rich in potassium chloride. A hydrate of magnesium-potassium sulphate is formed according to the following equation:

$$2\ KCl + 2\ MgSO_4 + \text{water} \rightarrow MgSO_4.K_2SO_4\ \text{hydrate} + MgCl_2.$$

The double salt crystallizes out and is separated from the solution by filtration. The cake obtained is treated with a saturated solution of potassium chloride and potassium sulphate crystallizes according to the following equation:

$$2\ KCl + MgSO_4.K_2SO_4\ \text{hydrate} \rightarrow MgCl_2 + 2K_2SO_4 + \text{water}$$

The mother liquor which remains after filtration of potassium sulphate is recycled to the first stage of the process.

In a similar process, potassium sulphate is produced from langbeinite and potassium chloride in the USA. In France potassium sulphate is prepared by treating potassium chloride with sulphuric acid in a Mannheim furnace (a cast iron muffle oven). Gaseous hydrogen chloride which is released during the reaction is absorbed in water.

Potassium sulphate is a white crystalline product. Only 7 g of potassium sulphate dissolve in 100 g water at 0° C. Its solubility in water at 100° C is 24 g.

Most potassium sulphate is used as fertilizer. Due to its tendency to complex salt formation it is used for the production of alums (see p. 525). It is also used as a setting time accelerator in gypsum wallboard production.

The most important producers of potassium sulphate are Germany, France and the USA, respectively producing 175000, 190000 and 130000 metric tons in 1962 (in terms of K_2O).

The imports of the United Kingdom are as follows:

	1955	1957	1959	1961	1963
In long tons of K_2SO_4	14000	16000	25000	22000	28000
In £	275000	307000	438000	369000	466000

The prices of potassium sulphate in 1965 in the USA were as follows:
Potassium sulphate, min. 50% K_2O, agricultural grade $ 36 to $ 42 per short ton;
Potassium sulphate, crystalline $ 0.32 per lb.

10.11.2 Potassium carbonate

Potassium carbonate (potash, K_2CO_3) was formerly obtained (for use mainly in washing) from the ash obtained by burning wood and the like. At the present time wood waste is used, and also sunflower stalks in Russia, tobacco stalks in Java, and wine lees in France. Potash is also obtained from molasses washing from the effluent water, from wool scouring and also from potassium sulphate or chloride.

The method of preparation from potassium chloride by electrolysis to caustic potash, and then passing in CO_2, is very simple. The Solvay process for sodium carbonate cannot be used for potassium carbonate because of the high solubility of potassium bicarbonate although the Leblanc process could be used.

Potassium chloride can also be reacted with magnesium carbonate ($MgCO_3.3H_2O$) at a suitable temperature to form the double salt $KHCO_3.MgCO_3.4H_2O$, and then by addition of more water to the solution and heating, magnesium carbonate is precipitated, while potassium carbonate and bicarbonate remain in solution; the carbonate can finally be extracted by filtering off the precipitate and evaporating down the solution.

Among the methods for obtaining potassium carbonate, that involving the production of potassium formate deserves consideration. In this, potassium sulphate, milk of lime and generator gas (which consists largely of carbon dioxide, carbon monoxide, and nitrogen from the air used in combustion) are allowed to react in autoclaves at 200° C and 32 atm. Potassium formate is produced, together with the highly insoluble calcium sulphate. Reaction equation: $K_2SO_4 + 2 CO + Ca(OH)_2 \rightarrow 2 KOOCH + CaSO_4$. The reaction mixture is passed through filters, which remove the calcium sulphate, while the formate solution passes through to be further purified, e.g. by passing in carbon dioxide to precipitate calcium carbonate resulting from any calcium salts remaining in solution. Any potassium sulphate, which is not converted, also crystallizes out. After filtration, the liquor is evaporated down, so that potassium formate crystallizes out; this is calcined, and thus converted into potassium carbonate of 99.5% purity.

Crude potassium carbonate may be obtained by calcining a mixture of molasses and lime, the composition of the resulting ash is not constant, since it depends on the salt content of the water used in the sugar refining, but it is estimated to contain on the average 35% of potassium carbonate, 8% potassium sulphate, 20% potassium chloride, and 20% sodium carbonate. The different salts are extracted from the ash, partly by conversion to bicarbonates followed by fractional crystallization.

Potassium carbonate is used mainly for the production of other purified potassium compounds, among which is potassium nitrate. About a quarter of the output is used for potash glass, which is a hard glass. Much is also used in wool scouring. It is also used as baking powder in gingerbread production, with the addition of tartaric acid so that carbon dioxide is liberated easily.

It should be remembered that, outside the English-speaking countries, the word potash is used exclusively to mean potassium carbonate K_2CO_3.

The production of potassium carbonate in the USA was about 30 000 tons in 1963.

The exports of potassium carbonate from the major producing countries in Europe are as follows:

	1955	1957	In long tons 1959	1961	1963
Belgium-Luxembourg	1 800	2 000	2 800	1 500	2 400
France	7 500	9 100	9 100	14 000	16 000
Germany, East	9 100	9 900	9 500	8 000	10 000
Germany, West	5 500	3 600	5 400	7 000	8 000

The following quantities were imported into the United Kingdom:

	1955	1957	1959	1961	1963
Long tons	5 400	5 400	4 800	5 500	5 800
£	333 000	353 000	301 000	334 000	339 000

Anhydrous potassium carbonate sells at about $ 8.50 to $ 9.55 per 100 lb, and the hydrated form (chiefly monohydrate 83 85%) at $ 6 8 per 100 lb. The pure bicarbonate sells at up to $ 0.35 per lb (USA prices in 1965). In the UK potassium carbonate (96-98%) was sold at £ 85 per long ton in 1965.

10.11.3 Potassium hydroxide

Potassium hydroxide (caustic potash, KOH) was known in ancient times, being prepared from wood ash with slaked lime and water; the solution was then used in soap manufacture. At the present time, the raw materials are potassium chloride and carbonate. The production is completely analogous to that for caustic soda. Weight yields in the mercury and diaphragm cells are higher than for sodium hydroxide because of the difference in molecular weights, so that 56 parts of KOH are obtained against 40 parts of NaOH for the same current usage.

The older lime process is still much used, the reaction being as follows:

$$K_2CO_3 + Ca(OH)_2 \rightarrow CaCO_3 + 2 KOH.$$

The properties of caustic potash are similar to those of caustic soda, but more concentrated solutions can be obtained; it is more expensive than NaOH, because of the dearer raw materials. Caustic potash is used mainly in the manufacture of potash glass, soft soap, and potassium compounds; a relatively large amount is used in organic syntheses.

The largest producer of potassium hydroxide is the USA. Production in that country was 120 000 long tons in 1963. Quantities of about 30 000 to 35 000 tons per year are produced in France and East Germany.

Imports into the United Kingdom are shown in the following table:

	1955	1957	1959	1961	1962
In long tons	2 500	1 600	1 800	1 900	1 900
In £	178 000	124 000	130 000	141 000	142 000

Solid caustic potash (88-92%) sold at $9-11 per 100 lb in 1965, whilst 45% liquor sold at $ 3.70 per 100 lb. The price of potassium hydroxide pellets USP grade was $ 0.34 to $ 0.38 per lb.

10.11.4 Potassium peroxide

Potassium peroxide (K_2O_2) is a product similar to sodium peroxide (Na_2O_2) but, on account of the higher price, is used only in certain military gas masks which completely regenerate the exhaled air. Potassium peroxide not only provides oxygen but also absorbs all the carbon dioxide and water produced in respiration. It is prepared from pure potassium, which is carefully oxidised.

10.11.5 Potassium persalts

Potassium forms two persulphates derived from peroxymonosulphuric acid and peroxydisulphuric acid respectively. The peroxydisulphate can be readily prepared by electrolysis at a high current density of a mixture of potassium sulphate and potassium hydrogen sulphate the reaction being:

$$2KHSO_4 \rightarrow K_2S_2O_8 + H_2$$

or it can be made by adding potassium bisulphate to an electrolysed solution of ammonium bisulphate (see hydrogen peroxide). The peroxydisulphate, commonly called perdisulphate can be hydrolysed to yield the more unstable peroxymonosulphate (permonosulphate):

$$K_2S_2O_8 + K_2O \rightarrow KHSO_5 + KHSO_4$$

Permonosulphate is being developed as a household washing agent as the triple salt $KHSO_4.K_2SO_4.2KHSO_5$.

Potassium perdisulphate is quite stable in the solid crystalline form, but in solution in the presence of a catalyst, e.g. silver peroxide, it is one of the most powerful oxidizing agents available. It is practically unaffected by exposure to the atmosphere and only hydrolyses slowly in aqueous solution at room temperature. Potassium perdisulphate is a true persalt since the active oxygen derives from the anion and not from a perhydrate group in which H_2O_2 is an adduct of the salt. It was at one time made in large quantities for hydrolysis to hydrogen peroxide. Nowadays it is one of the major polymerization initiators because of its powerful oxidizing power, e.g. in the butadiene-styrene copolymerization. It is also used in cotton printing for oxidizing certain dyes (ammonium peroxydisulphate is also used for this purpose). The list price in the USA in 1963 was $ 0.18-0.22 per lb in drums.

Peroxydicarbonate ($K_2C_2O_6$) can be made by electrolysis of potassium carbonate in an analogous way to the perdisulphate as can also the perdiphosphate ($K_2P_2O_8$).

The more common commercial percarbonate is the potassium carbonate perhydrate $K_2CO_3.H_2O_2$, made by allowing carbonate to react at low temperature (8° C) with hydrogen peroxide. Perhydrates of phosphates can be made similarly. Before and during the second world war the German capacity for percarbonates was 7 200 tons per annum.

All salts of this type (including those of sodium and ammonium) decompose easily, with the evolution of nascent oxygen; they can therefore be used as oxidizing and bleaching agents. Perphosphates are used in this way for bleaching flour; they are the more suitable for this purpose in that, after the bleaching has been completed, the phosphorus has a favourable effect on the yeast. Persalts are also used in solution in boiling caustic soda for colouring copper and its alloys black.

10.11.6 Potassium metasulphite

Potassium metasulphite ($K_2S_2O_5$, also known commercially as potassium meta-bisulphite) corresponds with sodium pyrosulphite (see sodium bisulphite) and is prepared in the same manner from sulphur dioxide and potassium carbonate. The solution obtained is evaporated to dryness and the resulting metasulphite is ground. Like the sodium sulphites it is used in the preservation of wine, fruits etc. Large quantities are used in fixing solutions for photographic purposes. The dry salt sold at about $0.27 per lb in 1965.

10.11.7 Potassium nitrate

Potassium nitrate (saltpetre, KNO_3) is, like potassium carbonate, one of the oldest chemical products. It was, many centuries ago, an important constituent of fireworks in China. It was obtained in India by the method still used. During the summer dirt and loose earth are scraped off the roads and from the clay huts. The quantities thus obtained are extracted with water in a pond with a clay floor, and the solution obtained is evaporated down, either over a fire or by the sun. On cooling, a crude form of potassium nitrate crystallizes out, which is sold to the refining factories. The mother liquor left behind, together with the last extract obtained and the residue filtered off, are kept until the following season, so that, in spite of the crude technique used, very little nitrate is lost. In the refining plants, the crude salt is dissolved and filtered, the separation of the nitrate from common salt being effected in the same way as in the conversion method described below. The crude salt is also used as a potassium/nitrogen fertilizer. The Indian government is making efforts to revive this industry and increase its output, in part by the introduction of modern equipment.

In earlier centuries, saltpetre was also obtained in Europe by scraping the walls of stables and houses. This often took place at the orders of the rulers to meet the needs of the army (for manufacture of gunpowder). Sometimes saltpetre plantations were arranged, in which earth rich in chalk, humus, dung or animal remains, was heaped into piles, which were protected against rain. Liquid manure was regularly poured over them, and wood ash was also mixed in. As a result of bacterial action, certain decomposition processes took place, which led to the formation of potassium nitrate. The salt crystallized out on the windward side of the heaps and was scraped off to be sold and purified. This method of production became obsolete after the Napoleonic wars, and other saltpetre such as Bengal saltpetre was not used again until about 1860. Nowadays sodium nitrate and potassium chloride are used as raw materials for the production of potassium nitrate. When solutions of the raw materials are added to one another at room temperature, no reaction takes place, since the ions of the four substances are present in the solution, in which they are all soluble. However, use can be made of the fact that the solubility of sodium chloride differs only slightly at $0°$ C and $100°$ C, while that of potassium nitrate increases markedly at the higher temperatures (see the solubility curves in fig. 10.30).

The reaction is obtained by adding large equal quantities of solid sodium nitrate and potassium chloride to a cold saturated solution of potassium nitrate and sodium chloride. On heating the mixture the following double decomposition conversion takes place:

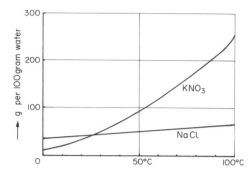

Fig. 10.30 Solubility curves of solutions of sodium chloride and potassium nitrate in water.

$$NaNO_3 + KCl \rightarrow KNO_3 + NaCl.$$

This reaction is possible since many more potassium and nitrate ions can dissolve in the solution at higher temperatures, but only a little more sodium and chlorine ions. Sodium chloride crystallizes out and is removed by filtration. Potassium nitrate, which remains in solution at the higher temperatures, comes out of solution in the form of fine crystals by cooling. Before cooling some water or pure saturated potassium nitrate solution is added in order to prevent the crystallization of any sodium chloride. The fine potassium nitrate crystals are filtered off and freed completely from common salt by careful washing with cold water or pure potassium nitrate solution; after this the crystals are dried by hot air in countercurrent flow. For very pure potassium nitrate, repeated dissolving and crystallization is necessary.

Saltpetre can also be prepared by passing synthetically produced nitrogen peroxide and oxygen into a solution of potassium chloride; a solution of saltpetre in hydrochloric acid and nitric acid is then obtained, the two acids being easily separated and removed by heating.

In contrast with sodium nitrate, potassium nitrate is not hygroscopic and for that reason it is used for the manufacture of gunpowder, sodium nitrate being too hygroscopic. It melts at a temperature of 334° C and gives off oxygen on heating above this temperature.

The purest potassium nitrate is used in the manufacture of gunpowder. It is also used in some matches. Less pure material can be used for fertilizers and in the glass and glazing industry, and also for improving the ripening of cheese. Potassium nitrate is used in mixtures with sodium nitrate (55% KNO_3, 45% $NaNO_3$, melting point 223° C) as a fused salt heat transfer medium.

Important exporters of potassium nitrate are West Germany and Chile. The exports from these countries are as follows:

	1955	1957	*In long tons* 1959	1961	1963
Germany, West	7 000	8 500	9 600	11 600	12 700
Chile	67 000	51 000	86 000	67 000	

The United Kingdom imports the following quantities:

	1955	1957	1959	1961	1962
In long tons	1280	1200	2740	3370	3400
In £	61800	66400	136000	165000	160000

In 1965 the price was $ 9.50 to $ 17.00 per 100 lb in the USA and the price in the UK was £ 62 to £ 65 per long ton.

10.12 LITHIUM AND ITS COMPOUNDS

10.12.1 Occurrence and concentration of lithium

Lithium was given this name because its Swedish discoverer (1817) thought that it occured exclusively in rocks (the Greek word *lithos* means stone). The first electrolytic process for the isolation of lithium was used in 1855.

Lithium is found mainly in the following minerals:

Amblygonite (an aluminium-lithium-fluorophosphate); this is used mainly for the preparation of fluxes of low melting point for earthenware, enamel and opal glass.

Lepidolite (an aluminium-potassium-lithium fluorosilicate) is also used for frit for enamels, and for dissolving aluminium oxides in glass.

Petalite (an aluminium-lithium silicate) is used mainly for clay casting mixtures, and for certain types of glaze. Spodumene (an aluminium-lithium silicate) is used in the preparation of frit for sanitary ware.

Amblygonite, petalite and spodumene can be leached out with concentrated sulphuric acid at a temperature of 250° C. Before leaching out, petalite and spodumene are heated to 1100° C to convert the minerals into modifications which can be attacked by sulphuric acid. Lithium sulphate is formed by treating with the acid and this can be dissolved in water. Dissolved iron compounds and alkaline earth compounds are precipitated as lithium carbonate by means of soda. (Lithium carbonate is less soluble than the carbonates of sodium and potassium.)

Spodumene and lepidolite can be leached out with water after heating with limestone at a temperature above 850° C.

The wastes of these processes already form enormous hills. These wastes consist mainly of calcium and aluminium compounds. Attempts are being made to use them in the production of cement.

Lithium compounds also occur in the soda of Searles Lake. Originally these lithium compounds formed a waste product extremely difficult to deal with. It was found possible to concentrate the salts to a content of 21.5% lithium carbonate (the mixture is known as 'licons'). The initial concentration is very low, but is increased by allowing the solution of lithium compound, together with a number of other salts to evaporate down *in vacuo*. A salt mixture containing dilithium sodium phosphate then crystallizes out, from which the lithium concentrate can be obtained by flotation. This concentrate is then treated with sulphuric acid, so that sulphates are produced from which finally, lithium carbonate is precipitated by means of carbon dioxide.

Lithium compounds are also present, to the extent of 0.5% in the ash from certain types of coal and it is possible that it will be worth while to extract the lithium compounds from this ash, since at present it is already economic to operate with minerals containing 1% of lithium. The ash can be treated with acids without further concentration.

10.12.2 Metallic lithium (Li, atomic weight = 6.94)

Lithium is prepared commercially by electrolysis of a mixed melt of anhydrous lithium chloride and potassium chloride (see also sodium, p. 406). Lithium is a silvery white metal which is harder than the other alkali metals but softer than lead. Its melting point is 186° C. Lithium is the lightest of the metals, its density being 0.53. Ordinary lithium contains 92.5% lithium of atomic weight = 7. The atomic weight of the remainder is 6 (see isotopes p. 622).

Lithium metal can be made into an emulsion in the same way as sodium (see p. 406); this is possible also with lithium hydride. The emulsions are very reactive chemically and are important catalysts for producing organic polymers such as synthetic rubber. They are also used to prepare alkyl lithium compounds used in organic synthesis and polymerisation processes.

Lithium is also used in metallurgy. In general, metals and alloys are hardened if small quantities of lithium are added to them. Alloys of lithium, aluminium and lead are very hard, such an alloy being a constituent of 'Bahnmetal' (see vol. III); alloys of lithium with magnesium are also produced. Molten metals can be refined by means of lithium. Copper having a high electric conductivity is obtained by deoxygenating molten copper with lithium vapour. It has also been suggested that lithium be used for removing sulphur and oxygen from cast iron and steel. Lithium metal is allowed to evaporate in carburisation and decarburisation furnaces for steel, so that it can combine with all the oxygen and/or sulphur present.

Lithium metal (and also lithium compounds) became of great importance during the second world war. The metal is produced on a larger scale at the present time for use in nuclear engineering, e.g. for the production of tritium and lithium deuteride for the hydrogen bomb and for use as heat transfer fluid in nuclear reactors. For these purposes the isotopes of lithium are separated (see isotope separation, p. 627; tritium production, p. 641). Lithium appears to be better than sodium as a liquid metal heat transfer medium in nuclear reactors because of the smaller size of its atom and its lower cross-sectional area for the capture of thermal neutrons (see nuclear reactors, p. 648).

10.12.3 Lithium compounds

Lithium hydride (LiH) is prepared by the direct union of the elements. In wartime lithium hydride was important because by adding water hydrogen could be easily obtained from it for filling balloons, thus avoiding the need for the difficult procedure of transporting compressed hydrogen from place to place. It is an important reducing agent in organic chemistry.

Lithium borohydride (LiBH₄) also forms hydrogen with water and it, too, is an important reducing agent in organic chemistry.

Lithium aluminium hydride (LiAlH₄) can also be used in this way, and is employed particularly in the preparation of various silanes (see Silicones).

Lithium peroxide (LiO₂) was used in wartime as a source of oxygen (see also potassium peroxide).

Lithium hydroxide (LiOH) is prepared from the carbonate by the action of slaked lime. In the pure state it is used to increase the capacity and resistance to mechanical shocks of alkaline storage batteries. It is also required in appreciable amounts for the production of lithium stearate and other lithium soaps, of which the usage is markedly increasing as an important constituent of top grade lubricating greases. It sells as the monohydrate at about $ 1.15 per lb (dry basis).

Lithium chloride (LiCl). The strongly hygroscopic lithium chloride is prepared by treating lithium carbonate with a hydrochloric acid solution, followed by evaporation of the solution obtained. Anhydrous lithium chloride is the starting material for the production of metallic lithium. In solution lithium chloride prevents ice deposition on the cooling chambers of ice machines (see p. 193). An aqueous solution (containing 35-40% lithium chloride) is used extensively for humidity control in air conditioning. Lithium chloride is also used in the production of glass of low expansion coefficient. Certain welding fluxes also contain lithium chloride; in aluminium welding its function being to decrease the melting point and to clean the metal (oxygen scavenger).

Lithium hypochlorite (LiClO) is available in powder form for use in solution as a bleach; the powder is stable and completely soluble in water. The percentage available chlorine is very high (122%).

Lithium fluoride (LiF), when of high purity, can be melted and then on very slow cooling forms a monocrystal; this is set in plaster, and cut into pieces with a diamond saw; the pieces are shaped into lenses and polished with tin oxide or titanium white. In this way lenses are obtained which are of importance for apparatus using ultraviolet light. Monocrystals weighing 4 kg have been obtained.

Lithium carbonate (Li_2CO_3), as already indicated, can be obtained in a very pure state from solutions containing lithium salts, by adding a carbonate (such as soda). Lithium carbonate is the starting material for the production of other lithium compounds for chemical, ceramic and metallurgical uses. As a constituent of glass and enamel it lowers the melting point, and it increases the chemical resistance of these materials.

Lithium aluminate, borate, cobaltate, manganate, silicate, fluoride, etc., obtained from lithium minerals, are also made into glass, glazes and enamel.

Organolithium compounds can be obtained, which are analogous to those of sodium (see p. 464); their reactivity lies between that of the analogous compounds of sodium and magnesium. They affect, in particular, the way in which a polymerization takes place, and for this reason are used in the polymerization of isoprene to give a material which is very close in properties to natural rubber. A plant operating in America produces 500 kg of n-butyl lithium per month, which is taken up mainly by the synthetic rubber industry. It is also used for the preparation of certain methacrylates.

10.12.4 Statistics

The world production of lithium minerals is shown in the table on p. 484 in short tons (the minerals contain about 3-9% Li_2O).

Smaller quantities of lithium minerals are produced in Brazil. The USA is an important producer of lithium minerals (and lithium compounds from Searles Lake). The total output is not known but it may be of the same order of magnitude as that of Rhodesia (about 6000 tons per year in terms of LiO_2). The production of metallic lithium in the USA is estimated at about 200 tons per year. The imports of lithium minerals by the major importing countries is shown in the table on p. 484.

World production in short tons (lithium minerals)		1956	1958	1960	1962	1963
World total (estimate, exc. USA)		125000	96800	102000	—	—
Canada	Spodumene	2400	1930	100	250	330
Rhodesia	Eucryptite	650	400	1330	870	1160
	Amblygonite	84600	1840	—	40	50
	Lepidolite	13500	64700	15500	21200	16200
	Petalite	4460	13200	63300	21700	30000
	Spodumene	5600	5240	7690	1500	2200
South-West Africa	Amblygonite	830	530	160	140	160
	Lepidolite	1140	1040	970	1800	110
	Petalite	3680	7400	3910	1000	400
Republic of Congo	Amblygonite	2000	10	2570	—	—
(formerly Belgian)	Spodumene	70	—	—	—	—

Imports (lithium minerals)	1956	1958	In long tons 1960	1962	1963
UK	7100	6000	10500	3400	3200
Germany, West	2200	4900	10100	10300	10000
Netherlands	1900	5800	4200	3000	3200
United States	57300	139700	92000	19000	19000
Japan	—	600	3000	4000	3000

The consumption of lithium compounds in the USA is estimated as follows:

	1951	In short tons of LiO_2 equivalent 1956	1960
Lithium greases	160	600	900
Ceramics and glass	160	460	900
Welding fluxes	60	240	320
Air conditioning and refrigerating	60	300	400
Alkaline storage batteries	80	120	140
Military and nucleonics	—	350	530
Other	80	60	80
Total	600	2130	3270

The prices in the USA of the most important forms of lithium were in 1965: metallic lithium $9.0 to $11.0 per lb; lithium carbonate $0.50 to $0.58 per lb; lithium chloride (techn.) $0.87 to $0.92 per lb; (pure) $1.24 per lb; lithium hydride $9.50 per lb.

10.13 CAESIUM AND RUBIDIUM

Caesium (Cs, atomic weight = 132.91) and rubidium (Rb, atomic weight = 85.48) were discovered by spectroanalysis by Gustav Kirchoff in 1860.

These two elements usually occur together in the form of compounds particularly in granite and granite pegmatites. Rubidium does not occur as an essential constituent of any known mineral yet it is found as a minor element in so many minerals that it is sixteenth in abundance in the earth's crust. Caesium which ranks as the thirty-seventh most abundant element is the principal component of pollucite and a minor element in a wide variety of minerals. As much as 3.5% of either element may be present in such minerals as rhodonite, triphythite, lithiophyllite, lepidolite, carnallite, beryl, leucite, spodumene, petalite, zennivaldite, micas and potash felspars. Caesium and rubidium also are found in mineral spring brine, bitterns, saline waters and saline deposits. Average sea water contains 0.2 milligrams of caesium and 2.0 milligrams of rubidium per litre.

Pollucite, a hydrated caesium aluminium silicate, is the only known mineral that contains caesium as essential and major constituent. The mineral may contain up to 42.5% Cs_2O but usually averages about 25%. Rubidium is often present in pollucite in quantities as high as 3% Rb_2O. As pollucite and quartz are difficult to distinguish from one another in the field it is possible if not probable that many deposits remain to be discovered.

Caesium metal unlike sodium, potassium or lithium cannot be prepared by the electrolysis of the molten chloride. It is therefore prepared by a metal reduction of one of its salts or of the hydroxide. The metals which may be used include iron, calcium and magnesium. The metal vapour thus produced is entrained in a stream of pure dry hydrogen from which it is condensed.

Calcium carbide has also been used as a reducing agent under vacuum at 700-900° C. Caesium can also be prepared as the amalgam by electrolysis of a solution of a caesium salt with a mercury cathode. The metal is extracted from the amalgam by means of liquid ammonia. One US manufacturer obtains caesium bromide from ores by extraction with hydrobromic acid. The bromide obtained in this way is purified by a liquid-liquid extraction process based on the use of liquid bromine. The metal obtained from bromide purified in this way is exceptionally pure (99.9%). The metal can be made on a scale of several pounds per day.

The methods for the preparation of rubidium metal are very similar to those for caesium metal. Small amounts for laboratory use are prepared by calcium reduction of the chloride under vacuum. It can be prepared also by electrolysis of the fused hydroxide using a diaphragm, or of the fused chloride using an iron cathode and graphite anode or by reduction of the chloride with calcium carbide.

Rubidium is more volatile than potassium, giving rise to a blue vapour. On exposure to air it rapidly becomes coated with a grey-blue oxide film and in other ways shows the extreme reactivity of the alkali metals.

Caesium is the most reactive of all known elements and shows strong ionizing tendencies. It reacts with ice down to a temperature of −116° C. Its melting point is 28.5° C which makes it the most fusible of the alkali metals. It readily forms organo alkyl compounds, e.g. trimethyl caesium.

Rubidium and caesium form alloys with other alkali metals. With mercury they form a series of amalgams which can be used for hydrogenation purposes.

Caesium forms the compound Na_2Cs with sodium, and an uninterrupted series of solid solutions with rubidium, and alloys with alkaline earth metals. The last alloys can be used instead of caesium for many purposes and are more easily handled. Alloys of caesium with antimony, bismuth and gold are photoelectric.

The current production of caesium in the USA is only a few hundred pounds per annum but is expected to increase. It is available for laboratory uses in 'porcupines' which are glass vessels containing fused-on capsules with separate quantities of caesium in each. By this means small quantities of the metal can be used without risk of contaminating the remainder.

The current list price for caesium metal is 375 dollars/lb in lb quantities or $ 1 per gm for smaller lots. Rubidium costs $ 360 per lb.

The caesium halides are very transparent to infrared rays and therefore are very suitable for use in infrared spectrometers. The hydroxide can be used in alkaline accumulators which require to be exposed to very low temperatures. The isotope Cs^{137} occurs in the fusion product effluent from the recovery of spent nuclear fuel from which it may be obtained by base exchange in clays. Clay tablets containing 1540 curies of radiation with a half-life of thirty-seven years can be purchased for radio isotope applications (see also radioactive elements, p. 642). The tablets are contained in stainless steel containers.

The caesium atom is highly magnetic and can be made to vibrate by magnetic fields varying at suitable high frequencies. The energy absorbed by the caesium can be detected and from the peak of the absorption curve the frequency of vibration of the atoms can be calculated. This forms the basis of the so-called atomic clock. The error in time-keeping of such a clock, is only 1/400th part of the error in ordinary clocks.

At present the two elements find their principal usage in infrared lamps, telescopes, binoculars, spectrometers, photoelectric cells, vacuum tubes, scintillation counters, frequency and time standards, medicines and in ceramics. Possible uses for the future include utilization as ion type rocket engine fuel for interplanetary travel, as plasma in thermionic convertors to change heat to electrical energy, and as a heat transfer medium in nuclear power systems.

CHAPTER 11

The Alkaline Earth Metals and their Compounds

11.1 INTRODUCTION

The alkaline earth metals form the second main group of the periodic system. This group comprises the elements beryllium, magnesium, calcium, strontium, barium and radium. These elements are known as the metals of the alkaline earths, because the oxides of magnesium, calcium, strontium and barium have an alkaline reaction, like the alkali metal oxides, and they resemble the 'earths', the historical name for infusible oxides of various elements which are unaffected by strong heating, e.g. alumina.

The alkaline earth metals are bivalent in all their compounds. Calcium, strontium, barium, radium and their compounds have similarities in their chemical properties. barium, radium and their compounds have several corresponding chemical properties. The hydroxides are moderately strong bases and very slightly soluble in water. Barium hydroxide is even a very strong base. Magnesium resembles more the elements of the second subgroup of the periodic system (especially zinc). Magnesium hydroxide is also slightly soluble in water but it is a weak base.

The properties of beryllium are more related to those of aluminium.

Elemental beryllium has a metallic character but, like aluminium, it is amphoteric in its compounds. Thus its hydroxide can react as a base (like other metal hydroxides) and as an acid (like the hydroxides of metalloids).

Radium is a radioactive element and is discussed in the radioactive elements chapter. Metallic magnesium is very important in the metallurgical industry. For this reason it is considered in connection with the metals (see vol. III).

11.2 MAGNESIUM COMPOUNDS (Mg, atomic weight = 24.32)

For metallic magnesium, see vol. III.

11.2.1 History and occurrence

Some naturally occurring products containing magnesium compounds, such as soapstone and serpentine, were known in the Stone Age. Vessels of these products have been found. The Greeks and Romans produced non-combustible cloth and lamp wicks from asbestos. Black was the first who showed (in 1755) that there is a difference between the constituents of calcium and magnesium sulphates. Before that time nothing was known about magnesium compounds. This can be seen from the fact that several quite different minerals were also named 'magnesia', e.g. magnetite (iron oxide, named magnesius lapis) and pyrolusite (manganese oxide, named magnesia nigra). It was again Davy who, in 1808, prepared magnesium amalgam (electrolytically) for the first time.

Magnesium compounds are about as widely dispersed naturally as those of calcium, the total amount of magnesium occurring in the earth being of the order of 2% by weight. Magnesium is found in the form of carbonate in magnesite and dolomite (see rocks and refractories vol. II), as silicate (see under asbestos, talc, meerschaum and mica), as the chloride, sulphate and bromide in sea water, and also in kieserite and carnallite (see potassium compounds). Magnesium is an essential constituent of plants and animals (see fertilizers in vol. VII).

11.2.2 Magnesium oxide

Magnesium oxide (magnesia usta, MgO) occurs in small quantities naturally as the mineral periclase. Magnesium oxide is mainly produced by calcining (burning) magnesium carbonate (magnesite), basic magnesium carbonate and magnesium hydroxide. Depending on the kind of starting material and the method of burning, several grades, for various specific purposes, are prepared.

Dead-burned magnesia (sinter magnesia) is produced by heating magnesium carbonate (magnesite), magnesium hydroxide or magnesium chloride at a temperature of about 1 400°-1 700° C. Large rotary kilns, lined with magnesite or magnesite-chrome brick are used for this purpose. The magnesium oxide obtained is a dense material, consisting of sintered microcrystals which is of great importance in the manufacture of basic refractory bricks (see vol. II). A dead-burned and sintered product is necessary for this purpose. For this reason the sintering temperature of magnesium oxide (which is above 2 000° C) must be lowered, in some cases, by adding ferric oxide. However most natural magnesites contain sufficient quantities of impurities. Dead-burned dolomite is also used in the production of refractories (see vol. II).

Caustic-burned magnesia is produced by calcining magnesium carbonate (magnesite) or magnesium hydroxide at lower temperatures. Magnesium carbonate decomposes at temperatures of about 600-700° C. For a rapid decomposition temperatures of 800-900° C are used. Unlike dead-burned magnesia, caustic-burned magnesia is reactive. This product is used for the production of various magnesium salts, e.g. magnesium chloride, for the production of Sorel cement (see p. 493), and for the production of heat insulating materials.

Highly reactive grades of caustic-burned magnesia are prepared by calcining pure precipitated magnesium hydroxide or basic carbonate at a temperature of about 600° C. The resulting product still contains some carbon dioxide and moisture and has a lower specific gravity. For this reason it is named *light* magnesia (magnesia usta levis) in contradistinction with *heavy* magnesia (magnesia usta ponderosa) which is obtained by burning the same pure starting materials at 800-900° C. These products are used as fillers in cosmetics, as heat insulation material, as vulcanization accelerators for rubber, as an ingredient of pharmaceuticals (e.g. antacid stomach powder) and for the production of magnesium compounds. Heavy and light magnesia can also be used for the production of metallic magnesium by thermal reduction (see vol. III).

Dolomite, a double salt of calcium and magnesium carbonate can be decomposed partially at a temperature of about 800° C. Nearly, all the magnesium carbonate is converted into reactive magnesium oxide, but calcium carbonate is not converted into calcium oxide at this temperature. The product obtained is used in water purification and in the production of magnesium hydroxide and carbonate (see pp. 490 and 492).

The properties of magnesium oxide depend upon its origin. The specific gravity depends on the temperature of calcining. Dead-burned magnesia has a specific gravity of 3.5-3.6, and the specific gravity of very light magnesia may be 2.9. The melting point of pure magnesium oxide is about 2 800° C but it is lowered considerably even by traces of impurities. By fusion it is possible to obtain a material containing larger crystals than the dead-burned magnesia. The product obtained by fusion possesses the unusual property of being flexible; this could be of the greatest importance, since it might result in the possibility of making ceramic products which would be less brittle than those made of ordinary materials. (See further vol. II, refractories.)

Reactive grades of magnesium oxide are slowly converted to the basic carbonate (4 Mg CO₃. Mg(OH)₂.xH₂O) with carbon dioxide and moisture from air. But they can be regenerated by calcining.

The USA produced the following quantities of magnesium oxide in 1963:

Dead-burned magnesia 713 000 short tons (value $ 44 400 000) from minerals, e.g. dolomite, magnesite etc. 20%

from magnesium hydroxide or carbonate obtained from sea-water 80%

Caustic-burned magnesia 135 000 short tons (value $ 7 800 000)

from minerals: 50% from sea-water: 50%

USP grade (pure) and technical magnesia: light 3 300 short tons; heavy 3 800 short tons.

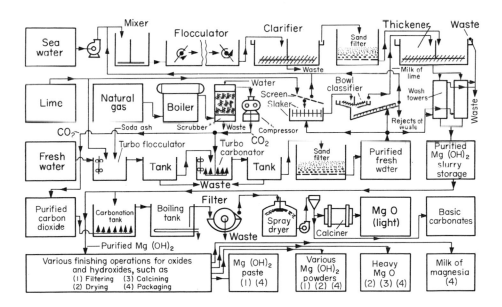

Fig. 11.1   Flow diagram for the production of magnesium hydroxide from sea water.

In the USA magnesium oxide was sold at the following prices in 1965: dead-burned magnesia, $ 46 per ton; technical heavy magnesia, $ 52 to $ 60 per ton; technical light magnesia, $0.26 to $0.30 per lb; USP grades light and heavy $0.39 to $0.40 per lb.

11.2.3 Magnesium hydroxide

Magnesium hydroxide (magnesia magma, $Mg(OH)_2$) can be prepared by hydration of magnesium oxide. However it is mainly produced from sea-water. Sea-water contains, per cubic metre, 4.17 kg of magnesium chloride, 1.67 kg of magnesium sulphate and 0.067 kg of magnesium bromide.

The sea-water is pumped at high tide to the magnesia factory (see fig. 11.1) from a point where it is relatively pure through wooden or cast-iron pipelines. It is first sterilized by passing in chlorine. The water is subsequently purified so as to remove all colloidal particles and other objectionable substances (see clarifying of water, p. 126); this is effected by stirring in milk of lime, which first combines with all the dissolved carbon dioxide, and then converts salts of iron, manganese, etc., together with some magnesium compounds, into insoluble hydroxides or oxides.

The slurry is now passed into large settling tanks, in which the impurities settle down into the conical bottom portion; clear, pure sea-water remains on top. This clear water is withdrawn from the top of the vessel and passed through a sand filter which removes the remaining (and finest) suspended particles. Only then is it possible to begin to extract the magnesium, which is effected by stirring pure milk of lime into the pure sea-water as this flows down into a tank with a conical bottom. The water and the milk of lime are well mixed at the inlet, so that the calcium hydroxide converts all the magnesium salts into insoluble magnesium hydroxide; this is finely divided and sinks slowly towards the conical bottom of the large tank from which it can be removed for subsequent treatment. Flocculating agents may be added to assist the settling of the slurry.

The sludge from the settling tank after filtration must be freed from sea-water and this is a difficult operation because of the colloidal nature of the sludge. One method is to extrude the sludge through small orifice plates and allow the extruded threads to fall through a series of tall columns through which passes a countercurrent flow of water. The soluble salts are thereby removed from the sludge by osmosis and diffusion, and pass out in the overflow, which is filtered to prevent loss of any entrained magnesium-hydroxide. The washed solids are removed from the base of the first tower and passed to the series of similar towers or decanters. The purified slurry of magnesium hydroxide (milk of magnesia) is finally de-watered by filtration on rotary vacuum filters and dried.

Plants of this type are both very extensive and very complicated, on account of the large mass of material to be handled, the numerous treatments required and because they also have to provide for the calcination of chalk for the production of lime.

Modifications of the process described above are also used for the production of magnesium hydroxide.

Calcined dolomite ($CaCO_3.Mg\ CO_3 \xrightarrow{heat} CaO.MgO$), slaked with pure water is increasingly used in the above process instead of slaked lime. The calcium hydroxide thus produced acts in the manner described above, while the magnesium hydroxide from the dolomite makes the precipitate richer in the desired product.

An enriched solution of Ca^{++} and Mg^{++} is sometimes prepared from sea water by treating the latter with a zeolite (a sodium aluminosilicate, see p. 136). The zeolite charged with calcium and magnesium ions is treated with 15% sodium chloride brine so that the sodium ions replace the calcium and magnesium ions which pass into the brine. Magnesium hydroxide is then produced from this brine by treatment with milk of lime, and settles out as a thick pulp.

Magnesium hydroxide is also prepared by precipitation from mother liquors containing magnesium salts, e.g. waste liquors from the potash industry (see p. 472) and concentrated wastes from common salt production (see p. 421).

The majority of the magnesium hydroxide produced is converted into dead-burned and caustic-burned magnesia (see magnesium oxide). Magnesium hydroxide is also used for the neutralization of acids in the chemical industry. Due to the semicolloidal nature of the precipitated product, magnesium hydroxide slurries are sometimes used as such, e.g. for the production of magnesium chloride or carbonate. Magnesium hydroxide for pharmaceutical purposes is prepared for sale in the following different forms.

1. Milk of magnesia with 8% $Mg(OH)_2$ (e.g. packed in bottles).
2. The milk of magnesia can be heated with steam and thickened in a Monel metal filter to give a 30% paste.
3. This paste can be sold as such, or it can be spray dried, after suitable dilution, to give the dry hydroxide.

Like magnesium oxide it is used as antacid stomach powder.

The USA produced 431 000 short tons of magnesium hydroxide in 1963 (excluding magnesium hydroxide converted into magnesium oxide in the same plant). Pure magnesium hydroxide was sold at $0.24 to $0.25 per lb in 1965. Substantial quantities of magnesium hydroxide are also produced in the United Kingdom, especially from sea-water. Production figures are not published. The total value of all magnesium compounds produced was close to £ 5 million in 1958.

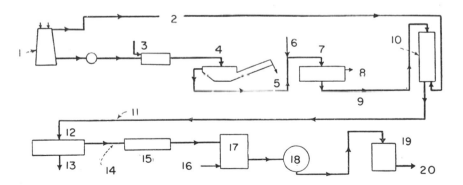

Fig. 11.2 Flow diagram for the production of magnesium carbonate from Dolomite for the production of insulating units with asbestos.
1. Oven for calcining dolomite; 2. CO_2 (purified); 3. Crusher (MgO + CaO); 4. Classifier; 5. Removal of grains; 6. Water; 7. Thickener; 8. Limewater; 9. $Mg(OH)_2$ + $Ca(OH)_2$; 10. Saturator; 11. Solution of $Mg(HCO_3)_2$ and precipitated $CaCO_3$; 12. Thickener; 13. $CaCO_3$; 14. Solution of $Mg(HCO_3)_2$; 15. Preheating; 16. Steam; 17. Precipitation *in vacuo* of $MgCO_3.3H_2O$; 18. Filter; 19. Carbonate storage; 20. To dryer.

11.2.4 Magnesium carbonates

Magnesium carbonate (magnesia alba Mg CO₃) occurs, as already stated, as magnesite and in the form of dolomite (MgCO₃.CaCO₃). Fairly pure magnesium carbonate can sometimes be prepared from magnesite by mechanical ore treatment methods, e.g. screening, flotation etc. Much magnesium carbonate is produced by direct carbonation (i.e. treatment with carbon dioxide) of magnesium hydroxide slurries, e.g. obtained from sea-water. A similar method is the precipitation of magnesium carbonate from solutions of magnesium salts with soda. This process is used for recovery of magnesium carbonates from mother liquors remaining from the production of potassium salts (especially in Germany). Magnesium carbonate is also prepared from caustic-burned dolomite (see magnesium oxide). The burned product (MgO.CaCO₃) is slurried in water and carbonated with the flue gases obtained from calcination (burning), under a pressure of 75 p.s.i. (see fig. 11.2). The resulting slurry contains magnesium bicarbonate, MgHCO₃, in solution, and calcium carbonate and other impurities in suspended form. The solids are removed from the solution by filtration. Magnesium can be precipitated from the solution as a basic carbonate (4MgCO₃.Mg (OH)₂. x H₂O and 3 MgCO₃ . Mg(OH)₂. x H₂O) by boiling, or as the neutral carbonate Mg CO₃ . 3H₂O by aeration. In a similar way pure magnesium carbonate can be prepared from magnesite.

In general neutral magnesium carbonate trihydrate is precipitated from solutions, etc., when precipitation is performed at temperatures below 50° C. At higher temperatures the basic carbonates are formed. Usually the neutral carbonate is converted into basic carbonate by heating the suspension, because normal magnesium carbonate trihydrate has a tendency to decompose to basic carbonate. Several grades of basic carbonate, having different bulk densities, can be obtained. The lightest forms are obtained at high dilutions and low temperatures (about 60° C), the heavy forms from more concentrated solutions at higher temperatures (about 90° C). The bulk density also increases with increasing heating period.

The carbonates are also known as magnesia, which can give rise to confusion since this name refers also to magnesium oxide. The names magnesia alba levis and magnesia alba ponderosa are used for light carbonates and heavy carbonates respectively. The carbonates are white crystalline powders which are very much less soluble in water. The melting point cannot be given since they begin to lose carbon dioxide at temperatures above 350° C.

Magnesium carbonates are used in toothpaste, dusting powder, medicinal preparations, fireproof paint, paper, synthetic rubber compositions, e.g. neoprene, and in table salt (and some other materials) to keep it free flowing. Besides the large quantities of magnesite and dolomite used in the refractory industry (see vol. II) the largest portion of magnesium carbonate (i.e. basic carbonate) is used in the manufacture of thermal insulation plates and shapes.

Insulating shapes are obtained by mixing the correct type of magnesium carbonate with water, a relatively small amount of asbestos being mixed in as a strengthener, while calcined gypsum is also often added.

After this the material must be poured quickly into heated oiled moulds, in which it rapidly solidifies. The material is then removed from the moulds, pressed and dried. This method of treatment ensures that there is no alteration in size, so that the pieces require no subsequent trimming, which was not the case with earlier techniques.

A process is now being adopted in which the material is impregnated with water-repellant substances, so that it remains in good condition even in extremely wet conditions.

The pieces contain 85% magnesium carbonate and more than 10% of asbestos, which acts only as a refractory binding agent. When used for pipe insulation they are fixed on to the pipes either by means of steel bands or with wire. They may also be made in a tubular form. The tubes are sawn lengthwise in such a way that they can be bent so as to become almost flat. They can then be easily applied to a pipe, since they are elastic, and become tubular again on being released. This type of construction makes applying and removing pipe insulation (e.g. for inspection or repair) very easy.

The world production of the mineral magnesite was about 9 million short tons in 1963. Nearly 105 million tons were produced in Austria and nearly 3 million tons in the USSR (see refractories, vol. II). The USA produced 530000 tons of magnesite in 1963 and the production of precipitated carbonates was 12000 tons in the same year. The price of the latter was \$ 0.12 to \$ 0.15 per lb in 1965. In the UK it was sold at £ 97 per long ton.

11.2.5 Magnesium chloride

Magnesium chloride (Mg Cl_2) occurs naturally in deposits of potassium salts, e.g. in carnallite (see potassium chloride, p. 466) and in sea water. Magnesium chloride is produced in several ways. In Germany it is obtained from the mother liquors resulting from the recovery of potassium chloride (see potassium chloride). These mother liquors, which contain up to 28% magnesium chloride have largely been regarded as a waste product, since it is very costly to obtain pure magnesium chloride from it. The mother liquors are often cooled first to crystallize sodium sulphate (see waste liquors of potassium chloride production, p. 472). Magnesium chloride is obtained by evaporating the remaining liquors in open pans or multiple effect evaporaters. Submerged flame heaters are sometimes used (see phosphoric acid). Sodium chloride, sodium sulphate and magnesium sulphate crystallize out and are removed. Ferrous iron is removed by oxidation with a chlorate and precipitation with lime. Impure magnesium chloride is obtained as a glassy mass by cooling the solution, which is evaporated to a density of 1.435. The solution is often solidified on rotating cooling drums from which the salt layer can be removed by scrapers. Pure magnesium chloride hexahydrate ($MgCl_2.6H_2O$) is obtained by repeated recrystallization.

Magnesium chloride hexahydrate is also obtained from salt lakes such as the Dead Sea (see production of potassium chloride).

Large quantities of the chloride are also obtained from the magnesium hydroxide paste produced from sea water (see p. 491). This is treated with hydrochloric acid and the solution obtained is then evaporated and so converted into solid magnesium chloride hexahydrate.

Dehydrated magnesium chloride is prepared by separating the water of crystallization in a series of large, strongly heated rotary kilns through which hot gases are passed. The final stages of the dehydration are done under an atmosphere of hydrogen chloride or chlorine as otherwise basic chlorides would be formed. In large-scale plants partial dehydration is performed by spray drying. The anhydrous salt is melted and cast into blocks, which are packed so as to exclude all air.

Thus magnesium chloride is available in the anhydrous form and as the hexahydrate.

The melting points are 715° and 117° C respectively. The solubility in water at 20° C is 55g $MgCl_2$ per 100g water. Both the anhydrous chloride and the hexahydrate are very hygroscopic. Solutions are highly corrosive to steel; many types of steel develop cracks in contact with such solutions, as a result of 'stress corrosion'. The nickel alloy Inconel (see vol. III) is generally used for equipment in which these solutions are to be handled.

Large amounts of anhydrous magnesium chloride are used for the electrolytic production of magnesium metal (see vol. III). Magnesium chloride is also used in strong solution (because of its hygroscopic character) to bind dust on roads and in mines (see also calcium chloride, p. 497). A solution of strength 22° Bé is used in the manufacture of Sorel cement (see vol. II). Magnesium chloride is also used in dry batteries and in the fireproofing of wood, e.g. for mine timbers and railroad sleepers (ties).

The USA produced 290000 tons of magnesium chloride in 1963. The prices in 1965 were $ 0.12 to $ 0.15 per lb for the anhydrous product and $ 0.03 to $ 0.05 per lb for the hydrate. The corresponding prices in the UK were about £ 60 and £ 25 per long ton.

11.2.6 Magnesium sulphate

Magnesium sulphate (heptahydrate (Epsom salt, bitter salt, Mg $SO_4.7H_2O$) was first discovered in 1695 and obtained from the mineral water at Epsom.

The most important sources of magnesium sulphate are the mineral kieserite ($MgSO_4$) and the residues of the potash industry from which potassium salts are leached (see occurrence and refining of potassium chloride). In these residues magnesium is also available as kieserite.

Magnesium sulphate heptahydrate is obtained from these materials by dissolving in water at 70° C, filtration and crystallization by cooling. Magnesium sulphate is also produced by treating magnesium oxide, hydroxide or basic carbonate with sulphuric acid (especially in countries having no deposits of kieserite).

Magnesium sulphate heptahydrate is the most important commercial form of magnesium sulphate. Anhydrous magnesium sulphate can be obtained by heating the heptahydrate in a rotating drum at about 500° C. The anhydrous form is hygroscopic and hardens (like gypsum) by mixing with a little water due to the formation of the heptahydrate. The solubility is 27g $MgSO_4$ per 100 g water at 0° C and 56 g $MgSO_4$ per 100 g water at 70° C. At higher temperatures the solubility decreases due to the formation of less soluble hydrates (compare the solubility of sodium carbonates).

Magnesium sulphate is used in a finishing composition for the conditioning or dressing of cotton, as an important constituent of the viscose silk bath (4-4½ tons of magnesium sulphate are used in Germany per ton of viscose silk), as a mordant for fixing certain basic dyestuffs on wool, and as a constituent of fireproofing compositions. The anhydrous sulphate is used as a drying agent for organic solvents. Magnesium sulphate also has medical applications. It is an analgesic and cathartic. Small quantities of magnesium sulphate are used for the production of magnesium trisilicate which is an antacid stomach powder. The naturally occurring silicate (meerschaum or sepiolite) does not act in this way. In the USA magnesium sulphate was sold at $ 2.15 to $ 3.15 per 100 lb in 1965, and in the UK at £ 19 per long ton.

11.2.7 Organo-magnesium compounds

Magnesium was the first metal from which organo-metallic compounds were prepared; this was achieved by Grignard in 1900, and they are still referred to as 'Grignard compounds'; they are produced on a large scale at the present time. Pieces of magnesium (obtained, for example, by sawing or milling) in the complete absence of water (e.g. in ether) are contacted with an organic chloride, bromide or iodide. With ethyl chloride ($CH_3.CH_2Cl$), the compound ethylmagnesium chloride ($CH_3.CH_2. MgCl$) is formed.

Grignard compounds react readily with a range of compounds containing functional groups such as active hydrogen and halogen and functional groups containing double

bonds, e.g. $>C = O$ (aldehydes, ketones, carboxylic acids), $>C = S$, $C{\Large\langle}^O_O$

(carbon dioxide), $C{\Large\langle}^S_S$, $-C{\Large\langle}^O_{Cl,}$ $S{\Large\langle}^O_O$,$-C-O-C-$, $-C \equiv N$ and $-N = N-$,

the Grignard compound adding across a double bond with the magnesium oriented away from the carbon centre. Examples are:

a. $CH_3MgI + CH_3COCH_3 \rightarrow CH_3\underset{|}{C}(CH_3)_2 \xrightarrow{H_2O} CH_3\underset{|}{C}(CH_3)_2 + Mg(OH)I$

Grignard   acetone $OMgI$ OH

compound   Grignard addition   tert. butyl alcohol

                        compound

The reaction of the Grignard addition compound with water yields an alcohol with an added alkyl (methyl)group.

b. $CH_3MgBr + C_6H_5CHO \rightarrow C_6H_5 \underset{|}{C}H CH_3 \xrightarrow{H_2O} C_6H_5 \underset{|}{C}HCH_3 + Mg(OH)Br$

Grignard   benzaldehyde $OMgBr$ OH

compound

The latter compound can be dehydrated to form styrene ($C_6H_5CH - CH_2$).

c. A reaction which led to important developments in silicones is:

$$2 CH_3MgCl + SiCl_4 \rightarrow (CH_3)_2 Si Cl_2 + 2 MgCl_2$$

$$n (CH_3)_2 Si Cl_2 + n H_2O \rightarrow ((CH_3)_2 SiO) n + 2 n H Cl.$$

The polymer chain is thus linked through a series of siloxane ($-SiO-$) groups.

Until recently, these compounds were made in the laboratory just before use, but certain companies have now begun to produce them on a large scale for sale.

Methyl magnesium carbonate is also produced, and this is used for the preparation of alpha nitro-acids and alpha amino-acids from nitroparaffins (see vol. IV).

Special operating conditions are always necessary in plants making Grignard compounds, such as good ventilation, the use of a nitrogen atmosphere, etc. because of the dangers associated with the use of ether.

Attempts are now being made to avoid using ether by starting with organo-sodium compounds dissolved in hydrocarbons; these can be converted into the magnesium compounds by the use of anhydrous magnesium chloride and also into organo-lithium compounds by using lithium chloride.

11.3 CALCIUM AND ITS COMPOUNDS

11.3.1 Calcium (Ca, atomic weight = 40.08)

Calcium occurs commonly as carbonate, silicate and sulphate (see marble, chalk, limestone, marl, silicates, gypsum). The total amount of calcium contained in the earth is about 3.5% by weight. A beautiful, crystalline form of the carbonate, called Iceland spar, deserves special mention; it sometimes forms very beautiful trigonal crystals in the shape of a rhombohedron. The non-transparent, or milky form, is called calcite (of which, e.g. marble is made up). A rhombic calcium carbonate is known as aragonite. In apparently non-crystalline form, calcium carbonate is known principally as chalk and limestone (see under these headings). It is also an important constituent of shells, egg shells and pearls. In bones it is always associated with calcium phosphate, for which reason finely ground bone meal can be of importance in cattle raising as promoting growth and milk production (milk is of particular importance on account of its calcium and phosphorus content).

Calcium is an important constituent of cell membranes, and plays an essential part in many physiological processes; it is responsible, e.g. for the clotting of blood. Calcium is taken up into the body from the highly complex organic constituents of food.

Calcium metal was first prepared by Davy in 1808; Black had found as early as 1756 the relations existing between chalk, quicklime and slaked lime.

Calcium is produced electrolytically from molten calcium chloride contained in a graphite crucible serving as anode, while the cathode takes the form of an iron pipe. This pipe is withdrawn from the bath at regular intervals, carrying the liberated calcium with it, and this in turn is removed in pieces ('carrots') of irregular size, and packed in well-sealed boxes. During the second world war, appreciable amounts were obtained by reducing pure lime with aluminium under vacuum, the liberated calcium being vaporized as a result of the high temperature used. Calcium powder is now produced by heating the carbide *in vacuo* at temperatures in the range 800-1 400° C.

Calcium is a soft metal, melting at 810° C. Its specific gravity is 1.55 at 20° C. Calcium is very reactive, e.g. with water it rapidly forms hydrogen and slaked lime, for which reason it can be used (particularly in powder form) for the manufacture of porous concrete. Calcium is not used on a large scale for this purpose because it is too expensive. At high temperatures calcium reacts also with hydrogen, nitrogen, boron and silicon to form stable nitrides, borides, carbides and silicides.

Calcium has a very high affinity for oxygen, hence its use as reducing agent in metal production. It is used for removing oxygen from metals such as steel, copper and nickel. At the same time it removes sulphur from these metals. Up to the present time, briquettes made from calcium with which steel turnings of the metal to be treated have been used for the deoxidation. However the powder seems to be increasingly used for this purpose since tubes of the metals to be treated can be filled with calcium powder and conveniently added to the molten metal. When used in molten lead, calcium removes also any bismuth present.

A silicon-calcium alloy has become of importance for the removal of oxygen from steel (see also silicides, p. 545). Pure aluminium can also be added to this alloy. The alloys, contained in a steel pipe, are placed in a Martin oven, so as to ensure that it reaches the steel underneath the slag layer.

Calcium is also used for the reduction of oxides of rare metals (especially uranium oxide and thorium oxide and since it is even able to remove traces of oxygen from gases, calcium is also used as a 'getter' in radio valves.

The most important application of calcium is based on its hardening action in metals. It is alloyed with lead for use in covering cables, and, with the addition of lithium in bearing metals. It is also used as a substitute for antimony in the lead used in accumulators, in which 0.1% of calcium then replaces 12% of antimony, while the life of the accumulator is appreciably greater, the current loss smaller, and the formation of harmful vapours is avoided. Calcium is also a constituent of certain types of chromium-nickel steels, and also of aluminium and magnesium alloys.

The world output of calcium is probably less than 1 000 tons per annum. In the USA it is sold at $2.00 per lb (1963). The much more expensive fine powder sells only in a small way.

11.3.2 Calcium compounds

a. Calcium chloride ($CaCl_2$) is almost invariably obtained as a waste product (in Solvay soda factories) for which disposal is difficult. Only relatively small amounts of the waste (which contains besides calcium chloride, various impurities such as sodium chloride and compounds of iron, magnesium and manganese) are purified and find any useful application. Pure calcium chloride is obtained from distiller blow-off liquors in the Solvay process by first freeing the aqueous solution from magnesium, manganese and iron compounds, by boiling with calcium carbonate, which precipitates the carbonates of the three metals. After filtration the excess calcium carbonate is converted into calcium chloride by means of hydrochloric acid. The clarified solution is evaporated down in multiple-effect evaporators (see common salt, p. 418) under vacuum, to crystallize the sodium chloride. After removal of the sodium chloride crystals, the liquor is further evaporated in a single effect evaporator to give a liquor which contains about 70% calcium chloride (by weight). This liquor is solidified in flakes on a drum drier and is further dried in a rotary drier. The resulting product is sold as 70-72% calcium chloride (it approximates in composition to $CaCl_2.2H_2O$). A fraction of the output is converted into anhydrous calcium chloride by heating (e.g. for use in fused chloride melts). Calcium chloride is packed in dampproof multi-ply sacks and sacks with polythene lining.

Both the anhydrous form and the dihydrate are very hygroscopic (even a solution of calcium chloride in water can attract moisture), hence their use as a drying agent for air, other gases and liquids. However, calcium chloride cannot be used to dry moist ammonia because it forms an addition compound. Because of its strong attraction for water, calcium chloride is also used for stabilizing unpaved road surfaces and keeping them dust free. It is also used for preventing dust formation in piles of coal, and in mines, and for producing a heavy solution for use in coal washing (the solution with 50% CaCl₂ has a density of 1.5). In America the inner tracks of heavy tractors are partly filled with a non-freezing solution of this substance. Piles of sand are sprayed with calcium chloride to prevent freezing. The addition of 2% calcium chloride speeds up the setting of concrete. In cold parts of the world the reserve supplies of water needed for fire fighting are kept liquid by the addition of calcium chloride.

Mixtures of calcium and magnesium chlorides are also commercially available as hygroscopic materials.

By adding 15-25 lb (dry basis) calcium chloride crystals to a ton of the pulp used for making board, a better quality is obtained than would otherwise be possible. It is probable that the positive Ca^{++} ions neutralize the negative fibres, causing them to aggregate more readily.

The production of calcium chloride in the USA was as follows:

| | In short tons | | |
	1958	1960	1963
Solid and flake (77-80% CaCl₂)	529 000	556 000	679 000
Liquid (40-45% CaCl₂)	201 000	210 000	235 000

It is estimated that the quantity used in the USA in 1963 was divided up approximately in the following proportions:

Dust control (roads and in mines)	25%
De-icing of highways in winter	30%
Concrete treating	13%
Industrial uses	10%
Brine refrigeration (cooling purposes)	5%
Other uses	17%

The most important exporting countries are Germany, Belgium and the USA. The exports of the United Kingdom are shown in the following table:

	1955	1957	1959	1961	1962
In long tons	6 200	5 100	6 400	7 800	6 500
In £	106 000	100 000	119 000	148 000	131 000

In the USA calcium chloride was sold at the following prices (in 1965):
flakes (77-80% CaCl₂), $ 34 per short ton; liquid in tanks, $ 14 per short ton. In the UK a solid grade containing 70-72% calcium chloride was sold at £ 17 5s 0d per long ton.

b. *Calcium hydride* (CaH₂) can be easily produced from the elements (see also p. 72). With water it is easily decomposed into lime and hydrogen. For this reason it was used in wartime as a source of hydrogen for balloons. Hydrogen in this form (canned hydrogen) is easy to handle. Calcium hydride is also used for the deoxygenation of metals and as a reducing agent.

c. *Calcium sulphide* (CaS) can be obtained by reducing gypsum with carbon, by heating calcium carbonate with sulphur, and from milk of lime and hydrogen sulphide. Rotary kilns, heated to 1 000° C are commonly used in the method of production from gypsum, the mixture of gypsum with coal being heated for about $1\frac{1}{2}$ hours. The product is then allowed to flow into tanks, into which flue gases are passed in order to prevent oxidation.

Calcium sulphide reacts with water according to the equation:

$$2CaS + 2H_2O \rightarrow Ca(OH)_2 + Ca(SH)_2$$

The hydrosulphide ($Ca(SH)_2$) acts as a solvent, especially for hair, for which reason it (and other sulphides) is used in cosmetics and in tanneries as a depilatory.

Calcium sulphide, when pure except for the admixture of a small quantity of bismuth, is distinctly phosphorescent (see p. 672).

d. *Calcium polysulphides* can be prepared by boiling milk of lime with sulphur, or exhausted material from coal gas purification with chalk; in the latter case, the mixture also contains iron oxides. The product, and also a mixture of it with thiosulphate is used as an insecticide and plant fungicide.

e. The calcium salts of *gluconic* and *lactic acid,* and of *amino-acids* are used in appreciable quantities for medicinal purposes.

f. *The other calcium compounds* are considered in connection with the groups of commercial materials having similar applications or groups of compounds containing other corresponding elements. For calcium nitrate, calcium cyanamide and calcium cyanide see nitrogen compounds. For calcium phosphates see phosphorus compounds. Calcium sulphate (gypsum) and calcium carbonate (limestone chalk, marble etc.) are discussed in the rocks chapter (vol. 11). For calcium carbide p. 538, for calcium hypochlorite see bleaching powder, p. 232, and for calcium oxide (quick lime) and calcium hydroxide (slaked lime) see lime and concrete.

11.4 STRONTIUM AND ITS COMPOUNDS

Strontium (Sr atomic weight = 87.63) took its name from the place where strontium compounds were first discovered (Strontian in Scotland). Metallic strontium was first prepared by Davy. The most important strontium minerals are the carbonate (strontianite) and the sulphate (celestine), which are found mainly in Great Britain and Russia. The properties of this element resemble closely those of calcium, which it can replace, e.g. in bones, and hence the danger of accumulation in bones of the strongly radioactive Sr^{90}, which is formed by the explosion of nuclear weapons.

The metal is used mainly as a getter in radio valves (tubes).

Strontium hydroxide ($Sr(OH)_2$) is the most important compound, but the demand for it is decreasing. It is prepared from purified celestine, which is heated with sodium carbonate so that the mineral is converted into strontium carbonate and sodium sulphate, the latter being dissolved in water. The solid residue is mixed with sawdust and compressed to form briquettes; on heating to 1 500° C the carbonate decomposes and strontium oxide remains. The hydroxide $Sr(OH)_2$ is obtained by then slaking with water.

The hydroxide was formerly used for beet sugar refining. Insoluble strontium disaccharate is formed when strontium hydroxide is added to a sugar solution. Sugar is recovered from the saccharate by treating with carbon dioxide (see also Sugar vol. VII). Strontium hydroxide is also used for the preparation of the nitrate and of other strontium salts, which were used in fireworks and light signals on account of the pretty red flames produced. Certain salts are used medicinally.

In recent times it has become of importance principally for the preparation of strontium soaps required for lubricating greases which remain unaltered after repeated heating and cooling, are resistant to water and hydrocarbons, and protect bearings and shafts against corrosion. These soaps, and also the naphthenate, are being used increasingly as stabilizers for vinyl resins.

The United Kingdom is an important producer of strontium minerals. The world production is shown in the following table:

			In long tons		
	1955	1957	1959	1961	1963
World production (estimated)		13 000	11 000	11 000	15 000
United Kingdom (celestite)	4 750	6 900	6 000	8 700	9 000
Mexico (celestite)	1 790	1 800	2 270	2 400	6 000
Morocco		270	390	—	·—
Pakistan (celestite)	300	850	660	420	380
Italy		1 100	320	1 000	

Strontium minerals are also mined in the USA, USSR, Poland, Germany and Argentina.

The United States imported the following quantities:

	1955	1957	1959	1961	1963
In long tons	5 500	5 800	7 300	8 900	14 500

Strontium carbonate sold at about $ 0.19 to $ 0.35 per lb and the hydroxide at $ 0.40 per lb in 1965.

11.5 BARIUM AND ITS COMPOUNDS

11.5.1 Barium (Ba, atomic weight = 137.4)

Barium was obtained, in a pure state, for the first time in 1901. Barium compounds have been known for a long time (the seventeenth century) and are noteworthy for their high specific gravity. The most important minerals are heavy spar (barytes, barium sulphate) and witherite (barium carbonate). The name barytes, given to the heavy mineral spar, comes from the Greek word for heavy. Similarly the metal, which was obtained as an amalgam for the first time by Davy (1809), was given the name barium.

Metallic barium is obtained from fused barium chloride by electrolysis. It can also be made by a metal (e.g. aluminum) reduction process under vacuum. The metal strongly resembles calcium, but reacts more violently with certain substances, including oxygen and hydrogen. It is used in the production of certain nickel alloys, and as a 'getter' in radio valves.

11.5.2 Barium sulphate

Barium sulphate (barite, barytes, heavy spar, $BaSO_4$) is the most important barium mineral. It occurs in a rather pure state. The most important deposits occur in Germany. Very pure deposits are found in Mexico and Brazil.

The best kinds of heavy spar contain 98% $BaSO_4$, and those with a $BaSO_4$ content of less than 94% are not economic to process. Heavy spar to be used in the coal or methane reduction process must not contain more than 2.5% of SiO_2, 1.5% of Fe_2O_3, and 1% of fluorides (see below).

When silica is to be removed purification with hydrofluoric acid is used; this converts silica into silicon tetrafluoride which with caustic soda gives sodium fluorosilicate (for sodium fluorosilicate see p. 216).

The commercially available barite is a moderately soft crystalline product. It can have a red, yellow, grey or green colour depending on the impurities. Very pure barium sulphate (blanc fixe) is a white crystalline product. It is prepared by precipitating barium sulphate from solutions of barium salts by adding sodium sulphate. Barium sulphate is only slightly soluble in water. Its specific gravity is 4.5.

Crude barite is used for the production of barium compounds (barium carbonate, chloride, pure sulphate etc.). Since barium sulphate is only slightly soluble in water, acids and alkalis, it is converted into barium sulphide which dissolves in acids due to decomposition. The reaction is caused by heating crude barite with coal. The barium sulphide obtained is the starting material for the production of almost all barium salts and the pigments blanc fixe and lithopone. The latter is prepared by adding zinc sulphate to a solution of barium sulphide. Blanc fixe and lithophone are used in white paints (see pigments, vol. V).

Blanc fixe is also used in paper, linoleum, oilcloth, natural rubber and cosmetics.

Sometimes crude barite is finely ground and purified with sulphuric acid. The product obtained is used as a filler in cheap paints etc.

Coarsely ground barite, with reduced iron content, is used in glass manufacture (e.g. for the image tubes of television sets). The melting point of the glass is reduced by adding small quantities of barite. However, barium carbonate is often preferred for fine glassware because of its higher purity.

Finely ground barite is added to drilling muds in oil well development. Due to its high specific gravity barium sulphate increases the weight of the drilling mud considerably (see also barium carbonate).

After the second world war, the world output of barium minerals (mainly barite) increased from about 1 million tons (in 1946) to 3 millions tons (in 1956). The world production has been constant in recent years. The most important producers of barite produced the following amounts as shown in the table overleaf.

The consumption of crude barite in the USA is shown in the following tables:

	1956	In 1 000 short tons 1959	1961	1963
For ground and crushed barite	1 840	1 227	1 224	1 048
For lithophone	31	170	167	152
For barium chemicals (inc. blanc fixe)	165			
Total consumption	2 036	1 396	1 391	1 200

The end uses of ground and crushed barite in the same years were as follows:

	1956	In 1 000 short tons 1959	1961	1963
Well drilling	1 421	1 154	942	907
Glass	33	12	31	56
Paint	21	17	16	35
Rubber	22	19	24	28
Other	6	7	23	3

As shown before, the consumption of barite in the United States is much higher than the production. About 0.5 million tons of barite per annum must be imported.

The imports into the United Kingdom were as follows:

		1955	1957	1959	1961	1963
Ground barite	in 1 000 long tons	22	19	18	15	28
	in £	293 000	314 000	302 000	271 000	286 000
Unground	in 1 000 long tons	50	27	19	23	
	in £	316 000	181 000	129 000	139 000	

The prices of barite in the United States were in 1965:
crude barite, $ 30 per short ton; floated and bleached barite $ 49 to $ 93 per short ton; blanc fixe, $ 156 to $ 175 per short ton.

The prices of bleached barite and blanc fixe in the UK were £ 20 and £ 36 per long ton in 1963.

Barite production	1938	1948	In 1 000 short tons 1956	1959	1961	1963
World (estimated)	1 200	1 400	3 100	3 100	3 100	3 200
Canada	–	95	320	240	190	180
France	20	45	60	95	95	80
Germany, West (*inc. Germany, East)	520*	150	450	490	520	460
Greece	40	20	30	140	80	90
Italy	50	60	100	130	160	120
Mexico	–	–	240	320	270	280
Peru	–	–	10	10	120	140
United Kingdom (inc. witherite)	90	100	90	70	90	60
USA	330	770	1 350	870	730	800
USSR	70		110	130	160	220
Yugoslavia	–	–	100	120	120	120

11.5.3 Barium carbonate

Barium carbonate ($BaCO_3$) is found, particularly in England, as witherite. It is also found in the dumps of certain coal mines, and is obtained from the material in these dumps by sorting on a belt. After grinding, the finest material is subjected to flotation with oleic acid and waterglass; together with the witherite, a good deal of finely divided and easily usable coal is thus recovered.

Synthetic barium carbonate is usually prepared from heavy spar as described above (p. 501) by reducing this with coal, and treating the barium sulphide thus obtained with carbon dioxide. Hydrogen sulphide is liberated at the same time, and this can be converted into sulphur or sulphur dioxide. If sodium carbonate is used sodium sulphide can be recovered as a by-product.

Finely divided barium sulphate, treated with a solution of sodium carbonate at a pressure of 5 atmospheres and a temperature of 200° C, is converted into barium carbonate and potassium sulphate, since under these conditions barium carbonate is even less soluble than barium sulphate.

All barium compounds are poisonous, including barium carbonate, since this dissolves in the acid present in the stomach; barium sulphate, however, being insoluble even in acid, can be ingested without danger (cf. use in radiology).

Barium carbonate is used as a flux in glass, as an additive for clay to prevent sweating after firing (see barium chloride, p. 504), as a rat poison, for the preparation of very pure barium sulphate and lithopone, for the preparation of other barium compounds, and as a filler in rubber and linoleum.

Barium carbonate is also added to drilling muds (see vol. III). Muds of this type are used for drilling through gypsum formations, the function of the barium carbonate being to prevent the formation of anhydrite on the drilling bit when it becomes heated above the transition point of the gypsum. It does this by means of the double decomposition reaction $CaSO_4 + BaCO_3 \rightarrow BaSO_4 + CaCO_3$.

The output of synthetic barium carbonate in the United States was about 66000 short tons in 1963. It was sold at about $ 112 per short ton in the USA in 1965.

11.5.4 Barium oxide, hydroxide and peroxide

Barium oxide (BaO) has so far been obtained by the decomposition of barium carbonate to barium oxide and carbon dioxide in the electric arc at temperatures of 1 200-1 365° C; it appears, however, that better quality material is obtained at a temperature of 915° C. For this purpose, the carbonate is heated by burning a methane/air mixture, the combustion gases and the carbon monoxide formed at the same time (partially by reduction of the carbon dioxide liberated) maintain the material in a fluidised state. In this way, oxide of purity 90-92 % is obtained.

Barium oxide is mainly used for the production of barium hydroxide $Ba(OH)_2$ and barium peroxide. Barium oxide as such or mixed with CaO and SiO_2 is used as emitter on cathodes of radiovalves. The method used for the production of *barium peroxide* is analogous to that for sodium peroxide (see p. 459). The amounts of barium peroxide produced are decreasing steadily, however, as a result of the introduction of new methods of producing hydrogen peroxide (see p. 195). It is used for the control of pH-value in nickel-plating baths by which both ions of any ferrous sulphate present are precipitated, the iron as ferric hydroxide and the sulphate as barium sulphate, without new ions being introduced. This process is used mainly in the production of enamelled goods, in cases where the metal is to be previously nickel-plated to ensure adhesion of the enamel.

Barium hydroxide is produced by treating barium oxide with hot water. This product is used for the production of barium soaps which are additives for high temperature lubricants.

The US production of barium oxide in recent years has not been published. In 1957 the production was about 30 000 tons. Barium oxide was sold at about $0.12 per lb in 1965.

11.5.5 Barium chloride

Barium chloride ($BaCl_2$) can be obtained from a dispersion of the sulphide in water by heating and reacting with calcium chloride, or barium carbonate can be dissolved in hydrochloric acid, and the chloride crystallized out. The chloride is used principally for the preparation of other pure barium salts, e.g. the sulphate. When mixed with clay and water, barium chloride converts magnesium and calcium sulphates present to insoluble barium sulphate. Thus it prevents sweating of ceramic objects after firing (which would be caused by diffusion of calcium and magnesium sulphate to the surface of the objects). A 2% solution in water is used as a rat poison. The purest grade is important in chemical analysis for the detection of sulphates in solution.

11.5.6 Barium nitrate

Barium nitrate ($Ba(NO_3)_2$) can be prepared by introducing barium carbonate and nitric acid into a solution which is saturated with barium nitrate in the same manner. Crystalline barium nitrate is obtained. Barium nitrate is used in fireworks (producing a green flame), green flares and detonators. Its price was $0.16 per lb in 1965.

11.5.7 Barium titanate

Barium titanate ($BaTiO_3$) has become of great importance. Ceramic bodies of this compound are prepared by mixing finely powdered barium carbonate and titanium dioxide and heating to 1 350° C. The calcined mass is then ground very finely, mixed with a plastic binder, and formed to the desired shape by extrusion, pressing or film casting. The shaped body is then heated to burn off the plastic and sintered by firing. Finally the fired material is polished to shape to final tolerances.

Barium titanate has a number of crystalline forms each of which is stable over a particular temperature range. One of these crystal forms (the tetragonal) has ferroelectric properties since it exhibits spontaneous electrical polarization (i.e., it can be polarized by means of an electric field). This polarization, being permanent, can be reversed by the application of an electric field in the opposite direction. Due to this phenomenon a barium titanate crystal has an extremely high dielectric constant and it is piezoelectric.

In a piezoelectric crystal the electric polarization changes when it is mechanically strained. The direction and magnitude of the change depend upon the amount and the direction of the strain. This effect makes it possible to convert a mechanical vibration (e.g. sound) into an alternating electric current. Since the converse effect is also observed an alternating electric current, applied to the crystal, can be converted into a mechanical vibration.

Other examples of piezoelectric materials are Rochelle salt, quartz (see vol. II) and other perovskite minerals (barium titanate is a commonly studied example of this group).

Ceramic bodies of barium titanate are polycrystalline. In this form the crystals are randomly orientated so that, although it is piezoelectric on the crystallite scale it is devoid of this property in the mass. It has been found that the most successful method of polarizing the crystallites of the ceramic, prepared as described above, is to allow the ceramic to cool under the influence of a high intensity electric field. In this way it is possible to align the tetragonal crystallites (which are formed below 105° C) permanently in the direction of polarisation so that a permanent electric polarization is imparted to the ceramic material. This is analogous to the basic magnetization possessed by a permanent magnet and, like it, can only be removed or reversed at room temperature by the application of a relatively high electric field. It is because of these attributes together with the very high electrical resistance of the ceramics that they are referred to as ferroelectric. Barium titanate ceramics which have been permanently polarized exhibit piezoelectric properties similar to those of single crystals. At a temperature above 105° C the tetragonal crystal form transforms to the cubic phase, which is not polarized. By analogy with demagnetization the temperature of the phase change at which polarisation vanishes is called the Curie point.

Ceramic barium titanate has become of great importance in electronic applications. It is used in gramophone pick-ups, crystal microphones and telephones, ultrasonic apparatus (e.g. ultrasonic drills) and strain gauges of various types. In all cases a mechanical vibration (e.g. sound) is converted into an electric vibration (or conversely). Ultrasonic generators often use mixtures of lead zirconate with barium titanate, the advantage of the mixture being a much higher Curie point.

Because of their high dielectric constant (of the order of 1 000 times that of water), ceramic bodies of barium titanate can be used in capacitors, e.g. in radio sets (10-12 per set) and television sets (up to 50 per set).

In the USA 4 000 tons of barium titanate was used as early as 1955.

CHAPTER 12

The Boron-Aluminium Group of the Periodic System

12.1 INTRODUCTION

The boron-aluminium group of the periodic system (the third main group) is formed by the elements, boron (B), aluminium (Al), gallium (Ga), Indium (In) and thallium (Tl). The last three members of this group are rare elements.

Boron and aluminium are trivalent in their compounds. The other elements of this group can form compounds in which they are present in the trivalent or in a lower valence state. The tendency to form trivalent compounds decreases from boron to thallium. Thallium is even more stable in its monovalent state than in the trivalent state.

Boron is of distinctly non-metallic character and its oxide (B_2O_3) has an acidic character. The other elements of the boron-aluminium group are typical metals. The corresponding oxides of aluminium, gallium, indium and thallium (Al_2O_3, Ga_2O_3, In_2O_3 and Tl_2O_3) are amphoteric although the basic character predominates. With acids, these oxides form salts containing trivalent positive metal ions, M^{+++}, and with strong bases they can form compounds containing negative ions having the general formula $M(OH)_4^-$. The oxide of monovalent thallium, Tl_2O, has a strongly basic character.

Chemically, gallium and indium show close resemblance to aluminium in their compounds. Like aluminium, the sulphates of these elements form double sulphates with alkali metal sulphates (alums, see also p. 525). Boron and thallium compounds are quite different in their behaviour.

12.2 BORON AND ITS COMPOUNDS

12.2.1 History and occurrence

Borax which is the most important boron compound has been recovered from Asian salt lakes since ancient times. In China it was used in borax glases before A.D. 300. In the late thirteenth century borax was imported for the first time into Europe as a flux under the name *tincal*. The present name borax is derived from the word 'burag' which was used as a general term by the Arabs to denote a flux in soldering and melting processes.

In 1702 Homberg for the first time liberated boric acid from borax by heating it with sulphuric acid. Boric acid was soon used as a pharmaceutical under the name *sal sedativum*. Elemental boron was first prepared and recognized as an element independently by the English chemist Davy (in 1807) and the French chemists Gay-Lussac and Thénard (in 1808).

Boron does not occur free in nature, but is always combined with oxygen in the form of boric acid and borates. Small quantities of boron compounds are widely distributed in the earth's crust and in the seas and oceans. In the form of a boric acid solution, larger concentrations of boron usually occur in small lakes formed by hot springs in volcanic regions e.g. in Tuscany (Italy). Boric acid is volatile in steam and thus it is leached out from volcanic rocks etc. and condenses together with water at colder places in the neighbourhood of hot springs. It is believed that the boron contained in similar springs must have been the chief source of the commercial borate deposits.

The most important concentrated deposits of borates occur in the USA in California and Nevada. Important deposits are also found in Turkey, Tibet, USSR and the South American states Argentina, Chile and Peru. The commoner borate deposits consist of one or more hydrated borates of sodium, calcium or magnesium which have been formed by evaporation of surface water of lakes etc. in hot and dry regions. No borate deposits have been formed in regions where the climate has always been moist enough to maintain drainage to the sea.

The largest solid borate deposit occurs in the Kramer district of the Mojave Desert in California and consists of kernite (Rasorite, $Na_2O.2B_2O_3.4H_2O$) and borax ($Na_2B_4O_7.10H_2O$). This deposit covers an area of 6 by 1.5 km and has a thickness of about 30 m. It is estimated that it contains 80 million tons of ore. The Searles Lake deposit and brine in the same desert contain borax. Colemanite and pandermite (calcium borates) are important constituents of the Turkish borate deposits. Colemanite also occurs in Chile and in California and Nevada in regions surrounding the enormous kernite and borax deposits. Sodium calcium borates (boronatrocalcite and ulexite) are important boron minerals of the South American deposits, while calcium and magnesium borates (e.g. ascharite) are important constituents of the commercial deposits in the USSR.

12.2.2 Mining of borate minerals

The kernite *(Rasorite)* and borax deposit in the Kramer district was first worked by underground mining which was very costly. The room-and-pillar method was used, in which the rich ore was mined, while poor ore was left behind in the form of thick columns which acted as supports for the roof. This wasteful method had to be employed because all the ore won had to be taken to Wilmington, about 250 km from the mine, for purification, which would be too costly for low-grade ores. For this reason it was decided to build a refinery at Boron (this town took its name from the element) and to convert the mine to open-pit working. About 8 million tons of overburden had to be removed for this purpose, an operation which took two years and cost $20 million for labour and materials.

A view of the pit is shown in fig. 12.1. The open pit measures 400 x 600 m with a depth of over 60 m (1 300 x 2 000 x 175 ft respectively). Previously enormous lorries were used to bring the ore out of the mine, but the position was changed in 1960 by the construction of a conveyor belt of total length of over 400 m (1 300 ft).

Fig. 12.1   Open pit borax mine at Boron (California).

The minerals have an average B_2O_3 content of 25%. They are broken into small lumps and, after analysis, piled up into four separate large heaps. Quantities of minerals from these heaps are mixed in such proportions that a product of nearly constant B_2O_3 content is obtained. The mixture is passed to 60 000 ton storage piles which are located above subterranean tunnels, so that removal is easy. From these piles the mixture passes to fine crushers and is calcined to produce 'prepared *Rasorite*'.

The borax of the Searles Lake brine which contains about 2% of this product is recovered by pumping the brine to an evaporation and selective crystallization plant. The mother liquor resulting after precipitation of sodium bicarbonate (see soda ash, p. 451) is evaporated in triple-effect evaporators to crystallize most of the sodium chloride, burkeite (double salt of sodium carbonate and sodium sulphate) and sodium sulphate. The resulting liquor is cooled rapidly to precipitate potassium chloride. Owing to the fact that borax crystallizes very slowly, the remaining solution becomes super-saturated in borax. The latter is precipitated by seeding to form a crude sodium tetra-borate pentahydrate which is purified by recrystallization.

Colemanite, boronatrocalcite and ulexite are found in underground mines. Most of the US colemanite and ulexite mines are inactive now because the production of boron compounds from kernite and borax is considerably cheaper.

In contrast to the other boron minerals which are grainy and sandy, the Turkish pandermite is a relatively hard rock, comparable with marble, so that mining and crushing are expensive. For this reason pandermite ore has been superseded by colemanite which is also found in Turkey.

The production of crude borate minerals in the most important producing countries is shown in the following table (see overleaf):

| | 1956 | *In '000 long tons* | 1962 | 1964 |
		1959		
Argentina	20	11	14	
Chile	9	6	4	3
Turkey	33	79	112	126
USA	486	554	577	693

Borates are also produced in Germany, Iran, Tibet and the USSR. In addition mineral boric acid is recovered in Italy (see p. 512).

In the USA the whole borate mining industry is under the control of three large companies of which the US Borax and Chemical Corporation is the most important, followed by the American Potash and Chemical Corporation, which exploits Searles Lake. The trade mark of the first company (twenty mule team) is very well known; this dates from the time when all the borate minerals still had to be transported from the desert with mules.

The major importers of boron minerals (crude and purified) are France, Federal Germany, Italy, Japan and the United Kingdom which imported 70000, 68000, 60000, 27000 and 50000 long tons respectively in 1964.

12.2.3 Elemental boron (B, atomic weight = 10.82)

Boron can be obtained practically pure by electrolysis of boron oxide (B_2O_3) dissolved in fused potassium chloride and potassium fluoroborate. A strongly heated graphite crucible forms the anode, while an iron rod of very low carbon content is used as the cathode, on which boron is deposited. When the boron-covered rod is removed, it is quickly covered with dry salt to prevent oxidation of the boron at the high temperature prevaling. After cooling, the boron can easily be removed from the iron.

Amorphous boron is most commonly prepared by the reduction of boron oxide with magnesium, and very pure crystalline boron can be obtained by reduction of boron trichloride with hydrogen in an electric arc between cooled tungsten electrodes.

A zone-melting process makes it possible to produce a strong, homogeneous and very pure rod from powdered boron. For this purpose the powder is mixed with boric acid solution and heated to dryness. The resulting grains of boron, surrounded by boric acid, are pressed into a rod which is heated to decompose the boric acid into boron oxide. The boron oxide binds the powder into a strong rod, which is then subjected to zone-melting (see silicon, p. 544). A narrow zone of the rod is strongly heated by high frequency induction and as the rod is raised, the molten zone descends, while boron crystallizes out above the narrow zone. The boron oxide vaporizes at the high temperature of 2 100° C which is used.

Elemental boron exists in two modifications. The amorphous form ranges from yellow to brown and the crystalline form is usually greyish-black and is very hard (hardness $9\frac{1}{2}$ on Mohs' scale). Boron melts at 2 300° C and boils at about 2 600° C. Boron is a semi-conductor, the electrical resistance of which decreases with increasing temperature. The electrical resistance decreases considerably when carbon is present as an impurity.

Boron is stable in air at room temperature but oxidizes at higher temperatures. At temperatures of about 700° C it burns in air with a red flame (in oxygen it burns with a green flame). In a nitrogen atmosphere, boron forms boron nitride which is also formed in a side reaction if boron is allowed to burn in air. In a hydrogen atmosphere boron is quite stable even at red heat.

Natural boron is composed of two stable isotopes with mass numbers of 10 and 11. The boron 10 content is about 19%. Boron 10 has a high neutron absorbing power without the production of hard gamma rays, hence the use of boron in nuclear reactor shielding. Owing to this property boron must not be present in the graphite used as a moderator in nuclear reactors. Boron may be used in reactor shielding in the form of a coating on plastics or aluminium or as a dispersion in plastics or concrete.

The boron 10 isotope has much higher neutron absorbing properties than boron 11 and is 20 times more effective than lead against thermal neutrons. The boron 10 isotope can be separated from ordinary boron by fractional distillation of a complex of boron trifluoride with dimethyl ether.

Boron is used as an additive in high purity silicon and germanium to control the electrical conductivity of these materials for rectifier and transistor purposes. In the chemical industry boron is used for the production of borides.

The most important consumer of boron is the metal industry. In its pure form boron is used as a deoxidizer and degasifier in metallurgical reactions (boron is very reactive with oxygen and nitrogen at high temperatures).

Boron is also used as a coating on soft base metals to provide hard, wear-resisting and corrosion-resisting surfaces. A metal may be coated by spraying a mixture of small boron crystals and waterglass on to the metal surface. After drying, the boron crystals are fixed in the metal surface by melting the latter with an oxyacetylene burner or atomic hydrogen torch.

In the form of 'master alloys' boron is used as an alloying agent. For this purpose boron is not isolated in a pure form but is prepared in the form of alloys by reducing boric acid or boron oxide with aluminium at high temperatures in the presence of the desired metal. Thus ferroboron containing about 16-20% boron, 2-6% aluminium (excess of reducing agent) and 74-82% iron is prepared by melting the oxide-aluminium mixture with iron. Other master alloys are manganese-boron and nickel-boron.

Amounts of boron up to 0.003% in steel increase the hardenability of the latter; the depth of hardening when quenched increases. As a consequence of the high neutron absorbing power of boron, steels containing larger amounts of boron are used as control rods in nuclear reactors. Amounts of boron up to 0.001% in malleable iron castings act as an accelerator of the annealing time. Cast iron containing 0.05% boron is used for grain rolls etc. since the boron increases the chill depth of cast iron (for chilling see vol. III).

Substantial amounts of boron are also incorporated into hard alloys for cutting tools. In hundredths of one per cent boron greatly improves the electrical conductivity of copper and aluminium.

The production and consumption of elemental boron is low. The US production may be of the order of 1 000 lb per year. Amorphous boron is sold at prices of $10 to $20 per lb; the US price of pure crystalline boron amounts to several hundreds of dollars per lb.

12.2.4 Boric acid

The recovery of boric acid (orthoboric acid, H_3BO_3) on an industrial scale from the hot water springs in Tuscany was started in 1815 and although borax and kernite

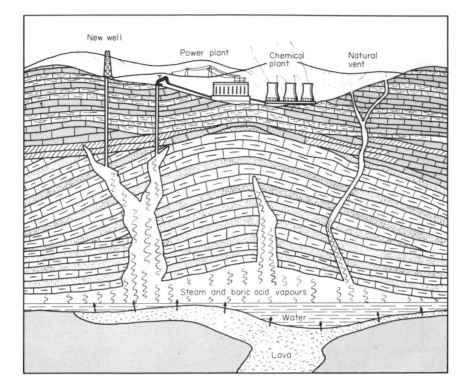

Fig. 12.2 A schematic cross-section through the boric acid containing steam wells at Larderella (Italy).

became the most important source of boric acid in this century, important quantities of boric acid are still produced in Tuscany. Over very long periods of time, the steam containing about 0.05% boric acid has ascended through the naturally existing cracks in the ground and has formed lagoons containing 0.4% boric acid. It is believed that the high pressure steam leaches the acid from a magma reservoir occurring at great depth (see fig. 12.2).

Formerly boric acid was recovered from the lagoons and from the steam which ascends through the natural springs. More recently deep bore-holes have been made down to the steam-bearing strata, in the same way as in drilling for oil. The wells yield steam at 4 atmospheres pressure at 180° C. This steam is the present source of boric acid and at the same time a source of energy which is used to generate electricity in turbines and to evaporate the boric acid solutions. The highly corrosive steam from the wells is passed through the heating coils of boilers to convert fresh cold water into steam which drives the steam generators of an electric power station. The natural steam condenses and the resulting solution of boric acid is concentrated by heating with steam from the wells. Crude boric acid (containing 95% H_3BO_3) crystallizes from the concentrated solution on cooling. The crude acid can be purified by recrystallization.

In the USA and several other countries boric acid is produced from kernite, borax, colemanite, ulexite etc. by adding a hot concentrated or dilute solution of sulphuric acid until the resulting solution or slurry is weakly acidic. Solids such as clay and gypsum (precipitated by treating calcium borates with sulphuric acid) are removed by filtering the hot solution. Boric acid is precipitated from the clarified hot solution by cooling. The mother liquor is worked up to recover sodium sulphate or recycled to the reaction vessel in which the borate ore is treated with sulphuric acid.

In the USA boric acid is also produced from some Searles Lake brine of which the borate content is too low to permit an economical recovery of borax in an evaporation process. In these cases brine is liquid-liquid extracted with a solution of a methylol phenol in kerosene. Borax dissolves in the organic liquid and is extracted from it by agitation with a dilute sulphuric acid solution from which boric acid is then obtained by evaporation and crystallization.

Boric acid forms white waxy plates which melt at 170.9° C in an enclosed space. Its solubility in cold water is relatively low but increases considerably at higher temperatures (5 g of boric acid dissolve in 100 g water at 20° C, and 40 g in 100 g water at 100° C). Boric acid is soluble in polyhydric alcohols owing to complex formation. Usually the complex solutions have a stronger acid reaction than the free boric acid which is a very weak acid. When heated at temperatures above 70° C boric acid decomposes to form metaboric acid (HBO_2) and water. When heated at red heat boric acid decomposes to form boron oxide (B_2O_3) and water.

The largest users of boric acid are the enamel and glaze industries. In the glass industry, boric acid is used for the production of optical glass and borosilicate glass. It is used in making glass in place of borax when it is desired to limit the alkali content. In the metal industry boric acid is used in electroplating solutions, in welding and brazing fluxes and for the production of elemental boron master alloys.

Boric acid is a preservative. For this purpose it is used in hides, woods, textiles, adhesives etc. In many countries its use as a preservative in food is not permitted since it is believed that it is rather toxic. It is, however, sometimes used in limited amounts in certain foodstuffs.

Dissolved in water, boric acid forms the 'boracic solution' used as a mild antiseptic in medicine (e.g. for washing the eyes). Boric acid is also incorporated in powders, ointments and bandages which are used on inflammations and minor cuts of the skin and mucous membranes.

Boric acid is used in textiles to make them non-inflammable, in organic synthesis as a catalyst, in photography, in scouring compositions, in latex base paints and in luminescent screens.

The US production of boric acid was nearly constant at 100 000 long tons per year during 1959 to 1964 inclusive. The production in Italy declined from 3 400 long tons in 1958 to 300 long tons in 1964 but the exports increased from 1 400 tons to 6 000 tons in the same period on account of the stock. The imports of boric acid into the United Kingdom were about 3 500 long tons per year in the period from 1958 to 1964 inclusive; in the USA the price of boric acid in 1965 was $106 to $193 per short ton depending on grade and purity. In the United Kingdom the prices were £70 to £89 per long ton.

12.2.5 Borax

Before 1890 more borax was obtained from boric acid than from all other raw materials put together, but since then the position has changed completely owing to the discovery of enormous borate deposits in California and Nevada. Nowadays the major raw materials of borax are the US material kernite, the crude sodium borates from

Searles Lake and the Turkish borates colemanite and ulexite. Borax is no longer made from boric acid which is more expensive than borax itself.

The production of borax from kernite and other sodium borates comprises a recrystallization process. The crude mineral is dissolved in hot water and mixed with sodium silicate to precipitate iron hydroxide and slimy materials. The resulting slurry which also contains impurities such as sand and clay, is filtered. To avoid clogging of the filters by organic matter which is present in kernite, the latter is usually calcined (prepared *Rasorite*) to destroy the organic matter before processing. Borax is precipitated from the clarified aqueous solution by cooling in crystallizers.

Borax is produced from calcium borates and calcium sodium borates (ulexite, colemanite etc.) by treating these minerals with a solution of a mixture of sodium carbonate and sodium bicarbonate. Usually the process is performed in autoclaves heated with steam. The resulting solution contains about 25% borax and 4 to 5% sodium carbonate and, in addition, a suspension of calcium carbonate and impurities such as clay and sand. The solution is clarified by filtering in a filter press and borax is crystallized on cooling. The remaining mother liquor is recycled to the autoclaves.

In the processes mentioned above, technical borax having a purity between 95 and 99% is obtained. Borax may be purified by dissolving technical borax in hot water and cooling the solution. Two crystalline forms of borax can be obtained by crystallization from a hot solution. At temperatures above 61° C sodium tetraborate pentahydrate ($Na_2B_4O_7.5H_2O$) (also named tincalconite) crystallizes and at temperatures below 61° C sodium tetraborate decahydrate ($Na_2B_4O_7.10H_2O$) crystallizes. The latter is the most common form of borax.

Nowadays anhydrous borax is of increasing importance. It is obtained from hydrated borax by heating it at temperatures between 350 and 400° C. The resulting melt is cooled to a glassy mass which is crushed in jaw-crushers. In a modified process, the major portion of the water of crystallization is removed by heating at temperatures between 70 and 90° C before heating at 400° C. Owing to the fact that the major portion of water is removed the borax does not dissolve in its water of crystallization; instead, the liberated water produces a foam of borax. The foamy borax can be crushed more easily than the massive form.

Ordinary borax ($Na_2B_4O_7.10H_2O$) forms colourless prismatic crystals on which a white turbid surface is formed under atmospheric conditions owing to weathering. Borax is only slightly soluble in water at low temperatures, but the solubility increases rapidly at higher temperatures (1 g anhydrous borax dissolves in 100 g water at 0° C and 52 g at 100° C). The solubility curve of borax shows a discontinuity at 61° C owing to the conversion of the decahydrate into the pentahydrate. Unlike the decahydrate, the pentahydrate does not weather when exposed to air.

Anhydrous borax is a hygroscopic glassy product which melts at 742° C ± 1° C. With metal salts and metal oxides, molten anhydrous borax forms characteristic coloured glassy bodies (borax beads), hence the use of borax in analytical chemistry for the detection of some metals. In glass manufacture it has the advantage over the hydrate that it does not form froth or foam.

About one half of the world output of borax is used in the production of glassware, porcelain and glazes. In general borax operates as a strong flux and its presence in glass and ceramics increases their resistance to sudden fluctuations of temperature, mechanical shock and chemical attack. The effect of the boron oxide, B_2O_3, content of the glass is to reduce its thermal expansion. Hence its use in glass for borosilicate heat-resisting ware, laboratory apparatus, cathode-ray tubes, chemically resistant glass etc. Borax also increases the refractive index of glass and for this reason it is used for the production of optical glass.

Borax is a non-selective herbicide which is used to destroy plant life especially on areas surrounding commercial crops. Owing to its flame inhibiting properties borax is also used as a weed killer in the vicinity of oil refineries and lumber yards. In the USA borate solutions are sprayed from aircraft over wide strips during forest fires to stop the fire. Its use in wood, paints, paper, textiles, straw for roofs and packing cases, etc. is based on the combined preservative and flame-proofing properties (as with boric acid). Owing to its preservative properties in combination with its mild alkaline reaction, borax is used also in the chrome tanning of leather. Because of its insecticidal and fungicidal properties borax is used to control fly larvae in the poultry industry, to destroy insect larvae, black beetles etc. and to prevent blue and green mould on citrus fruits which are washed with a borax solution. In smaller quantities, borax is used as a fertilizer on soils deficient in available boron which is necessary for the healthy growth of many crops.

Important quantities of borax are also used in various cleaning compositions either as a major constituent or in addition to soap or synthetic detergents. Cleaning compositions containing borax as a major cleaning agent are commercially available in the USA under names such as 'boraxo' or 'braxo'. When used as a cleaning agent for metals borax leaves a residual film on the metal surface which acts as a rust preventive.

In the cosmetic industry borax is used as an emulsifying agent in creams etc. Borax is also used in photographic developers, in electroplating of metals, in fluxes for metal melting, brazing and welding, in wire drawing, in explosives to provide a safety factor and in medical preparations. Borax is also the raw material for the production of almost all boron compounds. (Exceptions are those boron minerals which are directly converted into boric acid in one step.) Hence the primary borax production nearly corresponds with the p roduction of borate minerals (see p. 508).

The prices of various forms of borax were as follows in 1965:

	USA $ per short ton	UK £ per long ton
Technical anhydrous	83-92	59
Technical pentahydrate	58-64	56
Technical decahydrate	44-50	44-49

12.2.6 Other borates

Ammonium borates are prepared by reacting boric acid in aqueous solution with ammonia. Various ammonium borates can be formed depending on the quantity of ammonia added. Technically important ammonium borates are ammonium tetraborate $(NH_4)_2B_4O_7.4H_2O)$, and ammonium pentaborate $(NH_4B_5O_8.4H_2O)$.

These borates are used in electrolytic condensers and in fire retardant compositions.

Calcium borates occur in nature in the form of colemanite and pandermite (see p. 509). Technically important calcium borates are calcium monoborate dihydrate, $CaO.B_2O_3.2H_2O$, and calcium monoborate hexahydrate $(CaO.B_2O_3.6H_2O)$. These products, which are used in the ceramic industry, are produced by reacting borax with a mixture of calcium hydroxide and calcium chloride in water.

Barium borates are produced by treating borax with a mixture of barium hydroxide and barium chloride in water. The most important barium borates are barium metaborate dihydrate ($Ba(BO_2)_2.2H_2O$) and tetrahydrate ($Ba(BO_2)_2.4H_2O$), which like the calcium borates are used in the ceramic industry.

Various *zinc borates* may be precipitated from a borax solution by adding a solution of zinc chloride. These products are sometimes used in flameproofing textiles.

12.2.7 Sodium perborate

Sodium perborate or sodium peroxyhydrate ($NaBO_2.H_2O_2.3H_2O$) is prepared by electrolysis of an aqueous solution of borax and soda ash using platinum gauze electrodes. The perborate crystallizes from the resulting solution on cooling below $10°$ C. Sodium perborate may also be prepared by treating a borax solution with sodium peroxide or with an aqueous solution of sodium hydroxide and hydrogen peroxide. Sodium perborate may also be formed by an autoxidation process.

Sodium perborate is a white crystalline product which melts at $63°$ C with decomposition. If sodium perborate is fluidized with hot air it loses its water of crystallization and a product named sodium perborate monohydrate (sodium monoperoxyhydrate: $NaBO_2.H_2O_2$) is formed. The latter compound is quite stable at $63°$ C and its active oxygen can be set free in the nascent condition at temperatures above $100°$ C. About 2 g sodium perborate dissolve in 100 g water at $10°$ C and 13 g in 100 g water at $60°$C. Solutions in water are less stable than the anhydrous compound, but they can be stabilized by adding small amounts of sodium silicate (waterglass) or magnesium silicate.

Sodium perborate is mainly used in powders for washing and bleaching of textiles, especially in Europe. In the USA washing compositions prepared with sodium perborate are not used so much, probably because home laundering in the USA is commonly done in a lower temperature range in which sodium perborate is much less active.

The use of sodium perborate as a bleaching agent in the textile industry has declined considerably during recent years because it has been superseded by hydrogen peroxide, especially in bleaching cellulose materials such as cotton. However it is still used for bleaching of some textiles such as silk and velvet. In the textile industry sodium perborate is also used for the oxidation of the soluble leuco form of vat dyes to the insoluble fast vat dyes on cotton print goods.

Sodium perborate is used in tooth pastes, in hair washing compositions and in compositions for medical foot baths. Small quantities of manganese, copper, vanadium or molybdenum salts are added to foot washing compositions to promote the decomposition of the perborate in aqueous solution at lower temperatures. Since sodium perborate has also some germicidal action, it is also used in disinfectant soaps.

In the USA the price of sodium perborate was $0.15 to 0.25 per lb in 1965 ($300 to 500 per short ton). In the United Kingdom it was sold at £122 per long ton.

12.2.8 Diborane

Diborane (B_2H_6 or $(BH_3)_2$) is the simplest boron hydride. Various other boranes are known, but perhaps with the exception of pentaborane (B_5H_9), they are not of commercial importance.

Diborane can be prepared by contacting gaseous boron trifluoride or boron trichloride with sodium hydride or calcium hydride at a temperature of about 180° C:

$$2 BF_3 + 6 NaH \rightarrow B_2H_6 + 6 NaF.$$

Diborane can also be prepared by reacting a solution of boron trifluoride or boron trichloride in ethyl ether with a solution of lithium hydride, lithium aluminium hydride or lithium borohydride in ethyl ether.

Diborane is a poisonous gas which liquefies at about −93° C. The main toxic effect on breathing it is due to damage to the lungs. About 0.1 p.p.m. of diborane in air is the maximum allowable concentration for daily exposure. Pure diborane is fairly stable at room temperature in a dry atmosphere, but at temperatures of about 40-50° C it ignites or detonates spontaneously with a high flame speed and an extremely high heat of combustion. For this reason diborane must be handled in an oxygen-free atmosphere:

$$B_2H_6 + 3O_2 \rightarrow B_2O_3 + 3H_2O.$$

In the presence of small quantities of other boranes, such as tetraborane (B_4H_{10}) or pentaborane (B_5H_9) the ignition temperature drops considerably.

When heated in an oxygen-free atmosphere at higher temperatures, diborane decomposes to form a mixture of higher boranes. In the presence of water diborane decomposes rapidly to form boron oxide and hydrogen.

Diborane is one of the boron compounds used as a starting material for the production of various alkyl and aryl boranes by reaction with olefins.

Just like diborane, the alkyl and aryl boranes are readily oxidized, the lower members even ignite spontaneously in the presence of air. Unlike diborane the alkyl and aryl boranes are stable in the presence of moisture.

Diborane, pentaborane and various alkyl and aryl boranes are being extensively explored in respect of their properties as high energy fuels and some of these compounds are being used in propellants for rockets and other guided military missiles. Although boranes supply much more energy than the same weight of hydrocarbon fuels, the use of mixtures of boranes and hydrocarbons as a fuel for jet planes or motor vehicles is limited by the fact that the common engine construction materials must be modified to resist the more corrosive fuels containing substantial quantities of boranes. Only small percentages of some organic boron compounds are used as additives in motor fuels as anti-knock agents.

Owing to the fact that it decomposes in water with development of energy and the liberation of hydrogen (which can be burnt at the same time), diborane is of interest as a fuel for rockets to be launched under a water surface.

In industry diborane is used for the production of a series of trialkyl and triaryl boranes which are used as catalysts for the polymerization of vinyl compounds. Diborane itself is a suitable catalyst for the polymerization of olefins and epoxides, for the copolymerization of styrene and butadiene and for some cracking reactions.

Owing to the formation of elemental boron when it is heated in an inert atmosphere, diborane is used to produce extremely hard boron coatings on metals and ceramics by heating these materials in an atmosphere of diborane. Diborane is also used in selective hydrogenation and reduction of organic compounds.

12.2.9 Alkali borohydrides

Sodium borohydride ($NaBH_4$) is the most important metal borohydride. It may be prepared by passing hydrogen into an emulsion of sodium in oil to produce a dispersion of sodium hydride (NaH), and adding methyl borate ($B(OCH_3)_3$) to the reaction mixture to form sodium borohydride and sodium methylate:

$$2\,Na + H_2 \xrightarrow{\ 300°\,C\ } 2\,NaH$$

$$4\,NaH + B(OCH_3)_3 \xrightarrow{\ 250°\,C\ } NaBH_4 + 3\,NaOCH_3$$

Sodium borohydride may also be prepared by passing diborane through a solution of sodium methylate in methyl alcohol. Sodium borohydride may be separated from the reaction mixtures by extraction with liquid ammonia or an alkylamine and evaporating off the solvent. The extraction process may also be performed by means of water having a weak alkaline reaction. The aqueous solution is sold as a 12% solution.

Sodium borohydride is a colourless crystalline product which is stable in a dry atmosphere at temperatures up to 300° C. The product decomposes without melting at higher temperatures. In a moist atmosphere a dihydrate having a melting point of about 37° C is formed. Sodium borohydride is soluble in water (about 55 g dissolve in 100 g water at 25° C) and in various alcohols and amines. In aqueous solutions at pH = 7, sodium borohydride decomposes slowly, in weak alkaline solutions it is stable and in weak acidic solutions it decomposes rapidly.

Sodium borohydride is used as a reducing bleaching agent for wood pulp and cellulose textile materials. In organic syntheses sodium borohydride is used as a selective reducing agent. It reduces peroxides and carbonyl groups of ketones, aldehydes, lactones and acid chlorides without affecting various other compounds such as carboxylic acids, carboxylic acid anhydrides, amides and nitro compounds. The reduction of carbonyl groups (into alcohol groups) is of importance in the oxo-alcohols industry. Oxo-alcohols used in plasticizers must be free from carbonyl groups to avoid discoloration of the plastics in which the plasticizers are to be incorporated. Sodium borohydride may also be used for removing traces of peroxides in textiles returned after a bleaching process. It has also been proposed to use sodium borohydride as a blowing agent in polyvinyl foam production.

In the USA solid sodium borohydride was sold in 1965 at prices between $8 and $14 per lb depending on the quantity delivered. In the form of an aqueous solution it was sold at $7.50 per lb (100% basis).

Potassium borohydride may be precipitated from an aqueous solution of sodium borohydride by adding potassium hydroxide. The properties and uses of potassium borohydride are similar to those of sodium borohydride.

Unlike the latter, potassium borohydride is completely stable in air under normal atmospheric conditions. Its reducing power is somewhat lower than that of sodium borohydride.

Lithium borohydride may be prepared from lithium hydride and methyl borate (compare sodium borohydride). Its reducing power is higher than that of sodium and potassium borohydride. Its uses are similar to those of the other alkali borohydrides.

12.2.10 Boron nitride

Boron nitride (BN) may be prepared by heating boric oxide or boric acid with an alkali cyanide or by heating boric oxide with ammonia or ammonium chloride.

Boron nitride, resulting from any reaction mentioned above, is a finely divided white crystalline powder having a low bulk density (100 g per litre). Boron nitride sublimes at a temperature of about 2 500° C and under nitrogen pressure it melts at about 3 000° C. Boron nitride is quite stable at temperatures up to 3 000° C under a hydrogen or nitrogen atmosphere. In the presence of oxygen, carbon dioxide or chlorine it decomposes at temperatures of about 700° C. In the presence of carbon or metals, boron carbide and metal borides are formed respectively at temperatures of about 2 000° C. Boron nitride does not resist boiling water, particularly when the water has an acidic reaction. The resistance of boron nitride to water can be increased by a heat treatment process in which the surface area of boron nitride decreases owing to increasing particle size.

Owing to its low bulk density and the fact that it is not heated by induction currents, boron nitride powder is used as a thermal insulator for high-frequency induction furnaces. A temperature gradient of about 2 000° C can be reached through a layer of powder of 1 inch thickness maintained under high vacuum.

Sintered boron nitride is resistant to thermal shock, hence its use for the production of crucibles and other heat-resistant objects such as vessels for molten glass etc. These are made by sintering boron nitride in moulds under pressure. Boron nitride is also used as an electrical insulator for high voltages.

The common form of boron nitride has a graphite structure (hexagonal crystal structure) and like graphite it has a low coefficient of friction. Hence its use as a high temperature lubricant, e.g. in glass moulds as a release agent. At temperatures of about 1 350° C under a pressure of about 60 000 atm, boron nitride is converted into a cubic crystal structure. This modification which is named 'borazon' has a higher resistance to oxygen and is almost as hard as diamond (hardness 10 on Mohs' scale). Borazon is used as a high temperature abrasive.

12.2.11 Some other boron compounds

Boron oxide (B_2O_3) is prepared by heating boric acid at red heat. The resulting product is a colourless, brittle, glassy solid which is very hygroscopic. Just like glass it has no definite melting point but softening starts at about 325° C. It is used in the enamel, glaze and glass industries, for the production of elemental boron, boron master alloys, borides, boron carbide, boron nitrides and boron halides and for any other high temperature process in which boric acid cannot be used since it decomposes to form water at high temperatures.

Boron trichloride (BCl_3) is prepared by treating a finely divided mixture of boron trioxide and carbon with chlorine gas at temperatures between 900 and 1 000° C. Boron trichloride is a colourless gas which decomposes in moist air. It is used as an intermediate for the production of other boron compounds and as a catalyst for organic syntheses and polymerization processes. It has also been suggested that boron trichloride might be used as a source of boron for the gaseous boriding of metals.

Metal borides are compounds of metals and boron. Borides of almost all metals are known but the borides of the elements of the subgroups 4, 5 and 6 of the Periodic System are of special interest. Metal borides, like metal carbides, belong to a class of compounds termed 'interstitial'. Their composition is not determined by the ordinary valencies of the particular metal and boron. This feature is seen in such formulae as TiB_2, VB_2, CrB_2 and WB for some metal borides.

A metal boride may be prepared by mixing powders of boron and the required metal, followed by sintering at temperatures between 1 300 and 2 000° C. Metal borides are also prepared by treating a mixture of boron oxide and a metal oxide with a reducing agent (such as aluminium, magnesium, silicon, boron, carbon or boron carbide) at high temperatures. A metal boride also results from electrolysis of a fused salt containing boron oxide and a metal oxide.

Metal borides are of great interest because of their marked metallic properties. They have high melting points (between 1 100 and 3 000° C), extreme hardness (usually 8-9 on Mohs' scale), high electrical conductivity, high thermal conductivity, high thermal neutron cross-section and relatively low coefficient of thermal expansion. In addition the borides of the subgroup elements 4, 5 and 6 have high chemical inertness, but in general they do not resist hot concentrated sulphuric acid, nitric acid and other oxidizing agents, and they are also decomposed by a melt of an alkali hydroxide, peroxide or alkali metal carbonate.

Owing to their high thermal and chemical stability, some of the borides are used as construction or coating materials for parts of rocket and jet engines, jet turbines, spray nozzles for fuels, and other equipment which is submitted to the combined effects of high temperature and chemicals. Because of their extreme hardness, some borides are used for the production of cutting tools and for promoting the wear resistance of machine components. Other borides are very useful in the nuclear reactor field.

In the USA zirconium boride and titanium boride, which are among the most important borides, were sold in the form of powders at prices between $ 10 and $ 12 per lb in 1963.

Boric acid esters are produced by reacting boric acid, boric oxide or boron chloride with an alcohol or phenol, and removing the water formed during the reaction (compare production of esters in general in vol. IV.)

Boric acid esters undergo rapid hydrolysis in the presence of moist air, and the lower alkyl borates are also inflammable in air. For this reason boric acid esters should be stored and handled in a dry nitrogen atmosphere. In nitrogen boric acid esters are quite stable at high temperatures, e.g. methyl borate resists a temperature of about 470° C.

Boric acid esters are important as additives in hydrocarbon fuels and lubricants. Depending on the kind of ester and hydrocarbon, the boric acid esters are effective as anti-knock agents, to prevent icing, to improve the oxidation resistance and inhibit microbiological attack.

Owing to their high cross-section for neutron capture, various boric acid esters are used in nuclear shielding materials and in neutron detecting devices.

Some boric acid esters are effective epoxy-resin curing agents. Lower alkyl borates are also useful as fluxes in welding.

Boron trifluoride and *boron carbide* are also important boron compounds. They are discussed in ch. 7, Halogens, p. 215 and in vol. II, Abrasives respectively.

12.3 ALUMINIUM COMPOUNDS (Al, atomic weight = 26.98)
(for Metallic aluminium see vol. III)

12.3.1 Aluminium hydroxide and hydroxyoxide

Aluminium hydroxide (alumina hydrate, alumina trihydrate, $Al(OH)_3$) and aluminium hydroxyoxide (alumina monohydrate, $AlO(OH)$) occur in nature in bauxite. Bauxite which is the important source of aluminium and its compounds, consists of aluminium hydroxide, aluminium hydroxyoxide, aluminium oxide (Al_2O_3) and various impurities such as iron oxides, silicon dioxide and silicates. Although the terms monohydrate and trihydrate are used commonly, aluminium hydroxides do not contain water of crystallization but only oxide and hydroxide groups.

Aluminium hydroxide is produced from bauxite by heating it with a concentrated sodium hydroxide solution at temperatures between 150° and 250° C at a pressure between 5 and 35 atm, to form a solution of sodium aluminate. The major portion of impurities, such as iron hydroxide, is precipitated by diluting the resulting solution which is kept at a temperature above 90° C. The solution is clarified and aluminium hydroxide is precipitated from the strongly alkaline solution by further dilution with water, cooling to 50° C and seeding with previously formed aluminium hydroxide (the Bayer process, see aluminium in vol. III). The resulting solid is filtered and dried at a temperature of about 100° C.

The aluminium hydroxide produced in the Bayer process is one of the crystalline modifications of aluminium hydroxide (α-alumina trihydrate) which also occurs in certain bauxites e.g. (the mineral gibbsite or hydroargillite). Another crystalline product named bayerite (β-alumina trihydrate) may be prepared from a sodium aluminate solution by precipitation at room temperature at a pH of 10-13. Although this product is named bayerite, it is not formed in the Bayer process.

An amorphous form of aluminium hydroxide (alumina gel) is prepared by precipitation from an aluminium salt or sodium aluminate solution at a pH below 7. If the precipitation process is performed at pH 9, the resulting product is a crystalline modification of aluminium hydroxyoxide named boehmite. (This compound also occurs in European bauxites).

The products resulting from the processes mentioned above are more or less porous white powders having a hardness between 2.5 and 4 (Mohs' scale). The particle size, pore size and specific area depend on the method of preparation and can be predetermined from a wide range of possibilities. (Compare the production of silica gel, p. 553). For example, dried boehmite presents a powder of agglomerated micro crystals having a specific surface area ranging from 200 to 400 m^2/g and an average pore diameter between 50 and 100 Å. Dried gibbsite obtained in the Bayer process consists of relatively spherical particles which have a diameter of 50 to 100 microns and a relatively low specific area (about 10 m^2/g depending on the reaction conditions).

Aluminium hydroxide resists temperatures up to about 140° C. Decomposition into aluminium oxide and water begins at about 140° C but is complete only at a temperature above 500° C. Aluminium hydroxide dissolves in acidic and strongly basic solutions to form aluminium salts (containing Al^{+++} ions) and aluminates (containing $Al(OH)_4^-$ ions respectively.

Reaction equations: $Al(OH)_3 + 3H^+ \rightarrow Al^{+++} + 3H_2O$

$Al(OH)_3 + OH^- \rightarrow Al(OH)_4^-$

or according to an older conception:

$$Al(OH)_3 + OH^- \rightarrow AlO_2^- + 2H_2O$$

Thus aluminium hydroxide has an amphoteric character although the basic character dominates. Aluminium hydroxide is almost insoluble in water and in slightly alkaline solutions (up to pH9).

Aluminium hydroxide and hydroxyoxide are the starting materials for the production of aluminium oxide and other aluminium compounds. Aluminium hydroxide is also used in the manufacture of glass, glazes and ceramics. In glass it increases the mechanical strength as well as resistance to thermal shock, weathering and chemicals. In finely divided form aluminium hydroxide is used as a filler in paper, plastics, rubber and cosmetics. Aluminium hydroxide may also be used as a soft abrasive for polishing relatively soft materials such as brass and plastics. Pastes of aluminium hydroxide are used as anti-acids in medicine.

In the USA the production of aluminium hydroxide (excluding amounts converted into aluminium oxide or aluminium in the same plant) was 234000 short tons in 1964. Its price in 1965 was about $0.03 to $0.80 per lb depending on the purity.

12.3.2 Aluminium oxide

Aluminium oxide (alumina, Al_2O_3) is prepared from aluminium hydroxide or hydroxyoxide by heating it to remove most of the water of constitution.

Activated alumina is prepared by controlled heating of the various forms of aluminium hydroxide or hydroxyoxide at temperatures between 400 and 800° C. (In a similar way activated bauxite is prepared from bauxites which contain gibbsite as the major constituent.) The resulting white porous powders have a pore diameter of about 20 to 100 Å, a pore volume from 0.20 to 0.90 cm³/g and specific surface area between 50 and 400 m²/g depending on the starting material, the heating temperature and the duration of heating. In contradistinction to aluminium hydroxide, activated alumina can be dissolved in acid and basic solutions only by strong heating.

The most important use of activated alumina is as a selective adsorbent. It belongs to the group of solids which have the greatest affinity for water. Water may be removed from almost any product down to a retained water content of one p.p.m. by volume. Hence it is used for drying various gases and liquids. Examples are air and its constituents, chlorine, sulphur dioxide, hydrocarbon gases, gasoline, oils, aromatic hydrocarbons and chlorinated hydrocarbons. Activated alumina also shows selective adsorbing properties for constituents in non-aqueous mixtures. Hence its use for the separation of higher hydrocarbons from methane and in chromatography.

Activated aluminas also find applications in catalysis, especially as a support for catalysts. Aluminas for catalytic reactions must be very pure and for this purpose they are washed with acidified water before or after heat treatment. Activated alumina having high specific surface area catalyses dehydrating reactions such as the conversion of alcohols into olefins. Other activated aluminas having lower specific surface area are used for the production of dehydrogenating catalysts which are important in olefin syntheses.

Platinum, nickel or a metal oxide (molybdenum oxide, chromium oxide, vanadium oxide, silver oxide etc.) on a support prepared from activated alumina are widely used as catalysts in dehydrogenation, desulphurizing, cracking, isomerization, selective hydrogenation and polymerization processes (e.g., for the conversion of hydrocarbons in the petroleum industry).

In the USA about 61 000 short tons of activated alumina were produced in 1964.

Calcined alumina is prepared by heating any form of aluminium hydroxide at temperatures between 1 000 and 1 300° C in a rotary kiln. The resulting product is an extremely hard white powder having a specific surface area from 0.5 to 50 m^2 per g. This form of alumina, which is often named α-alumina, has a much lower adsorptive power than activated alumina, it occurs in nature as corundum (see Abrasives, vol. II). A product, prepared by calcining aluminium hydroxide in the presence of soda, is named β-alumina although it is not another crystalline modification of alumina but a product containing alumina and sodium aluminate. Calcined alumina is almost insoluble in acidic and basic solutions at room temperature. Its resistance to acids and bases is even higher than that of activated alumina.

Calcined alumina is used for the production of metallic aluminium, in the production of glass and enamel and in the production of ceramics having a high mechanical strength and resistance to high temperatures, chemicals and thermal shock. In metallurgy, calcined alumina is also used in slags to control the melting temperature. Because of its extreme hardness (9 on Mohs' scale) calcined alumina is used as an abrasive (e.g. for polishing steel).

Calcined alumina is also used for the production of heat resisting objects such as muffles, crucibles and thermocouple sheets. For these purposes alumina is shaped by extrusion or pressing followed by sintering at a temperature between 1 600 and 1 850° C. When heated at temperatures above the melting point (2 040° C) in an electric arc furnace, calcined alumina is converted into 'fused alumina'. This product is crushed and ground after solidification. It is used as an abrasive (see synthetic corundum in vol. II) and as a constituent of refractories.

In the USA about 5.3 million short tons of calcined alumina were produced in 1964. By far the major portion (about 80-90%) was used for the production of aluminium. In the USA calcined alumina (technical) was sold at $0.05 to $0.08 per lb in 1965.

12.3.3 Sodium aluminate

Sodium aluminate ($NaAlO_2$) is the only commercially important aluminate. It is formed as an intermediate in the production of aluminium hydroxide. Technical grades may be obtained by evaporating solutions withdrawn from the Bayer process for the production of aluminium hydroxide, but purer products are prepared by treating pure aluminium hydroxide with a boiling caustic soda solution and evaporating the resulting solution of sodium aluminate. Sodium aluminate is a white crystalline product. Commercial products usually contain an excess of caustic soda.

Sodium aluminate is widely used in industrial and potable water treatment, e.g. in lime-soda softening processes for boiler water and in clarification processes of low-turbidity waters (see water purification, p. 126). Sodium aluminate is also used in the production of alumina catalysts (see under aluminium hydroxide and activated alumina above). In the paper industry sodium aluminate is used to improve sizing operations and in the metal industry it is used to coat one side of a steel surface in order to make single-side galvanized steel. The sodium aluminate layer protects the steel surface from the galvanizing treatment.

12.3.4 Aluminium chloride

Anhydrous aluminium chloride ($AlCl_3$) is prepared by passing chlorine gas over a layer of aluminium powder or aluminium chips heated to red heat. Aluminium chloride sublimes on the cooler parts of the reactor. The resulting product usually contains some ferric chloride which cannot easily be removed by fractional sublimation because the difference between the sublimation temperatures of the two chlorides is too small. A pure product is usually prepared from refined aluminium.

Pure anhydrous aluminium chloride is a white hygroscopic powder which fumes in moist air and sublimes at a temperature of about 180° C. The commercial products usually have a yellow or brown colour owing to the presence of iron impurities. Aluminium chloride dissolves easily in water with the development of much heat.

Anhydrous aluminium chloride is used as a condensation catalyst in alkylation and acylation of organic compounds (Friedel-Crafts reactions). The most important condensation reactions are the reaction of benzene with alkyl chlorides to produce alkyl benzenes e.g. dodecyl benzene (which are intermediates in detergent production), the reaction of benzene with ethylene to produce ethyl benzene (which is an intermediate in styrene production), the reaction of isobutylene with isoprene (which is used to produce butyl rubber) and the reaction of aromatic compounds with acid chlorides or acid anhydrides to produce anthraquinone derivatives (which are intermediates in dye production), and diaryl ketones and aralkyl ketones (which are used in the perfume industry).

Anhydrous aluminium chloride is also a catalyst for the production of ethyl chloride from ethylene and hydrochloric acid. Ethyl chloride is a starting material for the production of tetraethyl lead and ethyl cellulose. In the petroleum industry aluminium chloride is used as an isomerization catalyst for the production of liquid fuels.

In the USA about 26 000 short tons of anhydrous aluminium chloride were produced in 1964. About 30% of the production was used for the production of anthraquinone dyes, 25% as a catalyst in ethyl benzene production and 15% for detergent production. In the USA anhydrous aluminium chloride was sold at $0.11 per lb in 1965.

Aluminium chloride crystal (aluminium chloride hexahydrate, $AlCl_3.6H_2O$) may be prepared by adding aluminium hydroxide and concentrated hydrochloric acid (or hydrogen chloride gas) to a concentrated aluminium chloride solution containing excess of hydrochloric acid. The resulting solid aluminium chloride is separated from the mother liquor by filtering and the filtrate is recycled into the reactor.

Aluminium chloride crystal is a hygroscopic colourless or yellowish white crystalline product. It is also commercially available in the form of a saturated solution which contains about 35% aluminium chloride (32° Bé solution). Both the solid and the solution are used in the soap industry for salting out glycerol lyes. Hydrous aluminium chloride is also used in the production of deodorants, antiseptics, aluminium hydroxide gel, pigments, photo fixing baths, wood preservatives and roofing granules.

In the USA in 1964 about 29 000 short tons of hydrous aluminium chloride were produced, over 50% of which was used in the production of soap, deodorants and antiseptics. The USA prices in 1965 were (a) crystal: $10.30 to $21 per 100 lb, (b) solution 32° Bé: $2.80 to $3.95 per 100 lb.

12.3.5 Aluminium sulphate

Aluminium sulphate (paper makers alum, 'alum', $Al_2(SO_4)_3.18H_2O$) is produced by treating aluminium hydroxide or bauxite with sulphuric acid near the boiling temperature of the solution. The resulting solution is clarified and sold as such or converted into solid aluminium sulphate by concentrating the solution and pouring it into moulds in which it solidifies to form blocks of hydrated aluminium sulphate on cooling.

Aluminium sulphate is available in a pure form (prepared from pure aluminium hydroxide) and in an impure form (prepared from bauxite). The formula $Al_2(SO_4)_3.18H_2O$ has traditionally been written for the commercial products but it is believed that these products contain many different hydrates. Pure aluminium sulphate is a colourless or white solid which is easily soluble in water. About 87 g dissolve in 100 g water at 0° C and 1132 g in 100 g water at 100° C.

Aluminium sulphate is used mainly in the paper industry and in water and sewage treatment. Aluminium sulphate has almost superseded sodium and potassium alums (see below) which were formerly used for the same purposes, in the USA it has even borrowed the name 'alum'.

In the paper industry aluminium sulphate is used for the clarification of process water, and as a setting agent in sizing and dyeing of paper. In water treatment, aluminium sulphate is added to turbid water and the resulting solution is neutralized to precipitate aluminium hydroxide which is a flocculant for the various solid impurities in turbid water.

Other uses of aluminium sulphate include the production of chemicals, pharmaceutical products, fire extinguishing solutions and the deodorizing mineral oils, the tanning of leather and dyeing wool with alizarine dyes (aluminium sulphate is a mordant which fixes alizarine on textiles). Aluminium sulphate is also used for the production of a basic aluminium sulphate, 'light alumina hydrate', which is produced by adding sodium carbonate solution to a solution of aluminium sulphate at pH 5. The resulting light powder is used as a bodying agent for lithographic ink.

Owing to the fact that about 4 kg of aluminium sulphate are needed in sizing 100 kg of paper, the demand for aluminium sulphate is enormous. In the USA, the production of aluminium sulphate was close to 1 million short tons in 1964. The UK is also an important producer of aluminium sulphate. The exports from the UK were:

	1957	1959	1961	1963	1964
In long tons	34 600	30 300	33 500	24 400	36 600

The price of aluminium sulphate in the USA was $44 to $48 per short ton for technical grade and $76 per short ton for iron-free grade in 1965. In the UK technical aluminium sulphate was sold at £17-21 per long ton.

12.3.6 Alum

Potassium aluminium sulphate (potassium alum, alum, $KAl(SO_4)_2.12H_2O$) is a double salt of potassium sulphate and sodium sulphate. Its name alum is derived from the latin 'alumen' which was once used for various compounds having astringent properties. Nowadays the name alum without any addition usually refers to potassium aluminium sulphate. It is also used for other double sulphates, but usually in combination with an additional indication, e.g., sodium alum, ammonium alum, iron alum $(KFe(SO_4)_2.12H_2O)$ and chrome alum $(KCr(SO_4)_2.12H_2O)$.

Potassium alum is prepared by dissolving aluminium hydroxide in sulphuric acid to form a concentrated solution of aluminium sulphate from which potassium alum is precipitated by adding potassium sulphate.

It forms white crystals melting at 105° C. Its solubility in water is relatively low; about 8 g of the anhydrous salt dissolve in 100 g water at 30° C.

Potassium alum is used for the same purposes as aluminium sulphate, although its commercial importance has decreased considerably owing to the fact that aluminium sulphate can be produced more cheaply. Since potassium alum precipitates easily in the form of pure crystals, it is sometimes obtained as an intermediate in the production of pure aluminium compounds from very impure bauxite or clay. Because of its astringent properties potassium alum is used in medicine. In the USA potassium alum was sold at $4.80 to 5.70 per 100 lb in 1965.

Sodium alum ($NaAl(SO_4)_2.12H_2O$) and *ammonium alum* ($NH_4Al(SO_4)_2.12H_2O$) are prepared in a similar way to that used for potassium alum. In the USA sodium alum is important in baking powders. Outside the USA the commercial importance of sodium alum is low although it may be used for the same purposes as aluminium sulphate and potassium alum. Ammonium alum is not used in baking powder but, like sodium alum, small quantities are used in water purification, in paper sizing, as a mordant in dyeing and in medicine.

12.3.7 Aluminium nitrate

Aluminium nitrate ($Al(NO_3)_3.9H_2O$) may be produced by treating aluminium hydroxide with nitric acid solution. It is separated from the resulting solution by evaporation and crystallization. Aluminium nitrate forms colourless hygroscopic crystals and melts at 73° C. It is used in the textile industry as a mordant, in the production of catalysts and in the production of filaments for incandescent lamps. Aluminium nitrate is also used as a salting out agent in solvent extraction processes for the recovery of nuclear fuels from nuclear reactor wastes.

12.3.8 Aluminium nitride

Aluminium nitride (AlN) is prepared by heating aluminium powder in an atmosphere of ammonia, or by heating aluminium powder containing small quantities of an alkali nitrite or fluoride in a atmosphere of nitrogen.

Like boron nitride, aluminium nitride is an extremely hard solid (9-10 on Mohs' scale) and it resists gases such as oxygen and carbon dioxide at temperatures up to 800° C. In an inert atmosphere (nitrogen or argon) it can be heated at temperatures up to 2 000° C before decomposition occurs.

Aluminium nitride is used as an abrasive and for the production of sintered refractory materials.

12.3.9 Aluminium formate

Aluminium triformate ($Al(OOCH)_3.3H_2O$) and aluminium diformate or basic aluminium formate ($Al(OH)(OOCH)_2.H_2O$) are prepared in the form of aqueous solutions by treating a solution of aluminium sulphate with equivalent proportions of formic acid and lime. Reaction equation:

$$Al_2(SO_4)_3 + 4\,HCOOH + 3Ca(OH)_2 \rightarrow 2AlOH(OOCH)_2 + 3CaSO_4 + 4H_2O.$$

Solid white powders of aluminium triformate and diformate may be obtained by filtering the resulting solution and evaporating to dryness, e.g. by spray-drying. By far the most important product of commerce is a solution of aluminium diformate which may be obtained by the same process; a solution containing 8.5% of Al_2O_3 equivalent is commonest. To prevent the development of turbidity on standing, aluminium diformate solutions are stabilised by adding small quantities of an acid other than formic acid, e.g. acetic, propionic or adipic acid.

Aluminium diformate precipitated from an aluminium formate solution and aluminium hydroxide formed by drying aluminium diformate have water repellent properties. For this reason the largest quantities of aluminium formate solutions are used in waterproofing compositions for textiles, paper and other materials. In the textile industry aluminium diformate is also used as a mordant in printing patterned fabrics. In some cases aluminium formates are preferable to the sulphate in textile and paper sizing operations because formic acid, which results from hydrolysis of aluminium formate, is harmless to the fibres. Aluminium formates are also used in anti-perspirant and cosmetic compositions since they have a bactericidal action.

12.3.10 Aluminium acetates

Aluminium acetate (aluminium triacetate, $Al(OOCCH_3)_3$) may be prepared by treating metallic aluminium with a hot acetic acid solution containing some acetic anhydride. Aluminium triacetate precipitates from the resulting solution on cooling. Aluminium acetate may also be prepared by adding solid aluminium chloride to a hot mixture of acetic acid and acetic anhydride. Aluminium triacetate precipitates from the resulting solution on cooling. It is sold both as a solid and a solution.

Aluminium triacetate is a white powder which decomposes at a temperature below the melting point. It is soluble in water but the resulting solution is not very stable; on standing a gelatinous precipitate is formed owing to hydrolysis. The solution can be stabilized by adding tartaric acid.

Like aluminium formate, aluminium triacetate is used in the dyeing of textiles as a mordant and in waterproofing textiles, paper, leather and other materials.

Aluminium diacetate ($Al(OH)(OOCCH_3)_2$) may be prepared in the form of a solid by treating a sodium aluminate solution with glacial acetic acid. Commercial solutions may be prepared by reacting aluminium sulphate with acetic acid and lime (compare the production of aluminium formate, above).

Aluminium diacetate solutions are used for the same purposes as the triacetate. In addition solutions of aluminium diacetate are used in medicine as antiseptic and astringent agents. Solid diacetate, mixed with talc, is used in antiseptic and deodorant ointments and powders.

12.4 THALLIUM COMPOUNDS

Thallous sulphate or thallium sulphate (Tl_2SO_4) is the most important commercial thallium compound and is prepared by dissolving metallic thallium in hot sulphuric acid and cooling the resulting solution (for metallic thallium see vol. III).

Thallous sulphate is an odourless and tasteless poisonous solid and for this reason it is used in rodenticides and insecticides. Bread crumbs or wheat grains etc. coated with a paste containing thallous sulphate, sugar and water are used to destroy rats. Small quantities of thallous sulphate are used in the production of thallium compounds for use in cosmetics and pharmaceuticals. However these uses are limited on account of the extremely poisonous nature of thallium compounds. Production figures for thallium and its compounds are not available, but annual production in the USA has been estimated at 5-10 tons. In the USA, thallous sulphate was sold at $5 to $10 per lb in 1965.

CHAPTER 13

The Carbon-Silicon Group of the Periodic System

13.1 INTRODUCTION

The carbon-silicon group of the periodic system is formed by the elements carbon, silicon, germanium, tin and lead. All these elements are di- or tetravalent in their compounds. Thus monosulphides and disulphides (except lead disulphide), mono- and dioxides, tetrahalides and gaseous tetrahydrides of these elements are known. (Dihalides are formed only by germanium, tin and lead.) In addition some unstable compounds of trivalent carbon are known. The tendency to form tetravalent compounds decreases from carbon to lead and the tendency to form divalent compounds increases. The compounds of tetravalent carbon and silicon are stable unlike the compounds of these elements in the divalent state which are usually unstable. Germanium has a greater tendency to form divalent compounds than carbon and silicon but the compounds of tetravalent germanium are more stable. The stability of tin compounds in the di- and tetravalent states is about equal, whereas lead is most stable in its divalent state.

Elemental carbon and silicon have a distinctly non-metallic character; germanium, tin and lead are metals. Corresponding to the behaviour of the elements in other main groups of the Periodic System, the acidity of the oxides decreases from the lighter elements to the heavier while the basic character increases. This feature is strengthened in the carbon-silicon group by the fact that the stability of the lower valence state increases in the same direction. When an element forms several oxides, the lower oxides are usually more basic, or less acidic, than the higher oxides. Thus the dioxides of carbon and silicon and the mono- and dioxides of germanium have acidic character, whereas the oxides of tin and lead are amphoteric, i.e. they can form salts with both acids and bases. However, tin dioxide is predominantly acidic, while the monoxides of tin and lead are predominantly basic. With strong alkali solutions stannites e.g. sodium stannite (Na_2SnO_2) and plumbites e.g. sodium plumbite (Na_2PbO_2) are formed from the monoxide of tin and lead respectively. With acids stannous hydroxide ($Sn(OH)_2$) and lead hydroxide ($Pb(OH)_2$) are precipitated from solutions of these sodium salts. The dioxides of the elements of the carbon-silicon group react with bases to form carbonates, silicates, germanates, stannates and plumbates respectively (e.g. Na_2CO_3, Na_2SiO_3, Na_2GeO_3, Na_2SnO_3 and Na_2PbO_3). These silicates, germanates, stannates and plumbates are also known as metasilicates etc., as distinct from orthosilicates etc.

which can be formed from the same oxides (e.g. Na_4SiO_4, Na_4GeO_4, Na_4SnO_4 and Na_4PbO_4).

With the exception of the salts of the alkali metals, carbonates, silicates, germanates, stannates and plumbates are almost insoluble in water. The corresponding acids of these salts cannot be obtained in a free state. Oxides are liberated when acids are added to solutions of the alkali metal salts; gaseous carbon dioxide, jelly-like precipitates of hydrated silicon dioxide, germanium dioxide and tin dioxide and a precipitate of hydrated lead dioxide are obtained respectively. The names carbonic acid, silicic acid, germanic acid and stannic acid are often used for the corresponding dioxides.

The salts of di- and tetravalent tin, in which tin is present as a cation (Sn^{++}, Sn^{++++}), are named stannous and stannic salts respectively, e.g. stannous chloride ($SnCl_2$) and stannic chloride ($SnCl_4$). Similarly the names plumbous and plumbic salts are sometimes used for salts of di- and tetravalent lead in which lead is present as a cation, (Pb^{++}, Pb^{++++}).

13.2 CARBON AND ITS COMPOUNDS (C, atomic weight = 12.01)

13.2.1 Occurrence

Carbon is very widely distributed in various forms in nature, although the abundance of carbon in the earth's crust is low compared with oxygen, silicon and most common metals. Carbon compounds are widely distributed in the earth's crust especially in the form of carbonates such as calcium carbonate (see e.g. limestone and marble, vol. II), calcium magnesium carbonate (see dolomite, vol. II), ferrous carbonate (siderite) and zinc carbonate (smithsonite).

There is no living organism, vegetable or animal, in which carbon compounds do not play a vital part. Thus almost all technical materials of vegetable and animal origin (e.g. wood, rubber, oils, fats and leather) consist of carbon compounds. Again, the products of decay of vegetation in nature are found in the form of anthracite, bituminous coal, brown coal, lignite and peat, and the products of decay of animal remains in the form of petroleum, ozokerite (natural wax) and asphalt. All these products result from decomposition processes (carbonization) whereby the carbon content of the vegetable or animal matter increases owing to elimination of other elements, e.g. hydrogen, oxygen and nitrogen, which were originally combined with the carbon. Most organic substances also undergo such a carbonization process when they are strongly heated. This can be seen in the black colouration which is due to the formation of finely divided carbon when, for instance, bread is over-toasted. Coal, petroleum etc. are the result of carbonization processes which have taken place in the course of geological ages. These products nowadays provide the bases of various chemical industries. (See Solid mineral fuels, vol. II and Petroleum products, vol. IV.)

In the air carbon occurs in the form of carbon dioxide. Although the concentration in the air is low (about 0.03% by volume), the total amount of carbon in the air considerably exceeds that present in all vegetable and animal life (see Air, ch. 3 and carbon dioxide, p. 533). Elemental carbon is also found in nature in the form of diamond and graphite (see vol. II). Graphite and diamond are both crystalline modifications of carbon. Graphite forms soft and grey hexagonal crystals in which layers of carbon atoms are arranged in regular hexagons. Diamond forms extremely hard and colourless regular crystals in which the carbon atoms are arranged tetrahedrally and equidistant. All other forms of carbon obtained by thermal decomposition of carbon compounds are black. It was formerly considered that black carbon was an amorphous modification of carbon, but in 1917 it was discovered by Debye and Scherrer that black carbon is identical in structure with graphite; but it is very finely divided. Coke, wood charcoal, animal charcoal, lamp-black (soot), and gas-retort carbon are the most important forms of amorphous carbon (see coal vol. II and petroleum vol. IV).

Both diamond and graphite burn to form carbon dioxide in air (diamond burns at 800° C). The formation of carbon dioxide in this manner proves that diamond consists of carbon. Diamond can be converted into graphite by heating it at a temperature of 1 900° C in the absence of air. It is also possible to make diamonds from graphite, which for this purpose must be heated at still higher temperatures under extremely high pressure followed by rapid cooling to avoid the reformation of graphite. In 1955 the General Electric Company (USA) prepared small diamonds (diameter up to 1/16 of an inch) at a temperature of 2 500° C and a pressure of 100 000 atmospheres. Examination by X-ray diffraction showed that these synthetic diamonds were identical with natural ones.

Owing to the ability of carbon atoms to combine together in rings and chains, carbon is unique among the elements for the number and variety of its compounds; silicon forms chains and rings to a smaller extent. About 600 000 carbon compounds are known, compared with about 40 000 compounds from all the other elements together. Before the development of synthetic chemistry it was believed that the intervention of a living organism was essential for the formation of many of the carbon compounds e.g. urea. In this way a branch of chemistry known as 'organic' chemistry grew up. Except in their complexity there is no essential distinction between these 'organic' compounds (see vols. IV to VIII) and the simpler substances, e.g. carbon disulphide, carbon monoxide, carbon dioxide, the metal carbonates, cyanogen compounds, and the like, which are usually dealt with in text books of 'inorganic' chemistry. (For carbon disulphide see ch. 8, for metal carbonates see the various metal compounds and for cyanogen compounds see ch. 9.)

13.2.2 Carbon monoxide

a. Occurrence. In nature carbon monoxide gas (CO) occurs in volcanic gases. Small amounts of monoxide are found in carbonaceous materials such as coal and coal lignites. Owing to slow oxidation of coal, carbon monoxide also occurs in mines. Since carbon monoxide results from the incomplete combustion of carbonaceous fuels, appreciable amounts of this gas may be discharged into the air and locally the carbon monoxide content of the air may increase considerably, especially in city streets, vehicular tunnels, garages (owing to the presence of up to 12% carbon monoxide in the exhaust gases of automobiles) and in houses (owing to incomplete combustion of gas and inadequate removal of combustion gases from stoves etc.). However the very small carbon monoxide content of the entire atmosphere of the earth does not increase considerably since carbon monoxide is slowly converted into carbon dioxide.

Large quantities of carbon monoxide are produced in the form of mixtures with other gases. The commercial importance of these mixtures, such as coal gas, coke oven gas, producer gas and water gas, is very great (see gas mixtures, vol. II).

b. Production. Pure or fairly pure carbon monoxide is produced and used to a limited extent. It is prepared chemically by passing carbon dioxide over coke at about 1 000° C. The carbon dioxide is formed by passing oxygen over coke at a hotter part of the same furnace.

Carbon monoxide is also obtained from a gas mixture, such as water gas (which consists of approximately equal amounts of carbon monoxide and hydrogen) either by selective absorption or by low-temperature liquefaction and fractionation.

In the most important selective absorption process the carbon monoxide contained in the gas mixture is absorbed in a ammoniacal solution of a cupric salt (preferably copper carbonate or copper formate) by scrubbing with the solution at high pressures (about 200 atm.) in a packed column. Carbon monoxide is then recovered from the liquid by releasing the pressure:

$$Cu_2(NH_3)_4{}^{++} + 2\,CO + 2\,NH_3 \rightleftharpoons Cu_2(NH_3)_6\,(CO)_2{}^{++}$$

At high pressures the equilibrium reaction is forced towards the right and complexions are formed in the solution. At low pressures the reaction moves back to the left and carbon monoxide is released again.

Any gas used for the production of carbon monoxide must be free from solids, sulphur compounds and carbon dioxide to prevent the formation of a sludge, which would plug the packed absorption column, and to prevent the decomposition of the absorbent. Carbon dioxide would form solid ammonium carbonate with ammonia present in the absorbent, and sulphur compounds would form solid copper sulphide.

Solids in the starting material are removed by electrostatic precipitation or by washing with water. Sulphur compounds and carbon dioxide may be removed by scrubbing with monoethanolamine or an alkali carbonate solution. The use of starting materials containing acetylene must be avoided since acetylene forms the very explosive copper acetylide with the copper ions present in the absorbent. Acetylene can be removed from the gas mixture by scrubbing it with concentrated sulphuric acid.

A low temperature liquefaction process for the separation of carbon monoxide from a gas mixture needs a starting material which is free from carbon dioxide and water. After removal of the carbon dioxide the gas mixture is carefully dried and liquefied by compression, cooling and expansion in many stages (see liquefaction of gases, p. 43). All constituents, such as oxygen, nitrogen and methane, but not hydrogen, liquefy with the carbon monoxide. The liquid is fractionated to yield carbon monoxide of at least 98% purity.

c. Properties. Carbon monoxide is a colourless, odourless and poisonous gas which liquefies at − 191.5° C and solidifies at − 205° C. The poisonous effect of carbon monoxide is based on the fact that it is absorbed and bound by the haemoglobin in the red blood cells and thus carbon monoxide reduces the capacity of the blood to carry oxygen. Very small concentrations cause only a slight headache but concentrations above 200 p.p.m. in air are harmful and concentrations above 0.5% in air are deadly when inhaled for a few minutes. Since carbon monoxide is a constituent of almost all exhaust gases from internal combustion engines and furnaces, fatal inhalation of carbon monoxide often occurs in rooms, garages and other places which are inadequately ventilated. (See also ch. 3 gaseous pollutants.)

Traces of carbon monoxide in a gas can be detected by passing the gas through a paper wetted with a solution of palladous chloride which becomes black when carbon monoxide is present in the gas, owing to the precipitation of metallic palladium. Reaction equation:

$$PdCl_2 + CO + H_2O \rightarrow Pd + 2\,HCl + CO_2.$$

Other gases, such as hydrogen sulphide, also produce a black coloration and for this reason a confirmatory test is required. (See also Safety in industry, vol. III, ch. 13.)

Carbon monoxide burns in air with a blue flame and is converted into carbon dioxide. Mixtures with air containing 16-74% carbon monoxide are explosive at room temperature; only a spark is required for ignition. Carbon monoxide also reacts with chlorine to form phosgene ($COCl_2$), with metals to form metal carbonyls (e.g. nickel carbonyl, $Ni(CO)_4$) and with hydrogen to form alcohols, aldehydes, fatty acids etc. The last reaction is the basis of the Fischer-Tropsch process for the production of methanol (CH_3OH) from hydrogen-carbon monoxide mixtures (see Gas mixtures, vol. II and Alcohols, vol. IV).

d. Uses and statistics. Isolated carbon monoxide is used for the production of various organic compounds including methyl formate and ethylene glycol. 'Inorganic' compounds produced with carbon monoxide are phosgene and the metal carbonyls. Metal carbonyls are formed by treating finely divided metals or metal salts with carbon monoxide (usually at pressures of about 200 atm and temperatures between 150 and 250° C).

Metal carbonyls are used in powder metallurgy and for the production of metal catalysts since metal carbonyls can be decomposed to form extremely finely divided metals (see also Iron pentacarbonyl, p. 587, and Powder metallurgy, vol. III). Carbon monoxide also plays a role in the Mond process for the recovery of nickel from ores containing copper, cobalt and iron. In one stage of the process, nickel is removed from the mixture of minerals in the form of nickel carbonyl (see nickel, vol. III).

Production of carbon monoxide, pure or contained in gas mixtures (excluding the enormous quantities of carbon monoxide contained in gaseous fuels), in the USA was estimated at about 1.5 million short tons in 1963. Only about 10% was produced in the pure form.

13.2.3 Carbon dioxide

a. Occurrence. Carbon dioxide (CO_2) is widely distributed in nature. Free carbon dioxide occurs in air at a concentration of about 0.03% by volume. The carbon dioxide in air is an important product in the life cycle of animals and plants. Plants are able to take up carbon dioxide from air and to convert it into carbohydrates with simultaneous liberation of oxygen (see Air, ch. 3, p. 587). Carbon dioxide also occurs in volcanic gases and in some natural gases associated e.g. with mineral springs, earth fissures. Like carbon monoxide it is a constituent of all waste gases resulting from the combustion of carbonaceous materials. Chemically combined carbon dioxide occurs in the form of carbonates especially calcium and magnesium carbonates (see Calcareous minerals and rocks, vol. II).

b. Production and purification. Carbon dioxide is usually produced as a by-product in various processes. It is recovered from gases developed in limestone calcination (see Lime, vol. II), the combustion of carbonaceous material and fermentation processes. Large quantities of carbon dioxide are developed during the fermentation of materials such as molasses, corn and potatoes in the production of beer, industrial alcohol and distilled beverages. Carbon dioxide is also obtained as a by-product in the production of hydrogen for the synthesis of ammonia (see the water gas shift reaction, under hydrogen production, p. 64). Sometimes carbon dioxide is recovered from gases of volcanic origin and natural gases having a very high carbon dioxide content.

Sometimes carbon dioxide is recovered from gas mixtures by a low temperature liquefaction process, but usually it is separated from the gas mixture by passing it through a packed column, countercurrent to an aqueous solution of sodium carbonate, potassium carbonate or an ethanolamine (mono-, di- or triethanolamine).

The sodium carbonate and potassium carbonate processes are based on the following equilibrium reaction:

$$CO_3^{--} + H_2O + CO_2 \rightleftharpoons 2 HCO_3^-$$

At low temperatures (e.g. room temperature) carbon dioxide is absorbed to convert carbonate ions into bicarbonate ions. The reaction is made to proceed to the left by heating the resulting bicarbonate solution in a boiler. Carbon dioxide is then released and is collected after removing any water by passing through a condenser. The remaining carbonate solution is passed through a heat exchanger and returned to the absorber. In the heat exchanger the hot carbonate solution is cooled by the cold bicarbonate solution which is transported from the absorber into the boiler. In this way the heat is recovered since the cold bicarbonate solution is heated before it enters into the boiler.

The ethanolamine process for the absorption of carbon dioxide is basically the same as the carbonate process. It is based on the following equilibrium reaction (using monoethanolamine):

$$2 HOC_2H_4NH_2 + H_2O + CO_2 \rightleftharpoons (HOC_2H_4NH_3)_2CO_3$$

At temperatures up to 65° C the reaction quickly proceeds to the right and at temperatures above 100° C the reaction moves to the left. Thus carbon dioxide is absorbed at lower temperatures and liberated again at higher temperatures.

Carbon dioxide recovered by any method mentioned above, usually contains small quantities of impurities such as hydrogen sulphide which is removed by passing the gas through a layer of active carbon or through a solution of an oxidizing agent, such as potassium permanganate or potassium dichromate, in which the hydrogen sulphide is oxidized to sulphur. Carbon dioxide obtained from fermentation processes often contains impurities such as alcohols, aldehydes and acids as well as hydrogen sulphide. These impurities are removed by washing the gas with water, dilute alcohol solution, potassium dichromate solution or by adsorption on active carbon, depending on the impurity contained in the gas.

  c. Properties. Carbon dioxide is a colourless gas with a weakly acidic taste and a slight odour. At atmospheric pressure it solidifies without liquefying at a temperature of −78.5° C. It can be liquefied only at a temperature between −56.6° C (triple point temperature) and 31° C (critical temperature) by compressing it to the corresponding pressure. The triple point pressure is 5.2 atm and the critical pressure is 73 atm.

  Carbon dioxide is not very reactive at ordinary temperatures. However in aqueous solution, it forms the weak acid H_2CO_3, which forms salts (carbonates) and esters with bases and alcohols respectively. A solid hydrate, $CO_2.8H_2O$, precipitates if a highly concentrated aqueous solution (made at elevated pressures) is cooled.

Carbon dioxide which is a normal constituent of exhaled air is considered to be non-poisonous. Concentrations up to 0.5% are not really harmful, but higher concentrations may be. Concentrations above 5% by volume of carbon dioxide in air may be fatal if inhaled for a few hours, and concentrations above 30% may be fatal even within 30 minutes. For this reason care must be taken to provide sufficient ventilation when carbon dioxide is handled, especially as carbon dioxide tends to accumulate at lower parts of a room because it is approximately $1\frac{1}{2}$ times as heavy as air.

d. Liquefaction and storage of liquid carbon dioxide. Carbon dioxide is often stored and transported in the liquid form. Bulk quantities are usually compressed to about 20 atm, liquefied by cooling to about $-20°$ C in a refrigerant-cooled condenser and stored in large refrigerated and insulated tanks containing up to 50 tons. Smaller lots of carbon dioxide are usually stored and transported at room temperature under a pressure of about 75 atm in tall cylinders containing up to 50 lb. The cylinders are filled by means of a compressor which compresses cold carbon dioxide gas, withdrawn from the liquid carbon dioxide stores at $-20°$ C, to a pressure of about 75 atm. The heat developed in the compression stage is used to evaporate a further portion of cold liquid CO_2.

In both liquefaction processes the carbon dioxide is pre-cooled after the last compression stage and filtered in the gaseous phase to remove water and any entrained lubricating oil. The purified carbon dioxide is further cooled to form liquid carbon dioxide.

e. Solidifying carbon dioxide. Sometimes small quantities of solid carbon dioxide ('dry ice') are prepared from liquid carbon dioxide, stored in a cylinder, by allowing it to flow rapidly out of the cylinder. Owing to the decreasing pressure, the carbon dioxide which escapes from the cylinder expands suddenly and freezes to a snow-like solid (Joule-Thomson effect, see p. 43). This process in its simplest form cannot be used for the production of large quantities of solid carbon dioxide since less than one-quarter of the carbon dioxide is recovered as a solid; the remainder is lost.

In industrial processes for the production of solid carbon dioxide means must be provided to prevent losses of gaseous carbon dioxide. In one such process, the Carba process, liquid carbon dioxide (cooled at about 15° C) is fed into a pressure chamber by means of a feed valve. Owing to the fact that the pressure in the chamber is kept at about 20 atm, part of the liquid carbon dioxide evaporates and the remaining liquid cools to a temperature of $-20°$ C. As soon as the pressure chamber is filled to the predetermined level, the pressure is reduced to 5 atm (slightly below the triple point). A further portion of liquid carbon dioxide evaporates and the remaining carbon dioxide is cooled to $-57°$ C and solidifies. The pressure is then reduced to atmospheric pressure which causes further evaporation of carbon dioxide and further cooling of the remaining solid carbon dioxide (to $-79°$ C). Gaseous carbon dioxide evolved in each expansion step is compressed again and recycled.

Carbon dioxide can also be solidified by releasing the pressure in one step to atmospheric pressure, but solidification in the neighbourhood of the triple point is usually preferred since a more compact body of solid carbon dioxide results. Before discharging the solid carbon dioxide from the pressure chamber, it is compressed into a more compact block.

Unlike liquid carbon dioxide, dry ice cannot be stored for a long time since it undergoes continuous loss owing to sublimation. For this reason solid carbon dioxide is usually produced at the time it is sold and it is transported in insulated containers or by means of specially insulated rail cars and trucks.

f. Uses. Most of the carbon dioxide produced is used as dry ice in refrigeration and carbonation processes.

Food and ice-cream refrigeration and conservation absorb the largest amounts. Dry ice can be mixed with the material to be refrigerated since it can easily be sawn into small pieces and it evaporates without leaving any liquid residue. Crushed dry ice is also mixed with various materials to make them brittle before grinding and pulverising or to cool materials which do not resist heat of friction. For example, 'Hamburger' meat, DDT and scrap plastics are ground in this way. Dry ice is also used to chill aluminium rivets which remain soft if kept with dry ice; at room temperature, they harden rapidly. Moulded rubber articles are also chilled with dry ice in a tumbling drum, so that a thin rind becomes brittle and can be removed easily. In laboratories, solid carbon dioxide is a common source of 'cold' for various processes on a small scale.

Although dry ice is still the most important form of carbon dioxide for refrigeration processes, it has been replaced by liquid carbon dioxide in many cases. The liquid form is usually injected into the material to be refrigerated. Owing to the decreasing pressure, carbon dioxide evaporates and expands rapidly and the heat required is withdrawn from the surrounding matter. Uses in which liquid carbon dioxide has partially replaced dry ice include 'Hamburger' meat grinding, cooling of chemical reaction mixtures by direct injection of carbon dioxide into the reaction system etc.

The most important outlet for liquid carbon dioxide is the carbonated beverage industry. For such carbonation liquid carbon dioxide is vaporized at the point of use and in its gaseous form is introduced into beer, sparkling wine and beverages. Other carbonation processes include the introduction of carbon dioxide under pressure into rubber and plastic compositions to produce foamed products on releasing the pressure.

Important quantities of liquid carbon dioxide are also used as a fire extinguishing agent, especially in hand-type extinguishers. Carbon dioxide is also used to produce an inert atmosphere in stores in which inflammable matter is kept.

In the chemical industry, carbon dioxide gas is used as a chemical reagent for the production of urea, aromatic oxycarboxylic acids (e.g. salicylic acid), basic lead carbonate, barium carbonate, ammonium bicarbonate, potassium carbonate and soda ash in the Solvay process. Carbon dioxide is also used in sugar refining and as a neutralizing agent, e.g. for neutralizing alkaline solutions in the textile industry and for neutralizing alkaline waste waters. In the foundry industry carbon dioxide is used for hardening of sand cores and moulds which are made from sand and waterglass.

Since liquid carbon dioxide has a pressure of about 75 atm at ordinary temperature, it is also used as a source of power. It is used in aerosol sprayers, for spraying paints and chemicals and for dispensing beer and beverages.

Other uses of carbon dioxide include painless killing of animals before slaughtering, rodent control in food stores, for therapeutic baths and respiratory stimulation. The last application is based on the fact that the breathing rate is controlled by the carbon dioxide present in air or oxygen; increasing carbon dioxide concentration causes an increase in the breathing frequency. For this reason up to about 5% carbon dioxide is added to oxygen for artificial respiration.

In the graphite-moderated nuclear reactors at Calder Hall (Britain) carbon dioxide gas is used as a cooling agent in the heat exchange equipment.

g. Statistics. The total production of carbon dioxide in the USA increased from 750000 short tons in 1954 to 1112000 short tons in 1964. In the same period the production of liquid and gaseous carbon dioxide increased from 190000 short tons to 690000 short tons, but the production of solid carbon dioxide decreased slowly from 560000 to 422000 short tons. In 1964 about 50% of all carbon dioxide sales in the USA was used for food refrigeration, about 25% for beverage carbonation and about 10% in the chemical industry.

In the USA liquid carbon dioxide was sold at $90 per short ton depending on the quantity delivered and solid carbon dioxide was sold at $50 to $100 per short ton in 1965. In the UK the price of solid and liquid carbon dioxide was $4\frac{1}{2}$ d per lb in 1965.

h. Literature

I. KUPRIANOFF, *Die feste Kohlensäure*. Stuttgart, Ferdinand Enke Verlag, 1953.
M. VOLLENWEIDER. *Fabrication et applications industrielles du anhydride carbonique*. Paris, Dunod, 1958.

13.2.4 Phosgene

Phosgene (carbonyl chloride, carbon oxychloride, $COCl_2$) was prepared for the first time by Davy in 1812 by the reaction of carbon monoxide with chlorine under the influence of light. The name phosgene is derived from the Greek words for 'light' and 'to produce'.

On an industrial scale phosgene is prepared by passing a mixture of pure carbon monoxide and pure chlorine under a pressure of about 3 atm over activated charcoal at 40-50° C. The reaction, which proceeds rapidly with the development of much heat, is conducted in iron tubes which are cooled with water. The resulting product is collected from the tubes and stored under pressure in iron containers.

Both the starting materials, chlorine and carbon monoxide, must be pure. Sulphides should not be present as they produce sulphur chlorides. Water, hydrogen and hydrocarbons must be absent in order to avoid the formation of hydrochloric acid, which may poison the catalyst (activated charcoal). Slight excess of carbon monoxide is used since chlorine is an undesirable impurity in phosgene.

Phosgene is a colourless, very poisonous gas and it has a characteristic and strong odour. The odour which is sometimes described as similar to that of new mown hay is even perceptible at very low concentrations (0.5 to 1 p.p.m.). At temperatures below 7.5° C phosgene condenses to a colourless liquid. Its melting point is −128° C. It dissolves in many organic liquids. Commercial products usually have a pale yellow to green colour when liquid, owing to the presence of impurities.

Phosgene is one of the most dangerous gases used in industry. Brief inhalation of air containing only 50 p.p.m. is fatal. The maximum safe concentration for working exposure has been set at 0.1 p.p.m. Inhalation of lethal concentrations does not cause any immediate irritation of the respiratory passages and consequently a protective reflex action does not occur. However, some time after inhalation of the gas the capillaries in the walls of the lung alveoli become permeable and allow the blood plasma (liquid) to escape into the air space of the lungs. The remaining blood volume decreases and in addition it becomes thickened since the corpuscles (containing haemoglobin) do not pass the permeated alveoli. The last effect is the most dangerous consequence of phosgene inhalation since the oxygen circulation decreases.

Phosgene may be considered to be 'carbonic acid chloride' of which the chlorine atoms are very reactive with various elements and compounds. In the presence of water phosgene hydrolyses rapidly to form carbon dioxide and hydrogen chloride. The latter reacts with the metal of any container in which phosgene is stored and the hydrogen evolved may cause dangerously high pressures in the container. For this reason care must be taken that no water can penetrate into the phosgene containers.

The largest quantities of phosgene are used for the production of isocyanates, which are starting materials for the production of polyurethanes. Isocyanates may be produced, for example, by treating an amine salt with phosgene in a toluene solution to form a carbamyl chloride (RNHCOCl), which when heated decomposes to give an isocyanate, (RNCO). Reaction equations:

$$RNH_2.HCl + COCl_2 \rightarrow RNHCOCl + 2HCl$$

$$RNHCOCl \rightarrow RNCO + HCl.$$

The reaction conditions depend on the isocyanate to be prepared. Phosgene is also used as a starting material for the production of pesticides, herbicides, triphenylmethane and aminoazo dyes, pharmaceuticals, softeners, carbonate esters and polycarbonates. In World War I phosgene was used as a poison gas.

In the USA about 155000 short tons of phosgene were produced in 1964. About 72% was used for the production of isocyanates and 18% for the production of pesticides and herbicides. The price of phosgene in the USA was $0.16 per lb in 1965.

13.2.5 Calcium carbide

a. History. Calcium carbide (CaC_2) was prepared for the first time by R. Hare in 1840, although its chemical composition was not recognized until 1862 by Wöhler. Industrial production started in 1895 and was based on a process developed independently by Moissan in France and Willson in the USA. Industrial production was initiated by the demand for a light source (the well-known carbide lamps) but the carbide light was soon superseded by other light sources. At the beginning of the twentieth century the production of calcium carbide increased only because of its consumption for acetylene welding and for calcium cyanamide production.

b. Production. The production of calcium carbide is based on the endothermic equilibrium reaction between calcium oxide and carbon which is performed in an electric arc furnace. Reaction equation:

$$CaO + 3C \rightleftarrows CaC_2 + CO$$

At temperatures above about 1650° C, the reaction proceeds to the right. At temperatures below 1400° C metallic calcium is formed in the reaction mixture, according to the following reaction equation:

Fig. 13.1 The top section of an open arc furnace.

$$CaO + C \rightarrow Ca + CO$$

At temperatures of about $2\,500°$ C any calcium carbide formed decomposes to form the elements calcium and carbon; however, usually the temperature does not increase above $2\,200°$ C in the furnaces commonly used.

Both the starting materials calcium oxide and carbon (coke), must be pure since impurities are not eliminated in the process and the resulting calcium carbide cannot be purified economically. About 550 kg of coke and 920 kg of calcium oxide are needed to produce a metric ton of calcium carbide.

Although the principle of the calcium carbide production process has only changed slightly since it was developed in 1895, the electric arc furnaces and other equipment have been improved and changed considerably.

Today most furnaces are of the submerged arc type using continuous, self-baking Söderberg electrodes (see electrodes, vol. II). A Söderberg electrode comprises a metal tube filled with a hot mixture of coal tar and calcined anthracite which passes slowly downwards through the tube in which it is baked by means of the heat of the furnace. The baked section which extends into the reaction mixture is consumed continuously and new electrode material is introduced from time to time at the top of the electrode tube.

Furnaces of large capacity use three electrodes placed in a triangle and fed with three-phase current. The ends of the electrodes extend from 2 to 4 ft below the surface

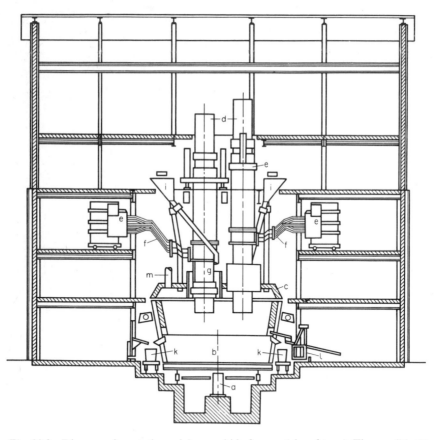

Fig. 13.2 Diagram of a rotating calcium carbide furnace (closed type). The crucible (b) rests on the rotating mechanism (a). The Söderberg electrodes (d) can be slipped downwards through the apertures in the cover (c). Electric power is supplied to the electrodes by means of transformers (e), leads (f) and contact shoes (g). The raw materials are fed into the furnace by feed chutes (i) and the calcium carbide formed is passed into the tapping receivers (k) by means of the tapping device (1). Carbon monoxide formed in the reactor is withdrawn by means of outlet (m).

Fig. 13.3 The top section of a rotating calcium carbide furnace (closed type).

of the unmelted charge which covers the molten mixture of calcium oxide and calcium carbide. In this way part of the heat is generated by the electrical resistance of the solid surface layer, which also protects the melt against attack by the nitrogen in the surrounding air (see below).

The furnace consists of reinforced steel, lined with several layers of refractory brick. The bottom is usually covered with a hearth made of carbon blocks. The side walls of the furnace are provided with tapholes just above the carbon hearth. The furnaces may be divided into two basic types: (i) the open furnace, in which the carbon monoxide formed burns with air to carbon dioxide (see fig. 13.1.); and (ii) the most commonly used closed furnace in which carbon monoxide is recovered. The furnace may be stationary or it may rotate under a stationary cover which bears the electrodes. (See fig. 13.2 and fig. 13.3; compare the electric arc furnace for phosphorus production p. 364).

Calcium carbide is withdrawn from the furnace in the form of a melt (temperature 1 900-2 100° C) and is cast into cast-iron cylinders or else poured on to conveyors. Although the melting point of cast iron is much lower than that of calcium carbide, iron does not melt since the quantity of heat transported to the iron surface is too low owing to the very low thermal conductivity of molten calcium carbide. After solidification the calcium carbide is treated on a breaking table, crushed in jaw crushers and passed through finer crushers to form lumps of the desired diameter.

   c. Properties. Calcium carbide is a transparent and colourless solid when pure. However, pure calcium carbide is a rarity which may be prepared on a laboratory scale by thermal decomposition of pure calcium cyanamide under vacuum. Commercial calcium carbide usually has a steel grey colour and contains about 70 to 85% CaC_2. The major impurity is calcium oxide. The melting point of the commercial product ranges from 1 800° C to 2 100° C depending on the composition.

Calcium carbide reacts with many elements and compounds. It is remarkable that calcium carbide does not react easily with a number of very reactive concentrated acids and reactive elements, but it reacts rapidly with relatively inactive materials such as water and nitrogen. In the presence of water (even with moisture in the air), calcium carbide decomposes to form acetylene ($CH{\equiv}CH$) and calcium hydroxide. Reaction equation:

$$CaC_2 + 2H_2O \rightarrow C_2H_2 + Ca(OH)_2$$

The reaction is highly exothermic and may become violent. Owing to the fact that acetylene is a poisonous and highly explosive gas, care must be taken that no moist air can penetrate into the containers in which calcium carbide is stored. For the same reason the atmosphere around furnaces and other equipment in a calcium carbide plant must be checked periodically and, if necessary, ventilated in order to avoid explosions.

The reaction of calcium carbide with nitrogen produces calcium cyanamide ($CaCN_2$). Reaction equation:

$$CaC_2 + N_2 \rightarrow CaCN_2 + C.$$

This reaction is initiated by heating to about 1 000° C and then it proceeds by itself since much heat is developed.

d. Uses and statistics. The major portion of calcium carbide is converted into acetylene (see acetylene, vol. IV) for the production of various compounds, including neoprene, vinylchloride, vinylacetate, acrylonitrile and trichloroethylene. Outside the chemical manufacturing field, acetylene obtained from calcium carbide is used for oxyacetylene welding and cutting.

Calcium carbide is used as such in metallurgy, e.g., for degraphitizing, desulphurizing and deoxidizing of iron and steel and for the production of nodular graphite in iron.

Another important application of calcium carbide is for the production of calcium cyanamide which is used as a fertiliser and also as starting material for the production of melamine, dicyandiamide and other nitrogen compounds.

The world capacity of calcium carbide was over 9 million metric tons in 1962. The capacity of some important producing countries in 1962 is shown in the following table:

In '000 metric tons annually			
Canada	550	Japan	1 200
France	450	UK	365
Germany (West)	1 200	USA	1 100
Italy	400		

Production in the USA in 1964 was about 1 million short tons. About 75% was used for the production of chemicals derived from acetylene, 16% was used for the production of calcium cyanamide, melamine and other nitrogen compounds derived from calcium cyanamide and the remaining 9% was used for all other purposes (including exports).

In the USA calcium carbide was sold at $171 per short ton in 1965. Its price in the UK was £40 17s 9d per long ton in the same year.

13.3 SILICON AND ITS COMPOUNDS

See also vol. II Glass, Ceramics (silicates and silicon nitride), Cement and concrete, Abrasives (silicon carbide), Silica and silicate minerals and rocks, and vol. IV Organo-silicon compounds and silicones.

13.3.1 Silicon (Si, atomic weight = 28.09)

In the seventeenth century it was discovered that the suitability of minerals, such as flint, sand and quartz, for the manufacture of glass was due to the presence of a particular substance which was called 'vitrifiable earth' (later 'siliceous earth'). In 1808 Berzelius tried to reduce siliceous earth by heating it with iron and carbon. He obtained ferrosilicon which is the most important form of silicon used in metallurgy today (ferrosilicon is an alloy of iron and silicon which contains silicides of iron, see vol. III). Elemental silicon was prepared for the first time by Berzelius in 1822 by treating silicon tetrafluoride with metallic potassium. He also discovered that silicon is converted into 'siliceous earth' by combustion and thus he proved that siliceous earth is an oxide of silicon (silicon dioxide, silica).

Next to oxygen, silicon is the most abundantly distributed of the elements, but it does not occur in the free state in nature on account of its affinity for oxygen. It is almost invariably found as silicon dioxide or compounds derived from silicon dioxide (see silica and silicate minerals). The principal source of silicon and its compounds is sand.

Silicon is prepared by reducing pure sand, silicon dioxide, with carbon (coke) in an electric furnace at 1 700° C. The resulting melt is cooled to solid silicon and crushed. The purity is usually 98%. This reduction can also be performed with magnesium; the reaction product must be washed with water to remove magnesium oxide.

Silicon is a lustrous grey crystalline solid melting at about 1 420° C. Although it shows a metallic appearance, its crystal lattice structure is not that of a metal but is similar to the lattice structure of diamond. Silicon also exists as black glistening plates (like graphite) and as a brown micro-crystalline powder (the so-called amorphous form), but both of these forms of silicon also have the lattice structure of diamond. The grey form is obtained by slowly cooling a melt of silicon and the black form by rapidly cooling the melt. The brown powder is obtained in the reduction process with magnesium. Silicon is a semi-conductor; the electrical resistivity of pure silicon at 0° C is about 60 000 ohm-cm.

Coarsely crystalline silicon is not very reactive. It is almost insoluble in acids and resists oxidation by air at temperatures up to 500° C. Oxidizing agents attack silicon at temperatures above 200° C. The finely divided form of silicon is much more reactive and is easily combustible in air. All forms of silicon react readily with dilute caustic alkalis to form a silicate and hydrogen. Silicon alloys with molten metals with which it forms compounds called silicides, e.g. magnesium silicide (Mg_2Si), but in some cases it is merely dissolved in the molten metal and separates again on cooling. Thus silicon can be recrystallized from molten aluminium or silver.

Silicon of 98% purity is a starting material for the production of silicon tetrachloride and organo-silicon compounds (see p. 545 and vol. IV). It is also used in the production of alloys with copper, aluminium, magnesium and nickel. Elemental silicon is also a constituent of refractory materials for furnace linings. In the furnace it oxidizes to silicon dioxide. Sometimes cermets are also prepared with elemental silicon (a cermet in a sintered metal oxide, metal carbide etc. with a binding metal, having the character of ceramics, see vol. II).

Since extremely pure silicon is a semi-conductor, it is used for electronic purposes. Silicon of 98% purity cannot be used as such. For this purpose it must be highly purified and this can be done by repeated zone refining of a rod of silicon.

Zone refining or zone melting is a process in which a rod of solid material is slowly passed through a small heated zone in which a temperature above the melting point of the solid material is maintained. When the material leaves the zone it crystallizes in a purer state than the starting material. The impurities remain in the molten zone and are collected at one end of the rod. To get very pure material the rod is slowly passed through a large number of heated zones. Heating may be performed by electrically heated coils or by applying a high-frequency electromagnetic field.

In this process various impurities can be removed from silicon, with the exception of boron. For this reason boron is often removed, before the zone refining, in a chemical process involving the conversion of the silicon into a silicon compound such as silicon tetrachloride, silicon tetraiodide or trichlorosilane ($SiHCl_3$). These compounds are purified by distillation, recrystallization or other physical method. The purified compounds are then converted into polycrystalline silicon by heating with hydrogen (silicon tetraiodide is converted into silicon by thermal decomposition). In a following zone refining process silicon can be purified to contain less than one part of impurities in 10000 million parts of silicon. In zone refining all discontinuities in the lattice of the material disappear with the formation of a large single crystal of silicon. In a modified process, developed by Bell Telephone Laboratories, USA, boron is removed by zone refining of a silicon rod in a stream of hydrogen and water vapour, thus forming boron oxide in the molten zone. The boron oxide vaporizes and condenses on the wall of the cooled tube surrounding the silicon rod.

Like various other semi-conductors, very pure silicon can be used for the production of rectifiers and transistors. The resistivity of the material is often controlled by the incorporation of traces of phosphorus, arsenic, or boron in it. The change in resistivity with a change in quantity of impurity added is shown by the following data (the contents of other impurities are much lower):

	Contents: p.p.m.	Resistivity
Transistor silicon	0.1 phosphorus	1 Ohm-cm
Rectifier silicon	0.002 phosphorus	50 Ohm-cm
Rectifier silicon	0.003 boron	50 Ohm-cm
Rectifier silicon	0.001 boron	100 Ohm-cm
Silicon for research purposes	0.00002 boron	10000 Ohm-cm

Silicon has replaced germanium in various types of transistors and rectifiers since silicon transistors and rectifiers can resist an operating temperature of about 200° C as compared with those made from germanium which resists temperatures only up to about 75° C. Pure silicon is also used as a photoresistor since its resistance changes with a change of the intensity of the light falling on it. Very pure silicon also shows photoelectric properties; hence its use in solar batteries for the conversion of solar energy into electrical energy, in pyrometers for measuring infrared radiation, for measuring visible light, and in photocells.

In 1964 production of elemental silicon (96-99%) in the USA was 69 000 short tons. The production of ferrosilicon and other silicon alloys (5-95% silicon) was 473 000 short tons gross weight in the same year. The consumption of elemental silicon in the USA was 58 000 short tons in 1964; 46 000 short tons were consumed for aluminium base alloys and 9 000 short tons for chemical compounds and silicones.

About 48 short tons high purity silicon were produced in the USA in 1964 (38 short tons polycrystal and 10 short tons single crystal). In 1962 about 46 tons high purity silicon were used for the production of 150 million diodes and 22 million transistors.

In the USA in 1964 the price of high purity silicon (polycrystal) ranged from $60 to $70 per lb and single crystal $600 per lb; silicon 98% $0.19 per lb.

13.3.2 Metal silicides

Just as carbon forms carbides with various metals, silicon forms silicides. Metal silicides are usually prepared by reduction of a mixture of a metal oxide and pure sand with carbon in an electric furnace. The preparation requires great experience, because a number of side reactions can take place at the same time, e.g., carbides can be formed. The metal silicides form crystals with a metallic lustre and high melting point. The silicide often alloys with excess of the metal; thus the composition of these products varies.

Silicides of calcium, manganese and magnesium are important de-oxidizers of molten open-hearth steel. Magnesium silicide is also used for the production of nodular cast iron, and silicides of boron, chromium, manganese, vanadium, titanium and zirconium are used for alloying with iron and steel.

Alloys of silicon with aluminium (aluminium silicide is not formed), alloys of calcium silicide with aluminium (e.g. 'alcasil'), alloys of silicon, aluminium and manganese (e.g. 'simanal') are also used as deoxidizers for steel. (For the very important ferrosilicon see vol. III.)

13.3.3 Silicon tetrachloride

Silicon tetrachloride ($SiCl_4$) was first prepared by the direct union of silicon and chlorine and modern production methods are based on this reaction. Chlorine is passed through granules of silicon, ferrosilicon or silicon carbide at red heat, but the reaction temperature, in the case of silicon, can be lowered to about 150° C by adding finely divided cobalt or copper cobalt as a catalyst. Silicon tetrachloride can also be prepared by passing chlorine through a mixture of silicon dioxide and carbon at a high temperature.

Pure silicon tetrachloride is a colourless liquid, boiling at 57.5° C. The technical product is often yellowish, owing to the presence of some ferric chloride. Silicon tetrachloride is very stable thermally, but chemically it is very reactive, e.g. with water it is decomposed to form hydrated silicon dioxide and hydrochloric acid. Alcohols also react readily with silicon tetrachloride to form alkyl silicates and hydrochloric acid (see tetraethyl silicate).

Owing to its reactivity silicon tetrachloride became important as a starting material for the production of silicon containing esters (especially tetraethyl silicate, $Si(OC_2H_5)_4$) and for the production of many other organo-silicon compounds (see silanes, siloxanes and silicones, vol. IV). Silicon tetrachloride is also used for the production of extremely pure silicon and pure colloidal silica. In war silicon tetrachloride has been used for making smoke screens.

In 1965 price of silicon tetrachloride in the USA was \$0.15 to \$0.20 per lb depending on its purity.

13.3.4 Tetraethyl silicate

Tetraethyl silicate (ethyl orthosilicate, tetraethoxysilane ($C_2H_5O)_4$ Si) is prepared by reacting silicon tetrachloride with ethyl alcohol, according to the following equation: $SiCl_4 + 4C_2H_5OH \rightarrow Si(OC_2H_5)_4 + 4HCl$. The hydrogen chloride formed during the reaction escapes.

Tetraethyl silicate is a colourless to pale yellow liquid, boiling at 168° C. Unlike tetramethyl silicate, tetraethyl silicate does not produce serious damage to the eyes. However, on inhalation, the vapours of tetraethyl silicate are toxic and like other silicon compounds may cause silicosis.

Tetraethyl silicate hydrolyses slowly when mixed with water in the presence of small quantities of an acid. Partially hydrolysed tetraethyl silicate forms gels or viscous products which are used in silicate paints for sealing and moisture-proofing stone. With water these gels hydrolyse to form silicon dioxide which is water repellent and blocks the pores in the stone. In a similar way tetraethyl silicate is used for filling cracks in bricks and other stones. A mixture of tetraethyl silicate with sand yields a heat resisting paste which can be used for the manufacture of moulds and cores for metal casting. Silicic acid-ester cement or putty is made by mixing finely ground quartz, sand or refractory brick with tetraethyl silicate, an alkaline material and alcohol. The mixture sets to a solid mass in 15-90 minutes, depending on the alcohol content. This cement is used mainly for the production of small refractory articles and for cementing together electric heating elements.

A mist of very finely divided and very pure silicon dioxide can be prepared by combustion of tetrasilicate vapours with oxygen. This mist can be deposited on the inside of lamp bulbs to improve the diffusion of light. The treatment cost per bulb is very low since the coating is only of the order of 0.1 to 1 micron in thickness.

The production of tetraethyl silicate in the USA was 2015 short tons in 1962 and its price in 1965 was \$0.65-\$0.66 per lb.

13.3.5 Sodium silicate, soluble glass, waterglass

a. History. Sodium silicate was known to both van Helmont and Glauber in the seventeenth century. Solutions of sodium silicate were named 'Oleum silicium' by Glauber. The production of sodium silicate by melting a mixture of quartz and sodium carbonate was reported by Guyton de Morveau as early as 1777. Modern industrial production of sodium silicate is based on the scientific work of J. N. von Fuchs in the first half of the nineteenth century. In 1835 Sheridan obtained a patent, British Patent

6 894, for a method of preparing a detergent composition containing sodium silicate. In the USA sodium silicate became important during the civil war of 1861-65 because it could be used in soap compositions to replace rosin which was only available in the southern States.

    b. Production. Sodium silicate is usually prepared by melting mixtures of pure sand and sodium carbonate at about 1 400° C in ordinary glass-melting furnaces fired with gas or oil (see Glass, vol. II). The following reaction takes place:

$$Na_2CO_3 + nSiO_2 \rightarrow Na_2O.nSiO_2 + CO_2 \uparrow$$

The ratio of the constituents ($Na_2O:SiO_2$) varies from 2:3 to 1:4. The materials, which must be free from water, are mixed and fed continuously at one end of the furnace. The sodium silicate produced passes slowly to the other end of the furnace and falls directly into the buckets of an endless conveyor which ascends like an escalator. As the melt travels up this conveyor it cools and solidifies. At the highest point the buckets are inverted and emptied, and the lumps of solid anhydrous sodium silicate are transported to storage or to dissolvers.

    A waterglass solution is readily obtained either by treating the solid lumps in an autoclave with steam under a pressure of 5 atm at 140° C, or by passing molten sodium silicate directly into water in a slowly rotating drum at atmospheric pressure. In both types of dissolvers, the solutions must be effectively diluted since overconcentration may cause the formation of solid hydrated masses in the equipment. The resulting solution is usually turbid, owing to unmelted sand and impurities, the major portion of which settles out rapidly in large settling tanks. The remaining fine solids are removed by means of a filter press.

    Non-crystalline hydrated solids which dissolve more rapidly than the anhydrous sodium silicate are produced from pure sodium silicate solutions by evaporation in multi-effect evaporators, followed by drying on a drum dryer or in a spray dryer. Crystalline hydrated solids are prepared by evaporating seeded solutions of sodium silicate in multiple-effect evaporators under carefully controlled conditions. Caustic soda is added to adjust the $SiO_2:Na_2O$ ratio. The crystals are separated from the mother liquor by centrifuging.

    In Europe sodium silicate is often produced from siliceous sand, carbon and sodium sulphate; the sulphate provides a cheap source of the necessary alkali. The carbon added to the mixture reduces the sulphate to sulphite and sulphur. The main reaction may be represented by the following equation:

$$2Na_2SO_4 + 2C + nSiO_2 \rightarrow 2Na_2O.nSiO_2 + S \uparrow + SO_2 \uparrow + 2CO_2. \uparrow$$

The amount of carbon is critical. If too much coke is used, a dark brown colour results from polysulphides and ferric sulphide (formed from traces of iron compounds which are present in the sand). If insufficient carbon is present, a destructive effect on the fire-brick lining of the furnace occurs owing to formation of a corrosive layer of molten sodium sulphate on the melt of sodium silicate. In addition the resulting sodium silicate is less pure. To obtain a product which is as pure as possible, the sodium silicate is withdrawn from the lower levels of a furnace carrying a deep bed of molten sodium silicate. In general sodium silicate obtained from sodium sulphate is less pure than that made from sodium carbonate.

Sodium silicate solutions having a SiO_2:Na_2O ratio up to 2:1 can also be prepared by dissolving sand in liquid caustic soda at elevated temperatures, usually under pressure. However, this process is commercially less important.

c. *Commercial products and their properties.* Several non-crystalline, anhydrous, vitreous sodium silicates, having varying silica:alkali ratios and water contents, are available in the form of white to grey-white lumps or powders. Anhydrous and hydrated products obtained by evaporating solutions of sodium silicate form either transparent vitreous solids or colourless crystals. The most important crystalline products are sodium metasilicate pentahydrate ($Na_2O.SiO_2.5H_2O$ or $Na_2SiO_3.5H_2O$), which melts at 72°, and sodium sesquisilicate ($3Na_2O.SiO_2.11H_2O$ or $Na_3HSiO_4.5H_2O$), which melts at 88° C. The melting points of the anhydrous compounds are 1 089° and 1 122° C respectively.

The SiO_2:Na_2O ratio of commercial solutions varies from 1.6:1 to 3.75:1. The total solids content varies from 37 to 54% by weight and the specific gravity from 37° Bé to 69° Bé. At the highest concentration such solutions are often syrupy. The types which are rich in silicon dioxide show high viscosity even at a relatively low concentration. Syrupy solutions of sodium silicate are coagulated by adding dehydrating agents. With acids, colloidal hydrated silicon dioxide is precipitated owing to decomposition of the sodium silicate (see silicon dioxide, p. 553).

Both solid and liquid sodium silicates are marketed as so-called 'neutral glass', with a low alkali content, and 'alkaline glass', with a high alkali content. These names are misleading since all sodium silicates are alkaline. Highly alkaline solutions containing sodium orthosilicate ($2Na_2O.SiO_2$ or Na_4SiO_4) are also known. These solutions can be prepared by adding sodium hydroxide to commercial sodium silicate solutions; solid products can be obtained by evaporation.

d. *Uses.* (i) For making other silicon compounds: the largest outlet for sodium silicate lies in the production of other silicon compounds, especially silica gel (silicon dioxide) for use as a catalyst, adsorbent and filtering material. Important quantities of sodium silicate are also used for the production of insoluble silicates of calcium, magnesium, aluminium (see synthetic zeolites, ch. 4, p. 136), copper, lead zinc, etc.

(ii) In detergents. The second largest consumer of sodium silicate is the detergent and soap industry. The cleansing action of sodium silicate solutions is due to their alkaline reaction and their surface-active properties. Sodium metasilicate and sodium sesquisilicate are especially used in washing powders, mixed with soap or synthetic detergents, for washing textiles etc. In war time large amounts were used as fillers in soap to effect a saving of the latter. Sodium silicates are excellent wetting agents for metal and earthenware surfaces; hence their use in cleansing compositions for washing bottles, earthenware, metal containers etc. The cleansing action is also applied in the cleaning of rough castings which are sprayed with fine, powerful jets of the solution, often at high temperatures; even strongly adherent casting sand can be removed in this way. Owing to its surface-active properties, sodium silicate is a component of suspension liquide used for ore purification (flotation), for the purification of china clay and for the separation of arsenic from industrial wastes.

(iii) In adhesives. The third large-scale application of sodium silicate is based on the marked adhesion of solid sodium silicates to various materials such as glass, wood (adhesive for veneer), metal and paper. Large amounts of sodium silicate are used as in adhesives for making fibre board and corrugated paper board, where it is used in the form of a syrupy solution which sets by loss of moisture. The solutions may be used either as such or as a mixture with pipe-clay, starch etc. The setting time can be accelerated by applying heat. Sodium silicate solutions are also used for the production of abrasive coated paper (sandpaper). A layer of adhesive is applied to the paper which is dried after pressing granules of sand into the adhesive layer. Large quantities of sodium silicate are also used for sealing paper box-flaps.

(iv) As a binder. Sodium silicate is used also as a binder for various powders and granular materials to form bricks or other moulded objects. Setting of binders may occur either by loss of mosisture or by the formation of silica gel or heavy metal silicates. Owing to the resistance of silicates to high temperatures, sodium silicate is used as a fire-resistant binder for asbestos and other insulation materials. The binding of finely divided abrasives to form abrasive stones is also of importance. Acid resistant and refractory materials in finely divided form can also be bound in a similar way. Dry mixtures of sodium silicate with metal salts (e.g. alum) are commercially available as 'acid cement'. If this is mixed with water, chemical reactions take place to yield silicon dioxide and silicates, which are not attacked by acids. This binder is therefore used for the manufacture of acid-resistant bricks which can be used as a lining for tanks. Sodium silicate can also be used as a binder in coal briquettes.

Sodium silicate is used as a binder in paints for coating plaster, stucco and cement. It is also used for colouring slate or rock granules; the granules are treated with a mixture of a pigment and a sodium silicate binder. The coloured granules are spread on asphalt or the like and embedded to provide a decorative and fire resisting coating for roofs. Fluorescent materials can be attached to the inside surface of glasses for fluorescent lamps by dusting them over a moist coating of sodium silicate applied to the inside surface.

Sodium silicate is being used increasingly in the manufacture of moulds and cores for metal casting. These cores are made from sand and a solution of sodium silicate and then treated with carbon dioxide to form a gel of silicon dioxide from the sodium silicate so that the mould can be handled (see casting of iron, vol. III).

Of importance also is the process in which rocks or stones which are not completely adherent to one another are strengthened; this may be effected by injecting a sodium silicate solution in the neighbourhood of the weak spots. There is then injected at the same point a solution of calcium chloride which reacts with sodium silicate to form an insoluble calcium silicate of high load-bearing strength. A solution of aluminium sulphate or other compounds which form insoluble silicates with sodium silicate can also be used. Sodium silicate can also be incorporated into concrete for the formation of a hard, dust-free surface.

(v) As a cement. Mixtures of sodium silicate with several other materials are used as cement. A somewhat arbitrary distinction between adhesives and cement is that the former are applied as a thin fluid film to unite surfaces nearly in contact, whereas the latter are viscous or plastic mixtures which occupy more space between the

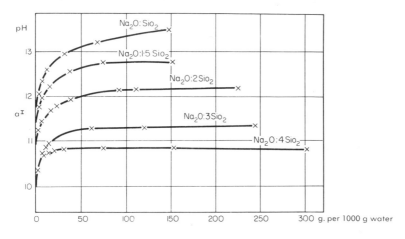

Fig. 13.4 Hydrogen-ion concentrations (pH values) of solutions of 5 types of waterglass (sodium silicate). A large proportion of the curves takes the form of (almost) horizontal lines, which show that the pH value changes hardly at all as the solutions become stronger, so that they have a marked buffering effect.

materials they bind. Silicate cement is usually a mixture of sodium silicate (preferably with a $SiO_2:Na_2O$ ratio 3.3:1) with an inert filler, such as quartz, sand, barytes, refractory brick-dust etc. In addition, the mixture must contain a substance which reacts rapidly with the silicate, e.g. sodium silicofluoride or calcium chloride. These cements harden rapidly when mixed with water and are excellent for use on cement or concrete floors to which tiles are to be cemented. The cement should be brushed on the joints with hydrochloric acid to neutralize any alkali which is liberated. If the floor is liable to come into contact with sulphuric acid, potassium silicate is preferred to sodium silicate so as to prevent the formation of hydrated sodium sulphate crystals which destroy the cement owing to expansion. Potassium sulphate forms only anhydrous crystals which occupy a smaller volume.

(vi) Miscellaneous uses. Small quantities of sodium silicate are used for various other purposes. Thus sodium silicate is used for waterproofing stone etc. Stone, which is permeable to moisture, is sprayed with a sodium silicate solution and then with hydrochloric acid to precipitate silicon dioxide in the pores, thus blocking them up. Common salt is formed at the same time and must sometimes be leached out by washing with water. For this reason sodium silicate is often replaced by organic silicates such as ethyl silicate.

Wooden barrels or cases for oils and fats are treated internally with a solution of sodium silicate. After drying, the layer of solid sodium silicate formed prevents the passage of material from the wood into the contents and vice versa. For certain packaging applications, paper or cardboard is sprayed with a sodium silicate solution to make it grease-resistant.

Sodium silicate is also used as a protective coating. Small quantities of sodium silicate added to cleansing compositions containing soda ash prevent corrosion of aluminium and tin when cleaned with these compositions. A protective coating is formed by surface reactions and further corrosion is prevented.

Copper wires can be insulated by passing the wires through a solution of sodium silicate followed by heating the wires. A highly insulating layer is then formed, which is resistant to bending and adheres strongly to the wire.

Eggs can be preserved by placing them in a 3% solution of sodium silicate. A gel of silicon dioxide is formed in the presence of carbon dioxide from air. The rate of coagulation can be speeded up by stirring in a little hydrochloric acid. The eggs retain their flavour better than when lime is used for their preservation.

Sodium silicate can also be used as a buffer since the pH of its solutions does not change over a large range of concentrations (see fig. 13.4).

e. Statistics. The production of sodium silicates (in metric tons overall weight) by a few important producing countries is shown in the following table:

	1958	1960	1962	1964
	In metric tons overall weight			
France liquid	134000	150000	178000	208000
solid	70000	74000	87000	87000
Germany (West)	198000*	238000	261000*	254000*
Japan	122000	167000	201000	—
USA liquid and vitreous (anhydrous basis)	431000	448000	498000	508000
Metasilicate pentahydrate	178000	174000	181000	—
Orthosilicate (anhydrous)	35000	35000	36000	—

(*All silicon compounds in terms of SiO_2 excluding silicon carbide and silicones.)

The United Kingdom produces more than enough to cover home demand. The following quantities were exported:

	1958	1960	1962	1964
In long tons	17200	15000	21200	19200
Value	£312000	£308000	£411000	£427000

The consumption of liquid and vitreous sodium silicate in the USA classified according to use is shown by the following breakdown for 1964:

In % by weight			
Catalysts and silica gel	35	Refractory, ceramic use	2
Detergents and soap	15	Textile industry	2
Boxboard and adhesives	13	Welding rod coating	1
Pigments (e.g. for rubber)	12	Foundry core binder	1
Water treatment	2	Roofing granules	1
Paper industry	2	Other uses	12
Metal ore flocculant	2	Total	100

Sodium metasilicate is mainly used in detergents and soaps.

In the United Kingdom sodium metasilicate was sold at £30 per long ton.

In the USA sodium silicate was sold at the following prices in 1965:

	per 100 lb
Sodium silicate liquid 40° Bé, Na_2O/SiO_2, 1:3.2	$1.20-1.70
Sodium silicate solid	$3.40
Sodium metasilicate pentahydrate	$4.45-6.70
Sodium orthosilicate	$6.70-7.65
Sodium sesquisilicate anhydr.	$5.70-6.20

f. Literature

J. G. VAIL. *Soluble silicates. Their properties and uses,* 2 vols., American Chemical Society Monograph Series, No. 116, New York, Reinhold Publishing Corporation, 1952.

N. A. DE BRUYNE and R. HOUWINK. *Adhesion and adhesives,* Amsterdam, Elsevier Publishing Company, 1951.

13.3.6 Potassium silicate

Potassium silicate is prepared in a similar way to sodium silicate. A vitreous product results. Usually the molar ratio $SiO_2:K_2O$ varies from 1:3.3 to 4.2, approximately corresponding with the formula for potassium tetrasilicate ($K_2Si_4O_9$ or $K_2O.4SiO_2$). Potassium silicate may be used for the same purposes as sodium silicate, which is usually preferred because it is cheaper. In some circumstances potassium silicate shows advantages over sodium silicate (see also silicate cement, p. 549). For example, it has much less tendency to form a white efflorescence when used in paints; hence its use in e.g. water paints, for coloured mural paintings. Potassium silicate is preferred as a binder in the manufacture of carbon arc-light electrodes to avoid the intense yellow colour of the light caused by sodium and its compounds. Potassium silicate is also used for coating welding rods; the potassium silicate coating yields a weld metal of higher tensile strength and lower elongation than does the corresponding sodium silicate. Television tubes to be coated with luminescent materials are cleaned with potassium silicate and then coated with the luminescent material using potassium silicate as a binder. An extremely pure silicate is required for this purpose.

In the USA potassium silicate glass grade was sold at $18 per 100 lb in 1965.

13.3.7 Synthetic insoluble silicates

(For naturally occuring silicates see silicate minerals, vol. II.)

Aluminium silicates, ($Al_2O_3.nSiO_2$) are precipitated by mixing solutions of sodium silicate and aluminium sulphate. The composition of the aluminium silicates depends on the reaction conditions; this is true also for other artificially prepared insoluble silicates. Aluminium silicates are used in the sizing of paper, for the production of ultramarine (see pigments in vol. V) and as a filler in rubber. Carefully purified aluminium silicates are used as catalysts and catalyst supports especially in petroleum refining. The best known artificial aluminosilicates are the zeolites prepared by mixing solutions of sodium silicate and sodium aluminate to form a hydrous gel of composition corresponding to the formula $Na_2O.Al_2O_3.nSiO_2.xH_2O$ (see ion exchange, p. 136).

Calcium silicates ($CaO.nSiO_2.xH_2O$) are prepared by mixing solutions of sodium silicate and a soluble calcium salt. The resulting hydrated calcium silicates are used as fillers for rubber and as an adsorbent for decolorizing and purifying mineral oil, sugar solutions, fermented beverages etc. (See also Ceramics, Glass and Cement, vol. II.)

Magnesium silicates ($MgO.nSiO_2.xH_2O$) prepared by mixing solutions of sodium silicate and magnesium salts are used for decolorizing oils, for stabilizing emulsions of mineral oils and for preventing the rancidity of soaps. Magnesium silicates are also used in boiler water treatment, as pharmaceuticals (anti-acids, control of stomach ulcers), as stabilizers for peroxides and as extenders for house paints.

Copper silicates ($CuSiO_3.H_2O$ and $CuSiO_3.2H_2O$) can be precipitated by adding sodium silicate to an ammoniacal copper solution. These silicates are used as pigments and as insecticides.

Anhydrous *lead silicates,* prepared by roasting lead oxide with silica, are used as pigments. Lead silicates are also used to protect rubber against attack by sunlight since they are opaque to ultra-violet radiation.

Zinc silicates prepared by any method mentioned above are used for the production of phosphors (see ch. 16).

13.3.8 Silicon dioxide (synthetic amorphous silica)

Silicon dioxide (silica, SiO_2) occurs naturally in various forms and degrees of purity. See silica minerals: quartz, quartzite, sand, gravel, chalcedony, flint (stones), opal, agate, tripoli and diatomite (vol. II).

Artificially prepared silicon dioxide is also available in various forms generally known as silica gel, silica aerogel and colloidal silica. These products are amorphous (see quartz for crystalline modifications of silicon dioxide and their properties). Silica gel was already known in 1640 to van Helmont who reported that it is precipitated by adding an acid to a solution prepared by dissolving silica in caustic alkali. In the USA the commercial production of silica gel was started in 1920. Other forms of synthetic silica were prepared for the first time at the beginning of the second world war.

a. Silica gel. Silica gel is prepared by mixing a sodium silicate solution with a mineral acid. A concentrated dispersion of very finely divided particles of hydrated silicon dioxide (a hydrosol of silica or silicic acid) results:

$$Na_2SiO_3 + 2HCl + nH_2O \rightarrow 2NaCl + SiO_2.nH_2O + H_2O.$$

Owing to polymerization of silica molecules, the hydrosol is converted into a white jelly-like precipitate (silica gel). The resulting gel is broken up mechanically, washed with water to remove salt and dried. In the last stage of the process, the polymerization of silica is completed and partially dehydrated microporous granules are formed. Various silica gels having a wide range of physical properties can be prepared by modifying the reaction conditions such as concentration, pH, reaction temperature, temperature of the washing water, drying temperature etc. For example, the pore diameter of the gel can be enlarged by heating the gel in an autoclave before drying. Two typical members of the group of silica gels are known respectively as regular-density and low-density silica gel. The differences in the physical properties are shown in fig. 13.5. The regular density type has a higher adsorption capacity for water vapour

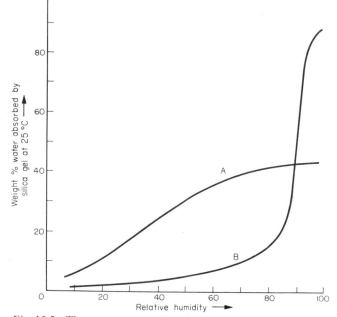

Fig. 13.5 The water vapour adsorption capacity of two types of silica gel.

silica gel	A regular density	B low density
bulk density	0.7	0.7
true density (specific gravity) of amourphous silica	2.2	2.2
surface area in m²/g	750-850	300-350
pore diameter in Å (average)	22-26	100-150
loss on ignition at 1000° C in % (water content)	6	3-4

and other vapours than the low density type, but the opposite is true in the vicinity of saturation pressure of the vapour to be adsorbed.

Owing to its high adsorption capacity for water vapour, silica gel is widely used to dry air and other gases (see air conditioning, p. 113; dehydrating agents, p. 112; drying of gases to be liquefied, p. 45). Silica gel saturated with water can be regenerated by heating at temperatures up to 175° C. Silica gel is also used for drying organic compounds in the liquid phase, especially halogenated refrigerants such as Freons. Since silica gel is selective in its adsorbing properties it is used in chromatography. Columns filled with a silica gel of relatively fine particle size are used to separate hydrocarbon mixtures in the petroleum industry and various pharmaceutical preparations in the pharmaceutical industry.

Silica gel is also used in catalyst mixtures, e.g. synthetic silica-alumina, silica-magnesia and silica-zirconia are used as catalysts in oil cracking. Silica gel is also a support for various other catalysts, e.g. a platinum-silica gel catalyst can be used for the oxidation of sulphur dioxide to sulphur trioxide and vanadium pentoxide on silica gel catalyses the oxidation of naphthalene to phthalic anhydride.

b. Silica aerogel. Silica aerogel closely resembles silica gel. It is prepared by washing a wet hydrogel with a low-boiling, water-miscible organic liquid, e.g. a low boiling alcohol. In this way all the water is removed and replaced by the alcohol. The resulting product is heated in an autoclave and dried. Usually a relatively fine powder (particle size 0.5 to 5 microns) having very large pores results, since shrinkage of the pores in the gel structure during drying is avoided owing to the fact that the surface tension of the alcohol is much lower than that of water. In the USA aerogels of this type are available under the name 'Santocel' (Monsanto Chemical Co) and 'Syloid' (Davison Chemical Co).

Owing to its macroporous structure, the bulk density and the water-vapour adsorption capacity of aerogel are lower than those of silica gel. Silica aerogel is used in electrical and thermal insulation (especially low temperature insulation), as a filler for some synthetic rubbers (e.g. silicone rubber) and paper, as a thickener and thixotropic agent for polyester and epoxy resins and as an inert diluent and anti-caking agent for insecticides. Varnishes, lacquers and films can be flatted to any degree of lustre from semi-glosses to dead flats by incorporating aerogel.

c. Colloidal silica (or activated silica). Colloidal silica is a very finely divided silica (particle size 0.01 to 0.02 microns) which can be prepared in various ways.

In the oldest process finely divided silica is precipitated by adding an acid to a solution of sodium silicate. The formation of a gel structure is prevented by diluting the resulting dispersion, by adding a precipitating salt, by quick setting at high pH or by freezing. The product is available in the form of an aqueous dispersion or as a dry solid. Aqueous dispersions are usually prepared by deionizing a dilute solution of sodium silicate by means of cation or base exchange resins.

In another process, developed in Germany, colloidal silica is obtained by the combustion of silicon tetrachloride in a mixture of oxygen and hydrogen. A smoke consisting of silicon dioxide and hydrogen chloride gas is obtained. The silicon dioxide, which is divided too finely to settle as such from the gas stream, is allowed to agglomerate by passing it through a series of large-diameter pipes from which the product is passed into cyclones to separate the solids from the hydrochloric acid gas.

Very pure colloidal silica can be obtained by combustion of tetraethyl silicate, but this process is very expensive owing to material costs.

Colloidal silica is available as a white powder and as a milky suspension under various trade names. In the USA precipitated colloidal silica is known under trade names such as 'Hy-Sil' (Pitsburg Plate Glass Co) and 'Si-o-Lite' (Mallinckrodt Chemical Works). Colloidal silica prepared by burning silicon tetrachloride is known under the trade names 'Aerosil' (Degussa, Germany), 'Cabosil' (G. L. Cabot, USA) and 'DC silica' (Dow Corning Corp., USA). Unlike silica gel and aerogel, colloidal silica is not porous and thus its adsorption capacity for vapours and liquids is very low. When agitated with water colloidal silica forms stable dispersions. Colloidal silica has similar applications to those of silica aerogel. In addition it is used as an aid to coagulation in water treatment and as a thickener for various liquids (inks, cosmetics, lubricating oils and greases, floor polishes etc.). Colloidal silica can also be used in paints to retard settling of high density pigments and to produce a matt finish. In rubber and plastics it is used to increase their tensile strength and in polyurethane foams to increase the compression strength. Silica dispersions can be used for spraying on clean carpets and other fibrous materials; the silica covering remains adherent to them. For this reason, the fibres can then not easily pick up any other substances e.g. dirt. It is remarkable that the silica particles, once embedded, resist removal by vacuum cleaners or carpet sweepers.

Colloidal silica and silica aerogel can be made water-repellent by heating them with an alcohol and potash in an autoclave at 375° C, followed by cooling in an atmosphere of alcohol vapour. The resulting product is used as a thickener for greases and as a reinforcement for silicone rubber.

In the USA the various forms of silica are sold at prices between $0.20 to $1.60 per lb depending on their properties.

13.4 TIN COMPOUNDS (Sn, atomic weight = 118.69)

13.4.1 Tin oxides
Stannous oxide (tin oxide, SnO) is prepared by mixing solutions of an alkali and stannous chloride to form a white precipitate of stannous hydroxide, $Sn(OH)_2$, or hydrated stannous oxide and converting the latter into the oxide by heating it at about 100° C in absence of air. Stannous oxide is usually a blue-black substance which decomposes at 385° C to form stannic oxide and tin. Stannous oxide and hydroxide have marked tendency to pass into the corresponding stannic compounds, hence their use as reducing agents, e.g. in vat dyeing and dye printing of cotton. Stannous oxide is also used in the production of other stannous salts. Ruby glass can be obtained by adding small quantities of a mixture of stannous oxide and a copper or gold compound to flint glass. In the USA stannous oxide was sold at $2.20 to 2.40 per lb in 1965.

Stannic oxide (tin dioxide, SnO_2) occurs naturally as the mineral cassiterite, which is used for the production of metallic tin (see vol. III). Cassiterite is not used as a starting material for the production of tin compounds because of its rather inert nature.

Artificial stannic oxide is produced in various ways. In one process molten tin is oxidized in air, either by passing air over the melt or by 'atomizing' tin by means of high-pressure steam followed by burning the 'atomized' tin in air. Stannic oxide can also be prepared by hydrolysing stannic chloride by means of steam at high temperatures, or by calcining hydrated stannic oxide which in turn is obtained from sodium stannate (see below).

Stannic oxide is a white crystalline solid which sublimes at about 1 800° C. It is used to make white enamels, glazes and glassware opaque. A pink glaze can be obtained by melting a mixture of stannic oxide, calcium oxide and chromium oxide with the glaze composition. This mixture of oxides is also used as an overglaze colour on faience earthenware. Stannic oxide and also a sintered product of lead oxide and stannic oxide (lead stannate or tin ash) are used, under the name of 'putty powder', for polishing glass, metal and stone such as marble and granite. In the USA stannic oxide was sold at $1.88 to 1.89 per lb in 1965.

13.4.2 Tin halides
Stannous chloride (tin salt, tin dichloride, $SnCl_2$) is prepared in the form of an anhydrous salt by reacting impure molten tin with chlorine or hydrochloric acid gas. Stannous chloride monohydrate is obtained by dissolving tin in hydrochloric acid solution. Both salts are white crystalline products. The monohydrate melts at 37.7° C and the anhydrous salt at 247° C. Solutions of stannous chloride tend to hydrolyse.

Hydrolysis is prevented by adding a small amount of hydrochloric acid. Stannous chloride is used for the production of other stannous salts. Because of its strong reducing power stannous chloride is used as reducing agent in the production of organic chemicals, in silvering mirrors, in vat dyeing and dye printing of cotton and in the production of Cassius purple for colouring glazes (see gold compounds, ch. 14, p. 574). Stannous chloride is also used as a catalyst in organic chemical syntheses, as an anti sludging agent in lubricating oils and as a perfume stabilizer in soaps. Stannous chloride is also used in tinning of metals and in tin coating of paper. In the USA, stannous chloride was sold at $1.48 to 1.84 per lb in 1965.

Stannic chloride (tin chloride, tin tetrachloride, butter of tin, $SnCl_4$) is usually prepared by the chlorination of impure molten tin. Stannous chloride may also be formed but stannic chloride can be separated from it easily, since it is a gas at the operating temperature. Stannic chloride forms a colourless, fuming, caustic liquid boiling at 114° C. It can be converted into a semi-solid mixture of hydrates by adding water. Hence the name 'butter of tin' which is a commercial product. Stannic chloride is used in the textile industry as a mordant in printing and for sizing silk. Before the second world war sizing of silk accounted for most of the world's consumption, but after the second World War less natural silk was produced and consequently the consumption of stannic chloride decreased rapidly. Stannic chloride is used also for the production of fuchsine, colour lakes and blueprint papers. The production of organo-tin compounds from stannic chloride is of growing importance today. In the USA stannic chloride (anhydrous) was sold at $1.18 to 1.20 per lb in 1965.

Stannous fluoride (SnF_2), a white crystalline powder, is prepared by dissolving stannous oxide in hydrofluoric acid. It is used in dentifrices as an agent for decreasing the incidence of dental caries.

13.4.3 Stannous sulphate

Stannous sulphate ($SnSO_4$) can be crystallized from a solution prepared by dissolving stannous oxide or tin in sulphuric acid. It is a white crystalline solid which decomposes at temperatures above 360° C. Solutions of stannous sulphate are used in the tin plating of steel wire before drawing. The coated wire passes more easily through the die than the uncoated wire. Stannous sulphate is also used in electroplating of steel strip. In the USA stannous sulphate was sold at $1.55 to 1.89 per lb in 1965.

13.4.4 Stannates

Sodium stannate ($Na_2SnO_3 \cdot 3H_2O$ or $Na_2Sn(OH)_6$) is obtained on a large scale in an alkaline detinning process for recovering tin from tin plate scrap. In this process tin is leached by dissolving in a hot solution of caustic soda and sodium nitrate (see vol. III). Sodium stannate is also prepared by fusing cassiterite with caustic soda. Sodium stannate is a white or colourless crystalline product which slowly absorbs carbon dioxide from air to form sodium carbonate and hydrated stannic oxide. It dissolves in cold water, but its solubility decreases with increasing temperature. Sodium stannate is mainly used in tin plating and for the electrolytic production of tin. It is used also as a mordant in dyeing and for production of stannic oxide. A jelly-like precipitate of hydrated stannic oxide ($SnO_2 \cdot nH_2O$) is formed by adding an acid to a solution of sodium stannate. The hydrated product can be converted into the anhydrous compound by calcining it. In the USA the price of sodium stannate was $1.03 to 1.11 per lb in 1965.

Other stannates such as the stannates of barium, calcium, magnesium and lead can be precipitated from a sodium stannate solution by adding a soluble salt of the corresponding metal. These stannates may also be prepared by fusing metal oxides with stannic oxide. The resulting products are used in glass and in ceramic bodies for electronic apparatus (e.g. dielectrics for capacitors etc.).

13.4.5 Organo-tin compounds

Tetra-alkyl and tetra-aryl tin compounds can be prepared by reacting stannic chloride with an alkyl or arylmagnesium halide in diethyl ether according to the following equation in which R represents an alkyl or aryl group:

$$SnCl_4 + 4RMgCl \rightarrow R_4Sn + 4MgCl_2$$

The most important tetra organo-tin compounds are tetrabutyl, tetraoctyl and tetraphenyl tin, which are the starting materials for various other organo-tin compounds. Tetrabutyl tin and tetraphenyl tin are also used as polymerization catalysts. Tetraphenyl tin is a corrosion inhibitor in transformer oil.

Trialkyl and triaryl tin chloride can be prepared by heating a mixture of stannic chloride and a tetra-alkyl or tetra-aryl tin compound in molar proportions of 1:3:

$$3 R_4Sn + SnCl_4 \rightarrow 3 R_3SnCl + RCl.$$

The resulting trialkyl or triaryl tin chloride can be converted into the corresponding *oxide or hydroxide* by heating it with 20% caustic soda solution. These oxides and hydroxides are the starting materials for the production of other trialkyl tin and triaryl tin compounds (e.g. the acetates are obtained by treating them with acetic acid). Trialkyl tin and triaryl tin compounds show an anti-microbiological activity. Thus *tributyl tin oxide* and *tributyl tin acetate* are used in textiles, paper and plastics as a rodenticide and in water paints, adhesives and plastics for mildew control. Salts such as tributyl tin naphthenate can be used in oil paints. In paper making tributyl tin oxide is also used to combat slime-forming micro-organisms. Tributyl tin oxide can also be used in wood preservation but it cannot be used as a fungicide in agriculture, since it is strongly toxic to plants. *Triphenyl tin hydroxide* and *triphenyl tin acetate* are suitable for use in agriculture.

Dialkyl tin dichlorides are prepared by heating a mixture of equimolar portions of stannic chloride and tetra-alkyl tin. Reaction equation:

$$SnCl_4 + R_4Sn \rightarrow 2 SnR_2Cl_2 + 2 RCl$$

Dialkyl tin dichlorides can be converted into the corresponding oxides by heating them with 20% caustic soda solution. The resulting oxides are starting materials for the production of various dialkyl tin salts which are usually prepared by treating the oxides with acids. *Dibutyl tin dilaurate, dimaleate, dodecyl mercaptide* and various other dibutyl tin salts are used as stabilizers in polyvinylchloride and other halogen containing compounds. The dibutyl tin salts are also used as catalysts in polymerization processes (e.g. for the production of silicones). *Dioctyl tin salts* are used for the same purposes. Since these are less toxic than the corresponding dibutyl tin compounds, they are also used as stabilizers in polyvinylchloride sheets for packaging food. As stated above, the trialkyl and triaryl tin compounds are used as biocides and the dialkyl tin compounds are used as stabilizers for polyvinylchloride (p.v.c.) etc. *Dibutyl tin dilaurate* is also used for curing worms in chickens.

13.4.6 Statistics

The world production of tin was 280 000 long tons in 1965 (including recovered tin). The consumption of tin in its compounds is estimated at about 2 to 4% (excluding tin compounds which are obtained as intermediates in tin production). The world production of organo-tin compounds was estimated at 1 800 long tons in 1965. This is about 3% of the total consumption of tin compounds.

The consumption of tin in the USA and UK is shown in the following table (in long tons):

	1955	1957	1959	1961	1963	1965
UK : total	23 000	22 000	21 000	22 000	22 100	21 000
for chemicals	1 100	1 100	1 300	1 700	1 800	1 600
USA: total	91 000	83 000	78 000	79 000	80 000	85 000
for chemicals	1 700	1 600	1 900	2 100	2 500	2 900

The UK exported the following quantities of tin dioxide:

	1955	1957	1959	1961	1962	1954
In long tons	360	430	460	540	520	406
Value	£343 000	£311 000	£322 000	£440 000	£415 000	£427 000

13.5 LEAD COMPOUNDS (Pb, atomic weight = 207.19)

13.5.1 Lead sulphide

Lead sulphide (PbS) is found in nature as the mineral galena which is the principal material for the production of lead (see lead ores and metallic lead, vol. III). Sometimes galena is found in the form of pure black crystals with a metallic lustre. Artificial lead sulphide can be prepared by passing hydrogen sulphide through a solution of a lead salt or by heating the salt in sulphur vapour.

Formerly galena crystals were important as rectifiers in radio engineering. Since pure galena is a photoresistor in infrared light, it is used in infrared radiation detectors for observing people in the dark and for the detection of heat radiation of rockets, jet planes etc.

13.5.2 Lead monoxide

Lead monoxide (yellow lead oxide, litharge, PbO) is formed by roasting the lead ores (lead sulphide etc.) in air. The resulting crude product is an intermediate in the production of metallic lead (see vol. III).

Lead monoxide for use in the chemical industry is produced by oxidation of molten lead with air at a temperature above 550° C. In the Barton process molten lead is fed into a mechanical furnace provided with stirring paddles. The molten lead is stirred and splashed by the paddles and thus treated with air which is fed in through a pipe in the cover of the furnace. The resulting mist of finely divided lead monoxide, and a little lead, escapes with the air and is collected in condensing chambers in which it is rapidly cooled. The major portion of the escaping lead falls back into the furnace, since the mist passes through an upright shaft before entering the condensing chambers. The resulting crude product, containing 1 to 3% metallic lead, is finely ground and sold as such. The ground lead oxide may be stirred for some hours at 700° C in the presence of air to convert the remaining lead into lead monoxide. After removal from the reactor the hot oxide must be cooled rapidly to a temperature below 300° C to prevent its oxidation to minium, Pb_3O_4. In another process molten lead is 'atomised' in a shaft furnace. The very finely divided lead falls down through an air stream and passes through a zone heated at 1 400° C in which lead evaporates and burns to very finely divided lead oxide, which is cooled rapidly by passing it through the cold zone of the shaft furnace.

The lead monoxide obtained in the processes described above is a powder consisting of yellow orthorhombic crystals (β-lead monoxide or massicot) melting at 884° C. Its solubility in water is low (1.2 mg dissolve in 100 g water at 20° C). Lead monoxide can also form red to orange-red tetragonal crystals (α-lead monoxide or litharge). The latter is the stable modification of lead monoxide at room temperature, but the yellow form is stable since the conversion velocity is extremely low at room temperature. At temperatures above 500° C the yellow modification is stable, hence its formation in the production processes. The red modification can be obtained by cooling a melt of lead monoxide. The inner part of the solidified mass cools very slowly and is converted into the red form. The outer part of the cake which cools rapidly consists of yellow oxide and protects the inner part from oxidation by air. There is a tendency to use the name 'litharge' also for the yellow oxide since the latter is preferred for commercial use today on account of its higher reactivity.

Like other lead compounds which are sufficiently soluble in digestive juices, lead monoxide is very toxic. The daily output of normal persons is about 0.3 mg and the daily intake of lead in the food of American adults is of the same order of magnitude. Thus accumulation of lead in the human body can occur when the intake increases. For this reason care must be taken that the lead content of beverages and food does not exceed predetermined quantities (about 0.1 to 2 p.p.m. depending on the kind of food are permitted). Lead pipes and vessels must not be used in preparing and storing food.

The most important use of lead monoxide is for the production of plates for storage batteries. The impure lead monoxide obtained in the Barton process (see above) is more widely used for this purpose than completely oxidized lead monoxide. Lead monoxide is also important for the production of lead compounds, e.g. lead acetate and various lead pigments such as minium (red lead oxide), basic lead carbonate (white lead), lead chromate, lead titanate etc. (see also pigments, vol. V). Nowadays lead monoxide itself is no longer important as a pigment. Lead monoxide is also a starting material for the production of lead arsenate (see p. 399) and for the preparation of sodium plumbite solutions (by dissolving lead monoxide in caustic soda) for removing sulphur in gasoline. Lead monoxide is also a component of litharge glass, glazes and enamels and a compounding ingredient in rubber manufacture.

In the USA lead monoxide was sold at \$360-380 per short ton in 1965 (\$0.18-0.19 per lb). The price in the UK was £ 142 5s per long ton in 1965.

13.5.3 Other lead oxides

Trilead tetraoxide (minium, red lead oxide, Pb_3O_4) is considered to be lead plumbate (Pb_2PbO_4), i.e. a lead salt of orthoplumbic acid (H_4PbO_4). It is prepared by oxidizing lead monoxide in air at a temperature of about 450° C. In order to avoid the decomposition to lead monoxide the reaction mixture must not be heated above 530° C. Processes for the oxidation of metallic lead to minium in one step have also been developed but are used only to a limited extent. In one of the one-step processes, lead is evaporated in a rotary kiln and cooled to 500° C to get a mist of lead which is oxidized to very finely divided minium.

Minium is a bright orange-red powder which is insoluble in water but soluble in acids. It decomposes at temperatures above 530° C.

Minium is used as a pigment in paints for the protection of metal surfaces and for the production of lead dioxide. Like lead monoxide, minium is also used in the production of storage battery plates and in the production of glass and ceramics.

In the USA the price of minium was $360-400 per short ton in 1965 ($0.18-0.20 per lb). In the UK the price was £140 5s per long ton in the same year.

Lead dioxide (brown lead oxide, lead peroxide, lead superoxide, PbO_2) can be prepared in various ways. By electrolysis of a solution of a lead salt, lead dioxide is deposited on the anode of the cell. It can also be prepared by treating minium with nitric acid to form lead nitrate and an insoluble powder of lead dioxide. Lead dioxide is also obtained by oxidizing an aqueous slurry of minium with chlorine or bleaching powder.

Lead dioxide forms brown to black crystals which decompose to lower oxides and oxygen when heated to about 300° C.

Lead dioxide is used as an oxidizing agent in the production of dyes and intermediates. It is used in matches and explosives as a source of oxygen. Electrodes of lead dioxide for storage batteries are obtained by charging batteries equipped with lead electrodes (see batteries, vol. II).

In the USA lead dioxide was sold at $0.60 per lb in 1965.

13.5.4 Lead acetates

Lead acetate (plumbous acetate, $Pb(OOCCH_3)_2.3H_2O$) is prepared by dissolving lead monoxide in hot dilute acetic acid. On cooling large white crystals of the trihydrate are precipitated. The solubility in 100 g water is 200 g at 100° C and 46.5 g at 15° C. This product loses its water of crystallization at 75° C and dissolves in it. The anhydrous salt can be obtained by evaporating the water at higher temperatures. Because of its intensely sweet taste (followed by a metallic after-taste), the very poisonous lead acetate is also known as 'sugar of lead'.

Lead acetate is a starting material for the production of other lead salts such as basic lead carbonate (see pigments, vol. V) and lead driers for paints (e.g. lead naphthenate, lead linoleate and lead resinate). Lead acetate is also used in medicine, in the lead-coating of metals and with alum in dyeing and printing cotton as a mordant.

In the USA lead acetate was sold at $540-600 per short ton in 1965. Its price in the UK was £180 per long ton in 1965.

Basic lead acetate ($Pb(OOCCH_3)_2.nPbO.3H_2O$) is prepared by dissolving sufficient lead monoxide in hot dilute acetic acid or by treating a solution of lead acetate with lead monoxide. A crystalline product is obtained on cooling the solution. Basic lead acetate is a starting material for the production of other lead salts. Solutions of basic lead acetate are used in medicine for poultices and washes.

Lead tetra-acetate (plumbic acetate, $Pb(OOCCH_3)_4$) is prepared by dissolving minium in warm glacial acetic acid, followed by cooling. The resulting colourless, crystalline product is used as a highly selective oxidizing agent in organic syntheses, e.g. for the production of aldehydes from glycols.

13.5.5 Other lead compounds

Lead nitrate ($Pb(NO_3)_2$) is obtained by dissolving lead or lead monoxide in hot dilute nitric acid. Crystalline lead nitrate results on cooling. Like lead acetate, lead nitrate is used in dyeing and printing cotton as a mordant and in matches and pyrotechnics as a source of oxygen.

Calcium plumbate (Ca_2PbO_4) is an orange to brown crystalline powder which is used in making safety matches and pyrotechnics.

Basic lead carbonate (white lead), basic lead sulphate, lead cyanamide, lead chromate and other lead pigments are discussed under pigments (see vol. V). For lead arsenate see p. 399, for tetraethyl lead see petrol or gasoline in vol. IV, and for lead salts of organic acids (e.g. lead naphthenate) see vol. V Dryers.

13.5.6 Statistics

Considerable amounts of elemental lead are used for the production of its compounds. These uses in the USA and the UK are shown in the following table:

	UK				USA			
	1960 metric tons	%	1962 metric tons	%	1960 metric tons	%	1962 metric tons	%
Lead monoxide (for storage batteries)	36600	9.5	35700	9.3	161200	17.4	174100	18.0
Tetraethyl lead	27100	7.0	27300	7.1	148600	16.0	152900	15.9
White lead	8300	2.2	8400	2.2	7700	0.8	6500	0.7
Minium	—	—	—	—	68000	7.3	67900	7.0
Other compounds	27600	7.2	25800	6.7	16300	1.8	15200	1.6
Total for chemicals	99600	25.9	97200	25.3	401800	43.3	416600	43.2
Total lead consumption for all purposes	384500		385000		926400		964000	

The total use of lead for the production of lead monoxide is higher than the portion for storage batteries since a large portion of lead monoxide is produced as an intermediate for the production of the lead compounds shown in the table (with the exception of tetraethyl lead). The USA imports important quantities of lead monoxide and lead pigments as shown by the following figures:

		In long tons		
1956	1958	1960	1961	1964
5000	7600	13800	15800	26600

Exports of lead monoxide and lead pigments by some important exporting countries are shown in the following table:

	In long tons				
	1956	1958	1960	1962	1964
Belgium-Luxemburg	3200	3300	4000	4900	3700
France	4500	4700	7300	4800	6300
Germany (West)	9900	7900	9700	9900	9300
Mexico	6000	8800	14700	22000	32000
United Kingdom	4100	5600	6000	7500	5800

.

CHAPTER 14

Compounds of the Subgroup Elements of the Periodic System

14.1 COMPOUNDS OF COPPER, SILVER AND GOLD

Copper, silver and gold form the first subgroup of the periodic system and are considered to be noble metals (although copper is much less noble than silver and gold). Thus they stand in marked contrast with the elements of the first main group (the alkali metals) which are among the most active of the elements. In this respect copper, silver and gold resemble more the preceding elements in the periodic system (nickel, palladium and platinum of the eighth subgroup). Like the metals of the eighth subgroup they have a strong tendency to combine with sulphur but a low tendency to combine with oxygen. However the alkali metals have great affinity for oxygen.

The oxides and hydroxides of copper and silver have a weak basic character, but gold has an amphoteric character in its compounds. Thus gold oxide (Au_2O_3) can be dissolved in both concentrated strong acids and bases, e.g. with hydrochloric acid, gold trichloride ($AuCl_3$) and with potassium hydroxide, potassium aurate ($KAuO_2$. $2H_2O$) is formed.

Copper and silver can form compounds in the mono-, di- and trivalent state and gold in the mono-, tri- and tetravalent state. Compounds of trivalent copper and silver and tetravalent gold are rarities. Copper is most stable in the divalent state and gold in the trivalent state. Silver is usually monovalent. Besides silver difluoride and silver oxide (AgO) only complex compounds of bivalent silver are known. The compounds of monovalent copper, silver and gold resemble each other. These compounds are either highly insoluble or form complexes, with the exception of some silver compounds (e.g. the nitrate which is soluble in water). The monovalent and divalent copper compounds are named *cupric* and *cuprous* compounds respectively. However the name 'copper compound' is often given to the compounds of divalent copper since the monovalent copper compounds are much less stable. Similarly the mono- and trivalent gold compounds are sometimes named *aurous* and *auric* compounds but the most stable compounds of trivalent gold are usually named 'gold compounds' (e.g. gold oxide means auric oxide or gold trioxide).

14.2 COPPER COMPOUNDS (Cu, atomic weight = 63.54)

14.2.1 Copper oxides

Cupric oxide (CuO) is prepared in several ways. Copper scrap or copper powder is oxidized to cupric oxide by contacting with oxygen at a temperature up to 850° C. In another process cupric oxide is precipitated from a boiling aqueous solution of a cupric salt (e.g. cupric sulphate) by means of a hot solution of sodium hydroxide or sodium carbonate. Cupric oxide can also be produced by dissolving metallic copper or oxidized copper ores in an ammoniacal ammonium carbonate solution. The resulting solution of complex cuprous ammonium carbonate is oxidized to a blue solution of complex cupric ammonium carbonate by passing oxygen through it. Cupric oxide can be precipitated from this solution by boiling to get rid of ammonia and carbon dioxide.

Cupric oxide is a black crystalline solid which is insoluble in water. It dissolves in acids with the formation of cupric salts. At temperatures above 900° C it decomposes to cuprous oxide and oxygen.

Cupric oxide is a starting material for the production of other cupric compounds. It is also used for the production of green, blue and black glass and enamels (compare nickel oxide, p. 589 and cobalt oxide, p. 588). Cupric oxide has catalytic properties. Hence its use as a catalyst in organic synthesis.

In 1965 the prices of cupric oxide were £ 420 per long ton in the UK and $ 0.59 per lb ($ 1300 per long ton) in the USA.

Cuprous oxide (Cu_2O) is prepared by heating copper at a temperature above 900° C in the presence of oxygen or by heating a mixture of copper (powder or scrap) and cupric oxide at a temperature between 500 and 600° C in an oxygen-free atmosphere. Cuprous oxide can also be prepared in an electrolytic process. If a solution of an alkali metal halide or an alkaline earth metal halide is electrolysed with copper electrodes, copper from the anode is oxidized to cuprous oxide. The particle size of cuprous oxide can be predetermined by varying the temperature and the pH of the electrolyte solution. The finer sizes are yellow and the coarser are deep red. The latter form is also obtained in the other processes described above.

Cuprous oxide is insoluble in water but soluble in hydrochloric acid with the formation of cuprous chloride. Cuprous oxide does not form cuprous salts with sulphuric acid and nitric acid since cuprous sulphate and cuprous nitrate are not stable in the presence of water, but decompose to cupric salts and metallic copper. Cuprous oxide forms colourless complexes with ammonia; for this reason it is soluble in ammonia and in solutions of ammonia compounds. These solutions are strong reducing agents since the cuprous complex is easily oxidized to a cupric complex.

Cuprous oxide is mainly used in anti-fouling paints (in which the red form is preferred), in fungicides (particularly the yellow form) and for the production of red enamels, glazes and glass. Cuprous oxide has also rectifying properties. It is formed *in situ* on copper surfaces for use in electronics etc. In the USA cuprous oxide was sold at $ 0.60 per lb in 1965.

14.2.2 Cupric hydroxide

Cupric hydroxide ($Cu(OH)_2$) may be produced by dissolving copper in ammonia which is aerated. The equipment may be similar to that for the production of cupric sulphate (see fig. 14.1). Excess of ammonia is removed by passing air through the solution at a temperature below 30° C. Cupric hydroxide precipitates (at temperatures above 60° C a precipitate of cupric oxide is obtained; compare production of CuO by means of an ammoniacal ammonium carbonate solution).

Cupric hydroxide is a blue or bluish-green powder which is converted into black cupric oxide at temperatures above 100° C. Like cupric oxide, it dissolves in acids with the formation of cupric salts. Similarly to cuprous oxide, it dissolves in ammonia, due to the formation of cupric ammonium complexes. Solutions of cupric hydroxide in ammonia are used in the cuprammonium process for the production of rayon (see vol. VI). Cupric hydroxide is also used as a mordant in textile dyeing and as a pigment (e.g. Bremen blue). In 1965 cupric hydroxide was sold at $0.53 per lb in the USA.

14.2.3 Copper halides

Cupric chloride ($CuCl_2$) is prepared by reacting metallic copper with chlorine at a temperature of 400-500° C. A hygroscopic yellowish-brown powder is obtained. Cupric chloride dihydrate $CuCl_2 . 2H_2O$ can be obtained by treating cupric hydroxide with hydrochloric acid and evaporating the solution obtained, or by mixing solutions of cupric sulphate and barium chloride and evaporating the solution obtained after removal of the precipitate of barium sulphate. The dihydrate forms long green hygroscopic needles. Cupric chloride is used as a mordant in the dyeing of fabrics and as a green fire-producing agent in pyrotechnics. It is also used in the wet process method for recovering mercury from its ores (see vol. III) and in the petroleum industry as a deodorizing and desulphurizing agent and as an ingredient of isomerisation and cracking catalysts. In 1965 the price of anhydrous cupric chloride was in the United Kingdom £ 245 per long ton and in the USA $ 0.49 per lb (approximately $ 1000 per long ton).

Cuprous chloride ($CuCl$) can be prepared by reducing cupric chloride, e.g. by boiling a solution of cupric chloride with hydrochloric acid and copper turnings or by treating a solution of cupric chloride with sulphur dioxide. Cuprous chloride precipitates in the form of small white crystals. It must be stored in an oxygen-free atmosphere to avoid oxidation. Cuprous chloride is mainly used for the production of cupric oxychloride. It is also used for removing carbon monoxide and/or acetylene from gas mixtures. In the USA cuprous chloride was sold at $ 0.43 to $ 0.46 per lb in 1965.

Cupric oxychloride (basic cupric chloride, 3 $Cu(OH)_2 . CuCl_2$) is prepared by oxidation of cuprous chloride, e.g. by blowing air through a solution of cuprous chloride in a concentrated solution of sodium chloride (cuprous chloride is soluble in water in the presence of sodium chloride). Cupric oxychloride precipitates and is separated from the liquid by filtration. A similar solution of cuprous chloride and sodium chloride is obtained by roasting copper ores in the presence of common salt and leaching the roasted product with water (see copper, vol. III). Thus cupric oxychloride can also be prepared in one process from ores.

Cupric oxychloride is also prepared by treating cupric hydroxide with a solution of cupric chloride.

Cupric oxychloride crystallizes in the form of green needles. It is mainly used as a fungicide. It is also used as a pigment (Brunswick green) and for the production of rayon in the cuprammonium process (see vol. VI). In the United Kingdom cupric oxychloride was sold at £ 322 per long ton in 1965.

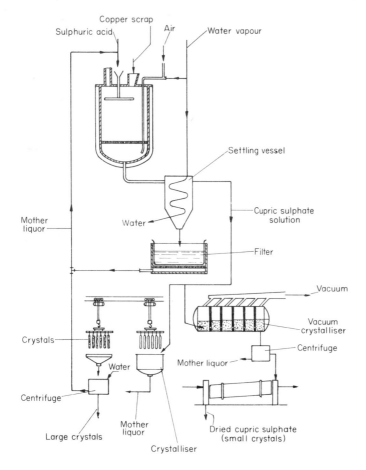

Fig. 14.1 Diagram of the production of cupric sulphate.

14.2.4 Cupric sulphate

Cupric sulphate (copper sulphate, $CuSO_4$) is prepared by dissolving copper containing materials in dilute sulphuric acid and evaporating the resulting solution. Several copper containing materials may be used, e.g. roasted copper ores, copper oxides and metallic copper. Metallic copper is dissolved in the so-called 'oxidizer process'. A lead-lined tower is filled with copper scrap or shot, and dilute sulphuric acid, heated at 75-90° C, is sprayed into the tower. At the same time air is passed through the copper scrap, countercurrently with the acid stream (see fig. 14.1). A solution of cupric sulphate is collected at the bottom of the tower. Insoluble substances are allowed to settle and are drawn off. In a modification of this leaching process, dilute sulphuric acid and air are pumped into the tower at the bottom and the overflow containing cupric sulphate and sulphuric acid is reheated and recycled until the acid concentration becomes too low to dissolve more copper. Cupric sulphate pentahydrate (blue vitriol, $CuSO_4 . 5H_2O$) is precipitated from the resulting solution by evaporation and cooling. In some plants a fine crystalline product is produced by means of vacuum evaporators.

In other plants the solution of cupric sulphate is allowed to cool slowly in large tanks. Large crystals (up to 20 cm diameter) crystallize on lead plates or copper wires suspended in the solution. In similar processes large amounts of copper refinery liquids are used, instead of sulphuric acid, for dissolving copper. These solutions are obtained in electrolytic refining of copper (see vol. III). The major constituents are sulphurric acid and cupric sulphate. The other constituents are impurities such as iron, nickel and arsenic. These impurities are also contained in the solutions of the processes previously described, when impure copper is used as starting material. Iron and arsenic are precipitated by adding cupric oxide or hydroxide until the pH is 3 to 3.5. Cupric sulphate is crystallized from the purified solution. Nickel is enriched in the mother liquor, which is recycled several times and can be recovered from the waste liquor.

Cupric sulphate pentahydrate forms blue crystals. When heated above 96° C a trihydrate, above 116° C a monohydrate, and above 150° C anhydrous cupric sulphate is formed. The latter is a greyish-white crystalline product melting at 200° C. About 21 g anhydrous cupric sulphate can be dissolved in 100 g water at 20° C.

Cupric sulphate is a starting material for the production of other copper compounds. The greatest use of cupric sulphate is as a fungicide. In the form of slurries with lime (forming a slurry of cupric hydroxide, gypsum and lime known as 'Bordeaux mixture') it is sprayed on potato, tomato, apple, pear, peach, grape, citrus and several other crops to control various plant diseases. Since 1885 Bordeaux mixture has been one of the most important fungicides for the control of plant diseases in vine culture (see also vines, vol. VII). Cupric sulphate is also used for the production of other insoluble cupric compounds such as basic cupric carbonate (Burgundy mixture, consisting of a mixture of cupric sulphate and soda ash), cupric phosphate, basic cupric sulphate, etc. These products are also used as fungicides but on a small scale.

Soluble copper compounds have also herbicidal and bactericidal properties. Thus algae and other micro-organisms in water reservoirs, water supply systems, swimming pools and lakes can be controlled by means of cupric sulphate. In Sudan cupric sulphate is used against bilharzia snails in irrigation canals. Canvas bags containing cupric sulphate are hung in the water stream to supply the cupric salt. In this way the growth of weeds is inhibited at the same time. Probably the control of the food of the snails (weed etc.) prevents their multiplication. Cupric sulphate is also used as such or combined with other compounds as a fungicide for wood preservation.

Cupric sulphate is also used in agriculture. About 20 to 50 lb of $CuSO_4.5H_2O$ per acre appear to meet most requirements of cultivated crops (see also fertilizers, vol. VII). In Australia and New Zealand small quantities of cupric sulphate are sprayed on the soil and plants to prevent copper deficiency in sheep. Copper is an important trace element in animal and human life: The human body for example needs about 1 to 2 milligrams per day. An excess of copper is harmful. For this reason wine, beer and ciders should not contain more than 7 p.p.m. and in general a copper content of 30 p.p.m. and more, in food, is not permitted. Cupric sulphate is also used in the mining industry as an activator in the flotation of lead, zinc and cobalt ore. The textile industry uses cupric sulphate in the cuprammonium process for making rayon, and in textile dyeing as a mordant. In the metallurgical industry cupric sulphate is used for copper plating (see vol. III) and in the petroleum industry it is used for removing organic sulphur compounds from petrol (gasoline) to improve the smell of the latter. (This process is known as sweetening process.)

Cupric sulphate is also a constituent of Fehling's solution. This solution consists of cupric sulphate, potassium hydroxide and tartaric acid. (A similar solution can be prepared with citric acid.) Fehling's solution has a dark blue colour due to complexes of bivalent copper and tartaric acid. A red precipitate of cuprous oxide is obtained from the blue solution by means of reducing agents such as aldehydes and monosaccharides, e.g. glucose (for aldehydes and monosaccharides, see vol. VII). For this reason the solution is used for the determination of aldehydes, glucose, fructose etc.

The production of cupric sulphate by the major producing countries is shown in the following table:

| | | In metric tons of pentahydrate | | | |
	1953	1956	1959	1962	1964
Belgium (exports)	14000	17900	22000	13000	6000
France	39900	55900	36800	25000	25000
Italy	79400	82400	75300	57000	—
UK (prod.)	45500	50900	32000	23000	26000
(exports)	46000	48800	31600	19000	18000
USA	66200	64100	36600	40000	40000
USSR (estimate)	—	50000	—	10000	10500

The world production in the same period is estimated at about 400000 tons per year. Cupric sulphate is widely used in wine-producing countries. Due to the development of other fungicides and the recovery of cupric compounds from the wastes of rayon manufacture by means of ion exchangers, the production of cupric sulphate did not increase during this period. Only small quantities are used in the United Kingdom and Belgium. Most of the output of these countries is exported. In the UK cupric sulphate was sold at £125 per long ton and in the USA at $300 to $500 per short ton in 1965.

14.2.5 Other copper compounds

Basic cupric acetates (verdigris blue and verdigris green) are prepared by the action of acetic acid on copper in the presence of air. The approximate formula of the green variety is $CuO.2\,Cu\,(CH_3COO)_2$ and the formula of the blue variety is $CuO.\,Cu\,(CH_3COO)_2$. These products are used as paint pigments and as insecticides and fungicides.

Cupric naphthenate, cupric 8-quinolinate and *cupric phthalate* are prepared from a copper salt and the corresponding sodium salt. These compounds are used as fungicides on a small scale.

Cupric gluconate and *cupric phenolsulphonate* are used in medicine. (See also cupric arsenite and cupric aceto arsenite p. 397.)

14.2.6 Literature

A. BUTTS. *Copper, the science and technology of the metal, its alloys and compounds.* New York, Reinhold, 1954. ACS monograph No. 122.

14.3 SILVER COMPOUNDS (Ag, atomic weight = 107.9)

14.3.1 Silver nitrate

Silver nitrate ($AgNO_3$) is prepared by dissolving purified silver (purity up to 99.97%) in pure nitric acid of medium strength (65%). The resulting solution of silver nitrate is evaporated until the concentration of silver nitrate is 85%. The latter is crystallized out by cooling and is separated by centrifuging. The silver salt obtained is purified by redissolving in hot distilled water and recrystallizing by cooling. A portion of the nitric acid is recovered by converting the nitrous vapours (nitrogen oxides), evolved during the reaction of silver with nitric acid, into nitrogen dioxide by adding oxygen. The mixture of nitrogen dioxide and excess oxygen can easily be collected in water to form nitric acid. Thus considerably smaller purification plants for the exhaust gases are needed. The equipment for the production of silver is made from chrome-nickel steel.

Silver nitrate forms colourless crystals having a melting point of 212° C. It is very soluble in water, 222 g dissolve in 100 g water at 20° C and about 950 g dissolve in 100 g water at 100° C.

Silver nitrate is the starting product for the preparation of the other silver compounds. Most of this salt is used in the photographic industry for the formation of light sensitive silver halides in gelatin (see the chapter on photography). Silver nitrate is also used for the manufacture of mirrors. For this purpose silver oxide is precipitated from a silver nitrate solution with potassium hydroxide. The silver oxide is redissolved by adding ammonia. The resulting solution is mixed with a solution of a reducing agent, such as a sugar or formaldehyde, and immediately poured on to a glass plate. From this mixture silver metal is precipitated on to the glass (see also vol. II). Residues of ammoniacal solutions of silver salts should be thrown away immediately after use or, if required, should be stored in carefully closed bottles only, since the very explosive silver azide (AgN_3, see vol. IV, explosives) may be formed in the solution after some time, especially at the edges of the liquid surface, due to evaporation of the solvent.

Silver nitrate can also be melted and cast into thin bars for the disinfection of wounds. This can be very painful, hence the name 'lapis infernalis'. Small quantities of silver nitrate are also used in indelible ink and in hair dyes.

During the second world war zeolites (sodium aluminosilicates) were treated with silver nitrate to produce silver zeolites (silver aluminosilicates), which were used as an ion exchanger for preparing small quantities of drinking water from sea water. The sodium ions of the salt from sea water are absorbed into the zeolite and the silver ions are given off. These latter ions immediately form a precipitate of silver chloride with the chlorine ions left in the water (see also purification of water, p. 136). For this purpose, aeroplanes, lifeboats and the like carry a stock of this type of ion exchanger.

The production of silver nitrate in the USA was 76 million troy ounces (of 31.1 g) in 1960 and 94 million troy ounces in 1963. About half the production was used for the production of sensitized paper and films. The output figures for silver nitrate in the UK are not published, but as shown by the following export figures, the total output must be considerable.

Silver nitrate (UK exports)	1955	1957	1959	1961
Ounces	204 500	218 800	127 700	374 700
£	45 300	47 300	29 400	77 900

In the USA the price of chemically pure silver nitrate was $ 0.94 per ounce in 1965.

14.3.2 Silver halides

Silver chloride (AgCl) is obtained by mixing a solution of silver nitrate with a pure potassium chloride solution in the dark. The resulting white precipitate is washed with water and dried (also in the dark). Silver chloride is very stable in the dark but decomposes slowly when exposed to the light, according to the following reaction equation:

$$2\ AgCl \rightarrow 2\ Ag + Cl_2$$

It assumes a dark colour owing to the formation of silver. Because of its light-sensitivity, silver chloride is used on a large scale in photography (see vol. VI).

Silver chloride will melt down to a yellow liquid at a temperature of 450° C. By cooling very slowly, large crystals can be obtained from the melt. These crystals are somewhat plastic-like metals and can be rolled into very thin plates. The crystals and the plates transmit visible light and infrared light up to a wavelength of 20 microns (200 000 Å). For this reason the large crystals of silver chloride are used for the manufacture of lenses and prisms destined for infrared measurements (such as spectral analysis in the infrared, infrared photography, etc.). Since silver chloride is sensitive to ultraviolet and part of the visible light, the lenses, prisms and plates are covered with a coating of silver sulphide which will freely transmit the infrared light but will retain the visible and the ultraviolet light.

Silver provided with a coating of silver chloride can be used as a cathode in electrical elements (batteries and accumulaters, see vol. II).

Silver bromide (AgBr) is prepared similarly to silver chloride by reacting silver nitrate with sodium bromide. Silver bromide is a light sensitive yellowish product and is used in light sensitive papers for photographic prints.

Silver iodide (AgI) is also used in photography. Under favourable circumstances the precipitation of rain from clouds can be initiated by nucleating them with crystals of silver iodide sprayed from an aeroplane.

The AgI crystals promote the condensation of the water present in the super-saturated clouds.

14.3.3 Silver oxide

Silver oxide (Ag_2O) is a brown powder, prepared by adding a solution of caustic soda to a solution of silver nitrate. The resulting precipitate is washed and dried.

A mixture of silver oxide with other metal oxides is used in gas masks for the absorption of carbon monoxide. A paint made from silver oxide, linseed oil and a hardening agent is sometimes used for printing resistors in printed circuits. Silver oxide mixed with antimony oxide is sometimes used in manufacturing yellow glass. The mixture is strewn on the glass and melted into it. Silver oxide on silver can also serve as a cathode in alkaline accumulators having lead anodes (see also accumulators, vol. II).

14.3.4 Silver cyanide

Silver cyanide (Ag CN) is precipitated from a solution of silver nitrate by adding a solution of potassium cyanide. An equivalent quantity of potassium cyanide must be used since silver cyanide is soluble in an excess of potassium cyanide due to the formation of complex salts.

A double salt (AgCN . KCN) can be obtained by dissolving silver cyanide in a solution of an equivalent quantity of potassium cyanide and evaporating the resulting solution. Both silver cyanide and the double salt are used in silver plating.

In the USA about 2 million ounces of silver cyanide were produced in 1963. Its price in 1965 was \$ 1.31 per ounce.

14.4 GOLD COMPOUNDS (Au, atomic weight = 197.0)

14.4.1 Gold trichloride

Gold trichloride (auric chloride $AuCl_3$) is prepared by passing chlorine gas over gold at a temperature above 200° C. The salt obtained sublimes and deposits in cooler parts of the reaction vessel in the form of red needles. Gold trichloride is very hygroscopic and is not stable in aqueous solutions. It has no commercial importance.

14.4.2 Chloroauric acid

Chloroauric acid (gold chloride, $HAuCl_4.3H_2O$) is prepared by dissolving metallic gold in aqua regia (a mixture of hydrochloric and nitric acid). A yellow crystalline product of the formula $HAuCl_4 . 4H_2O$ is obtained by evaporating the resulting solution (with repeated addition of hydrochloric acid to replace nitric acid). The commercial product contains about 50% gold, corresponding to the formula $HAuCl_4. 3H_2O$. It is obtained by drying the tetrahydrate. Chloroauric acid is amongst the most stable gold compounds and is commonly named 'gold chloride' in the trade and in the scientific literature. Gold plating (gilding) is the most important application of chloroauric acid. This process can be performed in several ways.

Gold mirrors can be precipitated on glass by reduction of a gold compound in the same way as silver mirrors. A solution of chloroauric acid in water is mixed with an alkaline solution of formaldehyde and poured on to glass.

Usually surfaces are gilded by electroplating and thermal plating. Cyanogen compounds of gold are used in the first process and several gold compositions prepared from chloroauric acid are used in the latter process. Thermal gold-plating is used for gilding metals, ceramics (china ware), glass and several other materials, and is based on the decomposition of gold preparations to metallic gold by heating. Several compositions are in use.

Chloroauric acid can be treated with a sulphurous oil (e.g. oil of rosemary treated with sulphur chloride, S_2Cl_2) to form a complex gold compound (gold resinate) which is diluted with an oil such as oil of rosemary or lavender. These compositions, called 'liquid bright gold' are applied to a surface and then fired at 400-450° C to form a bright gold layer.

Other compositions contain gold powder. The gold powder, suited for this purpose, is prepared by dissolving chloroauric acid in potassium hydroxide followed by adding mercurous nitrate to reduce the gold compound to finely divided metal. A composition named 'brown gold' is prepared by mixing finely divided gold with a flux (e.g. a mixture of bismuth nitrate and borax). This composition is dusted on a tacky surface. After firing a matt coating which must be polished (burnished) is obtained. Mixtures of liquid bright gold and brown gold, which must also be polished after firing, are known as 'burnished gold'.

A new development in thermal gold-plating is the production of gold alkyl mercaptides from chloroauric acid. These mercaptides decompose at 200 to 250° C to form a continuous gold film. The most important compounds are tertiary butyl, tertiary dodecyl, tertiary octyl and tertiary hexadecyl gold mercaptide. Due to their low decomposition temperature these compounds can also be used for gold plating some plastics (heat reflecting shields for missiles etc.). Research is aimed at finding compounds that require even lower decomposition temperatures, which would make it possible to gild materials which do not resist higher temperatures.

Chloroauric acid is also used in gold-toning of photographic prints and for the production of 'cassius purple' (gold-tin purple). Cassius purple is prepared as a brown powder by reduction of a solution of cloroauric acid with stannous chloride. A mixture of colloidal gold and tin oxide is obtained. This product produces brilliant rose, purple and carmine colours in glazes and glass (ruby glass) at temperatures between 850 and 1 100° C.

14.4.3 Gold potassium cyanide

Gold potassium cyanide $KAu(CN)_2$ is a very poisonous white crystalline product which can be obtained by dissolving chloroauric acid in potassium hydroxide and introducing potassium cyanide. Gold potassium cyanide is used in electroplating (electrogilding). Gold cyanide complexes play an important role in gold leaching and refining (see vol. III).

14.5 COMPOUNDS OF ZINC, CADMIUM AND MERCURY

Zinc, cadmium and mercury form the second subgroup of the periodic system. Zinc and cadmium are bivalent in their compounds. Mercury can be univalent and bivalent. The compounds are named mercurous and mercuric compounds respectively. Mercury is univalent in the electrochemical sense in mercurous compounds, but in fact it is also bivalent since mercurous compounds are invariably dimerized and always contain a pair of linked mercury atoms (e.g. mercurous chloride is $ClHg - HgCl$). Zinc and cadmium are more closely related to each other in their compounds than to mercury compounds. The hydroxides of zinc and cadmium, which can be precipitated from solutions of zinc and cadmium compounds respectively, are very sparingly soluble in water. Zinc hydroxide is amphoteric in character and cadmium hydroxide is weakly basic. Both hydroxides are dehydrated to stable oxides when heated. Mercury approaches the noble metals in properties. As with silver no hydroxide of mercury can be precipitated from solutions of mercury salts, but an oxide is obtained. Mercury oxides are weakly basic in character and are decomposed to mercury and oxygen if heated. The elements of the second subgroup are also related to magnesium. They correspond in their ability to form alkyl compounds readily, and several other corresponding compounds are known. This is very pronounced in the formation of double salts and complex salts that often have analogous compositions.

14.6   ZINC COMPOUNDS (Zn, atomic weight = 65.38)

14.6.1 Zinc oxide

Zinc oxide (ZnO) occurs naturally as zincite and it is also available from roasted zinc sulphide ores for the production of zinc (see vol. III). Industrial zinc oxide is prepared in the indirect or French process by evaporating zinc at a temperature of about 1 000° C in a retort or other chamber and burning the resulting zinc vapour with air or oxygen. French process zinc oxide (zinc white) is characterized by a high degree of chemical purity. It is very finely divided and has a bright white colour. In the direct or American process, crude roasted zinc oxide is reduced with a carbonaceous material in a furnace to produce zinc vapour which is burned with air (or oxygen) to zinc oxide in a combustion chamber (or in the same furnace). The resulting oxide has a purity of 98 to 99.5% and it is somewhat less bright than the French process oxide. The particle size can vary greatly but is usually larger than that of zinc oxide obtained by the indirect or French process.

The furnaces for the reduction of ore and evaporation of zinc are often basically the same as those for the production of metallic zinc (see vol. III). Besides these use is made of grate-type furnaces which consist of a block of several furnaces equipped with a grate. A bed of coal, spread on the grate, is ignited by residual heat from the previous charge and a layer of zinc ore mixed with coal is spread upon the ignited coal. Air is blown through the bed from below. An improved furnace is the travelling grate furnace provided with grates which form a continuous conveyor belt. This furnace was developed in the USA in 1920. At the feed end a layer of coal briquettes is spread on the grate, which moves into the furnace. The coal briquettes are ignited in a hot section of the furnace, which is heated separately with ignited fuel briquettes. The grate then

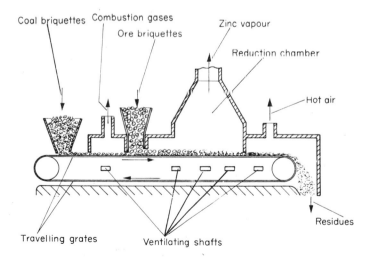

Fig. 14.2   Diagrammatic cross-section of a travelling grate furnace.

Fig. 14.3   Travelling grate furnace.

moves under an ore hopper, where a bed of ore briquettes is spread upon the coal briquettes. The residue is discharged on the opposite side of the furnace (see figs. 14.2 and 14.3).

A third type of zinc oxide is obtained by wet processes, e.g. by precipitation of zinc carbonate from zinc solutions and decomposition of the carbonate obtained. Zinc oxide obtained by a wet process is coarser and less bright than both French and American process zinc oxide.

Pure zinc oxide is a white powder which sublimes at about 1 900° C. It is insoluble in water, but, due to its amphoteric character, soluble in acids and in bases, forming zinc salts and zincates respectively. Zinc oxide is only slightly poisonous but inhalation of freshly prepared zinc oxide fumes is not without danger.

The largest quantities of zinc oxide (of all types) are used in the rubber industry as a filler and vulcanization accelerator. French process zinc oxide is also used in some fine paints and in salves, lotions and other cosmetics and pharmaceuticals. Besides its use in rubber, large quantities of American process zinc oxide are used as a white pigment in exterior house paints (see vol. V), in floor coverings etc. It is also incorporated in ceramics, where it acts as a flux and in ferrites to improve their magnetic and electrical properties. The brilliance of glass is increased by adding some zinc oxide. The use of zinc oxide for impregnating fabrics and textiles (e.g. high tenacity cord for use in tyres) is declining. Leaded zinc oxide (zinc oxide mixed with basic lead sulphate) is a paint pigment.

Wet process zinc oxide is mainly used in the rubber industry and for the production of zinc salts. Solutions of zinc oxide in phosphoric acid (forming of zinc phosphate solution) are used for applying phosphate coatings on zinc, aluminium and iron to protect them against corrosion. It also forms an excellent anchorage for paints on metal surfaces.

About 177 000 short tons of zinc oxide were produced in the USA in 1963. The rubber industry consumed about 45%, the paint industry 30%, and the ceramic and glass industry 6%. In 1965 zinc oxide was sold in the USA at $ 320 to $ 360 per short ton, and in the United Kingdom at £ 119 to £ 123 per long ton.

14.6.2 Zinc halides

Zinc chloride ($ZnCl_2$) is obtained by heating roasted zinc ores in the presence of common salt. Zinc (and also lead which is present in many zinc ores) is evaporated as chloride and condensed. The resulting product is treated with cold water to dissolve zinc chloride. (Lead chloride is very slightly soluble in cold water.) Traces of lead can be removed from the filtered solution by precipitation with sulphuric acid. Zinc chloride is obtained by evaporating the purified solution. Zinc chloride can also be obtained by dissolving roasted zinc ores or zinc scrap in hydrochloric acid, concentrating the solution obtained by evaporation.

Zinc chloride is available in the form of white granular crystals, as a 50% solution in water and as a glassy mass (e.g. cast into sticks). Its melting point is about 290° C and its boiling point is 732° C. Because of its hygroscopicity zinc chloride always contains some water (about 5%). About 430 g of zinc chloride can be dissolved in 100 g of water at 25° C.

Zinc chloride in an aqueous solution is used alone or in combination with phenol or sodium dichromate as a wood preservative, e.g. for railway sleepers. The same compositions are used for fireproofing timber. Zinc chloride is also used in the textile industry as a mordant in printing and dyeing textiles, for mercerizing cotton and for sizing and weighting textiles. Cellulose dissolves in a hot concentrated solution of zinc chloride. Hence the solutions can be used for carbonizing wool (i.e. removing plant remains) and for the treating of paper (e.g. production of parchment paper and vulcanized fibre). Concentrated solutions of zinc chloride are also used for soldering metals. On heating it liberates hydrochloric acid, which dissolves metallic oxides and keeps the metal surface clean. Because of its hygroscopicity zinc chloride is used as a dehydrating agent in organic chemical synthesis. Zinc chloride is also used in deodorants, in fungicides and in disinfecting and embalming fluids. Zinc chloride is also a constituent of the electrolyte in dry batteries.

In the USA about 25 000 tons of zinc chloride were produced in 1963. In the USA the technical granular grade was sold at $ 260 to $ 280 per short ton in 1965. The price of a corresponding grade in the UK was £ 105 per long ton.

Zinc bromide ($ZnBr_2$) can be prepared by passing bromine in a nitrogen stream over molten zinc at 600° C. Zinc bromide is a hygroscopic white or colourless crystalline product. About 470 g of zinc bromide can be dissolved in 100 g of water at 25° C. A solution of 77% zinc bromide in water is used as a radiation viewing shield, since it absorbs radioactive radiation. It is poured into the space between two strong plates of glass which form a double walled window for observing experiments with radioactive materials (see fig. 15.11 in nucleonics chapter).

Zinc fluoride (ZnF_2) can be prepared by adding hydrofluoric acid to a slurry of zinc oxide. A white crystalline solid, which is slightly soluble in water, is obtained. Its melting point is 872° C. Zinc fluoride is used in ceramic glazes and enamels and for the preservation of wood. In the USA it was sold at $ 0.50 per lb in 1965.

14.6.3 Zinc sulphide

Zinc sulphide (ZnS) occurs naturally as zinc blende in ores and is the main source of zinc and zinc compounds (see vol. III).

Pure zinc sulphide for industrial use is produced by precipitation from a solution of a pure zinc salt with hydrogen sulphide or sodium sulphide.

Zinc sulphide is a white crystalline product. When heated above 1 020° C in the absence of air it is converted into another crystal modification named wurtzite and it sublimes at a temperature of 1 180° C.

Zinc sulphide has good covering properties due to its high index of refraction. For this reason it is used in white paints (see vol. V). Lithopone, a mixture of zinc sulphide and barium sulphate, is also used in white paints. Lithopone is prepared as a mixed precipitate by reacting a solution of zinc sulphate with barium sulphide.

Like the sulphides of the earth metals, zinc sulphide can exhibit luminescence upon irradiation by light (see phosphors, p. 672) if it contains some traces of an activator such as copper, silver or manganese. However several other impurities such as iron, nickel and cobalt have a harmful effect upon its luminescence. Hence luminescent zinc sulphide must be prepared from extremely pure starting materials. The pure zinc sulphide is mixed with some sodium chloride and about 0.01 to 0.05% of an activator. The mixture is heated in an oxygen-free atmosphere at a temperature of 850° C (at a temperature of 1 250° C under pressure wurtzite, having different luminescent characteristics, is obtained). These sulphides are used in the manufacture of X-ray and television screens and for luminous watch faces.

14.6.4 Zinc sulphate

Zinc sulphate (white vitriol, white copperas, $ZnSO_4.7H_2O$) is prepared by leaching roasted zinc ores or other materials containing zinc compounds with sulphuric acid. The solution is then filtered and purified. In one purifying process, ferric sulphate ($Fe_2(SO_4)_3$) is added to the solution after oxidation of any ferrous iron present in the solution. Most of the impurities are precipitated together with ferric hydroxide if the solution is brought to pH 5 by adding zinc oxide. Other purification methods are also used (see also metallic zinc production, vol. III). Zinc sulphate heptahydrate crystallizes on evaporating the purified solution. The heptahydrate can be converted into the monohydrate by evaporating to dryness at temperatures above 70° C in a rotary kiln, in a spray dryer or on a drum dryer.

Zinc sulphate is commercially available as the heptahydrate (white crystals) and the monohydrate (a white powder) Anhydrous zinc sulphate can be formed by heating the monohydrate at a temperature above 238° C. The solubility in water is 54 g (in terms of $ZnSO_4$) in 100 g water at 20° C.

Zinc sulphate is used in viscose rayon spinning baths to form more plastic threads which can be stretched in the bath. Zinc sulphate is also used as a trace element in fertilizers and in animal feed, since zinc is of physiological importace. The human body contains about 2 g of zinc. The usual intake of zinc in the form of compounds is 10 to

15 milligrams per day. The same quantity is excreted. Cirrhosis of the liver, in individuals who regularly consume excessive amounts of alcohol, causes an above-normal excretion of zinc via the patient's urine. The depletion of the body's zinc store, which is fatal, can be prevented by the intake of about 20 mg zinc (in compounds) per day.

Zinc sulphate is the starting material for the production of lithopone. It is also a mordant in printing of cotton, a preservative for wood and skins and a constituent of galvanizing solutions.

In the USA about 60000 short tons of zinc sulphate were produced in 1963. The price of the monohydrate in 1965 was $ 185 to $ 200 per short ton. In the UK the heptahydrate was sold at £ 36 per long ton in the same year.

14.6.5 Zinc carbonate

Zinc carbonate ($ZnCO_3$) occurs naturally as the mineral smithsonite. It is prepared in a pure form by adding a soda solution to a solution of a zinc salt. A white precipitate of zinc carbonate is obtained. Basic carbonates may also be obtained, depending on the method of precipitation. Zinc carbonate is used in pharmaceutical preparations (e.g. salves), in rubber as filler and vulcanization accelerator, in ceramics and in paints.

14.6.6 Zinc dithiocarbamates

Zinc dithiocarbamates are prepared from a zinc salt and sodium dithiocarbamates. The products obtained are white powders and they can be represented by the following formula:

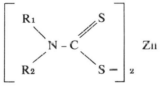

R_1 and R_2 may be hydrocarbon groups or hydrogen atoms.

Zinc diethyldithiocarbamate and zinc dibutyldithiocarbamate are non-toxic powders that are used as accelerators in rubber vulcanization.

Zinc dimethyldithiocarbamate (Ziram) and zinc ethylenebisdithiocarbamate (Zineb) may be harmful if inhaled and may cause irritation. These products are used as fungicides and insecticides. A complex of Ziram with cyclohexylamine is a less toxic fungicide and rat poison. It is said to be harmless to human beings. It has been suggested that paper boxes should be impregnated with it to save them from damage by rats.

14.6.7 Literature

C. H. MATHEWSON. Zinc. The metal, its alloys and compounds. New York, Reinhold, 1959. ACS monograph No. 142.

14.7 CADMIUM COMPOUNDS (Cd, atomic weight = 112.4)

The starting material for all cadmium compounds is metallic cadmium (see metallic cadmium, vol. III). Cadmium may be converted into cadmium oxide (CdO) by evaporation and burning the resulting vapour with air (compare the production of zinc oxide). Cadmium oxide may also be prepared by heating cadmium nitrate above its decomposition temperature. Cadmium oxide is a brown powder which is insoluble in water and alkalis but soluble in acids. It dissolves also in ammonia, due to the formation of complexes. Cadmium oxide is used for several purposes, e.g. in cadmium plating, in the negative electrode of nickel cadmium batteries, in ceramics as a pigment, and in the production of cadmium salts.

Cadmium salts are prepared by dissolving cadmium or its oxide in acids and evaporating to dryness. *Cadmium sulphate* ($CdSO_4$) is used in electrolyte solutions for the Weston standard cell (an electric element for electric potential measuring). *Cadmium bromide* ($CdBr_2$) and *cadmium iodide* (CdI_2) are used in sensitive layers for photo-engraving and lithography. *Cadmium chloride* ($CdCl_2$) is used as a catalyst and in photographic film emulsions as a fog inhibitor. *Cadmium nitrate* and *cadmium acetate* are applied on glass and porcelain to produce characteristic colour effects. Cadmium nitrate is also used in catalysts and in nickel cadmium batteries.

Cadmium salts are poisonous. They produce inflammation of the mucous membranes of the stomach, lungs etc.

Cadmium sulphide (cadmium yellow, CdS) is the most important cadmium compound. It occurs naturally combined with zinc ores especially as a solid solution in zinc sulphide (see volume III).

Commercial cadmium sulphide is prepared by passing hydrogen sulphide through an acid solution of a cadmium salt. Cadmium sulphide precipitates.

In a similar way cadmium sulphide may be precipitated from a solution of a cadmium salt by adding a solution of a sulphide. In general a yellow precipitate is obtained if a cold solution of low cadmium content is used. The precipitate is orange when a hot cadmium solution is used. This difference in colour is due to a difference in particle size and to the formation of different modifications. Cadmium sulphide sublimes at 980° C. It is insoluble in water and dilute acids. However it can be dissolved in strong acids.

Cadmium sulphide is used as a pigment in paints, artists' colours and printing inks. The pigment is also used for colouring vulcanized rubber, soaps, paper, ceramic glazes, glass etc. Other pigments containing cadmium sulphide are known as cadmium red (mixed cadmium sulphide and cadmium selenide) and cadmium lithopone (mixed with barium sulphate). (See also pigments and paints in vol. V.) Like zinc sulphide, cadmium sulphide has luminescent properties if it contains traces of an activator (see phosphors, p. 673). For this reason it is also used in luminescent paints.

A unique property of cadmium sulphide is its very strong photoeffect if it contains certain impurities. The resistance of a given mass of cadmium sulphide may change by a factor of 10 million on going from total darkness to 30 foot-candles of light. Hence cadmium sulphide is used in the production of photoresistors for measuring light intensities by recording an electric current which is passed through the resistor (e.g. for photo exposure meters and for flame control of oil fuelled furnaces). Conversely the resistors are also used in electronic circuits as variable resistors that are controlled by means of light. The resistors are prepared by mixing pure cadmium sulphide with traces of copper and gallium compounds which are homogeneously dispersed in cadmium sulphide by a heat treatment. The product obtained is compressed into small plates and sintered by heating.

14.8 MERCURY COMPOUNDS (Hg, atomic weight = 200.6)

14.8.1 Mercury chlorides

Mercuric chloride (corrosive sublimate, $HgCl_2$) is made on an industrial scale by bringing mercury into contact with a slight excess of chlorine in enamelled apparatus at a high temperature. The mercury burns in the chlorine atmosphere to a vapour of mercuric chloride which condenses in the cooler sections of the apparatus. It can also be made by heating a mixture of mercuric sulphate and common salt above 300° C, whereby the sublimate evaporates and sodium sulphate remains:

$$HgSO_4 + 2\ NaCl \rightarrow HgCl_2 + Na_2SO_4$$

A little manganese dioxide is added to the reaction mixture in order to prevent the formation of mercurous chloride. Mercuric chloride can be purified by dissolving in hot alcohol, followed by pouring into cold water to crystallize it out.

Mercuric chloride is a very poisonous white crystalline powder which is slightly soluble in water (7 g per 100 cm³ water of 20° C). It was well known by the alchemists in the Middle Ages. Mercuric chloride got the name sublimate because a considerable amount sublimes near its melting point and the vapour condenses, usually in the form of a solid on cold surfaces, due to the fact that the boiling point (302° C) and the melting point (280° C) of mercuric chloride are close together.

Mercuric chloride is used as a fungicide, disinfectant and sterilizing agent. Wood is preserved by soaking in an aqueous solution of sublimate. It is also used as a catalyst in many organic chemical processes. In photography mercuric chloride is used for intensifying negatives which are underexposed and consequently show silver images which are too thin. By treating the negatives with a mercuric chloride solution, the silver is converted into silver chloride and the mercuric chloride itself is reduced to the insoluble mercurous chloride which precipitates on the silver chloride. Metals are formed again by treatment with a reducing agent. In this manner the image on the negative has acquired a greater density because it has now been supplemented with mercury.

In 1965 mercuric chloride was sold at $ 10.11 per lb in the USA and in the UK at £2 14s 6d per lb.

Mercurous chloride (calomel, Hg_2Cl_2) can be prepared by heating an excess of mercury with chlorine gas, which gives rise to a mixture of mercurous and mercuric chloride (80% and 20% respectively). Mercuric chloride is removed by leaching with water. Mercurous chloride can also be prepared by treating a solution of mercurous nitrate with a common salt solution, thus causing mercurous chloride to precipitate. Mercurous chloride is a light-sensitive white crystalline powder which, in contrast to sublimate, is almost insoluble in water (0.2 mg in 100 cm³ water of 20° C).

Because of its toxicity and its insolubility in water it is used in anti-fouling paints applied to a ship's sides. Mercurous chloride is sometimes used in insecticides, fungicides and medicines. Mercurous chloride is also a constituent of the so-called calomel electrode, which consists of a solution of hydrochloric acid saturated with mercurous chloride over a layer of mercury and mercurous chloride. This electrode has constant and easily reproducible properties and is therefore used in electrochemistry as standard electrode for electrochemical measurements. Small quantities of calomel are also used in pyrotechnics.

In 1965 mercurous chloride was sold at $10.32 per lb in the USA; in the United Kingdom it was sold at £3 5s 6d per lb.

14.8.2 Mercuric oxide

Mercuric oxide (HgO) is obtained as red crystalline powder by heating mercurous nitrate. A yellow mercuric oxide is obtained by treating a solution of mercuric chloride or mercuric nitrate with alkali. The difference in colour is caused by a difference in crystal size. The yellow variety is finer than the red one and is, therefore, more reactive in chemical reactions. Mercuric oxide is a starting material for the preparation of various mercury compounds. It is further applied in medicines, antiseptics, fungicides and germicides, and as an ingredient of anti-fouling paints for the painting of ships' sides. Mercuric oxide is also used as a depolarizer in mercury batteries (Ruben Mallory cells).

In 1965 the red oxide was sold at $11.21 to $11.41 per lb in the USA, and in the United Kingdom at £3 8s 9d per lb. The yellow oxide is sold at about the same price.

14.8.3 Other mercury compounds

Mercuric sulphide (HgS) occurs naturally in a black and a red form. The latter is well known as the red pigment 'cinnabar' which can also be prepared synthetically, e.g. by heating mercury with a solution of potassium polysulphide. The black modification is converted into the red modification by sublimation (at 580° C). (See metallic mercury in vol. III and paints in vol. V.)

Mercuric nitrate ($Hg(NO_3)_2$) is produced by dissolving mercury in an excess of concentrated nitric acid while heating. A colourless hygroscopic crystalline monohydrate is obtained by evaporating and cooling the solution. Mercuric nitrate is the starting material for the production of other mercury compounds, and is also used for the production of mercuric fulminate (i.e. mercuric cyanate, fulminating mercury, $Hg(CNO)_2$) which is used as a detonator for military purposes (see explosives in vol. IV). Like mercurous nitrate, mercuric nitrate is used in medicine and in the tanning of hair destined for making felt for hats. The latter process has more than once led to serious poisoning, as mercuric nitrate, like all other mercury salts, is extremely poisonous.

In England its use for the felt process gave rise to the expression 'as mad as a hatter'. In 1963 mercuric nitrate was quoted at $6.44 per lb in the USA.

Mercurous nitrate ($Hg_2(NO_3)_2$) can be prepared by boiling an excess of mercury with dilute nitric acid. In addition to the applications already mentioned under mercuric nitrate, this product is also used for the preparation of mercuric oxide.

Mercuric sulphate ($HgSO_4$) is produced by heating mercuric oxide or mercury with an excess of sulphuric acid and evaporating the resulting solution. It is used in disinfectants, and as a catalyst in organic chemical processes.

Mercurous sulphate (Hg_2SO_4) can be obtained by electrolysis of dilute sulphuric acid using a mercury layer as anode. The salt obtained is sometimes used as a catalyst in the presence of sulphuric acid when oxidizing naphthalene into phthalic acid (see the production of phthalic acid, vol. IV).

Phenylmercuric compounds (merphenyl compounds) such as phenylmercuric acetate and the corresponding nitrate and chloride can be prepared by heating a mixture of the corresponding inorganic mercuric salt and benzene in the presence of a catalyst; for example, phenylmercuric benzene in the presence of boron trifluoride. Phenylmercuric compounds are used as fungicides (mildew-proofing agent), germicides, antiseptics, etc. They are used for the preservation of textiles, leather, paper, etc. Phenyl-mercuric oleate can easily be incorporated into oilbase paints, hence its use in anti-mildew house paints. Phenylmercuric borate is sold as a disinfectant under the trade name 'Merfen'.

14.8.4 Statistics

The world production of mercury increased from 5500 tons in 1952 to 9000 short tons in 1963. In 1963 about 3000 tons were consumed in the USA; about 75% was consumed in the form of metal, the remainder was consumed in the form of compounds as follows: pharmaceuticals, antiseptics, etc.: 4.5%, insecticides etc. in agriculture 4.5%, preservation (fungicides, anti-fouling paint etc.) 15%, catalysts 1%.

14.9 COMPOUNDS OF IRON, COBALT, NICKEL AND PLATINUM

Iron, cobalt, nickel and the platinum metals form the eighth subgroup of the periodic system. The platinum metals are ruthenium, rhodium, palladium, osmium, iridium and platinum; the latter being the most important platinum metal.

It should be noted that iron, cobalt and nickel show closer resemblance to each other than any of them does to the elements standing below them in the periodic system. This is due to the fact that atoms of cobalt and nickel have one and two electrons more respectively, not in their outer electron shell, but in an electron shell nearer the nucleus. (See atomic structure in the nucleonics chapter.)

It might be expected that the elements iron, ruthenium and osmium would display a maximum valence state of eight in their compounds as the electron structure of the preceding inert gases can only be reached if eight electrons are released. Similarly an even higher maximum valence state might be expected for the other elements of this group. However only ruthenium and osmium exhibit a maximum valence state of eight in their compounds. The maximum valence state of iron and platinum is six and that of cobalt and nickel is four. The tendency of these elements, to form compounds in the maximum valence state, is low. Thus iron is mainly di- and trivalent in its compounds (ferrous and ferric compounds respectively). These compounds can be converted into one another by reduction and oxidation. Cobalt and nickel are predominantly bivalent in their simple compounds and trivalent in complex compounds. Platinum is predominantly di- and tetravalent in its compounds.

The oxides of iron, cobalt, nickel and platinum have a basic character but ferrites, cobaltites and nickelites can be obtained by melting the corresponding oxides with strongly basic oxides. Except for the ferrites, these compounds are not of commercial importance. All the elements of the eighth subgroup and some of their oxides show well marked catalytic properties. They also have the property of forming several complexes with carbon monoxide of which iron pentacarbonyl is the most important. The property of the elements of the eighth subgroup of forming coloured compounds, is noteworthy.

14.10 IRON COMPOUNDS (Fe, atomic weight = 55.85)

14.10.1 Ferric oxides and ferric hydroxide

Ferric oxide (Fe_2O_3) occurs naturally in several minerals, e.g. haematite (Fe_2O_3) and limonite ($2Fe_2O_3.3H_2O$). It is also obtained as a by-product in the roasting of pyrites. These products are used for the production of iron and steel (see vol. III).

Industrial ferric oxide is obtained in various ways. It may be prepared by precipitation of ferrous hydroxide from a solution of ferrous sulphate by means of a base. The resulting slurry of ferrous hydroxide ($Fe(OH)_2$) is oxidized to ferric hydroxide ($Fe(OH)_3$) by aeration. After filtering, the latter is dehydrated by heating. Ferric oxide is also obtained by ignition of ferrous sulphate and by thermal decomposition of ferric oxalate or iron carbonyls.

Ferric oxide is a yellow-orange, red-brown or black powder depending on the temperature at which it is heated. At a temperature of about 1560° C it starts to decompose. When it has not been heated at too high temperatures, ferric oxide dissolves in strong acids with the formation of ferric salts. It is also soluble in oxalic acid. Hence the use of the latter to remove spots of rust. Ferric oxide forms 'ferrites' by melting with alkali metal hydroxides, oxides or carbonates (e.g. sodium ferrites $Na_2Fe_2O_4$ and $Na_2Fe_4O_7$). These ferrites are salts, unlike the compounds with divalent metals described below.

Commercially important substances also known as ferrites are prepared from ferric oxide and oxides of divalent metals. These ferrites have no salt character but are double compounds of the oxides having the character of ceramics. The ratio of ferric oxide to divalent metal oxide may vary. These products are semi-conductors and, like metallic iron, cobalt and nickel, they have ferromagnetic properties. For this reason the ferrites are used in electronic equipment. Examples of these ferrites are 'ferroxcube' (e.g. ferrites of manganese, zinc and/or nickel) having a high magnetic permeability and 'ferroxdure' (barium ferrites, $BaO.xFe_2O_3$) having permanent magnetic properties. Ferroxdure and ferroxcube are trade names of 'Philips N.V.' of Holland. Compare the natural occurring ferrite magnetite (= ferrosoferric oxide) which has also ferromagnetic properties (see below).

Ferric oxide is extensively used as a pigment for colouring rubber, paper, linoleum and ceramics. It is used in paint, e.g. for iron work (see pigments, vol. V). Ferric oxide is also used as a catalyst and it is a constituent (colcothar) of polishing agents for glass, precious metals and precious stones (jewellers' rouge).

The United States and the United Kingdom are important producers of ferric oxide. The production of industrial ferric oxide (chemically manufactured) in the UK was 88000 long tons in 1958 (including hydrated forms). Both the exports and imports of ferric oxide were 5000 to 6000 tons per year during 1958 to 1962. The production of chemically manufactured ferric oxide in the USA was 120000 short tons and of natural ferric oxide (paint grade) was 3400 short tons in 1963. The exports were 4000 long tons. This amount is considerably lower than the exports in 1947 which were ten times higher. In the USA ferric oxide was sold at $0.07 to $0.16 per lb depending on the colour in 1965.

Ferrosoferric oxide (magnetic oxide, $FeO.Fe_2O_3$) occurs naturally as magnetite which is used in the iron and steel industry. It is produced synthetically by heating iron in the presence of steam or by heating iron or ferrous sulphate in the presence of a limited quantity of air (partial oxidation). The resulting black powder is used as a pigment (see vol. V) and as a polishing agent. Ferrosoferric oxide is also formed on iron surfaces as a corrosion resistant film when iron is treated with molten potassium nitrate.

Ferric hydroxide ($Fe(OH)_3$) may be prepared, as described above, by precipitating white ferrous hydroxide from a solution of a ferrous salt and oxidizing the resulting slurry to ferric hydroxide. The resulting product is filtered and dried. Ferric hydroxide is an ochreous to red-brown amorphous powder. At a temperature above 500° C it loses water to form ferric oxide. It is insoluble in water, but dissolves in acids with the formation of ferric salts and in concentrated alkaline solution with the formation of ferrites (trivalent ferrates).

Ferric hydroxide is used as a pigment and as an adsorbent, e.g. for purifying water and in chemical processes. It is also used as a pharmaceutical preparation against arsenic poisoning.

14.10.2 Iron chlorides

Ferrous chloride ($FeCl_2$) is prepared by dissolving iron in a solution of hydrogen chloride in the absence of air and evaporating the solution. A blue-green crystalline hydrate ($FeCl_2.4H_2O$) is obtained. An anhydrous colourless product which is very hygroscopic can be obtained by passing dry hydrogen chloride gas over iron at red heat. Ferrous chloride is used as a reducing agent, as a mordant in dyeing textiles and as a starting material for the production of ferric chloride and pharmaceuticals.

Ferric chloride ($FeCl_3$) is prepared by passing chlorine gas over iron at red heat or by oxidizing anhydrous ferrous chloride by means of chlorine gas. Commercial solutions of ferric chloride are prepared by dissolving iron in a hydrochloric acid solution and oxidizing the resulting solution of ferrous chloride with chlorine gas. The hexahydrate ($FeCl_3.6H_2O$) crystallizes when the solution is evaporated. The hexahydrate forms orange-yellow crystals and the anhydrous salt consists of dark leaves which are green in reflected light and dark red in transmitted light. Both the anhydrous form and the hexahydrate are hygroscopic and very soluble in water. The solutions are very corrosive and thus they must be stored in bottles, carboys etc. Plastic-lined drums are also used. Ferric chloride is also soluble in many organic solvents such as methyl and ethyl alcohol, acetone, ether, benzene, pyridine and ethylamine but it is insoluble in glycerol. In its solutions, ferric chloride forms complexes with the solvent.

Ferric chloride is the most important ferric compound. The anhydrous salt is used as a catalyst (Friedel-Crafts catalyst) in organic synthesis, e.g. condensation reactions and chlorination of organic compounds (aluminium chloride is also used for this purpose). Solutions of ferric chloride are used for the chlorination of silver and copper ores (see vol. III), for the etching of copper in photoengraving (see vol. VI), as a mordant in textile dyeing, for the production of pharmaceuticals and as an oxidizing agent in chemical synthesis. Large quantities are used in water purification (see p. 126). Ferric chloride is a protein precipitant and thus it is used for the production of styptic cotton-wool.

In the USA about 47 000 short tons of ferric chloride hexahydrate were produced in 1963. In 1965 anhydrous ferric chloride was sold at $8 to $9 per 100 lb; in solution its price was $4 to $7 per 100 lb (100% basis).

14.10.3 Iron sulphates

Ferrous sulphate (copperas, green vitriol, $FeSO_4.7H_2O$) is mainly produced from 'pickle liquor'. The latter is a mixture of ferrous sulphate, sulphuric acid and water, which is obtained by dipping iron and steel in dilute sulphuric acid to clean it preparatory to a metal-coating process (e.g. galvanizing or electroplating). Scrap iron is added to the pickle liquor until the free acid content is reduced to 0.03%. The resulting solution is filtered, concentrated in triple effect evaporators and cooled in crystallizers. Ferrous sulphate heptahydrate crystallizes and is separated from the mother liquor by means of filters or centrifuges. The mother liquor is recycled. In a modification of this process the neutralized pickle liquor is concentrated with submerged combustion of gases as shown in fig. 14.4 (see also submerged flame evaporator for phosphoric acid).

A waste liquor which is similar to pickle liquor is obtained in the treatment of titanium ore with sulphuric acid, to separate titanium from the iron constituent present in the ore. This waste is also used for the production of ferrous sulphate.

Ferrous sulphate forms blue-green crystals. Its melting point is 64° C. It is very soluble in water but insoluble in alcohol. This property is used for the purification of ferrous sulphate by dissolving in water and adding alcohol to precipitate the pure product. A brown coating of basic ferric sulphate is formed on ferrous sulphate crystals which are exposed to moist air. Ferrous sulphate forms a double salt with ammonium sulphate (Mohr's salt) when a solution, containing both compounds is evaporated (compare ferric sulphate, p. 587).

Ferrous sulphate is the most important ferrous compound. It is the starting material for other iron compounds, e.g. ferric oxide and ferric hydroxide. It is also used for the production of alkali metal ferrocyanide and Prussian blue (see cyanogen compounds),

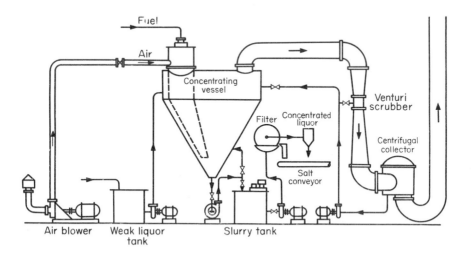

Fig. 14.4 Diagram of the production of ferrous sulphate from pickle liquor by means of submerged flame combustion. The fuel is burnt with air and the hot gas mixture is introduced into the concentrating vessel below the level of the pickling liquor. In this way the heat is applied for the evaporation of water from the pickling liquor.

for the preservation of wood, for water purification (see p. 126), and in the preparation of pharmaceuticals. A mixture with magnesium oxide is used as an antidote against arsenic poisoning. Ferrous sulphate is a constituent of writing ink and a reducing agent in chemical processes. Since ferrous sulphate etches aluminium it is used in cheap photomechanical reproduction methods, e.g. lithography.

Ferrous sulphate is obtained from wastes which cannot be discharged as such because they are corrosive. Thus the production is often higher than the demand. The production in the USA was 160 000 short tons in 1963 (in terms of $FeSO_4.7H_2O$). In 1965 its price in the USA was $0.09 to $0.10 per lb; in the UK it was sold at £3 7s 0d per ton.

Ferric sulphate ($Fe_2(SO_4)_3$) can be prepared by oxidation of ferrous sulphate with nitric acid, or by treating ferric oxide with sulphuric acid. Ferric sulphate can crystallize in a number of hydrates which are brown-yellow products. The anhydrous form, which is obtained from the hydrates by heating above 175° C, can be dissolved rapidly in water in the presence of some ferrous sulphate. In the absence of ferrous sulphate it dissolves slowly. Ferric sulphate is mainly used as a solution which is sold in glass bottles and wooden barrels. Like aluminium sulphate and chromium sulphate, ferric sulphate forms complex salts with potassium sulphate or ammonium sulphate. Pure ferric potassium alum ($KFe(SO_4)_2.12H_2O$) and ferric ammonium alum ($NH_4Fe(SO_4)_2.12H_2O$) are formed respectively by evaporation of a solution containing ferric sulphate and potassium or ammonium sulphate. These salts are used in analytical chemistry. Ferric sulphate is used for the purification of water, for the production of complex ferric cyanides (see p. 356) and for pickling stainless steel and copper. Ferric sulphate is also used as a mordant in textile dyeing and as a soil conditioner for alkaline soils. Ferric chloride hydrolyses in the soil forming sulphuric acid, which neutralizes the soil, and ferric hydroxide gel which improves its structure.

14.10.4 Iron pentacarbonyl

Iron pentacarbonyl ($Fe(CO)_5$) is the most important of a series of carbonyls. It can be produced by heating iron powder at a temperature of 200° C in the presence of carbon monoxide at a pressure of 220 atm. The reaction product is filtered and crude iron pentacarbonyl is obtained in the form of a yellow liquid. This is often used as such but it can also be purified by fractional distillation in a carbon monoxide atmosphere. Pure iron pentacarbonyl is a colourless liquid. Its melting point is −20° C and its boiling point is 104.6° C.

Large amounts of iron pentacarbonyl are used for the production of extremely fine iron powder by thermal decomposition of its vapour (see vol. III). It is also used for the production of red ferric oxide pigments (by burning it in air). The resulting ferric oxide can also be used for the production of ferromagnetic semi-conductors (ferrites). It has also been proposed to use iron pentacarbonyl as an anti-knock component for motor fuels but it is not much used, probably because of its tendency to deposit ferric oxide in the engine.

14.10.5 Pharmaceutical iron preparations

Ferrous tartrate and ferrous gluconate can be prepared by reacting ferrous sulphate with calcium tartrate and calcium gluconate respectively. Like pure ferrous sulphate these products are used in medicine, often combined with liver preparations and vitamins. These products are available in tablets, syrups, elixirs, etc., and are used for the treatment of iron-deficiency anaemia. This kind of anaemia is characterized by a decreased haemoglobin concentration in the blood. (Iron is a constituent of haemoglobin.) Iron deficiency anaemia is sometimes accompanied by a deficiency of iron in the vital metallo-enzymes.

Bivalent iron compounds are preferred for this purpose since bivalent iron is more easily absorbed in the blood than trivalent iron. In addition soluble salts of trivalent iron are protein precipitants and produce astringent and irritant effects on the mucous membranes (see also ferric chloride as styptic, p. 585).

14.11   COBALT COMPOUNDS (Co, atomic weight = 58.94)

Cobalt oxides are prepared by heating cobalt hydroxide or cobalt carbonate. The hydroxide and carbonate are obtained in the processes for the refining of concentrated cobalt ores (see vol. III). *Cobaltic oxide* (Co_2O) is formed when cobalt hydroxide or carbonate is heated at a temperature of about 300 to 400° C in the presence of an excess of air. When heated at 700 to 800° C the black *cobaltosic oxide* (Co_3O_4) is obtained and above 1000° C *cobaltous oxide* (CoO) is the resulting product. This product is usually dark grey due to the presence of cobaltosic oxide. Cobaltous oxide and cobaltosic oxide, being the most important cobalt oxides, must be cooled below 265° C in an oxygen-free atmosphere to avoid the formation of cobaltic oxide. These oxides are used for the production of metallic cobalt (see vol. III) and cobalt compounds. Like nickel oxide, cobalt oxides are used for the colouring of ceramic glazes and glass and for improving the adherence of enamel. Since they form blue silicates in glass, traces of cobalt oxides can be used for neutralizing the faint yellow colour of glass containing small quantities of impurities such as trivalent iron. Cobalt oxides are also used in the production of pigments for oil colour paints. These resemble the calcined products formed in glass and ceramic glazes. A fine blue pigment, Thenard's blue is essentially cobalt aluminate. Rinnmans green is a double oxide of zinc and cobalt oxide. Cobalt phosphate is violet. In 1965 cobalt oxide (black) was sold at $ 1.28 to $ 1.32 per lb in the USA, and in the UK at 7s10d per lb.

Cobalt chloride (cobaltous chloride, $CoCl_2.6H_2O$) is prepared by dissolving metallic cobalt, cobalt hydroxide, carbonate or cobalt oxide in a solution of hydrochloric acid and evaporating the solution. A pink hexahydrate crystallizes. When dried, anhydrous cobalt chloride, which is blue in colour, is obtained; it absorbs moisture from the air, becoming pink again. For this reason it is used in hygrometers and for moisture control of drying agents (see p. 113). It has also been used in invisible or sympathetic ink, which is almost invisible under ordinary conditions but becomes blue on heating. The most important application of cobalt chloride is its use for the production of dryers. Cobalt linoleate, cobalt resinate and cobalt naphthenate are prepared from the corresponding sodium salts and cobalt chloride. The resulting compounds promote the oxidation of unsaturated hydrocarbons, oils and fats with the formation of non-tacky substances. Thus they accelerate drying of varnishes, lacquers, printing inks, etc. containing the unsaturated compounds. In the USA the prices in 1965 were as follows: cobalt chloride, $ 0.97 per lb; cobalt linoleate (8½% Co) $ 0.72 per lb, and cobalt naphthenate (6% Co), $ 0.46 per lb.

Cobalt sulphate (cobaltous sulphate heptahydrate, $CoSO_4,7H_2O$) is obtained by dissolving cobalt oxide, hydroxide or carbonate in dilute sulphuric acid and evaporating the resulting solution. Like cobalt chloride it can be used for the production of dryers. It is also used for cobalt plating and as a trace element in fertilizers and animal feeds. Cobalt is essential in animals for the production of vitamin B12. Fatal diseases occur in sheep which graze in areas in which no cobalt or only a little is available (e.g. in New Zealand and Australia). Cobalt is applied by spraying a solution of cobalt sulphate on the soil or on plants. It has been suggested that tablets of cobaltic oxide and china clay or small tablets of cobalt should be inserted in the fore-stomachs of cattle and sheep. These pellets seem to remain in the digestive tract for some years, releasing the cobalt slowly. In the USA cobalt sulphate was sold at $0.65 to $1.15 per lb in 1965.

Cobalt nitrate (cobaltous nitrate hexahydrate, $Co(NO_3)_2.6H_2O$) is prepared by the action of nitric acid on cobalt oxide, hydroxide or carbonate. It is used for the production of supported cobalt catalysts (compare nickel nitrate). The catalysts are used in the synthesis of hydrocarbons from carbon monoxide and hydrogen in the Fischer-Tropsch process and for the production of alcohols and aldehydes from olefins, carbon monoxide and hydrogen in the oxo-process (see vol. IV).

Statistics. The world production of cobalt ores was 14 000 long tons in 1963 (in terms of Co). Seventy-five per cent of the world production is consumed in the form of metals and alloys, 13% in pigment, paints, inks and varnishes, 7% in ceramics, enamel and glass, and 5% for other purposes including catalysts and agriculture. The United Kingdom imported about 1 000 long tons of cobalt oxide and exported about the same quantity in the form of cobalt oxide and cobalt salts in 1963. The USA produced about 11 000 long tons of cobalt compounds in 1963 (gross weight, cobalt content 1 500 long tons) of which about 9 000 long tons were dryers, 600 long tons cobalt sulphate and 400 long tons cobalt oxide.

14.11.1 Literature

R. S. YOUNG. *Cobalt, its chemistry, metallurgy and uses.* New York, Reinhold, 1960. ACS monograph No. 149.

14.12   NICKEL COMPOUNDS (Ni, atomic weight = 58.71)

Nickel oxide (NiO). A crude form of nickel oxide (nickel oxide sinter) is produced by roasting of nickel ores as an intermediate in the production of metallic nickel (see vol. III). Pure forms of nickel oxide are produced by heating metallic nickel or nickel compounds (e.g. nickel nitrate or nickel hydroxide) in the presence of air. A black powder of nickel oxide is obtained from nickel salts at a temperature of about 400° C. This is converted into a greenish-yellow powder when heated at 900-1 000° C. Nickel oxide is used as a colouring agent in ceramic glazes and glass. Depending on the composition of the glass or ceramic glaze it forms silicates, borates, aluminates, etc., and brown, yellow, green-blue and violet colours are obtained. It is also used in enamel frits to strengthen its groundcoat adherence. Combined with ferric oxide, nickel oxide forms ferrites (see p. 584). Nickel oxide is also used as a catalyst. In 1965 the price of nickel oxide in the USA was $0.75 to $0.91 per lb.

Nickel hydroxide ($Ni(OH)_2$) is obtained by precipitation from a solution of a nickel salt by means of an alkali hydroxide. The green precipitate is filtered and dried. It is used in alkaline nickel-cadmium storage batteries. It is also used for the production of reactive nickel catalysts. (These can be prepared by reducing nickel hydroxide with hydrogen at a temperature between 200 and 500° C.)

Nickel chloride ($NiCl_2.6H_2O$) is produced by dissolving nickel in a hydrochloric acid solution and evaporating the solution. It forms green water soluble crystals which can be dehydrated at temperatures above 140° C. Anhydrous nickel chloride may also be prepared by passing chlorine gas over heated nickel. Nickel chloride is used for electroplating and for electrolytic refining of nickel.

Nickel sulphate ($NiSO_4$) is prepared by boiling finely divided nickel in sulphuric acid following by aeration when the acid strength decreases. Emerald green crystals of nickel sulphate hexahydrate crystallize on evaporating the resulting solution. Much nickel sulphate is obtained in processes for refining of metallic nickel (see vol. III). Nickel sulphate is used in electroplating baths and for the production of other nickel compounds, e.g. the hydroxide. Metals are sometimes dipped in a solution of nickel sulphate to improve the adherence of enamel on the metal surface. In 1965 the price of nickel sulphate in the USA was $0.30 to $0.38 per lb; in the UK it was sold at 2*s* 0*d* per lb.

Nickel nitrate ($Ni(NO_3)_2$) is produced by dissolving nickel in nitric acid and evaporating the solution. An emerald green crystalline hexahydrate is obtained. Nickel nitrate is the starting material for the production of very pure nickel compounds. It is also used for the production of nickel catalysts on a support. For this purpose a support such as silica or magnesia is impregnated with a solution of nickel and the resulting mass is heated to decompose nickel nitrate to nickel oxide and the latter is reduced to metallic nickel by means of hydrogen. The resulting catalyst is used for hydrogenating organic compounds, e.g. olefins and unsaturated oils and fats.

14.12.1 Statistics

The world production of nickel ores was 350 000 long tons in 1963 (in terms of Ni). About 30% was consumed in the USA. About 10% of the consumption in the USA was in the form of compounds. The US production of nickel sulphate hexahydrate was near 10 000 long tons in 1963 (2 200 tons in terms of Ni). The United Kingdom is an important producer of nickel salts and exported 500 long tons of nickel oxide and 5 000 long tons of nickel salts (including nickel sulphate) in 1963.

14.12.2 Literature

J. G. DEAN. 'The industrial growth of nickel compounds', *Industrial and engineering chemistry,* **51** (Oct. 1959), 40A-45A.

G. C. PRIDDY. *Caracteristiques et applications des principals sels de nickel.* Centre d'information du nickel Bruxelles, 1957.

14.13   PLATINUM COMPOUNDS (Pt, atomic weight = 195.1)

The most important platinum compounds are hexachloroplatinic acid (chloroplatinic acid, $H_2PbCl_6.6H_2O$) and its ammonium salt. Chloroplatinic acid is a complex compound of platinum tetrachloride ($PtCl_4$) and hydrochloric acid. It is often referred to as 'platinum chloride'.

Chloroplatinic acid is prepared by dissolving platinum in aqua regia (compare chloroauric acid) and evaporating the resulting solution. The evaporation is repeated, after adding hydrochloric acid, to expel the nitric acid. *Ammonium chloroplatinate* (($NH_4)_2 PtCl_6$) can be precipitated from a solution of chloroplatinic acid, by adding ammonium chloride. Chloroplatinic acid and ammonium chloroplatinate are usually formed in the recovery of platinum from ores and in platinum refining. The ammonium salt forms yellow cubes which are slightly soluble in water. It is particularly important for the production of platinum powder or sponge which can be obtained by heating ammonium chloroplatinate to redness.

14.14   MANGANESE COMPOUNDS (Mn, atomic weight = 54.94)

Manganese, technetium (Tc) and rhenium (Re) form the seventh subgroup of the periodic system. Technetium is unstable and does not occur naturally. It can be formed in nuclear reactions but it is not of commercial importance. Rhenium is a stable element but it belongs to the very rarest of the elements.

Manganese forms compounds in all valence states from one to seven inclusive. Compounds of monovalent and pentavalent manganese are rarities. Valence states of two, four and seven are the most common. The oxide of divalent manganese (manganous oxide, MnO) has a basic character and forms manganous salts with acids. These salts usually have a pink colour in solution. Manganic oxide (Mn_2O_3) containing trivalent manganese is also basic and forms manganic salts with acids but many of these are unstable. Compounds of tetravalent manganese are very unstable with the exception of manganese dioxide (MnO_2). This oxide has an amphoteric character. In its hexa- and heptavalent states manganese has an acid character and manganates (e.g. K_2MnO_4) and permanganates (e.g. $KMnO_4$) can be formed respectively. Manganates are salts derived from the hypothetical manganic acid (H_2MnO_4), and permanganates are derived from the relatively strong permanganic acid ($HMnO_4$). The manganates are usually deep green in solution and the permanganates form an intense purple colour.

14.14.1 Manganese dioxide

Manganese dioxide (battery manganese, MnO_2) occurs naturally as pyrolusite. It is among the most important sources of manganese and its compounds (see mining, ore concentration and metallurgy of manganese, vol. III). Pure grades mined as such or obtained by mechanical purification processes can be used as such for non-metallurgical purposes. Pure manganese dioxide is also obtained by chemical processing of crude manganese ores.

In one process finely ground ore is reduced to manganous oxide (MnO) by heating at 600° C for several hours in the presence of a reducing agent (e.g. a carbonaceous material or a reducing gas). The resulting product is leached with dilute nitric acid

(8-10%). Manganous oxide dissolves with the formation of manganous nitrate ($Mn(NO_3)_2$) which is crystallized by evaporating and cooling the solution after filtering. The mother liquor is recycled to the leaching stage. Manganous nitrate is converted into manganese dioxide and nitrogen dioxide by heating at 120 to 200° C. In a similar process a slurry of crude manganese dioxide is leached with nitrogen dioxide (instead of dilute nitric acid) without reduction process. This process is possible, since manganese dioxide, being insoluble in nitric acid, dissolves in nitrogen dioxide with the formation of manganous nitrate.

In another process crude manganese dioxide is reduced to manganous oxide and leached with sulphuric acid (Rhodochrosite, a natural manganous carbonate $MnCO_3$ is leached as such with sulphuric acid). Several impurities such as iron compounds can be precipitated by adding sodium hydroxide to the resulting solution of manganous sulphate ($MnSO_4$) until the precipitation of ferric hydroxide starts. Hydrated manganese oxide (manganic hydroxide, $MgO(OH)$) can be precipitated from the resulting purified solution by adding more sodium hydroxide and aeration. The resulting slurry is oxidized to manganese dioxide by continuing aeration for some hours. Manganous sulphate can also be oxidized to manganese dioxide by electrolysis of a solution of manganous sulphate. Manganese dioxide is precipitated on the anode.

These processes and several others, depending on the kind of starting materials, are also used for the concentration of low grade ores.

Manganese dioxide is a black or brown-black solid which forms crystals (usually tetragonal pyrolusite) or an amorphous or poorly crystallized powder. It is insoluble in water and oxidizing acids. It is an oxidizing agent, thus it reacts readily with reducing agents such as sulphur dioxide.

Important quantities of pure manganese dioxide are used in dry galvanic cells (batteries) as a depolariser. Polarization in a battery is caused by the formation of hydrogen at the positive electrode (anode) when it is in use. In the electrolyte solution, hydrogen suppresses the potential difference (voltage) of the battery. When the positive electrode is surrounded with a layer of manganese dioxide, the formation of hydrogen is prevented due to the oxidizing property of manganese dioxide (see also accumulators and galvanic cells, vol. II).

Manganese dioxide is used as a decolorizing agent in glass to neutralize the greenish tint caused by ferrous iron. Manganese dioxide is also used for producing brown glazes and for the production of dark brown or black bricks. Black bricks can be produced by adding finely ground manganese dioxide to clay which would otherwise burn to a terracotta colour. Frequently a surface colour is produced on bricks by blowing a mixture of manganese dioxide and salt on the surface of the clay body before firing.

Formerly manganese dioxide was also used as drying agent in linseed oil and other vegetable oils for paints and varnishes. Nowadays certain organic manganese compounds such as the naphthenate, resinate and linoleate are used for this purpose (compare also cobalt dryers, vol. V).

Due to its oxidizing property manganese dioxide can be used as an oxidizing agent in chemical processes (e.g. see manganous sulphate, p. 593, and concentration of uranium ores, p. 661). High grade manganese dioxide is the starting material for the production of other manganese compounds. In 1963 the world production of manganese ore (mainly crude manganese dioxide containing about 40% Mn) was about 16 million short tons gross weight, corresponding to about 6 million tons of manganese. It is estimated that only 500 000 to 600 000 short tons of manganese ore were for non-metallurgical purposes. In the USA about 28 000 short tons of manganese ore were consumed for dry batteries and 94 000 short tons in chemical processes and for the production of manganese compounds; manganese dioxide (83-87%) was sold at $ 144 to $ 148 per short ton in 1965.

14.14.2 Manganous sulphate

Manganous sulphate ($MnSO_4$) is prepared by evaporating manganous sulphate solutions obtained as described above for the purification of manganese dioxide. It is also obtained in a process for the production of hydroquinone from aniline. In one stage of this process aniline is oxidized to quinone with manganese dioxide in concentrated sulphuric acid:

$$2C_6H_5.NH_2 + 4MnO_2 + 5H_2SO_4 \rightarrow 2\ OC_6H_4O + 4MnSO_4 + (NH_4)_2SO_4 + 4H_2$$

Quinone is separated from the reaction mixture by distilling with steam and manganous sulphate can be recovered from the remaining solution. A commercial product containing some ammonium sulphate is obtained by filtering and evaporating the solution followed by spray drying.

Manganous sulphate forms pink crystals which are very soluble in water. Several hydrates are known.

The impure grades containing ammonium sulphate are used in agriculture. In certain areas in the USA (e.g. in Florida and Texas) manganous sulphate is added to neutral or alkaline soils containing too little manganese. It is said that manganese increases the yield of crops of tomatoes, potatoes and beans and combats chlorosis in various crops. Mixtures of manganous sulphate and ammonium sulphate or pure manganous sulphate are used in the electrolytic production of pure manganese. Purer manganous sulphate monohydrate is used for adding to feedstuffs such as chicken feeds.

In 1965 the US prices for manganous sulphate were: fertilizer grade (65%), $ 95 per short ton; technical (75-78%), $72 to $75 per short ton; feed grade, $85 per short ton.

14.14.3 Manganous chloride

Manganous chloride ($MnCl_2$) is produced by the reaction of hydrochloric acid with manganese dioxide. The latter oxidizes hydrochloric acid to chlorine and water and dissolves with the formation of manganous chloride according to the following equation:

$$MnO_2 + 4\ HCl \rightarrow MnCl_2 + Cl_2 + 2\ H_2O$$

The resulting still acid solution is neutralized by means of additional manganese dioxide, thus precipitating hydroxides of impurities such as iron and aluminium. Pink manganous chloride tetrahydrate crystallizes after filtration, evaporation and cooling of the solution. The product is dehydrated by drying above 200° C. The chlorine generated during the reaction of manganese dioxide with hydrochloric acid is absorbed in a slurry of lime in an absorption tower. To avoid generation of chlorine, rhodochrosite (manganese carbonate) is sometimes used as starting material.

Anhydrous manganous chloride is mainly used in the production of corrosion resisting magnesium alloys. The tetrahydrate is sometimes added to the electrolyte solution of dry galvanic cells to reduce their internal resistance and to make them more stable when stored.

In 1965 the price of anhydrous manganous chloride in the USA was $ 0.19 to $ 0.21 per lb.

14.14.4 Potassium permanganate

Potassium permanganate ($KMnO_4$) is prepared in two stages. In the first stage manganese dioxide (tetravalent Mn) is oxidized to a manganate (hexavalent Mn) as follows: finely ground manganese ore containing at least 60% manganese dioxide is mixed with a 50% solution of potassium hydroxide and passed through a series of rotary kilns. The first kilns are fired internally to a temperature of 350° C by burning hydrogen in a large amount of air. The last kilns are heated externally to a temperature of 250° C. The reaction product of each kiln is ground and moistened before passing through the following kiln. Air and steam are passed through the kilns. The reaction product is discharged from the last kiln as an impure melt of potassium manganate. The reaction may be represented by the following equation:

$$2 MnO_2 + 4 KOH + O_2 \rightarrow 2 K_2MnO_4 + 2 H_2O.$$

The yield is about 92 to 96%. Without the addition of steam the conversion is about 65%. It is said that dehydrated complexes, which are less reactive, are formed in the absence of steam.

In the second stage of the process, the melt of potassium manganate is dissolved in water, filtered and oxidized to potassium permanganate either in an electrolytic cell or in a chemical process. Electrolytic oxidation is usually performed in a cylindrical cell containing a number of concentric cylindrical anodes (nickel-plated). The cathodes consist of iron rods and are placed in the annular spaces between the anodes. The voltage of the cell is about 2.6 V and the current is 1 400 A. At the anode potassium manganate is oxidized to potassium permanganate and at the cathode water is reduced to gaseous hydrogen and hydroxyl ions (compare chlorates, p. 238). The result of these reactions may be represented by the following equation:

$$2 K_2MnO_4 + 2 H_2O \rightarrow 2 KMnO_4 + 2 KOH + H_2.$$

Thus the potassium hydroxide concentration of the solution increases. About 95% of the potassium manganate in a solution, containing 200 g per litre, is converted into potassium permanganate. The resulting solution is cooled to 10-15° C and potassium permanganate crystallizes. The latter is filtered and the remaining mother liquor is evaporated to recover a concentrated solution of potassium hydroxide, which can be used in the first stage of the process. During evaporation the last traces of potassium manganate, potassium permanganate and impurities precipitate and are removed. Crude potassium permanganate can be purified by redissolving and recrystallization. In a modification of the electrolytic oxidation process the slurry, obtained by digesting the melt of the first stage of the process with water, is electrolysed without filtering in a cell provided with a stirrer. The insoluble substances are removed after crystallizing and redissolving the permanganate.

In a chemical oxidation process, obsolete in Europe but still used in the USA, the filtered solution of potassium manganate is neutralized with carbon dioxide and heated.

Under these conditions two thirds of the potassium manganate is oxidized to potassium permanganate by the remaining one third which in turn is reduced to manganese dioxide. The latter is removed by filtering and returned to the first stage of the process. Solid potassium permanganate is obtained by cooling and filtration. An additional portion is obtained by evaporating the mother liquor in a double effect evaporator.

Potassium permanganate forms glittering dark purple crystals with a sweetish astringent taste. Its solubility in water is relatively low; at 20° C about 6 g dissolve in 100 g water. At a temperature of 240° C potassium permanganate decomposes with the liberation of oxygen. Because of its strong oxidizing action it must be stored and shipped in glass or steel containers. When potassium permanganate is heated in contact with organic substances, explosions can occur.

The uses of potassium permanganate depend on its oxidizing power. Important quantities are used for the production of saccharin and benzoic acid since potassium permanganate oxidizes the methyl group of toluene and toluene derivatives to a carboxylic acid group. Manganese dioxide is obtained as a by-product. Potassium permanganate is also used for bleaching and decolorizing several organic substances such as oils, fats, waxes and natural sponge. It is also used in textile bleaching, as a disinfectant and antiseptic and for staining wood. In 1965 potassium permanganate was sold in the USA at $0.24 to $0.45 per lb and in the UK at £236 10s per long ton.

14.15 COMPOUNDS OF CHROMIUM MOLYBDENUM AND TUNGSTEN

Chromium, molybdenum and tungsten (or wolfram) form the sixth subgroup of the periodic system of the elements. The elements of the sixth subgroup can function in all valence states from two to six in their compounds. In addition there are a few chromium compounds in which chromium is monovalent. In the most important compounds the elements of this group are hexavalent. Thus important trioxides of all these elements are available. The trioxides form salts with bases which are named chromates, molybdates and tungstates respectively. The compositions of these compounds are analogous to the sulphates but they differ from the latter in their strong tendency to form compounds which contain more than one equivalent of trioxide to one equivalent of base. Thus, besides chromates, there are also dichromates (corresponding with pyrosulphates), trichromates and tetrachromates. Polymolybdates and polytungstates which contain much more MoO_3 and WO_3 units per molecule of base, are also known. The strength of the acids derived from the trioxide (H_2CrO_4, H_2MoO_4, and H_2WO_3) decreases from chromium to tungsten.

Besides the compounds derived from hexavalent chromium, various compounds of bivalent and trivalent chromium are also known. These compounds resemble the corresponding ferrous and aluminium compounds respectively. Compounds of monovalent, tetravalent and pentavalent chromium are rarities. The other elements of the sixth subgroup form important compounds in their tetravalent state, e.g. molybdenum disulphide and tungsten carbide.

14.16 CHROMIUM COMPOUNDS (Cr, atomic weight = 52.01)

14.16.1 Sodium dichromate

Sodium dichromate ($Na_2Cr_2O_7 . 2 H_2O$) is produced from chrome ores (chromite, $FeO.Cr_2O_3$) containing 42-50% chromic oxide. The ore is ground until 90-98% passes through a 200 mesh sieve and is mixed with soda ash. Sometimes lime is also added. Either burned or hydrated lime may be used. The mixture is roasted at a temperature between 1 100 and 1 250° C in an oil-fired rotary kiln which is refractory lined. The mixture passes through the furnace within one to four hours. Under the given reaction conditions, the trivalent chromium in chromic oxide is oxidized to hexavalent chromium (in sodium chromate, Na_2CrO_4). Reaction equation:

$$2 Cr_2O_3 + 4 Na_2CO_3 + 3 O_2 \rightarrow 4 Na_2CrO_4 + 4 CO_2.$$

The resulting product is cooled and leached with water. If lime is used in the roasting process, the leaching process must be modified, since calcium chromate produced can not be leached with water. The leaching is then performed by heating with soda ash and water in an autoclave at a temperature above 100° C. Calcium chromate is converted into sodium chromate which dissolves in water. The slurry is clarified and the resulting solution contains 25% of sodium chromate or more and impurities such as sodium aluminate. The latter may be precipitated as aluminium hydroxide by neutralizing the solution with sulphuric acid, carbon dioxide or a solution of sodium dichromate. The solution obtained is evaporated to a concentration of 40 to 45% sodium chromate and is then treated with concentrated sulphuric acid. In this process, sodium chromate loses water and is converted into sodium dichromate according to the following reaction equation:

$$2 Na_2CrO_4 + H_2SO_4 \rightarrow Na_2Cr_2O_7 + Na_2SO_4 + H_2O.$$

Some sodium sulphate precipitates during the reaction. The slurry is concentrated in a multiple-effect evaporator. Crystallized sodium sulphate is removed in stages during the evaporation and sold as a by-product. Sodium bichromate is crystallized in vacuum crystallizers and separated from the mother liquor. The latter is returned to the crystallizer. The crystalline product obtained is dried and sold as technical grade. Pure grades are obtained by dissolving and recrystallization.

Sodium dichromate is a hygroscopic orange-red crystalline product which is very soluble in water. It is usually available as the dihydrate which can be converted into the anhydrous salt by heating. The latter melts at 356° C and decomposes at 400° C. Dust of sodium dichromate is very harmful. It causes irritation of the mucous membranes, eyes and skin.

Sodium dichromate is the starting material for all other chromium compounds. It is used as a tanning agent for leather, as a mordant for wool dyeing, as a preservative for wood (see sodium arsenate, p. 398) and as a fungicide. Sodium dichromate is also used for the production of various pigments such as chrome green, zinc chromate and lead chromate (see vol. V). With various colloids, such as glue, gum arabic and gelatin, it forms light-sensitive materials which are used in photomechanical reproduction (see photography, vol. VI). Sodium dichromate is also a corrosion inhibitor. For this reason it is used in cooling fluids, e.g. refrigerating brines and cooling water of automobiles. It is also used in boilers, in air washers and in oil well drilling muds to retard corrosion.

Several explanations have been given for the anti-corrosive action of sodium dichromate, but none seems to be quite satisfactory. In the metal industry sodium dichromate is used in baths for the pickling, etching or bright dipping of brass. It serves to balance the rates of dissolution of copper and zinc. Sodium dichromate forms protective coatings on zinc, cadmium and tin plate. Paints adhere better to steel and aluminium if these are coated with sodium dichromate.

The world production of sodium dichromate is not precisely known but it is said that more than 50% is produced in the USA. Total output in the USA was about 130000 short tons in 1963. This quantity was used for the following purposes (end uses).

	%		%
Pigments	38	Metal treating	10
Leather tanning	20	Wool dyeing	6
Chromic acid (e.g. for chromium plating)	17	Other uses and exports	9

Since sodium dichromate is the starting material for all chromium chemicals, the uses of other chromium compounds are included in the figures.

The production of sodium dichromate in the UK is not known but it may be of the order of magnitude of 10000 to 20000 tons.

In 1965 sodium dichromate was sold in the USA at $ 260 to $ 270 per short ton and in the UK at £ 102 per long ton.

14.16.2 Sodium chromate

Sodium chromate (Na_2CrO_4) may be obtained as an intermediate in the process for the production of sodium dichromate but it always contains some sodium sulphate which cannot be removed by recrystallization. For this reason almost all sodium chromate is prepared by heating a mixture of pure sodium dichromate and sodium carbonate in a moist atmosphere obtained by introducing steam in the air stream. After drying, a product containing 99.7% sodium chromate is obtained. This can be purified by recrystallization.

Sodium chromate forms yellow crystals. It melts at 792° C and is slightly hygroscopic. Sodium chromate is used for the same purposes as sodium dichromate but the latter is preferred because it is cheaper per unit of CrO_3. The price of sodium chromate in the USA in 1965 was $ 290 to $ 320 per short ton.

14.16.3 Potassium dichromate

Potassium dichromate ($K_2Cr_2O_7$) can be prepared by roasting chromite with potassium carbonate by a method similar to that for the production of the corresponding sodium salt. However it is mainly prepared by dissolving a predetermined amount of potassium chloride in a hot concentrated solution of sodium dichromate. Potassium dichromate crystals are formed when the solution is cooled.

Potassium dichromate is an orange-red crystalline product which melts at 397° C. Unlike sodium dichromate it is not hygroscopic. Partly for this reason but also because of its oxidizing properties it is used in safety matches and in pyrotechnics. It may also be used for the same purposes as sodium dichromate but it is more expensive. In 1965 it was sold in the USA at $ 380 to $ 400 per short ton and in the UK at £ 132 to £ 141 per long ton.

14.16.4 Chromium trioxide

Chromium trioxide (chromic acid anhydride, CrO_3) is erroneously known as chromic acid. It is prepared by mixing sodium dichromate with sulphuric acid in a steel tank equipped with a gate-type agitator. Reaction equation:

$$Na_2Cr_2O_7 + 2\ H_2SO_4 \rightarrow 2\ NaHSO_4 + 2\ CrO_3.$$

Heat is liberated and a molten mass having a temperature of 196° C is obtained. Chromium trioxide is heavier than sodium bisulphate and slightly soluble in the latter. Thus chromium trioxide collects at the bottom and can be drawn off. It is converted into flakes by passing between a pair of water-cooled rollers or by dropping on a cooled rotating drum.

Chromium trioxide is a dark red crystalline material. It melts at a temperature of 196° C and decomposes above this temperature. It is very hygroscopic and soluble in water. The freezing point of a 60.5% solution of chromium trioxide in water is − 150° C. In solution in water it acts as a solution of chromic acid (H_2CrO_4) and it can form chromates and dichromates with bases, but an acid having the formula H_2CrO_4 can not be separated from solution.

Chromium trioxide is a strong oxidizing agent, hence its use in organic synthesis. The bleaching of oils is another type of oxidation by means of chromium trioxide, e.g. montan wax and olive oil are bleached by emulsifying with sulphuric acid and dropping a concentrated solution of chromic acid into it. The chromium compounds are removed by washing with very dilute sulphuric acid followed by washing with water.

An important application of chromium trioxide is its use in chromium plating baths and in the anodizing of aluminium and its alloys (e.g. for aircraft construction). Very pure solutions of chromium trioxide are needed. These solutions can be purified by means of ion exchangers. Chromium trioxide is also used for etching metals and for the electrolytic production of metallic chromium. The production of chromium trioxide in the USA in 1963 was about 19000 short tons. In 1965 the price of technical chromium trioxide in the USA was $ 0.29 to $ 0.31 per lb; the pure grade was sold at $ 1.15 per lb.

14.16.5 Chromic oxide

As chromium can be di-, tri- and hexavalent in its compounds, three different oxides are known: chromous oxide (CrO), chromic oxide (Cr_2O_3) and chromium trioxide (CrO_3) having a basic, amphoteric and acidic character respectively. Only chromium trioxide (see above) and chromic oxide are of industrial importance.

Chromic oxide occurs naturally in the only important chromium mineral chromite ($FeO.Cr_2O_3$) which is the starting material for the production of metallic chromium, refractories (see vol. II) and sodium dichromate.

Commercial chromic oxide is produced by heating sodium dichromate with an excess of sulphur in a reverberatory furnace at low red heat. Small quantities of ammonium chloride and carbonaceous material (e.g. starch) are added to improve the colour of the reaction product. Reaction equation:

$$Na_2Cr_2O_7 + S \rightarrow Cr_2O_3 + Na_2SO_4.$$

The reaction mixture is washed with water to dissolve the sodium sulphate. After filtering and drying, chromic oxide is ground and packaged in paper bags. Chromic oxide is also produced by heating sodium dichromate with other reducing agents (e.g. coal).

Chromic oxide is a dark green amorphous powder. If heated above 900° C it is converted into a crystalline product which is insoluble in water and acids. Its melting point is near 2 000° C.

Chromic oxide is used as a catalyst. Especially chromic oxide-copper oxide catalysts are widely used, e.g. for the production of methanol. Chromic oxide is also used as a pigment (see vol. V) and for the production of green coloured glass. In 1965 in the USA the price of chromic oxide was $ 0.45 to $ 0.48 per lb.

14.16.6 Chromic hydroxide

Several processes for the production of chromic hydroxide (hydrated chromic oxide, $Cr_2O_3.xH_2O$) are used. Hydrated chromic oxide may be prepared by boiling a solution of sodium dichromate with sulphur (see also chromic oxide), by reduction of sodium dichromate with any carbonaceous material (e.g. sugar molasses) under pressure, and by melting sodium dichromate with boric acid and decomposing the chromium-boron compound formed by means of water.

Like chromic oxide, chromic hydroxide has a green colour. It can be dehydrated by heating at 400° C. Chromic hydroxide obtained by the methods previously described is slightly soluble in dilute strong acids and bases. However, chromic hydroxide which is freshly precipitated from a solution of a chromic salt with a base is even soluble in weak acids. This freshly precipitated hydroxide is an intermediate in the production of other chromic salts. The slightly soluble products are used as pigments (see vol. V). The chromic hydroxide obtained by means of boric acid is known as Guignet's green or emerald green.

14.16.7 Chromium chlorides

Chromic chloride (CrCl₃) can be prepared by passing a current of chlorine through chromic oxide, or a mixture of chromic oxide and carbon, which is heated at a temperature above 600° C. Pinkish-violet shimmering plates of chromic chloride condense in the cooler parts of the apparatus. Chromic chloride can also be prepared in solution by dissolving chromic oxide in concentrated hydrochloric acid. Basic salts are obtained by evaporating solutions of chromic chloride. Chromic chloride solutions are used as a mordant in the textile industry.

Chromyl chloride (CrO₂Cl₂) evaporates from a boiling mixture of sodium dichromate, concentrated sulphuric acid and common salt. Chromyl chloride condenses as a red liquid resembling bromine. Its melting point is −96.5° C and its boiling point is 116.7° C. It is a powerful oxidizing agent. Several combustible materials burn spontaneously when in contact with chromyl chloride. Chromyl chloride is used in the synthesis of organic chemicals.

Chromous chloride (CrCl₂) is prepared by reducing chromic acid with hydrogen or with zinc and hydrochloric acid. It is a very strong reducing agent.

14.16.8 Basic chromic sulphate and chrome alums

Basic chromic sulphate ($Cr(OH)SO_4$) is prepared by reducing sodium dichromate either with glucose or with sulphur dioxide. In the first process a solution of sodium dichromate and an excess of sulphuric acid is introduced into a lead-lined tank and mixed with glucose which is slowly added. The orange solution of sodium dichromate turns to green, due to the formation of trivalent chromium ions, according to the following reaction equation:

$$8\,Na_2Cr_2O_7 + 24\,H_2SO_4 + C_{12}H_{22}O_{11} \rightarrow 8\,Na_2SO_4 + 16\,Cr(OH)SO_4 + 12\,CO_2 + 27\,H_2O$$

A similar solution of basic chromic sulphate is obtained by contercurrently contacting a sodium dichromate solution with sulphur dioxide. Reaction equation:

$$Na_2Cr_2O_7 + 3\,SO_2 + H_2O \rightarrow Na_2SO_4 + 2\,Cr(OH)SO_4.$$

A solid mixture of basic chromic sulphate and sodium sulphate is obtained by evaporating and drying by means of a spray dryer or drum dryer. This mixture is sold as such. Pure basic chromic sulphate can be obtained by precipitating chromic hydroxide from the basic sulphate – sodium sulphate solution – by neutralizing with a base and dissolving the chromic hydroxide in sulphuric acid after filtration. This solution is evaporated.

Basic chromic sulphate is widely used for chrome-tanning leather. Several other basic chromic sulphates are known. They have a varying basicity and contain varying quantities of water of crystallisation. Like aluminium sulphate, chromic sulphates show a tendency to form double salts with potassium and ammonium sulphate.

Potassium chrome alum ($KCr(SO_4)_2.12\ H_2O$) is prepared by passing a stream of sulphur dioxide through a solution of potassium dichromate in dilute sulphuric acid (compare the production of basic chromic sulphate). Dark purple crystals are obtained by cooling the solution. The mother liquor is used again. Potassium chrome alum is used as a mordant in dyeing and printing cotton and as a tanning agent for leather (see vol. V).

Ammonium chrome alum ($NH_4Cr(SO_4)_2.12\ H_2O$) can be prepared from ammonium dichromate in the same manner as the potassium chrome alum. It can also be prepared by treating chrome ore with a hot mixture of sulphuric acid and ammonium sulphate. Ammonium chrome alum forms small purple crystals. It is used for the same purposes as the corresponding potassium alum.

14.16.9 Complex chromic salts of organic acids

Complexes of chromic salts and organic acids may be produced from basic chromic chloride and an organic acid e.g. stearic acid, glycollic acid or sorbic acid.

Stearatochromic chloride is formed from basic chromic chloride and stearic acid or sodium stearate. The following formula has been proposed for this complex:

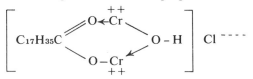

(see also complexes, p. 130). Stearatochromic chloride is known under the trade name 'Quilon'. It has surface active properties in aqueous solution. If it is applied on polar surfaces (e.g. surfaces of glass and cellulose) the latter become water repellent.

Complexes with p-amino benzoic acid can be used on surfaces as a barrier to ultra-violet light and methacrylato chromic chloride (having the trade name 'Volan') can be used as an adhesive for the production of glass-resin laminates. The complexes described above are commercially available as a solution in isopropyl alcohol.

14.16.10 Literature
M. J. UDY. Chromium. Vol. I Chemistry of chromium and its compounds. New York, Reinhold, 1956. ACS monograph No. 132.

14.17 MOLYBDENUM COMPOUNDS (Mo, atomic weight = 95.95)

Only a few few molybdenum compounds are of commercial importance.

Molybdenum disulphide (Molybdic sulphide, MoS_2) occurs naturally as molybdenite (molybdenum glance). It is the only commercial source of molybdenum and its compounds. Ores containing molybdenite are concentrated by grinding and flotation. The product obtained is the starting material for the production of molybdenum trioxide and metallic molybdenum (see vol. III). Technical molybdenum disulphide is produced from ore concentrates by repeated grinding and flotation. The resulting concentrate is heated in an oxygen-free atmosphere to remove water and oil from the flotation processes. The resulting product contains not more than 0.4% impurities which consist mainly of silica (sand). Pure molybdenum disulphide is obtained by treating the technical product with hydrogen fluoride, washing with water and drying. Molybdenum disulphide is a dark grey powder which is greasy to touch, like graphite. It sublimes at a temperature of 450° C and condenses as flat, thin and flexible leaves.

Technical and pure grades of molybdenum disulphide are used as lubricants especially for use at extreme pressure and high vacuum. It is used as such or mixed with grease or oil. Such lubricants are known under trade names such as Molykote and Moly-sylphide (see Lubricants, vol. IV). Molynamal is a lubricating enamel consisting of resin bounded molybdenum disulphide.

The world production of molybdenum ore was 76000 short tons in 1963 (in terms of MoS_2). About 72% is produced and about 50% is consumed in the USA. The United Kingdom imported 6300 short tons in 1963. It is estimated that about 5-10% of the world production is used in the chemical industry. The remainder is used for metallurgical purposes.

In the USA molybdenum sulphide (95% MoS_2) was sold at $ 1.40 per lb in 1965.

Molybdenum trioxide (MoO_3) is produced by roasting concentrated molybdenum ores at a temperature up to 650° C. The crude oxide is purified by sublimation at a temperature of about 1000° C. Molybdenum trioxide is a soft white powder which turns yellow if heated. Its melting point is 795° C and its boiling point is 1155° C but it begins to sublime in the neighbourhood of its melting point. Molybdenum trioxide dissolves in bases and forms molybdates. Thus it is used for the production of sodium and ammonium molybdate. Molybdenum trioxide is also a catalyst in the petroleum industry, e.g. for desulphurizing hydrocarbons and the oxidation of hydrocarbons to carboxylic acids. It is also used as a trace element in fertilizers and for the production of metallic molybdenum. The price of technical molybdenum trioxide in the USA was $ 1.75 per lb in 1965.

Sodium molybdate (Na_2MoO_4) is prepared by melting a mixture of soda ash and molybdenum trioxide. If molybdenum trioxide is dissolved in sodium hydroxide, a series of white complex salts, containing sodium hydroxide and molybdenum trioxide in a varying ratio, can be obtained depending on the pH and the reaction temperature. Sodium molybdate is used for the production of pigments especially 'molybdate chrome orange' which is a homogeneous mixture of lead chromate, lead molybdate and lead sulphate. Sodium molybdate is also used in fertilizers to provide plants with traces of molybdenum.

Ammonium molybdate ($3(NH_4)_2MoO_4.4MoO_3.4H_2O$) is prepared by dissolving molybdenum trioxide in an excess of ammonia. It is used for the same purposes as sodium molybdate, for the production of catalyst mixtures containing molybdenum trioxide and in analytical chemistry. It is also used for the production of phosphomolybdic acid (a complex of phosphoric acid and molybdic acid) which is used for the precipitation of basic organic pigments from their solutions (phosphomolybdic pigments or molybdenum lakes).

14.17.1 Literature

D. H. KILLEFFER and A. LINZ. *Molybdenum compounds, their chemistry and technology.* New York, Interscience, 1952.

B. H. DANZIGER et al. 'Industrial applications of molybdenum chemistry', *Industrial and engineering chemistry,* **47** (Aug. 1955), pp. 1492-1514.

14.18 TUNGSTEN COMPOUNDS (W, atomic weight = 183.9)

Tungsten trioxide (tungstic oxide, WO_3) can be produced from the minerals scheelite (calcium tungstate, $CaWO_3$) and wolframite (a tungstate of iron and magnesium) by heating them with a mixture of dry soda ash and sodium nitrate. The melt is leached with water to dissolve sodium tungstate. Crude tungstic acid ($H_2WO_4.H_2O$) is precipitated by adding hydrochloric acid to the solution after clarification. Tungstic acid is purified by dissolving in ammonia, filtering the solution and precipitating once again by means of hydrochloric acid. Tungstic acid is converted into tungsten trioxide by heating at a temperature of $1000°$ C. Tungsten trioxide is a yellow powder which melts at $1473°$ C. It is by far the most important of the tungsten oxides. It is used for the production of metallic tungsten (see volume III) and tungsten compounds. In the USA tungsten trioxide was sold at $ 2.25 per lb in 1965.

Sodium tungstate ($Na_2WO_3.2 H_2O$) is obtained by dissolving tungsten trioxide in a caustic soda solution followed by concentration and crystallization. Sodium tungstate is a white crystalline solid which is soluble in water. It is mainly used in tungsten metallurgy. Small quantities are used for fireproofing fabrics and cellulose. It is also used for the production of phosphotungstic acid (a complex compound of phosphoric acid and tungsten trioxide). The latter has the property of precipitating basic dyes from their solution and hence it is used in the manufacture of certain pigments for printing inks (compare phosphomolybdic acid, see above).

Calcium and *barium tungstate* can be precipitated from solutions of sodium tungstate by adding a solution of a calcium and barium salt respectively. These compounds are used in phosphorescent screens for X-ray photography.

Magnesium tungstate is a blue-emitting phosphor (see phosphors, p. 671).

Tungsten carbide (WC) is prepared by heating a mixture of tungsten (or tungsten oxide) and carbon at a temperature of about 1 500-1 600° C in an inert atmosphere. This product is a grey powder after crushing. It has a hardness approaching that of diamond and its melting point is about 2 800° C. These properties make it possible to use it in machine parts where resistance to wear is important and in tools and abrasives for machining metals and other hard materials. Examples of such applications are: bits used in rock drilling, dies for drawing metal wire and tools for cutting cast iron and other metals. For these purposes tungsten carbide is often mixed with cobalt powder and sintered (cemented tungsten carbide). Tungsten carbide coatings on steel are produced by melting the surface of the steel with an inert gas shielded arc and blowing tungsten carbide powder on the molten surface.

Tungsten carbide is the most important tungsten compound. This is illustrated by the following figures. The total consumption of tungsten products in the USA was about 5 000 long tons in 1963 (in terms of tungsten), 40% was consumed as tungsten carbide. The other chemicals accounted for about 3% of the tungsten consumption. The production and consumption of tungsten carbide in the United Kingdom has not been published but the production is more than enough to cover home demand. The exports were 150 long tons in 1962.

14.18.1 Literature

A. S. HESTER. 'Tungsten carbide', *Industrial and engineering chemistry,* **52** (February 1960), pp. 94-100.

14.19 VANADIUM COMPOUNDS (V, atomic weight = 50.95)

Vanadium is the first element of the fifth subgroup of the periodic system which consists of vanadium, niobium or columbium (Nb) and tantalum (Ta). Niobium and tantalum are mainly of importance in the metallurgical industry. Like tungsten carbide, niobium carbide and tantalum carbide are important constituents of cemented carbide cutting tools.

Vanadium can be di-, tri, tetra- and pentavalent in its compounds. The terms hypovanadous, vanadous, hypovanadic and vanadic are often used for the valence states from 2 to 5 respectively. However the nomenclature of vanadium compounds is subject to much confusion in the literature. The oxides of vanadium are amphoteric but vanadium monoxide (VO) is predominantly basic and vanadium pentoxide (V_2O_5) is predominantly acidic. Vanadium pentoxide forms vanadates with alkali metal hydroxides. Orthovanadates, pyrovanadates, metavanadates and complex polyvanadates are known (compare phosphates, p. 375).

Vanadium pentoxide and ammonium metavanadate (NH_4VO_3) are the most important vanadium compounds. These compounds are produced by roasting vanadium ores with common salt, followed by leaching with water. Crude vanadium pentoxide is precipitated from the resulting solution of sodium vanadate by adding dilute sulphuric acid. Vanadium pentoxide is purified by redissolving in a soda solution followed by precipitating in the form of ammonium metavanadate by adding ammonium chloride. Ammonium metavanadate is a white crystalline solid which can be decomposed to pure vanadium pentoxide and ammonia by calcining at about 300° C in the presence of air. Vanadium pentoxide is a yellowish-red product, melting at 660° C. It recrystallizes from the melt in the form of red needles. Like other compounds of pentavalent vanadium, vanadium pentoxide acts as an irritant to the respiratory tract and the eyes.

Vanadium pentoxide is a very important catalyst. The catalyst is often made by mixing ammonium metavanadate with a support such as diatomite, tripoli etc. followed by heating the mixture to form vanadium pentoxide on the support. The catalysts are used in several catalytic oxidation processes. The most important processes are the catalytic oxidation of sulphur dioxide to sulphur trioxide in the contact process for the production of sulphuric acid (see p. 286), and the catalytic oxidation of naphthalene to phthalic anhydride. Smaller quantities of vanadium pentoxide are used as a catalyst in the production of aniline black (a rich black dye) from aniline hydrochloride and a chlorate, in the manufacture of rubber and in drying of paints, varnishes etc.

Due to new motor traffic laws in some states of the USA, designed to reduce atmospheric pollution and 'smog' formation, it is expected that in future much vanadium pentoxide will be consumed as catalyst in catalytic afterburners for combustion gases of motor vehicles (see gaseous pollutants of air, p. 108).

Vanadium pentoxide is also used in glass-making. If about 0.02 % V_2O_5 is added, the glass remains colourless, but it filters out wavelengths below 3 590 Å (ultraviolet). In larger quantities, vanadium pentoxide produces a greenish-yellow colour in glass and glazes.

The world production of vanadium products in terms of vanadium pentoxide was about 15 000 long tons in 1963. About 50-60% was produced in the USA. It is mainly used for metallurgical purposes (see vol. III). Less than 10% of the world production is used in the chemical industry.

In 1965 the price of vanadium pentoxide in the USA was $ 1.15 per lb.

14.20 COMPOUNDS OF TITANIUM AND ZIRCONIUM

Titanium, zirconium and hafnium (Hf) form the fourth subgroup of the periodic system. In its behaviour hafnium is closely related to zirconium and it always accompanies zirconium in nature, but it is commercially far less important. Titanium and zirconium can be di-, tri, and tetravalent in their compounds. Only a few compounds of divalent zirconium and titanium and trivalent zirconium are known. The oxides of tetravalent titanium and zirconium are very non-volatile and very insoluble. They have an amphoteric character. However, titanium dioxide is more acidic than basic and zirconium dioxide is more basic than acidic. The oxides dissolve slowly in hot concentrated sulphuric acid and form titanium sulphate and zirconium sulphate respectively. These sulphates decompose when diluted with water. Titanates and zirconates can be formed by fusion of the oxides with alkali hydroxides or carbonates. Orthotitanates (M_4TiO_4), metatitanates (M_2TiO_3), orthozirconates (M_4ZrO_4) and metazirconates (M_2ZrO_3) can be formed. (M represents a univalent metal atom.)

14.21 TITANIUM COMPOUNDS (Ti, atomic weight = 47.90)

14.21.1 Titanium dioxide

a. Occurrence and ore purification. Titanium dioxide (TiO_2) occurs naturally as rutile. The principal economic deposits are found in Australia. Far smaller amounts are mined in the USA and South Africa and some other countries. Commercially important rutile is usually found in sands containing about 5% of this mineral. Rutile can be concentrated to 96-97% purity, after crushing, by passing through magnetic classifiers (removal of ilmenite, magnetite and/or monazite, see p. 612) followed by flotation and gravity concentration (removal of zircon and other minerals, see also ore classifiers, vol. I).

The main source of titanium dioxide is ilmenite, which may be represented by the formula $FeO.TiO_2$ although the composition is not always exactly constant (sometimes ferric oxide, Fe_2O_3, is also present in ilmenite). The name ilmenite is derived from the Ilmen mountains in the Ukraine (USSR) where the mineral was first discovered. Ilmenite occurs either as black sand in relatively pure grains together with other minerals (zircon, monazite, magnetite etc.) or as a massive rock mass usually associated with magnetite. The most important sand deposits are the black sands in India (Travancore), Australia and the USA, containing from 15 to 80% ilmenite. Ilmenite can be separated from the sands by magnetic classifiers (see also rare earths, p. 613). Large and

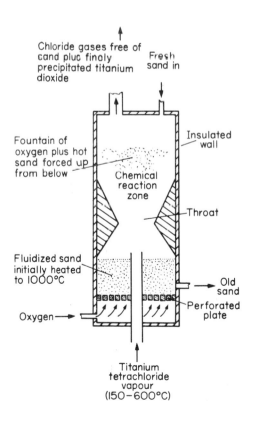

Chloride gases free of sand plus finely precipitated titanium dioxide

Fresh sand in

Fountain of oxygen plus hot sand forced up from below

Insulated wall

Chemical reaction zone

Throat

Fluidized sand initially heated to 1000°C

Old sand

Perforated plate

Oxygen →

Titanium tetrachloride vapour (150−600°C)

Fig. 14.5 Diagram of the production of titanium dioxide by reacting titanium tetrachloride with oxygen.

massive deposits of ilmenite-magnetite (titaniferous magnetite), containing about 20% TiO_2, occur in the USA, Norway and Canada. After crushing, this ore is treated in a similar way to the sands. In Canada large, massive deposits of ilmenite associated with haematite are also found. This ore mixture is treated in an electrothermal smelting furnace to produce pig iron and a slag containing about 65-70% titanium dioxide (titanium slag).

b. Production. Pure titanium dioxide is usually produced from ilmenite (and also from titanium slag) in the sulphate process. Ilmenite ore is crushed, dried in a rotary kiln and ground to a fine powder. The powder is mixed with a small quantity of antimony trioxide and added to concentrated sulphuric acid. The mixture is agitated by aeration and heated with direct steam to 110-120° C. The oxides react with sulphuric acid to form sulphates according to the following reaction equation:

$$FeO.TiO_2 + 2\ H_2SO_4 \rightarrow FeSO_4 + TiOSO_4 + 2\ H_2O$$

The reaction can become very violent due to the development of great heat. The solid mixture obtained, which is very porous as a result of aeration during the reaction, is dissolved in water or dilute sulphuric acid to a solution containing 120-130 g TiO_2 and 250-300 g ferrous sulphate per litre. Scrap iron is added to reduce any ferric iron to the ferrous state. The solution is clarified in one step by adding sodium hydrosulphide and a coagulant, such as glue, to precipitate antimony sulphide and suspended solid particles of silica, unreacted ilmenite, etc. The impurities are allowed to settle and the clarified liquid is decanted and pumped to vacuum crystallizers wherein it is cooled to 10° C to crystallize out a large portion (about 50%) of the ferrous sulphate. The remaining solution is concentrated in an evaporator to a solution containing 200-250 g TiO_2 and 180-250 g $FeSO_4$ per litre. (See also the process shown in fig. 14.5.)

Titanium dioxide is precipitated from the resulting solution by hydrolysis (decomposition of titanyl sulphate with water), which must be performed under carefully controlled conditions to ensure the formation of a suitable particle size and to avoid the occlusion of impurities. Usually the precipitation is controlled by nucleation (seeding). In one process a small quantity of hydrous titanium dioxide is precipitated by partially neutralising a small quantity of the solution under controlled pH conditions with caustic soda or soda ash followed by boiling. The resulting suspension is added to the bulk of the solution which is boiled until sufficient hydrous titanium dioxide is precipitated. (The titanium dioxide prepared previously promotes the formation of a precipitate with an uniform particle size.) After filtration and washing with water the product is calcined at temperatures up to 900° C in a rotary kiln.

c. Properties. Titanium dioxide is a white crystalline solid which is very stable at atmospheric conditions and insoluble in water and dilute solutions of acids, alkalis, etc. Its melting point is 1 825° C. Three crystal modifications named: anatase, brookite and rutile occur in nature, but only anatase and rutile are produced commercially. In the process described above anatase is obtained. This modification can be converted into rutile by calcining above 915° C. The conversion can be made to occur at lower temperatures (e.g. 400-500° C) by adding zinc and magnesium salts. The conversion into rutile takes place at 800-900° if the precipitation of titanium dioxide from titanyl sulphate solutions is controlled by nuclei of titanium dioxide prepared by precipitating from titanium tetrachloride. Both anatase and rutile have a high index of refraction (2.52 and 2.72 respectively).

d. Uses. Precipitated titanium dioxide is chiefly used as a white pigment. Due to its high refractive index it has a high opacity and covering power as compared with other white pigments. The pigment is used in white paints (see vol. V) and in the production of light-coloured linoleum, rubber, plastics and cosmetics (such as lipsticks and powders). Titanium dioxide pigment is also used as a filler and whitener in high grade printing papers. Since titanium dioxide is opaque to ultraviolet radiation, it is used in the formation of emollients and creams for protection against sunburn. Cotton is whitened by applying a coating of a composition containing titanium dioxide pigment and polyvinyl alcohol emulsion. When the rutile modification is used, cotton is protected against deterioration by sunlight. It is worth noting that the anatase modification accelerates the actinic deterioration of cotton. Synthetic fibres are delustred by incorporating titanium dioxide in the fibre-forming composition.

Both natural rutile and precipitated titanium dioxide are used for the production of titanium compounds, e.g. titanium tetrachloride, titanates, organic titanium compounds, etc. Titanium dioxide is also used in porcelain enamels to impart acid resistance. It also increases the bending strength of enamels since the enamel may be applied in a thinner layer due to the high hiding power of titanium dioxide. Ceramic bodies of titanium dioxide are used in resistors and capacitors for electronic equipment. Titanium dioxide is also used in welding fluxes and for coating welding rods since it stabilizes an electric arc and overcomes the tendency to sputter and flicker. Much natural rutile is used for this purpose.

Synthetic gem stones are produced by dropping droplets of molten titanium dioxide on to a movable pedestal on which the molten material solidifies (as so-called boule) in the form of a single crystal. This process (the Verneuil process) is also used for the production of synthetic sapphires and rubies (see vol. II).

Production of titanium concentrates		*In long tons gross weight*			
		1957	*1959*	*1961*	*1963*
Ilmenite:	World	2262000	2055000	2690000	2400000
	Australia	71000	84000	167000	203000
	Canada (incl. titanium slag)	736000	559000	1032000	817000
	India	296000	298000	171000	26000
	Fed. of Malaya	92000	73000	107000	147000
	Norway	207000	223000	306000	238000
	South Africa	3000	78000	88000	28000
	USA	676000	567000	699000	793000
Rutile:	World	139000	96000	115000	200000
	Australia	129000	82000	101000	184000
	USA	9600	8500	8000	11000
The UK and the USA imported:					
Ilmenite:	UK	225000	244000	273000	227000
	USA (incl. titanium slag)	411000	332000	175000	179000
Rutile:	UK	12000	7000	14000	18000
	USA	76000	21000	25000	43000

e. Statistics. The world production of titanium concentrates and the production by the major producers is shown in the table on p. 607.

In the USA 950 000 long tons of titanium concentrates (gross weight) were consumed in 1963 (corresponding with 540 000 long tons titanium dioxide); about 95% was used for the production of precipitated titanium dioxide (pigments), 2% for the production of metal (mainly via $TiCl_4$), 2% for welding rod coating and 1% for all other uses. About 62% of the precipitated titanium dioxide was used in paints, varnishes and lacquers, about 13% in paper manufacture, 5% in rubber and 5% in floor coverings (e.g. linoleum).

The proportional consumption classified according to use in European countries is approximately the same.

In 1965 precipitated titanium dioxide was sold in the UK at £ 163 to £ 173 per long ton (anatase) and £ 173 to £ 195 per long ton (rutile); the corresponding prices in the USA were $ 500 to $ 540 and $ 540 to $ 580 per short ton.

14.21.2 Titanium tetrachloride

Titanium tetrachloride ($TiCl_4$) is prepared by passing chlorine through a bed of briquettes or pellets prepared from titanium dioxide (natural rutile, precipitated titanium dioxide) and carbon at a temperature of 800° C. Titanium tetrachloride evaporates and is condensed by cooling. In a modification of this process the chlorine is passed through a fluid bed of finely divided titanium dioxide and carbon. Ilmenite can also be used in the latter process. In this case a mixture of ferric chloride and titanium tetrachloride evaporates. Ferric chloride can be condensed by cooling the vapours to a temperature between 150 and 300° C. Titanium tetrachloride condenses at temperatures below 136° C.

Titanium tetrachloride is a clear colourless liquid having a boiling point of 135.8° C. The liquid often has a yellow colour due to the presence of small quantities of ferric chloride. Titanium tetrachloride dissolves in water but aqueous solutions are readily hydrolysed to form a suspension of a hydrous titanium dioxide.

Titanium tetrachloride is mainly used for the production of metallic titanium (see vol. 504). Small quantities are also used for the production of titanium dioxide and for the production of organic titanium compounds. Several esters and salts can be prepared by reacting titanium tetrachloride with alcohols and carboxylic acids respectively. Esters such as tetra isopropyl titanate and tetra n-butyl titanate are used as adhesives and salts such as titanium stearate, which are readily soluble in many organic solvents, may be used as surface-active agents to disperse titanium dioxide, carbon black and other pigments in organic solvents.

In 1965 titanium tetrachloride was sold in the USA at $0.15 to $0.23 per lb.

14.21.3 Titanates

Titanates of the alkaline earth metals are prepared by sintering a mixture of titanium dioxide and an alkaline earth metal hydroxide or carbonate. These titanates are stable and insoluble in water.

Barium titanate ($BaTiO_3$) has important ferroelectric properties (see p. 504). *Strontium* and *calcium titanate* are used as an additive to barium titanate, to change its electric characteristics.

Alkali metal titanates can be prepared by melting titanium dioxide with an alkali metal hydroxide or carbonate. The alkali metal titanates are not stable, they hydrolyse in water to form titanium dioxide.

Recently a *potassium polytitanate* ($K_2O.6\ TiO_2$) has been prepared in a crystalline fibrous form for the first time. The fibres have an average diameter of 1 micron and a length of 1 mm to 3 cm. These fibres are able to diffuse and reflect infrared radiation to a high degree, due to their small diameter and the high refractive index. For this reason fibrous polytitanate can be used as a thermal insulator. The fibres are very stable against chemicals, are flexible and resist temperatures up to 1 200° C (the melting point is 1 375° C). Potassium polytitanate fibres are produced in the form of irregular masses and lumps. These lumps can be compressed into any shape desired. The fibres can also be dispersed in liquids. These dispersions are used to make temperature insulating papers and felts.

14.21.4 Literature

G. SKINNER, H. JOHNSTON and C. BECKET. *Titanium and its compounds.* Columbus, Ohio, Herrick L. Johnston Enterprise, 1954.

F. D. ROSSINI et al. *Properties of titanium compounds and related substances.* Washington, 1956.

14.22 ZIRCONIUM COMPOUNDS (Zr, atomic weight = 91.22)

14.22.1 Zirconium silicate

Zirconium silicate (zircon, $ZrSiO_4$ or $ZrO_2.SiO_2$) occurs very widely in soils, sands and rocks. It is the most important source of zirconium and its compounds. Commercial deposits of zircon occur associated with quartz, rutile, ilmenite, monazite and other minerals in sands. Important deposits are found in India (Travancore), USSR (Ukraine, Marinpol), Australia, USA, South Africa and Senegal. Zircon of about 99% purity can be isolated from the sands by subjecting them to the action of electrostatic or magnetic classifiers (see also processing of monazite p. 613, and ores, vol. III).

Pure zircon is a colourless crystalline product but natural zircon is found in various colours due to chemical impurities and to stresses caused by irradiation by radioactive elements with which zircon has been associated. At room temperature zircon is chemically inert and it is unaffected by aqueous reagents even at higher temperature. However it is attacked by aqueous alkali hydroxide solutions at 400° C (under pressure) and by molten alkalis. Zircon resists temperatures up to 1 550° C. Above 1 550° C it decomposes to zirconium dioxide and silica.

Zircon is a starting material for the production of zirconium compounds and metallic zirconium. Larger crystals of zircon are used in jewellery as gem stones. Colourless stones are almost as brilliant as diamonds. Zircon is widely used in the ceramics industry, e.g. for the production of chemically resistant ware, electric resistors and insulator bodies, porcelain, refractories and heat transfer pebbles. Zircon is also used as a catalyst for organic chemical reactions, as a pigment, and in compositions for coating foundry moulds.

14.22.2 Zirconium dioxide

Zirconium dioxide (Zirconia, ZrO_2) occurs naturally as baddeleyite. Large quantities of relatively pure baddeleyite are found in Brazil. Pebbles (known as favas) and enormous boulders are found in that country. Smaller quantities of less pure zirconium dioxide are found in the USA, Sweden, India and Italy.

Zirconium dioxide is also produced synthetically from zircon. Various processes are known.

In one process a mixture of zircon and carbon is heated in an electric arc furnace at a temperature above 1 400° C. Zircon decomposes and silicon monoxide is volatilized. The latter burns in air to form a dust of silicon dioxide (silica) which is collected in dust separators (see removal of dust from air, p. 99). Zirconum carbide, a dull grey solid remains in the furnace. Its approximate formula is ZrC but it contains also zirconium carbonitride which is formed with nitrogen present in air. Zirconium carbide can be burnt to zirconium dioxide and carbon dioxide by heating in air. Any nitrogen present in the carbide is released into the atmosphere. Zirconium carbide can also be burnt in chlorine to form zirconium tetrachloride ($ZrCl_4$) which sublimes into a condenser. Zirconium tetrachloride is either vaporized and burnt in air to form a dust of zirconium dioxide or dissolved in water and heated to precipitate hydrous zirconium dioxide. The latter is dehydrated by heating at 1 000° C.

Zircon can also be converted into zirconium tetrachloride in one step by heating briquettes of zircon and charcoal in a combustion tower at a temperature of 800-1 000° C in a chlorine atmosphere. Zirconium tetrachloride sublimes in a condenser (manufactured of nickel) in which the vapours are cooled to 250-300° C. Thus zirconium tetrachloride is an intermediate in the production of zirconia (zirconium tetrachloride is also used for the production of metallic zirconium, see vol. III).

In another process zirconium dioxide is prepared by melting zircon with sodium hydroxide to form sodium zirconate and sodium silicate. The latter is dissolved by treating with water, and zirconium dioxide can be obtained by decomposing the remaining sodium zirconate by means of a mineral acid. In similar processes zircon is heated with lime or soda ash.

Zircon always contains 0.5-3% hafnium which is not removed in the processes for the production of zirconium compounds. Thus the latter are not pure but usually the presence of hafnium is harmless. Hafnium can be separated from zirconium (if necessary) by liquid-liquid extraction of a solution of zirconium nitrate with tributyl phosphate. (Compare the purification of uranium, p. 663 and rare earths, p. 614).

Zirconium dioxide forms white monoclinic crystals which are unaffected by chemicals at room temperature. Zirconium dioxide is relatively hard and its melting point is 2 677° C.

Zirconium dioxide is used for the production of ceramics and refractories. It cannot be used as such at temperatures above 1 000° C since at this temperature it is converted into another crystal modification (tetragonal). This phase change (which is reversible when the temperature decreases below 1 000° C) is marked by a considerable dimensional change. At a temperature of about 1 900° C a second phase change occurs with the formation of cubic crystals. It is found that the cubic modification can be formed easily by heating zirconium dioxide in the presence of about 5% calcium or magnesium oxide. The cubic crystals are not converted again into tetragonal crystals when the temperature declines since the conversion velocity is too small (hence the name 'stabilized zirconia' for zirconium dioxide treated as described above). Zirconium dioxide is also used as an abrasive, as a polishing agent, as an activator for phosphors, as a pigment in enamels and glazes, as a filler for rubber and plastics, as a starting material for the production of zirconium metal, and as a catalyst in organic chemical reactions (e.g. vapour phase esterification reactions).

14.22.3 Statistics
The production of zirconium minerals by the major producing countries is shown in the following table:

		In long tons		
	1957	1959	1961	1963
Australia	88560	133360	136480	184000
Brazil (mainly baddeleyite)	1610	9680	6600	350
Nigeria	90	1120	740	790
Senegal	2900	8530	5300	3000
South Africa	—	5290	6790	2400
USA	50720	—	56000	—

The largest quantities of zirconium ores are imported by the United Kingdom, USA, Germany and France. In 1963 these countries imported 32000, 47000, 25000 and 19000 long tons respectively. In the USA about 92000 tons of zirconium minerals were consumed in 1961; 58% was used for ceramics and foundry moulds, 16.5% for refractories, 11% for metallurgical purposes and 14.5% for zirconium compounds, abrasives etc.

In the USA zirconium ore (97% zircon) was sold at $ 60 to $ 95 per short ton in 1965; the price of zirconium dioxide (99%) was $ 1.50 per lb.

14.22.4 Literature
W. B. BLUMENTHAL. *The chemical behaviour of zirconium*. Princeton, Van Nostrand, 1958.

14.23 THE RARE EARTH METALS AND COMPOUNDS

14.23.1 Introduction
The rare earth metals comprise the elements of the third subgroup of the periodic system and the lanthanide series. The third subgroup contains scandium (Sc), yttrium (Y) and lanthanum (La). The very rare radioactive element actinium (Ac) might also be included in the third subgroup but its only importance is due to its radioactivity. For this reason it is usually included with the radioactive elements. The lanthanide series comprises the elements of atomic number 58 to 71 inclusive as listed in the table on p. 612.

The lanthanide series is characterized by the progressive adding of electrons to inner electron shells. Since the electrons added are distant from the valence electrons, the chemical properties of the elements of the lanthanide series are closely related to

The lanthanide series	Symbols	Atomic number
Cerium	Ce	58
Praseodymium	Pr	59
Neodymium	Nd	60
Promethium (unstable)	Pm	61
Samarium	Sm	62
Europium	Eu	63
Gadolinium	Gd	64
Terbium	Tb	65
Dysprosium	Dy	66
Holmium	Ho	67
Erbium	Er	68
Thulium	Tm	69
Ytterbium	Yb	70
Lutetium	Lu	71

those of lanthanum. All the rare earth metals are usually trivalent in their compounds. Cerium can also be tetravalent in its compounds and compounds of divalent samarium, europium and ytterbium are also known.

The rare earth metals form solid, very involatile and very insoluble oxides having a basic character. Such oxides were formerly known as earths. These earths were named 'rare' because substantial amounts of ores containing these earths are found only in few places. They became of importance in 1890 when Auer von Welsbach invented the incandescent mantle (see p. 656).

14.23.2 Occurrence

Although the rare earth metals are considered to be rare they make up a larger fraction of the earth's crust than do many of the other elements which are generally regarded as 'common'. For example the earth's crust contains 40 p.p.m. cerium, 28 p.p.m. yttrium, 24 p.p.m. neodymium, 18 p.p.m. lanthanum and about 30 p.p.m. other rare earth metal compounds, but the earth's crust contains only 5 p.p.m. arsenic, 2.5 p.p.m. bromine, 0.5 p.p.m. mercury and 0.2 p.p.m. cadmium. This is due to the fact that the rare earths are present in very small amounts in almost all rocks with the result that the total quantity present exceeds the amounts of common elements which occur in more concentrated form in ore deposits.

With the exception of scandium and promethium, the rare earths always occur associated with each other in nature. (Scandium occurs in several ores, e.g. tin and tungsten ores, and promethium is an unstable radioactive element which does not occur naturally but can be formed in nuclear reactions.) The commercial minerals are monazite and bastnasite. Some pegmatic deposits of massive monazite occur in the Republic of South Africa, but usually monazite is found in sand deposits. The most important sand deposits are found in the USA, Brazil, India (Travancore), Ceylon, Nigeria, Malaysia and in Australian beach sands. The most important constituents of monazite are phosphates of lanthanum, cerium, praseodymium, neodymium and samarium. In addition it contains thorium phosphate and small quantities of the other rare earths. Bastnasite occurs in the USA (New Mexico and California) and in the Congo (formerly

Belgian) and consists of fluorocarbonates of the rare earth metals. It contains little or no thorium.

Monazite is an expensive ore and for this reason any process for treating the ore is likely to be a compromise between processes for recovering both rare earths and thorium with a good yield. Bastnasite is processed in the USA since the demand for rare earths exceeds the production from monazite.

14.23.3 Processing of ores

Due to its relatively high specific gravity (between 4.9 and 5.3), crushed monazite can be separated from various light minerals, such as sand, clay etc., by washing with water (see ores, vol. III). Monazite is often accompanied by various heavy ores such as zircon, rutile, ilmenite, magnetite and garnet. (The titanium ore, ilmenite, is the principal mineral of the deposits in Travancore. These deposits contain 65-80% ilmenite, 3-6% rutile, 4-6% zircon and only 0.5-1.0% monazite.) The heavy ores are removed and separated by a series of powerful electromagnets of varying intensity (see classifiers, vol. III). The weakest electromagnet removes magnetite from the mixture. Ilmenite is removed by stronger magnets and monazite is attracted by the strongest. The other impurities have no magnetic properties and are not attracted by the magnets. A concentrate containing 60% monazite is usually collected at the strongest magnets. It is concentrated to 95-98% by repeated washing and electromagnetic separation.

The purified monazite usually contains 15-16% lanthanum oxide, 27-33% cerium oxide, 3-4% praseodymium oxide, 9-10% neodymium oxide, 2-3% samarium oxide, 1-4% of the other rare earths, 4-9% thorium oxide and 26-29% phosphate in terms of phosphorus pentoxide. In addition small quantities of impurities such as alumina, lime, iron, uranium and silica are present.

The constituents or groups of constituents are separated by submitting them to chemical treatment. Various processes are in use, since the minerals, found in various deposits, usually present different problems in processing.

Monazite is commonly heated with concentrated sulphuric acid to convert the rare earth phosphates and thorium phosphates into water soluble sulphates. The resulting product is leached with water and filtered. Thorium can be precipitated from the solution obtained, e.g. as thorium pyrophosphate, by adding sodium pyrophosphate to the solution or as thorium hydroxide by partially neutralizing the solution. (Since thorium hydroxide is less basic than the rare earths it can be selectively separated from the solution at pH = 3 to 4.) The remaining solution is usually treated with ammonium oxalate to precipitate the oxalates of all the rare earth metals. After filtration the oxalates are decomposed to oxide by calcining in the presence of air. The resulting mixture is known as *technical cerium oxide* in the UK and as *rare earth oxide* in the USA.

The actual composition of technical cerium oxide varies with the source of the ore. A representative mixture contains 23% lanthanum oxide, 45% cerium oxide, 6% praseodymium oxide, 18% neodymium oxide, 3% samarium oxide and 5% yttrium oxide and other lanthanides. This mixture may be converted into technical cerium chloride or technical cerium nitrate (in the USA rare earth chloride or nitrate) by treating with hydrochloric acid or nitric acid respectively.

'Commercial cerium oxide' (impure cerium oxide, 92-95%) can be prepared by dissolving technical cerium chloride in water followed by precipitating the hydroxides

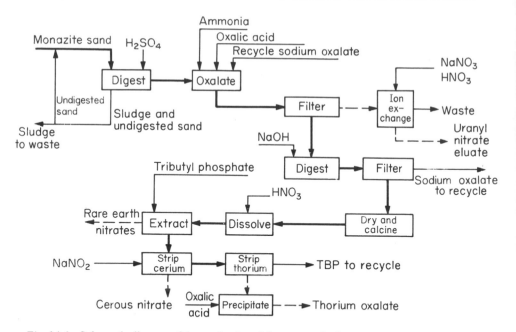

Fig. 14.6   Schematic diagram of the production of the rare earths from monazite sand.

with sodium hydroxide. As distinct from the hydroxides of the other rare earth metals, the hydroxide of tetravalent cerium is insoluble in dilute nitric acid. (Due to the calcining of the oxalates in the presence of air, cerium is present in the tetravalent state.) By adding dilute nitric acid to the mixture of hydroxides, cerium hydroxide forms an insoluble basic nitrate and can be separated from the solution of the other rare earth nitrates by filtering. The remaining solution can be converted into a mixture of nitrates, chlorides, carbonates or oxides by evaporating the solution or by precipitation. These mixtures are commercially named didymium nitrate, chloride, carbonate or oxide. A typical approximate composition of didymium oxide is: lanthanum oxide 45%, praseodymium oxide 11%, neodymium oxide 38% and other rare earths including yttrium 6%. The name didymium leads to much confusion since classically didymium means a mixture of praseodymium and neodymium.

In another process monazite is treated with a boiling solution of caustic soda or with molten caustic soda to form sodium phosphate and hydroxides of thorium and the rare earth metals. Sodium phosphate is leached with water and the hydroxides are dissolved in a mineral acid. The resulting solution is processed as previously described.

In a newer process (see fig. 14.6) monazite is treated with sulphuric acid, leached with water and filtered as described above. The resulting solution of sulphates is treated with ammonia, sodium oxalate and oxalic acid to precipitate the oxalates of thorium and the rare earth metals. Uranium sulphate remains in solution and is recovered from the solution after filtration (see p. 661). The precipitated oxalates are converted into hydroxides and sodium oxalate by digesting with sodium hydroxide. Sodium oxalate is recycled and the hydroxides are dried and calcined at 500° C to convert the hydroxides into oxides. At the same time 95% of the cerium (cerous hydroxide) is oxidized to its tetravalent state (ceric oxide). The oxides are dissolved in moderately concentrated nitric acid and contacted with tributyl phosphate in countercurrent. The latter is not miscible with the nitric acid solution but extracts thorium nitrate and ceric nitrate from it (compare the purification of uranium, p. 663). The remaining solution contains the nitrates of the rare earth metals with the exception of cerium (commercial didymium nitrate). The extract is treated with a solution of sodium nitrate which reduces ceric nitrate to cerous nitrate (trivalent cerium) and extracts it from tributyl phosphate, thus forming an aqueous solution of cerous nitrate. Thorium nitrate is extracted from tributyl phosphate by means of water or a 2% solution of nitric acid and can be precipitated by means of oxalic acid.

Bastnasite can be treated with sulphuric acid in a similar process as that for monazite but the processes are modified due to the fact that bastnasite contains fluorides. Bastnasite can also be leached with hydrochloric acid instead of sulphuric acid.

14.23.4 Separation and purification of the rare earths and metal production

Pure cerium compounds can be obtained by dissolving commercial cerium oxide in nitric acid and adding ammonium nitrate to the solution. A double salt of cerium nitrate and ammonium nitrate precipitates. This double salt can be purified by repeated recrystallization. The pure double salt is a starting material for the production of other cerium compounds. A solution of cerium oxide in nitric acid (ceric nitrate) can also be purified by extracting with an organic solvent such as tributyl phosphate or diethyl ether.

The other rare earths are separated from the cerium-free mixture (didymium oxide, didymium salts) in physical processes. Chemical processes cannot be used since the differences in chemical properties are very small.

The oldest method is fractional crystallization and precipitation in many stages. The rare earths are usually separated into a few groups by dissolving the mixture of oxides in sulphuric acid and adding sodium or potassium sulphate. Double sulphates of lanthanum, praseodymium, neodymium and samarium precipitate as double salts with a small portion of the other rare earths. The major portion of the other rare earths remains dissolved. The various rare earths are separated further by repeated crystallization of the nitrates, the double salts with ammonium nitrate or the bromates.

Since lanthanum forms the least soluble double ammonium nitrate, it can be separated commercially in purities as high as 99.97% by repeated crystallization.

The rare earths can also be separated from a mixture by absorbing a neutral nitrate solution in a cation exchange resin in the hydrogen form (e.g. a sulphonated styrene-divinylbenzene copolymer). The rare earths are then selectively eluted by means of a solution of citric acid or ethylenediamine tetra-cetic acid (EDTA) adjusted to a predetermined pH by means of ammonia. The stability of each complex formed from rare earths and citric acid or EDTA, is different. Thus the most stable complex is removed first and so on.

A more recent separation method is based on the selective extraction of rare earth nitrates from an aqueous solution by means of immiscible organic liquids such as alkyl phosphates and alkylamines. Countercurrent extraction methods are used.

The rare earth metals are obtained from the anhydrous chlorides either by electrolysis of the fused chlorides or by reduction with metals such as alkali metals, alkaline earth metals or aluminium. A metal mixture known as *misch metal* can be prepared by electrolytic reduction of a melt of technical cerium chloride.

14.23.5 Uses and statistics

Technical cerium fluoride (rare earth fluoride) is incorporated in the core of carbon rods used in electric arcs. It causes the latter to burn more evenly. In the USA, technical cerium chloride and acetate are used in the textile industry as waterproofing agents and fungicides.

Technical cerium oxide is used in glass polishing compositions, especially for polishing precision lenses. Such polishing agents must contain at least 45% cerium oxide since the latter is the effective constituent in polishing. Technical cerium oxide is also an efficient glass decolorizer. Cerium is present in the tetravalent state and oxidizes any iron to trivalent iron, while the didymium provides a complementary colour to that of the trivalent iron.

Pure cerium oxide is sometimes used as a decolorizer in high quality glass having a low iron content. Cerium oxide is also the essential component of lenses used to protect the eyes of furnace workers (e.g. Crookes' lenses). It produces a faint yellow colour which cuts out most of the ultraviolet and 30% of the heat rays.

Cerium salts are used in phosphors for cathode ray rubes. They activate alkaline earth metal phosphates and silicates. Cerium nitrate is used in the manufacture of incandescent gas mantles (see thorium, p. 658). Tetravalent cerium salts are used as oxidizing agents in analysis and as a catalyst in organic chemical preparations (catalytic cracking processes).

Didymium oxide (cerium-free rare earth oxide mixture) and small quantities of pure neodymium and praseodymium salts are used as a colorizing agent for porcelain and glass. They produce a mauve to red colour. When used in small quantities they are decolorizers of glass.

Lanthanum oxide is principally used for making optical glass of a very high refractive index and low dispersion (for photographic lenses).

Misch metal has pronounced pyrophoric properties. Hence its use in lighter flints and sparking toys. For this purpose misch metal is alloyed with 30% iron since it is too soft to be used alone. Misch metal is also alloyed with aluminium or magnesium to improve their tensile strength at high temperatures. These alloys are used in aircraft engine parts which have to resist high temperatures. The use of about 0.75% misch metal in cast iron improves its tensile strength and gives a nodular-graphitic iron that can replace carbon steels in some applications.

Some pure rare earth metals may be of value in the field of nucleonics, e.g. for reactor control and shielding. Especially yttrium may become important since it has the advantage of relatively small neutron absorption and of relatively high melting point (1 500° C).

Production of monazite concentrates	In long tons			
	1957	1959	1961	1963
Australia	443	331	1 544	1 940
Ceylon	134	84	213	–
Malaya (exports)	490	236	696	885
Malagasy Republic	295	–	449	600
South Africa	8 316	2 145	4 800	2 050
USA (inc. bastnasite)	–	1 021	–	–

The world production of monazite is not precisely known since the total output of the most important producing countries (India and Brazil) is no longer published for security reasons (because of the thorium content which is important in nuclear reactions). The production of monazite concentrates in several countries is shown in the table on p. 616.

India produced 5 200 long tons in 1938 and 1 600 long tons in 1945. Its production in 1959 was estimated at 1 500 long tons. Brazil exported about 100 long tons of cerium chloride in 1959, 1 400 long tons in 1961 and 850 long tons in 1963.

In the USA about 1 900 long tons of rare earths (in terms of oxides) were consumed in 1961; 23% were used for the production of misch metal, 21% for glass polishing and 13% in carbon arc lighting. The consumption of high purity metals was only 300 to 400 lb in 1961.

In the USA mixed rare earth oxalates (technical cerium oxalate) sold for about $ 1.15 per lb in 1965. Cerium oxide was priced at $ 1.85 to $ 1.90 per lb. The prices of separated oxides, salts or metals of the other rare earths ranged from $ 10 to $ 1500 per lb.

14.23.6 Literature

E. V. KLEBER and B. LOVE. *Technology of scandium, yttrium and the rare earth metals.* Oxford, Pergamon, 1963.

F. H. SPEDDING and A. H. DAANE. *The rare earths.* New York, 1961.

CHAPTER 15

Nucleonics and Radioactive Substances

15.1 ATOMIC STRUCTURE

It is common knowledge that all substances are composed of atoms. A substance which consists of only one kind of atom (including, as will be seen later, its isotopes) is called an 'element'. The atoms of the elements are capable of combination among themselves to produce the molecules of the chemical compounds, so that the elements (about 100) may be regarded as the raw materials of chemistry. From the further discussion of atomic structure it will become apparent, that the number of raw materials is actually much smaller, as all atoms are in turn made up of only a small number of different elementary particles.

An indication of the very small size of atoms is given by the fact that, for example one gram of hydrogen, the lightest element, contains 6×10^{23} atoms.

A simplified model of the atom may be obtained by regarding it as made up of a positively charged nucleus consisting of one or more positively charged particles (protons) and neutral particles (neutrons), which are all approximately of the same weight. One or more very much lighter negatively charged particles (electrons) move around this nucleus at a relatively large distance from it. The electric charge of an electron is equal in magnitude to that of a proton, and the total number of electrons moving around the nucleus is equal to that of the protons in the nucleus. For this reason, the atom as a whole is neutral. The atoms of a given chemical element all have the same number of protons and electrons and the atoms of different elements are different as far as the number of protons and electrons are concerned (and often also in respect of the number of neutrons) and are therefore of different weight.

The number of protons (and thus the number of electrons) in the atoms of the 90 elements found naturally varies from 1 in the case of hydrogen to 92 in that of uranium. These elements can be arranged in a series in which the number of protons is successively increased by one. (The two gaps in the series and also the places for the elements after the 92nd element are filled by elements produced artificially.) As a consequence, every element can be given a serial number which indicates the total number of protons in the nucleus and therefore also the number of electrons around the nucleus. These numbers are called the atomic numbers of the elements. For example, the element nitrogen has a nucleus containing seven protons with seven electrons

Table 1

LONG PERIOD FORM OF THE PERIODIC SYSTEM OF THE ELEMENTS

Key:

Atomic number
Atom symbol
Relative electronegativity
Atomic weight

At weight of
Natural isotopes
(x Radioactive)

98	98
101	99
	100
	101

Lanthanides

58	136 138 140 142	59 141	60 142 146 148 150	61	62 144 147 148 149 150 x152 154	63 151 153	64 152 154 158 160	65 159	66 158 160 162 164	67 165	68 162 164 166 167 168 170	69 169	70 168 170 174 176	71 175 x176
Ce		Pr	Nd	Pm	Sm	Eu	Gd	Tb	Dy	Ho	Er	Tm	Yb	Lu
1.1		1.2	1.2	1.2	150.43	1.2	1.2	1.2	1.2	1.2	1.2	1.2	1.2	1.2
140.13		140.92	144.27			152.0	157	158.93	162.46	164.94	167.2	168.94	173.04	174.99

Actinides

90 x227 x228 x230 x231 x234	91 x231 x234	92 x234 x235 x238 x239	93	94	95	96	97	98	99	100	101	102	103
Th	Pa	U	Np	Pu	Am	Cm	Bk	Cf	Es	Fm	Md	No	Lw
1.3	1.5	1.7	1.3	1.3	1.3	1.3	1.3	1.3	1.3	1.3	1.3	1.3	1.3
232.05	231	238.07											

moving around the nucleus, corresponding with its atomic number 7. The weight of the nitrogen atom is fourteen times the weight of a hydrogen atom and thus it can be inferred that the nucleus of the nitrogen atom must also contain seven neutrons.

The sequence of the elements mentioned above is found to contain periodically occurring elements whose chemical properties show considerable similarity with those of other elements placed earlier in the sequence. To obtain a clear picture of these features, the elements are usually arranged according to the so-called periodic system, in which the arrangement in order of increasing nuclear charge (i.e. increasing number of protons) is retained, but the elements are so set out in rows (periods) that the elements possessing corresponding properties are placed one below the other. This is known as the periodic table (see table 1, on p. 620).

The chemical properties of the elements depend upon the number of electrons and the orbits in which the latter are moving. The electrons moving around the nucleus of an atom may be supposed to follow circular and elliptical orbits. On the basis of important differences in the binding energy, the orbits of the electrons can be divided into a number of groups which are called the K, L, M, N, O, P and Q shells respectively. In this sequence the binding energy decreases and the distance from the nucleus increases. Since the binding energy is the highest in the inner shells, the shells are usually successively filled with electrons. The result is that a light atom, such as a nitrogen atom, which has a small number of electrons only contains electrons in the K and L shells and the other shells remain empty. For reasons of stability the outermost filled shell of an atom cannot contain more than 8 electrons.

Some of the electrons of an atom (especially those moving in the orbits of the outermost shell) can move in an number of different orbits. When all the electrons are travelling in the most stable orbits, the atom is said to be in its 'ground state'. If energy (in the form of heat, light, X-rays, radioactive rays etc.) is applied to the atom, one or more electrons may jump into another orbit in which they are less stable. The atom is then said to be in the 'excited state'. If more energy is applied, the electron will move still farther away from the nucleus.

This outward movement does not take place gradually, for not all orbits are possible ones. The electron should be considered as jumping from one orbit to another. If sufficient energy is applied the electron may be removed from the nucleus altogether. The atom then becomes an electrically charged particle known as an ion. An electron can be dislodged from the atom if the quantity of energy added is greater than the binding energy that keeps the electron in an orbit around the nucleus. Since the binding energy is the lowest in the outer shell, the electrons of the latter shell can be dislodged most easily.

In certain circumstances electrons can also jump into another orbit, or can even be dislodged, by another atom in the neighbourhood. An electron can jump into an orbit round both the atoms and thus bind the atoms together, or the electron can be dislodged from one atom and jump into an orbit round the other. In the latter case a positive and negative ion, which attract each other, are formed. In both cases a chemical bond is formed in a chemical reaction. Such a chemical bond can only be formed when the electrons can find orbits in which the binding energy is higher than in their original orbit. (The electron is forced to the most stable orbit.)

In this connection the atoms of the noble gases are of particular interest. These are also known as inert gases because they will scarcely enter into any chemical reaction.

They have an ideally stable electron structure which is characterized by the fact that that their outermost shell is always completely filled with electrons (see electron configuration of the inert gases table 2). The ideal electron structure proves to be so strong that atoms of the other elements try to acquire the structure of the inert gases by exchanging electrons.

Table 2

		ELECTRON CONFIGURATION OF THE INERT GASES				
Element	Total number of electrons		Number of electrons in the successive shells			
		K	L	M	N	O	P
		1s	2s 2p	3s 3p 3d	4s 4p 4d 4f	5s 5p 5d 5f	6s 6p 6d
Helium	2	2					
Neon	10	2	2 6				
Argon	18	2	2 6	2 6			
Krypton	36	2	2 6	2 6 10	2 6		
Xenon	54	2	2 6	2 6 10	2 6 10 –	2 6	
Radon	86	2	2 6	2 6 10	2 6 10 14	2 6 10 –	2 6 –

From the foregoing it is apparent that the chemical properties of the elements are, in the main, determined by the number of electrons that are present in the outermost orbits which are not yet completely filled with electrons. The nuclear charge also has an appreciable effect. A nucleus containing a larger number of protons is surrounded by a larger number of electrons and consequently the outermost electrons must find accommodation in orbits farther away from the nucleus, for which the binding energy is lower. This is one of the reasons why the chemical properties of the elements which are situated one below the other in the periodic table, while they do admittedly show similarities, nevertheless manifest many points of difference.

In contrast with the chemical properties, the occurrence and character of isotopes, radioactive radiation and nuclear reactions are mainly determined by the composition of the nuclei of the atoms as shown below.

15.2 STABLE ISOTOPES

15.2.1 History and occurrence

The conception of the chemical element as a substance which cannot be split into anything simpler was first put forward by Boyle in 1661 and remained unmodified in the development of chemistry for 250 years. In 1912 Thomson, from his experiments with the mass spectrograph, showed that many substances which had always been considered as elements were in fact mixtures of substances chemically similar but of different atomic weights. These different forms of an element are called *isotopes*.

As stated above the existence of isotopes in an element was first revealed in the mass spectrograph (see fig. 15.1). When an element in the gaseous state, or one of its volatile compounds under reduced pressure, is subjected to a powerful electric discharge, positive ions are formed by removal of one or more electrons from the atoms of the

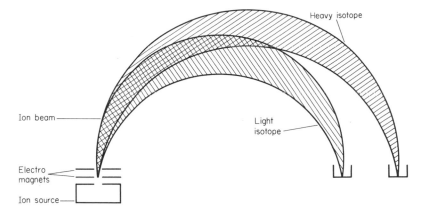

Heavy isotope

Ion beam

Light isotope

Electro magnets

Ion source

Fig. 15.1 Schematic diagram of a mass spectrograph.

element. These ions are accelerated in an evacuated chamber to a high velocity by passing them between electromagnets designed to give the ions a uniform speed. They then pass through an electromagnetic field which acts on them at right-angles to their original direction of travel. As a result the ions are deflected, the lightest undergoing the greatest and the heaviest ions the least deflection. A photographic plate receives them at their focus and a series of lines is formed each of which corresponds to atoms of the same mass. Measurement of the positions of these lines, relative to lines produced by atoms of another element which was deliberately added, enables the masses of the original atoms to be calculated.

When neon was examined in the mass spectrograph a line was observed corresponding to mass 20 and a fainter line to mass 22. The atomic weight of neon is 20.2 but a line corresponding to 20.2 was not obtained. It was concluded that neon has two kinds of atoms which have masses 20 and 22, present in proportions which give an average mass of 20.2.

The atomic weight of chlorine (35.5) has been repeatedly investigated because it is so far from a whole number. Examination in the mass spectrograph provided the explanation. There was no evidence for mass 35.5. The lines found correspond to masses 35 and 37, and ordinary chlorine is a mixture containing 3 atoms of mass 35 to every 1 atom of mass 37. Similarly copper with average atomic weight 63.54 consists of atoms of mass 63 and 65.

It is now established that about four out of five of the natural elements consist of mixtures of atoms which differ in their mass. As stated earlier, these different forms of the same element are called isotopes. There are two stable isotopes of chlorine and two of copper, but more than two may be present; in the case of tin there are in fact ten isotopes. On the other hand all the atoms of some elements have the same mass, i.e. isotopes are not present; examples are fluorine, sodium, aluminium and phosphorus.

Hydrogen has a stable isotope called deuterium. The nucleus of a hydrogen atom contains one proton only, but the nucleus of a deuterium atom contains both a proton and a neutron. Since a proton and a neutron have almost the same mass, the deuterium atom has atomic weight twice that of the hydrogen atom. It is common practice to indicate a particular isotope by writing its atomic weight at the upper left of the symbol, and the atomic number below it. e.g.,

$$^1_1 H, \quad ^2_1 D, \quad ^{16}_8 O, \quad ^{18}_8 O, \quad ^{20}_{10} Ne, \quad ^{22}_{10} Ne.$$

The atomic number is the net charge on the nucleus or the number of electrons in the surrounding orbits. The word 'heavy' is also used for a few isotopes, e.g. 'heavy hydrogen' instead of deuterium and 'heavy oxygen' for ^{17}O or ^{18}O. Similarly 'heavy water' is water formed from heavy hydrogen, D_2O.

The existence of isotopes is readily explained by the modern theory of atomic structure. In the case of neon the lightest isotope contains in its nucleus 10 neutrons and 10 protons; the electrons present make only negligible contribution to the mass, hence the atomic weight is 20. The heaviest isotope differs in that the nucleus contains 12 neutrons with the 10 protons. Additional mass is due to presence of 2 more neutrons. Hence the atomic weight is 22.

The isotopes of an element differ in their nuclear masses and in any properties which depend on these masses, e.g. rate of diffusion. But as the isotopes of an element have the same nuclear charge they have identical chemical properties. The last feature explains their belated discovery.

The discovery of isotopes by Thomson makes it possible to explain why the atomic weights of many natural elements differ significantly from whole numbers.

The atomic weight of an element is a ratio which is defined in various ways, e.g. the atomic weight has been defined as the number which indicates how many times the weight of the hydrogen atom is contained in the weight of the atom concerned. Alternatively one-sixteenth of the weight of oxygen atoms, or one-twelfth of the weight of the carbon isotope with 6 neutrons and 6 protons, is adopted as the basis of the system of atomic weights. Since the atomic weights of oxygen and the carbon isotope mentioned are approximately 16 and 12 respectively (calculated on hydrogen), this makes no significiant difference for the purpose of simple calculations.

As neutrons and protons have almost the same weight, the atomic weights of isotopes are approximately multiples of the atomic weight of hydrogen. Elements consisting of a mixture of isotopes (which contain a different number of neutrons in their atoms) may have an atomic weight which differs greatly from a whole number.

The isotopes always occur in the same proportions in the naturally occurring elements which fortunately makes it possible to consider the 'apparent' atomic weights of the mixtures of isotopes of an element as a characteristic property of the element.

The nuclear compositions of the isotopes of a few common elements are set out in fig. 15.2.

15.2.2 Separation of stable isotopes

Because the isotopes of an element have the same chemistry their separation by normal chemical means cannot be employed. Nevertheless a number of physical methods have been applied successfully and enriched stable (i.e. non-radioactive) isotopes of most elements are now available.

In the selection of a particular method an important factor is the quantity of enriched isotope required. For small quantities, or when the isotope desired is rare, the electromagnetic separator is used and is preferred also where an isotope of intermediate mass is to be selected from several others. For larger quantities, gaseous diffusion, fractional distillation, chemical exchange, thermal diffusion and ionic migration are employed;

Element	Symbol	Number of Protons	Number of Neutrons	Atomic Number	Chemical Atomic Weight of element	Abundance of naturally occurring isotopes %
Hydrogen (Protium)	$^1_1$H	1	–	1	1. 0080	99. 985
Deuterium	$^2_1$H	1	1	1		0. 015
Tritium	$^3_1$H*	1	2	1		minute
Carbon	$^{12}_6$C	6	6	6		98. 9
	$^{13}_6$C	6	7	6	12. 011	1. 1
	$^{14}_6$C*	6	8	6		minute
Oxygen	$^{16}_8$O	8	8	8		99. 76
	$^{17}_8$O	7	9	8	16. 000	0. 037
	$^{18}_8$O	8	10	8		0. 20
Chlorine	$^{35}_{17}$Cl	17	18	17	35. 457	75. 4
	$^{37}_{17}$Cl	17	20	17		24. 6
Uranium	$^{234}_{92}$U*	92	142	92		minute
	$^{235}_{92}$U*	92	143	92	238. 07	0. 71
	$^{238}_{92}$U*	92	146	92		99. 28

*radioactive

Fig. 15.2   Nuclear composition of some isotopes.

in most cases these exploit a countercurrent principle which multiplies many times each preceding separation. For the lighter elements fractional distillation and chemical exchange are the most efficient and of these the former is usually the cheaper. A thermal diffusion column has the advantages that it is simply constructed and can be used for most elements. Ionic migration is useful when the element cannot be easily gasified.

a. Electromagnetic separator. This apparatus employs the principle of the mass spectrograph (described above) with many refinements. One type (the 'calitron') separates 100 g isotopes daily and yields high enrichment of two adjacent isotopes, e.g. ^{206}Pb and ^{207}Pb. Stable isotopes of many elements have been obtained by this method for reserarch purposes, but it is expensive.

b. Gaseous diffusion. This is the most important large-scale process. It is based on the fact that light molecules diffuse more rapidly through a porous partition than heavy molecules, in consequence of which they become concentrated. To increase the separation, a cascade of stages may be built. This method was first used in 1920 to produce enriched ^{22}Ne, but it came into prominence in 1939 for the production of ^{235}U by diffusion of gaseous uranium hexafluoride which contains 1 part of $^{235}UF_6$ in 140 parts of $^{238}UF_6$. This separation is described on p. 665.

c. Fractional distillation. Small differences exist in the vapour pressures of liquid isotopes of an element as a result of which they can be separated to some extent by repeated distillation. The plant has a fractionating tower of much the same construction as that used for the separation of nitrogen and oxygen from liquid air. Heavy water (D_2O) can be separated from ordinary water (H_2O) by this process but the method is comparatively expensive. It is used for the separation from water of water containing heavy oxygen ($H_2{}^{18}O$), deuterium from liquid hydrogen (see heavy water production), ^{22}Ne from liquid neon, boron isotopes from boron fluoride and for the preparation of carbon monoxide enriched with ^{13}C or ^{18}O from liquid carbon monoxide.

d. Chemical exchange. Although the isotopes of an element have the same chemical properties, differences in their masses do exert a small difference on the concentrations of the various substances present when equilibrium is attained in suitable reactions. This influence is very marked only when the ratio of the masses of the isotopes concerned is large, e.g. in the case of ^1H and ^2H (or D) where this ratio is 2.

In an example ^{15}N becomes concentrated in ammonium nitrate to about 70% by causing ammonium nitrate solution to flow down a column against a countercurrent of ammonia gas: according to the following equilibrium reactions:

1 $\qquad\qquad$ $^{15}NH_3\,(gas) + H \rightleftharpoons {}^{15}NH_4{}^+$ (aqueous)
2 $\qquad\qquad$ $^{14}NH_3\,(gas) + H^+ \rightleftharpoons {}^{14}NH_4{}^+$ (aqueous).

The position of the equilibrium of reaction 1 is not the same as that of reaction 2. In this example reaction 1 shifts slightly to the right and reaction 2 shifts slightly to the left. The resulting net reaction is:

$$^{15}NH_3\,(gas) + {}^{14}NH_4{}^+\,(aq) \rightleftharpoons {}^{15}NH_4{}^+\,(aq) + {}^{14}NH_3\,(gas)$$

Countercurrent contact is readily achieved in conventional apparatus, e.g. packed columns.

^{13}C is similarly enriched in hydrogen cyanide by contacting hydrogen cyanide gas and sodium cyanide solution: ^{13}C content in the sodium cyanide is depleted. Another example is described below for production of heavy water. This method is one of the most satisfactory for isotopes of light elements.

e. Thermal diffusion. The isotopes to be separated are contained as gases in a cool, long, vertical tube down which passes an electrically heated wire. The lighter gas in the mixture diffuses preferentially towards the hot wire where it rises in a convection current, while the heavier gas streams downwards on the inner surface of the tube. Almost complete separation of ^{35}Cl from ^{37}Cl was effected with a tube 100 ft long and a temperature difference of $600°$ C. Almost pure ^{22}Ne and ^{18}O have also been prepared by this method.

f. Ion migration. The velocity of an ion in an electromagnetic field depends partly on its mass. Hence the isotopes of an element present in a solution or melt which is being electrolysed give ions of different velocities. This difference is exploited in the separation, for instance, of ^{7}Li and ^{6}Li by countercurrent migration. Molten lithium chloride is electrolysed; metallic lithium is deposited at the cathode and chlorine gas is liberated at the anode. The chlorine is recycled to the cathode where it reconverts lithium into lithium chloride. Under the conditions arranged the chlorine ions flow towards the anode with a velocity intermediate between the velocities of the ions of the lithium isotopes. The heavier $^{7}Li^{+}$ ions are washed back, while the lighter $^{6}Li^{+}$ ions make headway. The $^{7}Li^{+}$ ions thus become concentrated around the anode.

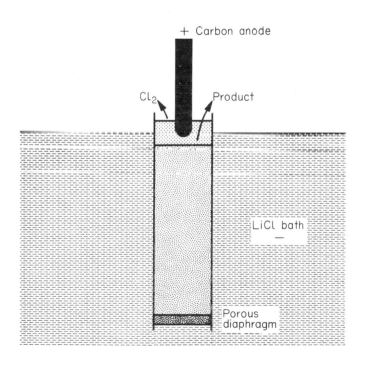

Fig. 15.3
Arrangement used by Klemm for the separation of lithium isotopes.

The plant may consist of a number of refractory tubes suspended in a bath of molten lithium chloride. They are closed at the bottom with porous diaphragms and filled with refractory packing to prevent convection of the molten salt. The anodes consist of carbon rods inserted into the upper ends of the tubes (see fig. 15.3).

g. Electrolytic separation. In the process for the electrolytic decomposition of water into hydrogen and oxygen, heavy water decomposes much more rapidly into deuterium and oxygen than common water into hydrogen and oxygen. Thus deuterium concentrates in the hydrogen gas (see below).

h. Separation by centrifuge. The mixture of isotopes in liquid or gaseous state is spun at high speeds. The heavier isotopes become concentrated near the periphery of the container and the lighter ones near the axis. This method has been used for enrichment of isotopes of selenium and germanium.

i. Gas chromatography. This technique applies countercurrent exchange between a stationary and a mobile fluid. In an example deuterium (D_2) is separated from a 1:1 mixture with hydrogen by passing the mixed gases up a column of palladium black on asbestos. The hydrogen is preferentially adsorbed while the deuterium passes on.

15.2.3 Uses

Isotopes such as D, ^{13}C, ^{34}S, ^{15}N and ^{18}O are used as tracers in chemical and biochemical processes. Usually radioactive isotopes are preferred since they are comparatively cheap and in addition they can more easily be detected due to their radiation (see p. 642). However, in some biological and medical researches the radioactive of radioactive isotopes may be undesirable. ^{15}N and ^{18}O are indispensable in studying organic reactions with tracers since radioactive isotopes of nitrogen and oxygen with a sufficiently large half-life are not available.

For example, ^{18}O has been used to study the reaction mechanism of esterification reactions. Starting from methyl alcohol containing the ^{18}O isotope and common benzoic acid, the resulting products are methyl benzoate and water:

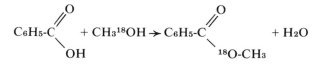

$$C_6H_5-C\overset{O}{\underset{OH}{\big\langle}} + CH_3{}^{18}OH \rightarrow C_6H_5-C\overset{O}{\underset{{}^{18}O-CH_3}{\big\langle}} + H_2O$$

After analysis of the reaction product, the ^{18}O isotope proved to be contained in the methyl benzoate molecules. From this it could be concluded that the -OH group of the benzoic acid and a hydrogen atom of the methyl alcohol form the water. In a similar way many reactions and molecular structures have been and are being investigated. Usually the specimens obtained from such investigations are assayed for their isotope content, e.g. by combustion followed by analysis of the products (CO_2, N_2 etc.) by mass spectrometry or by studying their infrared spectra.

Many applications of stable isotopes in nuclear technology are based on the fact that some isotopes absorb neutrons much more easily than other isotopes of the same element.

^6Li has a relatively high and ^7Li a very low neutron absorbing power. For this reason lithium is particularly suitable as a coolant in nuclear reactors after removal of the bulk of ^{6}Li. The latter is used for the production of lithium deuteride and similar products for the hydrogen bomb and other strategic nuclear objects.

Both the stable isotopes of boron, ^{10}B and ^{11}B have a high neutron absorbing power without the production of strong gamma rays and for these reasons natural boron (elemental or in the form of compounds) is used in nuclear reactor shielding and nuclear reactor controls. However since the neutron absorbing power of ^{10}B is higher than that of ^{11}B the isotopes are sometimes separated.

15.2.4 Heavy water

a. Occurrence and properties. Heavy water is an oxide of the hydrogen isotope deuterium analogous to normal water which is an oxide of normal hydrogen. Natural water contains about 0.015% by weight of HDO and D_2O molecules corresponding with 1 deuterium atom to 6 800 atoms of hydrogen. Hence common water must be concentrated 6 800 times to produce pure 100% D_2O.

The physical properties of heavy water differ from those of normal water. The freezing point of D_2O is 3.8° C, the boiling point is 101.4° C and the temperature of maximum density is 11.6° C.

b. Production. Heavy water can be produced commercially by the following processes.

Dual temperature chemical exchange. This is now the cheapest large-scale process. A plant in South Carolina (USA) has an annual capacity of 480 tons. Smaller plants are in operation in Sweden and Germany.

The reaction takes place between water and dissolved hydrogen sulphide both of which contain very small amounts of deuterium. The net reaction is:

$$D_2O + H_2S \rightleftharpoons H_2O + D_2S \text{ (or DHS + DHO)}$$

The equilibrium concentrations of the four compounds are sensitive to changes of temperature. The essential part of the plant is a pair of gas-liquid contacting towers; one operates at 30-40° C (the cold tower) and the other at 130-140° C (the hot tower). Water descends through the cold tower and then through the hot tower countercurrent to the hydrogen sulphide gas. In the cold tower the water becomes enriched in D_2O and the hydrogen sulphide becomes depleted of deuterium as the equilibrium shifts to the left. In the hot tower the equilibrium moves to the right and hydrogen sulphide becomes enriched in deuterium while the water becomes depleted of deuterium.

The enriched water is drawn off between the towers and the hydrogen sulphide which passes through both towers is recycled (see fig. 15.4.) The water in this way becomes enriched to 15% of D_2O in a few stages. This enriched water is concentrated up to 98% D_2O content by fractional distillation or by electrolysis. This is cheaper than further concentration by the foregoing process.

Electrolysis. In the electrolysis of natural water hydrogen is evolved at about ten times the rate of deuterium. The concentration of D_2O in the remaining water therefore increases as electrolysis proceeds. When this concentration of D_2O has increased 100 or more times, the gas evolved is markedly enriched in D_2. This gas is burnt in oxygen and the water thus obtained is mixed with electrolyte from an earlier stage and again electrolysed. By repeating the process many times 99.8% D_2O can be obtained.

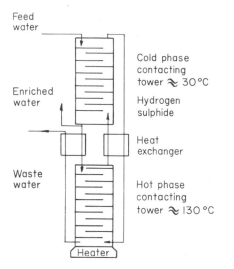

Feed water

Enriched water

Cold phase contacting tower ≈ 30 °C

Hydrogen sulphide

Heat exchanger

Waste water

Hot phase contacting tower ≈ 130 °C

Heater

Fig. 15.4 Flow sheet for the dual temperature chemical exchange process for heavy water production.

Nowadays instead of natural water, the starting material is water which has already been enriched to contain 10-20% D_2O by a cheaper process.

Electrolytic chemical exchange process. In this process, hydrogen gas obtained by electrolysis is contacted with water vapour in countercurrent at a temperature of 80° C and in the presence of a catalyst (Ni or Pt).

The reaction equilibrium of the reaction

$$HD + H_2O \rightleftharpoons H_2 + HDO$$

moves to the right under the reaction conditions mentioned above. The hydrogen gas and water vapour are contacted in a tower in which catalyst beds are alternated by bubble cap absorber plates which serve to bring the water vapour in the hydrogen gas into equilibrium with down-flowing feed water (see fig. 15.5). The water, which is enriched in heavy water, is electrolysed and the depleted hydrogen gas is drawn off. Pure heavy water may be obtained in this process, but usually water is enriched to 2.5% heavy water content. Since the catalytic exchange process involves the equilibrium between H_2O and HDO, the concentration of HDO to pure D_2O is highly impractical. Electrolysis or fractional distillation are used for further concentration of the heavy water.

This process is used in Canada and Norway. Heavy water is obtained as a by-product of hydrogen production. Since electrolytic hydrogen production is only employed when cheap electricity can be generated from water power, the application of this process is limited.

Fractional distillation of liquefied hydrogen. Hydrogen gas, obtained from water gas, producer gas, natural gas etc., is the starting material in this process. Impurities such as carbon monoxide and nitrogen are first removed by liquefaction. The resulting pure hydrogen is liquefied by further cooling (see liquefaction of gases, page 43).

In a primary distillation tower, the liquid hydrogen is fractionated into a bottom

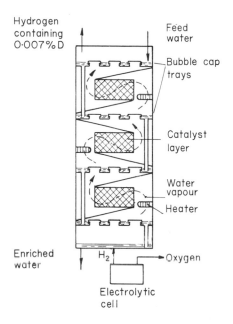

Hydrogen containing 0·007% D

Feed water

Bubble cap trays

Catalyst layer

Water vapour

Heater

Enriched water

H₂

Oxygen

Electrolytic cell

Fig. 15.5 Chemical exchange column for heavy water production.

product containing 5 to 10% HD and a top product which is free of HD. This is possible as the boiling point of deuterium hydride is 22.1° K (−250.9° C) and the boiling point of H₂ = 20.4° K (−252.6° C). The bottom product is fractionated in the upper column of a Linde double column (see the separation of gases p. 47). Nearly pure HD is obtained as the starting material mainly contains HD and H₂.

HD is drawn off, heated to room temperature in a heat exchanger and converted to a mixture of D₂, HD and H₂ in the presence of a catalyst. The gas mixture obtained is cooled in the same heat exchanger and fed to the bottom column of the Linde double column. At the bottom of this column liquid deuterium having a boiling point of 23.6° K can be drawn off (see fig. 15.6). Heavy water is obtained by burning D₂ after gasifying. This process is used in France, Germany, USSR and several other countries.

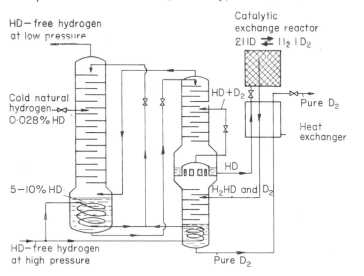

HD − free hydrogen at low pressure

Catalytic exchange reactor
2HD ⇄ H₂ + D₂

Cold natural hydrogen 0·028% HD

HD + D₂

Pure D₂

Heat exchanger

HD

H₂ HD and D₂

5−10% HD

HD − free hydrogen at high pressure

Pure D₂

Fig. 15.6 Flow sheet of a distillation plant for the separation of deuterium (D₂) from liquid hydrogen.

c. Uses and statistics. Heavy water is used as a 'moderator' in nuclear reactors producing for example plutonium from ^{235}U. The chain reaction which takes place requires the sowing down of fast neutrons. This is achieved by causing them to collide with material of low mass and low neutron absorbing power. Such a material is heavy water. Most materials are unsuitable as moderators because they absorb the fast neutrons and stop the chain reaction.

Several countries produce up to 20 tons of heavy water per year, which is sufficient for experimental purposes in research reactors. Power reactors may contain up to 1 ton of heavy water per MW of electrical capacity so that a 250 MW power reactor might require 250 tons of heavy water. Such heavy water moderated high power reactors are operated in the United States. The US sales of heavy water were 95, 86, 78 and 66 short tons in 1958, 1960, 1962 and 1964 respectively. The production capacity is much higher (see dual temperature chemical exchange process page 629). The concumption of heavy water in the UK is relatively low since the high power reactors in operation in the UK were graphite moderated (up to 1965).

d. Literature

H. LONDON. *Separation of isotopes.* London, Newnes, 1961.

J. O. MALONEY *et al. Production of heavy water.* New York, McGraw Hill, 1955.

P. T. WALKER. 'The production of heavy water in the United States', *The Industrial Chemist* **36** (1960) pp. 373-6.

E. W. BECKER. *Heavy water production.* Vienna, International Atomic Energy Commission, 1962.

15.3 RADIOACTIVITY AND RADIOACTIVE ISOTOPES

15.3.1 History

Following on Boyle's conception of the chemical element (see p. 622), Dalton stated in 1808 that an atom is a particle which can not be split into anything simpler. The refinement of this principle started in 1896 when Becquerel observed that a particle of uranium (or any of its compounds) constantly emits rays. He discovered that the radiation from uranium compounds was able to penetrate the light – excluding packaging of photographic plates and to act upon the latter in the same way as light.

Pierre and Marie Curie discovered in 1898 that pitchblende – a natural uranium ore – emits more powerful radiation than the uranium salts themselves. They came to the conclusion that the ore must contain another substance, and they succeeded in obtaining small quantities of the bromide of an intensely radioactive element which was given the name radium. P. and M. Curie also introduced the expression radioactivity.

Due to the investigations of Bragg, Royds, Rutherford and Soddy in the years between 1898 and 1913 the character and the mechanism of radioactivity was explained and it became known that radioactivity is the result of the spontaneous disintegration of the nuclei of unstable isotopes of an element to form isotopes with lower mass number or lower atomic weight. For example the naturally occurring isotope of uranium ^{238}U constantly emits rays and undergoes conversion first to ionium and then into a radium isotope, i.e. it is radioactive. The other natural uranium isotopes ^{234}U and ^{235}U and a number of natural isotopes of other heavy elements are also radioactive.

In 1934 T. and I. Joliot-Curie produced for the first time a radioactive isotope of the non-radioactive element phosphorus by bombarding aluminium with the radiation from radium. Now radioactive isotopes of most of the non-radioactive elements, (e.g. radioactive isotopes of carbon, sulphur, cobalt, iodine, gold etc.) can be produced artificially although they do not occur naturally.

15.3.2 Character and mechanism of radioactivity. In sharp contrast to the stable isotopes, the radioactive isotopes are characterized by a special feature called 'radio-activity' in which the *nuclei* of the elements are involved. When elemental sodium burns in chlorine gas to form solid sodium chloride transfer takes place of one electron from the orbit of each sodium atom to the orbit of a chlorine atom. Sodium ions (positively charged) and chlorine ions (negatively charged) are thus formed which then assemble themselves into tiny cubes of common salt. The important point now is that the components of *the nuclei* of the sodium and chlorine atoms *take no part in this chemical change*. This is true of most chemical reactions.

It is now known that many changes do involve these nuclei. A crystal of uranium or of any uranium compound, when wrapped in paper and left on a photographic plate in the dark slowly produces an image of the crystal on the plate. Some kind of ray is emitted by the uranium, and penetrates the paper. Investigation of similar effects with other elements, e.g. potassium, radium, thorium etc., shows that such emitted rays are of three kinds:

1. α-particles. These consist of the positive nuclei of helium atoms, $_2^4$He. They have atomic weight 4 and two units of positive charge. They ionize gases through which they pass and are able to penetrate thin aluminium foil, but they are stopped by a 1 mm thick aluminium sheet. When α-rays pass through a magnetic field they are slightly deflected.

2. β-particles. These are negative electrons. They are less effective than α-particles as ionising agents but have a greater penetrating power. In a magnetic field they undergo greater deflection than α-particles but in the opposite direction.

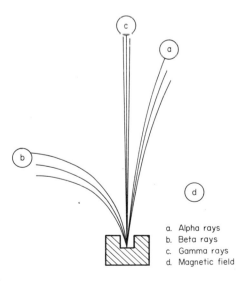

a. Alpha rays
b. Beta rays
c. Gamma rays
d. Magnetic field

Fig. 15.7 Diagram showing the radiation of radium. The rays emitted by a small quantity of radium (which is in a cavity in a block of lead) pass through an electromagnetic field. The heavy positive α-particles are deflected a little to the right. The light negative β-particles are strongly deflected to the left. The ϒ-rays undergo no deflection.

3. Υ-rays. These are not particles but consist of energy waves (electromagnetic radiation of extremely short wavelength). They travel with the speed of light and are still less effective ionising agents than β-particles. The penetrating power of Υ-rays is very high. They even partially penetrate a lead plate several centimetres thick. Since Υ-radiation is not composed of charged particles it is not deflected by a magnetic field (see fig. 15.7).

It has been established that the expulsion of α-particles, β-particles and Υ-rays takes place from within the nuclei of the decomposing atoms. Radium, like uranium, emits Υ-particles to form a gas called radon. Radium has atomic weight 226 and radon 222, while that of the expelled particle is 4. It seems obvious that a radon atom is formed from a radium atom by loss of a Υ-particle from its nucleus. Such a change is said to be 'radioactive'. It could not originate in the electrons which surround the nucleus.

β-particles are also expelled in many radioactive changes. They also originate in the nuclei and not in the surrounding orbits because they show a wide range of velocities. When β-particles *are* expelled from an orbital of an atom, e.g. by bombarding the element with monochromatic Υ-rays, the speed of travel of the emitted electrons is uniform. The production of β-particles within the nucleus is complex; it may be supposed that a neutron disintegrates into a proton and an electron.

Radioactive changes differ from the more usual non-radioactive type in that *(a)* they are irreversible and unaffected by temperature and pressure changes, *(b)* the energy liberated may be enormous and is in fact exploited in nuclear reactors as a new source of power, and *(c)* new elements are formed.

15.3.3 Units and detection of radioactivity

The unit of Υ-radiation is the Röntgen, which has been introduced for the intensity of X-rays (both Υ-rays and X-rays, or Röntgen rays are electromagnetic radiation of very short wavelength). The Röntgen (r) is based on the formation of ions in air as a result of the action of X-rays and indicates how much electric charge is formed in 1 cm³ of air.

A unit which can be used for all kinds of radioactive radiation is the curie. One curie is the quantity of radioactive substance which undergoes the same number of disintegrations (mutations)/s as 1 g radium which is in equilibrium with its disintegration products (the number of disintegrations in 1 g radium is 3.7 x 10^{10}/s). Based on this definition the intensity of radioactive radiation can be measured in curies. In this connection 1 curie is the intensity of radiation resulting from 3.7 x 10^{10} disintegrations per second. The curie does not show whether the radiation is of the same composition as that of radium. The proportions of the different forms of radiation may vary considerably for different isotopes.

Measurement of radioactivity is based on the fact that radioactive radiation is able to ionize gases. The most common measuring equipment is the Geiger counter (see fig. 15.8).

Basically the Geiger counter consists of a tube which is filled with gas (usually neon) under reduced pressure. The tube is internally provided with a positively charged axial wire (anode) which is surrounded by a cylindrical negative electrode (cathode). When radiation penetrates this tube, a portion of the gas is dissociated into positive ions and negative electrons and the tube becomes conductive. The result is an electric current pulse which ceases when all the ions and electrons are transported to the

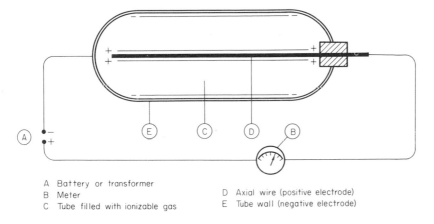

A Battery or transformer
B Meter
C Tube filled with ionizable gas
D Axial wire (positive electrode)
E Tube wall (negative electrode)

Fig. 15.8 Geiger counter. Ionisation of the gas, due to α, β and γ-radiation, causes a current to flow, so that deflection of the needle occurs. When amplified, this pulse can operate a mechanical counter.

cathode and anode respectively. The number of current pulses in a given time interval increases with increasing intensity of the radiation and can be detected by means of a galvanometer or earphone after amplification. In earphones a clicking noise is observed, the number of clicks per minute being a measure for the intensity of the radiation, but type of radiation cannot be determined in this way. Geiger counters are used, e.g. for the detection of radioactivity in the neighbourhood of nuclear reactors, for measuring the radioactivity of air and waste water, and for the exploration of radioactive ores.

A device for the detection of this type of radiation is the cloud chamber apparatus (Wilson's cloud chamber). This apparatus consists essentially of a cylindrical space which is closed on one side by a movable piston. This space – the chamber – contains gas under pressure and saturated water vapour.

When an electrically charged particle enters the chamber, it ionises the gas molecules that it encounters in its path. On expansion (by means of the piston), the gas in the chamber cools and the water vapour condenses. The vapour condenses preferably on the ions that have been formed, with the result that a 'cloud track' is produced which can be made visible by lateral illumination. The charged particle loses its ionizing capacity in the gas, and because of this the cloud track attains a certain length which is a measure of the velocity of the charged particle producing it.

By means of a magnetic field α and β-particles can be identified since these particles are deflected in opposite directions.

15.3.4 Natural formation of new elements

The equation for the disintegration of uranium (referred to above) may be written:

$$^{238}_{92}U \rightarrow {}^{4}_{2}He + {}^{234}_{90}Th + energy$$

The nuclear positive charge on the original uranium atom is 92 units and this becomes redistributed in the charges on the $_2$He and $_{90}$Th atoms. It might be inferred from the equation that the total mass of 238 units is similarly redistributed. In fact however the reaction proceeds with a slight loss of mass which appears in the kinetic energies of the He and Th atoms or in the form of Υ-rays.

The $_{90}$Th atom has atomic number 2 units less than that of the parent $_{92}$U atom. As the atomic number of an element controls its chemistry, and hence its position in the periodic table, the consequence of the disintegration of uranium is that a new element, thorium, has been formed. Uranium occurs in group VI and thorium in group IV of the periodic table.

The consequence of the loss of β-particles from a radioactive atom may be followed by referring to the behaviour of a thorium atom after it has been formed from uranium. It is also radioactive and spontaneously emits a β-particle. The change may be written:

$$^{234}_{90}\text{Th} \rightarrow \,^{0}_{-1}\beta + \,^{234}_{91}\text{Pa} + \text{energy}$$

The loss of the β-particle results in the formation of another new atom, protoactinium ^{234}Pa. The mass remains virtually unchanged because the β-particle (or electron) has very small mass compared with that of a proton. But the loss of one unit of negative charge increases the net positive charge on the nucleus and hence the atomic number, from 90 to 91. Protoactinium in fact occurs in group V of the periodic table.

Again a large amount of energy is emitted in consequence of a minute loss of mass. This energy is in part carried away by the fast moving electron and protoactinium atom and some appears in the form of Υ-rays.

The disintegration theory leaves little doubt that the natural radioactive elements are unstable and spontaneously change by emission of various particles and energy rays. The original radioactive element is thus converted into a new element which may or may not be radioactive. When all the known natural radioactive changes are surveyed, two main series appear which begin with uranium and thorium. Both these series end with an isotope of lead which is inactive. Lead has thus been formed in the earth's crust by the radioactive disintegration of other metals.

15.3.5 Radium

Radium forms with radon, thorium and uranium the group of radioactive elements of which commercially important quantities are recovered from natural products.

Radium is present in small quantities in all uranium minerals. It is in fact formed by the radioactive decomposition of uranium in several stages. Carnotite found in the USA contains about 10 mg of radium per ton. Pitchblende contains rather more. In recent years radium has become a by-product from the extraction of uranium for use as a fuel in nuclear reactors with the consequence that its price has fallen considerably.

Uranium ore is first digested with hot nitric acid to dissolve the uranium and radium compounds; on adding sulphate ions to the acid extract radium sulphate is precipitated together with sulphates of alkaline earth metals and lead. The lead is removed by boiling the mixture with sodium chloride or sodium hydroxide solution, the residual solid sulphates are fused with sodium carbonate and the carbonates of radium and alkaline earth metals are converted into their chlorides by treatment with hydrochloric acid. Fractional crystallization of these chlorides removes much of the barium; final separation is effected by the same means after conversion into the bromides with hydrobromic acid. The low content of radium in the original ore demands repeated treatments at the several stages.

Radium is often used in the form of its bromide or other salt. These salts are all

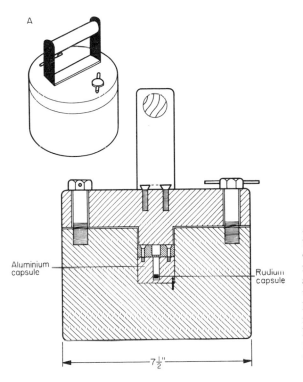

A

Aluminium
capsule

Rudium
capsule

$7\frac{1}{2}''$

Fig. 15.9 Illustration (A) and section of a holder (bomb), constructed
of tungsten alloy, for the storage of
radioactive substances. The radioactive substance is in a capsule
which is placed in an aluminium
holder. The latter in turn is accom-
modated in the thick-walled tungsten
holder. Both the aluminium and the
tungsten receptables are provided
with covers.

radioactive because of their radium content. They are usually stored in thick-walled
lead containers because of the serious effects of the radiation on human beings (fig. 15.9).

Radium is a relatively stable radioactive element. Its half life is about 1 600 years
which means that one half of any quantity of radium disappears in this time. The number
of primary disintegrations in a radioactive isotope is proportional to the quantity. Thus,
in the second period of 1 600 years, the remaining portion is again reduced to one half
and so on.

Chemically, radium belongs to the group of alkaline earth metals and its chemical
properties are closely related to those of barium.

As radium is used only because of its radioactivity its use in recent years has
decreased considerably because of its replacement by artifical radioisotopes (see below)
which are usually cheaper and more readily available.

The destructive effect of the emitted radiation on the living cell is utilized for
destroying malignant growths without seriously affecting the healthy tissue. Beams of
rays from the radium are directed on to the diseased tissue at various angles. Alternatively the radium is contained in the point of a needle which is inserted into the tissue.

The γ-radiation from radium is used for the irradiation of metals so as to reveal
presence of fractures for the inspection of weldings etc. In the case of welded pipes the
radium may be placed inside the pipe and x-ray film on the outside surface.

A minute porportion is mixed with a substance which emits light when irradiated.
(see phosphors p. 681). The luminous effect is used, for instance, on watch dials.

When γ-rays from a radium compound pass through air it becomes ionised and is
able to remove static electricity from surfaces. Threads of textiles etc. which have

become electrically charged during manufacture are relieved of their charge (and the possibility of spontaneous combustion) by passing them close to a container of radium.

Physical and chemical changes may be followed by incorporating radium in a solid. For instance when radium is incorporated in a mixture of silica (SiO_2) and lead oxide (PbO) it is found that its ability to emit radon is considerably reduced at 700° C. It is inferred that at this temperature a lead silicate with low radiating power is formed.

The use of radium and its compounds has not kept pace with the demand for radioactive materials. In the USA for example the production of radioactive materials increased from some hundreds of curies in 1946 to some millions of curies in 1965. No primary production of radium has been reported in the last five years. The small demand was met by imported radium salts and some recovered radium. The imports are shown in the following table.

US imports of radium salts	grams of radium content (i.e. curies)	Value $ 1000
1946-55 average	105	1700
1957	76	1061
1959	56	813
1961	13	185
1963	90*	726
1965	75*	700*

*Estimated

In 1965 radium was imported from Canada, Belgium-Luxembourg and the UK. Nearly 83% of the imports (over 84% of the total value) came from Oolen in Belgium where radium has been producted for many years.

The radium imports of the UK amounted to 30 g in 1958. More recent figures are not available, as now only the total quantity of imported radioactive substances is published.

In 1965 the price of radium in the form of salts was $16 to $21.50 per mg according to the radium content.

Literature
L. SANDERSON. '*Radium*'. *Canadian Mining Journal* **82** (Dec. 1961), pp. 57, 58.

15.3.6 Radon
Radon is the most important isotope of radium emanation, and is composed of a group of gaseous radioactive isotopes with mass number 86. Radon accompanies radium since it is formed by disintegration of the latter. The other radium emanation isotopes are formed by disintegration of other radioactive elements such as thorium and actinium.

Radon is separated from radium by heating an aqueous solution of a radium salt, e.g. bromide; hydrogen and oxygen are also evolved as a result of the action of the radioactive radiation on water. From these mixed gases radon is condensed into tiny tubes cooled in liquid air. The tubes are sealed by melting and provided with a gold or platinum coating to form the 'radon seeds' which are used in radiation therapy.

Like the other elements of group O of the periodic table, radon is a noble gas. It is radioactive and has a half life period of nearly four days. It remains therefore long enough to be handled unlike the other emanation isotopes which have half life periods varying from 10^{-3} s to about 1 minute. (Compare the half life of radium which is about 1 600 years.)

15.3.7 Production of artificial radioactive isotopes

As already stated the first preparation of these isotopes was in 1934 by exposing aluminium to α-particles, i.e. helium ions, from radium. A radioactive form of phosphorus was produced

$$^{27}_{13}\text{Al} + ^{4}_{2}\text{He} \rightarrow ^{30}_{15}\text{P} + ^{1}_{0}\text{n}$$

The nucleus of the bombarded aluminium atom absorbs the moving α-particle and a new atom is formed which disintegrates like a very unstable radioactive isotope into a radioactive isotope of phosphorus and a neutron.

By using neutrons and highly accelerated α-particles, protons and deuterons (i.e. heavy hydrogen ions) from a cyclotron, greater effects have been obtained. In the latter apparatus, electric discharges are produced in helium, hydrogen or deuterium in order to obtain charged particles which are accelerated in the same equipment by means of an electromagnetic field.

Progress in recent years has been so rapid that radioactive isotopes of almost all the elements have now been prepared. About 1 000 of them are known and about 200 are marketed. A few examples of such preparations follow.

a. Bombardment with α-particles. Many of the lighter elements, e.g. boron behave like aluminium

1
$$^{10}_{5}\text{B} + ^{4}_{2}\text{He} \rightarrow ^{13}_{7}\text{N}^{*} + ^{1}_{0}\text{n}$$

In this case radioactive nitrogen is obtained which is chemically indistinguishable from ordinary nitrogen.

Magnesium similarly produces radioactive aluminium.

2
$$^{25}_{12}\text{Mg} + ^{4}_{2}\text{He} \rightarrow ^{28}_{13}\text{Al}^{*} + ^{1}_{1}\text{H}$$

Like most artificial radio isotopes it is a β emitter.

b. Bombardment with neutrons. Nowadays by far the major portion of radioactive isotopes is produced by bombarding various stable elements with neutrons. On a small scale neutrons may be produced by bombarding beryllium with α-particles from radium.

$$^{9}_{4}\text{Be} + ^{4}_{2}\text{He} \rightarrow ^{13}_{6}\text{C}^{*} \rightarrow ^{12}_{6}\text{C} + ^{1}_{0}\text{n}$$

The asterisk indicates that the isotope is radioactive. For large scale isotope production, a nuclear reactor or atomic pile which provides both fast and slow neutrons, is a more effective source. Their velocity effects the reaction

3
$$^{63}_{29}\text{Cu} + ^{1}_{0}\text{n (slow)} \rightarrow ^{64}_{29}\text{Cu}^{*} + \gamma\text{-rays}.$$

The radioactive copper formed is mixed with the stable copper and cannot be separated from it.

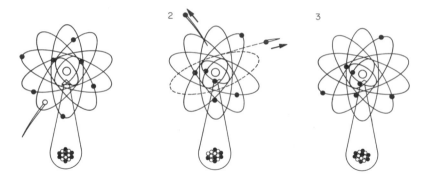

Fig. 15.10 Schematic diagram of the formation and disintegration of an isotope. 1. A stable nitrogen atom containing 7 protons and 7 neutrons in the nucleus is bombarded with a neutron which becomes lodged in it. As a result, a proton is dislodged from the nucleus, and at the same time an electron is dislodged from the electron shell. Thus, what is to all intents and purposes a ^{14}C atom has been formed. 2. The radioactive ^{14}C atom obtained in this way disintegrates and, in doing so, loses an electron. Hence a neutron is transformed into a proton. An electron is taken back into the electron shell. As a result, a stable atom of ^{14}N is once again obtained.

4
$$^{14}_{7}N + ^{1}_{0}n \text{ (fast)} \rightarrow ^{14}_{6}C^* + ^{1}_{1}H$$

Besides the radioactive carbon isotope, a hydrogen ion (i.e. a proton which may also be represented by $^{1}_{1}p$) is formed (see also fig. 15.10). Some other important nuclear reactions with neutrons are shown in the table on p. 641.

c. Bombardment with accelerated protons and deuterons. When neutron attack fails protons and deuterons may be more effective. Iron is thus converted into radioactive manganese by action of deuterons from a cyclotron

5
$$^{56}_{26}Fe + ^{2}_{1}H \rightarrow ^{54}_{24}Mn^* + ^{4}_{2}He$$

and magnesium into radioactive sodium

6
$$^{24}_{12}Mg + ^{2}_{1}H \rightarrow ^{22}_{11}Na^* + ^{4}_{2}He.$$

In general a nuclear reaction must be performed under carefully controlled conditions, since the reaction which occurs not only varies with the nature of the target and the bombarding particle but also with the energy of the latter. Several reactions may occur so that identification of the products may be difficult particularly if the target contains more than one isotope.

A simple case is provided by the bombardment of gold, which has only one isotope, with neutrons. Under carefully controlled conditions one of the following reactions may dominate.

$$^{197}_{79}Au + ^{1}_{0}n \rightarrow ^{198}_{80}Hg^* + ^{0}_{1}e \text{ (electron)}$$

$$^{197}_{79}Au + ^{1}_{0}n \rightarrow ^{198}_{79}Au^* + \gamma \text{ -rays.}$$

Table 3

PROPERTIES AND PRODUCTION OF SOME RADIOACTIVE ISOTOPES

Atomic no.	Element	Radioactive isotope	Properties			Reaction for production
			Radiation	½ Life	Waste product	
1	hydrogen tritium	$^{3}_{1}H$	β	1241 years	helium $^{4}_{2}He$	$^{6}_{3}Li + ^{1}_{0}n \rightarrow ^{3}_{1}H + ^{4}_{2}He$ bombardment of lithium with neutrons
6	carbon	$^{14}_{6}C$	β	5600 years	nitrogen $^{14}_{7}N$	$^{14}_{7}N + ^{1}_{0}n \rightarrow ^{14}_{6}C + ^{1}_{1}H$ bombardment of nitrogen with neutrons
15	phosphorus	$^{32}_{15}P$	β	14 days	sulphur $^{32}_{16}S$	$^{32}_{16}S + ^{1}_{0}n \rightarrow ^{32}_{15}P + ^{1}_{1}H$ bombardment of sulphur with neutrons
16	sulphur	$^{35}_{16}S$	β	87 days	chlorine $^{35}_{17}Cl$	$^{35}_{17}Cl + ^{1}_{0}n \rightarrow ^{35}_{16}S + ^{1}_{1}H$ bombardment of chlorine with neutrons
27	cobalt	$^{60}_{27}Co$	β, γ	5 years	nickel $^{60}_{28}Ni$	$^{59}_{27}Co + ^{1}_{0}n \rightarrow ^{60}_{27}Co + \gamma\text{-rays}$ bombardment of stable cobalt with neutrons
51	antimony	$^{124}_{51}Sb$	β, γ	60 days	tellurium $^{124}_{52}Te$	$^{127}_{53}J + ^{1}_{0}n \rightarrow ^{124}_{51}Sb + ^{4}_{2}He$ bombardment of iodine with neutrons
53	iodine	$^{131}_{53}I$	β, γ	8 days	xenon $^{131}_{54}Xe$	$^{130}_{52}Te + ^{1}_{0}n \rightarrow ^{131}_{52}Te + \gamma\text{-rays}$ $^{131}_{52}Te \rightarrow ^{131}_{53}J + \beta + \gamma\text{-rays}$
79	gold	$^{198}_{79}Au$	β, γ	2.7 days	mercury $^{198}_{80}Hg$	$^{197}_{79}Au + ^{1}_{0}n \rightarrow ^{198}_{79}Au + \gamma\text{-rays}$ bombardment of stable gold with neutrons
84	polonium	$^{210}_{84}Po$	α	138 days		$^{209}_{83}Bi + ^{1}_{0}n \rightarrow ^{210}_{84}Po + \beta\text{-rays}$ bombardment of bismuth with neutrons

15.3.8 Separation of radioactive isotopes and their handling

Usually the reaction product obtained as a result of irradiation is not one pure product, but it is a mixture of the starting material (the target) with one or more radioactive isotopes resulting from the mixture of isotopes in the target.

If a radioactive isotope is produced from another isotope of the same element, it is usually sold as a mixture with the target. Examples are $_{27}^{60}$Co (cobalt-60) obtained from elemental $_{27}^{59}$Co and $_{79}^{198}$Au (gold-198) obtained from elemental $_{79}^{197}$Au.

If the radioactive isotope is produced from an isotope of another element a separation process is often performed.

For example, the mixture of sulphur and radioactive phosphorus obtained by the irradiation of sulphur is separated by oxidizing both elements to sulphuric acid and phosphoric acid respectively. From this mixture the sulphate ions and phosphate ions can be separated with the aid of selective anion exchangers. Radioactive phosphorus thus becomes available in the form of phosphoric acid or a phosphate. In the case of other elements it is sometimes possible to employ fractional distillation.

Depending on the nature of the isotope and the purpose for which it is to be used, the isotope may be obtained in elementary form or as a compound.

Gaseous elements are often irradiated in the form of compounds. The production of $_{6}^{14}$C (carbon 14) by bombarding nitrogen with neutrons (reaction 4 in section 15.3.7) may be performed by bombarding a solid nitrate with neutrons. The nitrate is converted into a carbonate containing $_{6}^{14}$C from which carbon dioxide $_{6}^{14}$CO$_2$ is liberated by adding an acid.

A mixture of simple radioactive carbon compounds can also be obtained by bombarding beryllium nitride (Be$_3$N$_2$) and dissolving the resulting product.

Tritium ($_{1}^{3}$H) is obtained in the gaseous state from lithium. It can, however, be obtained in the form of compounds by bombarding a lithium compound in an organic solvent. As a result of collision with neutrons, the tritium atoms that are formed acquire a high velocity and are able to substitute hydrogen atoms of the molecules of the solvent. In this process radioactive tritium compounds such as methyl and ethyl alcohol are produced.

The processes involved in producing radioactive isotopes are cumbersome and expensive because elaborate precautions against radiation danger are necessary. The operations must be conducted behind screens which are impervious to radiation. The necessary instruments are actuated with manipulators (see fig. 15.11). The manipulations may be observed with the aid of television equipment or through windows with double glazing which enclose a liquid capable of absorbing the radiation. The radioactive substances are kept in thick-walled lead containers which are often stored under several yards depth of water, many of these isotopes are handled in a thick-walled steel, lead or tungsten holder which is provided with a closable 'window' through which the radiation emerges when required (see fig. 15.11).

15.3.9 Uses of artificial radioactive isotopes

Applications of artifical radioisotopes in medicine, biology, physics, chemistry and industry are very numerous and varied. They find use for the elucidation of living processes, the determination of the ages of geological strata and ancient objects, the investigation of air and water currents, testing and controlling the operation of industrial

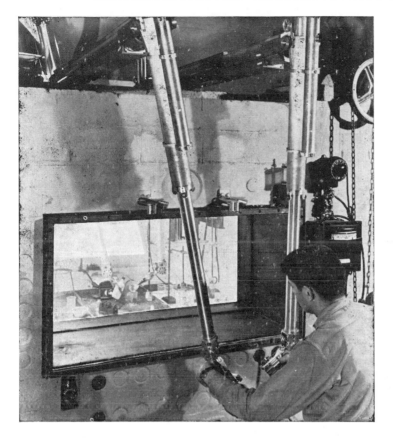

Fig. 15.11 Manipulator. When the manipulator arms in the foreground are actuated, a plastic bottle and a glass flask on the laboratory table in the dangerous space behind the window are manipulated. In this example a liquid has to be squeezed from the flexible plastic bottle into the flask for cooling. The window is composed of a number of plates of glass to prevent the escape of radiation.

machines, tracing the course of chemical reactions and bringing about particular reactions, for the sterilisation of micro-organisms and even for breeding new types of plants. Some indication of the scope and variety of these applications is obtained from the following examples.

a. Small quantities of sodium phosphate containing radioactive phosphorus are added to an animal's diet. Because it is an isotope, radioactive phosphorus behaves biochemically just like stable phosphorus. The radioactivity of various parts of the animal's body is measured at intervals. The route which the phosphorus takes in the body is thus established.

b. Radioactive cobalt (^{58}Co) has been used to investigate the function of the vitamin ^{12}B in the body and in the diagnosis of pernicious anaemia which occurs when the body is unable to absorb this vitamin. Radioactive iodine (^{131}I) is similarly used to investigate the function of the thyroid gland which produces an iodine compound.

c. To examine *absorption* by the skin of the widely used plasticiser tricresyl phosphate, a small quantity of this phosphate containing radioactive phosphorus (called a 'labelled' phosphate) may be rubbed on the palm of the hand. After a few hours radioactive phosphorus is found in the blood and is only slowly eliminated in the urine.

d. To determine the *adsorption* by charcoal of glucose from solvents, the glucose was 'labelled' with active carbon. This does not exchange with the carbon of the solvent or the charcoal, so that the specific activity of the glucose remains unchanged. Hence the specific activity of the charcoal during the adsorption is a measure of the amount of glucose adsorbed.

e. The *solubility* of an almost insoluble substance e.g. lead chromate, can be accurately determined. A radioactive lead compound is mixed with the lead chromate, a saturated solution prepared and the specific activity of a few millilitres of it is measured. From the known activity of the added lead the very slight solubility of the lead chromate can easily be calculated.

f. When radiation is passed through paper, plastic sheets, metal foils etc., it undergoes attenuation which varies with the thickness of the material. The thickness can thus be measured and arranged to actuate the mechanism so as to ensure uniform thickness in the product. A similar use is the detection of fractures in metal plates and pipes.

g. The direction and movement of underground water flow can be traced by adding a water-soluble compound of a radioisotope, e.g. ^{131}I, to one bore hole and taking samples at various times and intervals from surrounding bores. Similar techniques have been used to measure the porosity and flow rates of oil-bearing formations and to measure flow patterns in the surface waters of lakes and coastal regions.

h. The concentration of poisonous mercury in the air, e.g. near men making fluorescent lamps, is determined by adding radioactive mercury (^{197}Hg). A known volume of air is sucked through a cooled trap where the mercury condenses and its activity is measured. As little as 10^{-5} g of mercury is thus readily measured.

i. A radioactive metal (^{60}Co) may be included in the metal piston ring of an engine; radioactive assay of samples of oil drawn from the sump gives a measure of wear and erosion of the ring.

j. The mechanism of a chemical reaction can often be traced by adding a radioactive isotope to the reactants. For instance when ethylene, C_2H_4, is passed over hot metal oxides both ethylene oxide (C_2H_4O) and carbon dioxide (CO_2) are formed. If ethylene labelled with ^{14}C is used, the CO_2 formed has greater activity than the C_2H_4O. This observation shows that the CO_2 is formed directly from the C_2H_4 and not from the C_2H_4O as a secondary reaction.

k. In soil studies it has been shown by adding radioactive phosphorus that assimilation of phosphorus by plants is facilitated by presence of nitrogen compounds. This has led to the practice of adding nitrates to superphosphate fertilizers.

l. Controlled irradiation of some foods produces a pasteurising effect, but there is a tendency to reduce the vitamin content and alter the taste. Potatoes thus sterilized have been kept for eighteen months.

m. Carbon dating provides a method for ascertaining the age up to about 50 000 years of materials which contain carbon. It is based on the fact that carbon-14 is radioactive and is produced in the atmosphere by the action of neutrons which arrive in cosmic rays:

$$^{14}_{1}N + ^{1}_{0}N \rightarrow ^{14}_{6}C^* + ^{1}_{1}H$$

This carbon-14 has a half life of 5730 years. Its formation has continued at a constant rate for an extremely long time, even in relation to its half life. In consequence the atmosphere contains an equilibrium concentration which gives say x disintegrations per minute per g as measured in a sensitive counter. This equilibrium concentration is also present in all living plants and animals but at death no further exchange with the atmosphere can occur and the concentration of carbon-14 decreases. After 5730 years only $x/2$ disintegrations per minute per g will be recorded and after another 5730 years only $x/4$ and so on. The age of the sample can thus be estimated by measuring the specific activity of the carbon in it. The Dead Sea scrolls have in this way been dated to A.D. 40.

Outside the testing, investigation and research fields radioactive isotopes are used in radiation therapy, in luminous paints and for the removal of static electricity from surfaces (see uses of radium p. 637).

15.3.10 Statistics

In the USA the distribution of radioactive isotopes by the Atomic Energy Commission (AEC) and the Oak Ridge National Laboratory amounted to about 2 million curies in 1965 (including about 700000 curies of cobalt-60). This amount is four times the figure for 1961.

In 1961 the sales of a number of important radioactive isotopes by the AEC were:

	1961	
	curies	$
H 3	37000	75000
C 14	42	400000
P 32	130	140000
Co 60	71900	170000
Kr 85	3700	60000
J 131	300	100000
Cs 137	16100	30000
Ir 192	6300	40000
Po 210	1000	90000

The total amount of radioactive isotopes sold by the Oak Ridge National Laboratory and the AEC during the period 1946 to 1961 inclusive was 1560000 curies. In 1961 the USA exported radioactive isotopes to a total value of about $ 2 million and in 1964 to a total value of about $ 3 million.

Other major producers, besides the USA, are the USSR, GB, Canada and France. GB's exports of these substances in 1960 amounted to £550000 and in 1964 to £1.5 million.

The prices of radioactive isotopes in the USA can be deduced from the sales figures of the AEC. From the above table it appears that the price of carbon-14 was about $10000 per curie in 1961, whereas the price of tritium and cobalt-60 was only some $2 or 3 per curie.

15.4 NUCLEAR FISSION AND NUCLEAR REACTORS

15.4.1 Introduction

Nuclear fission is a nuclear reaction in which a heavy isotope is broken up into a number of medium weight fragments with the simultaneous development of large quantities of energy. The development of this important source of energy was made possible by the theoretical work of Einstein, who showed as far back as 1905 that matter is a form of energy. For the relation between matter and energy he derived his well-known equation: $E = mc^2$, where E denotes the energy, m the mass of the matter, and c the velocity of light ($= 3 \times 10^8$ m/s). From this equation it can be calculated that 1 g of matter would supply 25 million kWh of energy if it could be entirely converted into energy. On this theory, it must be inferred that in the transformation of a radio-active isotope into a stable isotope a certain quantity of matter will disappear because energy (in the form of radiation and moving particles) is emitted. Very accurate measurements of atomic weights confirm this.

Starting from the hydrogen isotope whose nucleus consists of one proton, we might expect the atomic weights of all other isotopes to be exact multiples of the atomic weight of the hydrogen isotope. It appears however that the atomic weight of all isotopes is in fact somewhat lower (mass defect). For the isotopes of the heaviest and the lightest elements the discrepancy is relatively smaller than for the isotopes of the medium-weight elements. In the case of deuterium (an isotope of hydrogen) and helium it is very slight.

As already stated a nuclear reaction in which energy is developed will be associated with a loss of matter and thus it is a transformation of an isotope with a small mass defect into one with a larger mass defect.

In the case of the natural disintegration of a radioactive isotope, the resulting stable isotope only has a slightly greater mass defect. The loss of matter associated with reactions of this kind is minute, so that the quantity of energy obtained is small. The loss of matter (and therefore also the gain in energy) is much greater when a heavy isotope is broken up into a number of medium-weight fragments with the greatest mass defect.

An example of such a process was found in 1939 when Hahn and Strassmann detected radioactive barium in uranium that had been bombarded with neutrons.

15.4.2 Mechanism of nuclear fission reactions

The effects obtained by bombarding heavy isotopes with neutrons depends on the energy of the neutrons employed and on the isotope bombarded.

a. Neutrons of low energy (slow or 'thermal' neutrons) are captured by the nucleus of the most abundant isotope ^{238}U:

$$^{238}_{92}\text{U} + {}^{1}_{0}\text{n} \rightarrow {}^{239}_{92}\text{U} + \gamma\text{-rays.}$$

A new isotope of uranium, $^{239}_{92}$U, is formed which, like most artifical isotopes, is a β emitter. This uranium isotope is spontaneously converted into a new element called Neptunium which does not occur naturally.

$$^{239}_{92}\text{U} \rightarrow {}^{239}_{93}\text{Np} + {}^{0}_{-1}\beta$$

Neptunium is also a β emitter and gives rise to another radioactive element called plutonium which again does not occur naturally.

$$^{239}_{93}\text{Np} \rightarrow {}^{239}_{94}\text{Pu*} + {}^{0}_{-1}\beta$$

Subsequently, more new elements with even higher atomic number are obtained by bombarding neptunium and plutonium with neutrons (see table 15.1). These new elements including neptunium and plutonium are called transuranic elements.

It must be noted that the electrons emitted are not derived from orbits around the nuclei, but are electrons formed in the nucleus itself by conversion of a neutron into a proton.

The naturally most abundant thorium isotope, $^{232}_{91}$ Th, also forms an isotope of uranium when it is bomvarded with slow neutrons

$$^{232}_{91}\text{Th} + {}^{1}_{0}\text{n} \rightarrow {}^{233}_{92}\text{U*} + {}^{0}_{1}\beta$$

The resulting radioactive uranium isotope does not occur in natural uranium.

b. When ^{235}U, which occurs in natural uranium (0.7%), or the artificial U^{235} or plutonium is bombarded by slow neutrons, the type of reaction is quite different. The nucleus of the target atom now breaks up into two large radioactive fragments together with release of more neutrons of high energy. One of the fragments usually has an atomic weight between 80 and 100, e.g. radioactive bromine, strontium or krypton, and the atomic weight of the other fragment usually ranges from 120 to 140, e.g. radioactive lanthanum, xenon or barium. Nuclear fission has taken place. For example:

$$^{235}_{92}\text{U} + {}^{1}_{0}\text{n (slow)} \rightarrow {}^{140}_{4}\text{Xe} + {}^{94}_{38}\text{Sr} + 2\,{}^{1}_{0}\text{n (fast)}$$

When xenon and strontium are formed two neutrons are released for every one used.

An important effect is that each released neutron can split another nucleus with the formation of more neutrons: thus they multiply rapidly at each collision with the consequence that a chain reaction is set up.

If not controlled in some manner the rate of the reaction will increase rapidly, the material will undergo almost instantaneous disintegration and an enormous amount of energy will be released.

c. As shown above the most abundant isotopes of uranium and thorium, ^{238}U and ^{232}Th, do not undergo nuclear fission with slow neutrons. This is due to the fact that the nuclei of these isotopes are more stable than those of the uranium isotopes mentioned under (b) and plutonium. (Because of their higher stability, they have a longer half-life time, which causes their greater natural abundance.)

^{238}U and ^{232}Th are fissible in the same way as ^{235}U when they are bombarded with fast neutrons (fast neutrons have a higher energy content due to their higher velocity).

To obtain a picture of what happens in a nuclear fission of the above kind it may be supposed that the cohesive forces which operate among the nucleons present within the nucleus produce a sort of artificial membrane which holds them together, much in the manner that the drops of a liquid are held together by surface energy forces. This membrane must be strong enough to resist the forces of electrostatic repulsion among the protons within the nucleus. As we pass from the lighter to the heavier elements, this electrostatic repulsion increases very rapidly because it is a long-range force. The cohesive forces however are only on contiguous particles, are short-range and increase only slowly. The consequence is that heavy nuclei have progressively less stability. The entry of a neutron into the uranium nucleus upsets this stability and the nucleus splits into smaller nuclei.

As already stated the release of a large amount of energy during such a fission is due to the destruction of a small proportion (about 0.1%) of the total masses of the reactants during the change. This may seem only a small amount but it can be shown using the Einstein equation $E = mc^2$ that 1 kg of uranium of which 1 g is destroyed produces about 25 million kWh of electrical energy. It is estimated that fission of uranium produces as much heat as the combustion of 3 million times the same weight of coal. The development of the power reactor could in due course provide energy which might well exceed that of all the fossil fuels (i.e. coal, oil and natural gas).

15.4.3 Nuclear reactors

A nuclear reactor is an assembly made of special material designed to sustain and control a neutron chain reaction in a fissionable fuel. The fuels used are enriched uranium, ^{235}U, ^{233}U and plutonium ^{239}Pu.

The reaction required is one which yields at each fission an average of one more neutron to produce the next fission. A difficulty is that many neutrons instead of continuing the chain become ineffective. This is due to the fact that neutrons move within a material much like the molecules of a gas and thus *(a)* they may be absorbed by ^{238}U and other materials or impurities, and *(b)* they may escape without making a collision. Loss due to *(a)* is reduced by choice of fuel, e.g. by using uranium in which the concentration of fissible ^{235}U has been increased artificially (enrichment of uranium see p. 664). Loss due to *(b)* is reduced by increasing, within limits, the amount of fuel; this feature exploits the fact that when the total weight of a solid is (say) doubled, its total surface is increased less than twofold.

Neutrons released by fission travel at high speeds but the probability of fission reaction with ^{235}U is greatly increased if the rate is slow or 'thermal'. Materials which are effective in this slowing down process are called moderators. They have low neutron absorbing power and include graphite, heavy water, beryllium, some hydrocarbons and some metal hydrides. No element of atomic weight greater than that of oxygen (16) has much significance as a moderator. If however ^{239}Pu or highly enriched ^{235}U is the fissile fuel, chain reactions become possible with fast neutrons and a moderator is not required.

In order to build a nuclear reactor, rods of enriched uranium (the fuel) are placed some distance apart in a space which is filled with the moderator. The concentration of ^{235}U in one rod and its size do not in themselves suffice to sustain a chain reaction. A group of fuel rods separated by a moderator can, however, sustain a chain reaction. This is because the neutrons retarded from any particular rod act upon the other rods or are reflected back into the same rod by the moderator. The nuclear chain reaction is started by means of neutrons from a radioactive isotope. Obviously, without any possibility of controlling the process it is not possible to maintain a constant number of collisions per unit of time because the conditions in the reactor are always changing as a result of the temperature rise, reduction of the quantity of fissile material etc. In order to make the reactor controllable, an excess of neutrons is employed. This excess (which therefore varies) might cause an increasing avalanche of fresh reactions with the development of tremendous amounts of heat resulting in an explosion. For this reason the varying excess is removed by installing, between the uranium rods, movable partitions or rods to absorb the excess of neutrons. The partitions and rods are composed of effective neutron absorbers such as cadmium or boron, and are moved mechanically in and out of the reactor. The extent of insertion is automatically controlled so that the reaction proceeds at the desired rate.

The heat released during the reaction in the uranium rods is removed by a coolant which flows through pipes placed in the moderator. The uranium rods are provided with a protective sheathing and are installed inside these cooling pipes. As the coolant usually becomes radioactive in consequence of the neutron bombardment to which it is subjected, the heat is transferred by means of a heat-exchanger to a second coolant which in turn transfers this heat to steam or gas turbines in a power station.

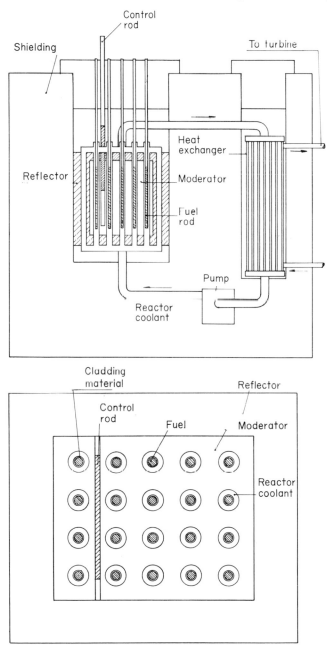

Fig. 15.12 Diagram of a solid-fuel nuclear reactor and a horizontal section through the left-hand part. The heat-exchanger is installed within the radiation shield (as a precaution in case the coolant becomes radioactive). Alternatively, in cases where the coolant becomes only slightly radioactive, the heat exchangers may be installed outside the shield. With such an arrangement, traces of radioactive matter can, for example, be removed from the coolant by means of filters before it emerges from the reactor.

A nuclear reactor is illustrated schematically in fig. 15.12. Only a few rods are shown in this diagram, but a large reactor may contain hundreds.

15.4.4 Reactor materials

Great difficulties arise in the choice of materials which are suitable for their particular purpose in the reactor and for protection against radiation. All these materials must be resistant to high temperatures and (excepting of course the fuel) they must resist the action of neutrons. These requirements severely restrict the selection.

The fissile material must resist the large temperature gradient between the centre of the rods and their surface. These fuel rods must emit heat readily at the surface and, since this heat is removed by means of a coolant, the fuel must not be attacked by the coolant. For these reasons uranium and plutonium are usually employed as the metals, as ceramics composed of their oxides or as alloys of highly enriched uranium with zirconium or aluminium: the rods are usually sheathed in a thin casing of zirconium, aluminium, magnox (a magnesium alloy) or stainless steel. These are known as cladding materials and serve also to prevent the scattering of radioactive products within the reactor.

The coolant must have high thermal capacity because it controls the temperature of the fuel and removes the generated heat for subsequent use. It must resist heat and radiation and moreover, absorb few or no neutrons. The following substances are used: water or other gases (air, nitrogen, carbon dioxide) under high pressure, and some molten metals (lithium, potassium, sodium). The advantages of using molten sodium are: (a) it has excellent heat-transfer properties; (b) it has much higher boiling point than water so that the pressure required to prevent boiling is less than in the case of water; (c) it is not expensive. On the other hand it tends to become reactive owing to formation of radioactive sodium $^{24}_{11}Na$.

One or more heat exchangers are often installed within the envelope of the reactor for the purpose of effecting the transfer of heat from the first coolant (which has become more or less radioactive) to a second coolant, which can be safely handled outside the reactor.

An important factor which is determined by the cladding material and the coolant, is the permissible operating temperature. If aluminium is used as the cladding material, the temperature in the fuel can in general not be raised above 230° C. If zirconium is used, with water as the coolant, an operating temperature of about 350° C is possible; with magnox cladding and carbon dioxide coolant the temperature can be raised to about 400° C and if a cladding of type 304 stainless steel is used, in conjunction with sodium as the coolant, an operating temperature of over 500° C in the fuel rods becomes possible.

To prevent loss of neutrons by leakage through the walls of the reactor, the core (which consists of fuel, coolant, moderator and control rods) is enclosed in a reflector made from material which has high reflective and low absorption capacity for neutrons. These properties are required also in the moderators referred to above.

The surroundings of the reactor may be protected from the radiation by enclosing it within a steel wall lined internally with boron-steel or a boron-aluminium alloy to absorb neutrons and provided with layers of lead or iron. The lead, iron and concrete absorb Υ-rays. Special concretes may be used with water content high enough to serve as neutron moderator and with added constituents, e.g. iron, barytes and boron ores, to increase their neutron and Υ-ray absorption.

Figure 15.13 shows one of the reactors at the Calder Hall power station designed to produce plutonium from uranium and simultaneously large amounts of energy. In this reactor the moderator consists of perforated carbon blocks. Fuel rods consisting of natural uranium, encased in a magnox cladding, are inserted in the channels formed in the moderator. Carbon dioxide under pressure also passes through these channels to cool the reactor.

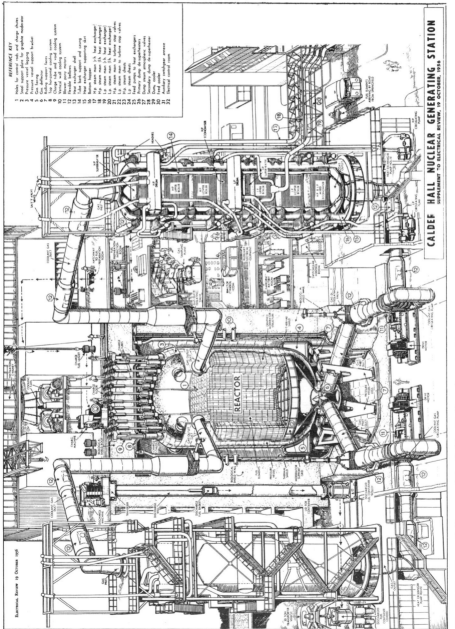

Fig. 15.13 General diagram of the Calder Hall nuclear reactors.

15.4.5 Classification of reactors

Although all nuclear reactors embody the same principle, four types of construction can be distinguished depending on the purpose for which they are designed. Some types serve two purposes.

a. Research and development. A reactor for this purpose is comparable to a pilot plant and may be built to provide a rich source of neutrons for the study of the small-scale bombardment of a particular substance and the behaviour of fuels and other materials, and for the production of radioactive isotopes. For these reasons such reactors are often provided with separate containers in which various substances can be placed. This reactor may also represent a test of a particular design and may be provided with a cooling system which is not concerned primarily with the economic recovery of heat.

b. Production reactors or conversion reactors. These are specially designed for producing a fissible material by means of the excess of neutrons obtained from nuclear fission of *another* fissible material. For example an excess of neutrons is produced by nuclear fission of ^{235}U contained in ^{238}U and these neutrons are used for producing ^{239}Pu from ^{238}U. Production reactors are based on the fact that it is less difficult to separate plutonium from uranium than to separate ^{235}U from natural uranium.

c. Breeders. In these reactors a fissible material is produced by means of neutrons obtained from nuclear fission of the *same kind* fissible material. $^{239}_{94}Pu$ (made in another nuclear reactor) is consumed to produce an excess of neutrons and the latter are used to produce more $^{239}_{94}Pu$ from $^{238}_{92}U$. The core contains natural uranium mainly $^{238}_{92}U$ mixed with $^{239}_{94}Pu$ and is surrounded by a 'blanket' of natural uranium. The fast neutrons emitted by the $^{239}_{94}Pu$ gradually lose their energy by collisions in this 'blanket' and by reflection back into the core. Eventually they have the energy necessary for recapture by $^{238}_{92}U$ followed by formation of $^{239}_{94}Pu$ and $^{239}_{93}Np$ by the following disintegrations.

$$^{238}_{92}U + ^{1}_{0}n \rightarrow ^{239}_{92}U + \gamma$$

$$^{239}_{92}U \rightarrow ^{239}_{92}Np + ^{0}_{-1}\beta$$

$$^{239}_{93}Np \rightarrow ^{239}_{94}Pu + ^{0}_{-1}\beta$$

Thus the reactor has produced more fuel. Breeder reactors are often dual purpose reactors which are designed to produce more fuel and, in addition, to enable efficient recovery of heat which is fed to an electric power station.

d. Power reactors and propulsion reactors. This type contains no special device for production of fuel or isotopes and may therefore be simpler and smaller. It is most appropriate for nuclear-powered ships. To minimize its size enriched fuel is used.

Other classifications of the reactors mentioned above are also common. According to one classification nuclear reactors are divided into (1) slow (or thermal) reactors and (2) fast reactors.

1. In a thermal reactor the velocity of the fast neutrons obtained in nuclear fission is decreased by means of a moderator. The fuel usually has a low content of fissible materials, e.g. slightly enriched uranium or plutonium in uranium.

2. The fast reactor contains little or no moderator and therefore operates with fast neutrons. The fuel usually has a far higher content of fissible material, e.g. highly enriched uranium. This type of reactor cannot be controlled by means of control rods, because the neutrons move at such high velocities that too few of them are captured by the rods. For this reason the nuclear chain reaction in the fast reactor is controlled by means of reflectors. For example, more neutrons can be allowed to leak away by moving the reflector elements away from the reactor core. The heavier moderators, such as beryllium and graphite are preferably used as reflectors, because on collision with and reflection by relatively heavy atoms the neutrons lose less of their velocity.

Classification of reactors is also often based on the coolant (boiling water reactor, pressurized water reactor, gas-cooled reactor, sodium-cooled reactor, etc.) or on the moderator (e.g. graphite-moderated reactor or heavy-water-moderated reactor).

Reactors may also be divided into heterogeneous and homogeneous reactors. Heterogeneous reactors are reactors using solid fuel non-uniformly distributed (e.g. in the form of rods as discussed in the preceding paragraphs). However a reactor may also be operated with fuel in liquid form. In such a reactor, for example, a solution of a uranium salt in water may be used. If the water also serves as the moderator the fuel is distributed uniformly in the reactor, hence the name homogeneous reactor (see also fig. 15.14). Hitherto homogeneous reactors have been built only for fairly low power outputs. The heterogeneous reactors using solid fuels are by far the most important.

The demarcations between the various types of reactors are often vague since there are many intermediate varieties and new types are continuously being developed.

15.4.6 Statistics

In Britain, twenty-four high-capacity power reactors were in operation in 1966, and six more were under construction. The total output of the reactors in regular operation then was more than 16000 MW (this represents the thermal output; the

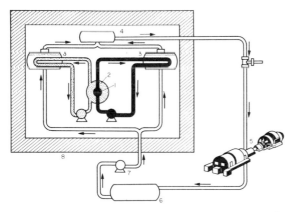

Fig. 15.14 Diagram of a liquid fuel nuclear reactor. (1) Central sphere with liquid fuel (which may be dissolved in the moderator). (2) Enveloping 'breeder' liquid in concentric sphere. (3) Heat exchangers. (4) Steam boiler. (5) Steam turbine with generator. (6) Condenser for exhaust steam. (7) Boiler feed-water pump. (8) Heavy shielding wall to prevent escape of radiation.

electricity output is about 4000 MW; it is probably the largest nuclear power output of any country in the western world).

These are all graphite-moderated uranium fuel reactors. In addition to the twenty-four reactors mentioned above, there were, in Britain, a reactor operating with a mixture of thorium carbide and the carbide of enriched uranium as the fuel, and a fast reactor operating with enriched uranium fuel. These reactors have lower outputs (20-60 MW). A reactor using heavy water as the moderator and designed for an output of 300 MW was under construction in 1966. The above figures do not include about twenty low-output research reactors. These use graphite, heavy water or ordinary water as the moderator.

Although the total number of nuclear reactors in operation in the USA is much larger than in the UK, the total output is considerably lower. This is due to the fact that in the USA the construction of reactors has been concentrated more particularly on units for scientific research and on power reactors for propulsion purposes rather than for the generation of power for large electrical power stations. In 1965, ninety-nine test, research and teaching reactors and fifty-six propulsion reactors (for submarines, etc.) were in operation. In addition twelve civilian nuclear power reactors with a capacity of 1060 MW electrical energy were in operation during 1965. In 1970 the number of civilian reactors will be increased to twenty-three with a total capacity of 7000 MW electrical energy.

15.4.7 Processing of nuclear reactor wastes

The major problem of nuclear reactor technology is that of disposal of radioactive waste.

When the fuel of a reactor has been in use for a time, large quantities of radioactive fission products will have formed in it, with the result that the properties of the fuel rods deteriorate. Their thermal conductivity is reduced, the rods begin to sinter and disintegrate into powder, the concentration of fissile material is diminished, etc. The fuel thus becomes unsuitable for further use and must be removed from the reactor.

To recover useful fuel from the mixture, the waste material, which is highly radioactive, is usually dissolved in nitric acid. From the solution obtained in this way the fuel can be extracted by means of liquid-liquid extraction with organic liquids which are immiscible with water, e.g. with a tributyl phosphate solution in hexane. This treatment is, in principle, the same as that used in the purification of uranium (see p. 663).

Uranium and plutonium (or thorium if present) dissolve in the organic liquid. The radioactive fission products remain behind in the aqueous nitric acid solution. After separation of the liquids, the plutonium compound in the organic liquid is converted into a trivalent plutonium compound with the aid of a reducing agent. The uranium compound can then be selectively extracted with water. Uranium and plutonium are obtained in the form of nitrates from the two liquids. These compounds in turn are converted into metal, alloy or oxide and re-used.

The aqueous nitric acid solution contains a mixture of radioactive isotopes with atomic weights ranging from 70 to 160. This solution constitutes the principal radioactive waste from the nuclear reactor. The most dangerous radioactive isotopes in this waste matter are strontium–90 and caesium–137, which emit powerful radiation and have half life periods of twenty-five to thirty years. Most of the other radioactive isotopes in this mixture lose their emissive power in about ten years.

Obviously, these dangerous waste products cannot simply be discharged into rivers, seas and the like. The only method of disposal at present known consists in depositing them in places where the radiation can do no harm. To this end they are usually concentrated. The principal method consists in the precipitation of the bulk of the radioactive substances by treatment with chemicals with which they form compounds which are insoluble in water. For example, the addition of ferric sulphate and sodium phosphate, followed by sodium hydroxide solution results in the formation of a radioactive slurry of basic phosphates of a large number of radioactive isotopes. Radioactive caesium can then be precipitated by the addition of potassium or ammonium aluminate.

Methods derived from ordinary waste water treatment technology are also applied, including filtration through absorbent clays such as montmorillonite.

The concentrated waste products are packed in watertight concrete boxes, which are then stored underground in worked-out salt mines and deep excavations, or they are sunk at sea in very deep water. As strontium-90 and caesium-137 are the most dangerous waste products, they are sometimes separated from the waste mixture and stored separately.

Radioactive waste products are in some cases processed into solid blocks which cannot be leached out by water. Thus, they may be mixed with cement, poured into barrels and, after hardening, stored away in the manner described above.

All manipulations, from removal of used fuel from the reactor to storage of the wastes, are performed with the aid of remote-controlled automatic equipment (see p. 642 and fig. 15.11). Automatic scoops deposit the waste products in boxes which in turn are handled by automatic cranes.

How great the problem of the storage of radioactive wastes is likely to become in the future is apparent from the following figures. Up to 1960, about 75 million gallons of wastes were disposed of in the United States. The cost involved is estimated at $ 100 million. The electricity output of nuclear power stations in 1960 was about 2 million kW. It is estimated that this figure will be increased a hundredfold in twenty-five years time, whereas twenty years ago no nuclear reactors existed at all.

Nowadays various radioactive isotopes are obtained by suitably processing radioactive waste matter. Since the waste mixtures consist of various isotopes of different elements, many isotopes can be precipitated from the solution with the aid of chemicals with which they selectively form insoluble products.

15.4.8 Nuclear weapons and nuclear fusion

Basically the atomic bomb consists of a power reactor in which the chain reaction is uncontrolled. It contains a neutron source and a number of fuel units which are individually too small to sustain a chain reaction. By moving the fuel units and the neutron source towards each other the neutron efficiency is increased and an uncontrolled chain reaction can start. The result is an explosion.

In the hydrogen bomb the great amount of energy released by an atomic bomb can be made combine to hydrogen nuclei (with no mass defect), deuterium, tritium, helium and/or lithium nuclei into nuclei with a much greater mass defect

$$\,^2_1\mathrm{H} + \,^3_1\mathrm{H} \rightarrow \,^4_2\mathrm{He} + \,^1_0\mathrm{n}$$

$$\,^2_1\mathrm{H} + \,^6_3\mathrm{Li} \rightarrow \,^4_2\mathrm{He} + \,^4_2\mathrm{He}$$

$$\,^2_1\mathrm{H} + \,^3_2\mathrm{He} \rightarrow \,^4_2\mathrm{He} + \,^1_1\mathrm{H}.$$

These reactions, known as nuclear fusion reactions, are associated with the release of a far greater amount of energy than in nuclear fission reactions. In addition to developing larger amounts of energy, nuclear fusion reactions have the advantage that no radioactive wastes are formed.

Unfortunately it has not yet proved possible to find a high energy source capable of starting a controlled fusion chain reaction between the very stable nuclei of hydrogen, helium and lithium atoms. For this reason nuclear fusion cannot yet be used in nuclear reactors.

15.4.9 Literature

R. LINDNER. *Kern- und Radiochemie*. Berlin, Springer Verlag, 1961.

D. J. CARSWELL, *Introduction to nuclear chemistry*. London, Elsevier, 1967.

G. FRIEDLANDER and J. KENNEDY. *Nuclear and radiochemistry*. New York, Wiley, 1956.

E. BRODA and T. SCHÖNFELD. *Technical applications of radiochemistry,* vol. 1. Oxford, Pergamon, 1966.

A. A. JACOBS, D. E. KLINE and F. J. REMICK. *Basic principles of nuclear science and reactors*. Princeton; London, Van Nostrand, 1960.

H. ADAM. *Einführung in die Kerntechnik*. Munich, Oldenbourg Verlag, 1967.

15.5 THORIUM

15.5.1 History and occurrence

Thorium was discovered by Berzelius in 1828. It acquired some practical importance in 1886 when Auer Von Welsbach discovered that a brilliant white luminescence is obtained by heating a mixture of thorium oxide and cerium oxide. This effect is used in the incandescent gas mantle.

Modern interest in thorium is due to its value as a potential source of uranium-233 (^{233}U) as a nuclear fuel and to the possibility of increasing the supply of fissionable material by breeding with thorium.

Thorium occurs in the earth's crust in an average quantity of 10 to 15 p.p.m. (about three times the average quantity of uranium). Many minerals containing thorium are known but most of them contain only traces of thorium. Important minerals are thorite (mainly thorium silicate), thorianite (mainly thoria, ThO_2) and monazite which consists mainly of phosphates of rare earths containing 4 to 18% of thoria. Only monazite sands are of economic importance and the largest deposits occur in India and Brazil. Other deposits are in the USA, South Africa and Indonesia.

15.5.2 Extraction of thorium compounds from ores

The extraction of thorium from monazite sands mainly involves the separation of thorium from large amounts of rare earths which are also present, and the removal of phosphates so as to produce either a pure thorium salt, e.g. oxalate or nitrate, or the oxide (ThO_2). Both acid and alkali extraction processes are used.

In one variation of the *acid* process, the monazite ore is treated with excess of hot concentrated sulphuric acid for several hours. Cold water is added to obtain a solution of mixed sulphates. Separation of thorium may be effected by several techniques, e.g. fractional crystallization and precipitation. In the latter thorium pyrophosphate is precipitated by adding sodium pyrophosphate to the solution. The rare earths are not precipitated by sodium pyrophosphate and may be recovered from the remaining solution. The precipitated thorium pyrophosphate is converted into thorium oxalate or sulphate which can be obtained in a pure state by repeated crystallization.

Solutions containing thorium and other salts may also be purified by liquid-liquid extraction, e.g. thorium nitrate is extracted with tributyl phosphate from solutions containing rare earths.

If separation of thorium and uranium is needed, the sulphuric acid leach of the compounds is treated with oxalic acid. Thorium and the rare earths are precipitated and uranium remains dissolved. Several combinations of extraction, separation and purification processes may be exploited depending on the nature of ore which is used.

In one variation of the *alkali extraction* process the ground monazite sand is digested with 50% aqueous sodium hydroxide for several hours. The slurry of mixed metal hydroxides thus obtained is diluted and filtered off, and then dissolved in hydrochloric acid; the resulting solution is partially neutralized with sodium hydroxide. The precipitate contains all the thorium and uranium in the sand but only a small amount of rare earths. It is redissolved in nitric acid and then solvent-extracted with tributyl phosphate to give pure thorium nitrate ($Th(NO_3)_4$).

15.5.3 Thorium oxide

This thorium compound is prepared by heating thorium hydroxide or some thorium salts, e.g. thorium oxalate or thorium nitrate. Thorium oxide is a white powder. It has the highest melting point (about $3220°$ C), of any available oxide and is more stable than any other. It may be fused in a carbon arc furnace. It is radioactive and toxic.

15.5.4 Thorium metal

Thorium metal powder is produced by the reduction of thorium oxide with calcium metal in a steel refractory-lined autoclave at $950°$ in an inert gas atmosphere:

$$ThO_2 + 2\,Ca \rightarrow Th + 2\,CaO.$$

The product is cooled and leached with dilute acetic acid to remove the lime and any unreacted calcium. The thorium powder obtained is washed, dried and vacuum sintered to give a dense, ductile metal having purity not less than 99.77%. The main impurity is oxygen.

In a modified process the thorium oxide is first converted into thorium fluoride (ThF_4), with hydrofluoric acid and the reduction with calcium is promoted by addition of zinc chloride.

Massive thorium having a high purity can be produced by thermal decomposition of thorium iodide or by electrolysis of a fused mixture of potassium fluoride, sodium fluoride and potassium fluorothorate ($KThF_5$), using a graphite crucible as anode and a molybdenum cathode.

Powdered thorium metal can be converted into massive metal either by sintering in an electric furnace in a high vacuum at $1300-1400°$ C or by melting in a beryllia crucible at a temperature between 1800 and $1850°$ C.

Thorium (atomic weight 232.04) is a radioactive metal with the colour of nickel. Its melting point is about 1 700° C, and boiling point 4 200° C. Its density is 11.4 g/cm³. Several natural radioactive isotopes of thorium are known, but the commonly occurring isotope is thorium-232. The half life of thorium-232 is 1.4 x 10¹⁰ years. The half life of the other thorium isotope is short with the exception of ionium (or thorium-230) which has a half life of 8 x 10⁴ years. Small quantities of ionium occur in uranium ores as it is a radioactive decay product of uranium-238. In its compounds thorium is tetravalent.

Thorium slowly tarnishes on exposure to air. It has excellent fabrication characteristics, i.e. it can be extruded, rolled, drawn, forged and machined, but it is found that its behaviour varies somewhat with the method of manufacture.

15.5.5 Uses

Thorium is chiefly used in the form of metal, oxide and nitrate. In spite of the widespread use of electricity for illumination, important quantities of thorium are consumed in the manufacture of incandescent mantles for gas lamps. Gas mantles are prepared by impregnating a combustible woven cloth with a mixture of 99% thorium nitrate and 1% cerium nitrate. On ignition a skeleton of thorium oxide, containing dispersed cerium oxide, is formed. As thorium oxide has very low heat conductivity, cerium oxide is heated intensively and glows with a bright white light.

In the USA important quantities of thorium metal are employed in the manufacture of light-weight heat-resistant magnesium alloys containing 3% of thorium. These alloys are used in the construction of satellites, missiles and supersonic aircraft.

Thorium metal and oxide are used in nuclear reactors as thorium can be converted into uranium-233 in breeder reactors. Uranium-233 can be employed as a nuclear reactor fuel (see nuclear fission and nuclear reactors, p. 647). Experimental nuclear power reactors, having an output of 20 to 40 MW and using alloys of thorium and enriched uranium or a ceramic mass of thorium oxide and uranium oxide, are in operation in the USA and the UK.

Thorium oxide is used in making refractory crucibles for melting metals, but an important competitor in this field is beryllium oxide.

Thorium metal is used as a catalyst for petroleum cracking and for oxidizing ammonia to nitric acid, sulphur dioxide to sulphur trioxide and carbon monoxide to water gas.

Small quantities of thorium metal are consumed in electrodes for cold cathode discharge tubes and electric arc lamps and in filament wires for electronic tubes to increase the life of the filament.

15.5.6 Statistics

The western world reserve of thorium was estimated at over 1.4 million short tons of thorium oxide in 1964 (considering only ores containing over 300 p.p.m. of ThO_2). An important reserve is available from Canadian uranium deposits (over 200 000 tons of thorium oxide, ThO_2). Concentrates containing 20 to 30% of thorium oxide were available at $1.75 to $2.25 per lb of ThO_2 content in 1964. The price for thorium oxide containing 97 to 99% ThO_2 ranged from $7.00 to $12.00 per lb nuclear grade. Thorium metal in quantities of 2 000 lb or more was available at $25 per lb.

World production of thorium is less than 2 000 short tons a year. The USA produced only about 50 short tons of thorium oxide, in 1964. The US consumption for purposes other than energy amounted to about 50 short tons in that year. Much larger quantities were imported from Canada, Australia, Ceylon, Malaysia, UK and South Africa and were mainly stored for energy purposes.

About 60% of the US consumption for non-energy purposes was used for the production of magnesium alloys and 30% for gas mantle manufacture. The remaining 10% was used for refractories, chemicals, medicinals and electronic products. The US investment of thorium for energy purposes in nuclear reactors has not been published.

15.5.7 Literature

C. A. HAMPEL. *Rare metals handbook,* 2nd edn. New York, Reinhold, 1961.
F. L. CUTHBERT. *Thorium production technology,* London, Addison-Wesley, 1959.

15.6 URANIUM

15.6.1 History and occurrence

The black mineral pitchblende, (which occurs in Bohemia, Saxony, East Africa and Colorado) was found by Klaproth in 1789 to be the oxide of a metal which he called uranium after the planet Uranus, then recently discovered. In 1896 Becquerel found that uranium salts are radioactive and thus began a new chapter in chemistry and physics.

Before 1939 uranium and its compounds were of little importance and apart from its use for the production of yellow glass scarcely any technology had been developed. After the discovery of nuclear fission by Hahn and Strassmann, uranium became very important economically, because of its use in generating electricity in nuclear power stations, and in military strategy because of its exploitation in nuclear weapons. In both these categories, use is made of the fissionable isotopes of uranium or plutonium which is itself made from uranium.

For security reasons most knowledge on the processing and use of uranium has been kept secret for a long time, but now data and techniques have been established for the successful use of uranium as a nuclear fuel. Many tons of uranium metal are annually converted into tubes, rods, sheets, plates etc., using ordinary mill equipment, in spite of the fact that it cannot be handled like iron, copper and other common metals because it is chemically reactive, radioactive and toxic.

Uranium may be found naturally on a wide scale. The most important uranium-containing minerals are the primary deposits of uraninite, which consists of uranium oxide (UO_2), and pitchblende, which has a higher content of oxygen (approximate formula U_3O_6) but the uranium:oxygen ratio differs from one deposit to another.

The primary uranium minerals are of magnatic origin. In various places in the earth's crust and at considerable depths, masses of magma occur, consisting of hot molten matter which penetrates through the crust and sometimes emerges at the surface, e.g. as lava in volcanic eruptions. Millions of years ago as cooling continued, solidification processes occurred at great depths and basic rocks crystallized out. A molten material remained, with a high content of acidic constituents (quartz, silicates, etc.), water and gases, in which the uranium compounds were retained in solution. This material was forced upwards towards the surface. At lower depths acid silicates containing uraninite crystallized out and the remaining melt was forced up into veins and solidified in the form of pitchblende, together with rocks containing silicon oxide. Deposits of this type are called hydrothermal veins because of their deposition from a liquid with a high content of water.

In addition to these primary deposits secondary deposits occur which were formed because pitchblende is somewhat soluble in acidic surface water. From such a solution, in conjunction with other substances, new minerals were formed, such as carnotite which is a hydrous potassium uranyl vanadate.

Many other uranium-containing minerals are known, but most of these contain so little that they have no economic importance. Up to 1952 uranium was produced chiefly from ores containing 1% or more of uranium oxide, but increasingly uranium is nowadays obtained as a by-product from rocks with a lower uranium content. Examples are the production of uranium from traces present in many phosphate rock deposits and in the waste material from gold mines. Uranium oxide in concentration as low as 0.01% can be extracted economically from these sources.

At the present time uranium is produced on a large scale in the US, Canada, South Africa, the Congo, Australia and the USSR (see fig. 15.15).

Uranium ores are often detected with the aid of a Geiger counter. Exploration carried out with an instrument of this kind enables sources of radiation and hence uranium ores to be discovered (see fig. 15.8, p. 635).

15.6.2 Extraction of uranium compounds from ores

Uranium ores vary so much in composition and complexity that extraction methods also vary. Published information concerning the processes is often restricted and details of the methods are often not available. Nevertheless general features can be recognised and include: (1) concentration of the ore, (2) leaching with perhaps prior roasting, (3) recovery of a uranium compound from the leach liquor usually by a precipitation process, ion exchange or solvent extraction.

1. The concentration may depend on the high gravity of the uranium ore compared with that of the other components. Flotation is not usually sufficiently selective.

2. Roasting with sodium chloride at 850° C is employed in the case of carnotite ores which are rich in vanadium. Sodium vanadate is formed which is removed by percolation with water. The roasting also destroys any organic matter and iron compounds are converted into acid-insoluble oxides.

3. Leaching with either acid or alkali converts the uranium present into soluble compounds.

a. With 50% aqueous nitric acid the nitrate of the hexavalent uranyl ion is formed:

$$U_3O_8 + 8\,HNO_3 \rightarrow 3\,UO_2(NO_3)_2 + 2NO_2 + 4H_2O$$

The slurry obtained is treated with a sulphate, with the result that a precipitate of alkaline earth sulphates and lead sulphate is formed and removed.

To promote the formation of a precipitate, an organic coagulant such as starch, carboxymethyl cellulose, 'separan' (a polyamide) or polyethylene oxide is added. Radium is obtained from the precipitate (white cake), which contains silicates and silica in addition to sulphates (see under radium, p. 636). Crude uranyl nitrate can be obtained from the solution by evaporation. Usually, however, evaporation is continued until a concentrated solution remains, which is further purified.

Fig. 15.15 Map of the world showing known deposits of uranium and thorium.

● Primary uranium ore (pitchblende and uraninite)
▲ Secondary uranium ore (carnotite and autunite)
▲ Uranium ore deposit of unknown size
★ Thorium (monazite)
☆ Thorium (thorianite)
○ Principal deposits

b. When ores are treated with a hot soda solution with a supply of air, uranium compounds are converted into soluble uranyl tricarbonate compounds:

$$2U_3O_8 + O_2 + 18\,Na_2\,CO_3 + 6H_2O \rightarrow 6\,Na_4\,[UO_2(CO_3)_3] + 12\,NaOH$$

After undissolved constituents, consisting of carbonates of various metals and silicates, have been removed by filtration, fairly pure sodium uranate (Na_2UO_4) can be precipitated from the solution by addition of sodium hydroxide.

This method is employed if the rock from which the uranium is extracted contains a high percentage of carbonates. In the USA it is sometimes applied to carnotite ores.

c. The extraction can also be performed with 50% sulphuric acid. The uranium compounds dissolve to form uranyl sulphate, which dissolves in excess of the acid. As a tetravalent uranium compound ion of low solubility is formed, an oxidising agent such as a ferric salt or manganese dioxide is added. This converts all the uranium into the soluble uranyl UO_2^{2+} state. After the insoluble constituents have been filtered off, an ammonium uranate can be precipitated by adding ammonia.

This method is frequently used for ores with a very low content of uranium, e.g. the wastes from gold mining (see fig. 15.16). The precipitation of an uranium salt with ammonia in this treatment is preceded by purification which involves ion exchange. In this process the solution in sulphuric acid is passed through a series of at least three columns filled with a granular ion exchanger, which consists of polystyrene containing quaternary ammonium groups, e.g. Amberlite IRA 400, Dowex 1, Permutit Fl, which are trade names of Rohm and Haas Company, Dow Chemical Company, and the

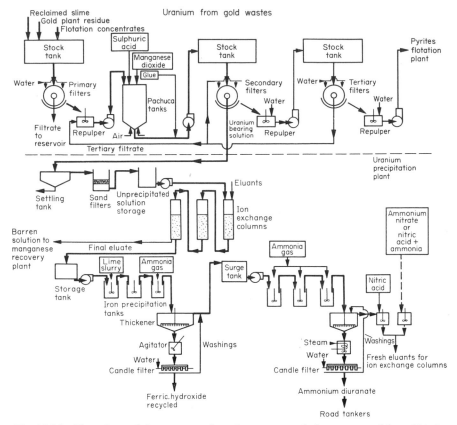

Fig. 15.16 Flow sheet of the recovery of uranium compounds from wastes of the gold industry in South Africa. The waste, made by filtering the solution before the ion exchange, is worked up again in a separate flotation plant (not shown) producing a useful concentrate from which valuable metals are won (e.g., iron from pyrites, etc.).

Permutit Company Ltd respectively. This exchanger adsorbs the negatively charged complex ions which have been formed in the solution from uranyl sulphate and the excess of sulphate ions. Impurities such as aluminium, calcium, magnesium, manganese and a large proportion of the iron remain in solution. A small proportion of the iron remains behind in the adsorbed uranium.

When the first column has become saturated with uranium, the uranium is dissolved from it by extraction with an acid nitrate solution. The regenerated column is re-introduced into the process, in which it now becomes the last column, and so on. By precipitation with ammonia, a uranate containing 85-90% U_3O_8 can be obtained from the solution, even though the original ore may contain only 0.1% U_3O_8 (see fig. 15.16). A continuous ion exchange process is illustrated in fig. 15.17.

15.6.3 Purification of uranium compounds

The principal methods of purification are liquid-liquid extraction processes. These are based on the selective solubility of uranyl nitrate in various organic liquids which are immiscible with water. The most important are diethyl ether and a solution of tributyl phosphate in kerosine or hexane. Other organic liquids, such as dibutyl phosphate, monodecyl phosphate, di(2-ethyl hexyl) phosphate and aliphatic amines with branched chains are also suitable for this liquid-liquid extraction.

1. In the diethyl ether extraction process two parts of ether and one part of the nitric acid solution of the uranium compound are mixed whereupon the greater part of the uranium dissolves in the ether layer which is separated and leached with small quantities of water. The leaching water, as also the water extracted with ether, is brought to pH 2.3 by the addition of caustic soda. Some impurities, such as phosphates, molybdates and vanadates, are precipitated. After the precipitate had been removed by filtration, the pH value of the solution is increased to 6. Uranium oxide is then precipitated, which is filtered off and again dissolved in nitric acid and processed again.

The leached ether layer, which contains the uranyl nitrate is extracted four times with distilled or de-ionised water, using each time one part of water to four parts of ether. The extracted ether can be re-used. The water, containing pure uranyl nitrate and nitric acid, is evaporated at 120 to 143° C. Uranyl nitrate hexahydrate ($UO_2(NO_3)_2.6 H_2O$) is obtained, with a yield of 99.8%. The impurities do not exceed about 50 p.p.m. The nitric acid vapours which are evolved in the process are recovered. Ether extraction may be applied as a continuous process in which the extraction is repeated after the excess of nitric acid has been removed.

2. In the tributyl phosphate-kerosene process, extraction is effected with a 15% solution of tributyl phosphate in kerosene. In principle it is the same as the extraction process with ether, except that more than twice as much organic liquid to the same quantity of nitric acid solution is employed. In re-extracting with water, one part of water to two parts of organic liquid is used. The uranium yield obtained is 99.9%.

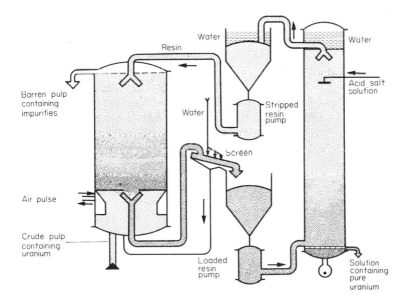

Fig. 15.17 Diagram of a method for the continuous winning of uranium compounds from waste materials with the aid of an ion exchanging synthetic resin. The ion exchanger is continuously regenerated.

Another purification process involves fractional distillation of uranium hexafluoride (UF₆). In principle this process consists of the reduction of hexavalent uranium compounds in solution, whereby tetravalent uranium compounds are formed. The tetravalent uranium ions are precipitated as uranium tetrafluoride (UF₄) by means of hydrofluoric acid from the solution obtained. The tetrafluoride is converted into uranium hexafluoride (UF₆), which is subjected to fractional distillation.

15.6.4 Production of metallic uranium

In many cases the initial substance used in the production of the metal uranium is purified uranyl nitrate hexahydrate. This substance is converted into uranium trioxide (UO_3: 'orange oxide') by heating it at 850° C in calcining kilns. The nitrous vapours evolved are collected and reconverted into nitric acid.

By treatment with hydrogen at 650° to 800° C uranium trioxide is reduced to uranium dioxide (UO_2: 'brown oxide'). Water is condensed from the resultant gas mixture and excess of hydrogen can be re-used. In more recent processes, reduction is effected with a mixture of nitrogen and hydrogen obtained by decomposition of ammonia.

A small proportion of the uranium dioxide as such is consumed in nuclear reactors. The greater part of the dioxide is converted into uranium tetrafluoride (UF_4: 'green salt') by bringing it into contact with hydrogen fluoride gas at 500° C (see also fig. 15.18). Uranium tetrafluoride is a green substance which melts at 1036° C.

This last-mentioned process, like the reduction of uranium trioxide to dioxide, can be carried out in various ways:

1. by passing the gas over beds of uranium compound (batch process);

2. by moving the uranium compound, with the aid of a conveyor worm, in counter current with the gas flow (stirred bed process);

3. by blowing the gas through the powdered uranium compound (fluidised bed process). The two last processes are continuous and cheaper.

Uranium tetrafluoride is reduced to metallic uranium with magnesium metal:

$$UF_4 + 2Mg \rightarrow U + 2 MgF_2$$

This process is carried out at 1650° C in a steel reactor provided with a lining of magnesium fluoride (which is also obtained as a by-product in the reduction process.)

The uranium obtained is a silvery-white lustrous metal which melts at 1130° C. It is relatively soft and can be shaped at room temperature by rolling, etc. Uranium is highly reactive, it reacts readily with air and moisture at room temperature, readily dissolves in dilute acids, and is attacked by hot water with liberation of hydrogen; for this reason it is encased in another metal when used in reactors.

15.6.5 Enrichment of uranium

Uranium consists of three isotopes: ²³⁸U (99.28%) ²³⁵U (0.71%) and ²³⁴U (0.006%). This mixture can be used in various reactors provided with a moderator. However, for some types of nuclear reactor it is necessary to increase the content of ²³⁵U; this is called 'enrichment' of uranium, (see also nuclear fission, p. 648). In cases where natural uranium or relatively slightly enriched uranium is employed, plutonium is usually recovered from the waste products. Enrichment of uranium therefore involves separation of its isotopes. At first sight this appears to be a very difficult process, since the isotopes all have the same chemical properties and the atomic weights differ relatively little from one another. The fact that there are small differences in the diffusion rates of gaseous compounds of the isotopes makes it possible to effect the separation.

For this purpose, uranium tetrafluoride is not directly converted into metal but into uranium hexafluoride (UF₆). Fluorine gas and powdered uranium tetrafluoride are brought together in a reaction tower at about 500° C.

The components react immediately. The hot gas mixture of the hexafluoride and fluoride thus obtained has its solid constituents (unconverted tetrafluoride etc.) removed from it and is condensed (see fig. 15.18). The condensed uranium hexafluoride is a solid substance which vaporises at 56° C (sublimation).

Isotope separation is achieved by causing UF₆ in the vapour phase to diffuse through a porous wall, behind which a vacuum is maintained in order to assist the diffusion process. The compound of ^{235}U diffuses a little more rapidly through the wall than does the heavier ^{238}U compound. On the other side of the wall a mixture slightly richer in ^{235}U is therefore obtained. This process is repeated hundreds of times in as many stages (cascades), each provided with a porous partition wall. In this way, by varying the number of cascades, any desired concentration of ^{235}UF₆ in ^{238}UF₆ can be obtained.

It should be noted that some possible complications are avoided because natural fluorine consists of only one isotope. If fluorine consisted of several isotopes, a number

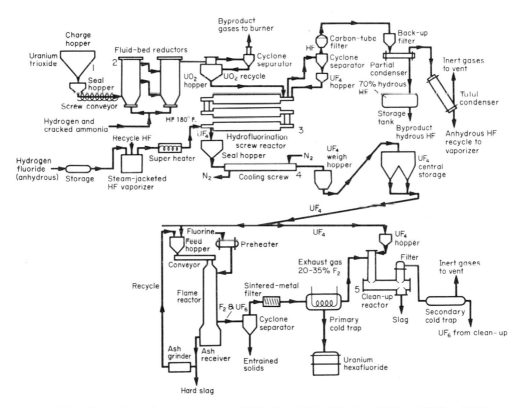

Fig. 15.18 Flow sheet of the preparation of UO₂ from UO₃, UF₄ from UO₂, and HF and UF₆ from UF₄ and fluorine.

of combinations with uranium would be possible, so that isotope separation would be much more difficult, or indeed impracticable.

In principle this separation by diffusion is a simple process, but in reality it requires elaborate apparatus. Buildings at Oak Ridge, USA, housing such apparatus are shown in fig. 15.19.

One result of having to build such installations has been the construction of much better and larger vacuum pumps. This in turn has led to substantial progress in other fields of application of vacuum technology, e.g. in the production of metals.

As the enriched uranium is used in the form of metal or oxide in nuclear reactors, the uranium hexafluoride must be converted into one of these substances. To this end it is reduced with hydrogen to the tetrafluoride and hydrogen fluoride. The uranium tetrafluoride obtained in this way can be converted into enriched uranium by the method already described.

Uranium metal is also produced from the uranium hexafluoride poor in ^{235}U which is obtained in the isotope separation process. This 'impoverished' uranium is converted into plutonium (see nuclear fission, p. 646); it can also be used for shielding against radiation from radioactive sources. A much smaller amount of material is needed for this purpose than of other materials such as lead, so that containers for radioactive substances, etc., can be constructed to much smaller dimensions.

The various processes outlined above in the extraction of uranium are summarized in the scheme on p. 667.

Fig. 15.19 View of the gaseous diffusion plant at Oak Ridge (Tennessee). At this diffusion plant uranium-235 and uranium-238 are separated.

THE EXTRACTION OF URANIUM

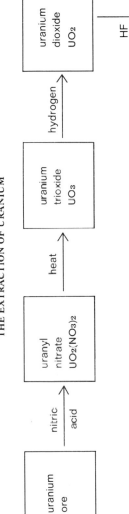
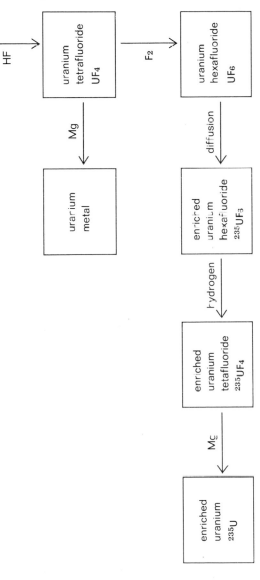

15.6.6 Statistics

The known uranium deposits in 1964 were estimated at 700000 tons (considering only ores which can be recovered at prices up to $10 per lb of U_3O_8). An estimate of the principal deposits (excluding the USSR) is given in the following table (the figures denote tons of uranium):

USA	150000	France	40000
Canada	200000	India	12000
South Africa	150000	Australia	10000

It should be noted, however, that as a result of new uranium discoveries and fresh calculations of the size of known deposits these estimates continually vary.

The world output of uranium minerals (expressed in long tons of uranium metal) and the output figures for the most important producer countries are as follows:

	1956	*1958*	*1960*	*1962*	*1964*
Canada	1700	10100	9700	6400	5200
Australia	–	500	1200	1100	300
France	90	490	970	1000	960
Congo Republic	–	1800	900	–	–
Gabon	–	–	–	350	430
South Africa	3300	4700	4900	3800	3400
USA	4500	9500	13400	12900	9000
World (including USSR)	16000	35000	40000	35000	27000

World output for 1940 was about 7000 tons (reckoned on uranium content), of which 4000 tons was supplied by what was then the Belgian Congo. It is estimated that the world's production will have diminished considerably by 1967; this decline is partly due to the fact that ores of increasingly poor quality have to be processed at consequently greater cost.

As appears from the above table the USA is the largest producer of uranium. In addition, that country imported some 6000 to 15000 tons annually during 1957-64, the greater part of which is stockpiled for strategic reasons.

Britain also imports substantial quantities of uranium ores. The actual quantities are not published, probably for security reasons. The importance of uranium to Britain can be inferred from the capacity of its power reactors, which generate electric power on a large scale. In 1963 the capacity was more than 4000 MW (thermal). The thermal output is expected to have risen to about 20000 MW by 1970. (The electrical output is approximately one-quarter of this figure.) These figures mean a consumption of 1000 to 1500 tons of natural uranium in 1963 and about 5000 tons in 1970. Part of this quantity will have to come from stockpiles now already existing.

In the power reactors some 600 kg of plutonium per year can be produced per 1000 MW of electrical capacity. This means that the annual output of plutonium in Britain will increase from 600 kg in 1963 to about 3 tons in 1970.

Apart from use for nuclear energy purposes, the world requirement for uranium and compounds is no more than 1 ton (reckoned as U_3O_8). In the main, this quantity is used for reagents and for the colouring of glass and glazes.

The average price of ore concentrate (impure U_3O_8) in the USA was $8 per pound of contained U_3O_8 in 1964. The South African price in 1961 was $10.70 per pound. The International Atomic Energy Agency of Euratom has received offers of uranium oxide at £3 18s per pound from South Africa. Prices for metallic uranium are substantially higher. In the USA about $20 per pound was paid for natural uranium in 1964. Uranium with 90% ^{235}U and 100% ^{233}U cost as much $7500 per pound.

15.6.7 Literature

C. D. HARRINGTON and A. E. RUEHLE. *Uranium production technology.* New York, Van Nostrand, 1959.

Reactor handbook, 2nd ed. New York, US. Atomic Energy Commission, vol. 1, *Materials,* 1960; vol. 2, *Fuel reprocessing,* 1961.

W. D. WILKINSON. *Uranium metallurgy.* New York, Wiley, 1962.

Engineering and Mining Journal. Nov. 1966, pp. 77-94; Dec. 1960, pp. 79-89.

J. H. GITTUS. *Uranium.* London, Butterworths, 1963.

CHAPTER 16

Luminescent Materials

16.1 SOLID INORGANIC LUMINESCENT MATERIALS

16.1.1 Definitions and history

All substances emit light when sufficiently heated. In the case of gases a spectral line pattern is observed, while solids and liquids emit a more or less continuous spectrum. This phenomenon is due to the fact that electrons, raised to orbits of higher energy by the absorption of heat, subsequently fall back into smaller orbits while losing energy in the form of light. This form of light production is always accompanied by the absorption and development of a large excess of heat.

Luminescence, however, is light emitted without rise of temperature when suitable substances are 'excited' by radiation or other means. Luminescence may be produced, for example, by absorption of electromagnetic radiation such as light (photoluminescence). Other exciting agencies are electron bombardment (cathodoluminescence), friction (triboluminescence) and chemical reaction (chemiluminescence).

It many cases luminescence only persists while the material is actually being excited, but some materials continue to emit radiation for considerable periods after the excitation has ceased. Emission limited to the excitation period is known as fluorescence, and the emission which persists after excitation is known as afterglow or phosphorescence.

Fluorescence was observed for the first time in 1570 in an extract of certain timbers and of chlorophyll from leaves. It was noticed that the colour of a sunbeam changes after transmission through such an extract. Phosphorescence was well known in the tenth century to Chinese painters who prepared phosphorescent pigments from oyster shells. In 1603 the alchemist Vincentius Casciarolus of Bologna ignited a mineral (now known to be heavy spar, barium sulphate) with coal, and discovered that the resulting product (barium sulphide) glowed in the dark. This material was named phosphor, after the Greek word 'phosphoros' meaning lightbearer.

The element phosphorus, which was discovered about 60 years later, derived its name from the fact that it glows in the dark (chemiluminescence caused by surface oxidation).

Nowadays the name phosphorus is restricted to the element, and the name phosphor is used for all solid materials showing luminescence. Of the latter group, the phosphors

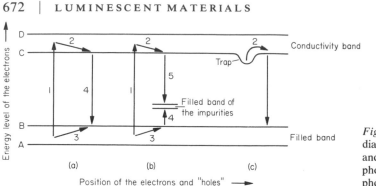

Fig. 16.1 Energy diagram for excitation and emission of a photoconductive phosphor.

showing photoluminescence or cathodoluminescence are the most important.

The character of luminescence was recognized for the first time in 1852 by Stokes, who discovered that a phosphor which absorbs light emits light of higher wavelength.

16.1.2 Mechanism of luminescence

Like thermal radiation, luminescence is caused by the passage of electrons from one orbit to another but this form of light emission is characterized by the fact that only small amounts of heat are developed or absorbed (hence the term 'cold-light emission').

Luminescent solids may be photoconductive or non-photoconductive, and the explanation of the phenomenon is somewhat different in the two cases.

a. Photoconductive phosphors. In one group of luminescent solids, a number of sulphides, selenides, tellurides and some oxides, the occurrence of luminescence is closely related to the phenomenon of photoconductivity, in which certain substances are insulators in the dark and conductors in the light.

The mechanism of excitation and luminescent emission in a very pure photo-conductive phosphor can be explained by means of section (a) of fig. 16.1, in which the permitted energy levels of the electrons are represented by bands. (In gaseous products an electron can only move in a restricted number of orbits, of which the energy levels may be represented by horizontal lines; but in solids each permitted orbit is extended to a larger zone, due to the influence of surrounding atoms and molecules. For this reason the energy levels of the electrons in a solid must be extended to bands.) The lower energy band in fig. 16.1 (AB) represents the energy level of the outermost electrons of the phosphor atoms in a non-excited state. In the non-excited state each atom of the phosphor has a certain number of electrons on this energy level (the energy band is filled, hence the term 'filled band'). No electrons can pass from one atom to another within this band, and the atoms can only take up more electrons if the latter have a much higher energy level. For this reason a non-excited photoconductive phosphor is an insulator, since there are no available free electrons.

If atoms of a photoconductive phosphor absorb energy (e.g. light) one or more electrons may be raised into a higher energy level, at which the movement of the electrons to other atoms is possible. The result of the movement of excited electrons into the higher energy band is a number of empty places ('holes') in the filled band. These holes can then be filled up with electrons from surrounding atoms, with the simultaneous formation of new holes. In fact the result is a displacement of the holes. The new holes can in turn be filled up with electrons from the surrounding atoms, resulting in a further displacement of the holes. Thus the holes can be said to travel through the filled band. This movement of electrons and holes can be accelerated by means of an electric field, and causes the conductivity of the excited phosphor. Consequently the corresponding higher energy band of a photoconductive phosphor is known as the conductivity band.

Due to attractive forces, the electrons (negative) in the conductivity band and the holes (positive) in the filled band lower their potential energy by moving towards each other to the borders of the conductivity band, and to the filled band within the region (BC) of energy levels in which no electrons can occur in a pure photoconductive phosphor (see fig. 16.1). A small portion of the energy absorbed is evolved in the form of heat as a result of the declining potential energy. Since electrons cannot occur in the zone (BC) between the two bands they can only jump back to the filled band, and the remainder of the absorbed energy is simultaneously emitted in the form of electromagnetic radiation. The energy of the radiation is equal to, or smaller than, the energy absorbed. Electrons fall back from border to border but may be elevated from any energy level in the filled band to any energy level in the conductivity band. Thus a very pure photoconductive phosphor which absorbs energy in the form of electromagnetic radiation emits radiation of equal or longer wavelength, since the energy of electromagnetic radiation decreases with increasing wavelength.

For pure photoconductors such as pure zinc sulphide and strontium sulphide the electromagnetic radiation absorbed and emitted is ultraviolet. A photoconductor which contains foreign atoms (impure photoconductor) usually emits visible light (i.e. electromagnetic radiation of longer wavelength, and thus of lower energy content). This phenomenon can be explained by means of section (b) of fig. 16.1, in which the energy level of the outermost electrons of the impurity is represented by a band between the filled band of the pure photoconductor and the conductivity band. An electron may be raised to the conductivity band by the absorption of energy (e.g. ultraviolet), and the resulting hole may be filled by an electron from an atom in the neighbourhood: consequently a new hole is formed near the latter atom. In this way the hole travels to an impurity atom, and an electron from the impurity atom moves to the hole since the latter has a lower energy level. Thus the hole is situated at a higher energy level. The passage of the electron from the impurity is accompanied by the emission of radiation of long wavelength which may be visible or even infrared, depending on the energy level of the filled band of the impurity. Then the electron which has jumped to the conductivity band jumps back to the energy level of the electrons in the impurity atoms with the simultaneous emission of light of lower energy (and thus longer wavelength) than in the very pure photoconductor).

Thus the colour of the light emitted by a photoconductive phosphor can be changed by melting or sintering suitable impurities (named activators) in the latter. The most common impurities used in photoconductive phosphors are compounds of monovalent silver and copper.

In addition to the movement of electrons in the conductivity band there is another factor which influences the character of the luminescent emission. An atom which is excited has a larger diameter than a non-excited atom since one or more electrons of the excited atom move in an orbit at a greater distance from the nuclei. For this reason an

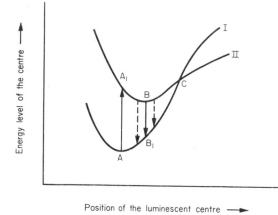

Energy level of the centre →

Position of the luminescent centre →

Fig. 16.2 Energy diagram for excitation and emission by a luminescent centre.

additional amount of the energy absorbed is used to change the position of the atoms. This energy is dissipated in the form of heat when the atom returns to its original position (see luminescence mechanism of non-photoconductive phosphors, below).

b. Non-photoconductive phosphors. Phosphors which are not photoconductive have a similar luminescent character to that of photoconductive phosphors. The mechanism differs, however, from the mechanism of the luminescence of the photoconductive phosphors in that the excited electrons do not reach a conductivity band, and for this reason the absorption and emission of energy is restricted to certain places in the solid, the so-called luminescent centres (consisting of atoms, ions or molecules). The behaviour of the luminescent centres can be explained by means of the energy diagram shown in fig. 16.2. The luminescent centres vibrate around a certain position in which the potential energy is minimal. At points removed from the minimal position the potential energy has a higher level (see curve I with minimum A in fig. 16.2). A luminescent centre which is excited by the absorption of energy vibrates also around a position in which the potential energy is minimal (see curve II with minimum B).

As shown in fig. 16.2, the excited centre has a higher potential energy (and another position, see curve II) than the same centre in the non-excited state (curve I). This is caused by the fact that the excited centre has a larger diameter than the non-excited centre since one or more of the electrons of the excited centre move in an orbit at a greater distance from the nuclei, and thus the excited centre no longer fits in the place of the same centre in the non-excited state.

The energy transfer during excitation and emission is shown by the transition A-A_1-B-B_1-A in fig. 16.2. The transition A-A_1 corresponds with the absorption of energy, resulting in an excited centre with a high potential energy. The transition A_1-B corresponds with a change in the position of the centre to lower its potential energy. The excess of energy is evolved in the form of heat. The transition B-B_1 represents the passage from the excited to the non-excited state with the simultaneous emission of electromagnetic radiation. From the position B_1 the luminescent centre returns to its original position with further loss of thermal energy.

This energy transfer also shows that the energy of the electromagnetic radiation is always smaller than the energy absorbed since a portion of the absorbed energy is ultimately dissipated in the form of heat. Thus, like the photoconductive phosphors, the non-photoconductive phosphors emit light of longer wavelength when they absorb radiation of short wavelength.

The wavelength of the radiation absorbed and emitted depends on the character of the luminescent centres, and the latter in turn depends on the structure of the solid and the types of atoms forming the centres. Some crystalline forms of tungstates, molybdates and uranyl compounds show luminescence in a pure state. Usually a non-photoconductive material does not emit visible light because the position of the excited and non-excited atoms differ so much that almost all energy absorbed is dissipated in the form of heat. However, some products which do not show luminescence in a pure state may be converted into luminescent materials by melting or sintering a small quantity of a suitable product (an activator) in them. In this way the product is provided with luminescent centres consisting of the foreign atoms and the surrounding atoms of the original product. For example, some silicates, phosphates and borates can be converted into luminescent materials by a suitable activator such as a compound of divalent manganese, lead or tin, or a compound of trivalent cerium or antimony.

16.1.3 Some properties of phosphors in relation to the luminescence mechanisms

a. Modification of luminescent emission.

The mechanisms of the emission by photoconductive and non-photoconductive phosphors suggest that it must be possible (in some cases) to modify the wavelengths emitted by modifying the structure of the phosphor or the type of activator.

The wavelenghts of the radiation produced by a phosphor can in fact often be modified by a suitable choice of the quantity and type of the activator. For example,

TABLE I

Some properties of non-photoconductive phosphors

Phosphor	Firing temp. °C	Cath.	X-rays	2537Å	3650Å	Colour of luminescence	3000Å	4000Å	5000Å	6000Å
Zn₂SiO₄–0·012 Mn²⁺ (Willemite)	1250	x	x	x		Green			5250	
β–Zn₂SiO₄–0·012 Mn²⁺ (molten and chilled)	1600	x	x	x		Yellow			5630	
0·8 ZnO. 0·1 BeO)₂. SiO₂–0·05 Mn²⁺	1250	x	x	x		Yellow			5300	
0·8 ZnO.0·1 BeO)₂. SiO₂–0·09 Mn²⁺	1250	x	x	x		Orange				6100
CdSiO₃–0·006 Mn²⁺	1200	x	x	x		Orange			5900	
Cd₂B₂O₅–0·012 Mn²⁺	800	x	x	x		Red				6250
Cd₂P₂O₇–0·02 Mn²⁺	1100	x	x	x		Red				6150
Cd₅(PO₄)₃ Cl–0·025 Mn²⁺ (Apatite structure)	850	x	x	x		Orange			5800	
β–Ca₂P₂O₇–0·001 Bi³⁺	1100	x	x			Red				6550
β–Ca₂P₂O₇–0·01 Sn²⁺	1100	x	x	x		UV	3550			
β–Ca₃(PO₄)₂–0·04 Sn²⁺	1200	x	x	x		White				6300
β–CaSiO₃–0·1 Mn²⁺ (Wollastonite)	1100	x	x			Orange				6100

——— Emission
‑ ‑ ‑ ‑ Absorption

TABLE I (continued)

Some properties of non–photoconductive phosphors

Phosphor	Firing temp. °C	Cath.	X-rays	2537Å	3650Å	Colour of luminescence	Emission — / Absorption --- (3000Å, 4000Å, 5000Å, 6000Å)
β-CaSiO₃–0·01 Pb²⁺	1000	x	x	x		UV	3450
β-CaSiO₃–0·01 Pb²⁺–0·1 Mn²⁺	1100	x	x	x		(UV) orange	6100
α-Ca₃(PO₄)₂–0·02 Mn²⁺	1250	x	x			Red	6500
α-Ca₃(PO₄)₂–0·05 Ce³⁺	1250	x	x	x		UV	3550
α-Ca₃(PO₄)₂–0·04 Ce³⁺–0·02 Mn²⁺	1250	x	x	x		(UV) red	6500
Ca₅(PO₄)₃(F.Cl)–0·1 Mn²⁺ (Apatite)	1000	x	x			Yellow	5700
Ca₅(PO₄)₃(F.Cl)–0·1 Sb³⁺	1000	x	x	x		Blue green	4850
Ca₅(PO₄)₃(F.Cl)–0·1 Sb³⁺–0·1 Mn²⁺	1000	x	x	x		Yellowish white	5700
CaWO₃–0·01 Pb²⁺	1000	x	x	x		Blue	4300
β-MgWO₃	1000	x	x	x		Blueish white	4030

calcium metasilicate containing 1 mole-% Pb^{++} emits ultraviolet radiation but calcium metasilicate containing 1 mole Pb^{++} and 10 mole-% Mn^{++} emits orange light in addition to ultraviolet radiation.

Sometimes two different modifications of one solid emit different wavelengths, e.g. manganese-activated zinc orthosilicate having the crystalline structure of the naturally occurring Willemite emits green light, but glassy zinc orthosilicate having the same chemical composition but another structure emits red light. More commonly a solid is a phosphor in only one modification.

b. Light spectrum of the luminescent emission. If a monatomic gas such as argon or neon is excited (e.g., by heating) it emits light of definite wavelengths (spectral lines) caused by the electrons falling from one energy level to the other. Since the quantities of energy emitted in any transition are always the same, the light emitted is of one characteristic wavelength.

Phosphors, however, emit light over a band of wavelengths (spectral bands) up to a width of about 200 Å (see tables 1 and 2). This is due to the fact that the position in which the potential energy of an excited atom is minimal differs from the corresponding position of the non-excited atom. The excited atom vibrates around its minimum B (see fig. 16.2) and may also return to the non-excited state from a position in the neighbourhood of the minimum B, with the consequent emission of a slightly different quantity of energy (and thus a slightly different wavelength).

c. Influence of the temperature on luminescent emission. Fig. 16.2 also explains why luminescence disappears at higher temperatures. At higher temperatures the excited atoms vibrate more strongly and may reach the potential energy curve of the non-excited atoms at point C. Then the excited atoms may return to their non-excited state without the emission of radiation. Thus for a phosphor there is a temperature region in which the luminescent emission decreases with increasing temperature. At the highest temperature of this range luminescence is abruptly quenched.

The temperature at which the luminescence of calcium tungstate is reduced by 80% is about 135° C. The corresponding temperatures for a manganese-activated zinc sulphide and a manganese-activated zinc orthosilicate are 320 and 445° C respectively.

d. *Duration of luminescent emission.* In many phosphors the states of the atoms are unstable, and consequently such atoms return rapidly to the non-excited state. Thus the luminescent emission extinguishes rapidly after the excitation has ceased. For the luminescent organic solids stilbene, anthracene and phenanthrene, for instance, the time required for the brightness of the luminescence to fall to one-third of the initial brightness is about 10^{-8}s after excitation with cathode rays. The corresponding times for luminescent zinc oxide, calcium tungstate and magnesium tungstate are 10^{-6}, 10^{-5} and 10^{-5}s respectively. For zinc silicate containing 1 mole-% manganese, cadmium silicate with 1 mole-% Mn, and cadmium borate with 0.5 mole-% Mn, the corresponding times are 0.015, 0.03 and 0.015 s respectively. The decay of the brightness is nearly exponential (i.e. the brightness recorded after the given time intervals decreases again to about one-third in the next equal time interval, and so on). Thus the brightness of the phosphors mentioned above decreases to 10 and 1% of the initial brightness after respective periods of twice and four times as long as the given time intervals. At very low brightness levels the decay is no longer exponential but occurs more slowly.

In long-lasting phosphorescent phosphors a relatively large portion of the atoms are stable in their excited states. It is believed that the more stable of the excited atoms are

TABLE 2

Some properties of photoconductive phosphors

Phosphor		Firing temp. °C.	Excitable by					Colour of luminescence	Emission / Absorption			
			Cath.	X-rays	2537 Å	3650 Å	4358 Å		3000	4000	5000	6000
ZnS−2% wt NaCl	Blende	900	x	x	x	x		Light blue	3400 4600			
ZnS−2% wt NaCl or 10^{-4} Al	Wurtzite	1200	x	x	x	x		Blue	3350 4500			
ZnS−4·10^{-5} Cu−2% wt NaCl	Blende	900	x	x	x	x		Green		5280		
ZnS−7·10^{-5} Cu−2% wt NaCl or 10^{-4} Al	Wurtzite	1200	x	x	x	x		Blue green		5160		
ZnS−10^{-4} Ag−2% wt NaCl	Blende	900	x	x	x	x		Blue	4550			
ZnS−10^{-4} Ag−2% wt NaCl or 10^{-4} Al	Wurtzite	1200	x	x	x	x		Dark blue	4350			
ZnS−0·034 Mn−2% wt NaCl		1000	x	x	x	x	x	Orange		5910		
0·58 Zn−0·42Cd) S−10^{-4}Ag−2% wt NaCl		900	x	x	x	x	x	Yellow	4080 5730			
0·50 Zn−0·50 Cd)S−10^{-4}Ag−2% wt NaCl or 10^{-4}Ga		950	x	x	x	x	x	Orange		5830		
CdS−10^{-4} Ga		950	x	x	x	x	x	Dark red				
ZnSe−2% wt NaCl		800	x	x	x	x	x	Red			6500	
ZnO		1000	x	x	x	x		(UV) green	3850			

retained in traps of lower energy level than the level from which they can return to the non-excited state. For this reason the excited atoms can return to the non-excited state only when the temperature is such that the thermal energy of the excited atoms is sufficiently high to allow the atoms to escape from the traps, and thus the duration of phosphorescence decreases with increasing temperature (see the simplified diagram in section (c) of fig. 16.1). When such an excited phosphor is strongly cooled (e.g. in liquid air) the phosphorescent emission disappears but on heating, the emission starts again.

In long-lasting phosphors the luminescent emission usually declines rapidly to about 30 to 10% of the initial brightness (exponential decay). Further decay occurs much more slowly (power law decay). Long-lasting phosphorescence is observed most strongly among the sulphide phosphors. For example strontium sulphide activated with bismuth shows bright phosphorescence for 10 to 20 h after excitation has ceased. The time required for the brightness of phosphorescence of ZnS-0.005 Cu (fired at 1 220° C), to fall to 1% of the initial brightness is about 6s: the corresponding time for ZnS-0.015 Ag (fired at 1 250° C), on the other hand is about 0.1 s and for manganese activated ZnS this time is only a few milliseconds. The times mentioned above apply only to phosphors excited by ultraviolet radiation of about 3 650 Å, since the phosphorescence time of long-lasting phosphors depends on the type of radiation (see fig. 16.3) owing to the fact that in general the proportion of relatively stable excited atoms decreases with decreasing wavelength (i.e. increasing energy of excitation), and is smallest for radiation with cathode rays (electron beams).

The distinction between fluorescent emission and phosphorescent emission (i.e. luminescence during and after excitation respectively) is quite definite but each phosphor shows phosphorescence (afterglow) in addition to luminescence, and the afterglow time varies from 10^{-8}s to several hours. According to a somewhat arbitrary and subjective, but practical classification phosphors with afterglows which are short, relative to the 0.1 s persistence of human vision, are described as fluorescent. However, other definitions are also used in the literature.

16.1.4 Production of phosphors

The most important step in the production of effective phosphors is the formation of extremely pure products. Some phosphors, such as a number of tungstates, phosphates and sulphides, may be prepared by precipitation from solutions of pure starting materials as shown in the following exemples:

calcium tungstate:	$(NH_4)_2WO_3 + CaNO_3 \rightarrow CaWO_3 + 2NH_4NO_3$
calcium phosphate:	$(NH_4)_2HPO_4 + CaCl_2 \rightarrow CaHPO_4 + 2NH_4Cl$
zinc sulphide:	$H_2S + ZnCl_2 \rightarrow ZnS + 2HCl$

As shown above, ammonium salts or free acids are preferred as starting materials to prevent the incorporation of undesired foreign metal atoms in the precipitate. The precipitates are carefully washed and dried, mixed with the activator, and fired to convert the mixture into the required crystalline or glassy modification (see the firing temperatures in tables 1 and 2). If the ammonium salts formed in the precipitation processes are not completely removed in the washing operation, they will certainly evaporate during firing. The activator is usually added in the form of a carbonate, nitrate, oxide or other salt with the same anion as the principal product. For example, tricalcium phosphate (calcium orthophosphate) activated with trivalent cerium and divalent manganese may be prepared by firing calculated amounts of dicalcium phosphate ($CaHPO_4$), cerium nitrate ($Cc(NO_3)_3$) and manganese carbonate ($MnCO_3$) to form a phosphor having the following composition:

$$Ca_3(PO_4)_2 - 0.04CePO_4 - 0.007Mn_3(PO_4)_2$$

The phosphoric acid liberated by the conversion of dicalcium phosphate into tricalcium phosphate replaces the volatile acids in cerium nitrate and manganese carbonate.

Other phosphors, e.g. silicates and cadmium borate, are prepared without precipitation by firing a mixture of pure starting materials such as oxides, carbonates and acids, as shown in the following examples:

Manganese-activated cadmium borate ($Cd_2B_2O_5.0.01MnO$) may be prepared by firing calculated amounts of CdO, H_3BO_3 and $MnCO_3$.

Manganese-activated zinc orthosilicate ($Zn_2SiO_4.0.01MnO$) may be prepared by firing calculated amounts of ZnO, Sio_2 and $MnCO_3$.

Manganese-activated cadmium chlorophosphate ($3Cd_3(PO_4)_2.CdCl_2.0.01MnCl_2$) is prepared by firing the following constituents in the given proportions:

$$9CdCO_3 + 6(NH_4)_2HPO_4 + CdCl_2 + 0.01MnCl_2.$$

16.1.5 Uses of phosphors

The most important use of phosphors is in connection with gas-filled electrical discharge lamps, in particular the tubular fluorescent lamp. The cylindrical glass tube of the fluorescent lamp contains mercury vapour at a pressure of about 0.005 mm Hg. An electric arc is produced in the tube by applying a sufficiently high voltage between the metal electrodes sealed in at each end of the tube. The major portion of the radiation energy of the arc lies in the region of the 2537 Å mercury line, which is invisible. This radiation is used to excite a combination of phosphors applied in the form of a thin coating on the inside of the discharge tube.

The phosphors are chosen from a group whose peak excitation (absorption) by radiation is produced by the 2537 Å mercury line. For the production of white light for general illuminating purposes, phosphors having a wide emission spectrum are preferred. For example, mixtures of blue and yellow emitting β-$Ca_3(PO_4)_2.0.04Sn^{2+}$, β-$MgWO_4$, calcium halophosphates and zinc beryllium silicates meet these requirements (see table 1). With these highly efficient phosphors the light yield is considerably higher than that of incandescent lamps consuming the same electrical power, since a much lower amount of the energy consumed is emitted in the form of heat (in a 40W incandescent lamp 4 to 5% of the energy consumed is emitted as visible light but in a 40W fluorescent lamp about 16 to 20% of the energy consumed is converted into visible light).

Coloured fluorescent lamps are based on the same principle but use is made of phosphors which emit light of the required colour. For example, calcium tungstate (1 mole-% Pb^{2+}) is used in the blue fluorescent lamps used in diazo type copying apparatus. A corresponding application is the use of phosphors in the so-called neon lamps used for display, advertising and stage effects.

Phosphors with a high emission yield at higher temperatures, such as the orange-red emitting magnesium germanate and barium strontium lithium silicate ($4BaO.SrO.Li_2O.4SiO_4. + Ce^{3+}.Mn^{2+}$), are used for the correction of the colour of high-

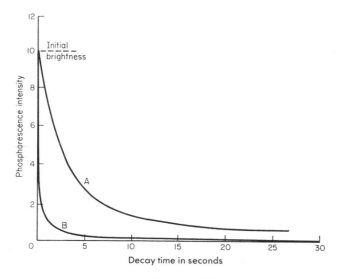

Fig. 16.3
Phosphorescence decay of a ZnS-CdS phosphor. A represents excitation by 3650 Å radiation. B represents excitation by cathode rays: the phosphor is excited to the same brightness in each case.

pressure mercury vapour lamps which are operated at about 300° C. These lamps emit a spectrum of ultraviolet (mainly 3650 Å mercury line) and blue, green and yellow spectral lines. White light is produced by converting the ultraviolet light into red light by means of the phosphors mentioned above.

The second important application of phosphors is in cathode-ray tubes such as television picture tubes, radar tubes and tubes for oscillographs, electron microscopes and other instruments.

Phosphors for television screens must show a very brief phosphorescence since pictures are formed with a frequency of 1/50 of a second, and each picture must extinguish before the following picture is formed. A mixture of phosphors emitting blue and yellow light is commonly used in black and white screens; e.g. a combination of silver-activated zinc sulphide emitting blue light, and a silver-activated zinc-cadmium sulphide emitting yellow or orange light (see table 16.2). Since heavy electron beam currents tend to blacken or burn the sulphides, zinc-beryllium silicate is a more satisfactory yellow component when a very high brightness is required. Colour television screens require the use of mixtures of three phosphors emitting a blue, green and red spectrum respectively. Manganese-activated zinc silicates emitting green light with a short phosphorescence time are widely used in tuning indicators in wireless sets.

For radar screens the colour of the light is less important than for television screens, but the choice of phosphors is restricted to those showing a long phosphorescence time. Since the time of bright phosphorescence is longer after excitation with ultraviolet radiation compared with cathode rays, the radar screens are provided with two layers of different phosphors. The phosphor of the inner layer is excited by cathode rays to emit ultraviolet light which excites the long-lasting phosphor in the outer layer to emit visible light.

Smaller quantities of phosphors are used for a number of other purposes. Some zinc-cadmium sulphide phosphors activated with silver are used in X-ray screens for visual examination inside the human body. The relatively high phosphorescence time of these phosphors is diminished by incorporating about 1 p.p.m. nickel in the phosphor. In a modern technique for mass X-ray chest examinations, a visual image is formed in a zinc sulphide phosphor on the luminescent screen by using a beam of high intensity X-rays for a very short time. The visible image formed on the screen persists for a longer time, and is photographed.

Very long-lasting phosphors are widely used for phosphorescent illumination, e.g. for illuminated instrument dials and for locating light switches, keyholes, bellbuttons, etc. in the dark. Phosphors mixed with a small quantity of radioactive materials as an exciting means are less commonly used for the same purposes. The use of phosphors in luminescent paints and lacquers, for road traffic signs, advertisement posters, etc. is of increasing importance.

16.1.6 Electroluminescent panels

Electroluminescence is the emission of light by a material under the influence of an alternating electromagnetic field. As the strength of the electromagnetic field increases electrons of the material are raised to a higher energy level, and as the strength of the electromagnetic field decreases these electrons fall back to their original energy level with the emission of light. The brightness of the light, which is, of course, intermittent, increases with increasing voltage and with increasing frequency of the alternating electromagnetic field. In addition, the colour of the light shifts to lower wavelengths with increasing frequency. For example, a zinc sulphide phosphor which emits green light under the influence of an alternating electromagnetic field of 50 c/s, emits light with a much more prominent blue component at frequencies of about 2 000 c/s.

The difference between photoluminescence and electroluminescence is essentially a difference in the means of excitation, but the light emission processes are believed to be very similar. The colour of the electroluminescent emission may be changed by activators similar to the activators in photoluminescent and cathodoluminescent phosphors. Some materials showing photo- and cathodoluminescence also show electroluminescence, e.g. zinc sulphide, cadmium sulphide and zinc oxide, but there are also electroluminescent phosphors which show no pronounced photo- or cathodoluminescence, e.g. silicon, silicon carbide and boron nitride.

Electroluminescence is utilized in the so-called electroluminescent panel which comprises basically a capacitor consisting of a phosphor dispersed in a dielectric between two conductive plates connected to an alternating voltage source (see fig. 16.4). One of the plates must be transparent to allow the passage of light, and usually comprises a glass plate coated with a transparent conductive oxide such as tin dioxide. The other plate may also be conductive but usually consists of a metal sheet coated with a white ceramic layer (light reflector) on the side which is in contact with the phosphor. The phosphor between the plates is usually a zinc sulphide (activated with copper or manganese compounds) suspended in a ceramic or a synthetic organic polymer.

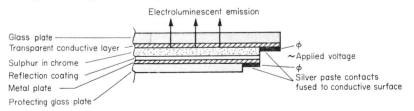

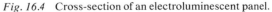

Fig. 16.4 Cross-section of an electroluminescent panel.

The most common electroluminescent panels emit green light, but panels emitting blue or orange light are also available.

Due to the uniformity of brightness over large areas and the thin plate form, electroluminescent panels are particularly suitable for lighting uses for clock, telephone and instrument dials, aircraft control and radio panels, decorative lighting, night lamps, darkroom safelights, photographic contact printers, etc. Electroluminescent panels are not suitable for room illumination since the intensity of the light produced is relatively small. At the frequency of the common sources of electricity (50 c/s) about 20 m² are needed to produce as much light as a 100W incandescent lamp.

16.2   OTHER LUMINESCENT MATERIALS

Besides the solid inorganic phosphors there are other groups of materials showing luminescence. Luminescence is even observed in gases such as the halogens and nitrogen dioxide, and in solutions. The most important luminescent materials outside the inorganics field are the organic products used as optical brighteners and luminescent dyes.

The first group does not absorb visible light and may be white or transparent with a blue fluorescence as a result of ultraviolet absorption. These products are used in the textile industry and in washing powders to compensate the more or less yellow colour of textiles. An important group of optical brighteners consists of nitrogen substituted aminostilbenes such as

(See organic dyes, vol. IV, and washing powders, vol. V.)

Luminescent dyes absorb light as do common dyes, the remaining light is reflected and causes the colour of the dye. However, in addition, the luminescent dye emits visible light (luminescence) as a result of ultraviolet absorption. This luminescence may have the same colour as the dye, and also another colour. A well-known luminescent dye is Rhodamine B which shows an orange-red luminescence in addition to the purple light reflection (see Organic dyes, vol. IV). Luminescent dyes are used in various paints and printing inks.

16.3   LITERATURE

G. F. J. GARLICK. *Luminescent Materials.* Oxford University Press, 1949.
P. PRINGSHEIM. *Fluorescence and Phosphorescence.* London, Interscience, 1949.
D. CURIE. *Luminescence in Crystals.* London, Methuen, 1963.

Index